Naval Science 2

Naval Science 2

Maritime History and Nautical Sciences for the NJROTC Student

Cdr. Richard R. Hobbs, USNR (Ret.)

Naval Institute Press
Annapolis, Maryland

Naval Institute Press
291 Wood Road
Annapolis, MD 21402

Library of Congress Cataloging-in-Publication Data

Hobbs, Richard R.
    Naval Science 2 : maritime history and nautical sciences for the NJROTC student / Richard R. Hobbs.
    p. cm.
    Includes bibliographical references and index.
    ISBN 1-55750-398-2 (alk. paper)
    1. Naval art and science—Juvenile literature.   2. Naval history—Juvenile literature.
    3. United States—History, Naval—Juvenile literature.   I. Title.
    V27 .H63 2002   2002001424

Printed in the United States of America on acid-free paper ⊗

09 08 07 06 05 04 03 02   9 8 7 6 5 4 3 2
First printing

To
Karen and Sarah,
there will always be hope for our world
as long as you are in it.
Thanks for being my inspiration.

Contents

Acknowledgments

One of the most satisfying aspects of my professional career throughout the past twenty years has been my association with the NJROTC program. I am convinced that this program represents one of the finest and most worthwhile endeavors to serve American youth in existence. Given my admiration for the program and the people who comprise it, preparing this textbook was certainly a labor of love.

Special thanks for their assistance with reviewing and critiquing this textbook in its formative stages are due the Chief of Naval Education and Training (CNET), NJROTC staff, and especially the 2000–2001 curriculum advisory committee members, who made many much-appreciated suggestions and recommendations concerning it. The professional staff of AmerInd, Inc., which prepared the audio-visual material that accompanies the various program texts, also provided many valuable recommendations. Other individuals who helped review various parts of the draft manuscript include Amanda Kirby, whose critique of the history section was extremely thorough and most appreciated; Karen and Sarah Mostellar, who provided wonderful inspiration as well as a student perspective on the draft manuscript; and Susan Sheperd, who graciously let me take much advantage of her knowledge of oceanography and earth science during preparation of the sciences section of the manuscript.

Finally, thanks are due the editorial, art, and production departments of the Naval Institute Press for their many contributions to the successful production of this volume, and to copy editor Karin Kaufman, whose excellent editing of the final draft contributed much to the final product.

Maritime History

Sea Power and Early Western Civilization

Sea power is the ability to use the sea to meet a nation's needs. It means being able to defend a nation's own sea-lanes, and the ability to deny an enemy the use of the sea in time of war.

Sea power played a major role in the development of early Western civilization. In many wars throughout history, a single major victory at sea made winning possible. Defeat of the enemy's fleet kept it from supplying its land forces. The victor was then able to attack the enemy's homeland, thus winning the war on land.

EARLY SEAFARERS

Early people feared the seas. They saw them as barriers. Gradually, however, they learned to use the water, both as a way to get food by fishing and as an easier way to travel and conduct trade. Travel by sea was faster, cheaper, and safer than travel over land. Before long the countries bordering the Mediterranean Sea that carried on the most trade became the richest and most powerful in that region.

The first European people to use sea power were the sailors and traders of ancient Crete, a large rocky island south of Greece. Some 4,000 years ago (2500–1200 B.C.) the Cretans dominated their neighbors on the shores of the Aegean Sea, countries now known as Greece and Turkey. This was inevitable because of Crete's geography. The island was too rugged for farming, and it sits right on the major sea routes of the eastern Mediterranean.

The Phoenicians were the next to master the sea in this region. From about 2000 to 300 B.C., their ships roamed throughout the Mediterranean, carrying tin from Britain, amber from the Baltic Sea, and slaves and ivory from western Africa. The Phoenicians established great ports at Tyre and Sidon in what is now Lebanon.

These port cities were at the end of the Asian caravan routes, which brought in the wealth of Asia. Phoenician ships carried this wealth to the coastal trading cities around the Mediterranean and to northern Europe. The Phoenicians also started colonies and trading stations, which grew into new centers of civilization. The Phoenician alphabet became the written language of traders, and they were the first to use money as a means to facilitate trade. Later, the Phoenician alphabet became the basis for our own alphabet. The greatest of the Phoenician colonies grew to be the empire of Carthage in North Africa, later the main opponent of Rome.

Next came the Greeks. Famous Greek authors—Herodotus, Thucydides, and Homer—wrote detailed, semifictional accounts of early sea power. One of the more well known of these tales is about the Trojan War. It is based on an actual series of conflicts fought between 1200 and 1190 B.C. to control the Hellespont, now called the Dardanelles (Turkish Straits), in order to take control of the Aegean–Black Sea trade. By 500 B.C., the Greek city-states had achieved a high level of civilization, and their trading ships and naval vessels sailed the entire Mediterranean. Many prosperous Greek colonies developed in Asia Minor (Turkey), Sicily, Italy, France, and Spain. They took over sea control from the Phoenicians.

Early trading vessels were clumsy craft, easy prey for armed robbers in smaller, swifter craft. So merchants began to crew vessels with hired seagoing soldiers to protect their ships and to patrol the seaways. Navies thus came into being, using special ships called *galleys* (which could be propelled by oars as well as by sails) crewed by trained fighting men.

GREECE VS. PERSIA

By 492 B.C. Greek expansion had run into the mighty forces of Persia (now Iran) moving westward into the eastern Mediterranean. The Greeks were able to hold off two Persian invasions in the next twelve years but then were forced to withdraw from their northern lands in Thrace and Macedonia. In 480 B.C. Xerxes, the Persian king, undertook a huge invasion to try to conquer the Greeks once and for all. Knowing that sea power would be necessary for a victory, Xerxes built a navy of 1,300

A galley of the type used in the Mediterranean circa 500 B.C. Galley tactics in fighting were simple: overtake, ram or grapple, board, and capture in hand-to-hand fighting. At other times galleys patrolled the sea routes over which most ships traveled.

galleys. This fleet followed his 180,000-man army westward around the coast of the Aegean Sea, guarding his flank and carrying his supplies.

Themistocles, the Greek commander, realized that the only way the Persians could be stopped was to break this Persian sea line of communication supporting Xerxes' army from Asia Minor. He convinced the Greeks to build a naval force of 380 *triremes,* a type of multi-decked war galley. Greek strategy was to hold the Persian army at bay at the narrow pass of Thermopylae, while the Greek fleet struck the Persian fleet in a series of hit-and-run attacks in the waters among the Greek islands. But a traitor showed the Persian army a secret mountain pass, which enabled the Persians to surround and destroy the Greek defenders at Thermopylae.

Xerxes' army now continued south to plunder the abandoned city of Athens. The Greeks took up new positions at the Isthmus of Corinth. Meanwhile their fleet moved south to the waters around the island of Salamis, near Athens, to protect their eastern flank.

Bad weather and the Greek hit-and-run attacks had by this time reduced the Persian fleet to 800 vessels. There were only 300 Greek triremes left to oppose them. Splitting his force, Xerxes sent 200 galleys to block the retreat of the Greek fleet around Salamis. The remaining 600 galleys moved directly against the Greek fleet in the narrow strait between Salamis and the shore. But in the narrow strait, the Persians lost the advantage of numbers, since only the lead ships had contact with the Greek

fleet, which was better armed. So the Greeks were able to prevail. About half the Persian fleet was sunk with great loss of life, compared to a Greek loss of only 40 ships. Xerxes watched the unfolding disaster from a throne set up on a hill overlooking the battle. Upon realizing his fleet was wiped out, he ordered his army to begin a long retreat.

Following this battle, there was a short period of peace and prosperity, thereafter known as the Golden Age of Athens. Theater, sculpture, writing, and philosophy flourished. The concept of democracy in government was born. Thus the foundations of Western civilization were laid, and the key event that made this possible was the sea battle of Salamis in 480 B.C.

During the next 150 years, Greek civilization moved steadily eastward, conquering most of what was the Persian Empire. Under Alexander the Great of Macedonia, Greek culture spread throughout the entire eastern Mediterranean. The great port of Alexandria in Egypt was established. Persia was driven from the seas, and the reign of the Phoenicians was ended. Macedonia became the world's greatest sea power, conquering most of the civilized Western and Middle Eastern world.

ROME VS. CARTHAGE

The Greeks controlled the eastern Mediterranean for the next two centuries. In the western Mediterranean, however, Greek expansion was checked by the rising sea

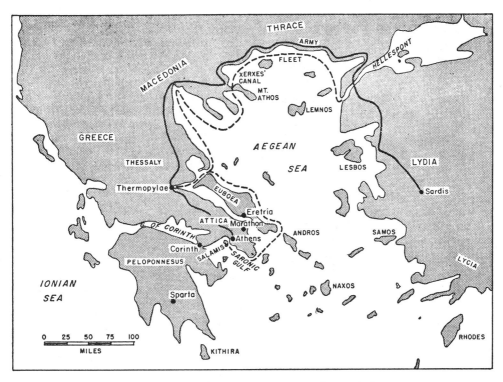

Route of the Persian fleet and army against the Greeks in 480 B.C.

power of Carthage, a city-state in North Africa founded in the late eighth century B.C. by the Phoenicians. But on the Italian peninsula, a new power was emerging: Rome. In 275 B.C., the Romans conquered Italy, including the Greek colonies in the south. In the process, they absorbed the Greek culture, helping to continue the advance of Western civilization. In their way, however, was a strong rival: Carthage. In 265 B.C., the first of several bitter con-

flicts between the two powers began in Sicily. Together these conflicts were known as the Punic Wars (*Punic* is a Latin variation of the word "Phoenician," or *Punicus*).

At the beginning of the Punic Wars, Rome saw what sea power and a strong navy could do. The Carthaginian navy protected Carthage from attack by the Romans, harassed Roman sea commerce, and plundered the Roman coast.

The Romans studied Greek sea tactics and eventually improved on them. As the Punic Wars progressed, Roman seamanship and tactics overcame the Carthaginians, driving them from the sea. The first Punic War gave Rome the island of Sicily as a province, and the second Punic War gave Spain to Rome. The third Punic War began with an amphibious invasion of North Africa. By the time it was over, Carthage had been burned, and Carthaginian power was destroyed forever.

THE *MARE NOSTRUM*

The Roman Empire was now free to spread throughout the Mediterranean. The Roman navy cleared the Mediterranean of pirates, moved and supported Rome's armies, and defeated any hostile fleets.

In the first century B.C., rebellious Romans and their Egyptian allies, under the command of Mark Antony and Queen Cleopatra, tried to overthrow the Roman Empire during the confusion following the assassination of Julius Caesar. The rebellion was crushed, however, in

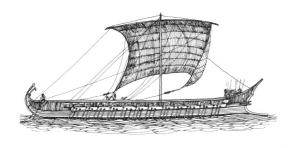

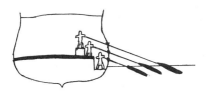

An ancient Greek trireme of the type that defeated the Persians at Salamis. There were three decks of oars and rowers, one above the other on each side of the ship. Often the rowers were slaves.

31 B.C. at a great sea battle near Actium (Greece). The Roman admiral Agrippa destroyed the Egyptian fleet with blazing arrows and pots of flaming charcoal. In an earlier battle at Naulochus, Agrippa had defeated Pompey, Caesar's other rival to power, and secured the western Mediterranean. The Battle of Actium put the whole eastern Mediterranean in the Roman Empire.

For more than five centuries after Actium, trade vessels could move freely from the Black Sea to Gibraltar with little fear. The Mediterranean had become the Roman *Mare Nostrum* (Our Sea) with all coasts, ports, and naval bases controlled by Rome. On land and sea the *Pax Romana* (Roman Peace) was established, the longest period of peace in world history. Roman law, government, art, language, and religion were firmly established in western Europe, the Middle East, and North Africa. Western civilization today can be traced to Rome and to the earlier Greek contributions.

THE MIDDLE AGES

Eventually, Rome's greatness began to decline, due to social, political, and economic breakdowns too extensive to discuss here. As Rome declined, the empire broke up into two parts. The Eastern or Byzantine Empire had its capital at Constantinople (after 1930 called Istanbul), and the Western Empire kept its capital at Rome. Barbarian invaders from northern and central Europe conquered Rome and deposed the last emperor in A.D. 476.

From then on, for the next thousand years, Europe was in constant turmoil, and there was a constant threat of Muslim/Arab expansion into the Mediterranean from northern Africa. The period of western European history from the fall of Rome until about the eleventh century has been called the Dark Ages, because of numerous invasions of barbaric tribes, incursions of North African Moors, religious bigotry, and a general lack of education among the masses of people. Only in the region around Constantinople, where much of the Roman tradition was preserved, was there a general advance of culture during this period. In the late eleventh century, the Crusades, religious-military expeditions to retake the Holy Lands from the Muslims, began gradually to hasten a reawakening of culture and education in western Europe. This movement flourished in the thirteenth through sixteenth centuries. This time is referred to as the Renaissance (the Rebirth) in western European history.

In the eastern Mediterranean, however, the Byzantine Empire, centered in what is now Turkey, defeated the advancing Muslims at Constantinople in A.D. 717. The Byzantines thereafter prospered and blocked additional westward Muslim overland expansion. The Muslims became largely content with piracy on the Mediterranean and with strengthening their control over their huge North African and Middle Eastern territories. Mus-lim fleets dominated the Mediterranean at this time. By the eleventh century, though, Christendom was ready to contest Muslim control. The Muslims were expelled from Sardinia and Sicily and pushed into southern Spain. The First Crusade, initiated by Pope Urban II in 1095, recaptured Jerusalem and nearly swept the Arabs from the Mediterranean.

Over the next 300 years, the religious fervor that had brought on the Crusades turned more to commercial expansion by the Italian states. Their merchant fleets took advantage of the Muslim retreat. Venice profited most from the increased trade and became the biggest center of commerce between Asia and Europe. It hired out ships to Crusaders and gave the Arabs commercial favors, thus profiting from both sides. Venice acquired Crete and Cyprus in the course of these events. By 1400 Venice was at the height of its power, with a fleet of 3,000 ships.

The north German port cities were on the opposite end of much of the Venetian trade. They formed the Hanseatic League, or the Hanse, which dominated the northern and western European economy. The Baltic and North Seas became to some degree in the north what the Mediterranean had been for centuries in the south.

But by now the Islamic cause had been taken over by the aggressive Ottoman Turks. They swept across the Dardanelles into southeastern Europe and captured Constantinople in 1453. The fall of the Byzantine Empire removed the barriers to Muslim advances into Europe. The Turks swept to the very gates of Vienna, Austria. Muslim fleets sought domination of the Mediterranean and control of the profitable east-west trade.

THE BATTLE OF LEPANTO

For some time the divided Christian states could not get organized to oppose the Turks, but after the Turkish conquest of Cyprus in 1570, fear of the Turks finally drew the states together. Spain and the Italian states agreed to combine their fleets for a conclusive battle with the Turks. The winner would have a significant effect on the course of Western civilization.

The Christian fleet, commanded by Don John of Austria, was composed of some 200 galleys, mostly Venetian and Spanish. The Ottoman fleet, commanded by Ali Pasha, numbered about 250 galleys. For their main offensive weapon the Turks still relied on the bow and arrow. Many Christian soldiers, however, were armed with the *arquebus,* an early type of musket. The opposing fleets came together in the Gulf of Lepanto (near Patras, Greece) in 1571. This was just a few miles south of where Agrippa had defeated Antony in the Battle of Actium sixteen centuries earlier. In the terrible battle that took place, the Christian navies crushed their Turkish opponents. Some 30,000 Turks died. All but sixty of their ships were captured or destroyed. Some 15,000 Christians cap-

The Battle of Lepanto in 1571 ended Muslim attempts to move farther into Europe and control the Mediterranean Sea.

tured earlier by the Turks and used as slaves to row the galleys were freed by the victory.

As a result of the Battle of Lepanto, the Turks never again seriously challenged control of the Mediterranean, although Muslim pirates continued to harass merchantmen on these waters for the next 250 years.

Lepanto was the end of the age of the galley. By the time of Lepanto, the Mediterranean had begun to decline as the center of world maritime activity. It had served for 2,000 years as the cradle of western European civilization and commerce. Its period of greatest influence was the age of the galley. But the Turkish hold on the Middle East had caused seafaring nations to seek new routes to Asia. The Age of Discovery had dawned. Columbus laid claim to the New World for Spain in 1492. Soon Portuguese, Spanish, English, Italian, French, Dutch, and Swedish seafarers were sailing across the Atlantic to new markets, new wealth, and new conflicts.

THE AGE OF DISCOVERY

The Age of Discovery was a new age of sea power. Brave explorers in wooden ships sailed the world's oceans and founded colonies while seeking religious freedom and fortunes for king and country. The hardships were great, but the lure of gold and adventure was greater. As before, the nations with sea power became rich and powerful. Inevitably, rivalries arose and wars were fought between opposing great powers.

The Portuguese were the first to seek a new sea route to the East Indies and the rest of Asia. Prince Henry the Navigator hired explorers to try to find a route to the East by sailing around Africa. Bartolomeu Dias rounded

the Cape of Good Hope at the southern tip of Africa in 1488. This proved that a sea route to Asia existed. Vasco da Gama sailed from Portugal to India in 1498, opening a Portuguese trade route to the Indies and China and establishing colonial trading sites. Portugal's leadership was brief, though, for it was soon overwhelmed by neighboring Spain.

Contributing about $5,000 in royal jewels, Queen Isabella financed Christopher Columbus on his first voyage of discovery. It certainly was the most profitable investment in history. Columbus landed in America and thus helped put Spain into a position of European leadership. Through sea power, Spain established a huge empire. Millions in gold, silver, and jewels poured into the royal treasury. Treasure-laden ships sailed in groups escorted by warships to protect them against pirates and privateers of rival nations. This was an early example of a *convoy*, a method used centuries later in World Wars I and II to protect merchant shipping.

At the time, national wealth was thought to be measured by the amount of treasure in the royal vaults. The total wealth of the world was considered to be a fixed quantity. Thus, to become richer and more powerful, a nation had to make some other nation poorer through capture of its trade and colonies. This *mercantile theory* kept the world in almost continuous conflict well into the 1800s.

ENGLAND CHALLENGES SPAIN

In 1570 Pope Pius V called upon King Philip II of Spain to drive the Muslims from Europe and the Mediterranean. At the same time, the pope asked Philip to crusade against the "heretic and usurper" Queen Elizabeth I in Protestant England. Having proved himself and his great fleet at Lepanto, Philip accepted this task.

Elizabeth, on the other hand, wanted to protect her throne against the Catholic Mary Queen of Scots. She began to strengthen England's defenses against the attack she knew would soon come from Spain. After securing England's flank by an alliance with the king of France, she secretly released her fortune-seeking seamen to raid Philip's treasure ships from the New World, a practice called "privateering." And she began rebuilding her navy.

The privateering of the English "seadogs"—Sir Francis Drake, Martin Frobisher, and Sir John Hawkins—was extremely successful and pleased the queen. In 1578 Sir Francis Drake, the most famous of the English raiders, sailed his *Golden Hind* into the Pacific through the Strait of Magellan and raided Spanish cities and shipping along the west coast of South America. He returned to England in 1581 via the Cape of Good Hope, laden with gold, silver, and jewels worth half a million pounds sterling (equal to many millions of today's dollars). Queen Elizabeth accepted the treasure and knighted Drake on the quarterdeck of his ship.

Elizabeth had a significant advantage in her superb seamen. The widespread privateering had created a group of men who had great knowledge of ships and the sea. With these seadogs in command of the world's best sailors, England prepared to meet Spain in a great contest for supremacy on the seas.

DEFEAT OF THE SPANISH ARMADA

In the early summer of 1588 Philip sent forth what he believed to be an unbeatable naval armada. Its purpose was to stop the English raids on his ships and ports and to bring England back into the Catholic Church. The Spanish Armada consisted of a fleet of 124 galleons with 1,100 guns. It was crewed by 8,000 sailors and carried 19,000 soldiers, all under the command of the Duke of Medina-Sidonia.

To oppose it, the English had reinforced the queen's 34 men-of-war with 163 armed merchantmen, 16,000 men, and 2,000 guns. The English fleet was under the overall command of Charles Howard, lord admiral of England.

So the scene was set. The Armada had fewer guns, but had superior total firepower. The English had smaller ships and long-range culverins (a type of cannon). The English had an advantage in maneuverability, clear decks, and range. King Philip's orders were to "grapple and board and engage hand to hand." But the English intended to fight with guns alone, for they carried fewer soldiers. The sailors and marines doubled as antiboarding defenders and cannoneers.

During their first encounters in the English Channel, each side used more than 100,000 rounds of shot. Spanish fire had little effect because of the distance kept by the English ships. The English pounded the Spanish ships, causing many casualties on the packed decks but little damage to the hulls.

Ignoring a chance to attack the English off Plymouth, the Spaniards sailed on up the channel. The English picked away at them with little effect. But by the time Medina-Sidonia sought rest and resupply in the neutral French port of Calais, he found that he had fired all of his heavy shot. During the night, Howard sent eight fireships into the Spanish ships anchored at Calais, forcing the Spaniards out in confusion during darkness. The next day the English and their Dutch allies attacked without fear of the now-silent Spanish guns, facing only the small border-repellers and muskets.

However, the English supply system also proved to be inadequate. After Howard had sunk two Spanish ships, driven three onto the rocks, and littered the enemy decks with casualties, he too ran out of ammunition. But the Spanish were already on the run. With the wind against them and the English behind them, the Spaniards fled northward into the North Sea, intending to round Britain and Ireland to get home.

If the English ammunition had held out, they probably would have crushed the Spanish Armada then and there. As it was, hunger and thirst, storms, and poor navigation finished the task for the English. About forty of the Spanish ships sank at sea, and at least twenty were wrecked on the rocky shores of Scotland and Ireland. In October, only about half of the great naval force that Philip had confidently sent to conquer England returned to Spain.

The failure of the Armada marked the beginning of Spain's decline. The defeat of the Armada was a signal to seafaring nations, especially England, France, and the Netherlands, to strike out for colonies and commerce around the world. The fact that these efforts often involved taking over territories and trade routes claimed by the king of Spain made little difference to the mariners. They did not attempt to conquer Spanish colonies in Central and South America. But pirates and privateers often plundered the Spanish Main, stretching from Colombia and Panama to the islands in the Caribbean. Asia, Africa, and North America east of the Mississippi River were considered wide open for colonization and trade.

ENGLAND BUILDS ITS EMPIRE

England's efforts at colonization in the seventeenth century were paid for by private groups who received charters (licenses) for that purpose from the Crown. The first successful colony in North America was founded in 1607

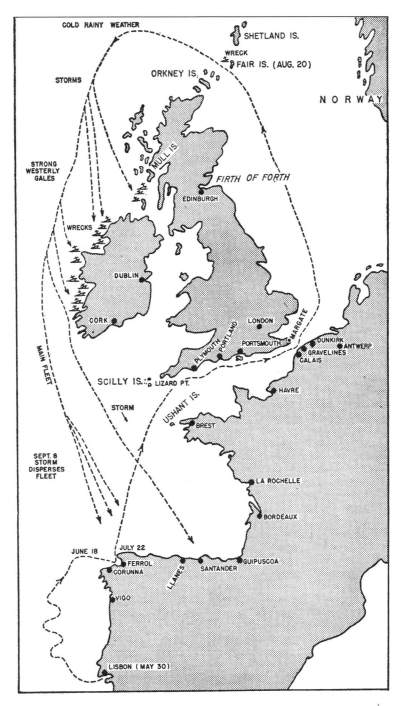

The route of the Spanish Armada, 1588. The British defeated the Armada in the English Channel near Calais, after which the Spanish fleet fled northward around Britain and Ireland to try to return home.

at Jamestown, Virginia. Later colonies in Massachusetts, Pennsylvania, and Maryland were begun by groups seeking religious freedom. The last colony on the East Coast was Georgia (1732), whose settlers volunteered as a way to get out of debtors' prisons.

With the English, French, and Dutch all eagerly seeking colonies, conflict was inevitable. Between 1665 and 1674, the English and Dutch fought three fierce naval wars. The English were the winners, and one of their gains was the Dutch colony of New Amsterdam, which the English soon renamed New York. Between 1689 and 1763, the English fought a series of wars with the French, now their only serious rival at sea. During the Seven Years' War (1756–63), known in America as the French and Indian War, the two powers fought what amounted to a world war, with land and sea battles occurring in almost every part of the globe. England's ultimate victory gained it many new possessions, the main one in North America being Canada.

Whatever may have been happening among the superpowers, throughout this period of nearly two centuries the colonies existing in a thin strip of cultivated land on the East Coast of North America did so only because of the sea. It was across the Atlantic Ocean that all of the settlers had come, bringing with them only the bare necessities of life and their Old World traditions. And it was across this same ocean that additional colonists, livestock, and hardware came, to sustain and expand what the hardy first folk had begun. The sea provided them with an industry, particularly in New England, where they soon discovered some of the richest fishing grounds in the world. Virginians used the sea to send large quantities of tobacco to the Old World, which had taken an almost instant liking to it. Within and among the colonies, the inland rivers and coastal waters became waterborne highways. On these highways the products of inland regions were traded for imported goods and sent on their way to the larger coastal communities and then overseas, primarily to England.

Born of the sea, maintained by the sea, and enriched by the sea, England's American colonies had grown in population to more than 1.5 million people by 1760. By 1775, they had grown to 2.5 million. American seamen and American-built ships made up about one-third of the entire English merchant marine. With the Treaty of Paris in 1763, the war in North America between France and England ended. England was supreme, and its navy and merchant fleets controlled the world's seas.

Chronology

2500–1200 B.C.	Crete dominates Mediterranean
1200 B.C.	Trojan War
480 B.C.	Battle of Salamis
275 B.C.	Rome conquers Italy
31 B.C.	Battle of Actium
476	Last Roman emperor deposed
1095	First Crusade
1492	Columbus discovers America
1571	Battle of Lepanto
1588	Spanish Armada defeated
1607	Jamestown colony established
1756–63	French and Indian War

Study Guide Questions

1. What is meant by a nation's sea power?
2. A. How did navies start?
   B. What was their purpose?
3. What was the major type of warship used in ancient times?
4. Why did ancient Crete develop into the first sea power in the Mediterranean?
5. How did the Phoenicians contribute to Western culture?
6. Which great Middle Eastern empire was the main enemy of ancient Greece?
7. What was King Xerxes' invasion plan against Greece?
8. What was the Greek plan of battle at the Battle of Salamis?
9. A. Who followed the Greeks as the leader in Western culture?
   B. Which country was their principal enemy during their rise to power?
   C. What were the wars between these countries called?
10. What two sea battles won the Mediterranean for Rome after Caesar's death?
11. What is the period of western European history from the fall of Rome until about the eleventh century often called?
12. A. Which of the Italian states became a great commercial and naval power during the Crusades?
    B. How did it do this?
    C. What organization of ports dominated the trade of northern Europe at the same time?
13. What happened in 1571 to end the threat of control of the Mediterranean by the Moors?
14. What happened by the time of the Battle of Lepanto that caused the Mediterranean to decline as the center of world maritime interest?
15. Which country led the way to the Age of Discovery with early explorations around Africa?
16. What changes occurred in Spain as a result of the discovery of the Americas?
17. Which country rose to oppose Spain as the leading sea power in the sixteenth century?
18. For what purpose did the Spanish Armada sail in 1588?
19. A. Which country challenged English colonialism in North America first?
    B. What was the outcome of these wars in America?
20. What was the main result of the French and Indian War in America?

Vocabulary

sea line of communication	rebellion
grapple	piracy
invasion	privateers
plunder	convoy
flank	mercantile theory
galley	ammunition
Mare Nostrum	maneuver
armada	

2

The American Revolution, 1775–1783

The Seven Years' War was fought from 1756 to 1763. During this war, Britain captured French and Spanish colonial possessions around the world, mainly because of its superior naval strength. Chief among these possessions were Canada and Florida in North America and India in Asia.

England's prime minister during these years, William Pitt, planned the naval strategies that made it possible for England to win half the world by the war's end. The prime ministers after Pitt, however, allowed the Royal Navy to decline somewhat in the years after the war. On the other hand, France began to rebuild its navy immediately.

PRELUDE TO REVOLUTION

While England and France were busy fighting each other in the Seven Years' War, the American colonies grew and prospered. When the war was over, British officials looked to the colonies as a way to raise money to help pay off the debts built up during the long war. They felt the colonies had benefited unfairly. They believed that, unlike Englishmen at home, the colonists had not borne their share of the taxes and restrictions. England thus passed the Revenue Act and began enforcing taxes on sugar imports to the colonies in 1763. Then, by the Stamp Act of 1765 and other similar acts, it tried to reassert Parliament's power in the colonies. The colonists thought all this was unfair and soon became upset over the way Britain was treating them.

In 1767 Parliament passed the Townshend Act, which taxed paper, lead, and tea. All over the colonies people protested. Anti-British feelings were especially strong in Boston. There, on the evening of 5 March 1770, an angry crowd of protesters led by an African American named Crispus Attucks gathered and began to taunt British soldiers. One thing quickly escalated to another, and in a scuffle that followed, the soldiers shot and killed Attucks and several other people—considered the first casualties of the American Revolution. The incident was played up in the press and soon became known as the "Boston Massacre." It made many colonists want to seek revenge.

Three years later, irate Bostonians disguised as warlike Indians boarded a merchant ship and dumped some British tea into the harbor rather than pay taxes due on it. Parliament soon responded to this "Boston Tea Party" with the Coercive Acts, which closed the port of Boston, abolished the right of the people of Massachusetts to select their own council, and restricted other civil liberties.

These were the events that led to the American Revolution, which began at Lexington and Concord in April 1775. "The die is cast," wrote King George III. "The colonies must either triumph or submit." There was no longer the possibility of a peaceful settlement.

PROBLEMS FOR BRITISH SEA POWER

The Royal Navy, in 1775 the mightiest in the world, soon found out that it would not be easy to fight the Americans. For one thing, the British had been getting much of their shipbuilding materials, such as tar, pitch, turpentine, and timber for masts and hulls, from the colonies. Now, of course, the colonies would not supply these materials to England. The British also soon found that many officers in the British Army and Navy believed the Americans were English citizens and refused to fight against them.

Another force that had earlier been on England's side was now turned against it: the *privateers*, the armed American merchant ships that had helped the British win the French and Indian War. Now these *privateersmen*, with the blessing of the Continental Congress, set out to capture British ships and goods.

The 1,800-mile-long American coast presented a big problem for the British. How could they defend their merchant ships from privateers in English waters, patrol the American coastline to keep ships from supplying the colonies with arms and other goods, and at the same time supply British land troops with the weapons and other things they needed?

THE BIRTH OF THE AMERICAN NAVY

In July 1775 the Continental Congress petitioned King George III to restore liberty to the colonies in a final attempt to avoid war with England. Despite the difficulties facing the British, the king refused to accept the petition, and the colonists knew that they must prepare for war.

George Washington, who had been a British colonial officer in the French and Indian War, had taken command of the Continental Army surrounding Boston on 3 July 1775. Washington knew he could not wage war without a navy. "Whatever efforts are made by land armies, the navy must have the casting vote in the present conflict," he said.

Just the month before Washington had taken command, a group of Maine backwoodsmen under Jeremiah O'Brien won the first real sea fight of the Revolution. The Patriots captured a small British merchant sloop, and then they used her to capture the British armed cutter *Margaretta* and all of the supplies the ship was taking to British troops in New England.

This action was similar to most of the naval warfare done by the colonies throughout the war. Every colony except New Hampshire commissioned ships, and Virginia and South Carolina had fairly large squadrons. Nearly all of these ships were small. They operated all along the Atlantic seaboard, in river mouths, bays, and coves. They carried on coastal commerce and attacked British supply boats and parties whenever the opportunities and odds were favorable. But most important, they kept open the coastal lines of communication on which so much of the life in the colonies depended.

Partly because of this "coastal cavalry" force, the Continental Congress was reluctant to establish a navy. Many representatives thought that no warships built and manned by colonists would be able to stand up to the powerful ships of the Royal Navy. Still, the colonies needed supplies to wage war, and capturing them from British ships was a good way to get them. When Congress learned that two unescorted transport ships loaded with supplies for the British army in Quebec had sailed from England, it decided that the time had come to launch the Continental Navy.

On 13 October 1775 the Continental Congress took the step that the U.S. Navy regards as its official birth. It approved a plan for buying, fitting out, and arming two vessels, the *Andrew Doria* and the *Cabot*, to intercept the British supply ships. Two larger ships, the *Alfred* and the *Columbus*, soon were added. These ships were not only to attack British transports but also to protect and defend the colonies.

Sketch of a U.S. frigate of the late eighteenth and early nineteenth centuries.

The Continental Congress quickly enlarged its Navy even more. New men-of-war were built, and merchant vessels were converted into fighting ships. Privateers also helped. They captured some 2,200 British vessels by war's end. After the war, many privateer captains became famous in the U.S. Navy.

George Washington himself commissioned seven ships to capture some of the supplies that were streaming in to the British troops in Boston. In November 1775 his "navy" took muskets, shot, and a huge mortar, which Washington's poorly armed forces needed desperately, from the British ships.

On 10 November 1775 the Continental Congress established a Marine Corps of two battalions. These men helped man the new Navy. The Marine Corps still celebrates this date as its birthday.

In the early days of the Revolution, men were eager to serve in the Continental Navy. As the war continued, however, recruiting them became more difficult, due to a combination of stricter discipline, low pay, and the rewards that could be obtained by privateering. Sometimes the Continental authorities even resorted to the practice of impressment to crew the ships; men were forced to serve by taking them on board against their will. Finding men to serve in the Continental Navy was a problem throughout the war, and ships were often unable to go to sea because they lacked crews.

FIRST NAVAL OPERATIONS

The first Continental naval squadron was composed of six small schooners, brigs, and sloops donated by several states and assembled at Philadelphia. They were placed under the command of Esek Hopkins, a Rhode Islander. On 22 December 1775 the first American naval flag was raised on one of them, the *Alfred*, by the senior lieutenant in the Continental Navy, John Paul Jones. More would be heard of him later.

In February 1776 Congress directed Hopkins to take his squadron to the Virginia Capes to neutralize any loyalist craft he might find there. But in keeping with his independent New England spirit, once at sea, Hopkins decided to go after bigger game. He sailed straight for New Providence (later Nassau) in the Bahamas, where he was able to overcome two British forts and take more than eighty artillery pieces, powder, and naval stores.

On their way home, the squadron captured several British ships loaded with more British arms, which they took to Washington's troops as well. The expedition was not without casualties, however. Just after midnight on 5 April, the squadron happened upon the twenty-gun British corvette *Glasgow* off New England. After damaging many of the squadron's ships, the *Glasgow* escaped, even though she was outnumbered six to one.

This incident showed in many ways what kind of navy the Continental Congress had gathered. For the most part, the squadron captains were privateersmen who could not cooperate with each other, teach their men gunnery, or maintain squadron discipline. One of the captains, Tom Hazard of the sloop *Providence,* was dismissed for cowardice, and his ship was given to Lieutenant Jones.

A few weeks later, when Hopkins took the squadron south to Providence, Rhode Island, troubles began to multiply. Several of the ships began to break down, an epidemic of smallpox sent a hundred men ashore, and General Washington wanted another hundred men he had loaned to the squadron returned. There was no

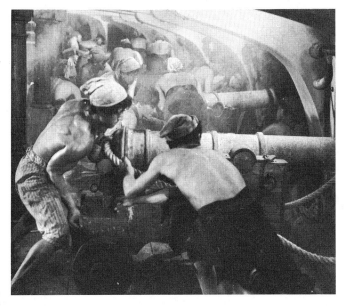

Action on the gunnery deck of an American frigate during the Revolutionary War.

money to pay those who were left. It was nearly impossible to recruit men for such duty, when the crews of the coastal privateersmen got better shares of the prizes they captured plus quick payoffs for their efforts.

Thus, the Nassau expedition turned out to be the last time American ships would put to sea as a squadron during the war. Later, various officers who had been in the squadron set out by themselves in their ships and took on many British ships in hard-fought individual actions.

One such officer was Lieutenant John Paul Jones. With his sloop the *Providence,* in a single month, August 1776, he captured sixteen enemy vessels and destroyed many others. Later, as captain of the makeshift frigate *Alfred,* Jones cruised off the New England coast and raided enemy shipping and fishing in that area. One of the ships he captured carried British winter uniforms, and soon 10,000 American soldiers were wearing them. John Paul Jones would become legendary among early American naval leaders.

THE BATTLE OF LAKE CHAMPLAIN

In the fall of 1775, the American Patriots under General Benedict Arnold attacked Quebec in Canada, but they could not capture the city. The Americans stayed and bombarded the city through the winter. In the spring, when the ice melted on the St. Lawrence River, British reinforcements arrived by ship, forcing the Patriots to retreat toward the colonies. The British, under Generals Sir Guy Carleton and John Burgoyne, pursued them.

When Arnold and his men reached Lake Champlain in June 1776, he assembled a ragtag flotilla of sixteen craft. In response the British constructed their own naval force, and by October, they were ready to proceed against the Americans.

Strength was not on Arnold's side, but he outfoxed the British. At Valcour Island on 11 October he hid his flotilla until the enemy fleet sailed past before a strong north wind. Then the American force attacked from downwind, forcing the British to turn and attack against the wind. Over the next two days the Americans inflicted much damage on the superior British fleet, though they lost most of their ships in the process. Afterward the Americans ran their few surviving craft ashore and burned them, then escaped into the woods. By this time winter was approaching, and Carleton had to return to winter quarters in Canada.

This action could not be considered a "victory" in the usual sense because Arnold lost all his ships. However, the Patriots were able to stop the southerly British advance and thus gain time to regroup and train their forces until the following spring.

Meanwhile, the Second Continental Congress had signed the Declaration of Independence on 4 July 1776, making the colonists' rebellion a revolution. The Patriots were more determined than ever to be free from British rule.

WASHINGTON SAVES THE CAPITAL

While General Arnold was fighting the British on Lake Champlain, farther east things were not going well. The British general Sir William Howe held the city of Boston. The Americans placed cannon on Dorchester Heights overlooking the city in March 1776, but the colonial militia did not have enough gunpowder to engage Howe's troops and enter the city. Also, the Continental naval forces there were not large enough to stop the British from evacuating by sea. Thus Howe's troops and 1,000 loyalists escaped in ships to Halifax, Nova Scotia, to await reinforcements.

After the reinforcements arrived, General Howe sailed south from Nova Scotia with the main British army to join British generals Sir Henry Clinton and Charles Cornwallis at New York on 5 July, the day after the Declaration of Independence was signed. Five hundred British ships anchored off Staten Island. The Americans did not have a single warship, and the few small craft they had could not keep the enemy out of New York. Altogether, the British landed more than 30,000 well-equipped and well-trained troops. Washington's opposing troops numbered only about 20,000, and many of them were untrained militiamen.

By late fall, General Howe's superior forces had driven the Patriots from Long Island and then from White Plains, New York. General Washington's army fled again and again before the advancing British. By December 1776 the American forces were reduced to only about 2,000 men because of casualties and desertion, and also because most of those whose enlistments had run out went home to take care of their families for the winter.

Washington and his remaining troops were cold, hungry, and tired. They badly needed a victory to regain the momentum and sustain the revolution. As his men crossed the Delaware River to escape the enemy yet again in late December, Washington devised a bold plan. He ordered his men to take all boats from the New Jersey side of the river to the Pennsylvania side. Then, on Christmas night, in a raging sleet storm, the nearly frozen American soldiers quietly rowed through the ice floes on the river back to the New Jersey shore. Their surprise attack on the enemy troops (Hessian soldiers who were German mercenaries) at Trenton was a huge success. One week later, Washington surprised the British again, this time at Princeton, and his men won another complete victory.

The British then returned to New York for the winter, while Washington and his troops wintered in Morristown, New Jersey. They had saved the colonial capital at Philadelphia from the enemy, but more important, the tide was turning. The Patriots would be ready to fight again with the coming of spring.

THE CRUCIAL YEAR: 1777

British forces poured across the Atlantic into America during the winter, spring, and early summer of 1777. The British prepared to use the same three-pronged plan of attack that had failed the year before because of the delays caused by the naval operations on Lake Champlain. General Burgoyne would move south from Montreal with 8,000 men to the Hudson Valley. An army of pro-British Tories and the Indians would advance eastward from Lake Ontario. The main army, commanded by Howe, would march north from New York City. The three forces were to meet in Albany, New York, after destroying all Patriot forces in their paths, thus splitting the colonies in half.

Burgoyne moved south and recaptured Fort Ticonderoga in early July, but in late August Patriot militia beat the Tories and Indians near Fort Stanwix. The plan probably still would have worked if Howe had proceeded according to plan. But he decided to take Philadelphia en route to meeting Burgoyne at Albany.

On 25 August 1777 Howe landed 15,000 men on the shores of the Chesapeake Bay about 50 miles south of Philadelphia. Howe's use of water transport had kept Washington guessing about his intentions for two months. When he finally received word that Howe's armada of 260 ships had entered the Chesapeake, Washington quickly moved most of his army south of Philadelphia to Brandywine Creek. But the Americans were no match for the superior British forces, and after a two-day battle on 10 and 11 September, the British marched in triumph into Philadelphia as the Continental Congress fled. Howe then quartered his army comfortably in Philadelphia for the winter, while Washington's men faced terrible cold and hunger at Valley Forge, northwest of the city. However, as events were to turn out, although Howe had taken Philadelphia, by not following the British plan he contributed to the eventual defeat of the British in the colonies.

THE TURNING POINT: THE BATTLE OF SARATOGA

Burgoyne was now by himself in northern New York, and he was in trouble. His supply line was stretched through the wilderness, and his men were running short of food. Through the summer of 1777 militiamen from New York and New England constantly harassed his troops.

Almost in desperation, on 19 September Burgoyne marched his men European-style through an open field to try to break through the American lines near Saratoga, New York. They made easy targets for American sharpshooters, who were firing from behind trees. When the British retreated, the Americans followed, only to be driven back by British bayonets. The two forces took turns advancing and retreating. On 7 October Burgoyne led his trapped Redcoats in a final attempt to break through American lines. Once more, Daniel Morgan's riflemen mowed them down. The British retreated when General Benedict Arnold led a charge. Burgoyne had lost 1,200 men and was surrounded by a total of 15,000 American militiamen and regulars under Major General Horatio Gates. Burgoyne finally surrendered on 17 October 1777.

Saratoga marked the turning point of the war in two ways. First, after Burgoyne's defeat, the British government was less willing to carry on the war. Lord North, England's prime minister, offered to repeal the British tax laws that had caused the war if the Patriots would stop fighting and remain under British rule. But by now the leaders of the Revolution were dedicated to winning freedom for a new nation.

Even more important, the American victory at Saratoga now brought the French into the war on the American side. A few months after declaring independence, the Continental Congress had sent Benjamin Franklin to France. He tried to convince the French that joining the American cause was the best way for them to take world leadership away from England. After Saratoga, the French finally decided that the Americans had a chance of winning the war, and they signed a treaty of friendship with the former colonies on 6 February 1778. In June France declared war on England and began actively helping the Patriots win their freedom. A year later Spain joined the war as France's ally, followed by the Netherlands in 1780.

The naval battle on Lake Champlain had set the stage for Saratoga. Saratoga helped bring France and, later, Spain and the Netherlands into the war on the American side. These allies made American victory and independence possible.

THE WAR AT SEA

American naval efforts in American waters during the war were mostly just a nuisance to Britain. By 1780 only a few of the forty converted merchantmen and thirteen frigates built for the Continental Navy remained in American hands. Though these vessels captured many British ships, they did not affect the outcome of the war. The small naval forces of the coastal states were also largely ineffective, as British ships were able to sail freely up and down the coast throughout most of the war.

American privateers were the biggest problem for the British in the offshore waters of the Atlantic. They hurt British trade in the West Indies, delayed troop transports bringing reinforcements, and captured arms and supplies that the colonial forces badly needed. However, privateering also took away men, ships, and weapons that the Continental Navy could have used. Despite the problems they caused, the privateers did not greatly harm the British war effort. Washington had been right when he said that naval power would decide the outcome of the war, but in the end, it was French, not American, naval power that made the difference.

The American naval record in more distant waters, however, was impressive. The tiny Continental Navy and several American naval heroes won glory overseas during the war. The most famous of them was John Paul Jones, who took the war to European waters with inspiring results.

Jones received command of the new eighteen-gun *Ranger* in June 1777 and sailed to France. In the spring of 1778 Jones took the *Ranger* around Britain and Ireland, where he captured HMS *Drake* and several merchant ships.

One year later, Jones was given command of an old forty-two-gun converted French merchantman, which he renamed the *Bonhomme Richard* in honor of Benjamin Franklin, who had written *Poor Richard's Almanac*. In August 1779 Jones sailed in command of a small squadron that included the American frigate *Alliance*, which

John Paul Jones was one of the first naval heroes of the new American Republic. As the inscription on his tomb under the Naval Academy chapel reads, "He gave to our Navy its earliest traditions of heroism and victory."

The *Bonhomme Richard*, commanded by Captain John Paul Jones, engages HMS *Serapis*, a powerful British frigate, on 23 September 1779.

carried thirty-six guns, and three smaller French vessels. The captain of the *Alliance* was an unpredictable Frenchman named Pierre Landais.

On 23 September 1779 Jones's squadron was trailing a large English convoy off the northeast coast of England when its two escorts approached at dusk. The British warships were the fifty-gun HMS *Serapis,* under Captain Richard Pearson, and the twenty-gun *Countess of Scarborough.* Jones immediately ordered an attack, but the small French ships turned away. Later, though, the French frigate *Pallas* took the *Countess* after a sharp fight.

The *Richard* and the *Serapis* both began to fire broadsides as soon as they came into range. Early in the exchange, however, two of Jones's 18-pounder cannons exploded on the lower gun deck, killing all the crewmen there and blowing a huge hole in the deck above. Jones saw that his only hope was to lay the *Richard* alongside and take the *Serapis* by boarding. He ordered grapples heaved, and then he seized one of the forestays from the British vessel and tied it to the *Richard*'s mizzenmast himself. For the rest of the battle, the two ships swung together stern to bow and bow to stern, their guns firing directly into each other.

After two hours of fighting, the crew of the *Richard* had cleared the topside weather decks of the *Serapis,* but the *Richard* was full of holes. At this point the *Alliance* reappeared. A glad shout went up from the Americans, but it was quickly drowned out when the *Alliance* fired a broadside that ripped into the *Richard* instead of the *Serapis.* The *Alliance* fired two more broadsides into the *Richard,* and then withdrew. Landais later told a friend

that he had hoped to become the victor by sinking the *Richard* and capturing the *Serapis* himself. Jones later brought charges against Landais, and he was dismissed from the French Navy.

The *Richard* slowly began to sink. At this point Captain Pearson of the British ship asked if Jones was ready to strike. Jones replied with the immortal words, "I have not yet begun to fight!" At about 2130 hours an American seaman dropped a grenade through an open hatch on the *Serapis.* The grenade hit powder cartridges in the British vessel, and the explosions killed many of her gunners.

Jones's crew now came topside to fight hand to hand. The fighting continued for an hour, until at 2230 Captain Pearson tore down his flag with his own hands. He had been shaken by the explosions and the ferocity of the hand-to-hand fighting and was afraid his tottering mainmast would collapse.

The battered *Richard* went down two days later, and Jones raised the American flag on board the *Serapis.* Then, avoiding the British ships that were trying to find him, he sailed his squadron and prizes to Holland.

THE CLOSING CAMPAIGNS

With France its enemy, Britain could no longer concentrate all its efforts in the colonies. The British were now determined to stand on the defensive in the north, mount an offensive in the south, and take the war to the West Indies.

Sir Henry Clinton, who was put in command of the British forces in the colonies, abandoned Philadelphia and moved his army through New Jersey to reinforce New York City. Meanwhile the French vice admiral Comte d'Estaing was on his way to America with a French fleet of twelve ships. Had he arrived sooner, he could have caught General Howe, who was transporting Clinton's artillery and supplies on the Delaware River. But d'Estaing arrived too late, and Howe completed his transit of the Delaware on 28 June 1778. Howe delivered Clinton's supplies the next day, and then he stationed frigates in New York Harbor to warn of the approach of the French naval forces.

When d'Estaing arrived off New York on 11 July, General Washington offered to launch a land attack while d'Estaing attacked by sea. But the French ships could not get into the shallow harbor, so d'Estaing sailed away to the Caribbean, where he remained for over a year.

D'Estaing returned to the colonies in September 1779 to help the Americans try to recapture New York. On 9 October French ships and troops, together with American troops, launched an attack, but the British held them off. D'Estaing returned to France with his fleet.

In Morristown, Washington's troops were suffering through their most difficult winter. Confident that these troops were not a threat to New York City, Clinton mounted a major offensive in the south in February 1780. His large fleet set sail for Charleston, South Carolina, and surrounded the American forces there. The city had held off the British for three years, but Clinton's new force was overwhelming, and the city's defenses soon broke down. On 12 May the entire garrison of 5,000 men surrendered to the British. The last Continental naval squadron was captured in Charleston Harbor at about this time, so the Continental Navy was never again an effective fighting force.

In August 1780 Clinton received word that a French fleet bringing 5,500 soldiers had arrived in Newport, Rhode Island. He left General Lord Cornwallis, who had come with him, in command in the south and hurried back to New York. Cornwallis defeated General Gates's forces at Camden, South Carolina, and took the city in mid-August. Then Cornwallis moved into North Carolina, and Washington could do nothing to stop him.

In October General Nathaniel Greene's troops defeated a Tory force at King's Mountain, South Carolina, and in January 1781 General Morgan destroyed a British force under General Tarleton at Cowpens. Cornwallis followed Morgan and Greene through North Carolina. He won a battle at Guilford Courthouse, but he lost so many men that he had to retreat. Cornwallis retreated to Wilmington, North Carolina, and asked the Royal Navy to send help to him there. When help did not arrive, he disobeyed Clinton's orders and led his troops into Virginia, where he would soon be trapped.

THE BATTLE OF YORKTOWN

Cornwallis successfully raided some areas in Virginia, then he followed Clinton's orders to entrench his army at Yorktown, on the Chesapeake Bay, late in the summer. The Marquis de Lafayette, an influential young Frenchman who had been appointed a general in the Continental Army in 1777, immediately sent word of Cornwallis's move to General Washington. Lafayette and General "Mad Anthony" Wayne commanded about 5,000 ragged militia in the area, and these troops kept Cornwallis under observation.

In the meantime, French general Comte de Rochambeau, who had brought troops to Newport a year earlier to aid Washington, learned in May 1781 that reinforcements were not coming. In spite of this, he and Washington agreed to battle Clinton's superior troops in New York. Washington wrote to the French minister to ask him to urge Admiral de Grasse, in command of French naval forces in the West Indies, to come north from the Caribbean to join the New York operation.

On 14 August 1781 the letter on which everything hinged arrived at Washington's headquarters. De Grasse reported that he would arrive in the Chesapeake with more than twenty-five warships and 3,000 troops in September. Four days later, Washington ordered 4,500 Americans and General Rochambeau's French army of 5,500 to march from New York to Yorktown. He left enough men behind to protect West Point and to keep Clinton busy in New York. The French fleet sailed south from Newport. Washington hoped to bring all these land and sea forces together to battle the British at Yorktown.

On 5 September the American and French troops passed through Philadelphia, and General Washington learned that de Grasse was in Chesapeake Bay. On the evening of 14 September Washington and Rochambeau greeted Lafayette and Wayne at Williamsburg, Virginia, and then set up siege lines around Yorktown. The next morning the land forces learned that off the Virginia Capes, de Grasse had driven the British fleet back to New York on 5 September, and that the French fleet from Newport had arrived with artillery and supplies on 10 September. The stage was now set for the attack against Cornwallis.

Twenty thousand French and American troops attacked Yorktown on 9 October. For eight days the combined land forces fired artillery at the British while the French fleets bombarded the city. American forces also stormed two key defensive positions and kept the British from fleeing across the York River to Gloucester. The British fleet that had retreated to New York returned to the Chesapeake with Clinton and 6,000 British troops one week too late to help Cornwallis. He had surrendered his entire army of 7,600 men to General Washington on 19 October 1781.

The British loss at Yorktown marked the end of the fighting in the colonies. The war then shifted to the West Indies, the Mediterranean, and India. England, tired of war, now faced the powerful combined forces of France, Spain, and the Netherlands in Europe.

In February 1782 Lord North resigned, and the new pacifist cabinet in Parliament decided not to launch any more offensive attacks in North America. England sent a representative to Paris to discuss peace with the Americans there. The American delegation, headed by Benjamin Franklin, John Jay, and John Adams, insisted on American independence. England still held New York, Charleston, and Savannah in the colonies, but the pressure in Europe was working to the Americans' advantage.

The treaty that the Americans and the British drew up gave the colonies their full independence. They would not be under British rule or protection in any way. The colonies received a territory that extended west to the Mississippi, north to the Great Lakes, and south to Florida. The U.S. Congress declared the war over on 11 April 1783, but it was not until 3 September that the American and British representatives signed the Peace of Paris.

The small Continental Navy was generally ineffective throughout the war in the face of what was then the most powerful navy on earth. But it was plain that sea power had played a major role in America gaining its independence. Much of the artillery and other supplies used by the Continental Army came from prizes captured at sea and were delivered by sea routes of supply. Though no one won the battle off the Virginia Capes in 1781, the French fleet prevented the British from helping Cornwallis, leading directly to his surrender. To many Americans, it had become obvious that to keep its freedom America needed a navy of its own.

Chronology

1775	Revolution begins
13 Oct. 1775	Congress establishes Navy
11–13 Oct. 1776	Battle of Lake Champlain
25 Dec. 1776	Washington crosses Delaware
17 Oct. 1777	Burgoyne surrenders at Saratoga
6 Feb. 1778	France allies with America
23 Sept. 1779	Jones defeats *Serapis*
12 May 1780	Charleston surrenders
9–19 Oct. 1781	Battle of Yorktown

Study Guide Questions

1. As a result of the Seven Years' War, whose worldwide colonial possessions did Britain obtain?

2. A. Why did the British Parliament begin to lay burdensome taxes on the American colonies?
   B. What happened in 1773 as a result of the Townshend Act?

3. What did the British response to the Boston Tea Party lead to in April 1775?

4. What naval materials did the colonies supply to the British Navy?

5. When was the Marine Corps established?

6. What were the problems of recruiting a crew in the early Continental Navy?

7. How did the American invasion of Canada in 1775 turn out?

8. A. Who was the American commander at the first Battle of Lake Champlain in 1776?
   B. What was the important outcome of the battle?

9. A. What was the overall British plan to defeat the Americans in 1777?
   B. What happened?
   C. Why was the Battle of Saratoga vital to the American cause?
   D. What were the names of the opposing generals in this battle?

10. Who was the great American diplomat who brought about the French alliance early in 1778?

11. Who was the greatest American naval hero of the Revolutionary War?

12. A. Where did John Paul Jones have his famous battle with HMS *Serapis*?
    B. What was the name of the ship commanded by Jones?
    C. What was Jones's strategy in the fight?

13. What was Jones's famous reply when the British captain asked if he was ready to strike his colors?

14. A. What crucial naval battle made victory at the Battle of Yorktown possible?
    B. Who were the American and French commanders at Yorktown?

15. A. After Yorktown, where did the British concentrate their war effort?
    B. When did the war officially end?

Vocabulary

impressment	desertion
artillery	reinforcements
delegation	grenade
powder cartridge	topside
weather decks	broadside
forestay	mainmast
mizzenmast	militia
garrison	

3

The Growth of American Sea Power, 1783–1860

When the Treaty of Paris ended the Revolutionary War in 1783, the new nation was badly in debt. The government did not have authority to raise money through taxation, so there were no funds for maintaining ships or building new ones. In 1783, when the *Alliance* was sold, the old Continental Navy passed into history. The officers and men who had served in the Continental Navy returned to their peacetime jobs of merchant shipping and ship-building.

American merchant mariners and shipbuilders soon found, however, that the British were not going to make life easy for them. The British government issued Orders in Council that sought to keep Americans out of the East Indies trade, limited exports to England, and made it illegal for British subjects to buy ships built in America.

Thus, American merchants had to find new overseas markets for their trade. Some looked to China, but it was far away, and getting there took a lot of time and money. Now that the protection of the British flag was removed, American ships trading in the Mediterranean and eastern Atlantic region became subject to harassment by pirates from the Barbary states of Morocco, Algiers, Tunis, and Tripoli. They had been capturing ships and crews for ransom in these waters for hundreds of years. European nations such as Britain, France, and the Netherlands had long paid these states tribute money so they could sail these waters in safety, but the United States had no such arrangements. In 1784 and 1785 three American ships were seized by the Barbary pirates. The United States concluded a treaty of peace and friendship with Morocco in 1786, but no agreements were reached with the other Barbary states for another ten years.

A NEW AMERICAN GOVERNMENT

In 1789 the Articles of Confederation were replaced by the U.S. Constitution. The Constitution authorized Congress "to provide and maintain a navy," but other needs in the new nation were more pressing. Besides, a war had started between Portugal and Algiers, and this made it possible for American merchantmen in the Mediterranean to join with Portuguese and Spanish convoys for protection. The need for a navy seemed less urgent.

One of the first acts of the new U.S. government helped American merchants. The government decided to impose tariffs (taxes) on incoming foreign shipping, which gave an immediate advantage to U.S. shipping. Additionally, British West Indian planters needed and began welcoming U.S. ships and the goods they carried, despite the Orders in Council that prohibited such trade.

With these incentives, U.S. shipping and shipbuilding grew rapidly until 1793. In that year Portugal and Algiers declared a truce, and soon thereafter, a pirate fleet captured ten U.S. ships in the Mediterranean. In addition, in 1790 the Napoleonic Wars had broken out in Europe, and France had declared war on Britain. British warships then began to seize neutral vessels trading with France, and French privateers began capturing neutral vessels trading with British possessions such as the West Indies. The time had come for the United States to give serious consideration to building a navy.

THE NAVY ACT OF 1794

Not all Americans were in favor of building a navy. Those who lived inland did not want to be taxed for something they felt would benefit mainly those who lived along the coast. So the Navy Act that Congress eventually passed in 1794 provided for only six frigates, and their construction would stop if the United States made peace with Algiers. In 1796 this happened, but President Washington convinced Congress to allow work on three of the frigates to be completed. The *United States* and *Constitution*, both forty-four guns, and the *Constellation*, thirty-eight guns, were launched in 1797.

The British realized early in their war with Napoleon's France that they would need trade goods carried in U.S. ships, and so they stopped seizing them.

The British and the Americans worked out their other maritime differences in Jay's Treaty, which the two countries signed in 1797.

The French were outraged by this agreement, and they increased their raids on U.S. ships. In one year French privateers in the West Indies and along the U.S. Atlantic coast seized over 300 U.S. merchant ships. In the fall of 1797 President John Adams sent three representatives to Paris to try to work out a settlement. The French wanted these men to pay a huge bribe to begin the talks, but they refused. Americans everywhere responded to the French demand with the slogan "Millions for defense, but not one cent for tribute!"

The French XYZ affair, as this came to be called, put Congress in the mood to finish building the six frigates authorized in 1794. The *President,* forty-four guns, and two thirty-six-gun ships, the *Congress* and the *Chesapeake,* were soon launched, along with some smaller vessels. On 30 April 1798 Congress established the Navy Department. The following month, it allowed U.S. vessels to seize armed French ships that were found cruising in U.S. coastal waters. The United States had started an undeclared naval war, the Quasi-War with France.

QUASI-WAR WITH FRANCE, 1798–1800

As commander in chief, President Adams made sure that U.S. seamen were well paid and well fed. Therefore, the Navy had plenty of recruits from the merchant marine (commercially owned and operated shipping). Many of the fifty ships that eventually made up the wartime Navy also came from the merchant marine.

Adams had men and ships. Now he needed a leader. He chose a merchant shipper from Maryland, Benjamin Stoddert, to be his first secretary of the navy. Stoddert immediately ordered his warships to patrol the Atlantic coast. The first American prize was the *Croyable.* Captured in July 1798, this privateer was renamed the *Retaliation* and put in service in the U.S. Navy.

That same month, Congress extended its authorization and allowed U.S. ships to capture armed French ships on the high seas. Stoddert was then able to send a series of expeditions to the West Indies, where most of the French privateers were based. The first mission, led by Commodore John Barry, captured only two privateers because most of the French ships were able to escape into shallow water where the U.S. vessels could not follow. In the second expedition, which arrived in the fall of 1798, Lieutenant William Bainbridge was defeated in the *Retaliation,* which was returned to French hands.

After the U.S. Navy cleared U.S. coastal waters, Stoddert sent twenty-one ships in four squadrons to the West Indies. There, U.S. vessels were allowed to use British bases and had the support of the Royal Navy. U.S. officers and seamen learned many useful things as they served with what was then the finest navy in the world.

Commodore Thomas Truxtun was one of the Americans who worked hard to profit from the lessons learned from the Royal Navy. In his ship the *Constellation,* Truxtun fought the two most famous battles of the Quasi-War. The first took place in February 1799, when the *Constellation* encountered the French frigate *Insurgente* while on patrol in the Caribbean. After a brief fight the *Constellation* holed *Insurgente's* hull so many times that her captain had to surrender. In the second battle a year later, the *Constellation* fought the French frigate *Vengeance* to a draw after a five-hour battle off Guadeloupe.

Finally, in October 1800, after more than two years of undeclared war, a peace treaty was signed between France and the United States. One of the provisions in the treaty was a very unpopular clause canceling U.S. claims against the French for attacking U.S. merchant ships. Partly because of all the uproar the treaty caused, Thomas Jefferson was able to defeat John Adams in the presidential election of 1800.

During the war, the U.S. fleet had grown rapidly. U.S. exports had risen to more than $200 million, and the income from imports was more than $22 million. The Navy had spent only $6 million to protect this commerce from the French. It was clear that the Navy benefited New England shipping, but it also benefited the economy of the entire nation.

WAR WITH TRIPOLI AND THE BARBARY PIRATES, 1801–1805

As part of his campaign for the presidential election of 1800, Jefferson had promised to reduce government spending. The Navy cost the country over $2 million every year, so after he was elected, making the Navy smaller was one way for Jefferson to keep his promise. He began to sell off smaller naval ships.

Then the Barbary pirates began to cause more trouble. When the frigate *George Washington* arrived in Algiers with a tribute payment in September 1800, the dey of Algiers (the Algerian leader) ordered Captain William Bainbridge to take passengers and the tribute payment to the sultan in Constantinople. When Bainbridge refused, the dey aimed the guns of the fortress at the frigate and forced Bainbridge to carry out his orders. After this incident, other Barbary states increased their tribute demands. Jefferson refused to pay them. In May 1801, when the United States did not meet the tribute demands of the pasha (ruler) of Tripoli, he declared war on the United States.

That summer, the twelve-gun schooner USS *Enterprise* blockaded the port of Tripoli for eighteen days and then left for Malta. On the way she met and defeated a Tripolitan cruiser, the *Tripoli.* Other U.S. warships convoyed U.S. merchantmen through the Mediterranean.

But by the end of summer, most of the crews' enlistments were running out, so the squadron had to return home.

A more powerful squadron was prepared for the next year. This squadron arrived in the spring of 1802, under the command of Richard Morris. The Americans were able only to capture one Tripolitan cruiser and destroy another. Morris's blockade of Tripoli was not effective, and Tripoli refused to lower its price for peace. Embarrassed by these failures, President Jefferson ordered Morris replaced by Commodore Edward Preble.

The officers serving Preble at first did not like their commander because he was very strict. After seeing their leader in action, however, the officers were proud to be called "Preble's Boys." Preble was at first worried because his officers were all younger than thirty. "They have given me nothing but a pack of boys!" he said. But the young officers' aggressive spirit and quick minds soon won Preble's respect.

When Preble arrived in Gibraltar in September 1803, he found that Morocco had broken its treaty with the United States by capturing a U.S. vessel. He quickly sent the *Philadelphia* under Captain Bainbridge and a schooner to blockade Tripoli. Then he assembled a powerful force in the Moroccan port of Tangier. The emperor of Morocco was impressed by Preble's display of strength, and after that he kept his treaty with the United States.

THE *PHILADELPHIA* INCIDENT

While she was blockading Tripoli, the *Philadelphia* had run aground and been captured. Her crew of more than 300 were then held for ransom. Unfortunately, the Tripolitans were able to free the U.S. vessel from the reef she was on, and they anchored her near the guns of the castle.

Commodore Preble's squadron arrived off Tripoli in December. Preble saw that the *Philadelphia* was too closely guarded to be recaptured, but he wanted to destroy her so that Tripoli could not use her.

Lieutenant Stephen Decatur Jr. volunteered to lead a raiding party into the harbor to burn the *Philadelphia*. On 16 February 1804 Decatur and his men slipped into the harbor in a captured Tripolitan ketch renamed the *Intrepid*. Decatur disguised himself in Maltese dress and stood next to his vessel's Sicilian pilot. Some of his seventy volunteers, also in disguise, stayed on deck, but most hid below.

As the *Intrepid* came near her target, a Tripolitan guard warned the vessel to stay away. The pilot told the guard that the *Intrepid* had lost her anchors in a storm and asked to be allowed to tie up. The guard agreed, but then, just as the *Intrepid* was passing her lines, the guard became suspicious and shouted, "Americanos!"

Decatur immediately ordered, "Board!" and led his men over the side. The few Tripolitan guards on duty in the *Philadelphia* put up little fight. Several were killed, and the rest jumped overboard. Decatur's men set fire to the ship, and the *Philadelphia* was soon engulfed in flames. The Americans then reboarded the *Intrepid* and returned safely to the squadron, despite being fired upon by the Tripolitan fort and several warships.

When news of the exploit reached the United States, Decatur was hailed as a hero and given a captain's commission. At twenty-five he was the youngest man to reach that rank in the short history of the U.S. Navy.

The burning of the captured frigate *Philadelphia* on 16 February 1804.

Stephen Decatur, promoted to captain at age twenty-five by President Jefferson as a result of his heroism during the war with Tripoli in 1804, was the youngest to achieve this rank in U.S. naval history.

ATTACK ON TRIPOLI

During the summer of 1804, Preble tried to convince the pasha of Tripoli to release the crewmen of the *Philadelphia,* but he refused. Preble decided he would have to use force. He obtained half a dozen gunboats plus some other craft from the king of Naples and attacked Tripoli on 3 August. Nine Tripolitan gunboats came out to attack them. The Tripolitans were ready to board and fight hand to hand, but the Americans surprised them by leaping into the lead Tripolitan vessels and fighting wildly.

Decatur and his men captured the first enemy gunboat while the squadron kept the others away. During the battle, Decatur broke off the blade of his cutlass and would have been killed if a seaman named Reuben James had not thrust his own head under a sword meant for Decatur.

As Decatur was towing his prize out of the harbor, he learned that his younger brother James had been shot as he stepped on board to take control of another enemy gunboat that had surrendered. That gunboat was trying to escape when Stephen Decatur overtook her, boarded her, and killed her captain in a hand-to-hand fight.

By the time Preble called an end to the battle, the Americans had captured three enemy gunboats. Following this attack, the pasha of Tripoli offered to return the U.S. crewmen for $150,000 in ransom money and to demand no more tribute. Preble rejected the offer and ordered his forces to bombard Tripoli. The Americans continued the bombardment during the next few weeks, but the enemy gunboats never again came out to fight the U.S. vessels.

President Jefferson and the U.S. public were spurred to action by Preble's feats. They hoped that a final victory would end the war with Tripoli and make all of the Barbary states stop demanding tribute. Jefferson sent a powerful U.S. naval force to the Mediterranean, and he ordered Captain Samuel Barron to replace Preble. The United States gave Preble a hero's welcome when he returned to Washington.

The U.S. naval forces kept Tripoli blockaded through the early part of 1805, and plans were made for a better blockade and more attacks on the city in the summer, when more gunboats were to arrive from America.

In the meantime, however, William Eaton, a bold U.S. naval agent to the Barbary states, devised a scheme to topple the pasha from his throne. He convinced the pasha's dethroned older brother, Hamet, to join a ragtag army of about 400 men he had put together. In return, Eaton agreed to restore Hamet to the throne.

Eaton's army, which included a few U.S. marines, marched 600 miles across the Libyan desert in early March 1805. Along the way, 700 additional men joined to help Hamet's cause. This force captured the Tripolitan city of Derna with the help of two brigs and a schooner from the naval squadron. (The phrase "to the shores of Tripoli" in the Marine Hymn refers to this operation.) Eaton held the city for several weeks, and then came word that the war was over. In return for $60,000 in ransom and a promise that the United States would no longer support his brother, the pasha agreed to a treaty that released the captive crew members and ended all tribute payments. Eaton did not want to break his promise to Hamet, but the United States was anxious to end the war.

Some Americans were pleased by the treaty with Tripoli. They believed the ransom was reasonable and should be paid to free the captives, who had suffered for a year and a half. They also welcomed the end of tribute paying. The Americans who did not like the treaty thought that more attacks on Tripoli would have forced it and the other Barbary states to accept treaties that were more favorable to the United States. As it turned out, the Americans who opposed the treaty were correct.

TRIPOLI'S LESSONS

Between 1803 and 1805 the only vessels built for the U.S. Navy were small gunboats. President Jefferson did not favor building large seagoing ships because he believed the Navy should protect the U.S. coastline, not carry out attacks on the high seas.

Other nations immediately saw this "gunboat diplomacy" as a weakness. The dey of Algiers again began capturing U.S. ships and making slaves of their crews and passengers. The British began impressing U.S. seamen to serve in the Royal Navy in England's war with France.

Impressments and other British actions against the United States led to the War of 1812. During that war the forces of the United States were too busy to take steps against Algiers. But on 2 March 1815, less than two weeks after the peace treaty ending the War of 1812 went into effect, Congress declared war on the Barbary states.

In the Algerine War, as it was called, the dey's fleet was quickly defeated by a powerful U.S. naval squadron commanded by Stephen Decatur, now a commodore. U.S. victory and the end of our troubles with the Barbary states finally came in 1816.

The lesson offered by the war with Tripoli has two parts. First, giving in to demands for tribute and ransom (appeasement) usually only leads to more demands. Second, a weak navy invites aggressive actions by enemies. Refusing to give in to demands and maintaining a strong navy help to keep a nation out of war.

AMERICA MOVES TOWARD WAR WITH ENGLAND

As mentioned previously, throughout the 1790s Napoleon Bonaparte's France had been at war with most of Europe. In 1797 he attempted to conquer Egypt, but he was defeated by Britain's Admiral Lord Nelson at the Battle of Abu Qir Bay in August 1798. Still, he was able to seize control of the French government in 1799, and the following year he forced Spain to cede to France the Louisiana Territory in America. In 1802 the British and French agreed to peace in the Treaty of Amiens, but Napoleon knew that further conflict with the British was inevitable. Besides, the Louisiana Territory was far away and difficult to administer. So in 1803, as a way to finance his anticipated war against England, Napoleon sold the Louisiana Territory to the United States for $15 million. Napoleon also hoped that this would cause the United States to look with favor toward France in its coming struggle with Britain, which began again later in 1803.

For two years following the outbreak of war between France and Britain in 1803, the U.S. merchant marine made great profits as the leading remaining neutral carrier of ocean commerce. But in 1805 that changed. At the Battle of Trafalgar that year, the British fleet under Admiral Nelson smashed the combined fleets of France and Spain, France's ally, making Britain ruler of the seas. At the Battle of Austerlitz in December 1805 in Austria, Napoleon crushed the combined Austrian and Russian armies, which made France master of the European continent. England and France then struck against each other's sea lines of communication, an action that inevitably would involve the United States.

Once again, as had happened in the mid-1790s, U.S. merchant ships were subjected to harassment and capture as prizes on the high seas. British Orders in Council closed French ports to foreign shipping, and French decrees ordered French privateers to seize any ships trading with England or carrying British goods to continental European ports. Nevertheless, U.S. merchants continued to make great profits by trading desperately needed supplies with both sides.

Gradually, however, American sentiment turned against the British because of increasing incidents of impressments as the war dragged on. According to British naval custom, if short of crew, British warship captains could stop any British merchantmen and take the men needed to fill their crews. But problems arose when the British began seizing seamen off U.S. ships, claiming they were deserters from the Royal Navy. This may have had some basis in fact, for conditions in the Royal Navy were often bad, and U.S. merchant seamen made good wages. It was not uncommon for British warships to lose a significant part of their crews to desertion whenever they visited an American port during these years.

THE *CHESAPEAKE* AFFAIR

Bad as the growing number of impressments on merchant ships was, irate feelings against the British became even more inflamed when a U.S. warship was boarded and some of her crew were forcibly removed. In 1807 the U.S. frigate *Chesapeake*, thirty-six guns, was set upon by the HMS *Leopard*, fifty guns, off Cape Henry, Virginia. The *Chesapeake* was fired upon and forced to surrender, after which the British took four of her seamen. One was soon hanged as a British deserter.

The nation was outraged, and there were many demands for a declaration of war against England. President Jefferson, however, was greatly opposed to any American involvement in the European wars. So he tried to stop the movement toward war by having Congress pass an embargo (stoppage) of exports of needed raw materials and food to Europe. He hoped that this would force the European powers to respect U.S. rights.

All that the embargo did, however, was cause severe economic strain for U.S. shipping companies in New England and for farmers in the South and West. Soon smuggling became rampant, further draining revenue from the government. And neither Britain nor France stopped impressing American seamen or seizing U.S. merchant ships. By 1812, the English had taken over 900 U.S. ships and had impressed more than 6,000 U.S. citizens into duty with the Royal Navy. France had seized over 500 U.S. merchant ships.

FINAL MOVES TOWARD WAR

James Madison became president in 1809. The next year congressional elections brought into office young "War Hawks" from the South and West. These men called for an end to pacifism and urged an invasion of Canada as punishment for the outrages at sea. They also wanted to expand U.S. territory. Madison did not want war, so he urged Congress to make one last try to halt the harassment at sea. Congress passed a bill stating that the United States would cease importing from any nation that did not do away with restrictions on U.S. trade.

In response, Napoleon quickly repealed all French decrees against U.S. shipping, hoping this would bring the United States into the war against Britain if the British did not follow suit. Britain did not repeal the Orders in Council, so Madison enforced the law against importing British goods. This angered the British and made them think that the United States was teaming up with France against them. Britain kept up the impressment of sailors on the high seas and harassment of U.S. ships, and "Freedom of the seas!" became the War Hawks' slogan. Britain and the United States were moving toward war.

Matters reached the boiling point in April 1811, when the British frigate *Guerrière*, thirty-eight guns, stopped a U.S. merchantman off New York and impressed one of the ship's seamen, a native of Maine. Commodore John Rodgers was sent to sea in the forty-four-gun *President* to protect U.S. shipping. On the evening of 16 May off the Virginia capes, the *President* came upon a ship that refused to identify herself. It is unclear who fired first, but the *President* soon silenced the stranger by pouring broadsides into her. The ship drifted away in the night, but the next morning Rodgers saw her a short distance away in great distress. The ship turned out to be the British sloop of war HMS *Little Belt,* twenty guns. She managed to limp into Halifax, Nova Scotia, with thirty-two dead and wounded crewmen. Rodgers was hailed as a hero for getting revenge for the *Chesapeake.*

Also in 1811, the British incited Tecumseh, a Shawnee Indian chief, to unite the tribes in the old Northwest Territory against white settlers. The usual horrors of Indian warfare took place in the Indiana and Ohio Territories. In November 1811, General William Henry Harrison led a well-trained U.S. frontier army against the Indians at Tippecanoe Creek in Indiana. He won an important victory, and Tecumseh fled to Canada to join British forces.

New England senators and congressmen did not want to go to war, for in spite of the harassment at sea, their voters back home would get rich if only one ship in three made it to port. But the War Hawks, under the strong leadership of Henry Clay, Speaker of the House, and Senator John C. Calhoun, finally persuaded Madison to ask Congress to declare war. On 18 June 1812 the United States declared war on Britain, for impressment, interference with neutral trade, and British plots with the Indians in the Northwest.

THE WAR OF 1812

The U.S. Navy in 1812 had only sixteen ships, seven of them frigates. Many were in need of repairs, and all were short of crew. Wood for shipbuilding and stores had been used up. Several hundred useless little gunboats built by Jefferson lay rotting in rivers and harbors along the East Coast. The same congressmen who voted the nation into war had, only seven months before, voted down a plan to build a dozen large ships-of-the-line and twenty frigates.

Britain, on the other hand, had more than 600 men-of-war, including some 250 ships-of-the-line and frigates. Fortunately for the United States, most of this fleet was in Europe blockading the ports of Napoleon's France. Faced with these odds, the U.S. naval strategy was clear: try to protect the nation's sea trade while harassing the British Navy and sea commerce with small squadrons and individual commerce raiders.

In the early days of the war, U.S. land forces launched an invasion into Canada, but because it was poorly planned and met with stiff British and Canadian opposition, it was unsuccessful. The Canadians captured

a U.S. fort at Mackinac Island in Lake Huron, giving the British control of the upper Great Lakes region. Then the British chased the Americans out of Detroit, built a fleet on Lake Erie, and helped Tecumseh and his Indian allies continue fighting in the Northwest Territory.

THE WAR AT SEA

Things at sea went considerably better for the United States at first. Several significant victories were won by American warships in one-on-one encounters with British men-of-war. The first of these occurred on 19 August 1812, when the USS *Constitution,* commanded by Captain Isaac Hull, one of Preble's Boys, encountered HMS *Guerrière* off the coast of Nova Scotia. Of all British ships, Americans hated *Guerrière* most, because of her role in impressing American seamen a year earlier.

Captain Dacres of the *Guerrière* opened fire first, but Hull calmly told his gunnery officers to wait. By 1800 hours, Hull had brought the *Constitution* to within 100 yards of his opponent. With both ships running before the wind, he ordered his first broadside fired. Exchanges of broadside after broadside followed. Dacres saw his shot rip through the rigging or bounce harmlessly off the heavy oaken hull of the American ship, earning for her the nickname "Old Ironsides." The U.S. captain first aimed his fire at the enemy ship's waterline, making gaping holes that let water pour inside. Next he aimed at the masts. Within twenty minutes the *Guerrière*'s mizzenmast had been knocked off. It was soon followed by the foremast and mainmast. The battle was over, and Dacres surrendered. The *Guerrière* sank the next day.

Although at the time Americans called this one of the greatest battles of the war, in reality it was not of great importance. Though surprised and dismayed, the British

Seamen and gunners of the USS *Constitution* cheer at the start of action with the British frigate *Guerrière.* British shot bounced off the hull of the U.S. ship, giving her the name "Old Ironsides."

The USS *Constitution* defeats the British frigate *Guerrière* on 19 August 1812, pounding her to a hulk that would sink the next day.

could easily afford to lose one frigate in battle. But for Americans this was a great boost to morale. On the day Hull returned to Boston, word had been received of bad U.S. defeats in the land battles to the west. Detroit had fallen almost without a fight, and the Indians had captured Fort Dearborn (Chicago) and massacred everyone in it. The victory of the *Constitution* was indeed cause for joy.

OTHER HIGH SEAS BATTLES

In October 1812 another famous battle took place far across the Atlantic. The frigate *United States*, forty-four guns, under the command of Stephen Decatur, met the British frigate *Macedonian*, thirty-eight guns. In two hours Decatur wore the enemy down and captured the ship, a valuable prize.

In December the *Constitution*, now under the command of Captain William Bainbridge, defeated the British frigate *Java*, thirty-eight guns, off the coast of Brazil. In February 1813 Captain James Lawrence in the sloop of war *Hornet* met and sank the brig HMS *Peacock* off British Guiana.

The opening months of the war at sea had given the Americans much success. Not only had three British frigates and several smaller men-of-war been beaten, but Lloyd's of London, the major insurer of British merchant ships of the time, reported that nearly 500 merchant ships had been captured by Yankee privateers and commerce raiders.

Despite these victories, the U.S. Navy also suffered some significant losses. The most important of these happened on 1 June 1813, when the HMS *Shannon*, thirty-eight guns, under command of Captain Philip Broke, defeated the USS *Chesapeake*, thirty-six guns, now commanded by Captain James Lawrence, off Boston Harbor. During the conclusion of the fierce fifteen-minute battle, Lawrence was mortally wounded, and while being carried below, he cried out the immortal words "Don't give up the ship!" More than 200 men were dead or wounded on both sides. The *Chesapeake* was sailed into Halifax, Nova Scotia, by a prize crew, followed by the *Shannon*, pumps going to keep her afloat. Captain Lawrence died on the way.

BRITISH SEA POWER PREVAILS

The early victories at sea had given the United States new pride and respect. By 1813, however, the British had driven the French from the sea, and they were therefore able to increase the number of ships patrolling the U.S. coast and blockading U.S. ports. Once they returned from their victories, hardly any of the American warships could get to sea again for the duration of the war. Thus, after 1813 most of the burden of fighting the British at sea fell to the privateers. More than 500 of them were commissioned during the remainder of the war, most from Massachusetts, New York, and Maryland. Though they carried the war to the British and captured over 1,300 vessels by war's end, they could not take the place

A modern-day member of the crew of the USS *Constitution*, now in Boston Harbor. The ship is a popular historical attraction, and she is kept in sailing trim. She is the oldest U.S. ship still in commission.

Captain James Lawrence in the USS *Chesapeake* uttered some of the most famous words in U.S. naval history, when, fatally wounded aboard the USS *Chesapeake* during its battle with HMS *Shannon* in 1813, he told his crew, "Don't give up the ship!"

of a powerful navy. They could do nothing to stop the British blockade of East Coast ports. Consequently, by 1814 U.S. exports had fallen in value to only about one-tenth of what they had been in 1811. A Boston newspaper gave a gloomy picture of conditions at the time: "Our harbors blockaded; our shipping destroyed or rotting at the docks; silence and stillness in our cities; the grass growing upon the public wharves."

The Jeffersonians had claimed that no enemy could gather enough ships to blockade the entire U.S. coast, so it was not necessary to have a seagoing navy to protect seagoing commerce. The United States and its merchant marine paid a stiff price for that mistake.

THE GREAT LAKES CAMPAIGNS

After war had broken out in June 1812, there began on Lake Ontario a shipbuilding race between the British naval commander Sir James Yeo and his American counterpart, Commodore Isaac Chauncey. Both men had tal-

ent for building and organizing, but neither was willing to fight without overwhelming superiority. The result was a series of naval skirmishes throughout the war on the lake that decided nothing, and blockade efforts that lasted only until the other side built a new and bigger ship. This went on until war's end, when both sides had two-decker 58-gun men-of-war and were building 110-gun dreadnoughts, larger than any in service on the ocean at the time. None of these, however, saw any significant action during the war.

Because control of Lake Erie was key to control of the entire Northwest Territory, both sides saw it as an important objective in the early days of the war. Detroit had been surrendered to the British at the outbreak of war, and the British had control of the entire Northwest Territory down to Ohio, where American general William Harrison was sustaining a difficult defense against the British and their Indian allies. The British had a small squadron of armed vessels on the lake, but the Americans had no warships there at all. To remedy this situation President Madison sent a contingent of shipwrights to Presque Isle (now Erie, Pennsylvania) to begin building a small U.S. fleet there. Later, twenty-seven-year-old Captain Oliver Hazard Perry was sent there to take operational command.

When Perry arrived in the spring of 1813, he found things in a bad state. Work had begun on two twenty-

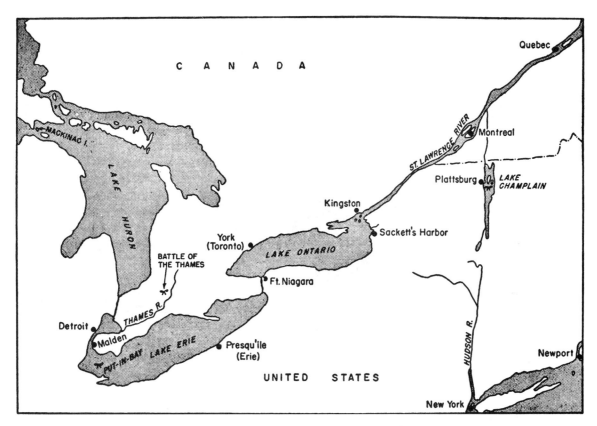

Campaigns of the eastern Great Lakes in the War of 1812. Principal actions were fought on Lake Erie and Lake Champlain.

gun brigs that would be better than anything the British had on the lake, but winter delayed their completion and fitting out until July 1813. Perry named one brig the *Niagara,* and the other the *Lawrence* for his good friend the late captain of the *Chesapeake,* and chose it for his flagship. Meanwhile, Commodore Yeo sent Commander Robert Barclay, a distinguished Trafalgar veteran, to command the British Lake Erie squadron.

After overcoming one obstacle after another, Perry finally went on patrol in August with his two brigs and seven other vessels. When Barclay sighted Perry's squadron, he beat a hasty retreat to his base at Malden on the northwest corner of Lake Erie to await completion of a new flagship, the twenty-gun brig *Detroit.* Perry moved west and consolidated his forces at Put-in-Bay in a group of islands opposite Malden.

By September things at Malden were getting desperate, as some 14,000 Indian allies of the British there were running out of food. It was imperative that Barclay move promptly to regain control of the sea lines of communication through Lake Erie to Malden. So, early on 10 September, despite knowing he was going against a superior force, Barkley sailed forth to meet Perry in a battle that would ultimately decide the fate of the entire Northwest Territory. Besides the *Detroit,* he had the ship *Queen Charlotte,* seventeen guns, and four smaller vessels.

Sighting the British, the American squadron came before the wind and approached the enemy. Flying from the masthead of the *Lawrence* was Perry's blue battle flag, inscribed with Captain Lawrence's dying command: "Don't Give Up the Ship." Perry took some punishment from the *Detroit*'s long guns. Then at close range he opened up with his carronades and rifle fire from a contingent of Kentucky marksmen manning the tops of his rigging. Soon nearly every man topside on the British ship, including most of her officers, was dead. If Lieutenant Elliot in command of the *Niagara* had done the same to the *Queen Charlotte,* the battle would have quickly been over. But Elliot harbored a grudge that he, not Perry, should have been placed in command of the squadron, and he chose to remain out of the *Charlotte*'s range. So for the next two hours Perry and the *Lawrence* battled four British vessels that gradually shot her to pieces and killed or wounded half her crew. At that point Perry had himself rowed through a hail of fire to the *Niagara* and took command from Elliot.

With his fresh new flagship, Perry steered across the British line, firing double-shotted broadsides for which the British had no real defense. One by one the British ships struck their colors, and at 1500 Barclay surrendered the remainder of his squadron. After returning to his shattered flagship *Lawrence,* Perry wrote the now-famous

The Battle of Lake Erie during the War of 1812. Oliver Hazard Perry is rowed from his damaged flagship, the *Lawrence*, to take command of the *Niagara*, from which he won a decisive victory.

dispatch about the victory to General Harrison: "We have met the enemy and they are ours." Lake Erie was now firmly under American control. The Kentuckians pursued the retreating British and Indians, defeating them in the Battle of the Thames. Tecumseh was killed in this battle, ending support for the British cause. Detroit was thus recaptured, and the Northwest Territory was secured, eventually becoming the states of Ohio, Indiana, Illinois, Michigan, Wisconsin, and part of Minnesota.

THE FINAL YEAR OF THE WAR

As war was breaking out between the United States and Britain in 1812, the British and their allies were beginning to achieve success against Napoleon's forces in Europe. In December 1812 Napoleon's armies in Russia were virtually annihilated. His defeat at Leipzig in October 1813 and his abdication of the French throne in April 1814 freed more and more British assets for deployment in the war against America. A large expedition against Louisiana was prepared. Another force was assembled to proceed to the Chesapeake Bay and attack Washington, D.C., and Baltimore.

In the summer of 1814 ships of the Royal Navy entered the Chesapeake Bay, swept aside a little flotilla of Jeffersonian gunboats, and landed 4,000 troops without opposition on the west bank of the Patuxent River. From there they marched on Washington, overwhelming the militiamen trying to defend the city on 24 and 25 August. After government officials, including President Madison,

fled in panic, the British set fire to the White House, the Capitol, and other public buildings. They did this partly in retaliation for Americans burning several towns in Canada earlier in the war, as well as for the effect they thought such action would have on American morale. The Americans burned two warships at the Washington Navy Yard to keep them from falling into enemy hands.

The British next turned their attention to Baltimore. They regarded this city as a "nest of pirates" because it was the home port of a great many privateers that had been raiding British merchantmen at sea. A British army of nearly 5,000 men stopped before the city's defenses to wait for a fleet of frigates and bomb vessels to silence Fort McHenry, which was located at the entrance to the harbor.

The night-long bombardment that began the evening of 13 September failed to bring down the U.S. flag waving defiantly over the fort. Francis Scott Key, a U.S. civilian being held aboard one of the British vessels, witnessed the stirring sight and wrote the words of "The Star-Spangled Banner," which later became our national anthem. Unable to get past the fort, a few days later the British reboarded the troops on their ships and sailed away.

In the Montreal area, in the summer of 1814 Sir George Prevost, governor general of Canada, had 12,000 troops, including four brigades fresh from the Peninsular campaign against Napoleon. They were preparing to advance down into the United States along the old Lake

Thomas Macdonough's victory at the Battle of Lake Champlain, September 1814. The U.S. victory caused the British to retreat into Canada and sign the Treaty of Ghent, ending the War of 1812.

Champlain route, used by Burgoyne during the Revolution. To oppose them the United States had only 1,500 troops, stationed at Plattsburg on the western shore of the lake. A small naval squadron under the command of Master Commandant Thomas Macdonough, another of Preble's Boys, assisted in the American defense.

Prevost delayed his invasion in order to wait until the British gained control of the lake. Otherwise American naval guns would be able to dominate the lakeside road that Prevost had to use, and the American squadron could prevent use of the lake as a sea line of communication along which to resupply his invasion force. The British quickly built a naval flotilla made up of the frigate *Confiance,* thirty-seven guns, three smaller warships, and twelve gunboats to challenge Macdonough for control of the lake. Completely outgunned, Macdonough hastily built the twenty-six-gun corvette *Saratoga,* the twenty-gun brig *Eagle,* two sailing vessels, and ten gunboats, all in a little more than a month.

Macdonough anchored his ships in Plattsburg Bay, a deep inlet on the western side of the lake, to await the British attack. He placed his ships close enough to shore that his line could not be circumvented. Then he ran out spring lines (ropes at sharp angles) from the sterns so that the ships could be swung around and the guns brought to bear from both sides. On 11 September the British squadron under command of Captain George Downie sailed south to do battle with the American fleet. When he learned that the British were outside the bay, Macdonough called his men to quarters and, imitating Nelson's famous message at Trafalgar, hoisted a message to his fleet: "Impressed seamen call on every man to do his duty."

Downie's squadron sailed south in line abreast to attack the Americans. Soon all vessels of both squadrons were engaged in furious gunfire. During the first few minutes a broadside from the *Saratoga* into the British flagship *Confiance* dismounted one of her guns, which rumbled across the deck and crushed Downie to death. When the engaged broadsides of both flagships were about smashed to silence, Macdonough swung his ship 180 degrees, thereby bringing a fresh broadside to bear on the *Confiance.* With water rising in her hull, and her commander killed, the British flagship surrendered, as did the rest of the British squadron a short time later. Over two hours of close fighting had cost both sides hundreds of casualties. For the second time in the war, and only the second time in history, an entire British fleet had been defeated. Prevost beat a hasty retreat back to Canada the next morning.

Macdonough's victory had a profound effect on peace negotiations, which had been taking place in Ghent for some time. The Duke of Wellington offered his opinion that the cost of any new offensive would vastly outweigh any probable gains, and that peace should be made at once, without demands for territory. The British government dropped their demand for territorial concessions and so notified the delegates at Ghent, thereby paving the way for conclusion of a peace treaty by year's end. On Christmas Eve 1814, the Treaty of Ghent was signed. It made no mention of impressments, or of neutral shipping rights at sea, the main reasons given by Madison for declaring war. These issues were no longer important, since the British had repealed the Orders in Council and the war in Europe was over.

CONCLUSION OF WAR

News traveled slowly in the early nineteenth century. Thus, even though the peace treaty ending the war had been signed in Europe, fighting continued in America. The British expedition to Louisiana had finally arrived off the mouth of the Mississippi River on 8 December 1814, after having been delayed several weeks by privateer actions in the Azores. Soon the British had swept through a flotilla of gunboats and sailing vessels arrayed against them, and on 23 December, they landed 8 miles below New Orleans and began skirmishing with U.S. general Andrew Jackson and his defenders. By the end of the first week in January, more than 8,000 British veterans under Major General Sir Edward Pakenham were ashore and ready to attack. Upstream, Jackson's force had grown to 4,000 men, including a contingent of ex-pirate Jean Lafitte's men and a naval battery manned by gunners from the disabled schooner *Louisiana.*

On 8 January 1815 Pakenham foolishly marched his men in a frontal assault against Jackson's strong position between the Mississippi and a swamp where he had dug in to prevent encirclement. Jackson's riflemen firing from behind cotton bales and earthworks mowed the British down. When the smoke cleared, Pakenham and over 2,000 of his troops were dead or wounded, and the rest were in flight.

The peace treaty finally arrived in the United States on 11 February, and Congress ratified it six days later. By and large, the treaty was welcome in both countries, since they had much more to gain from trade with each other than from war. The U.S. Navy had won new respect throughout the world. American diplomats were again treated with respect. The victories of the navy both at sea and on the Great Lakes united the nation and started a great naval tradition. The United States at last stood as an equal among the powers of the world, respected as never before.

THE UNITED STATES ADVANCES AS SEA POWER PROSPERS, 1815–1860

The nation and the Navy emerged from the War of 1812 stronger and more confident than ever. Within a few months of the Battle of New Orleans, hundreds of U.S. merchantmen plied the world trade routes. A large naval squadron sailed to the Mediterranean in the war with Algiers to wind up the unfinished business with the Barbary states. After so doing, the United States kept up its presence in the Mediterranean regularly until the Civil War.

Many changes were to come in the business of seafaring. The Navy now enjoyed prestige and popularity because of its successes in the war. For the first time, the Navy was able to build up after the end of a war, with public support. Piracy demanded the attention of the Navy, especially in the Caribbean and Mediterranean. The desire to stop the international slave trade added other patrol duties. Commercial trade grew rapidly. Whaling became a major industry in New England ports. And some of the most "romantic" days in the history of sailing were about to unfold. American clipper ships would soon become the queens of the sea.

The age of technology began to have an effect on life at sea. The science of oceanography came into being. Better instruments, mapping, and clocks improved navigation and helped American firms compete for world trade. Steam propulsion came into the world of sea power. With it came the screw propeller, iron hull, armor, and heavy ordnance with the first rifled barrels. No major wars, and consequently no major sea battles, were fought between 1815 and 1860. For the first time, wars in Europe did not directly affect American progress. Americans went their way, across the seas and across the continent.

PIRACY AND PROTECTION

The chief task of the U.S. Navy between 1815 and 1860 was promoting and protecting U.S. overseas commerce. American trade increased fivefold during the period. American traders were everywhere on the globe. Often the traders sailed into areas of rebellion and turmoil—the type of situation in which piracy flourishes.

After taking care of Algeria, along with Morocco, Tunis, and Tripoli, in naval operations during 1815 and 1816, the United States signed treaties with the Barbary states that stopped the need to pay tribute. American squadrons continued their presence in the Mediterranean, however, operating from a base in Port Mahon, Minorca, to make sure that the deys and pashas did not revert to their old ways.

When revolts against Spain began in South and Central America in the early nineteenth century, piracy increased in the West Indies. Some of the new South American countries issued *letters of marque* (official documents commissioning vessels as privateers) to their ships. However, many of these ships began piracy against all shipping. This affected American shipping, for at this time New Orleans was developing into the second-largest port of the nation. This was a result of the westward migration and agricultural expansion in the Mississippi Valley.

Jean Lafitte was the most notorious American pirate. He established his base on an island at the mouth of the Mississippi River. He and his men had been given pardons because of their assistance to General Jackson at New Orleans in 1815, but they returned to piracy after the war. The Navy was given the job of wiping out the pirates. At the same time, it had to deal with the Latin American governments and colonies from which many of the pirates came.

Between 1815 and 1822, nearly 3,000 merchant ships were attacked by pirates in the West Indies. Merchants, ship owners, and insurance companies demanded an end to these attacks. In 1819, Congress authorized President James Monroe to launch a campaign against the pirates. He sent Oliver Hazard Perry to Venezuela to talk with President Simon Bolivar about stopping the letters of marque. Bolivar agreed, but the piracy did not stop. The new governments had no power to stop the marauders already on the seas. Perry contracted yellow fever during his mission, and died the same year at the age of thirty-four.

Piracy continued to flourish. By 1822 the damage to American trade in the Caribbean became so great that the United States decided to put an end to the pirates once and for all. A West Indies Naval Squadron, under the command of Commodore James Biddle, was sent to the area. Biddle captured or destroyed thirty pirate vessels in less than a year, but his large ships could not pursue the smaller pirate vessels into the coves close to shore where many lurked. Spanish officials in Cuba and Puerto Rico refused Biddle permission to pursue pirates who beached their vessels and escaped ashore. Yellow fever and malaria caused many deaths in the American crews.

In 1822 David Porter took command of the West Indies Squadron. Porter learned from Biddle's operations. He gathered a squadron of smaller vessels, gunboats, and the first steam-powered paddle wheeler to be used in naval operations. He then followed the pirates into the coves and inlets for the next two years. His larger ships escorted merchantmen at sea. By mid-1826 a new commodore, Lewis Warrington, had succeeded in driving Lafitte and other pirates out of the Caribbean. For the first time in three centuries, the ships of all nations could sail those waters without fear of being plundered.

WHALING

Colonial Americans had begun whaling in the early 1700s. Sailing out of New Bedford, Nantucket, and other New England seaports, whalers flourished until the Civil War. After the War of 1812, the whaling industry grew rapidly. Between 1830 and 1860, many fortunes were made by the owners of whaling vessels. By 1846 the Americans had over 700 whaling ships, about three-quarters of the total world's whaling fleet.

A whaleboat with a harpooner in the bow is rowed toward a whale, with the whale ship standing by behind. The whaling industry was profitable, but whaling was a dangerous job with severe living conditions.

Life aboard the whaling ships was primitive and dirty. Many crewmen died from disease and injuries, but the lure of profits from a share of a successful voyage pushed men on. Many sea stories of the era have been passed down from writers of the day and have become a part of American history and adventure. Probably the most famous of these stories is *Moby Dick*, by Herman Melville.

The era of American whaling ended with a series of important developments. The principal products made from whales were whale oil for lighting, whalebone, spermaceti for candles, and ambergris for perfume. In 1859 oil was discovered in Pennsylvania, giving momentum to the fledgling petroleum industry. Petroleum could be distilled into kerosene and used for lighting and heating. Later, lighting by natural gas dealt the final blow to whalers. The flexible whalebone used for hoopskirts, corset stays, buggy whips, and umbrella ribs was replaced by other materials as dress styles and needs changed. During the Civil War, Confederate raiders attacked and destroyed many Northern whaling fleets, and the trade never revived. Weather and the Arctic ice claimed most of the surviving American whaling fleet in the 1870s.

THE MERCHANT MARINE

The American colonists had designed and built ships since the earliest days of settlement. By the mid-1800s,

British investors were buying fishing vessels to harvest the huge schools of cod, haddock, and pollock along the New England coast and on the Grand Banks of Newfoundland. Favorable tax rules encouraged the industry, which soon became the largest in early New England. The cod was so important to Massachusetts that a huge wooden carving of the fish was made and hung in the state house in Boston in 1798. It is still there today.

By the end of the eighteenth century, American merchant ships had begun the trade to Hawaii, China, and the Orient. They explored the Pacific coast up to the Columbia River and helped establish the later claim of the United States to Oregon.

Soon after the War of 1812, American seaborne trade began a rapid expansion. By the mid-1820s American ships were carrying most of the passengers and freight that crossed the North Atlantic. By the late 1830s several competing transatlantic passenger and freight companies were operating regularly scheduled service between Europe and the United States. They used a type of sailing ship developed in New England called *topsail schooners,* which combined speed, seaworthiness, and easy handling with ample cargo space. The ships engaged in this service became known as *packet ships.* Also, a service connecting New York, Charleston, New Orleans, and the Mexican port of Veracruz had begun. Most of the freight carried to Europe was raw materials, especially cotton, tobacco, indigo, and naval supplies from the South. From Europe, the ships brought back English cutlery, hardware, fine clothing, books, wines, luxury goods, and manufactured products.

The packet ships were the most amazing vessels of their day. Captained by expert mariners and crewed by the toughest men ever to put to sea, these packets had luxury features for rich passengers. Quarters were cramped but finely finished. Some even carried farm animals so that there were fresh meat, eggs, and milk at meals. Because the prevailing winds between America and Europe blow from west to east, it took about twenty-four days to complete the run to Europe and thirty-eight to forty-three days for the return trip. These packet ships gave America world leadership in the building and operation of sailing ships. Not even the English could contest the American position. America held onto its transatlantic supremacy until the mid-1800s, when steamships began replacing sails.

As the numbers of well-to-do passengers declined and ships became bigger, the packets began carrying immigrants. Often the living conditions were terrible. Immigrants were packed in like sardines, without sanitary facilities and with poor food. Sometimes, up to 10 percent of the immigrants died in the "tween deck spaces," as they were called. Nevertheless, the packets brought hardy immigrants to the United States at a time when they were badly needed for the country's industrial de-

velopment. This was probably the most lasting effect of the packets.

The British had developed a profitable three-cornered trade between Britain, North America, and the British West Indies during the years immediately following the War of 1812. British ships carried manufactured products to America. There they loaded up with lumber, salt fish, flour, and livestock and sailed to the Indies. Offloading these trade goods, they reloaded with raw materials for British factories and sailed back to England. American ships were prohibited by British law to trade in the Indies, so this part of the British transatlantic trade prospered, even with growing American competition in other areas.

THE SLAVE TRADE

Unfortunately, another much less praiseworthy and more infamous *triangular trade* developed during the 1700s: the slave trade. This persisted until the mid-nineteenth century, despite laws in both the United States and Britain to the contrary. Much of the wealth and prosperity of New England in the eighteenth and early nineteenth centuries was founded on the slave trade. The rich businessmen and shipowners and their families never saw the loads of human misery for which they were responsible.

In North America this triangular slave trade most often originated in the New England colonies, from which the slave ships sailed, loaded with rum made in New England's distilleries from West Indies molasses. The ships sailed to West Africa, where the rum was exchanged for slaves, and the slaves were taken to the West Indies and sold. Then another cargo of sugar and molasses would be carried back to New England. The equatorial route across the Atlantic Ocean from Africa was called the Middle Passage. Many slaves died during this voyage due to the terrible conditions on board the slave ships. Over 15 million black Africans were transported to slavery in the Americas over this route.

Following the War of 1812, the British made treaties with most European nations that allowed Royal Navy ships to search and capture any of their vessels involved in the slave trade. The United States refused to sign such a treaty, partly because of their recent sad experience with British impressment of sailors. But it was also a result of political pressures in Congress by southern planters and New England slavers, who were becoming wealthy through the illegal trade. The result was that other nations' slavers would often hoist the U.S. flag when the Royal Navy was in the area on antislavery patrol.

In 1819 the U.S. Navy was authorized to conduct antislavery patrols off the African coast in the Gulf of Guinea. It was here that the slave-trading posts were set up in what now are the countries of Liberia, Ivory Coast, Ghana, and Togo. In 1820 a federal law was passed that defined the carrying of slaves as an act of piracy, making it punishable by death. At the same time, the Navy was assigned the task of helping resettle freed blacks in a new country they named Liberia, in recognition of the liberty of the freed slaves. These people named their capital Monrovia after President James Monroe, who helped them start their new country.

The antislavery patrols were not very successful. Involvement in the Liberian venture and the unpopularity of the patrol in Congress were the main reasons. The campaign against piracy in the Caribbean, which was going on at the same time, was given more support than antislavery operations. In 1824 the United States withdrew its patrol because of a dispute with the British over rights of visit and search at sea. As soon as the patrol had gone, the slavers again took cover under the American flag, much to the frustration of the Royal Navy.

Not until the Webster-Ashburton Treaty with Britain in 1842 did the United States send a formal African squadron to cooperate with the British in stopping the slave trade. This effort too was only half-hearted. American naval officers considered the slave trade a terrible business and wanted to stamp it out. But they were handicapped by lack of support in Congress, which was heavily influenced by the southern proslavery politicians. Also, American juries often failed to convict captured slavers, making the Navy's task even more difficult.

Between 1845 and 1850 the U.S. Navy captured only 10 slavers, carrying about 1,000 captives. The Royal Navy took more than 400 prizes with 27,000 African captives in the same period. Clearly, the American naval squadron made only a small dent in the slave traffic. Both Americans and British returned the captives to Africa, where they were freed. American ships and capital, as well as foreign ships illegally flying the Stars and Stripes, continued the slave trade until the start of the Civil War in 1861.

THE MEXICAN WAR

Americans began moving into Texas in the 1820s, when that territory was still a part of Mexico. By 1835 nearly 30,000 Americans had moved into the area, and many problems had started with the Mexican government. After a year of skirmishing, Texans declared their independence and organized the Republic of Texas with its "Lone Star" flag. In February 1836 Mexican forces under General Santa Anna entered Texas and overran a small Texan garrison at the Alamo near San Antonio, killing all the defenders. Rallying under the cry "Remember the Alamo!" Sam Houston and 800 Texans routed the Mexican army and captured Santa Anna at the Battle of San Jacinto about six weeks later. In April 1836 Santa Anna recognized Texan independence.

Texas remained a "hot spot" during the next ten years, however. American settlers poured into Texas, and the new government claimed the Rio Grande as its southern border. In 1845 Texas was admitted to the Union, and U.S. troops under General Zachary Taylor moved to garrison the Rio Grande boundary. In April 1846 a Mexican force crossed the river and attacked elements of Taylor's command, inflicting a dozen casualties and capturing some soldiers. Taylor responded by invading Mexico and capturing the border town of Matamoros. A few days later, President James K. Polk called on Congress to declare war on Mexico. Both houses of Congress voted by a large majority for war on 13 May 1846.

A four-ship naval squadron in the Pacific, under command of Commodore John Sloat, was operating off the coast of California when war was declared. Sloat's forces went ashore at Monterey, the capital of Mexican California, occupied the city without a fight, and raised the American flag. A day later, on 8 July 1847, another naval force, under the command of Commander John Montgomery, took possession of Yerba Buena (later San Francisco). The naval forces then joined land forces that had fought their way across the New Mexico–Arizona territory into California, defeating poorly organized Mexican forces on the way. The little American army proceeded to capture Los Angeles, San Diego, Santa Barbara, and other California settlements. The Mexican defense force signed the Treaty of Cahuenga in early 1847, giving California to the United States.

The United States had now brought the entire Southwest under the protection of the American flag, and for all practical purposes had won the war. The Mexican government, however, did not recognize the American victories, so President Polk planned to carry the war into the heart of Mexico. Zachary Taylor's army, though greatly outnumbered, spent the next few months defeating Mexican forces in a number of battles in northeastern Mexico. This was not enough to conclude the war, so Polk ordered General Winfield Scott to assemble an army of 14,000 men to take the capital, Mexico City.

Since Mexico had no navy, there were no sea battles. Nevertheless, sea forces had to carry out the operations leading to a successful end to the war. Scott's army was loaded in army transports and sailed to join with the Navy's Home Squadron, which was blockading Mexico's east coast. The transports and the Home Squadron met at Veracruz in March.

In the largest U.S. amphibious operation carried out before World War II, over 100 ships landed the American force without losing a man. Included in the landing were 1,200 sailors and marines. As the ground forces surrounded Veracruz, the Navy took up bombardment positions off the major Mexican fort. A naval battery was

The landing of 12,000 American troops under General Winfield Scott at Veracruz during the Mexican War in 1847. The landing was made without casualties while U.S. ships fired on shore batteries in the fort and city.

sent ashore to aid the army in its bombardment of the city. The fort and the city were pounded into submission in less than two weeks.

With the port in American hands and supply lines clear, Scott and his army swept into Mexico. A series of tough engagements were fought before the Army and Marines captured Mexico City on 14 September 1847. It is this military operation that is remembered in the beginning line of the Marine Hymn, "From the Halls of Montezuma."

The Treaty of Guadalupe-Hidalgo ended the Mexican War in February 1848. By its terms, Mexico recognized the U.S. annexation of the New Mexico–Arizona Territory and California, and set the Rio Grande as the U.S.–Mexican border. The United States had now reached its second seacoast. This realized the American "Manifest Destiny," the dream of a country stretching from coast to coast, and was the most important result of the Mexican War. As always, such a great victory meant both immense benefits and increased responsibilities for the American people. A navy would now have to be maintained in the Pacific to defend the nation's new shores and to protect the many merchant ships that were soon to ply the trade routes to Asia.

THE CLIPPER SHIPS

Just as the Mexican War was about to start in 1845, the most colorful and dramatic era of sailing ships began.

The square-rigged clipper ship *Rainbow* slid down the ways in New York that year. The era of the clipper ships was beginning.

As early as 1784 American ships had been taking part in the China trade. By 1825 American trade with China was second only to that of England, and the U.S. Navy established the East Indian Squadron to protect American ships and interests in the Pacific. In 1840 this rich commerce stopped during the Opium War between China and Britain. Trade was reopened in 1842, when Commodore Lawrence Kearny sailed into Canton, China, with the USS *Constellation* and USS *Boston* of the East India Squadron. Kearny used a combination of courtesy, firmness, fairness, and show of force to lay the foundation for a successful trading treaty that was signed by China and the United States a year later.

The trade with China always involved a race against time. In the early days it took as much as a year and a half for a round trip between New England and China. The Chinese trade offered tea, silk, porcelain, ivory, and other luxuries. Profit was so great that one successful trip would pay for a ship. But time was important, especially for tea, which could spoil on a long trip. Therefore, Yankee shipbuilders sought to build a ship that would cut the sailing time to China. The *clipper ship* was their answer. The clippers were the most beautiful ships ever to sail the seven seas; in their time, they were also the fastest. By the 1850s, American "China clippers" were sailing from New York to Hong Kong in about ninety

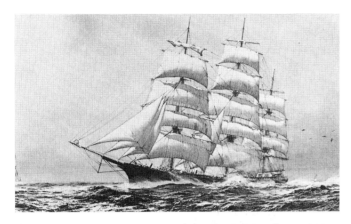

Clipper ships were the "Queens of the Seas" from about 1845 to 1855.

days. In 1845, the *Rainbow,* mentioned earlier, was the fastest ship in the world, having made the trip home to New York from Canton in eighty-eight days.

At the same time the China trade began to make great fortunes in New England, the Mexican War ended, opening up the Pacific Coast to American shipping. Later that year, gold was discovered in California. Now the clipper-ship builders had another great demand: to bring supplies and passengers to San Francisco. The beautiful ships were used to haul thousands of gold seekers between East Coast ports and California.

The clippers had their greatest year in 1853, when 145 of them sailed for San Francisco. In all, 161 clippers were launched between 1850 and 1855. Then the ship-building boom collapsed. Clippers were expensive to build and keep up. Their rapid decline was caused partly by the completion of a railroad across the Isthmus of Panama in 1855. This made the long, dangerous trip around South America unnecessary. Over the much shorter distance, larger and slower ships could haul bulk cargoes and more passengers much more cheaply. With profits down, the fast clippers could not carry enough cargo to make further construction of this type of ship worthwhile.

Other things happening in America and the world at this same time also affected merchant shipping. Steamships began to overtake sail as the preferred means of sea transport. Then, in 1858, the first transcontinental stagecoach made the trip from St. Louis to San Francisco. This brought a complete change of attitude in America.

In the early years of the nation's independence, young, energetic Americans and businessmen had turned toward the sea for adventure and fortune. Now the great expanse of the American West beckoned. Farms, cattle, mining, lumbering, land speculation, and railroads captured America's imagination. And in the late 1850s the turmoil of the Civil War was about to break loose, turning the people's attention to internal affairs.

As the clipper ships moved off the American historical stage, all other aspects of American life began to change.

OPENING THE DOOR TO JAPAN

With the reopening of the China trade in 1842, the next objective of American Sailors was Japan. After a brief relationship with Portuguese traders and missionaries in the late sixteenth and early seventeenth centuries, Japan had driven all foreigners out of the country. Except for Chinese traders and a few Dutch envoys on an island in Nagasaki Harbor, no foreigners were allowed in Japan during the 215 years after 1637. In fact, a Japanese law in 1825 decreed that any foreign ship that attempted to anchor in a Japanese harbor was to be destroyed. Any seamen coming ashore were to be arrested or killed. Any Japanese who left to visit a foreign country was to be killed upon his return. Such isolation, of course, kept Japan in a feudal state, with few technological, scientific, or social advances.

Cultural misunderstandings impeded U.S.–Japanese relations as well. When the U.S. East India Squadron tried to open the trade door in 1846, Commodore James Biddle was treated in an insulting manner. When pushed by a Japanese guard, he chose not to make an issue of the matter. He was not aware that this caused him to "lose face"—a major shortcoming in Asian culture. Afterward the Japanese would not even consider talking with such a "weak" individual, so Biddle's trade proposals were rejected and his ships were towed out to sea.

Two years later, when the Navy sloop *Preble* called at Nagasaki to pick up fifteen shipwrecked American whalers, the commanding officer found the Japanese still bragging about their "victory" over Biddle. Commander James Glynn decided quick action was the only answer to such behavior. He threatened to bombard Nagasaki if the whalers were not released within two days. The whalers were safely turned over, and the *Preble* sailed away without further problems.

But the lure of the Japanese market, the need for a coaling station for ships crossing the Pacific to China, and demands for protection of shipwrecked sailors caused America to want an open door to Japan. President Millard Fillmore chose Commodore Matthew Calbraith Perry to head a naval squadron to Japan. Perry, the younger brother of Oliver Hazard Perry, the hero of Lake Erie, was the perfect man for the job. He had more diplomatic experience than any other naval officer. He had forty-four years of naval service and had taken part in most important naval actions since 1808. Perry's mission was to carry a letter from the president to the emperor of Japan and to conclude a treaty that would satisfy all three main American interests.

Perry's seven ships sailed in November 1852 from the United States and met in Hong Kong the following spring. Leaving three ships in Okinawa, he entered Japanese waters with his steam frigates and anchored at the entrance to Tokyo Bay on 8 July 1853. The Japanese had never seen steamships, and they could not fail to be impressed with the fact that Perry had all guns loaded and readied for action.

Having arrived, Perry put into practice all the things he had learned from previous attempts to trade and negotiate with the Japanese. He ordered away the Japanese guard boats and refused to deal with anyone whose rank was lower than his own. He made it clear that he would entrust President Fillmore's letter only to a member of the imperial family. For a week the commodore refused to allow himself to be seen, while the Japanese fretted and debated about what was to be done.

Finally, on 14 July the Japanese sent the Prince of Izu, one of the imperial counselors, to act on the emperor's behalf. They set up a fine pavilion on the shore to receive Perry. Perry moved his squadron closer to shore, where the Japanese could easily see that this mission of peace was well supported by the equipment for war. Perry realized the importance of ceremony and "face" in the conduct of affairs with the Japanese.

A thirteen-gun salute echoed over the anchorage as Perry stepped into his barge. One hundred marines in well-starched dress uniforms, a company of seamen, and two Navy bands preceded the barge in fifteen gunboats, serving as a guard of honor. Perry was flanked by two huge African American seamen who served as bodyguards, the first blacks the Japanese had ever seen. In front of them marched two young midshipmen carrying

the president's letter in a beautiful rosewood box. After the letter was delivered to the prince, Perry announced that the squadron would depart for China in a few days but would return in the spring with more ships for a reply to the president's letter.

He returned in February with a much larger squadron. The Japanese had been convinced by the first visit that America was a nation worthy of trade. When the Americans returned, more ceremonies took place, and there were exchanges of gifts. The Americans were given silks and carvings and other handicrafts. The Japanese received firearms, tools, clocks, stoves, a telegraph, and even a one-quarter-size locomotive complete with tender, coach, and circular track. The track was quickly laid and the Japanese envoys were treated to rides on the little cars, with their robes flying in the breeze as the train went around at 20 miles per hour.

After more than a month of detailed talks, the Japanese and Americans signed the Treaty of Kanagawa in March 1854. It provided for the opening of the ports of Shimoda and Hakodate to American shipping, the protection of shipwrecked American seamen, start-up of an American consulate at Shimoda, and granting of most-favored-nation status (reduction or elimination of trade barriers such as tariffs, and other favorable trade provisions) to the United States. This latter provision enabled a trade agreement to be signed two years later. That completed the opening of Japan to commerce with foreign nations.

The Perry mission was regarded as the most important "peacetime battle" of the nineteenth century for the

The second landing of Commodore Perry and his officers to meet the Imperial Commissioners at Yokohama, Japan, in February 1854. The Treaty of Kanagawa was signed in March, opening several Japanese ports to American shipping. Other parts of the treaty led to a trade agreement opening Japan to trade with the United States and other nations.

U.S. Navy. Perry was showered with honors upon his return to America. The great American author Washington Irving wrote of his exploit, "You have gained yourself a lasting name, and have won it without shedding a drop of blood or inflicting misery on a human being." Truly a new era was about to dawn for America as a trading nation in the Pacific, and the U.S. Navy had helped make it possible.

Chronology

1783	Treaty of Paris
1789	U.S. Constitution adopted
1794	Navy Act passed
1798–1800	Quasi-War with France
1801–5	War with Tripoli
1807	*Chesapeake* affair
1812	War of 1812 begins
19 Aug. 1812	*Constitution* vs. *Gurrière*
10 Sept. 1813	Battle of Lake Erie
24–25 Aug. 1814	Washington burned
11 Sept. 1814	Battle of Lake Champlain
13 Sept. 1814	Baltimore attacked
24 Dec. 1814	Treaty of Ghent
8 Jan. 1815	Battle of New Orleans
1830–60	American whaling flourishes
1846–48	War with Mexico
1845–55	Era of the clipper ships
1854	Treaty of Kanagawa with Japan

Study Guide Questions

1. What occurred in the United States in 1789 that enabled Congress to authorize construction of a navy?
2. What were the names of the first three U.S. frigates?
3. When was the Navy Department established by Congress?
4. Who was the U.S. naval officer who fought the two most famous battles of the Quasi-War with France?
5. A. What was the outcome of the war?
   B. Why was John Adams defeated in the next election?
6. How did the term "Preble's Boys" come into being?
7. A. What was the *Philadelphia* incident?
   B. Who was the hero of the exploit?
8. A. How did William Eaton finally get the war against Tripoli to end in 1805?
   B. What phrase in the Marine Hymn refers to this operation?
9. Why was American public opinion divided on the Tripolitan treaty?
10. What was President Jefferson's "gunboat diplomacy," and how did it affect U.S. national interests?
11. What are the lessons of the war with Tripoli concerning naval power?
12. What caused American sentiment to turn against the British in the years leading up to the War of 1812?
13. What was the *Chesapeake* affair?
14. What was the U.S. naval strategy for the War of 1812?
15. A. What naval battle fought in August 1812 helped sagging U.S. spirits?
    B. Who was the U.S. naval officer involved?
    C. What famous nickname was the USS *Constitution* given because of this battle?
16. What famous battle cry was uttered by Captain James Lawrence in the battle between the USS *Chesapeake* and HMS *Shannon*?
17. What was the result of the British blockade of U.S. ports during the War of 1812?
18. What was the result of the Battle of Lake Erie?
19. What famous song was written during the British attack on Baltimore in 1814? Who wrote it?
20. What was the significance of the Battle of Lake Champlain in 1814?
21. When and where was the peace treaty ending the war signed?
22. A. Why was the Battle of New Orleans fought after the peace treaty was signed?
    B. Who was the U.S. general who won the battle?
23. What benefit did the U.S. gain from the War of 1812 around the world?
24. What task was of prime importance to the U.S. Navy following the War of 1812?
25. What caused the U.S. whaling industry to decline in the years before 1860?
26. What was the infamous triangular trade carried on in the Atlantic from pre-colonial times to 1860? Describe the route and the cargoes carried.
27. What action caused the United States to declare war on Mexico in 1846?
28. What was the "Manifest Destiny" in the United States in the mid-1800s?
29. What happened to cause the era of the clipper ships to end?
30. What was the outcome of Perry's mission to Japan in 1853–54?

Vocabulary

ransom	tribute money
expedition	concession
embargo	massacre
smuggling	boycott
skirmish	waterline
letter(s) of marque	harpoon
clipper ship	schooner
most-favored-nation status	triangular trade
lose face	

4

The Civil War, 1861–1865

By the late 1840s the United States had crossed the North American continent, a result of both the Mexican War and the lure of gold and fertile farmlands in the western territories. The Canadian boundaries had been established in Oregon Territory. The U.S. Navy had beaten the Barbary states in the Mediterranean and the pirates in the Caribbean. The threat of a foreign attack on U.S. territory had been eliminated, so American maritime interests concerned themselves with overseas trade. Clippers, whalers, and packet ships loaded with immigrants caught the imagination of Americans. But one other thing haunted American life and commerce: slavery.

Although the importation of slaves had been illegal in the United States since the early 1800s, the slave trade continued by unlawful means. Slavery became a major political issue as new states joined the Union from the western territories. There were repeated debates and compromises on the issue of slavery in Congress.

The issue was both moral and commercial. Slavery had become the main support of the South's agricultural economy. Tobacco, rice, indigo, and, above all, cotton depended on hand labor. Thus the plantation system, in which slaves provided that labor, developed. The North, on the other hand, had an industrial economy based on water power and coal for energy. These conflicting interests inevitably would lead to civil war.

In the presidential election of November 1860, the newly formed Republican party nominated Abraham Lincoln. The party opposed admitting any more slave states from the western territories. The Democrats had two candidates, one from the North and one from the South, neither of whom gained a majority. As a result, Lincoln won, even though he got only 26,000 of over a million Southern votes and no southern electoral votes. On 20 December South Carolina carried out its threat to secede from the Union, based on the idea that the election results did not represent the will of the Southern people. In early January 1861 the Union steamer *Star of the West* attempted to enter the harbor of Charleston, South Carolina, to resupply Union troops

at Fort Sumter. The ship was fired on, and she retreated out of range.

Six other Southern states soon followed South Carolina's lead. In February the Confederate States of America was formed, with Jefferson Davis as its first president. The Confederacy at this point consisted of South Carolina, Mississippi, Florida, Alabama, Georgia, Louisiana, and Texas.

A great shuffling of personal loyalties now began within the officer corps of the U.S. Army and Navy. They had to choose between the flag they were sworn to protect and their home ties to the Southern states. For many, the home ties proved to be strongest. They resigned their commissions and headed south to serve the Confederacy. Among many others were Robert E. Lee, who had been recognized as the Army's most promising officer, and Matthew Fontaine Maury, the Navy's first oceanographer. Union feeling was much stronger in the Navy enlisted rates, however. Most of the experienced career petty officers, boatswain's mates, gunners, quartermasters, and leading seamen stayed with the Union.

Southern militias quickly took over many federal forts and bases throughout the South, leaving only four remaining in Union hands: Fort Pickens at Pensacola, Fort Taylor at Key West, Fort Jefferson on the Tortugas, and the forts in Charleston Harbor. Due to their remote positions and strength, the first three were beyond immediate danger. The Civil War was to start, however, at Fort Sumter in Charleston.

The South Carolinians set up batteries facing the fort and on 1 April notified Confederate president Davis that all was in readiness. On the eleventh, General Pierre Gustove Beauregard demanded that Fort Sumter surrender. Major Robert Anderson, USA, garrison commander, refused. At dawn on 12 April, Beauregard fired the first shot of the American Civil War. Fort Sumter returned the fire. The next day the administration buildings were set on fire by hot shot and the magazines threatened, so most of the powder had to be wet down or thrown into the harbor. On the fourteenth, Anderson hauled down the flag. The fort was evacuated and the troops carried away by a small Union naval force that had been standing by off the harbor entrance.

On 15 April President Lincoln called for 75,000 volunteers for three months to suppress the rebellion. News of the fall of Fort Sumter brought Arkansas, Tennessee, North Carolina, and Virginia into the Confederacy, but the western counties of Virginia left that state and came back into the Union as West Virginia.

RESOURCES AND PREPARATIONS

The United States Army had only about 16,000 regulars in uniform when the Civil War began. It was composed mostly of volunteer state militiamen. Of the 31 million Americans, however, 22 million lived in the North, while only 9 million, including 3.5 million slaves, lived in the South. The North's greater population would prove decisive. Before the war ended, the North had over 2.5 million men in uniform, including some 200,000 African Americans. The Confederates put about 1 million men in uniform.

In heavy industry, the North was overwhelmingly superior to the South. The South had little industry except some textile manufacturing. The South had no foundries or metal works to make heavy guns, and few skilled workers. The transportation system was inadequate, especially the railroads, which were barely able to handle peacetime needs. The North had an efficient rail system that was in full operation.

There were no major shipyards in the deep South, and few merchant seamen. Even though the Union Navy was not prepared for the war, it was able to build and grow. The Confederacy had no navy at all when the war began. It tried to build naval ships and armored gunboats called ironclads for harbor defense, and fought valiantly, but it could never match Northern sea power.

Despite its agricultural economy, the South was not self-sufficient in food. Much of the plantation land was used to grow cotton and tobacco, of value only if it could reach a market. Large areas of the South were dependent on the importation of foodstuffs from other areas, particularly Texas and Arkansas. When the Mississippi River fell under Union Navy control in 1863, food from the West was cut off. This, along with the Union naval blockade of Southern ports, had the Confederacy on the verge of starvation by the time the war ended.

In the face of these odds, one could rightfully question why the South would ever want to fight a war. There were many answers to such a question, some of them based on emotions and wishful thinking, but they were persuasive enough to cause many Southerners to hope for a victory. In the first place, neither side expected a prolonged war. The South thought the North would quickly tire of casualties and war expenses. It also be-

lieved Northern politics to be so unstable that the Union would never be able to fight as one unit. The border states—Maryland, Delaware, Kentucky, and Missouri—while remaining in the Union, were at least partially sympathetic to the Confederate cause. For example, they supported both sides with troops.

The Southern leadership had no idea of the economic demands of modern war, so it was not able to foresee its battlefield needs. One very important belief in the South was that the Northern blockade would cut off "King Cotton" from British and French markets, forcing those countries to help the Southern cause for economic reasons. This proved to be a vain hope, though there was much sympathy for the South in Europe. When exports of cotton from the South dwindled, Europeans turned to alternative sources of supply in Egypt and India.

In spite of these handicaps, however, the South had some undeniable strengths. Key among these was the high quality of its officer corps, most of the finest of whom had recently worn the blue uniform. Also, the South was a vast territory, not easily invaded or held by anything other than a large and expensive army. Finally, the majority of Southerners were very loyal to the Confederate cause, a fact that gave the Southern leaders much comfort and enabled them to fight on against great odds. For a comparison of the assets of the North and South, and the advantage the North had over the South at the start of the Civil War, see table below.

NAVY ROLE: BLOCKADE

When the war started, Jefferson Davis knew that the South must get help abroad. In order to force the economic issues, he authorized privateering on 17 April, granting letters of marque to ships of any nation that would prey on Northern shipping. He also declared an embargo on cotton, keeping it in the South in the hope that prices would rise for later sale to blockade runners.

Lincoln's immediate response was to begin a naval blockade of all Southern ports from the Virginia Capes to

Comparison of North and South in 1860		
	North (%)	*South (%)*
Population	71	29
Wealth produced	75	25
Farm acreage	65	35
Value of crops	70	30
Railroad mileage	72	28
Factories	85	15
Iron production	96	4
Bank deposits	81	19

Texas. Davis figured that Lincoln's action would so anger the British and French merchants and textile businesses that foreign privateers would be attracted to the Southern cause, tempted by the great profits that could be made. Second, he believed that this would eventually force the British and French to at least recognize and assist the South, if not openly join it as allies.

Davis was wrong on both scores. Both British and French shipyards built fast schooners and cruisers for the South to use as blockade runners, but they observed the Union blockade themselves. Trade with the North was far more important to them than trade with the South. Furthermore, in addition to new sources of cotton in Egypt and India, the Europeans already had huge inventories of raw cotton from the 1860 crop. Davis undoubtedly would have helped the Confederate cause much more if he had tried to ship out all the cotton he could before the Union blockade could become effective. This might have built up some cash reserves for purchasing war materials that could have been smuggled in by blockade runners.

Proclaiming a blockade and making one effective are two different things, however. When Lincoln gave his Navy the task, he had three ships in commission in home waters to blockade and patrol 3,550 miles of Confederate coast with 189 harbors and navigable river mouths. Gideon Welles, Lincoln's secretary of the navy, was a man who understood naval administration and the role of the Navy. He began a shipbuilding program and bought and adapted many vessels of the American merchant marine. By December 1861, Welles had 264 vessels in commission and had established an adequate blockade off all the major cotton ports: Wilmington, North Carolina; Charleston; Savannah; Pensacola; Mobile; Galveston; and the entrances to the Mississippi River.

Every kind of ship, tugboat, and even paddle-wheel ferryboat was commissioned, equipped with one or two guns, and staked out along the Southern coast. They quickly stopped Confederate coastal shipping and made privateering and blockade running a hazardous business. Crews were recruited from every walk of life and often put to sea without any training. However, in most ships, career men or merchant mariners served as a nucleus of trained men, and they quickly whipped the new men into shape. Men learned fast when they were under shore-battery fire, and they were kept busy trying to stop enemy blockade runners throughout most of the war.

The expansion of the blockade, however, presented one problem. The farther from Union territory the ships were, the more dependent on coal and other supplies they became. Consequently, a plan was developed to establish a series of bases at strong points along the Confederate coast. These would be captured by amphibious assault, garrisoned strongly, and then used to support

the blockade. By the end of 1862, amphibious actions had secured Port Royal, South Carolina; Hatteras Inlet, North Carolina; and Jacksonville, St. Augustine, and Pensacola, Florida. Once these bases were established and the blockade was tightened around Florida, that state was practically put out of the war because its inland transportation was so poor. The loss of Florida deprived the South of its salt mills, which were essential for the preservation of ham and bacon for Southern troops. The Confederates were never able to get rid of these naval bases deep in their territory. These coastal actions, though not as well known as several of the major land battles, were ultimately significant factors in the Union victory.

One of the key lessons learned by the Navy in its successful amphibious actions was that even the finest forts ashore were vulnerable to accurate naval gunfire. The man largely responsible for the improvement of naval ordnance at this time was Commander John Dahlgren. He developed larger smoothbore guns that fired round shot with heavy charges. These shells were excellent for destroying gun emplacements and fortified sites along the shore.

DEFEATS AND DIPLOMACY

The First Battle of Bull Run in July 1861 had ended in a Northern defeat just a few miles from Washington, D.C. The battle put an end to any ideas of a quick victory over the Confederacy. Lincoln extended enlistments from the original three months to three years. The battered Northern Army of the Potomac dug in around the capital, expecting a Confederate attack that never came.

By October the South was anxiously hoping that British and French ships would run the blockade in order to pick up the cotton crop that had just been harvested. In order for this to happen, the South needed the Confederacy to be recognized as an independent nation. To try to accomplish this, Davis sent two ambassadors to Europe on a British steamship, the *Trent*, sailing from the West Indies. James Mason was en route to England, John Slidell to France. They were, however, intercepted on 8 November by Captain Charles Wilkes and his Union sloop *San Jacinto*. Wilkes overhauled the British ship, stopped her on the high seas with shots across the bow, and removed Mason and Slidell by force, an action in direct violation of international law.

As a result of this affair there were immediate cries for war in England, and the English fleet was mobilized. However, the matter was settled by diplomacy by having the prisoners released to British custody. France, which was planning to take advantage of the Civil War by sending an expeditionary force to Mexico, also came near to recognizing the Confederacy. Naval events, however, caused both nations to hold off.

RIVER CAMPAIGNS

Bull Run had temporarily stopped military activity in the east, but not in the upper Tennessee and Mississippi River Valleys. Events were about to take place that would foretell the defeat of the Confederacy.

In February 1862 a joint force of Navy gunboats and Union Army volunteers under the command of a little-known brigadier general, Ulysses S. Grant, captured Fort Henry in north-central Tennessee. The river Navy was a development of the times, adjusting to the circumstances of the war. The Union river gunboats became the first ironclads in the United States. Grant conceived of them as mobile artillery. Under Commodore Andrew Foote, the Navy's river squadron demolished Fort Henry and

had already accepted its surrender when Grant's army arrived.

Grant then marched overland for an attack on Fort Donelson some 12 miles away on the Cumberland River, while four ironclads and two wooden gunboats moved against the river face of the fort. Here the Navy foundered because the twelve large guns comprising the fort's battery were on high bluffs overlooking the river. The Confederate shots fell on the unarmored upper decks of the ships, putting them out of action. Grant took the fort from the land side after attacking its fortifications for several days.

Grant next moved up the Tennessee River to Pittsburg Landing and was attacked at Shiloh in April. But for the covering gunfire from two gunboats, Grant's left

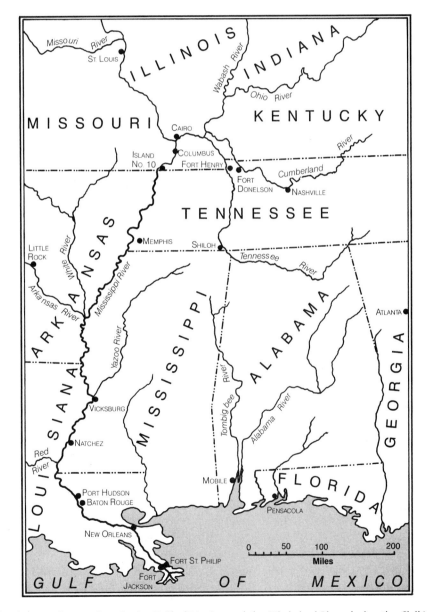

The theater of operations in the Gulf of Mexico and the Mississippi River during the Civil War.

flank would have been destroyed and the battle lost. The gunboats fired into the Confederate positions all night, one shell per minute. The next morning when Grant attacked, it was this section of the Confederate line that broke, giving Grant his costly victory.

The Confederates now had to abandon their big fortress at Columbus, Kentucky, since all river transport to the place had been stopped. While Grant rested from Shiloh, the Union general John Pope kept up the pressure and moved on down the Mississippi River to Island No. 10, where the river swings in an **S**-curve at the Kentucky-Tennessee line. There was a major Confederate fortress guarding the route south on the river.

On 4 April the Union gunboat *Carondelet* succeeded in running the Confederate batteries, placing herself in position to destroy the enemy guns on the Tennessee side. Pope's men could now cross behind her, and Island No. 10 surrendered on 7 April with 7,000 prisoners. All of western Kentucky and much of western Tennessee were now under federal control. The Union forces consolidated and made preparations to move on Memphis.

THE BATTLE FOR NEW ORLEANS

New Orleans was the South's largest and most important port city. While Grant was making a military name for himself by winning the strategically important central Mississippi Valley, another of the great Union heroes of the war began his move on this key city. Flag Officer David Glasgow Farragut assembled his fleet in mid-April: one frigate, four sloops, a paddle-wheeler, twelve gunboats, and twenty schooners. Farragut had been in the Navy for fifty years, having served continuously

Admiral David Farragut would emerge from the Civil War at age sixty as the Union's most famous naval hero.

since the War of 1812. This was to be his biggest battle yet.

He navigated the fleet through the delta to a Confederate log barrier several miles upriver. Here there were two forts, Fort Jackson on the left bank and Fort St. Philip on the right. On the sixteenth of April, he started a steady fire on the forts, which was to last for five days. Then he sent a raiding party to destroy the barrier. They were successful in making a small gap so ships could get through in single file. On the twenty-fourth, just after midnight, the fleet started the dangerous trip.

Farragut organized the assault force in three divisions, plus one division of mortar boats under the command of Commander David Porter, which was to remain at the barrier and protect the rear. At 0340 the assaulting divisions arrived at the barrier and started to take heavy fire from the forts. The Union warships received numerous hits but plowed through the hail of fire into the midst of the Confederate defensive fleet. Once through the barrier, the superior Union fleet blasted the defenders out of the water, sinking a dozen vessels. Farragut proceeded up the river to New Orleans and anchored his fleet off the quays of the port. The next day, the city surrendered, and the bypassed forts quickly gave up.

The South's leading port was now in the hands of the Union. It was a disaster for the Confederacy. The British and French, who had been thinking about recognizing the South, now thought differently. After all, if a major port could not be held, there did not seem to be much chance that the Confederacy could survive. Thereafter, they no longer seriously considered recognizing the South, though shipyards in both nations continued to build blockade runners and cruisers for the Confederacy.

Union naval forces and supporting armies now converged from both the north and south on Vicksburg, Mississippi, the major remaining Confederate fortress on the river. A major naval battle—the only real fleet action of the war—was fought in the Mississippi at Memphis, Tennessee. The entire Confederate river navy was destroyed, except for the unfinished ironclad ram *Arkansas*, which had been towed south into the Yazoo River. By late 1862 Grant had arrived to surround Vicksburg, and Farragut had brought his blue-ocean fleet past Vicksburg. The high bluffs prevented serious naval bombardment of the city, so the Navy patrolled, transported Union troops, protected the Army's flanks, and prevented Confederate relief of the city. The city's defenses were strong, however, and Vicksburg did not surrender until 1863.

THE *MONITOR* AND THE *MERRIMACK*

As the Union was sealing off the Confederacy with the blockade, the Confederates made plans to break out. They had captured the USS *Merrimack,* a new steam frigate burned and scuttled by Union forces when they withdrew from the Norfolk Navy Yard. The Confederates raised the vessel, placed her in drydock, and set about converting her into the first Confederate ironclad. Stephen Mallory, the Confederate secretary of the navy, directed the plan. Mallory believed the vessel to be the best means of driving the Union blockaders from the mouth of the Chesapeake and reopening Norfolk as a cotton port.

The ship could make only 4 knots and drew too much water for safe navigation in the rivers, but she was something entirely new and a real danger to any wooden vessel. Her main deck was overlaid with a casemate framed with twenty-inch pine beams, four-inch oak planks, and two layers of iron plates. The sloping sides of the casemate were to be smeared with tallow so solid shot would bounce off harmlessly. Recommissioned as the CSS *Virginia*, she mounted three 9-inch Dahlgren guns, two 6-inch rifles in broadside, and two 7-inch rifled pivot guns. A heavy iron ram was fitted on her bow.

When the work was nearly completed, Commander Franklin Buchanan, a former U. S. naval officer who had been the first superintendent of the U.S. Naval Academy, was named commanding officer of the *Virginia*. He mustered a crew of about 350 men. If the ship could get under way in time, the five wooden Union Navy ships blockading Norfolk and the lower Chesapeake could be smashed to matchwood, and the Union troops in Newport News and Fortress Monroe in Hampton Roads would have to evacuate.

Work continued from May of 1861 to the end of February 1862, the project slowed by the lack of iron plate and other metal parts. In early March, the *Virginia* was finally ready to fight.

In August 1861 spies brought word to Lincoln that the Confederates had raised the *Merrimack* and were working to build an ironclad ram. Navy secretary Welles appointed an Ironclad Board, and Congress was persuaded to appropriate $1.5 million for construction of ironclad steamships. The Navy itself was slow to accept the idea, however, because most of its older officers held the highest positions. Nevertheless, Welles pushed the project through. John Ericsson, a Swedish-born builder in Brooklyn, New York, was awarded the contract to build the vessel after President Lincoln commented favorably on his sketches.

Ericsson worked feverishly on his design, incorporating in it as many as forty new patents. The craft had only a foot or so of freeboard, so as to present a very small target. Her battery was two Dahlgren 11-inch guns in a heavily armored turret. The deck was armor plated also, and an overhang protected the screw and rudder. Through steam power, the fourteen-ton turret could be rotated 360 degrees. The *Monitor* was commissioned on 25 February 1862, with Lieutenant John L. Worden, USN, as commanding officer. After a brief testing, the ship was ordered to Hampton Roads, near the entrance to Norfolk Harbor.

THE BATTLE OF HAMPTON ROADS

In early March, the North and South appeared to be in an unstable balance in the east, though things had begun to

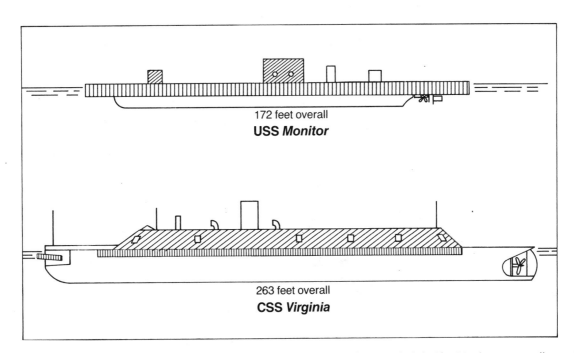

This comparison chart shows the difference in size between the USS *Monitor* and the CSS *Virginia*. The *Monitor* was smaller and more maneuverable, but the *Virginia* had more guns.

go badly for the Confederacy in the west. President Lincoln finally persuaded General George McClellan to plan a move on Richmond from the south, landing his forces at Fortress Monroe and moving up the peninsula to the Confederate capital. Only the threat of the CSS *Virginia* hung over the optimistic expectations of the Union commander. If the *Virginia* got loose in Hampton Roads, it would not only doom the wooden blockade vessels but also destroy his whole plan to move on Richmond.

On 8 March the *Virginia* steamed out from the Norfolk Navy Yard and headed down the Elizabeth River toward the anchored Union blockade ships, the USS *Cumberland* and the USS *Congress.* As the *Virginia* moved toward the two ships, the *Cumberland* began firing, but the shots merely bounced off the sloping iron sides. Buchanan fired a few shots, but his intent was to ram. The *Virginia* plowed into the side of the *Cumberland*, then backed off. The Union sloop sank quickly, taking with her more than a third of the crew. The ship's crew fought gallantly right to the end. The *Virginia* suffered only two casualties but lost her ram when backing off the sinking ship.

Buchanan then turned on the *Congress*, which had run aground while trying to escape to the protection of Union shore batteries. The ironclad slowly and carefully placed herself in position to rake the Union ship. Finally, at a range of only 150 yards, she threw one rifled shell after another into the trapped ship. The *Congress* became a flaming wreck, with many of her crew killed and wounded. Her commanding officer was killed, and his successor ordered the colors struck to end the slaughter. Buchanan ordered Confederate boats to accept the surrender and take off the crew as prisoners. In this operation, however, some Confederate sailors were killed by Union troops on shore. In retaliation Buchanan ordered the *Congress* bombarded with red-hot shot. While topside to observe this, Buchanan was hit in the leg by a Union Minié ball and had to be relieved in command by Lieutenant Catesby Jones.

Jones now turned his attention to the USS *Minnesota,* another blockader run aground. But this ship was too far into the shoal waters to be accurately fired upon. The *Minnesota* was hit several times by the *Virginia* and some small Confederate ships from the James River squadron that had joined the fight since they were no longer blockaded. After three hours of trying to get closer, the *Virginia* broke off and retired to an anchorage under Sewell's Point in Norfolk. She had suffered only minor damage, and she was ready for action again the next day.

The *Monitor*, meanwhile, had been laboring in heavy seas toward Hampton Roads. She arrived the night of 8 March, her entrance to the area lit by the burning *Congress.* Worden was directed by the senior Union officer

present afloat to take up position near the *Minnesota* to protect her from further damage.

Early in the morning of 9 March, Union sailors saw the exhaust of the *Virginia* as she came out of her anchorage. The Confederate ship took a different channel so she could get much closer to the *Minnesota.* Worden pulled up anchor and placed the *Monitor* between the *Virginia* and the helpless wooden vessel. Then began a ferocious four-hour gunnery duel at close range between the two ironclads. The *Monitor* kept so close that the *Virginia* had trouble bringing a gun to bear. The Union ship, much smaller and drawing only twelve feet of water, was much more maneuverable, but even with her larger guns, she could not penetrate the Confederate's armor. Finally Jones broke off with the *Monitor* and concentrated on the *Minnesota,* quickly setting the ship on fire.

Now, however, the *Virginia* went aground. The *Monitor* closed in, believing she could finish the Confederate off. Jones, however, shifted his fire from the *Monitor*'s turret to the small pilothouse forward. A lucky shot exploded ahead of the viewing slits, temporarily blinding Worden and seriously wounding him in the face. Lieutenant Samuel Greene, the executive officer, was in the turret. It took him twenty minutes to get the word and proceed to where he could conn the ship. In the meantime, the helmsman kept steering Worden's last order, which was to "sheer off." As a result, the *Monitor* withdrew toward Fortress Monroe, during which time the *Virginia* freed herself from the bottom. The *Virginia* had been damaged and was leaking badly at the bow. Even though the *Monitor*'s shots had not penetrated the iron plates, many were cracked, as was much of the wooden superstructure. Jones decided to retire to the shelter of the Norfolk Navy Yard for repairs.

The battle thus came to an indecisive end. But clearly, the age of ironclad vessels had arrived. With it, a whole new set of naval tactics had to be developed by the world's navies. The timely arrival of the *Monitor,* and numerous other Union vessels, including other ironclads, enabled General McClellan to launch his peninsular campaign against Richmond. Norfolk was captured, and the *Virginia* was blown up by her own crew to prevent capture. The *Monitor* sank a year later in a gale off the Carolina Capes, taking down a part of her crew. She would be an important influence in naval ship design for more than forty years. (The wreck of the *Monitor* was located in 1973, and various parts, including her anchor, propeller, and engine, have been recovered. Future plans call for possibly salvaging her turret.)

LEE GAINS TIME

McClellan had launched his attack on the Virginia peninsula on 17 March 1862, only a week after the famous Battle of Hampton Roads. Lincoln realized that the war would not end before Lee and his Army of Northern Virginia were crushed, despite the Union victories in the west. By 5 April, McClellan had landed some 121,500 blue-coated soldiers of his Army of the Potomac on the peninsula and had begun his advance from Fortress Monroe after taking Yorktown. A month later Norfolk was taken. But the slow Union advance enabled Lee to gather his forces and prepare the defenses before Richmond.

In a series of sharp engagements called the Seven Days' Battles, Lee pushed McClellan back from Richmond. By August, McClellan had to evacuate the peninsula and reorganize the defenses of Washington. In September, Lee crossed the Potomac into Maryland in the first invasion of the North. He hoped to detach Maryland from the Union and move into Pennsylvania. He wanted to impress the North with the horrors of war and gain diplomatic recognition and military aid from the European powers by this grand undertaking.

On 17 September at Antietam Creek near Sharpsburg, Maryland, however, Lee met McClellan's reorganized and reequipped army in the bloodiest one-day action of the entire war. Over 12,000 thousand Union and 13,000 Confederates fell in battle that day. Lee was forced to withdraw to Virginia. The immediate threat to Maryland, Washington, and the North was stopped, but Lee had gained some time and prolonged the life of the Confederacy.

THE EMANCIPATION PROCLAMATION

Antietam was an expensive victory for the North, but it served to hearten the Union. Lincoln took the opportunity to announce his preliminary Emancipation Proclamation on 22 September 1862. He promised freedom to all slaves within the territories still in rebellion on 1 January 1863. He was in no position to enforce such an edict, but it was a great psychological move. Although it did nothing to free slaves in the border states, or in Confederate areas controlled by the Union, the proclamation rallied many Northerners who were only lukewarm about continuing the war. It also made a significant difference in European attitudes. The war now became a cause for the liberation of the slaves, which Europe favored, not just a war to save the Union, toward which most Europeans were indifferent. It thus ended any chance that France or Britain would intervene in favor of the South in the war.

Also, many liberated slaves joined the Union forces. Lincoln's proclamation could not enforce freedom for slaves in the Confederacy, of course. But the Emancipation Proclamation encouraged the passage by Congress of the Thirteenth Amendment to the Constitution in 1865, which finally ended slavery in the United States.

VICKSBURG

Farragut had arrived off the Mississippi River fortress of Vicksburg in May 1862, after running north from New Orleans. He quickly discovered, however, that this "Gibraltar of the Mississippi" could not be taken by the Navy alone. He called for at least 12,000 troops to storm the city from the landward side before the Confederates could fully prepare for such an assault. An army never came, however, and the Confederate buildup continued. Finally, Farragut had to return to New Orleans because the depth of the water began to fall as summer progressed. A large stretch of the southern Mississippi returned to Confederate control by the end of the year because of this lack of coordination between the Army and Navy.

In October Rear Admiral David Dixon Porter was given command of the naval forces on the upper Mississippi. He called for many more ships and guns. Porter worked out a scheme with Grant and General William Tecumseh Sherman to put a pincers movement against Vicksburg. He figured the Confederates could not defend the city equally well from two directions. But the scheme failed when Grant's supply line and stores were destroyed by Confederate cavalry. Without Grant's forces, the Confederates were able to concentrate on Sherman, and the campaign failed.

In early 1863 the Navy tried again, first with Porter, then with Farragut and Porter, but without success. In April Grant arrived. He moved south of Vicksburg on the western shore of the Mississippi, and then had the Navy ferry him across the river to attack the southern defenses of the city, while Sherman moved in from the north. Direct assaults on the now impregnable fortifications failed, and Grant settled in for a siege of the city.

For forty days and nights, Porter's mortar boats rained destruction on Vicksburg, while the Army tightened its noose. Vicksburg's defenders took shelter in caves and lived on horse meat and rats. Finally, weakened by starvation, the 31,000 Confederates surrendered on 4 July 1863. Four days later the fort at Port Hudson surrendered, and the Mississippi River was clear of all Confederate forces from Illinois to the Gulf of Mexico. The Confederacy was split. Grant paroled the Vicksburg prisoners and sent them home under a pledge to take no further part in the war.

TURNING POINT

Despite the Union victories in the Mississippi Valley, General Lee and his Army of Northern Virginia were still very much in the war. In May 1863 Lee took on the Army of the Potomac at Chancellorsville, Virginia, and won a resounding victory over Northern general Joseph Hooker. Lee lost his most talented general officer at Chancellorsville, however. "Stonewall" Jackson was accidentally killed by his own men in the darkness as he returned from a reconnaissance mission.

The victory spurred Lee on to plan another invasion of the North. It was a desperate gamble to crush the Union's will to carry on the war. Taking an army of 75,000 men, he marched up Virginia's Shenandoah Valley and emerged near the town of Gettysburg, Pennsylvania, on 1 July. At Gettysburg he ran into a Union Army of 90,000 men under the command of General George Meade. There followed one of the bloodiest and most decisive battles of the war.

After initial Confederate successes on 1 July, the two generals spent the next day probing for weaknesses in each other's lines. Lee took control of the town, while Meade took control of strong defensive positions in the hills south of it. Desperate fighting took place as Lee tried to outflank the Union line on Cemetery Ridge and Culp's Hill. The Confederates were thrown back after fierce hand-to-hand fighting.

On 3 July Lee ordered an all-out frontal assault against Cemetery Ridge after an intensive two-hour artillery barrage. At about 1400, a force of 15,000 men in gray, most under the command of Major General George Pickett, moved in front of the ridge and began a charge across an open field into the very teeth of the Union lines. Artillery and small-arms fire cut down thousands. Some managed to reach the Union lines but were killed or thrown back. Pickett's failed charge decided the battle. Lee was forced to begin his retreat back to Virginia that night, leaving 20,000 casualties on the field.

The North had now achieved two great victories on successive days—Vicksburg and Gettysburg. The tide of the war had changed; there was no longer any hope of the South winning. Lee's task now was to try to keep his army intact by avoiding major battles, and to try to arrange a settlement that would keep the Confederacy alive.

CHARLESTON

From the beginning of the war, Secretary Welles and the North looked upon Charleston as the hotbed of secession. Especially galling was Fort Sumter, where Union forces had been humbled in the first battle of the war. Charleston was not as important as New Orleans, Wilmington, or Mobile, but it was of high symbolic value to both sides. The Union Navy had blockaded it since the start of the war. Charleston Harbor was defended by well-placed fortifications. It was impossible to approach the harbor entrance without coming under fire from these forts. Further, the main ship channel

went directly past Fort Sumter. Confederate generals Beauregard and Ripley were engineers who had laid out an extensive earthen and sandbagged defensive system that was far more efficient than masonry forts. They emplaced many heavy guns of the latest design with rifled barrels that fired shot of great penetrating power. Underwater they had placed obstacles such as heavy piles, a log and chain boom, rope barriers to foul propellers, and a field of torpedoes (mines).

In addition to these defenses, inside the harbor the Confederates had built two ironclads, which periodically made destructive forays out into the Union's wooden blockade fleet. With the experience of the *Monitor* and the *Virginia*, both sides had begun an ironclad building program. The North believed that its new ironclads could force their way into the harbor at Charleston. Union admiral Samuel DuPont decided to launch a naval attack on 7 April 1863 with nine ironclads. The ships were slow in getting started, and the lead ship became fouled in her own minesweeping apparatus. The column plodded up the channel, anchoring periodically to avoid running aground.

On arrival at the first barrier, the entire column became a target for the most accurate and concentrated fire yet seen in the war. The Confederate generals had pre-aimed their guns and could hardly miss. Hundreds of Southern shells hit the ironclads. The ironclad *Keokuk* was sunk after being struck more than ninety times. The other monitors made it out, jarred, jammed, and damaged, but with only one death.

Although the monitors had withstood the punishment, their own fire on the Confederate works was ineffective. Fort Sumter had been hit fifty-five times, but its fighting efficiency was unscathed. The earthen works were undamaged. DuPont had served well on the blockade station for over two years, but he had attempted the impossible. The admiral reported to Lincoln that Charleston was impregnable to naval attack alone, and that a major amphibious assault involving large army units was necessary. Both the president and the Navy Department reluctantly agreed, but the political pressures were such that DuPont was relieved shortly thereafter.

Admiral John Dahlgren arrived on the scene as DuPont's relief. The Army sent down General Gillmore of the Corps of Engineers. Together, the two hoped to place Charleston under siege and force its surrender. Thereafter, a series of land and sea assaults took place. Several of the outer islands were taken by amphibious landings, but only after weeks of terrible casualties were the forts secured. The guns were then turned on Fort Sumter, which was reduced to rubble. The Confederates refused to surrender, however, and several naval and amphibious assaults on it failed during the next year.

THE DAVIDS AND THE *HUNLEY*

During the attacks on Charleston, the Confederates devised two new kinds of war vessels: the "David" and a submarine. Davids were old gunboats cut close to the water line, covered with iron plating, and armed with a charge of gunpowder attached to the end of a long spar protruding from the bow. The vessel was supposed to ram a Union ship hard enough that the spar would stick like a spear, then back off while the explosive was detonated by yanking a long cord. A number of Union vessels were attacked in Charleston Harbor by the Davids. The powerful Union ironclad *New Ironsides* was badly damaged.

Since the Davids had some success, the Confederates began working on a more sinister vessel in Mobile, Alabama. This was the CSS *Hunley,* the world's first submarine warship. It was designed to pull a torpedo fastened at the end of a line into the side of an enemy ship after the submarine had gone under the ship.

The *Hunley* was built of a section of iron boiler about forty feet long, four feet wide, and four feet deep. The bow and stern each contained a ballast tank that could be flooded to make the vessel submerge and pumped out to make her rise. A set of leather bellows provided for air circulation. A small conning tower on top had four tiny glass observation ports through which the captain could see where he was going. The vessel was powered by eight or nine men turning a crankshaft attached to a propeller at the stern. During the first sea trials in Mobile, the *Hunley*'s crew had drowned. The vessel was shipped by rail to Charleston, where three more crews drowned in trials. General Beauregard prohibited her from being submerged again, and tactics were changed to make the *Hunley* operate more like a David, attacking with a spar torpedo.

On the night of 17 February 1864, the *Hunley* crept out of the harbor and headed toward the Union blockade line. Approaching the Union sloop *Housatonic,* the *Hunley*'s commanding officer, Lieutenant George Dixon, rested the men and then had them flood the ballast tanks to the point where the deck was awash. Then they cranked hard to plunge the spar torpedo into the ship's side. But something went wrong after the spar was set, and the charge exploded before the *Hunley* could get away. The *Housatonic* sank in less than five minutes, carrying down the *Hunley* and her fifth brave crew. This was the first undersea boat to sink an enemy ship in battle. No other attempts were made to build a submarine during the Civil War. (The CSS *Hunley* was raised in August 2000 from about thirty feet of water off Charleston, South Carolina, and transported to that city. Remains of her crew have been found still aboard, and further salvage efforts are expected to continue until about 2005.)

CONFEDERATE PRIVATEERS, BLOCKADE RUNNERS, AND CRUISERS

Although the Confederates commissioned several privateers during the early days of the war, by mid-1862 most had been sunk or captured by Union naval forces. Their efforts were hampered somewhat by the Declaration of Paris of 1856. The declaration, signed by all major European countries except Spain, declared privateering illegal. Early on, however, the Southern privateers forced many Union ships to transfer to foreign registry to avoid them. Thus began a great decline in the American merchant marine that has persisted to this day.

Another much more profitable Confederate maritime enterprise that arose during the war was blockade running. By some estimates as many as 1,500 blockade runners saw service during the Civil War. The more successful ones were specially designed fast side-wheeler steamships with low silhouettes, collapsing funnels, and shallow draft. They operated out of ports such as Wilmington, North Carolina, and many other shallow harbors along the Confederate coastline. Because the Union did not have sufficient ships to effectively blockade the entire 3,500-mile Southern coast until near the end of the war, blockade running was a very profitable business worth the risks involved. Salt that usually sold for $6.50 a ton would bring $1,700 a ton in Richmond, and coffee jumped from $249 a ton to $5,500. Even in 1863, when the Union blockade was beginning to make its presence felt, the odds of capture were only one in four. In 1864 blockade runners brought in from foreign markets, among other commodities, 8 million pounds of meat, 1.5 million pounds of lead, half a million pairs of shoes, and 69,000 rifles and 43 cannon. All this was paid for by $5 million worth of cotton they exported that year.

The most effective Confederate Navy effort against Union shipping was commerce raiding by commissioned naval cruisers. These cruisers were mostly foreign-built with foreign crews and Southern officers. After capturing their prizes, the cruisers simply burned them. They continued the decline of the Northern merchant marine begun by the privateers. Some shipping companies went out of business. Over 600 American ships transferred to foreign registry, more than half of these in 1863, when the Confederate cruiser CSS *Alabama* run amok on the high seas.

The cruisers did achieve their primary purpose for the South: weakening the blockade. Over 100 Union ships were kept busy tracking down a dozen Confederate raiders.

CAPTAIN SEMMES AND THE *ALABAMA*

The most famous and successful of the Confederate cruiser skippers was Captain Raphael Semmes. His first

Confederate admiral Raphael Semmes commanded the Confederate commerce raider *Alabama* during the Civil War. He and *Alabama* drove most Union commercial shipping from the North Atlantic during much of the war.

ship, the CSS *Sumter,* captured seventeen Union ships before being cornered by the Union Navy in Gibraltar. Semmes sold her and made his way to England. There he learned a new cruiser was being built in a British shipyard for a Confederate agent, without British government approval.

On her trial run, the ship was sailed to the Portuguese Azores, where officials looked the other way when a chartered British ship transferred a battery of six 32-pounders and other armament to the ship. Semmes then took the ship outside territorial waters to perform a ship-commissioning ceremony. He read his Confederate Navy orders, mustered his crew of volunteers and English and Irish adventurers, and raised the Confederate ensign. Now the CSS *Alabama* was a ship of war.

Semmes took twenty ships in the North Atlantic over the next two months, then sailed to the Caribbean. He captured a number of ships there, and then moved into the Gulf of Mexico. Off Galveston he tricked a Union gunboat away from other Union Navy support and quickly sank her. For eighteen months Semmes cruised the world's oceans—the Caribbean, South Atlantic, Indian Ocean, Bay of Bengal, and South China Sea. His crew exhausted and his ship badly in need of repairs, he brought the *Alabama* into the French port of Cherbourg on 11 June 1864 and requested docking.

In the harbor, the *Alabama* was spotted by the American consul. He telegraphed Captain John Winslow of the U.S. sloop *Kearsarge*, then off Holland. Three days later the Union ship arrived off Cherbourg. French authorities now refused Semmes docking rights, so he refueled and

challenged Winslow to a single-ship duel outside French territorial waters.

On 19 June the *Alabama* steamed out of port, following the *Kearsarge* into international waters. A French ironclad followed and anchored at the 3-mile limit, and an English yacht, the *Deerhound,* stood by to observe the action. Thousands of spectators lined the shore to see the battle. The ships fired a number of broadsides without much effect because of the long range. Then the *Kearsarge* came about, and the two ships steamed in a broad circle half a mile apart seeking to rake each other. Soon the *Kearsarge* took control of the situation. The *Alabama* did not have the speed, and much of her ammunition was ineffective. After an hour of battle, the *Alabama* was sinking, while the *Kearsarge* was only slightly damaged.

Semmes tried to beach his ship, but Winslow cut in front and raked the *Alabama* again. Water rushing into the Confederate ship extinguished her boilers, and Semmes struck his colors. As the *Alabama* began to sink, the *Deerhound* came in to pick up survivors. Semmes and forty of his crew were taken to England, escaping capture.

The *Alabama* had captured seventy-one Union ships during her commerce raiding, destroying most at sea. The Northern steamship lines suffered huge losses. Because the raider was built in Britain, the British government later had to pay $15.5 million in claims as the result of an international court ruling in Geneva, Switzerland.

Other Confederate raiders also enjoyed much success against Northern shipping. One, the CSS *Shenandoah,* commanded by Captain James Waddell, wreaked such havoc among Union whaling ships in the Aleutian Islands near Alaska that she all but destroyed the American whaling industry. Altogether the raiders sank about 5 percent of all Union merchant ships that sailed during the war. Costly as this was, these losses did not have much effect on the outcome of the war, mainly because more and more cargo was carried by neutral ships safe from Confederate attack. However, American merchant shipping was dealt a blow from which it never recovered.

THE BATTLE OF MOBILE BAY

Following their victories at Vicksburg and Gettysburg, the Union armies shifted their attention to central Tennessee. In several fierce battles around Chattanooga, Grant opened the northwestern door to Georgia. Promoted by Lincoln to become supreme commander of all Union forces, Grant now went to Virginia to command the Army of the Potomac. He left General Sherman in command of the western army, with orders to march on Atlanta, Georgia.

The impending Atlanta campaign pushed ahead Admiral Farragut's plans to close off the last of the Confed-

The most famous of the Confederate raiders was the CSS *Alabama*, commanded by Captain Raphael Semmes. After capturing fifty-four Union vessels during commerce raiding, the *Alabama* was finally sunk off Cherbourg, France, in a fierce engagement with the U.S. Navy sloop *Kearsarge*. Above, sailors in the *Kearsarge* cheer as Semmes strikes his colors. Note the 11-inch Dahlgren gun in the center.

eracy's Gulf ports, Mobile, Alabama. Sherman figured that a naval assault on Mobile would cause the Confederates to move units defending Atlanta to the Gulf. In July 1864, therefore, Farragut was given additional monitors and an amphibious troop contingent to besiege and capture the forts guarding the entrance to Mobile Bay.

Mobile was a strategic port for the South. It had been the leading cotton-shipping port of the United States before the war. Accordingly, the Confederates had prepared defenses for the harbor stronger than any other on their coast. Three strong forts guarded the outer entrance to the bay. Fort Gaines on Dauphine Island and Fort Morgan protected the main entrance. Ships had to pass directly under the guns of Fort Morgan to enter Mobile Bay. Pilings formed a submerged obstruction 2 miles long from Fort Gaines toward the main channel. A triple line of 200 moored torpedoes (mines) extended that barrier to within a quarter of a mile of Fort Morgan. A buoy marked the eastern end of the minefield, which left only a 150-yard-wide channel for blockade runners.

Key to the Mobile defenses was a brand-new Confederate ironclad, the CSS *Tennessee,* from which Admiral Buchanan flew his flag. The ship, though better built than the CSS *Virginia,* still had design flaws. It had only 6 knots of speed, its steering chains were exposed on topside, and its gun-port shutters easily jammed. Three other small gunboats completed the little Confederate fleet with a total of 16 guns, compared to Farragut's bat-

tle force of eighteen ships and 159 guns. In the morning of 4 August 1864 Farragut landed army units on Dauphine Island to lay siege to Fort Gaines. The next day his fleet started up the channel, with the monitors closest to Fort Morgan, and the other ships lashed together in pairs, larger ships facing the fort. The Union monitors were no faster than the *Tennessee,* but they had heavier armor and 15-inch and 11-inch Dahlgren smoothbore guns, compared to the Confederate's 7-inch and 6.4-inch rifles. The Union monitor *Tecumseh* headed the van, her commanding officer concentrating his attention on the *Tennessee* rather than his navigation. He ran into a huge mine that exploded and ripped out her bottom. The ship sank almost instantly, taking most of her crew of 100 down with her.

The other monitors kept going, however, in order to avoid disaster. As it was, the wooden frigates headed by the *Brooklyn* heard confused reports about objects in the water ahead and stopped right in the middle of the channel. The whole federal line was in danger of colliding with one another.

Farragut now was faced with the most important decision in his career. He climbed into the rigging of his flagship, the USS *Hartford,* and surveyed the scene. He saw that he must go ahead into the danger of the minefield or turn back with a major naval defeat on his hands. He took a calculated risk, figuring that most of the mines had been in the water so long that they were probably

Battle of Mobile Bay—the crucial moment. Admiral Farragut orders his fleet to bypass the sinking monitor *Tecumseh* and go through the Confederate minefield into Mobile Bay, past Fort Morgan.

ineffective due to leakage. His voice shouted out the now-famous words "Damn the torpedoes!" Then he ordered Captains Jouett of the gunboat alongside and Drayton of the *Hartford:* "Four bells! Captain Drayton, go ahead! Jouett, full speed!"

The ships moved through the minefield, often bumping and scraping the easily seen black mines. Not a single one detonated. The entire Union battle line swept into the bay, and into the charging Confederate force.

Admiral Buchanan tried desperately to ram one of the Union's wooden ships, but it skipped out of his way. Buchanan wanted to keep the Union ships bunched up at the entrance where the fort's guns could be brought to bear. Two of the Union monitors rammed the *Tennessee,* damaging themselves more than their enemy. The *Hartford* now unleashed a full broadside into the *Tennessee.* By this time, all of the ships had moved several miles north of Fort Morgan, so the fort's guns could not help the Confederate ships. Now the Union ships started closing in. The Confederate gunboat *Selma* was forced to surrender, the *Gaines* was sunk, and the *Morgan* escaped to the city. The *Tennessee* retired under the guns of Fort Morgan.

Farragut anchored the Union fleet 4 miles north of Fort Morgan and ordered the crews to breakfast. They had barely finished when Buchanan charged forth again. He wanted to sink the *Hartford.*

The Union ships weighed anchor, surrounded the Confederate, and began to fire point-blank. Buchanan could do little but maneuver slowly. He got off some

good shots, but his ammunition was poor and often did not fire. Gradually, the *Tennessee*'s gun ports were jammed and the steering chains cut. The stack was shot away, so her gun deck was filled with suffocating heat and fumes. Admiral Buchanan was wounded. As the entire Union fleet closed in for the kill, Buchanan authorized the *Tennessee*'s captain to surrender. It was the end of the Confederate navy. The forts quickly surrendered. No serious attempt to capture the city itself was made until the spring of 1865, but the war had now passed the city by, and it was lost to the Confederacy.

Sherman, who had been moving slowly toward Atlanta, now broke loose and defeated the Confederates in three sharp battles. The city fell on 2 September 1864. He then set out with 60,000 shock troops with light rations, living off the countryside, and in what became known as "Sherman's march to the sea," cut a devastating path 60 miles wide to the coast, wiping out the Confederacy's last agricultural area. Savannah fell in December, and he surged northward into the Carolinas. Charleston fell on 18 February. Grant's master plan had now confined Lee to the Petersburg-Richmond area. Wilmington, North Carolina, connected to Richmond by rail, was now the only port still open to Confederate blockade runners.

FORT FISHER

Fort Fisher was the key to Confederate defenses at the mouth of the Cape Fear River in North Carolina. Wilmington was located up the river. The port continued to receive a trickle of foreign war supplies through the winter of 1864–65 despite the Union blockade. An attempt to capture Fort Fisher was made in late December, but this was unsuccessful because the Army supplied a force that was less than half the number requested by the Navy for an amphibious assault. General Grant was so dissatisfied with the Army general's performance that he sent him home.

Both sides prepared for the next assault. The Confederates heavily reinforced Fort Fisher and repaired and extended the fortifications. Meanwhile, Grant sent General Alfred Terry to head an 8,000-man Army landing force, the number the Navy had requested in the first place. With Admiral Porter's fleet bombarding in direct support, Terry's force landed on 13 January 1865 and dug in north of the fort, cutting off any hope of help from Wilmington. Terry had his men dig trenches and works to within 500 yards of the fort, while Porter's fleet rained shells on the besieged defenders.

On 15 January the Navy renewed its firing. A Navy landing force of 1,600 sailors and 400 marines then landed on the sea face of the fort, in coordination with an attack by Terry's army from the north. The Navy–Marine Corps effort was repulsed with over 300 casualties, and the survivors regrouped on the landing beach. The Army succeeded in breaching the northern parapets just as the defenders were recovering from the naval assault. Calling for fleet support, Terry's forces moved forward with naval bombardment just ahead. Caught between Terry's forces and the naval landing force, the 1,800 Confederate survivors surrendered.

When Navy secretary Welles informed Lincoln of the victory at Fort Fisher, the president suddenly realized, "Why, there is nothing left for your ships to do!" And that was true.

The Fort Fisher expedition was of special interest since it was the only successful large-scale joint amphibious attack against a strongly fortified position during the war. It showed the value of heavy supporting fire by ships. It also showed that well-planned Army-Navy assaults could be successful against even the best defenses.

Strategically, the capture of Fort Fisher blocked Wilmington, thus ending the Navy's primary role in the war. Despite occasional setbacks, the Navy had accomplished every job it had been assigned on the rivers in the west and on the Gulf and Atlantic coasts, and had driven the Confederates from the seas. The final act of the war was about to take place between Lee and Grant near Richmond.

LEE SURRENDERS

Grant was now in a position to outflank the defenses of the Richmond-Petersburg position. He kept up relentless

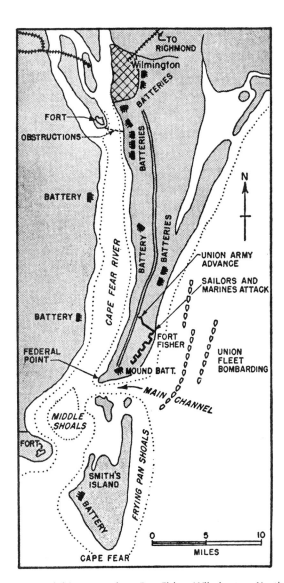

The naval amphibious assault on Fort Fisher, Wilmington, North Carolina. This was the only successful large-scale, joint amphibious attack against a strongly fortified position during the Civil War. It showed that well-planned Army-Navy assaults could be made on the best defenses.

attacks through the winter, suffering heavy casualties. Grant's losses, however, were quickly replaced. Though Lee suffered fewer losses, he had no reserves on which to call. In desperation, Lee launched a final attack on Grant's lines on 25 March 1865. He was repulsed with heavy losses and forced to abandon Petersburg. On 9 April, at Appomattox Court House, Virginia, Lee surrendered his command to General Grant in the parlor of Wilmer McLean's home.

Like Lincoln, Grant sought only to conclude the war and return the nation to peace. He gave Lee's men food and allowed them to keep their horses for the spring plowing. He paroled the Confederate officers and men on their word and sent them home. But for a few skirmishes, the war was over. On 14 April 1865 the now retired major general Robert Anderson raised the same flag over Fort Sumter that he had lowered as major exactly four years earlier. On 10 May Jefferson Davis was captured near Irwinville, Georgia, by a detachment of the 4th Michigan Cavalry. The Confederate government ceased to exist. The Union was preserved.

AFTERMATH OF THE CIVIL WAR

Nearly 540,000 servicemen from both sides died during the Civil War, the nation's most costly wartime toll. About $5 billion was spent by both sides. Destruction in the South was devastating, and it was stricken with poverty and famine for many years. The spirit of defeat oppressed the people even longer.

Many changes occurred during the war. Because of the scarcity of whale oil, for example, petroleum, which had been discovered at Titusville, Pennsylvania, in 1858, was used to make kerosene for lamps throughout the nation by war's end. Food canning was developed by Gilbert Van Camp in Indianapolis. The Union Army soon was living on canned meats and vegetables. Mines came into being as an effective weapon of war. Some thirty-five Union ships were sunk by Confederate mines, more than from any other cause. Torpedoes on the ends of spars were tried. Ironclad ships were proven effective. The idea of a submarine, though not entirely successful, was resurrected. Balloons were used as observation platforms, not with much success, but the idea of aerial reconnaissance began.

Medical care of wounded men received great attention, and the U.S. Navy fitted out its first hospital ship, the *Red Rover,* a side-wheeler put into service in 1862 at St. Louis on the Mississippi River. It was staffed by female nurses and had operating rooms, elevators, bathtubs, and ice vaults. Dorothea Dix and Clara Barton, who later founded the American Red Cross, recruited both men and women to perform nursing duties at the battlefronts and in Army hospitals.

Cameras were used to record the sights and scenes of men and battle for the first time. Railroads and telegraph, though existing before the war, became indispensable communication links.

The Navy itself had grown to more than 600 ships, including sixty armored ironclads and monitors. Nearly 60,000 officers and men were serving in a Navy that had numbered only about 9,000 at the start of the war. That the Navy played a vital role in the victory of the Union is unquestionable.

Confederate general Robert E. Lee proved to be the superior tactician in the field, but the overall grand strategy of the Union under Lincoln and Grant gradually forced him into submission because of lack of men, food,

and military supplies. Despite the final defeat of Lee in Virginia, the battles around the edges of the Confederacy were really the decisive ones. The Navy played a relatively small role in the holding and maneuvering actions in the eastern theater, except for the final battle for Fort Fisher, which sealed Lee's fate at Petersburg and Appomattox.

The Confederacy's attempts to sustain itself by interior lines of communications, as Continental strategists advocated, failed in the face of the superior naval power around it. Movement by sea forces proved to be faster than movement by land forces over the poor roads and railroads of the South. These are geopolitical and strategic lessons on sea power versus land power that have been studied by generations of strategists since the Civil War.

Chronology

12	Apr.	1861	Civil War begins
8	Nov.	1861	*Trent* affair
9	Mar.	1862	*Monitor* vs. *Merrimack*
24	Apr.	1862	New Orleans surrenders
17	Sept.	1862	Battle of Antietam
1–3	July	1863	Battle of Gettysburg
4	July	1863	Vicksburg surrenders
17	Feb.	1864	CSS *Hunley* sinks *Housatonic*
19	June	1864	CSS *Alabama* sunk
5	Aug.	1864	Battle of Mobile Bay
15	Jan.	1865	Ft. Fisher surrenders
9	Apr.	1865	Lee surrenders

Study Guide Questions

1. What were the two different economies that had developed in the North and South?
2. What political development caused the Southern states to secede from the Union?
3. What was the significance of the Fort Sumter surrender?
4. In spite of the odds, why were many in the South persuaded that they would be able to establish the Confederacy as an independent nation?
5. What maritime miscalculations did Jefferson Davis make in the early days of the war?
6. How did the U.S. Navy set about accomplishing its blockade?
7. What was the Navy's amphibious strategy to support the Union blockade?
8. A. What was the *Trent* affair?
    B. How was it settled?
9. What were the military and diplomatic gains achieved by the Union victory at New Orleans?
10. What was the great significance of the battle between the USS *Monitor* and CSS *Virginia?*

11. What was the great significance of the Union victory at Vicksburg?
12. What great battle was the turning point of the war in the East?
13. Why was the Confederate effort with privateers unsuccessful?
14. A. What was the principal effect of the Confederate cruisers?
    B. Which cruiser was the most successful?
15. What was the result of commerce raiding by the cruiser CSS *Shenandoah?*
16. A. What command decision did Admiral Farragut have to make at Mobile after the ironclad *Tecumseh* was sunk?
    B. What was Farragut's famous order?
17. How did Grant use Sherman's striking force to set up his master plan to end the war?
18. What was the importance of Fort Fisher at Wilmington, North Carolina?
19. What were some of the major developments and inventions that came about during the Civil War?
20. What were the geopolitical and strategic lessons of the Civil War in regard to sea power versus land power?

Vocabulary

secede
monitor
shock troops
Emancipation Proclamation
ironclads
bombardment
diplomatic recognition
blockade
tactician
interior lines of communication

foray
detonate
besiege
pincers movement
turret
artillery barrage
parapet
blockade runner
calculated risk

5

The Rise to World Power Status, 1865–1914

The usual postwar demand to save money quickly reduced the U.S. Navy in size after the Civil War. Ships were expensive. So they were tied up at piers, and their sailors went back to the farms and factories or headed West to seek adventure and fortune. Within five years the fleet had dwindled from nearly 700 ships to fewer than 200. Only 50 of these were in commission, and most were already obsolete.

The decline persisted, despite calls for a stronger Navy and merchant marine by concerned naval officers and other farsighted people. There was a great increase in overseas trade, but the new steamships were not flying the U.S. flag.

In 1871 the crews of several shipwrecked American trading vessels were murdered by Korean armed forces. In response, the U.S. Asiatic naval squadron launched an amphibious assault on five forts guarding the approaches to Seoul, the capital of Korea. They captured the forts after inflicting heavy casualties. The purpose of this was to show the Koreans that the United States wanted no further uncivilized actions against American merchantmen. The point was made forcefully, and such attacks did not occur again. Advocates of a stronger Navy pointed to this as an example of the need for new and better ships, but Congress did not authorize any. In 1881 a treaty was negotiated between the two countries, the first such treaty that Korea had signed with a Western nation. A naval officer was the American representative at the negotiations.

In 1873 there was a brief threat of war with Spain. The Spanish authorities captured a Cuban ship crammed with revolutionaries seeking to make Cuba independent. The ship was illegally flying the U.S. flag in order to avoid interference. The Spaniards shot many of the conspirators, some of them Americans. But the issue was settled when Spain paid some money to satisfy American claims. By that time the U.S. fleet had shrunk even further and was in no shape to take on any enemy navy.

In addition to decreasing the Navy's size, Congress and some older officers also wanted the fleet to go back to sail because of the cost of coal. Existing boilers and engines were replaced with smaller ones or removed. Captains were warned that if too much coal was used, they might have to pay for it themselves.

In Europe this was a time of technological progress, much of it stimulated by studies of naval actions during the Civil War: the development of self-propelled torpedoes, improved armor plate, large rifled guns, and powerful engines. In 1873 the British launched the prototype (preliminary model) of the modern battleship; it could steam to America and back without refueling. But a series of secretaries of the navy did nothing to stop the decline of U.S. sea power.

By 1878 fewer than 6,000 men remained in the U.S. Navy, most of them foreigners. There were too many officers in the upper ranks, and few ships to assign them to, resulting in slow promotions and little incentive for younger officers. By 1881 the U.S. Navy ranked twelfth in the world, and over 80 percent of its men were not U.S. citizens. Naval officers often had to learn four or five different languages to communicate with their crew. There was no place to go but up.

EDUCATIONAL RENAISSANCE

Following the Civil War there were some important advances made in the professional training and education of U.S. naval personnel, both officer and enlisted. These were accomplished through the dedication, professionalism, and loyalty of a handful of superb officers.

The Naval Academy, which had been moved to Newport, Rhode Island, during the war, was returned to Annapolis, Maryland, in 1865. Under new superintendent Admiral David Porter and commandant Lieutenant Commander Stephen B. Luce, the academy acquired a brilliant staff of young administrators and instructors who were veterans of the war. They raised academic standards, expelling midshipmen who did not measure up. They instituted an honor system, set up a program of athletics, and encouraged creative expression and healthy social activities. By 1869 the academy's engineering curriculum and physics department had achieved a high academic reputation, which continues to this day. In the early 1870s the department attracted a brilliant young immigrant from Germany named Albert Michelson, who, after graduating and serving as an instructor at the academy, went on to head the department of physics at the University of Chicago. He became the first American recipient of the Nobel Prize for Physics in 1907 for discovering the speed of light.

In 1873 the U.S. Naval Institute was established on the grounds of the Naval Academy. Composed of officers and civilian instructors at the academy interested in reform, the institute's purpose was to advance professional and scientific knowledge about the U.S. Navy, other world navies, and the maritime industry. It soon became a major forum for ideas to improve the fleet. In 1875 it began publishing a journal called the U.S. Naval Institute *Proceedings*. The *Proceedings* was a leader in criticizing the condition of the fleet, pointing out both the commercial benefits and naval requirements of a strong American maritime force. This professional journal is still the foremost naval and maritime publication of its type in the world. Eventually the Naval Institute also became an important publisher of books on naval matters.

Also in 1875, Luce, now a commodore, was instrumental in starting a system of training naval enlisted men on station ships before they were transferred to training vessels to be taught gunnery and seamanship. This was the forerunner of the Navy's modern training system for enlisted men.

In 1884 after a brilliant career in sea billets (job assignments aboard ships), including the Naval Academy training squadron, Luce convinced the secretary of the navy to establish the Naval War College in Newport, Rhode Island. Luce had argued that naval warfare of the future would require senior officers well schooled in the broad principles of grand strategy, modern fleet tactics, naval history and policy, and international law. The college was the first institution of its kind in the world. Among the excellent officers selected by Luce for the first Naval War College staff was Captain Alfred Thayer Mahan, professor of naval history, who would soon make history himself.

Today's naval training programs for both officers and enlisted personnel stem directly from Commodore Luce's efforts. He also started fleet exercises as a means of battle practice, and until his death in 1917 at the age of ninety, he fought tirelessly for improvements in ships and gun design. His work contributed immensely to improving the morale of the service following its post–Civil War decline.

MAHAN AND SEA POWER

In 1886 Commodore Luce was ordered to sea duty again, and Captain Alfred Thayer Mahan was appointed to relieve him as president of the Naval War College. As Mahan studied naval history in preparation for assuming his duties, he became convinced that the importance of sea control in human history had never been fully appreciated or properly communicated. From this time on he became one of the foremost proponents of sea power as a means to achieve world power status. In 1890 he published his findings in *The Influence of Sea Power upon History, 1660–1783*, which became world famous as the foremost text on sea power and naval strategy. He published two more studies in 1892 and 1897.

Mahan argued that it was command of the sea that had enabled Britain to create its empire, reap the profits of maritime commerce, and defeat the land powers that tried to challenge it on the trade routes of the world. He believed that a seafaring nation could, if led by an enlightened and dynamic government, use the sea to become a world power. For the United States, or any other nation desiring to become a world power, the lesson was clear: national survival depended on control of the sea. The country needed to build a fleet of ships that could defeat any enemy fleet at sea and break up any blockade that might be deployed against it. To support this fleet, overseas bases were needed anywhere sea communications might be threatened. And, for security purposes,

Rear Admiral Alfred Thayer Mahan had a profound influence on naval strategy and tactics worldwide for the first quarter of the twentieth century after publication of his book *The Influence of Sea Power on History* in 1890.

such bases would best be located in overseas colonies under control of the aspiring maritime power.

Mahan's work was a brilliant study of maritime history and naval strategy. It immediately received acclaim worldwide, especially in Europe and the Far East, where it was used to help justify the large naval construction programs in which the major nations in these regions were then engaged. It also seemed to justify the new imperialism that had become rampant among these nations in the last part of the nineteenth century. Mahan was honored by the queen of England and given honorary degrees. German kaiser Wilhelm II ordered that copies of Mahan's work be placed on all ships of the German Navy. The Japanese government provided copies to all its army and naval officers, political leaders, and schools. At home, Mahan's ideas were welcomed by advocates of a strong navy—in particular, by a rising young politician named Theodore Roosevelt—and by proponents of American expansion across the Pacific, the annexation of Hawaii, and the building of a canal across either Nicaragua or Panama.

POSTWAR FOREIGN NAVAL DEVELOPMENTS

During the years following the American Civil War, the British began using iron for all new warship construction. In 1872 the French introduced the use of steel, and soon the British followed suit. Other improvements in armor, propulsion, and armament followed. As a result of their naval building programs, the British had become the preeminent naval power in Europe by the 1890s. Meanwhile, the Germans, not wanting to fall too far behind the British, embarked on a strong naval building program of their own in order to challenge for control of the North Sea region. Simultaneously they began imperialistic moves into the western Pacific, taking control of several of the islands there in order to establish colonies and bases.

In the Pacific the island nation of Japan had been made aware of the advances in Western naval and other military technology by the contacts with American commodore Matthew Perry in the 1850s, which opened the door to trade with the West. The strategic problem facing Japan in the last half of the nineteenth century was in many ways similar to that facing Britain in Europe. Both were island nations located off continents that were dominated by aggressive land powers. What Japan feared most during these years was the emergence of China as a naval power and the march of Russia toward ice-free ports in the region.

The Japanese had realized that neither of these potential adversaries could bring full strength to bear against them as long as they remained in control of the seas in the western Pacific. Thus, Japan too had begun a vigorous naval shipbuilding effort in the latter part of the nineteenth century. Because of its naval superiority, Japan defeated China in the Sino-Japanese War of 1894–95, forcing the Chinese to withdraw from Korea, surrender to Japan the islands of Formosa and the Pescadores, and relinquish control of Port Arthur in Manchuria. Later, the Japanese gained worldwide acknowledgment as the major power in the region when they defeated the Russian Far Eastern fleets during the Russo-Japanese War of 1904–5, gaining control of southern Sakhalin Island as a result. It is worth noting that in both these conflicts, the Japanese launched major preemptive naval attacks on enemy forces prior to formal declarations of war.

THE UNITED STATES REBUILDS ITS NAVY

Partly in response to the naval building programs overseas, and partly to ensure a foreign market for growing quantities of U.S. manufactured goods, in the early 1880s pressure began to mount for the United States to rebuild its Navy and merchant marine. Both had been suffering from neglect since the end of the Civil War. Congress established the Naval Advisory Board in 1881, and in 1883 it authorized the building of three new protected cruisers of the latest European design. These were followed in 1886 with authorizations for America's first battleships, the *Texas* and the *Maine*. Though these proved suitable only for coastal defense, they provided a means for American shipyards to learn how to build modern warships. They also helped establish the American steel industry because of the steel armor plating used in these ships. By the end of the 1880s, American shipyards were producing fine cruisers such as the *New York* and *Olympia*, which compared favorably with any in the foreign navies.

The building program continued into the 1890s, spurred on by Mahan's publications on sea power. The Naval Act of 1890 called for the construction of three new first-class battleships—the *Indiana, Massachusetts,* and *Oregon*—plus additional cruisers, torpedo boats, and gunboats. In 1892 Congress authorized the battleship *Iowa,* which was somewhat heavier and faster than the *Indiana* class. In 1897, one of the greatest American proponents of Mahan's views on sea power, Theodore Roosevelt, became assistant secretary of the navy in the McKinley administration. Roosevelt firmly believed that war with Spain over Cuba was inevitable, and he insisted that the U.S. fleet continue to be built up to maximum readiness. Thus, at the eve of the Spanish-American War in 1898, the United States had a fleet that was respectable by any measure: four first-class battleships, two second-class battleships, two armored cruisers, ten protected cruisers, and a number of gunboats, old monitors that could be used for coastal defense, and torpedo boats.

THE SPANISH-AMERICAN WAR OF 1898

For years Americans had resented Spain's harsh rule over Cuba, the most important Spanish colony in the New World. Cuban revolutionaries had been inciting insurrections against this rule for more than twenty years, which by 1895 had resulted in a state of near anarchy and open rebellion. Spanish authorities had been ruthless in their attempts to suppress the rebellion and retain control of the island, resulting in the killing of thousands of civilians. Partly in response to this human suffering, and certainly because of economic concern over some $50 million worth of American investment in sugar cane plantations and $100 million in annual sugar trade, support grew for the United States to intervene in Cuba, perhaps even to annex it from Spain, by force if necessary. Yellow journalism (stories written to incite an emotional response) in U.S. newspapers, including publication of a letter stolen from the Spanish ambassador describing President McKinley as "weak," further whipped up American feelings in support of war with Spain.

In February 1898 McKinley sent the battleship USS *Maine* to Havana to protect American lives and property. On the evening of 15 February a tremendous explosion ripped the *Maine* apart, sinking her in minutes, and killing 266 of her 354 officers and crew. Most Americans at the time immediately blamed the Spanish for the ex-plosion, even though the Spanish government expressed sympathy and denied any part in the incident. Several studies in recent years have indicated that the probable cause was spontaneous combustion in a forward coal bunker, which set off ammunition in a nearby magazine. In any event, the loss of the *Maine* brought the nation to the brink of war with Spain.

Although both nations tried to head off war with further negotiations over the next couple of months, neither had much doubt that war was inevitable. On 19 April Congress passed four resolutions: declaring Cuba free and independent, demanding withdrawal of all Spanish forces, guaranteeing that the United States would not annex Cuba, and directing the president to use American armed forces to enforce these resolutions.

Under the leadership of Assistant Secretary of the Navy Theodore Roosevelt, the Navy prepared for war. Recognizing that the Spanish-owned Philippine Islands in the Pacific region could become a key U.S. base to protect its Asian trade, in late February Roosevelt cabled Commodore George Dewey in his flagship *Olympia* at Hong Kong to make ready the U.S. Asiatic Fleet to attack the Spanish fleet at Manila. Roosevelt backed up the instruction by rushing the cruiser *Baltimore* across the Pacific with a load of shells and arranging for the purchase of two British vessels to be used as colliers (coal resupply ships). Because Cuba would be a primary objective of the

Remember the *Maine!* Sunk in the harbor of Havana, Cuba, by an explosion of unknown origin, the loss of the *Maine* set off the war of 1898 with Spain. Above, the *Maine* rests on the bottom on 16 February 1898, the morning after she blew up.

war and Puerto Rico a close second, the bulk of the U.S. fleet was concentrated in the Atlantic. In mid-March the new battleship *Oregon*, just being completed in San Francisco, was ordered to leave immediately and begin an amazing 15,000-mile trip in sixty-six days to join the U.S. Atlantic Fleet by way of Cape Horn.

The Spanish government alerted Admiral Cervera, commander of the home fleet, to prepare to sail to the Caribbean to defend the colonies, destroy the American fleet and naval base at Key West, and blockade the American coast. Though Cervera pointed out that his fleet was not ready to take on the superior U.S. Atlantic Fleet, he reluctantly steamed from Cadiz, Spain, to the Cape Verde Islands on 9 April with four cruisers and two destroyers.

News of his sailing immediately caused a war scare all along the U.S. East Coast. To calm the frightened populace, the Navy hauled out some of its obsolete Civil War monitors and stationed them in various port cities for harbor defense, and the Army placed several old Civil War cannons along the coast. Also, a so-called Flying Squadron with a battleship and three cruisers under Commodore Winfield Schley was detached from the Atlantic Fleet and based at Norfolk for protection of the Atlantic seaboard, should Cervera's ships proceed there. The main part of the fleet, consisting of three battleships and three cruisers under Rear Admiral Sampson, was ordered to Key West, ready for offensive operations against Cuba and Puerto Rico.

On 22 April the Navy Department directed Admiral Sampson to set up a blockade of Cuba. On 25 April Congress declared that a state of war had existed with Spain as of 21 April. On the twenty-ninth, Admiral Cervera's fleet left the Cape Verdes and steamed to the defense of Puerto Rico. Cervera knew the poor state of his ships and the lack of training of his crews; he firmly believed he was sailing into destruction. Other European countries, however, believed that Spain would defeat the United States in a long war. Alfred Thayer Mahan predicted that America would win in "about three months."

OPERATIONS IN THE PACIFIC

News of the formal declaration of war reached Commodore Dewey by cable in Hong Kong the day after the cruiser *Baltimore* arrived with her load of ammunition. He was given twenty-four hours to get underway for the Philippine Islands and commence operations against the Spanish fleet at Manila. Besides the flagship *Olympia*, Dewey had three other cruisers, including the *Baltimore*, two gunboats, and a cutter. The Spanish squadron under the command of Admiral Patricio Montojo consisted of his flagship, the cruiser *Reina Christina*, and six other light cruisers and three gunboats, all of which were in poor condition. Montojo realized he would have no

chance at sea, so he planned to fight at anchor under the shore batteries at Cavite, a naval station south of Manila.

Shortly after midnight on 1 May 1898 Dewey's squadron slipped into the entrance of Manila Bay past the fortified island of Corregidor and made for Manila, 22 miles across the bay. As dawn broke, the enemy squadron was sighted off Cavite. Dewey in *Olympia* at the head of his column of ships immediately turned south and proceeded to within 5,000 yards of the enemy, at which point he gave the famous command to his ship's commanding officer, "You may fire when you are ready, Gridley."

With that the American ships began a series of oval-shaped firing runs past the Spanish ships, each ship firing both at the enemy ships and the shore batteries behind them. After two hours, Dewey retired for a time. When the smoke cleared, Dewey saw that the Spanish fleet was in shambles. All major vessels had been sunk or abandoned, and only a few gunboats remained. At 1100

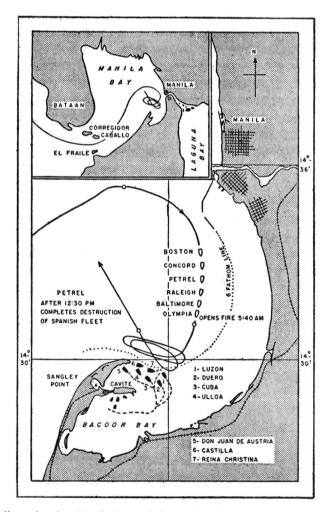

Chart showing Manila Bay and the maneuvers of Dewey's ships in their victory over Admiral Montojo's fleet, lying under the protective shore batteries at Sangley Point and Cavite Naval Base.

Dewey resumed battle, and in another hour, he had wiped out the remainder of Montojo's squadron. He then anchored off Manila to hold the Philippines against any outside interference.

Though the Spaniards had fought bravely, their lack of training, inferior firepower, and poor ammunition defeated them. Dewey's careful preparations for war at Hong Kong had paid off. The Americans, who had drilled regularly at gunnery, had made some 170 hits on the Spanish vessels. The Spaniards, who had not practiced at all, had only about 15 hits on the U.S. ships. When the news reached home, the nation was jubilant.

While waiting for troops to arrive from the United States off Manila, Dewey was confronted by five German warships that entered the harbor hoping to pick up some of the Philippines for their empire. Dewey stood his ground and threatened to fire on any ships that tried to interfere with him. The Germans sailed away. A year later, however, Germany bought the Caroline, Marshall, Mariana, and Palau Islands, and many others, from Spain. They would become fierce issues in later naval history.

En route to the Philippines, the USS *Charleston,* one of the escorts for the American troop convoy en route to Manila, stopped off at the Spanish island of Guam. Her commander took command of the colony in the name of the United States without firing a shot.

On 13 August the force of 11,000 Army troops arrived in Manila Bay. The Spanish colonial government surrendered after putting up only token resistance.

Admiral George Dewey engaged and destroyed the entire Spanish fleet at Manila Bay during the war with Spain in 1898, without a single American fatality and only seven wounded in action.

Thereafter began a three-year insurrection of the Filipinos, who wanted immediate independence. Finally, a workable American commonwealth administration was established that was supported by both Americans and Filipinos. The turning over of the Philippines to the United States by the eventual peace treaty would permanently involve the United States in the affairs of the Far East. The Republic of the Philippines received full independence after World War II.

Though not directly involved in the war, the Hawaiian Islands had become very important to the United States as a base for operations in the Philippines, and for growing American business interests in the Pacific. Some years earlier in 1894 the Americans in Hawaii had formed a provisional government and asked for immediate annexation by the United States. The request had been denied by President Grover Cleveland, who considered the Hawaiian queen the legitimate government. After Dewey's overwhelming victory in Manila Bay, however, the expansionists in Congress were so strengthened that by mid-1898 they were able to pass a joint congressional resolution for the annexation of Hawaii. In 1900 it became a U.S. territory, and in 1959 it became our fiftieth state.

OPERATIONS IN THE CARIBBEAN

As the foregoing events were taking place in the Pacific, in the Atlantic region Admiral Sampson assumed that Admiral Cervera would head directly for the Spanish port of San Juan, Puerto Rico, after leaving the Cape Verde Islands. This seemed logical because the Spanish fleet would have to replenish its coal after the transatlantic voyage. So, Sampson lifted the blockade of the Cuban coast opposite Key West and headed toward San Juan. Sampson's progress was slowed by two unseaworthy monitors, which had to be towed by his battleships. When he finally arrived off San Juan, there was no sign of Cervera. He spent time in a useless bombardment of San Juan's defenses, suffering eight casualties and some damage from the shore batteries.

While Sampson was using up his coal and ammunition off San Juan, the wily Cervera brought his fleet near the French island of Martinique for refueling. Refused entrance there by the French, he proceeded to the Dutch island of Curaçao. After refueling there, he sailed northwest toward Cuba.

The American consul in Martinique had cabled Washington as Cervera passed that island. The Navy Department then ordered Schley's Flying Squadron to sail from Norfolk to Key West. Cervera had thus in effect outmaneuvered the Americans by guessing that Sampson and Schley would do what they did. With the Atlantic Squadron split, the Spaniards successfully eluded them both and headed toward the back door of Cuba at

Santiago. Meanwhile, the *Oregon,* just entering the Caribbean after its circumnavigation of South America, stood a chance of steaming alone into the midst of the Spanish fleet.

Word of Cervera's stop at Curaçao, however, indicated that the *Oregon* was safe, and that Cervera was probably headed toward Cuba. There were three ports in Cuba large enough to handle Cervera's fleet—Havana, Cienfuegos, and Santiago. The Navy Department concluded that Cervera probably would try to reach Havana, possibly stopping at Cienfuegos for coal. Accordingly, Sampson ordered the Flying Squadron to go around the western end of Cuba to blockade Cienfuegos, while he guarded the approaches to Havana. Both the department and Sampson were incorrect again. Cervera had steamed directly to the isolated southeastern port of Santiago de Cuba, arriving on 19 May.

Meanwhile, Commodore Schley headed toward Santiago after determining that the enemy was not at Cienfuegos. But before arriving—and against Navy Department orders—he reversed course, intending to return to Key West for coal. The seas calmed on the night of 27 May, however, and he was able to take on coal from a collier at sea. His squadron finally arrived off Santiago de Cuba on the morning of the twenty-ninth. There he saw the *Cristóbal Colon,* Cervera's best cruiser, at the harbor entrance. He laid off the harbor for two days, then bombarded it for a few minutes at extreme range with little effect. On 1 June Admiral Sampson arrived with his squadron, plus the *Oregon.* As senior officer present, Sampson took command of all U.S. naval forces and established a close blockade of the port.

BATTLE OF SANTIAGO DE CUBA

Sampson arranged his blockaders in a semicircle off the harbor entrance, the battleships in the center and smaller ships on the sides. At night the ships came in closer and directed a searchlight on the channel lest a Spanish torpedo boat try a surprise attack. There was always the problem of refueling the blockading ships and concern that a hurricane might blow in and disperse them.

The coaling problem was partially solved on 10 June when a force of U.S. Marines from the *Oregon* went ashore at Guantánamo Bay and, after a week of fighting, drove away the Spanish garrison. This gave the fleet a secure anchorage only 40 miles from Santiago that could be used as a coaling and maintenance base. Guantánamo has been an important American naval base ever since under a treaty with Cuba.

Sampson now called on Washington to have Army troops land and take the Spanish batteries at Santiago, so he could go in with small boats and sweep the Spanish minefield before forcing an entrance to the harbor. The Army was eager to oblige, in order to take part in the war. On 20 June Major General William Shafter arrived with an Army expeditionary force of 16,000 men. He had orders to cooperate with the Navy and land near Santi-

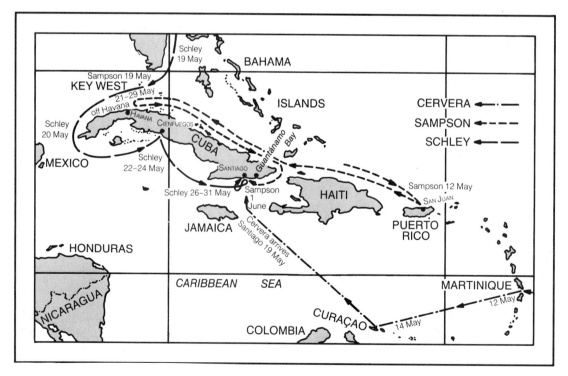

Maneuvers of the opposing U.S. and Spanish fleets in the Caribbean campaign of the Spanish-American War.

ago to capture the batteries. With naval assistance, Shafter landed at Daiquiri, 16 miles east of Santiago, on 22 June without opposition.

But Shafter had other ideas about how to conduct the operation. Instead of making his objective the Spanish batteries, he went charging into the jungle with the intent of capturing the city. He thought this would either force Cervera out into the waiting blockaders or cause him to surrender or be destroyed in the harbor.

Shafter's army found the going very rough and slow. His men were hampered by barbed-wire entanglements, poor trails, heatstroke, and typhoid fever. On 1 July the Spaniards made a strong stand at El Caney and San Juan Hill, inflicting nearly 1,500 casualties before retreating to the city's main defense lines. During this battle, Lieutenant Colonel Theodore Roosevelt's Rough Riders and a regiment of African American cavalrymen swarmed up nearby Kettle Hill on foot and threw the Spaniards off. (Roosevelt had resigned his post as assistant secretary of the navy in order to get into battlefield action.)

Shafter, shocked by his losses and ill with fever, considered retreating to escape from the Spanish forces, which were now much larger than his own. As a last resort, however, he called on the Navy to try to force the entrance of the harbor to relieve the pressure on his men. Sampson was very upset by this request, as it was asking him to risk the fleet in a narrow, twisting, mined channel to save the Army, when the Army had not proceeded on its mission of silencing the shore batteries. On Sunday morning 3 July, the exasperated Sampson turned over command of the blockading force to Commodore Schley and sailed eastward along the Cuban coast in his flagship, the cruiser USS *New York*, to meet personally with Shafter. The blockade had been further weakened that morning with the departure of the USS *Massachusetts* for Guantánamo to refuel.

Though the situation looked bad to the Americans, it looked worse to the Spanish. The Spanish authorities in Havana, feeling that Santiago would probably soon fall, had directed Cervera to escape at his first chance. Seeing the blockade weakened, the Spanish admiral chose this opportunity to try to escape. He realized his move was an unlikely gamble, but he thought that this was the only way to avoid surrender of his squadron without fighting. That, he felt, would result in a terrible loss of honor, severely damage the morale of all Spanish forces, and destroy Spain's reputation in Europe.

The *Infanta Maria Teresa*, Cervera's flagship, headed directly for the harbor mouth at 0935 on 3 July. She was followed at ten-minute intervals by three armored cruisers and two destroyers.

The American fleet, somewhat relaxed in Sunday blockade routine, was caught by surprise but quickly recovered. The Americans were under way toward the harbor entrance as the Spaniards exited and turned west to run along the coast. By now both sides were firing at each other, the American battleships concentrating on the *Teresa*. The enemy shells were missing the American ships, but soon the *Teresa* was in bad shape. Hit repeatedly by 8-inch and 12-inch shells, her wooden decks ablaze, she nevertheless led her battle line out of the harbor and tried to ram the cruiser *Brooklyn*, Schley's flagship, before turning west. The *Brooklyn*, on Schley's orders, turned sharply away to the east, crossing the bow of the *Texas* and almost causing a collision. The *Brooklyn* was then temporarily out of the fighting as she circled to recover her position. The confusion enabled the Spanish to clear the harbor, but soon the faster speed and superior firepower of the American warships made the Spanish ships blazing torches. They turned into the beach, one at a time, to run aground and surrender rather than to sink and lose all hands. As the *Brooklyn* and battleships *Texas* and *Oregon* cut down the Spanish cruiser *Vizcaya*, Captain Philip of the *Texas* called to his jubilant crew, "Don't cheer, boys, the poor devils are dying." The *Oregon* overtook the last and fastest Spanish cruiser, *Cristóbal Colon*, about 70 miles west of Santiago. With 13-inch shells slamming all around, the *Colon* ran onto the beach and surrendered. The two Spanish destroyers were cut to pieces by the battleship *Indiana* shortly after they

The Battle of Santiago de Cuba. Cervera came out of the harbor from anchorages behind Morrow Castle and ran into Schley's blockading force. All Spanish ships were sunk or beached, with only one American killed and one wounded.

cleared the harbor mouth and before they could fire a single torpedo.

Sampson, on the *New York,* steamed valiantly westward to try to get into the battle but never made it. A bitter dispute later arose between him and Schley over who deserved credit for the victory. Schley was also later roundly criticized for his tardiness in blockading Santiago and his wrong-way turn when Cervera emerged.

The entire action took a little more than three hours. One American was killed and another wounded. Spanish losses were heavy, over 300 killed and 150 wounded, with 1,800 captured, including Admiral Cervera. The Spanish fleet had been annihilated by a superior fleet, despite the latter's tactical errors and surprisingly poor marksmanship.

END OF THE WAR

The Battle of Santiago de Cuba had given the American people another Fourth of July victory. In only two months, the U.S. Navy had destroyed the Spanish fleets in both the Pacific and Caribbean. Santiago surrendered its 22,000 troops on 14 July to General Shafter, after a brief siege assisted by long-range naval bombardment. An expeditionary force was sent to Puerto Rico; it quickly overcame all resistance after capturing San Juan, the capital. American arms were victorious everywhere by the end of July, and the U.S. Navy made plans to cruise against the Spanish mainland. Before that happened the Spaniards sued for peace. The two countries signed a peace treaty in Paris on 10 December 1898. Spain recognized the independence of Cuba and turned over Puerto Rico, the Philippines, and Guam to the United States.

Notwithstanding the U.S. success in the war, there were several lessons learned from it. First, the war clearly showed that American military and political leaders had to understand the principles of naval warfare, as elaborated by Mahan. Second, the American people had to understand that to be effective, the Navy had to be a mobile seagoing organization supported from overseas bases. Defense of American cities against attack was not an objective of the Navy. Third, it was clear that a sound amphibious doctrine had to be developed and gunnery and fire control techniques had to be improved. None of the rather disorganized landings in Cuba, Puerto Rico, and the Philippines could have succeeded in the face of serious opposition. Gunnery at Manila Bay and Santiago de Cuba proved effective only against old ships and untrained crews. As Mahan himself warned, "We cannot expect ever again to have an enemy as entirely inept as Spain showed herself to be."

Probably the most important long-term consequence of the war was America's new overseas empire. The United States now had territories and bases that made a seagoing navy a necessity. The United States had become a formidable naval power. But the new possessions in the Pacific posed many problems.

Attempts to find solutions to these problems would dominate much of the U.S. Navy's thinking for the next forty years. Most perplexing was the issue of how to defend the Philippines against a militaristic, expansionist Japan. Located some 8,000 miles from the U.S. West Coast and only a few hundred miles from Japan, defense of the Philippine Islands would require naval superiority in Far Eastern waters. This, in turn, would require base facilities in the Pacific far beyond anything the United States had in 1898. Thus, in addition to annexing Hawaii, early in 1899 the United States laid claim to Wake Island, and later the same year it annexed part of the Samoa Islands, including a fine harbor at Pago Pago. In the face of growing anti-imperialist sentiment at home, however, that was as far as Congress could go.

Spain, having lost all her principal colonies, decided to divest herself of all her remaining empire and concentrate on domestic development. In 1899 she put up for sale all her remaining Pacific possessions—nearly a thousand islands. The United States was not interested, so Germany acquired many of them, including several located between the United States and the Philippines.

THE RISE TO WORLD-POWER STATUS

The first decade of the twentieth century saw major changes in the world balance of naval power. In the United States, the recent victories over Spain had kindled a national pride in the Navy and helped convince Congress to accept as a national goal the building of a navy that would be second only to that of Great Britain. The chief rivals of Britain and the United States soon became Germany and Japan.

While Mahan had provided the basic philosophy for the American rise to major power status in the years following the turn of the century, the forceful young leader who made it all happen was Theodore Roosevelt. Following the war with Spain, he had returned as a national hero and won the governorship of New York in 1898. Two years later he was selected as President McKinley's vice presidential running mate. When McKinley was assassinated in 1901, Roosevelt assumed the presidency. The brash young proponent of naval power who had done much to get the United States prepared for war with Spain four years earlier as assistant secretary of the navy was now the youngest president in American history. Roosevelt had always been openly enthusiastic about the idea of a large navy. In 1890 he had publicly stated that the United States needed "a large navy, composed not merely of cruisers, but containing also a full proportion of powerful battleships able to meet those of any other nation."

Beginning in 1903, the Navy began building two capital ships (large warships) a year, a trend that would continue for about the next fifteen years, through the Roosevelt administration and that of William Howard Taft, who succeeded him from 1909 to 1913. The size of these ships continually increased, both in displacement and armament. In 1905 Congress authorized the battleships *Michigan* and *South Carolina,* both of which would have eight 12-inch guns arranged in two pairs of turrets fore and aft.

Then in 1907 came a warship that would set the standards for all capital ships thereafter: the British battleship *Dreadnought.* Her main battery (primary armament) consisted of ten 12-inch guns mounted in five turrets, and because the U.S. ships were still on the building ways, this gave her two and a half times the firepower of any other battleship then afloat. She was also the first large ship to be powered by turbine engines, which gave her a maximum speed of 21 knots, faster than any other battleship. The *Dreadnought* became the type name for all big-gun battleships launched after her, and all the battleships with smaller guns that preceded her came to be called *predreadnoughts.* In 1912 the British pioneered the use of oil instead of coal as fuel for large battleships, with

the launching of the first battleships of the 27,500-ton *Queen Elizabeth* class. These developments were soon reflected in subsequent warships built by other world-class navies, including the United States.

Advances also were being made in other fields of naval technology. In 1900 Roosevelt urged the Navy to buy its first submarine, the *Holland,* named after her inventor. Submarines developed rapidly after this, in all of the world's major navies. Roosevelt was also a prime supporter of experiments with manned aircraft, which had begun in 1898, and culminated with the Wright brothers' first successful heavier-than-air flight at Kitty Hawk, North Carolina, in 1903. In 1910 Eugene Ely flew an airplane off a platform built on the bow of the cruiser USS *Birmingham.* A few months later, he made the world's first arrested shipboard landing in lines strung across the deck of the cruiser *Pennsylvania,* thus setting the stage for the development of the aircraft carrier.

But hardware was not the only area in which the U.S. Navy improved in the years following the turn of the century. The technology being incorporated into the newer ships demanded highly specialized and trained crews to operate them. Because of their relatively high standards of living and education, young Americans

A contemporary photograph of the British battleship HMS *Dreadnought.* She set the standards for all subsequent capital ships. At the time of her launching in 1907 she had two and a half times the firepower of any other battleship then in existence.

who enlisted in the Navy soon became very good sailors proficient in the new technology. And since the Navy was doing so many interesting things during these years, enlistment and reenlistment rates were high. By the time World War I broke out in 1914, U.S. naval personnel were among the world's best.

Though the American merchant marine could not compete very well in world markets due to wage competition and corporate taxes, the lack of commercial business in the United States had the advantage of keeping American shipyards interested in building quality warships. This produced a whole generation of shipyard constructors who were pretty much warship-building specialists. They were backed by a now-thriving steel industry that had grown mightily since the days, just twenty years earlier, when nobody knew how to produce rolled steel plate. These capabilities would stand the nation in good stead through two world wars in the twentieth century.

INTERNATIONAL RELATIONS

Toward the end of the nineteenth century, Great Britain, traditional enemy of the United States since colonial times, had begun to display a new friendship toward the United States. Britain alone of the major European powers supported American objectives during the Spanish War of 1898. In 1903 the British agreed to a settlement of the Alaskan-Canadian boundary favorable to America. They also conceded exclusive control of the proposed canal across Panama to the United States.

The same could not be said of Germany, however. There had been confrontations in Samoa since 1889. The Germans had challenged Commodore Dewey in Manila Bay in 1898 for control of the Philippines and had bombarded the Venezuelan coast to force settlement of international debts in 1902. Then in 1904 Germany threatened to collect debts in the Dominican Republic by force. In response to this latter action, Roosevelt proclaimed what came to be called the Roosevelt Corollary (extension of a previous doctrine) to the longstanding Monroe Doctrine of 1823, which prohibited foreign interference in the Americas. Roosevelt stated that the United States might feel obligated to intervene in any situation involving wrongdoing by or collapse of government in any Latin American nation to prevent foreign intervention. There followed several such interventions by the United States in various revolution-torn countries in the Caribbean during the following years.

Thus in a background of some hostility, Congress set out on a building program to surpass that of Germany, so that the United States, and not Germany, would be the one to have a navy second only to that of Great Britain. Germany continued to arouse American anger by the arrogant utterances of her kaiser, by the brutal way in which she developed her new colonies, and by her purchase from Spain of the Carolines, the Marshalls, and the Marianas in the Pacific, all islands located between the U.S. mainland and the Philippines. The leadership within the Navy prepared plans for possible war with Germany. In the process they assumed incorrectly that such a war would be solely a naval war, fought between capital ships of the two navies. This misconception heavily influenced the U.S. warship-building program in the early years of the twentieth century toward the construction of large battleships rather than cruisers and small destroyers. The latter would be sorely needed for escort duties and antisubmarine warfare during World War I.

In the Pacific region, when the Sino-Japanese War of 1894–95 showed the weakness of the Chinese government, several of the European powers began to move into the region, seeking to establish "spheres of influence" in China backed up by naval squadrons. This caused American merchants to fear that they would lose access to Chinese markets, unless the United States would establish a sphere of influence of its own in China. The U.S. government, however, was opposed to such a course of imperialist action. A solution was found by Secretary of State John Hay, who in 1899 drafted a paper calling for assurances from each power that China would be open to the trade of all friendly nations, a policy that came to be known as the "open door policy."

Hay's policy did not prove to be a final solution, however. To protect their interests, the major powers kept warships in the area, which caused the Chinese to become resentful. In 1900 this led a group of Chinese called Boxers to begin a campaign to rid their nation of foreigners by force. This campaign came to be called the Boxer Rebellion. Russia seized upon the opportunity presented by the Boxers to tighten her grip on Port Arthur, to occupy Manchuria, and to dominate Korea. This in turn led to conflict with the Japanese, and ultimately it led to the Russo-Japanese War of 1904–5. After the Battle of Tsushima, the Japanese government requested that President Roosevelt end the war. Though the resulting Treaty of Portsmouth did so in 1905, there was no provision in it for payment of war reparations to Japan, which angered the Japanese and soured relations between them and the United States.

In 1906 the Japanese were further agitated by a new San Francisco School Board policy of segregating the school children of Japanese immigrant laborers who had come into the area following the war with Russia. The situation was soon blown up into a full-scale international incident, and some in Japan threatened to go to war with the United States. The situation was resolved in 1907 only when Roosevelt persuaded the board to rescind its policy.

Later in 1907 Roosevelt wanted to impress the Japanese and the other major nations of the world with a demonstration of the sea power behind American diplomacy. Roosevelt had some years earlier expressed his concept of effective diplomacy by quoting an old African proverb: "Speak softly and carry a big stick." American sea power was Roosevelt's "big stick." In December Roosevelt sent sixteen of the most powerful U.S. battleships on a fourteen-month voyage around the world. It was a triumphant cruise of 46,000 miles, with stops in twenty foreign ports, including Japan. Painted white, the fleet was supposed to symbolize peace as well as strength.

The "Great White Fleet" was a success. The ships performed well, and their crews were excellent ambassadors of good will. The cruise provided good training for the fleet and showed that there was great need for bases and coaling stations in the Pacific. Though the voyage was overshadowed somewhat by the launching of the British *Dreadnought* battleship, it proudly demonstrated the might of America to the world.

The Japanese victory over Russia in 1905, plus the war scare in 1906–7, caused leaders in the Navy to begin to consider Japan a threat against American interests in the western Pacific, especially the Philippines. Accordingly, beginning in 1911 a series of color-coded war plans was developed by Navy and Army planners that would specify American strategy in the event of any future conflict with Japan. Collectively called War Plan Orange, these plans would eventually form the basis of U.S. tactics and strategy in the Pacific theater in World War II.

THE PANAMA CANAL

For over three centuries, Europeans and Americans had talked of a canal across the narrow Isthmus of Panama

Upon the return of the Great White Fleet to Norfolk in 1908, President Theodore Roosevelt went aboard the USS *Connecticut* to welcome the men home after their grand fourteen-month cruise around the world.

between the Atlantic and the Pacific. A dangerous journey of thousands of miles around South America would be replaced by a 50-mile trip across the isthmus if a canal could be built. The California Gold Rush that began in the 1840s stimulated ideas of a canal again. Many gold seekers sailed to Colon, hiked across the isthmus to Panama City, and picked up a ship for San Francisco. In 1855 Americans built a railroad across the isthmus for shipment of goods between the oceans.

In 1881 a French company headed by Ferdinand de Lesseps, the engineer who had successfully built the Suez Canal, started a Panama canal project. It was a disaster due to financial mismanagement and disease. By 1889 yellow fever and malaria had killed over 22,000 workers, and the project was canceled.

Mahan revived the idea of the canal in his writings on sea power. He foresaw the need to connect the Atlantic and Pacific so American naval and merchant ships could move quickly between the nation's coasts. The sixty-six-day trip of the battleship *Oregon* around South America during the Spanish-American War illustrated Mahan's point. It was clear that with new territories in the Pacific, the United States must have either a canal or two separate navies.

In 1901 a treaty was concluded with Great Britain in which the two nations agreed to total American control of such a canal (if built), including fortification and defense. In 1903 the United States purchased the construction rights, abandoned equipment, and the Panama Railroad from the French company. Now the United States had to secure treaty rights from Colombia. A preliminary treaty was worked out with a Colombian diplomat in Washington. However, the Colombian senate refused to approve the treaty, hoping to hold out for more money.

Colombia had made a mistake. The people of Panama wanted a canal for jobs. They had repeatedly revolted against Colombia to gain independence over the years, so they were easily convinced by Canal Company agents to revolt again. President Roosevelt, who had counted on the Colombian treaty, was anxious to build the canal. He sent the cruiser USS *Nashville* to the Panamanian city of Colon, supposedly to maintain "perfect neutrality and free transit" of the isthmus, according to the terms of an 1846 treaty with Colombia.

The *Nashville* arrived in November 1903, and the next day the Panamanian revolutionary government raised its flag. The rebels officially declared themselves the independent Republic of Panama on the fourth. When Colombian troops arrived by ship to put down the revolt, the commanding officer of the *Nashville* made ready his guns and politely told them they could not land because the presence of troops ashore would violate American treaty obligations to maintain "perfect neutrality." Within hours, the USS *Dixie* arrived with a force of

The battleships USS *Arkansas (left)* and USS *Texas (right)* go through the Gatun Locks in the Panama Canal in 1919, heading back to the Pacific Fleet after duty in the North Atlantic during World War I. The canal was opened in August 1914, just as the war began in Europe.

U.S. Marines to act as a police force ashore to assist the new government. On 6 November the United States formally recognized the Republic of Panama as a sovereign nation.

Fifteen days after the revolution, a treaty was concluded with Panama, which gave the United States a Canal Zone 10 miles wide "in perpetuity" for $10 million and a $250,000 annual payment. The treaty was ratified by the U.S. Senate on 23 November. (The canal was returned by the United States to Panamanian control on 31 December 1999.)

Construction of the canal began in 1904. The U.S. Army Corps of Engineers used all of its technical skill and organizing ability and built the canal in ten years. An average of 39,000 men worked daily. Building dams, they created Gatun Lake, 85 feet above sea level. By means of three sets of locks, each 1,000 feet long and 110 feet wide, ships are raised to the lake to transit the isthmus and then lowered again to sea level on the other side. The canal was opened on August 1914, just as the First World War began in Europe. The Navy now had its priceless canal. All of Mahan's criteria for America to become a major world power through sea power had been met.

Chronology

1865	Civil War ends
1873	Naval Institute established
1884	Naval War College established
1890	Mahan publishes Sea Power study
1898	Spanish-American War
1907	HMS *Dreadnought* launched
1907	Voyage of Great White Fleet
1914	Panama Canal opens

Study Guide Questions

1. What happened to the U.S. Navy after the Civil War?
2. What developments were taking place in foreign navies in the post–Civil War years?
3. A. When and where was the U.S. Naval Institute started?
   B. What is its purpose?
   C. What journal does it publish?
4. What were Alfred Thayer Mahan's principal arguments for sea power in 1890?

5. Why did pressure begin building for the United States to rebuild its Navy and merchant marine in the 1880s?
6. What ships comprised the U.S. fleet at the start of the Spanish-American War in 1898?
7. What happened in Havana Harbor that finally set off the war between the United States and Spain?
8. How was the U.S. Atlantic Fleet divided in response to Spanish admiral Cervera's sailing toward the Caribbean?
9. What was Commodore Dewey ordered to do with the Asiatic Fleet at Hong Kong at the start of hostilities?
10. A. Where did Commodore Dewey meet the Spanish fleet in battle?
    B. What was Dewey's famous order to start the battle?
11. A. Where was the major battle fought in the Caribbean Sea area?
    B. Who were the opposing commanders?
    C. What was the outcome of the battle?
12. What territories did the United States acquire from Spain as a result of the war?
13. Who was primarily responsible for the United States's rise to world power status in the early years of the twentieth century?
14. What naval development occurred in England in 1907 that would revolutionize warship design?
15. What events caused friction between the United States and Japan in the first decade of the twentieth century?
16. What was the name of the war plans drawn up beginning in 1911 to prepare for possible Japanese threats against the Philippines?
17. What was the "Great White Fleet," and what was its purpose?
18. A. What was the Roosevelt Corollary announced in 1904?
    B. Which nation was it initially directed toward?
19. What heavily influenced Congress to authorize building mainly battleships for the U.S. fleet during the pre–World War I years?
20. How had American interest in a Panama Canal developed?

Vocabulary

prototype	corollary
rifled guns	arbitration
honor system	cede
coal bunker	isthmus
primary objective	sphere of influence
circumnavigation	open door policy
collier	imperialism
Dreadnought	predreadnought

6

World War I, 1914–1918

The late 1800s and early 1900s were characterized by increasingly aggressive competition among the world's major powers for control of world resources and for economic, military, and political power. The naval building races that had begun between the European powers in the West and between Russia, China, and Japan in the East were one aspect of this competition. The United States came late to this naval building program, and it took part primarily because it was required as a condition of its rise to world power status.

In the Taft administration from 1909 to 1913, and even more in the early years of the Wilson administration that followed, the main focus of the United States was turned inward toward domestic reforms. The era was marked by a movement called progressivism, which focused on individual rights, engaging in antitrust legislation against big business, banking reform, conservation of natural resources, and nonintervention in the affairs of Europe unless U.S. interests were directly threatened.

Meanwhile, the European powers were engaged in a series of actions that would inevitably lead to war in 1914. Since the late 1800s imperialism had been rampant in both Europe and the Far East. The European powers competed with one another for colonies in Africa and the Pacific region, while Japan acquired Korea, Taiwan, and territory on the Chinese mainland as a result of its victories over China in 1895 and Russia in 1905. Diplomacy in Europe had been overtaken by militarism. This meant that the primary political preoccupation in the major nations was preparation for war rather than domestic programs. In countries with diverse populations, a series of nationalistic movements began to take place among ethnic minorities longing for independence. Finally, a series of entangling alliances arose. These alliances were designed to enhance the security of the participating nations, but they actually made war more likely because they made it mandatory for the major powers to defend one another in the event of attack by an opposition power.

Europe went to war on 28 July 1914, when Austria-Hungary declared war on Serbia. Within a week all the great powers of Europe had been drawn into the war because of the various interlocking defense treaties. On one side was the Triple Entente, consisting of France, Britain, Russia, and Serbia (referred to as the Allies); on the other side were the Central Powers, Germany and Austria-Hungary. At the end of 1914 the Ottoman Empire (modern-day Turkey) entered the war on the side of the Central Powers. In 1915 Italy joined the Allies, as did most of the North African nations by war's end. President Wilson wanted to keep the United States neutral in the conflict, though most Americans supported the British and French.

OPENING STRATEGIES

At sea the two main enemies were the British home fleets and the German High Seas Fleet. The British had two home fleets: the Grand Fleet based at Scapa Flow in the Orkney Islands of Scotland and the Channel Fleet. The mission of the twenty-four front-line battleships and battle cruisers of the Grand Fleet was to prevent the escape of German ships into the Atlantic, to guard the North Sea, and to engage and destroy the German High Seas Fleet in battle. The main task of the Channel Fleet, with seventeen second-line battleships, was to keep the English Channel safe for passage of British troops and supplies to France.

The German fleet was based in the estuaries of the Weser and Elbe Rivers. It was supposed to guard the German coast from British attack and defeat units of the British fleet whenever possible.

The Central Powers occupied the interior land position. They had an excellent railroad system to shift forces quickly to either the western front in France or the eastern front in Russia. They controlled the central agricultural areas of Europe. By contrast the Allies were geographically separated, and they lacked adequate communications. Thus Germany had a geographical advantage in the land struggle but was at a disadvantage at sea. Its ships would have to go through the North Sea to

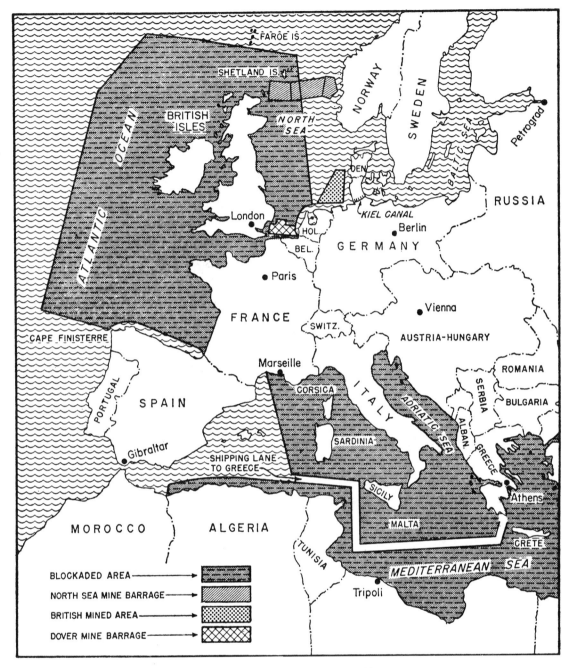

The European theater of operations, World War I.

get into the Atlantic, and this would be difficult in the face of the British fleet at Scapa Flow.

Britain, on the other hand, was absolutely dependent on imported foodstuffs for survival. She could, however, call on nearly half the world's merchant shipping and economic resources in every corner of the globe—as long as she controlled the oceans. At the outbreak of war the Germans intended to quickly defeat France on land, hold Russia at bay, and keep their High Seas Fleet intact as a bargaining chip at a peace conference. In the meantime, they also planned to hurt the British merchant and naval

fleets with far-ranging cruisers and raiders and to whittle down the strength of the home fleets in small actions.

In Britain there were two conflicting ideas on how to fight the war. One group wanted a peripheral strategy, depending mainly on the navy to blockade Germany and gradually weaken the German ability to fight by a series of amphibious operations. The continental Allied powers would carry the war to Germany on land. The other group wanted to place the main British army on the continent to assist France and drive toward the heart of Germany. The latter group won out. During the first months of the war, Britain was able to transport a quarter of a million troops across the channel into France because of her control of the English Channel. These troops were a key factor in helping to stop the first German offensive across Belgium toward Paris in September 1914. Thereafter both sides consolidated their positions and constructed miles of soggy, rat-infested trenches, from which the two sides faced each other across an empty no-man's-land stretching 350 miles across Europe. Periodically each side tested the other's lines by charging against them, only to be cut down by machine guns, a newly developed weapon. This condition of stalemate lasted for months, and the loss of life on both sides was appalling.

In the North Sea, meanwhile, the British and German navies fought several times, with the British victorious every time. After January 1915 the German surface forces mostly retired to port behind protective mine fields, where they stayed for most of the rest of the war.

THE PACIFIC THEATER

In 1898 Germany had acquired a naval base at Tsingtao, China, and had purchased many other Pacific islands from Spain in the years following. These were developed into coaling stations and colonies. Thus, when war broke out in 1914, half a dozen German cruisers were operating in the Pacific under Vice Admiral Graf von Spee. Japan had been resentful of the German presence in the region ever since Germany had been instrumental in forcing Japan out of Port Arthur at the end of the Sino-Japanese War. Japan had signed an alliance with Britain in 1902. Hence, when war was declared in 1914, Japan cited the alliance and demanded the withdrawal of German warships from China and Japan and the surrender of Tsingtao.

When war broke out von Spee was at Ponape in the Caroline Islands with four of his cruisers. Von Spee reasoned that if he lingered in the western Pacific he would eventually be hunted down, so he decided to proceed to the west coast of South America, where he could get support from friendly Chile. On the way he picked up two more cruisers at Easter Island. He arrived off Chile in October 1914.

The British had a force of cruisers operating off the coast of Brazil, home-ported at the British colony of Port Stanley in the Falkland Islands. Several of these sailed around the cape and engaged the Germans off Coronel, Chile, in November but were driven off with two cruis-

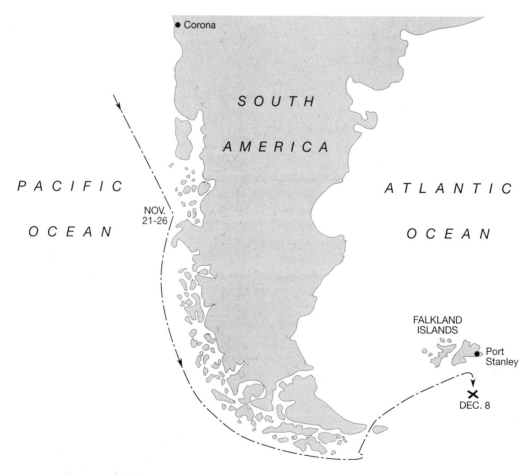

German admiral von Spee's route of attack on the Falkland Islands, December 1914.

ers sunk. Von Spee then decided to proceed around the cape to Port Stanley in December, hoping to capture the base and its coal supplies. The British, however, had sent two additional cruisers to the Falklands to join six others already there, so when von Spee arrived on 8 December, he found himself outnumbered. He tried to flee back west, but was overtaken and his ships were cut to pieces by the superior British force. This battle eliminated the last major German surface forces outside the North Sea.

GALLIPOLI AND JUTLAND

In late 1914 the British war command concluded that if they could force the Dardanelles and capture Constantinople, the Allies could then supply men and war materials through Russia to the eastern front, thereby ending the war in a matter of months. The key to this plan was to capture the Turkish peninsula of Gallipoli, which commanded the approaches to the Dardanelles and the Sea of Marmara.

Accordingly, but only after much delay, which allowed the Turkish defenders to reinforce and secure their positions, an amphibious assault was launched against Gallipoli in late April 1915. Because of a lack of experience, poor reconnaissance and bad planning, a lack of coordination, and ineffective naval gunfire support, the landings did not go well. Still, a sizable number of Allied troops were eventually landed. However, they were soon deadlocked in position by an equal number of Turks under the aggressive command of Mustafa Kemal, who eight years later would found the Turkish Republic. The stalemate continued until November 1915, when it became obvious that the campaign would not succeed. The Allied forces then began to withdraw, completing this operation by January 1916. Their successful withdrawal under fire is still considered to be one of the most remarkable amphibious evacuations in the history of modern warfare. As a result of the failed Gallipoli campaign, Bulgaria joined the Central Powers and helped Germany conquer all of the Balkan countries.

In January 1916 a new, more aggressive admiral was given command of the German High Seas Fleet: Vice Admiral Reinhard Scheer. He was determined to do selective battle with the British fleet in order to reduce its numbers and perhaps win control of the North Sea. Accordingly, in May the fleet sortied from its base at Jade Bay and proceeded toward the coast of southern Norway opposite Denmark's Jutland Peninsula to raid Allied shipping there. Altogether there were some 100 German ships, including 16 dreadnought and 6 predreadnought battleships and a number of cruisers and destroyers in scouting positions. Unknown to the German commander, however, the British Grand Fleet had sailed for the same area the day before from its bases at Scapa Flow and the Scottish firths (openings of rivers into the sea).

The Royal Navy had earlier broken the German naval code and had gathered radio intelligence that tipped them off about the German plans. Under the command of British admiral Sir John Jellicoe were about 150 ships, including 28 dreadnoughts and several squadrons of cruisers and destroyers.

First contact was made at about 1530 the afternoon of 31 May between opposing cruiser forces. Within minutes, two British cruisers had been sunk by German cruisers, which were superior in armor and armament. But the main action was yet to come. At about 1650, a division of four British dreadnoughts came into range with the German main body and began a running battle to the north, with Jellicoe's main body of twenty-four battleships proceeding to join the action from the northwest. About 1800 a long column of Jellicoe's battleships succeeded in "capping the T" on Scheer's force. (Capping the T is a classic naval tactic. A commander attempts to maneuver his column of warships into position at the head of a T with an enemy column moving up the stem of the T. This gives his ships full broadside capability against the enemy ships while the enemy ships can bring only their forward guns to bear.) Before they could do much damage, Scheer turned away to disengage. Jellicoe

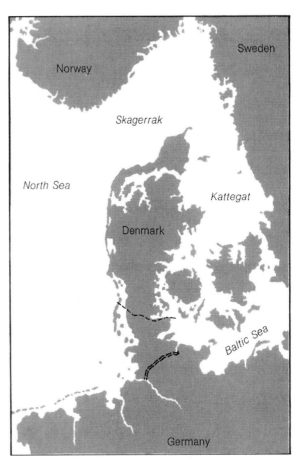

The North Sea–Skagerrak area, site of the Battle of Jutland.

refused to follow, fearing that his force might be led into minefields or waiting submarines.

Several times later that night and into the early morning hours the next day the two opposing fleets maneuvered close to each other. Several short but hard-fought encounters took place. Finally Scheer decided to preserve his remaining ships and to retreat in a south-easterly direction back to base, despite any British forces he might encounter along the way. At about 0230 Scheer succeeded in breaking through the British rear, with the loss of only an old predreadnought and two light cruisers. Jellicoe, again not wanting to risk the German minefields, decided not to pursue. The Battle of Jutland, as this action came to be called, was over. Scheer made it back to Jade Bay later that afternoon with most of his force intact. The British had lost six cruisers and eight destroyers, while the Germans had lost one old predreadnought, five cruisers, and five destroyers.

The Germans were pleased by their good showing against the world's most powerful navy. After Jutland, however, they did not want to risk their High Seas Fleet again, so it mostly stayed in port for the rest of the war. Gradually many of the fleet's personnel were transferred to the submarine force, which caused a severe loss of morale within the German navy. This in turn would ultimately contribute to the collapse of its fighting forces two years later. The Battle of Jutland was the final great action to be fought between surface forces in the Age of Steam.

In America, the Battle of Jutland shocked the Wilson administration. It demonstrated that the British fleet was not supreme, and that the United States might yet find itself facing Germany on the high seas without British protection. In response to the battle, plus a new threat of German U-boat warfare, in August 1916 a large new naval building program was rushed through Congress. Ten battleships, six battle cruisers, ten scout cruisers, fifty destroyers, and sixty-seven submarines were to be built within the next three years.

UNDERSEA WARFARE

When war broke out in August 1914, Britain imposed a blockade against Germany, hoping that this would deny vital foodstuffs and raw materials. But the blockade did not seriously hurt Germany at first because of previously stockpiled materials, development of substitutes, and imports from neutrals by way of the Baltic Sea. In response, in February 1915 Germany declared the waters around Britain and Ireland a war zone and warned that both Allied and neutral ships in the war zone would now be subject to attack by submarines and surface ships.

The German surface raiders were kept at bay by the British home fleets, but not so the German submarines,

or *U-boats,* as they were called. Beginning in February the U-boats sank an average of almost two ships per day. In May the *U-20* sank the British passenger liner *Lusitania* off the south coast of Ireland. Among the dead were 128 U.S. citizens. (Besides passengers, the ship was later determined to have been carrying war supplies to England.) Americans at home were outraged, but as Germany had calculated, the United States was not ready to go to war. President Wilson urged patience, and he demanded that Germany stop its unrestricted submarine warfare. In August a British passenger steamer was sunk with the loss of three American lives. This brought U.S. protests to the point of threatening war. In response to this, the German kaiser proclaimed that no more passenger liners would be attacked. This ended the first phase of U-boat warfare in the North Sea. For the rest of the year the Germans shifted the focus of U-boat warfare to the Mediterranean, where more than 100 Allied ships were sunk by year's end.

Early in 1916 the German general staff thought that the United States had become more understanding about German submarine warfare, and so they resumed attacks in the British Isles area. In March the unarmed French steamer *Sussex* was sunk in the English Channel by a U-boat that mistook her for a warship. Casualties included three wounded Americans. This led President Wilson to threaten to break diplomatic relations with Germany. The German government replied with the "*Sussex* Pledge," promising that henceforth international law would be followed. This required that notice be given and provisions be made for the safety of passengers and crew before a noncombatant ship could be torpedoed.

Admiral Scheer decided that U-boat warfare against merchant shipping could not possibly succeed under these circumstances, so he recalled most of his U-boats and directed that those left only attack Allied warships. He decided to try to use cruisers to lure British forces to locations where waiting U-boats could torpedo them. Thus it was that about a dozen German U-boats were deployed when the Grand Fleet sortied for the cruise that would lead to the Battle of Jutland.

By late 1916 the German general staff had begun to realize that Germany was losing the war simply because it had not yet won it. Time was on the side of the Allies. Germany could not continue this stalemate because the British blockade was beginning to hurt. The U-boat offered the only hope of immediate victory. A study by the chief of the German naval staff concluded that if major unrestricted submarine warfare were started by February 1917, Britain would be starved into submission by June, before the summer harvest.

The Germans calculated that even if American aid were started, it would be too late to do any good. They believed the Allies would not start convoys. And they figured Allied antisubmarine tactics would not be successful in combating the large number of improved German U-boats. They were to be proven wrong on each of these assumptions.

On 1 February 1917 the kaiser ordered his U-boat fleet to begin unrestricted submarine warfare in designated "barred zones" in the eastern Mediterranean and around Britain, France, and Italy. Any Allied or neutral ships found in these areas were liable to be sunk without warning. By the end of April, the Germans had sunk over 2 million tons of shipping, exceeding even their own estimates. Britain's economy and war industry were severely hurt. It quickly became clear that if the sinkings continued at this rate, Britain would soon have to surrender.

AMERICA DECLARES WAR

Top American naval officers had been strongly recommending that the Navy prepare for war ever since the European war started. There was powerful political opposition to this from Secretary of the Navy Josephus Daniels and from Congress, however. With Wilson's approval, Secretary Daniels had refrained from making any war preparations during Wilson's first term in office, concentrating instead on in-house reforms. In 1916 President Wilson had been reelected on a platform of staying out of the war. They felt that any buildup of the fleet would be contrary to that pledge. The shipbuilding program authorized in 1916 was plodding along without a sense of urgency, and this was as President Wilson and Daniels wanted it. The Navy was especially weak in destroyers and other small antisubmarine patrol craft, but the battleship fleet was adequate under the circumstances.

American public opinion had swung strongly to the side of the Allies by the end of 1916, mainly because of German U-boat warfare and American civilian casualties. When Germany proclaimed its policy of unrestricted submarine warfare in February 1917, President Wilson severed diplomatic relations and ordered American merchantmen bound for the war zone to be armed.

In early March, British intelligence intercepted a secret German note to Mexico. In it, Germany's foreign secretary, Arthur Zimmermann, tried to convince Mexico to join Germany in the event of war with the United States. In return, Germany would help Mexico recover land it had relinquished to the United States after the Mexican War, comprising the states of Texas, Arizona, and New Mexico. When the British revealed the contents of this note to the U.S. government, it caused an uproar. All remaining support for the German cause in Washington evaporated, even among those who had strongly supported neutrality. In late March, four American merchant ships were sunk by U-boats without warning off the British Isles. Wilson hesitated no longer. On 2 April he sent his war message to Congress, stating, "The world must be made safe for democracy. . . . The right is more precious than peace." On 6 April Congress declared war on Germany.

THE CONVOY SYSTEM

Shortly before war was declared, President Wilson had sent Rear Admiral William Sims to London to confer with the British. The ship on which he was traveling struck a German mine near Liverpool and he came ashore among the survivors. He proceeded to London, arriving a few days after the American declaration of war. He immediately went into consultation with Admiral Sir John Jellicoe, the first sea lord. Sims learned that Britain was losing the war and would have to surrender by October if the U-boat sinkings could not be stopped.

Sims was very surprised that the British had not started a convoy system to protect merchant shipping. This method of grouping merchantmen under destroyer escort had proven successful across the English Channel. But British admirals believed it unwise to bunch merchant ships at sea, fearing collisions and claiming that destroyers should not be used for such a "defensive" role. A group of younger British naval officers, however, had wanted to try the convoy. Sims conferred with them and was convinced that the convoy concept would work. He went directly to the British prime minister, David Lloyd George, and strongly recommended that the convoy be tried. The prime minister agreed and directed the admiralty to try it out.

In the meantime, Sims cabled President Wilson to send every destroyer possible to Britain to help in antisubmarine warfare. The first destroyers arrived in May. By July, thirty-seven American destroyers were in Britain assigned to antisubmarine work, mostly escorting convoys under British command.

Sims was appointed commander, United States Naval Forces Operating in European Waters. He concentrated on all aspects of antisubmarine warfare. He had to convince the top officers in the U.S. Navy, and Josephus Daniels as well, about the value of the convoy. While the British started convoys on 30 April at Sims's urging, it took the U.S. Navy until July before it accepted the idea. By that time the success of the convoy system had been proved in actual operations. Escorts of convoys sank more U-boats than ever before, convoys sailed without collisions, and port schedules were greatly improved. Convoys could sail on direct routes, not having to zigzag to avoid U-boats. This saved both time and fuel. From May onward, losses dropped steadily. Adoption of the

A British sailor on the stern of a torpedo boat destroyer prepares to drop depth charges on German U-boats in the North Atlantic.

convoy system was a key factor in saving Britain from defeat in World War I.

ANTISUBMARINE OPERATIONS

No one single method of warfare, however, could defeat the U-boats. In addition to the convoy, the following methods were used to finally bring the menace under control:

Surface Warfare. The destroyer came to be the main surface vessel designed for combating the submarine. Along with its guns and torpedoes, the destroyers also carried a new weapon called the *depth charge.* Designed by the British in the earlier part of the war, depth charges were canisters of TNT fitted with a device that would detonate at a preset depth. These could be rolled off the stern from racks or fired from simple launchers called "Y guns," so named because of their shape. By 1918 destroyers carried from thirty to forty depth charges, each containing 300 pounds of TNT. The United States built 273 destroyers during and immediately after the war.

Another ship designed by the U.S. Navy especially for antisubmarine warfare was the *submarine chaser.* This was a wooden vessel 110 feet long. Subchaser patrols were established in the North Sea, and across the southern end of the Adriatic Sea in the Mediterranean to bottle up Austrian submarines. Nearly 400 of these little ships were built, and they were very helpful in convoying and other antisubmarine functions.

It was not enough just to escort and patrol against lurking submarines, however. Locating the submarine under the water was the key to destroying it. In 1915 the *hydrophone* was invented. This device could pick up underwater noises and indicate their bearing but not the range. If two or three ships, each with a hydrophone, found a submarine, however, they could determine by cross bearings almost exactly where the submarine was located, drop depth charges, and destroy their prey. The subchasers were fitted with hydrophones in 1917 and proved to be even better equipped than the destroyers to hunt the U-boats. When three ships worked together in this manner, the system was called *triangulation.* This was the beginning of what is now called *sonar,* underwater sound equipment.

Mines. The blockade of German submarine bases with surface ships did not prove to be very effective. So, the Allies laid gigantic minefields to prevent U-boats from getting into the Atlantic. One of these minefields was laid across the Dover Strait, from England to Belgium. Because this field could be patrolled against German minesweepers, it proved to be the most effective. The Dover Strait Barrage destroyed at least twelve U-boats and completely closed the strait to German submarine traffic.

The largest minefield was the North Sea Mine Barrage, which ran from Scotland almost to the Norwegian coast. The laying of this minefield presented great problems, all of which were overcome with special equipment and hard work. When finished, the field had 70,200 mines, 56,600 of them laid by the U.S. Navy. There is no positive information available on how effective the field was. It is believed that at least one submarine was sunk and a number of others damaged.

The submarine chaser was a ship designed by the U.S. Navy especially for antisubmarine patrols in the North Sea and the Mediterranean. This squadron of sub chasers is getting under way to head for home at the end of the war.

A minefield, however, is often far more dangerous in the minds of those who must try to cross it than it may actually be. How many U-boats declined to try to make the trip through the minefield is unknown. It is documented that morale among the submariners was falling fast at this time, partly because of the minefields. And it was the German submarine force that led mutinies that undermined the whole German fleet as the war neared its end.

Air Warfare. Air operations had been carried out by the British against submarines since early in the war without much success. With the advent of the convoy, however, careful coordination of air patrols with convoy schedules began to pay off. The early airplanes flying these missions had no effective weapons to sink submarines, but they did attack and damage a number of them, and this served to discourage the U-boats. Improved weapons and detection methods would make the airplane an important antisubmarine weapon during World War II.

AMERICA'S ROLE

The U.S. Navy did not take part in the dramatic surface warfare actions that had occurred in the early years of the war. Our Navy's role was mainly to patrol and convoy the huge numbers of troops and enormous amounts of supplies needed by the ground forces on the western front after the American entrance into the war. By midsummer 1917, just a few months after the United States entered the war, 50,000 troops a month were crossing to France. A year later, 200,000 were crossing each month. All told, over 2 million Americans crossed the Atlantic to the war zone, and not a single troop ship or soldier was lost to U-boats.

On land, these American forces were vital in stopping major German offensives against the Allies in early 1918, and again in July 1918, during the Second Battle of the Marne. American forces, including over 25,000 marines, bore some of the heaviest fighting at Château-Thierry, Belleau Wood, and the Meuse-Argonne fronts and succeeded in throwing the Germans back. Large-caliber naval guns mounted on railway flatcars helped destroy German railroads, bridges, and ammunition dumps during the first Allied offensive in late summer 1918.

The American shipbuilding industry built several thousand merchant ships to carry supplies and war material to England and France. These supplies, along with the manpower and the highly successful convoy system of the U.S. Navy, were essential in helping the Allies to victory.

ALLIED VICTORY

Fortunately for the Allies, the Americans had entered the war at the decisive time. Russia had surrendered to the Germans in late 1917 after the Russian Revolution and terrible defeats on the eastern front. This released large numbers of German troops to the western front, where they outnumbered the Allies for the first time since 1914. New tactics and equipment—aircraft, tanks, and mobile artillery—had been adopted by the Germans. The Americans arrived just in time to help stop these fierce drives.

But Germany could not keep up its last offensives. It had temporarily avoided starvation with the capture of Romania and the Russian Ukraine in early 1916, but the British blockade gradually caused widespread famine and shortages of war material. By October 1918 its submarines were defeated, and the Allies were advancing rapidly toward Germany. Its High Seas Fleet began to mutiny because ships could not sortie without heading into certain death. The convoy system had not only destroyed the U-boats, it had also made the Allies overwhelmingly powerful on the sea and in the field. The German people were starving and near revolution. On 9 November 1918 Kaiser Wilhelm II abdicated and fled to exile in Holland. Two days later, on the eleventh hour of the eleventh day of the eleventh month, Germany surrendered to the Allies in a railway car near Paris.

Chronology

28 July	1914	World War I begins
8 Dec.	1914	Von Spee beaten at Falklands
25 Apr.	1915	Gallipoli assault
7 May	1915	*Lusitania* sunk by U-boat
31 May	1916	Battle of Jutland
1 Feb.	1917	Germany begins unrestricted sub warfare
6 Apr.	1917	America declares war on Germany
July	1917	Convoying begins to Europe; American troops arrive
3 Mar.	1918	Russia signs nonaggression treaty with Germany
11 Nov.	1918	Germany surrenders

Study Guide Questions

1. What was the main focus of the United States during the Taft administration from 1908 to 1913?
2. A. Which nations formed the Triple Entente in World War I?
   B. Which nations formed the Central Powers?
3. A. Which two navies were the principal enemies in World War I?
   B. What sea became the major area for hostilities in the Atlantic region?
4. A. What geographic advantage did the Central Powers have?
   B. What major geographical disadvantage did Germany's navy have?
   C. What great disadvantage did Britain have?
5. What strategy did the enemy navies set out to follow to win the war?
6. What major amphibious operation was carried out by the Allies in 1915–16?
7. A. Who was the commander of German surface forces in the Pacific when war broke out?
   B. When and where did the German threat in the Pacific region end?
8. What major battle took place in the North Sea in 1916? What were the results?
9. What did Germany do in 1917 to try to bring the war to a favorable conclusion?
10. What two events nearly caused the United States to go to war with Germany in 1915 and 1916?
11. What event in early 1917 caused all remaining congressional support for Germany to cease?
12. What tactic caused Allied shipping losses from U-boat attacks to decline after May 1917?
13. What new weapons began to be used by destroyers against submarines in World War I?
14. What weapon was used in large numbers to prevent egress of German U-boats into the North Atlantic?
15. What was the U.S. Navy's principal role in World War I?
16. What turned the tide of the war on land for the Allies in 1918?
17. When and where did Germany surrender to the Allies?

Vocabulary

neutrality	U-boat
stalemate	unrestricted submarine
stockpile	warfare
hydrophone	depth charge
minefield	sortie
mine barrage	triangulation

7

The Interwar Years, 1918–1941

After World War I was over, the victorious Allies conferred at Versailles, France. They imposed their demands on a defeated Germany the following June. The resulting Treaty of Versailles included a requirement that Germany pay reparations (payments for economic injury) to the Allies, eventually set at $33 billion, an amount far beyond Germany's ability to pay. This provision served to foster much resentment on the part of many Germans toward the Allies for years to come.

As part of the treaty inserted at President Wilson's insistence, the Allies agreed to form the League of Nations, an organization in which the nations of the world would join together to ensure peace and security for all. But because the league included a mutual defense provision, which stated that an attack on one would be defended by all, the U.S. Congress refused to accept the treaty, despite many attempts by Wilson to gain support for it. Finally, in July 1921, after Wilson had been replaced as president by Warren Harding, Congress passed a resolution to end the war and ratified separate peace treaties with the Axis powers that October.

Another treaty provision that was a severe blow to German morale was that most of the newer German warships had to be turned over to the Allies. Germany was allowed to retain only half a dozen predreadnought battleships and cruisers and twelve destroyers, but no submarines. However, before the Allies could take ownership of the forfeited vessels, the German navy succeeded in scuttling them all at Scapa Flow, where they had been ordered to proceed at the end of hostilities. The furious Allies then decreed that almost all of the remaining German navy's ships had to be turned over to the Allies.

NAVAL DISARMAMENT TREATIES

Soon after World War I a headlong rush "back to normalcy" had quickly made itself felt across the United States. Isolationism gained in favor. Naval building projects were vetoed as the country listened to the demands of pacifists to cut military spending. In 1921 there was a business recession, felt not only in the United States but also in other major industrial nations. It seemed to President Harding that it was time for the Allies to come to an agreement on arms limitations.

In November 1921 Britain, France, Italy, and Japan were invited to send representatives to a conference in Washington on naval disarmament. At the opening of the conference the United States stunned the conferees with sweeping proposals to drastically reduce the standing navies of each of the major naval powers. Among other things, the United States, Britain, and Japan would agree to a 5:5:3 ratio in battleship tonnage. After several weeks of negotiations, the Washington Naval Disarmament Treaty was signed. This limited the total tonnage of capital ships and placed limitations on the tonnage and armament of these ships and cruisers. The treaty limited battleships to nine 16-inch guns and cruisers to 8-inch guns. No limitations on total tonnage of cruisers were included.

As a concession to the Japanese, who felt that the treaty gave them third-rate naval status, a so-called nonfortification clause was inserted. This specified that no further fortifications in the Pacific area would be carried out by Japan, by the United States in any of its possessions west of Hawaii, or by the British anywhere east of Singapore and north of Australia. Another treaty negotiated simultaneously "guaranteed" the territorial integrity of China.

There were, of course, some Americans who voiced opposition to the treaty provisions. The United States would not remain one of the strongest naval powers in the world if it followed the agreements. But most Americans, concerned with the weak economy and wanting to stay isolated from events in Europe, could not be persuaded to spend money on warships. As might have been expected, soon after the treaty was signed, all the world powers except the United States began major heavy-cruiser building programs. The Japanese also proceeded to fortify major island bases in the Pacific, once they knew Britain and the United States would do nothing to contest such construction.

Additional naval disarmament conferences were held on several occasions in succeeding years, but none really accomplished anything of significance. For all practical purposes, there were no further treaty limitations on navies after 1936, when the ban on capital ship construction expired.

In 1928 American isolationism led to another unusual attempt to avoid international conflict, in the form of the Kellogg-Briand Pact. This was a treaty worked out between Frank Kellogg, Coolidge's secretary of state, and French foreign minister Aristide Briand. Under its terms fifteen nations tried to outlaw war by agreeing henceforth not to use the threat of war in their dealings with each other. Eventually more than sixty nations signed the treaty. Unfortunately, this idealistic treaty would soon be scrapped because it had no provisions for enforcement.

In the late 1920s and early 1930s Presidents Coolidge and Hoover, faced by the aggressive building programs of the Europeans and Japan, reluctantly put construction bills before Congress, but pacifists, isolationists, and others who naïvely wanted the U.S. to abide by the Kellogg-Briand Pact forced Congress to reduce the programs to virtually nothing. It was not until President Franklin Roosevelt was inaugurated to his first term in 1933 that any substantial American naval warship building resumed.

RISE OF THE DICTATORSHIPS

After a short period of prosperity immediately following World War I, the economies of much of the world, including the United States, had begun to waver in the 1920s. Periods of recession and labor unrest alternated with almost dizzying heights of prosperity. Europe's faltering economy collapsed because of widespread inflation, first in Germany and then in other major nations. Revolution swept across Russia, and riots and strikes erupted throughout Europe. Finally, in 1929, the U.S. stock market collapsed. The great world Depression was on.

In this climate of worldwide despair, anyone with a radical plan to end the depression—and a voice loud enough to be heard—could move crowds of disillusioned people to follow. Benito Mussolini had come into power in Italy in 1922, reawakening the grandeur of ancient Rome in the eyes of his followers. He inspired Italian workers to build up the country's military might so that he could reestablish Rome as the center of Mediterranean power. At the same time, Adolf Hitler, playing on the theme of German superiority, founded the Nazi Party in Germany. By 1932 the party dominated the German government. When unrest swept Berlin in 1933, Hitler was named chancellor.

During the early 1920s, Japanese moderates were fairly successful in keeping the militarists out of political

Adolph Hitler *(right)* rose to power in Germany and became chancellor in 1933. He campaigned on themes of national economic self-sufficiency and *lebensraum* (living space) for the German people.

control. However, in 1924 the U.S. Congress passed an immigration bill classifying the Japanese as undesirable Orientals. The bill prohibited them from entering the United States under any circumstances. The militarists were now able to arouse national resentment against the United States and political support for themselves. Once in control, the militarists selectively assassinated their political opposition and began to build up the Imperial armed forces.

By the early 1930s, the military dictatorships in Italy, Germany, and Japan were seeking to regain prosperity for their peoples by conquering their neighbors. The democracies—Britain, France, and the United States—refused to take effective countermeasures against these aggressive acts. This lack of military response helped bring on World War II.

In 1931 the Japanese leaders felt themselves sufficiently strong to invade China from their Korean bases. The United States and Britain protested the move as a violation of the Washington Treaty, but they did nothing more. A protest by the League of Nations did nothing to stop Japan's three-month conquest of Manchuria. Japan simply withdrew from the league. The militarists recognized that they had achieved the naval superiority to do whatever they wished in the western Pacific. And they had; the treaties had ensured that they would.

In 1935 Hitler withdrew Germany from the league and refused to continue abiding by all treaty limitations imposed on German armaments and military service. The Germans began rebuilding their armed forces, including capital ships and submarines for a new German navy. In response, the British got Germany to agree to naval building quotas limiting their number of surface warships to 35 percent of British tonnage, and submarines to 45 percent. Also in 1935 the Italians invaded Ethiopia, annexing that country in 1936 and renaming it Italian East Africa. When the League of Nations denounced that act as "bald aggression" and imposed some economic sanctions, Italy purchased war supplies from Germany, withdrew from the league, and with Germany formed the Rome-Berlin Axis.

In early 1939 Hitler abolished the Anglo-German naval limitation agreement, freeing Germany to begin building as many warships of whatever kind and tonnage it wanted. By the time war broke out in September 1939, when Hitler invaded Poland, the German Navy consisted of two 31,000-ton battleships, two 42,000-ton battleships nearing completion (the *Tirpitz* and *Bismarck*), three 20,000-ton pocket battleships, nine cruisers, a number of destroyers, and fifty-six submarines. Germany continued to build U-boats throughout the war at a furious rate. Before it was finally defeated in May 1945, Germany sent nearly 1,200 submarines into action against Allied shipping.

U.S. NAVY IN THE PREWAR YEARS

After the Washington treaties, U.S. Navy strategists changed their planning as reflected in War Plan Orange, the contingency war plan that had been developed for the Pacific some years earlier. In the event of war in the Pacific, the strategists' new plans included the necessity of making a comeback from an initial loss of bases in the Philippines and Guam. They saw that the Navy would probably have to fight its way back across the Pacific, operating for long periods far from its bases while seizing and converting enemy bases. The Navy faced three problems: (1) how to free the fleet from dependence on established bases, (2) how to isolate and attack enemy bases protected by land-based air units, and (3) how to invade and occupy heavily defended enemy bases.

The U.S. Marine Corps took on the task of working out problem number three. From this effort came the amphibious doctrine, which was put into effect in World War II. Amphibious operations emphasized the concepts of command and control, close air support, naval gunfire support, patrol tactics, and the development of new amphibian vehicles and landing craft. This amphibious capability, when expanded to meet the needs of the war, proved to be an unstoppable assault force. Many historians regard these amphibious tactics as the most far-reaching tactical innovations of the war.

During the same time, naval aircraft and aircraft carriers came into use on a sophisticated scale. Naval aviation was originally looked upon as merely a reconnaissance arm of the fleet. But this changed in 1921 when General Billy Mitchell proved in a test that an airplane

A biplane takes off from the *Langley*, the U.S. Navy's first aircraft carrier.

could sink a battleship with bombs. Mitchell's feat convinced Navy leaders to convert a collier into the Navy's first aircraft carrier, the *Langley*, and to get the treaty powers to consent to the United States building the carriers *Lexington* and *Saratoga*.

Finally, with carriers, their aircraft, and amphibious forces working far from established home bases, a logistic support system had to be devised that would keep these forces in operation. First, there was the problem of mobile fuel and supply support. This problem was solved by the development of highly versatile at-sea replenishment capabilities: support ships moved with the fleet and resupplied it while underway. This innovation is sometimes regarded as "the secret weapon" that strategists believed would win the Pacific war.

When a marine amphibious force captured new areas from the enemy, new bases on that captured territory would have to be built rapidly. For this task the Naval Construction Battalions (NCBs, or "Seabees") were developed. The Seabees were trained to create operating bases in any environment, from jungle to rocky atoll. These bases included all the materials and personnel needed to set up various kinds of facilities. Depending upon the needs of the area commander, the bases could be rapidly built as soon as the land was cleared. Shortly thereafter the base would be in full operation.

FINAL STEPS TOWARD WAR

By 1936 the League of Nations was little more than a squabbling group, neither able nor willing to halt the drift toward world war. The aggressive dictatorships had withdrawn their memberships. In 1936 Germany remilitarized the Rhineland, in defiance of the Treaty of

Versailles. In 1937 Japan launched a full-scale invasion of China, quickly conquering most of the eastern half of the country. During these Chinese operations, Japan repeatedly bombed U.S. missions, schools, churches, and hospitals, and even sank the U.S. Navy gunboat *Panay*. The United States limited its response to verbal and written protests. In 1938 Hitler invaded Austria. Betrayed by traitors from within, that nation became a province of Germany.

British prime minister Neville Chamberlain now decided that the only way to avert war was to come to some agreement with Italy and Germany. He undertook what has become known as a policy of "appeasement." Under this policy, Britain and France made a series of concessions to Hitler and Mussolini in return for "promises of peace." In one of these deals Britain persuaded the league to recognize the Italian conquest of Ethiopia, an act that effectively destroyed the league. Next, Britain and France agreed to the takeover of Czechoslovakia by Germany.

But when Hitler's next demand was for the free city of Danzig and a large segment of western Poland, Britain and France finally drew the line, abandoned the policy of appeasement, and aligned themselves with Poland. The Soviet Union, which had been angered by the British-French sellout on Czechoslovakia, now signed a nonaggression pact with Germany. Hitler was thus free of the Soviet threat from the east. On 1 September 1939 his armies invaded Poland in a massive offensive. Britain and France, henceforth referred to as the Allies, declared war on Germany two days later. World War II had begun.

AMERICAN DRIFT TOWARD WAR

Between 1935 and 1939, as the Washington disarmament treaties collapsed, the United States retreated into a policy of isolationism and neutrality. When the Europeans declared war on each other, President Franklin Roosevelt established the Neutrality Patrol, which had as its task the reporting and tracking of belligerent ships and aircraft approaching the United States or the West Indies. Actually, President Roosevelt regarded the Neutrality Patrol as a means of preparing for the war he saw coming. The patrol enabled him to refit some ships and recall reserves to active duty for training and assignment at sea.

The American people were certainly opposed to the totalitarian governments and aggression of the Axis powers and Japan, but they wanted to stay out of the war. As the Nazi blitzkrieg rolled over Poland and conquered Belgium, Holland, Luxembourg, Norway, Denmark, and France—all by June 1940—President Roosevelt began to see the defeat of Britain as a possibility. He asked for assurances that the British fleet would not be turned over to Hitler in that event. Prime Minister Churchill replied that he could not guarantee this, since

he probably would not be prime minister following a British defeat.

Faced with the potential loss of the Royal Navy, which in effect served as the first line of U.S. defense, Congress finally recognized the necessity of expanding the U.S. Navy as Roosevelt had requested. Congress passed the Two-Ocean Navy bill, authorizing the president to build for each ocean a fleet sufficient to meet American defense needs.

Events started to move faster for the United States. In September 1940 Roosevelt concluded a deal with Churchill in which Britain gave the United States bases in the West Indies, Newfoundland, and Bermuda. In return, Britain received fifty old destroyers and ten Coast Guard cutters. In March of the following year, the famous Lend-Lease Act was passed, allowing the United States to "loan" war materials to Britain. This put U.S. industry on a wartime production level, because, as Roosevelt declared, America had become the "arsenal of democracy." The United States later seized Axis ships in American ports, froze German and Italian assets in the United States, occupied Greenland, and took over the defense of Iceland from Britain.

In 1941 high-ranking U.S. and British officers met secretly in Washington and drew up what was called the ABC-1 Staff Agreement. This agreement put the U.S. Navy in the war on the side of the Allies, since by its terms the Navy would be sharing escort duties for transatlantic convoys to Britain. The agreement also called for meetings between American and British chiefs of staff in order to make strategic plans. A key decision to come out of the meetings was that the United States would make its principal military effort in the European theater, even if Japan made war on America. This decision was made because of Germany's greater military potential and because of the immediate danger faced by Britain.

In the meantime, the situation in the Pacific had also deteriorated. When France fell in 1940, the Japanese quickly declared a protectorate (a relationship of protection and partial control) over Indochina, taking control of the valuable rice crop and occupying the air and naval bases there. They also informed the Dutch authorities in the East Indies that the oil resources on those islands would now be developed "jointly" with them. It was clear that the Japanese were out to dominate the East Indies and its mineral resources. In reaction to this aggressive behavior, President Roosevelt immediately placed an embargo on the sale of aviation gasoline and scrap iron to Japan. Steel was added to the embargo two months later.

An embargo on oil was sure to be the next U.S. move. It came in July 1941, along with a freeze on all Japanese assets in the United States. Thus the Japanese could no longer pay in cash for Dutch East Indies oil. War was now inevitable. Japanese militarists would accept nothing less than full cooperation in their effort to conquer China—and America would not give it to them.

Though some earlier actions had taken place between German submarines and U.S. naval escorts, it was not until 16 October 1941 that the first casualties were sustained by the two undeclared enemies. On that date, a U.S. destroyer was damaged by a torpedo with the loss of eleven men. In early November a naval tanker and the destroyer USS *Reuben James* were sunk with heavy losses. That caused Congress to remove the last feature of the U.S. neutrality policy. U.S. merchant ships were now armed and authorized to carry lend-lease goods directly to Britain.

However, it remained for the Japanese to bring the United States totally into the war. On 7 December 1941, the Japanese launched a carefully planned surprise carrier attack on Pearl Harbor, Hawaii. The following day Congress declared war on Japan. On 11 December Germany and Italy declared war on the United States. The United States declared war on those countries that same day.

Chronology

1918	Treaty of Versailles
1921	Washington Naval Disarmament Treaty
1929	U.S. stock market collapses
1933	Hitler becomes German chancellor
1937	Japan invades China
1938	Germany invades Austria
1939	World War II begins in Europe
1940	France falls to Germany
1940–41	U.S. enacts Japanese embargoes; U.S. declares war on Axis powers

Study Guide Questions

1. What provision of the Treaty of Versailles ending World War I caused much resentment by the German people toward the Allies for years to come?
2. A. What was the League of Nations?
   B. What defense provision did it have?
3. What provision of the Treaty of Versailles dealt with the German navy?
4. A. What were the five major naval powers invited to the naval disarmament talks in Washington in 1921?
   B. What did the 5:5:3 ratio in the proposed disarmament treaty refer to?
5. Why did the United States not embark on any large warship building programs throughout the 1920s?
6. How did the worldwide economic problems of the 1920s allow the dictatorships to arise in Europe?
7. What did Hitler do regarding the German military forces shortly after assuming power in 1933?
8. In the Pacific, what three problems did the Navy and Marine Corps have to solve?
9. What did Billy Mitchell's test sinking of a battleship by aerial bombing cause Navy leaders to do?
10. Who are the Seabees, and what is their mission?
11. What was the British policy of "appeasement" toward Germany and Italy?
12. What action by Hitler's Germany in 1939 began World War II in Europe?
13. What was the decision reached at the ABC-1 Staff meeting in 1941 about the priority of fighting the war in the Atlantic versus the Pacific regions?
14. What were the final U.S. economic acts that made war with Japan inevitable?

Vocabulary

negotiations
reconnaissance
militarist
dictatorship
Seabees
appeasement
neutrality
protectorate

Rome-Berlin Axis
League of Nations
isolationism
disarmament
pacifist
belligerent
blitzkrieg

8

World War II: The Atlantic War, 1941–1945

When Germany invaded Poland in September 1939, the German Army used a revolutionary new tactic called *blitzkrieg* (lightning war). Rather than move overland on foot, German troops used motor vehicles and tanks to advance deep into enemy territory before the defenses could react. Germany overran western Poland by the end of the month. In mid-September, under terms of a nonaggression pact secretly negotiated with Hitler, the Soviet leader Stalin invaded and captured eastern Poland.

For the next six months the war entered a quiet phase, during which Germany massed troops and equipment along the Maginot Line, a massive system of fortifications along the border between France and Germany. Then in April 1940 Hitler invaded Denmark and Norway. In May German troops maneuvered around the Maginot Line and rapidly advanced across Belgium, the Netherlands, and France. All three of these countries were soon overcome.

British troops that had been sent into France to counter the initial German buildup now hastily retreated to the coastal city of Dunkirk on the English Channel. There, in an amazing operation over a nine-day period from late May into early June, nearly 340,000 English soldiers were successfully evacuated across the channel to England by a 900-vessel fleet of mainly civilian tugboats, yachts, and other small craft—all this in spite of continual air attacks by the German Luftwaffe (air force).

In June 1940 German troops entered Paris and France surrendered. An armistice between the two was concluded a week later. A new French government called the Vichy government was set up by Marshal Philippe Pétain. By terms of the armistice agreement, the Vichy government was given nominal sovereignty over the southeastern two-fifths of France not yet occupied by German military forces, and it controlled most of the surviving French military forces. Never recognized by the Allies, Vichy was in fact under German control throughout its existence, and it eventually collapsed with the defeat of Germany in 1945. Meanwhile, in London General Charles de Gaulle organized a resistance movement

called the Free French. They rejected the Vichy government and did what they could to support the Allies throughout the war. They eventually formed the nucleus of the Fourth Republican government headed by de Gaulle after the war.

In just three months Hitler had conquered most of western Europe, and German troops were massing along the coast opposite Britain, just 20 miles away across the English Channel. The threat of invasion was imminent. But Hitler first wanted to destroy the English will to resist. To accomplish this, over the next year he used the Luftwaffe to launch against Britain the greatest air assault the world had ever known.

In what has since become known as the Battle of Britain, as many as 1,000 sorties a day were carried out by Luftwaffe bombers against targets throughout all of England at first, then later concentrated against London. To counter them, Royal Air Force pilots flying the famous Spitfire fighters often flew six and seven missions a day, inflicting heavy losses on the attackers. Inspired by Prime Minister Winston Churchill, the British people never lost their will to resist, despite massive losses. By June 1941, when Hitler finally ended the bombing campaign, over 150,000 Londoners had been killed or injured. "Never in the field of human conflict was so much owed by so many to so few," said Churchill in praise of the courageous performance of the RAF.

In late 1940 Hitler sent General Erwin Rommel and his Afrika Korps into North Africa, where they had much early success in driving back the British and advancing into Egypt. For a year and a half after that, the North African campaign was a back-and-forth affair that depended on which side was being better resupplied at the moment.

In early 1941 both British and American intelligence began picking up information that Hitler was about to invade the Soviet Union, in spite of the nonaggression pact the Soviets and Germans had signed. Both governments informed the Soviets, but they chose to disregard the warnings. Then in June Hitler launched a major in-

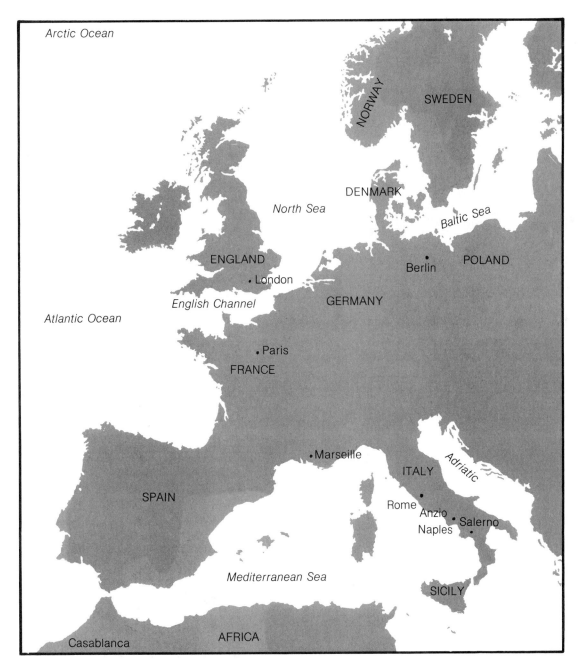

The European theater, World War II.

vasion of the Soviet Union, forcing it to join forces with the Allies. Over the next four years fighting along the eastern front in the Soviet Union would be some of the bloodiest the world had ever known. Altogether there would be over 25 million Soviet casualties and 5 million German casualties.

Despite these events taking place in Europe, the majority of Americans wanted no part in the European conflict. President Franklin Roosevelt, however, reelected for a third term in 1940, felt differently. As mentioned in the last chapter, he took many measures to prepare America

for war and to gear up American military industrial production to wartime levels.

The Japanese surprise attack on Pearl Harbor on 7 December 1941 stunned the American people and galvanized them into action. America was now ready to go to war. Three days after the Japanese attack, Germany and Italy joined Japan in declaring war on the United States. The second of two world wars had come to America.

A reorganization of Navy commands followed the Pearl Harbor attack and declarations of war. Admiral Ernest J. King became commander in chief of the U.S.

Admiral Ernest King, chief of naval operations during much of World War II, played a major part in formulating the strategy that led to victory in the Atlantic and the Pacific wars. His leadership was summarized in his statement, "I can forgive anything except for three things which I will not tolerate—stupidity, laziness, and carelessness."

fleet. He would also become the chief of naval operations in March 1942. It was under his guidance that the United States would contribute to the defeat of Germany in the Atlantic and achieve victory over Japan in the Pacific.

THE BATTLE OF THE ATLANTIC

When World War II broke out in September 1939, the German admiral in charge of U-boat operations, Admiral Donitz, tried to put as many submarines at sea as possible to disrupt the flow of food and war materials to Britain. At first he was hampered in his efforts by the small number of German U-boats (only fifty-six when war started) and by the distances they had to proceed in order to get to the western Atlantic sea-lanes from their bases in Germany. Once Norway and France had been conquered, however, the situation changed. While secondary bases of operation were established in Norway, Donitz personally supervised the construction of fortified submarine bases along the French Atlantic coast at Brest, Lorient, St. Nazaire, La Pallice, and Bordeaux. Submarines operating out of these bases could cut their transit time to the hunting grounds in the western Atlantic in half. Moreover, German submarine production was continually increasing. By July 1940 there were many more U-boats on station in the Atlantic at any given time than in the opening months of the war.

Because of a limited number of available escorts, and lack of any effective convoy operations, Allied losses to the U-boats began to mount rapidly. Admiral Donitz often used wolf-pack tactics, with as many as twenty or thirty U-boats coordinating their attacks. Often the targeted merchantmen were silhouetted by bright lights ashore all along the U.S. Atlantic seaboard. By fall of 1940, German U-boats were sinking about 300,000 tons of Allied shipping per month. German successes were making such a dent into oil supplies that fuel rationing had to be imposed in the northeastern United States.

A particularly difficult phase of the North Atlantic sea war involved the Allied convoys to the Russian port of Murmansk on the Barents Sea. During the German offensives into the Soviet Union in 1942 and 1943, Allied assistance to Soviet forces was slowed to a trickle. Sometimes less than 40 percent of a given convoy made it to Murmansk, but the perseverance of the Allied merchantmen and Allied escort ships finally broke Germany's efforts to destroy the convoys. Some historians believe that the supplies received through Murmansk were a decisive factor in preventing Russian surrender to the Germans during the war.

President Roosevelt and Prime Minister Churchill realized that little could be done against the Germans in Europe until the submarine menace had been brought under control in the Atlantic. Every effort was made to defeat the U-boats. By early 1941 enough escort vessels

A depth-charge attack on a German submarine in the North Atlantic.

had been built so that most merchant vessels could be convoyed at least part of the way on each side of the Atlantic. In addition, an improved radar was developed that allowed convoy escort ships to detect and track surfaced U-boats. By May 1941 the German Kriegsmarine's code had been broken by British code breakers, allowing the British to decipher Donitz's instructions to his wolf packs at sea and steer convoys away from them. Increasingly effective coastal air patrols inhibited U-boat operations off the U.S. Atlantic seaboard by late 1941 and in the Gulf of Mexico and off South America by 1942. British patrols flying out of Iceland did the same for the western approaches to Britain. Eventually all these efforts began to pay dividends. In 1940 twenty-six Allied vessels were sunk for every U-boat lost. By 1942 that ratio had been cut to thirteen to one. This was still serious, because by then the Germans were producing about twenty new U-boats per month, but the tide was turning. By 1943, with the addition of the escort carrier and hunter-killer groups, and sufficient numbers of escorts to accompany convoys all the way across the Atlantic, the rate of exchange had fallen to just two vessels lost for every U-boat sunk.

Thereafter, continued improvements in radio-direction-finding techniques and hunter-killer operations kept the U-boats pretty much under control and out of the Atlantic sea-lanes until the war's end in 1945. After the liberation of France in 1944, most U-boats operated from bases in Norway. Toward the end of the war, U-boats fitted with breathing tubes called snorkels (which permitted them to operate diesel engines while submerged) attempted a last blitz against Allied shipping in British waters. Some even patrolled once again in U.S. waters, but these efforts came too late to affect the outcome of the war.

Notable among U.S. antisubmarine group exploits was an incident involving the submarine *U-505* in June 1944. She had been tracked from the time she left her base in Brest until she headed home northward from a cruise in the south Atlantic. With this information Captain Dan Gallery and his group led by the escort carrier *Guadalcanal* intercepted *U-505* and blasted her to the surface with depth charges and hedgehogs. The defeated crew set demolition charges and abandoned ship, but before the U-boat could sink, a specially trained American salvage party boarded it. They disconnected the demoli-

A boarding party from the USS *Guadalcanal,* under the command of Captain Dan Gallery, captures the German submarine *U-505* in a hunter-killer operation on 4 June 1944. This was the first boarding and capture by U.S. naval forces since 1815.

tion charges, closed the sea valves, and captured the U-boat and her entire crew. They then pumped out the waterlogged boat and towed her to Bermuda. After the war the *U-505* was restored, and has since been on display at the Museum of Science and Industry in Chicago, Illinois.

In all, the Allies lost 2,775 merchant ships, amounting to 23 million tons during the Battle of the Atlantic. Of this, 14.5 million tons were sunk by German U-boats. The Germans entered 1,175 U-boats into the war, of which they lost 781. They used the capital ships they had at the beginning of the war and those completed during it as independent surface raiders. Though they scored some notable successes, most of these were eventually hunted down by the Allies and sunk or blockaded in port.

THE WAR IN EUROPE AND AFRICA

In the spring of 1942 the German armies were consolidating their positions in France and North Africa. Nowhere were things going well for the Allies. American military leaders and Stalin in the Soviet Union wanted to bring the war directly to Hitler with an invasion in Europe. But cooler British heads prevailed, convincing President Roosevelt that the Allies were not ready for such a major undertaking in the face of Hitler's superior forces.

Still, the Allies had to do something in order to recover the initiative. Winston Churchill proposed an invasion of French North Africa in order to take the pressure off British forces in Egypt. Field Marshal Erwin Rommel, the "Desert Fox" commanding the elite German Afrika Korps, was heading toward Suez, the loss of which would be extremely serious for the Allies. Churchill believed an Allied invasion would also have the secondary benefit of drawing German forces away from the beaches of Europe to Africa. Once there, they could not be easily returned to the continent because of increasing Allied control of the Mediterranean Sea area.

Operation Torch was planned for 8 November 1942. This became the first Allied offensive operation against the Axis in the European–North African theater. American amphibious forces making up the Western Naval Task Force were to come from East Coast ports and converge on French Morocco. They were to land on three beaches near the primary objective, the port of Casablanca.

Combined British and American forces making up the Central Naval Task Force would invade Oran, in Algeria. A third combined contingent, called the Eastern Naval Task Force, would seize Algiers. Lieutenant General Dwight Eisenhower was the supreme commander, and Admiral Kent Hewitt, USN, was the Amphibious Task Force commander.

The big question mark of Operation Torch concerned the Vichy French forces in the area. Would they resist the landings? The invasion thus became a political problem

Operation Torch, the invasion of North Africa by the Allies. Arrows show the landing sites. American forces landed at the three beachheads in Morocco while combined British and U.S. forces landed at the two Algerian cities.

as well as a military one. If the French decided to offer serious resistance, they might well be able to hold off the Allies until German reinforcements arrived. This could doom the invasion and set up a major disaster for the Allies in North Africa.

As it turned out, the French Navy and some shore batteries put up a spirited defense at Casablanca, but this was quickly eliminated by U.S. Navy gunfire. Little resistance was met in either Oran or Algiers. The French quickly surrendered and joined forces with de Gaulle's Free French (in accordance with secret orders from Marshal Pétain, the French leader in Vichy). In response, Hitler's armies immediately occupied the previously unoccupied parts of France.

Operation Torch, though anything but smooth, was completely successful in meeting all of its objectives. It showed, however, that the Allies were by no means ready to invade Hitler's Europe. Much more training, larger forces, and better equipment would be necessary.

The North African operations set up one of the first major defeats for the Axis. Shortly before the Allied landings in Morocco and Algeria, British field marshal Bernard Montgomery's Eighth Army routed the Afrika Korps at El Alamein, thus removing the threat to Suez.

The Allies then squeezed the Germans and Italians between them into Tunisia. In May the fighting in North Africa ended with the defeat and capture of the entire Afrika Korps, about 275,000 troops, and all of their remaining equipment. (Rommel escaped to Germany in the closing days of the campaign.) As an indirect result of the Allied victory in Africa, most of the main units of the Vichy French naval fleet were subsequently scuttled at Toulon.

ON THE EASTERN FRONT

In the winter of 1942–43 the Soviets had surrounded and defeated an entire German army at Stalingrad, an industrial city on the Volga River. They took 330,000 prisoners in one of history's most savage battles. The Battle of Stalingrad turned the tide on the eastern front. The Soviet advance, begun in February 1943, did not stop until the Red Army entered the German capital of Berlin two years later.

CASABLANCA CONFERENCE

In January 1943 President Roosevelt and Prime Minister Churchill met in the famous Casablanca Conference. They decided that before any major offensives were to succeed elsewhere, antisubmarine warfare in the Atlantic had to be given top priority. This was when merchant shipping losses along the U.S. East Coast were at their peak. Second, the Allied leaders agreed that the next offensive operation against the Axis would be an invasion of Sicily in July. The Mediterranean sea-lanes were now reasonably secure, except from land-based air attack. Finally, the leaders announced that the Allies would demand nothing short of the unconditional surrender of Germany, Italy, and Japan.

OPERATION HUSKY: INVASION OF SICILY

With the success of North Africa still fresh in the minds of all, Allied forces under the command of General Eisenhower prepared for a massive invasion of Sicily, code named Operation Husky. This was to be the first major attempt to take the home territory of an Axis nation. On 9 July 1943 the invasion took place on beaches on the southern side of the island. Admiral Hewitt again commanded the American amphibious forces, while Field Marshal Montgomery commanded the British Eighth Army. Over 580 ships landed and supported some 470,000 Allied troops on the island.

A force of newly developed amphibious ships and assault craft—LSTs, DUKWs, LCIs, LCTs, and LCVPs—took part. Axis tanks leading strong armored counterattacks were driven off the field by effective naval gunfire, thus allowing the Americans and British to advance.

Soon the 350,000 troops of Italian general Alfredo Guzzoni were in full retreat, chased by General George Patton's tanks and Montgomery's forces. Patton proved to be a masterful field commander, rapidly moving his armor to best advantage and chasing the retreating Axis armies toward Messina and an evacuation of the island. Only about one-third of the Axis armies escaped to Italy with their equipment.

By 17 August Sicily was under Allied control. Allied forces had sustained some heavy casualties at the hands of the German Luftwaffe, but the new amphibious ships, detailed training, planning, and rehearsals paid off handsomely.

The Sicilian campaign was a major triumph for the Allies, for it largely eliminated Italy from the war. King Victor Emmanuel II deposed Mussolini and put him into "protective custody." Marshal Pietro Badoglio, the new head of government, said publicly that he would continue the war against the Allies, but in private he began negotiations that would lead to surrender. In the meantime, Eisenhower's staff began immediate planning for the invasion of Italy itself.

OPERATION AVALANCHE: INVASION OF ITALY

On the eve of 8 September, just before the invasion of Italy at Salerno, the Italian government announced an armistice. Much of the Italian fleet steamed out of the northern ports of Genoa and La Spezia to surrender at Malta.

But the Allies still had to contend with the Germans. Montgomery's army had crossed the Strait of Messina to the mainland on 3 September without much opposition. The Germans, however, had sensed a landing planned for Salerno and had mined and fortified the beaches accordingly. When the landings, designated Operation Avalanche, occurred on 9 September, the amphibious forces of Admiral Hewitt and General Mark Clark met fierce German resistance.

German forces had the beaches zeroed in, and motorized vehicles and tanks were positioned overlooking the landing sites. The Luftwaffe was standing by to turn the beaches into an inferno. In spite of these defenses, a precarious beachhead was secured, but with heavy losses. The beachhead was repeatedly saved by naval gunfire support. Noting the reliance of Allied forces on the supporting warships, the Nazis hurled the bulk of their air power at these ships. The Germans introduced radio-controlled glide bombs, which caused severe damage to a number of British and American cruisers. Three destroyers were sunk, and many ships were damaged.

But the beachhead held. German tactical errors in the field halted their counterattacks in mid-September. A strategic error by Field Marshal Rommel withheld German reinforcements from the north—when they could probably have made the difference. On 16 September Montgomery's Eighth Army joined forces with Clark's Fifth Army, and the Germans withdrew to a new defense line north of Naples. That great port city was occupied by the Fifth Army on 1 October. The port was a shambles, and the harbor was cluttered with sunken, booby-trapped ships scuttled by the Germans. Clearance of the harbor was assigned to the Seabees, who managed to do it, despite incredible obstacles, within four months. Meanwhile, the Allies began their buildup for further movement northward.

ANZIO

The Germans had consolidated their forces at the Gustav Line, about halfway between Naples and Rome. To bypass these defenses, the Allies planned an "end run"—an amphibious assault on Anzio Beach, some 37 miles south of Rome. The planning was complicated by the fact that many of the Allied forces in the Mediterranean theater were being transferred to England in preparation for the great invasion of France across the English Channel.

Nevertheless, the landing was made on 22 January 1944 with only two reinforced divisions. The initial landing met with little resistance, but the Germans quickly moved in to stop any forward movement by the relatively small Allied invasion force. Allied reinforcements poured into the small area, but the Germans kept reinforcing their surrounding forces at a similar rate, building up powerful artillery defenses that continuously

The cruiser USS *Philadelphia* points her antiaircraft guns skyward while making a smoke screen off the Anzio beachhead.

pounded the enclosed Allies. A major seaborne supply route was established between Anzio and Naples over the next several months. As forces on both sides grew, Allied casualties rose to 59,000 men. One-third were lost from disease, exhaustion, and stress caused by severe battle fatigue and continuous rains.

The Allied force eventually grew to 90,200 Americans and 35,500 British, packed into a small beachhead. They were surrounded by 135,000 Germans who had placed their artillery so it could reach any part of the invasion site. It wasn't until the rains ceased in May that the Allies finally broke the German hold on Monte Cassino, the key fortress on the Gustav Line, and surged northward. The Germans broke off all contact at Anzio when this happened, and the victorious Allies swept unopposed into Rome on 4 June.

Two days later the focus of attention in Europe became coastal France, where the great cross-Channel operation against Hitler's *Festung Europa* (Fortress Europe) began. The rest of the Italian campaign received little public attention. Nevertheless, the fighting went on, as the Germans slowly but steadily retreated northward.

OPERATION OVERLORD: INVASION OF NORMANDY

Hitler had calculated that the Allies would be invading his Festung Europa no later than the spring of 1944. He ordered the commander on the western front, Field Marshal Karl von Rundstedt, and his deputy, Field Marshal Rommel, to build a great "Atlantic Wall" of concrete fortifications to keep the Allies out. Von Rundstedt felt that static defenses were useless against naval gunfire, so he organized highly mobile inland divisions, which could rush to any spot where an invasion occurred.

Rommel, on the other hand, felt that Allied air power would prevent the mobile divisions from getting to the seacoast. So he concentrated his efforts on beach defenses, counting heavily on mines. He also had concluded that the Allies probably would invade at the Normandy beaches, rather than at Calais, the English Channel's narrowest point. He was right. The Allies had begun to prepare for a major amphibious invasion of the Normandy coast, about 170 miles southwest of Calais, under the code name Operation Overlord.

In the early spring Eisenhower began a strategic air attack against Germany designed to eliminate aircraft factories and ruin the Luftwaffe. By April the raids had decimated the German air force to the point where the Allies could count on a thirty-to-one superiority over the Normandy beaches. Next, the Allied air forces struck at the railroad marshaling yards, bridges, and the trains and tracks themselves, wreaking such havoc that it was almost impossible for any military traffic to move by rail anywhere in France. These air attacks assisted the amphibious assault. In fact, the Allied air strikes in France and Germany *had* to be successful if Operation Overlord was to be a success.

D DAY AT NORMANDY

The invasion at Normandy was originally set for 1 May 1944, but Eisenhower postponed the date to 1 June in order to get an additional month's production of landing craft.

The physical conditions of tide, visibility, and weather all were of utmost importance to the planners. The tide was especially crucial. It had to be rising at the time of the initial landings, so the landing craft could unload and retract without becoming stranded. At the same time, the tide had to be low enough to expose sunken obstacles so underwater demolition teams could destroy them.

The Allies finally selected one hour after low tide for the first landings. This meant that each succeeding wave of boats would come in on higher tides, with less beach to cross. Only three successive days each month would provide the desired tidal heights. The closest dates to 1 June were 5, 6, and 7 June. Eisenhower selected 5 June as his first choice for D Day (debarkation day), and then chose H hours (times for operations to begin) from 0630 to 0755 for the best tidal conditions for each beach.

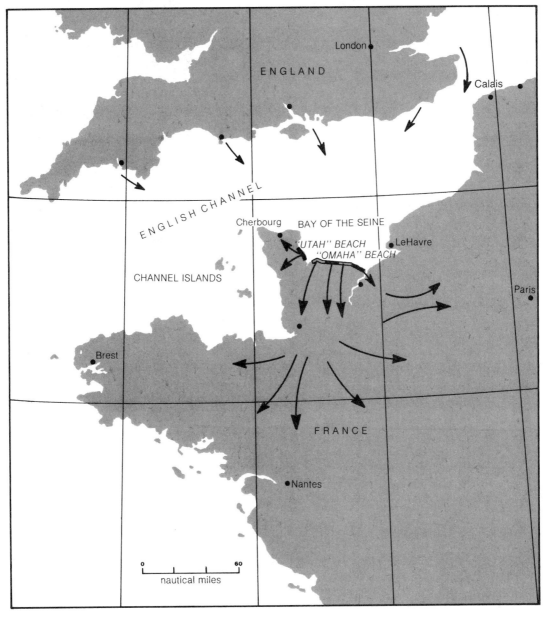

The Allied landing areas on D Day in Normandy. U.S. forces landed on Utah and Omaha Beaches; British and Canadians landed on Gold, Juno, and Sword. Breakout occurred in mid-August, and Paris was liberated on 24 August.

The invasion at Normandy. Troops wade ashore from LCVPs into withering German machine-gun fire.

The Allies planned to land on five beaches located between the Cotentin Peninsula and the Orne River mouth, near the city of Caen. The Americans were to land at Omaha and Utah Beaches on the right flank, and the British were to hit Gold, Juno, and Sword on the left flank. The principal objective of the landings, beyond establishing the beachhead itself, was to capture the port city of Cherbourg so the enormous flow of supplies could be handled quickly.

The landings took place on 6 June 1944—a day later than planned because of bad weather, which would have limited air support. In commemoration of the event, this date has been memorialized as "D Day" ever since. Minor opposition was encountered on four of the five beaches, but at Omaha Beach crack German troops were well dug in and opposed the landing fiercely, causing heavy casualties. Many of the Germans assigned to the other beaches had been lured inland to counter Allied paratroops—dropped there for just that reason. The bad weather of the fifth had in fact led the Germans to think that a landing would not occur under such conditions. But a hole in the clouds on 6 June proved to be their undoing.

The Allied troops consolidated their beachhead while expanding south and west to cut off Cherbourg on the Cotentin Peninsula. By the twenty-fourth the 40,000 Germans in Cherbourg were surrounded. A U.S. naval force of battleships, cruisers, and destroyers was called in to pound the heavily fortified Cherbourg into submission. The Germans put up a determined counterbattery action. The battleships prevailed, but not before three destroyers and the battleship USS *Texas* were hit. On 25 June the Germans surrendered Cherbourg, and the Allies began the salvage of the wrecked harbor. It was back in commission and receiving cargo within two weeks.

Throughout the Normandy invasion, the single most deadly weapon used by the Germans was the mine. The Germans had planted every kind of mine in the seas off Normandy: contact mines, which exploded upon impact; magnetic mines, detonated by the magnetic fields of steel ships; and pressure mines, set off by ships passing over them. The Allies used nearly 400 minesweepers to try to clear these mines in the days prior to the landings. Nevertheless, over 30 ships were sunk by mines during the invasion, and others were sunk in succeeding weeks as they ferried supplies across the channel.

Despite the mines and the German resistance ashore, the Allies advanced. Taking advantage of a weak spot in the German lines found by General Omar Bradley's First Army, General Patton drove through with the U.S. Third Army, creating a major breakout and trapping 50,000 German troops. On 24 August Paris fell, and General Eisenhower assumed command of the Allied ground forces on the continent. The Germans were in full retreat. A new Free French government under Charles de Gaulle replaced what was left of the Vichy regime.

Navy LSTs off-load cargo following the invasion at Omaha Beach at Normandy. Note the large number of Allied ships in the background and the barrage balloons tethered above the beach to deter air attacks.

OPERATION ANVIL: INVASION OF SOUTHERN FRANCE

Only one more invasion remained to be staged in the European theater. Operation Anvil was to take place on the French Riviera near Marseille. The operation had two objectives: to gain another port for supplies flowing into France and to serve as a diversion drawing German forces away from the primary beaches in Normandy. The landing was delayed until 15 August, however, because of a shortage of landing craft.

Admiral Hewitt was given the opportunity to conduct this first daylight landing in the Mediterranean. The assault was preceded by 1,300 bombers, which pounded the German defenses for nearly one and a half hours, and by over half an hour of heavy naval shore bombardment. The landing craft moved in under a canopy of missiles fired by amphibious ships. The missiles, naval gunfire, and bombing eliminated German resistance, and Free French and American forces quickly took the offensive. Within two weeks they had captured the port of Marseille, the naval base at Toulon, and the Riviera cities of Nice and Cannes. The Allies then surged northward through the Rhône Valley, joining with Patton's forces near Dijon on 12 September. Most of France, Belgium, and Luxembourg had been liberated, and the Germans were settling in behind their west wall, the Siegfried Line.

GERMANY IS DEFEATED

The rapid movement of Allied forces through France was made possible mainly because of the complete control of the air. When winter weather arrived, however, air cover was reduced because of poor flying conditions. On 16 December von Rundstedt launched a major counteroffensive, named the Battle of the Bulge, in the Ardennes area of Belgium. The Nazis made quick advances through a break in the U.S. lines before being stopped by massive attacks on their flanks by Allied armies. The Germans had surrounded elements of the U.S. 101st Airborne Division at the Belgian town of Bastogne. After several days of fierce fighting, the German commander demanded that the cutoff Americans surrender. The American commander, Brigadier General Anthony C. McAuliffe, gained instant and lasting fame for himself and his troops when he sent back one of the most eloquent replies in the annals of military history: "Nuts!" The terrible siege was broken on 27 December, when the U.S. Third Army, led by General George Patton, broke through the German lines. The Battle of the Bulge was Germany's last offensive.

In early 1945 the Allies resumed their attacks on the German Reich—Americans, British, French, and Canadians on the western and Italian fronts, and the Soviets on the eastern front. In March the Allied forces reached the Rhine River, and the U.S. Navy was called on to make its last direct contribution in the fight against Germany. Navy landing craft, which had been carried across Belgium by trucks and trains, helped ferry elements of Bradley's armies over the river in most of their initial crossings.

Then, on 7 March, the First Army captured the Ludendorff Bridge at Remagen, establishing a major bridgehead across the Rhine. The bridge held up for ten days under heavy German artillery fire. This was sufficient time for major forces to cross the river. The final push was now on from the west, while the Russians surged toward Berlin from the east. On 25 April U.S. and Soviet forces met at the Elbe River. They had cut Germany in half from west to east.

On 28 April Mussolini was captured and killed by Italian antifascist guerrillas while trying to escape to Switzerland. Two days later, Hitler, besieged in his bunker in Berlin by Soviet forces, committed suicide after naming Admiral Donitz as his successor. On 7 May 1945 hostilities ceased in Europe. The representatives of the German Army, Navy, and government signed the unconditional surrender document at Eisenhower's headquarters in a little red schoolhouse in Reims, France. World War II was over in Europe after five years, eight months, and six days of death and destruction.

Chronology

14 June 1940	France falls to Germany
7 Dec. 1941	Japan bombs Pearl Harbor
8 Nov. 1942	Allies invade North Africa
9 July 1943	Sicily attacked
9 Sept. 1943	Italy invaded
22 Jan. 1944	Anzio landing
4 June 1944	*U-505* captured
6 June 1944	D Day at Normandy
24 Aug. 1944	Allies liberate Paris
16–27 Dec. 1944	Battle of the Bulge
7 May 1945	World War II ends in Europe

Study Guide Questions

1. What was the Maginot Line in Europe?
2. What French city was the site of an amazing evacuation of trapped English troops in May 1940?
3. What actions took place during the Battle of Britain in 1940–41?
4. Who was the senior U.S. naval leader who took over the leadership of the U.S. Navy following Pearl Harbor?
5. What was the Battle of the Atlantic?
6. What was the German U-boat wolf-pack tactic?
7. Why was the German conquest of Norway and France important to U-boat warfare?
8. What famous antisubmarine group exploit was carried out under the leadership of Captain Dan Gallery in June 1944?
9. What factors finally led to the defeat of U-boat warfare in the Battle of the Atlantic?
10. What was Operation Torch?
11. What battle turned the tide for the Allies on the eastern front in 1942–43?
12. What was the most significant result of the Sicilian campaign of 1943 for the Allies?
13. Where did the Allies stage an invasion in January 1944 to try to accomplish an "end run" around the Gustav Line in Italy?
14. A. Where did the massive Allied invasion of northern France take place in June 1944?
    B. By what name has 6 June 1944 been called ever since?
15. What was the last major German offensive against the Allies?
16. When and where did Germany surrender to Allied forces?

Vocabulary

nonaggression pact	Maginot Line
Luftwaffe	subversive
wolf-pack tactics	D Day
silhouette	radio direction finding
snorkel	demolition charge
Vichy French	unconditional surrender
beachhead	"zero in"
paratroops	counterbattery fire
defense perimeter	demoralize

9

World War II: The Pacific War, 1941–1945

When the United States restricted the sale of oil to Japan in July 1941 in response to Japanese expansion into Indochina, the Japanese had to find an alternative source of oil. The Dutch East Indies were the only possible source of supply in the western Pacific region. Thus, American strategists reasoned that a Japanese military move into the Indies would be their next logical step. To deter such a move, President Roosevelt had directed that the battleships and aircraft carriers of the U.S. Pacific Fleet be based at Pearl Harbor, Hawaii. In October the civilian government of Japan fell and was replaced by a military government headed by General Tojo. In November a special Japanese envoy arrived in the United States to assist the Japanese ambassador in negotiations to resume the flow of western oil.

Unknown to the Japanese, the United States had an advantage in the negotiations because American code breakers had some months earlier succeeded in breaking the Japanese diplomatic code. Thus, Washington knew that a deadline for the negotiations had been set for late November, after which something ominous would happen. In late November a Japanese naval expeditionary force was sighted heading toward the Malay Peninsula, where they presumably would launch an invasion. But unknown and undetected was another Japanese force at sea. This one, which included all six of Japan's large carriers and numerous escort ships, was headed east across the Pacific toward Pearl Harbor, Hawaii.

THE ATTACK ON PEARL HARBOR

Masked by stormy seas and heavy rain, the Japanese strike force had approached to within 200 miles north of Oahu, Hawaii, by the early morning of Sunday, 7 December.

Because of a threat of subversive activity, most American aircraft at the air base at Pearl Harbor on Oahu had been lined up in neat rows to guard against sabotage. The eight battleships of the Pacific Fleet were all anchored at Battleship Row in the harbor to permit week-

end liberty. Fortunately, the two carriers *Lexington* and *Enterprise* then stationed at Pearl Harbor were out delivering planes to Midway and Wake Islands.

At 0600 the six carriers of the Japanese strike force turned into the wind and launched over 180 planes to attack the battleships and destroy the parked aircraft so that there could be no counterattack.

At 0800 the first of the attacking Japanese planes reached the harbor and radioed back the signal "Tora . . . Tora . . . . Tora," a code word meaning complete surprise had been achieved. At this time most American Sailors and airmen were finishing breakfast or just relaxing. Suddenly death and destruction began raining from the skies. The attack struck all parts of the harbor at once because all the Japanese pilots had predesignated targets. Within moments the battleship *Arizona* exploded and sank after a bomb set off her ammunition magazines. Soon all remaining battleships were sunk or badly damaged. By 0945 the attack was over. Altogether some 2,400 American servicemen had been killed and another 1,200 had been wounded. Nineteen ships had been sunk or severely damaged, including all eight of the battleships. Over 230 planes had been destroyed on the ground. Fortunately for the United States, a large tank farm near the harbor containing some 4.5 million barrels of oil was spared. Loss of this oil would have hindered later American naval operations even more than the damage done to the ships. Also, important repair yards and machine shops, which would make possible the eventual salvage and return to duty of fourteen of the nineteen ships disabled by the attack, were practically untouched.

Calling 7 December 1941 "A day which will live in infamy!" the next day, President Roosevelt asked Congress to declare war on Japan. Three days later Germany and Italy joined Japan in declaring war on the United States.

Despite the attack's apparent success at the time, the Japanese had made three serious miscalculations. First, they had counted heavily on the efforts of twenty submarines deployed in the area and five midget

Pearl Harbor, Hawaii, just before the Japanese attack of 7 December 1941. Ford Island lies in the center of the harbor. Hickam Field is off toward the upper left on the main shore. Battleship Row lies along the left side of Ford Island.

submarines launched for the attack. However, as far as is known, none of the midgets reached their targets, and the other submarines were never able to successfully interdict the sea-lanes between California and Pearl Harbor. Second, rather than demoralize their American enemy, as had the sneak attacks on their Chinese foes in 1894 and the Russians in 1904, the attack on Pearl Harbor roused and infuriated the American public in general, and the U.S. Navy in particular, as nothing else could have. Third, and perhaps most important, the attack forcibly altered the mind-set of the senior American naval leadership, which had until then believed that the dominant ships in naval warfare would be battleships. After Pearl Harbor, the U.S. and its allies had no choice but to build their offense in the Pacific around the aircraft carrier. The Japanese held to a belief in the superiority of a battleship-centered strategy until the end. History would show that the carrier, not the battleship, would be the dominant naval weapon in the Pacific in World War II, as it has been in all the major navies of the world ever since.

With the American fleet crippled in Pearl Harbor, the other parts of the Japanese master plan swung into action. Japanese forces landed on the Malay Peninsula to

begin their successful push toward the great British base at Singapore. They took Thailand without resistance. Their planes bombed U.S. air bases in the Philippines, and troops landed on the U.S. territories of Wake Island and Guam and at British Hong Kong. All these would fall to the Japanese by year's end.

Into the confusion of successive defeats in the Pacific came the new commander in chief of the Pacific Fleet, Admiral Chester W. Nimitz. He arrived at Pearl Harbor on Christmas Day and assumed command in a brief ceremony aboard a submarine on 31 December. It was up to him to win the biggest naval war the United States had ever faced. Nimitz was quiet and unruffled, inspiring confidence. There was no question who was running the show. Nimitz was to prove equal to the monumental task he had been assigned.

Admiral King's first instructions to Nimitz were clear: (1) cover and hold the Hawaii-Midway line and maintain communications with the U.S. West Coast, and (2) maintain communications between the West Coast and Australia by holding a line drawn north to south from Dutch Harbor in the Aleutian Islands of Alaska, through Midway to Samoa, then southwest to New Cale-

The USS *Arizona* burning and sinking after being hit by Japanese carrier planes on the morning of 7 December 1941. Over 1,100 of her crew were killed in the attack.

Admiral Chester Nimitz, with Admiral King, devised much of the Pacific war strategy. He personified the true meaning of the phrase "an officer and a gentleman."

donia and Port Moresby, New Guinea. The order was to hold the line against any further Japanese advance. Available forces were to be sacrificed in delaying Japanese advances in the Dutch East Indies in order to hold that defense line. Forces would be sent to the Pacific to reinforce as they became available. In the meantime, the United States was going to have to make a major effort in the Atlantic in order to keep the sea-lanes open to Britain and thwart the massive German threat facing the British and Soviet allies.

PACIFIC WAR PLANS

The fires had hardly been extinguished at Pearl Harbor in December 1941 before the U.S. Navy began to finalize both short- and long-term plans for the conduct of the war against the Japanese. The war in the Pacific was going to be primarily a naval war, and planning had already been done for the conduct of such a war. A contingency plan for an island-hopping campaign in the Pacific, called War Plan Orange, had been drawn up thirty years earlier by naval planners at the Naval War College in Newport, Rhode Island. It had been much refined in the years since.

Given the orders to hold the line of defense across the mid-Pacific and to protect the sea-lanes to Australia, Admiral Nimitz knew his task would be a grim one for the first months while small Allied naval forces fought a delaying action in the Dutch East Indies. But after that, there was no question in his mind that the U.S. Navy would have to take the offensive.

EARLY JAPANESE SUCCESSES

The Japanese moved quickly following their attack on Pearl Harbor. Within days they made landings in the Philippines to guard the sea-lanes of communications to their main objective, the oil of the Dutch East Indies. By mid-December they made their first landings near the oil fields on the island of Borneo, followed by an advance southward toward Java, the main island of the archipelago. Java was especially rich in the natural resources that Japan needed.

In January 1942 the ABDA (American, British, Dutch, and Australian) defense command was formed. Its headquarters was in Java. It was never very effective because of the small forces at its disposal and disagreements over what it should do. The Dutch considered defense of Java the principal goal; the British and Americans believed that a successful defense of Java was impossible, and that the best ABDA could do was delay the Japanese so they could not move their forces farther into the Southwest Pacific and isolate Australia. The Japanese methodically moved through the Indies, setting up airfields for land-based air support at each succeeding location they conquered. In mid-February Admiral Nagumo's carrier striking force arrived in the area. It raided Darwin, Australia's northernmost port, and supported an invasion of Portuguese Timor, thus effectively isolating Java from any major reinforcement.

The ABDA naval force under command of Dutch Admiral Karel Doorman made several attempts to stop the Japanese advance but was defeated in almost every

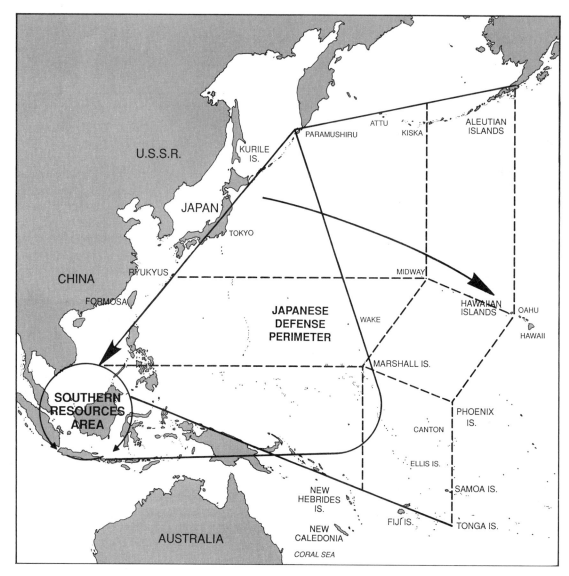

The Pacific theater, showing the Japanese defense perimeter.

encounter. The Battle of the Java Sea on 29 February all but eliminated the Allied force. The majority of ABDA ships, including the cruiser USS *Houston,* was sunk by aircraft and destroyer-fired torpedoes. The Allies fought gallantly, but they inflicted only minor losses on the Japanese before Nagumo's naval aircraft mopped up the opposition. Surviving Allied destroyers made it to Australia to fight another day.

The Japanese began landing on Java on 28 February 1942; by 9 March the island was forced into unconditional surrender. Before the end of March all of the Dutch East Indies were in Japanese hands, and the rich oil wells of Java, Borneo, and Sumatra were providing an inexhaustible supply of fuel and other resources. The Japanese had attained all of their objectives in the south, and at the same time they had conquered Burma and the Andaman Islands in the Indian Ocean. They had driven the battered British Indian Ocean Fleet into East African ports. They had accomplished all of their primary objectives in less than half the time they had planned, and with insignificant losses.

On 11 March, two days after the fall of Java, General Douglas MacArthur was ordered out of the Philippines by President Roosevelt. He slipped away from his command post on Corregidor in Manila Bay on a PT boat and made his way to the southern Philippines. From there he flew to Australia to take command of the defense of that nation. As he left the Philippines, he promised the Filipinos, in his now-famous words, "I shall return." In April and May the last Filipino and American defenders of the Philippines were overrun on Bataan Peninsula and Corregidor. The survivors suffered every form of human brutality as they were forced on a "Death March" from Bataan to their prison camps.

THE JAPANESE DEFENSE PERIMETER

The Japanese had now established their defense perimeter. Anchored by Rangoon in the Indian Ocean area, it included all of the Dutch East Indies and northern New Guinea on the south, extending to include Rabaul on New Britain and Kavieng on nearby New Ireland in the southwest. It then crossed the Pacific northward to newly acquired Wake, Guam, and the British Gilbert Islands. On the northern flank Japan was protected by bases in the Kurile Islands. Japan had also improved its many bases in the islands acquired from Germany during World War I—the Carolines, Marshalls, and Marianas. Japan made Truk in the Carolines into its "Pearl Harbor" of the central Pacific and developed Rabaul into a major forward base for further expansion southwestward. Only on the central perimeter, near Midway Island, did a gap exist. Admiral Yamamoto wanted to seal this gap, but the Japanese General Staff felt it was not necessary.

The Japanese hoped that their string of well-defended bases and their fine navy would be sufficient to keep the growing American strength at bay. They hoped to defeat newly arriving American forces bit by bit in a prolonged war of attrition. This, they hoped, would cause the American people to become disheartened and willing to make a compromise peace that would let Japan keep her newly acquired territory. But Admiral Nimitz, the U.S. Navy, and the American people would not let the Japanese achieve their hopes.

LIMITED OFFENSE BECOMES THE BEST DEFENSE

Admiral Nimitz knew that the Japanese were planning additional moves to the southwest. Unknown to them, the Japanese naval code had been broken by U.S. naval intelligence. Thus, on many crucial occasions throughout the war, Japanese plans were known ahead of time. This allowed successful countermeasures to be planned and executed. Nimitz felt that he could best defend the sea-lanes to Australia by attacking Japanese bases in the central Pacific with carrier task forces in a series of hit-and-run raids. This would cause much concern in the Japanese high command. Yamamoto himself was afraid that the Americans might even attempt a raid on Tokyo and endanger the emperor's life.

Vice Admiral William Halsey was selected as the man to strike the Japanese bases. He was to conduct raids at widely separated locations so as to cause the Japanese the most anxiety. Halsey even hoped to make them believe that there were more U.S. naval task forces in the region than they thought existed. Back home the press exaggerated the effects of the raids and greatly boosted American public morale, and so the raids achieved part of their purpose.

Then came an electrifying surprise U.S. attack on the Japanese home islands. In April 1942, Halsey's carrier striking force boldly sailed deep into Japanese waters with sixteen long-range Army B-25s lashed to the flight deck of the aircraft carrier USS *Hornet.* The plan was to launch the bombers on a one-way mission to the Japanese home islands as soon as the force approached within maximum range. On 18 April the all-volunteer pilots, led by Army Colonel James Doolittle, successfully took off when the force had come within 660 miles of Japan. They made air raids on Tokyo, Nagoya, and Kobe. None of the B-25s were lost over Japan. They then continued on into China, since they did not have sufficient fuel to return to the carrier. There the pilots crash-landed or parachuted to the ground. Most escaped in friendly Chinese territory, though some were captured and executed in Japanese-controlled areas.

The Japanese armed forces were humiliated. Their boast that the sacred territory of the Land of the Rising Sun would never be attacked was proved wrong. Yamamoto's plans to attack Midway in June in order to close the gap in the Japanese defense perimeter were now revived. Another Japanese move into the Coral Sea to cut the sea-lanes to Australia was put into action for early May. A third Japanese move, a two-pronged thrust into the Solomon Islands and toward Port Moresby in New Guinea, also was started. Nimitz, aware of these intentions through decoding of Japanese messages, planned his own actions carefully.

BATTLE OF THE CORAL SEA

Nimitz directed his carrier task groups to converge on the Coral Sea to stop the Japanese moves toward the Solomons. The *Lexington* and her group were sent to reinforce Rear Admiral Frank Jack Fletcher's *Yorktown* group.

On 8 May the Battle of the Coral Sea was fought. It was the first great combat between carrier forces, with neither fleet ever coming into sight of the other. Both groups launched their attack waves about the same time. The Japanese had several advantages: fliers with more combat experience, better torpedoes, and a storm front that partly concealed their movements. The opposing waves hit the two task groups almost simultaneously. The Japanese carrier *Shokaku* was severely damaged, and both the *Yorktown* and *Lexington* were hit. The *Lexington* was struck by two torpedoes, which ruptured her fuel lines and caused major explosions. The ship had to be abandoned and was later sunk by one of her own escorting destroyers.

The Battle of the Coral Sea turned back the Japanese advance for the first time in the Pacific war. Even though the American losses were somewhat greater, the strategic victory was clearly on the side of the United States. While only one Japanese carrier was sunk, another was

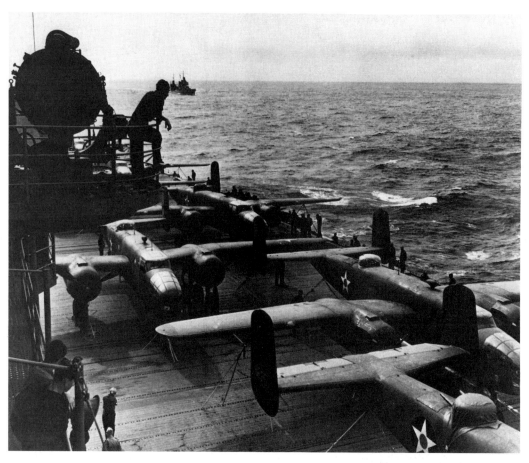

The Doolittle raid on Tokyo on 18 April 1942. B-25s are on the deck of the USS *Hornet*. The raid humiliated the Japanese armed forces, which had pledged that their homeland would never be attacked. When asked where the planes had come from, President Roosevelt said, "From Shangri-La," a mythical land of eternal youth in Tibet. Later in the war, a newly built U.S. carrier was given the name *Shangri-La* in memory of the attack. This book's author served aboard her before she was decommissioned in the early 1970s.

damaged, and the third lost so many aviators it was kept out of the Midway operation. Nagumo's Midway force would be short three carriers for the major action of Yamamoto's grand plan.

BATTLE OF MIDWAY

In mid-1942 Yamamoto's Combined Fleet had immense numerical superiority over Allied forces in the Pacific. But he devised a curious battle plan that split his forces into ten separate groups, spread all the way from the Aleutian Islands to Midway itself. The Japanese Combined Fleet was a huge armada of eleven battleships, eight carriers, twenty-three cruisers, and sixty-five destroyers. They were pitted against Nimitz's small force of three carriers, eight cruisers, and fourteen destroyers. The key to the impending action, however, was U.S. intelligence. Nimitz had deduced all the major movements in the Japanese plan through radio intercepts and code breaking. The Americans were not going to be surprised—much to the astonishment of the Japanese.

The first action occurred on 3 June 1942, with a Japanese diversionary attack on Dutch Harbor in the Aleutians. A scout plane ranging 700 miles to sea from Midway alerted the Midway defenders. Fletcher drew his two task forces in to within 200 miles of Midway and waited. Nagumo launched his first attack of 108 planes against Midway at dawn on the fourth. Fletcher located the Japanese force with patrol bombers and then ordered Rear Admiral Raymond Spruance in the *Enterprise* to attack while the *Yorktown* recovered the search planes.

At the same time, all aircraft on Midway took off to attack the Japanese force. The American planes proved to be no match for the Zero fighters and were quickly shot down. Nagumo now was faced with four hours of fast action and difficult decisions. His carriers were successively attacked by torpedo planes and bombers, none of which scored a hit and almost all of which were shot down. Then an American submarine penetrated his formation and fired torpedoes, all of which missed. Finally, the aircraft returning from the first Midway attack re-

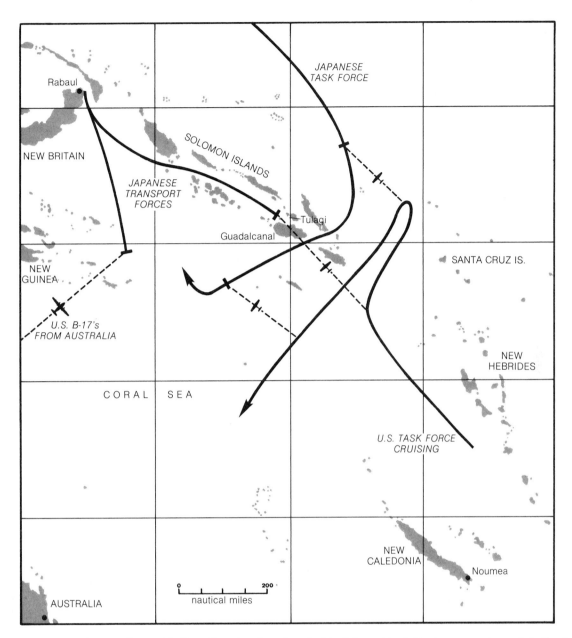

The Battle of the Coral Sea. This was the world's first all-carrier air and sea battle. It turned back the Japanese advance into the South Pacific and kept open the supply route to Australia.

ported that another attack was needed to destroy the runways there.

At almost the same time, Nagumo received word of the American carrier task force. He changed course to approach it and ordered that the bombs that had been loaded on aircraft for the second Midway attack be replaced with torpedoes for an attack on the U.S. carrier force. The bombs were left lying on the deck. At the same time, the first Midway attack wave returned, and Nagumo ordered that the planes be recovered before launching the second wave.

Nagumo's force was now attacked by three low and slow waves of U.S. carrier torpedo planes, all of which

were shot down in flames before they could score a hit. Their sacrifice would not be in vain, however. Nagumo had now turned back eight attacks in three hours without a scratch. But his luck had run out. About to launch the counterattack, the four Japanese carriers turned into the wind. At that moment another American wave of dive bombers from the *Enterprise* and *Yorktown* came screaming down on a high-altitude dive-bombing attack. They met almost no resistance from the Japanese combat air patrol, which had been pulled down to meet the previous American low-level torpedo attack.

The Americans caught the Japanese carriers with planes on their flight decks about to take off, other planes

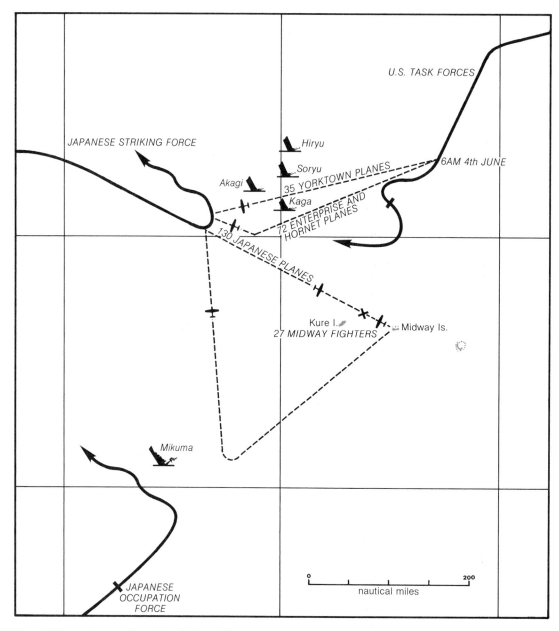

U.S. TASK FORCES

JAPANESE STRIKING FORCE

Hiryu

Soryu

35 YORKTOWN PLANES

6AM 4th JUNE

Akagi

Kaga

72 ENTERPRISE AND HORNET PLANES

130 JAPANESE PLANES

Kure I.

27 MIDWAY FIGHTERS

Midway Is.

Mikuma

JAPANESE OCCUPATION FORCE

0   200
nautical miles

The Battle of Midway. This was the turning point of the Pacific war. Not only did the Japanese lose four carriers, but more important, they lost the best of their carrier pilots.

refueling, and the off-loaded bombs lying around waiting to be returned to the magazines. American bombs hit the carriers *Soryo, Kaga,* and *Akagi* and turned them into flaming torches in minutes. Only the carrier *Hiryu,* farther north, escaped this attack. Her dive bombers followed the *Yorktown*'s planes back and stopped the U.S. carrier with three hits. Additional hits by torpedo planes caused Fletcher to abandon his flagship and turn tactical command over to Admiral Spruance.

About the time the *Yorktown* was being abandoned, her search planes discovered the *Hiryu* and reported her location and course. A short time later a wave of dive bombers from the *Enterprise* set the *Hiryu* on fire with

four direct bomb hits. Yamamoto was now without aircraft carriers to protect his main body of heavy warships. Though he ordered a counterattack during the night with four cruisers of his bombardment force, he canceled the Midway operation in the early hours of the morning, rather than have his surface force exposed to a daylight dive-bombing attack. He ordered his entire force to retire to the west.

The cruiser force now came under attack by a U.S. submarine, and in the process of dodging torpedoes, two of them, the *Mogami* and *Mikuma,* collided. On 6 June Spruance located the damaged ships and sank the *Mikuma.* The final action came when the *Yorktown,* which

The sinking USS *Yorktown* at the Battle of Midway.

A night battle in the Solomons. The battle for Guadalcanal raged day and night on the island, and in the seas surrounding it, for six months. Losses for both sides were heavy, but in the end, U.S. forces were triumphant and the Japanese had to pull back their defense perimeter.

was under tow after being abandoned, was sunk by a Japanese submarine. The spread of torpedoes also sank an escorting U.S. destroyer.

The Battle of Midway was the turning point in the Pacific war. The Japanese loss of four carriers and a cruiser was compounded by the loss of her best Japanese carrier pilots. This loss of pilots was one of the chief causes of Japan's ultimate defeat at sea. After Midway, new aviators sent to the carrier fleet were less prepared to face the growing number of well-trained American pilots.

Only the Japanese northern forces had achieved success in Yamamoto's grand plan. They had succeeded in occupying Kiska and Attu in the Aleutian Islands without resistance. But from then on, the Japanese would never be able to launch a major offensive.

THE BATTLES FOR GUADALCANAL

After the defeat of the Japanese at Midway, both Admiral Nimitz and General MacArthur believed that an Allied counteroffensive should be started while the enemy was still off balance. To the Japanese, the defeat indicated that they had to reinforce their advanced bases and bring ships and troops down to the southwestern perimeter of their defense line. The Solomon Islands thus became an objective of both sides.

For the Japanese, this meant building an airfield on the island of Guadalcanal so its aircraft could be used to cover their flank while they completed the conquest of New Guinea. For the Allies, it meant launching an operation to lessen the Japanese threat to the Australian sealanes, protecting Port Moresby on New Guinea, and establishing an advanced base from which to strike the Japanese base at Rabaul. All the earlier planning incorporated in War Plan Orange had proposed recapturing

the Philippines, if lost, by a drive across the central Pacific. However, the Japanese threat to the sea-lanes of communication with Australia diverted much of the Allied effort to the south.

When an American scout plane discovered the Japanese building the Guadalcanal airstrip, that island became the focal point of a series of naval battles, and a prolonged struggle between U.S. marines and Japanese forces, for the next six months. A force of marines landed on 7 August at Guadalcanal and nearby Tulagi. The seaway north of Guadalcanal used by the Allied task force staging the landings would become known as Ironbottom Sound because of the many ships sunk there during the campaign.

Within a few hours, the task force was under bombing attack from the Japanese base at Rabaul. After driving off the air attack, the U.S. carriers *Saratoga, Wasp,* and *Enterprise* retired because of heavy fighter-plane losses and the need for refueling. What the Allied force did not know was that a major Japanese naval force of cruisers was heading for the amphibious ships. They were coming down "the Slot," the passage between the major Solomon Islands from Rabaul.

It was now that the Japanese surface training in night operations would pay off for them. Catching the U.S. and Australian surface force completely unaware off Savo

The mud of the jungles of Guadalcanal made fighting there a terrible ordeal. U.S. forces had to fight not only the enemy but also the disease and discomfort of the hot jungle.

Island, Vice Admiral Gunichi Mikawa's cruisers gave the U.S. Navy the worst defeat it has ever suffered in battle: the U.S. cruisers *Astoria, Vincennes,* and *Quincy* plus the Australian cruiser *Canberra* were sunk, and the cruiser *Chicago* and two destroyers were heavily damaged. One thousand Allied sailors were killed.

With the Allied surface force shattered and the carriers away from the scene, the amphibious task force was forced to withdraw, leaving 16,000 U.S. marines on Guadalcanal without support and supplies. Only because the Japanese had no significant force ashore were the marines able to capture the airfield, which they renamed Henderson Field, and set up a defense perimeter. By 20 August the Seabees had the field in operation and the first planes were flying sorties and bringing in supplies.

When the Japanese learned that the Americans were repairing the airfield on Guadalcanal, they realized that they had to try to recapture that field. They began pouring troops onto the island at night, bringing them down the Slot by fast transports and destroyers with such regularity that the marines called the enemy ships the "Tokyo Express."

Japanese submarines were stationed at the approaches to Guadalcanal, and by early September, they had sunk the USS *Wasp,* damaged the USS *Saratoga,* and torpedoed the new battleship *North Carolina.* Japanese

forces continued to be heavily reinforced despite terrible casualties. By 15 October 22,000 troops were ashore.

Night naval battles and attacks by the Japanese Combined Fleet wreaked havoc on American forces. But the marines held, and they inflicted ten casualties for each one of their own men lost. Then, in the Battle of the Santa Cruz Islands on 24 October, Admiral Halsey gambled his carriers—and came out the loser. The *Hornet* was sunk and the *Enterprise* heavily damaged, leaving no operational U.S. carriers in the Pacific. In the process, however, two Japanese carriers and a cruiser were badly damaged and a hundred Japanese planes were shot down.

The naval Battle of Guadalcanal was now about to begin. On 12 November the Japanese started down the Slot with 11,000 troops jammed into eleven transports. Escorted by two battleships as well as many cruisers and destroyers, this was to be the last major attempt by the Japanese to relieve their army on Guadalcanal. In a night cruiser action, the American and Japanese naval forces clashed head-on in the darkness, with heavy losses sustained on both sides. Seven of the Japanese transports with 9,000 troops were sunk.

Another night naval battle off Guadalcanal was fought in late November, again resulting in severe damage to U.S. cruisers by Japanese "long lance" (very long range) torpedoes. But the Tokyo Express was slowly fading, and resupply of Japanese troops on the island was becoming more difficult. Extremely heavy casualties were inflicted on troop reinforcements by destroyers and PT boats.

The marines ashore continued their hard-fought advance, pushing the Japanese into the jungle interior. Finally, on 9 February 1943 the Japanese slipped out of the jungle, and 12,000 half-starved survivors made an escape on fast destroyers. Guadalcanal was secured.

STRATEGY OF 1943: CONTINUOUS PRESSURE

A consolidation and planning period took place following the success on Guadalcanal and other successes on New Guinea. Events in Europe dictated that it would be mainly up to U.S. forces, assisted when possible by Australian and New Zealand (ANZAC) forces, to prosecute the war in the Pacific against the Japanese. The program put into effect for the rest of 1943 and early 1944 called for the elimination of the Japanese outposts in the Aleutians; intensified submarine attacks on the Japanese lines of communication from the Indies; and the isolation of Rabaul, with MacArthur's forces assisted by the South Pacific naval forces. A two-pronged advance across the Pacific would then follow, with the objective of reaching the Luzon (northern Philippines)–Formosa–China coast geographic triangle by late 1944. From there, attacks against the Japanese home islands could be launched. One line of advance would proceed across the central Pacific by way of the Gilberts, Marshalls, Marianas, Carolines, and Palaus toward the Philippines or Formosa, using naval forces commanded by Nimitz. The other line of advance would be across the Southwest Pacific via the north coast of New Guinea to the southern Philippines, using combined U.S. and Allied forces under the overall command of MacArthur. In the early part of 1943 there was also hope that the Nationalist Chinese army and other Allied forces under Chiang Kai-shek, the Allied commander in the China theater, could fight their way through Burma to the Chinese coast as well. Later in the year, however, these hopes were abandoned when it became obvious that the poorly equipped and badly organized Chinese army would not be able to overcome the stiff resistance of Japanese occupational forces in the region.

The reconquest of Attu and Kiska in the Aleutian Islands took place over the summer months of 1943. By August the Aleutians had been fully returned to American control, and they were never again threatened by the Japanese. Ground forces used in the attacks were redeployed to the central Pacific. Though some thought was given to establishing a third line of advance across the North Pacific via these islands, the Joint Chiefs finally decided that the foggy, cold North Pacific with its rocky islands was not suitable for such a major offensive.

THE SUBMARINE WAR IN THE PACIFIC

The submarine war in the Pacific was in many ways a mirror image of the Battle of the Atlantic. In the Atlantic it was the goal of German U-boats to interdict Allied shipping in order to strangle Britain, but in the Pacific the roles were reversed. It was the American submarines that attempted to gain a stranglehold against Japanese shipping. In this endeavor they were aided somewhat by the Pacific geography, where shipping lanes to Japan from their sources of supply in Malaya, Borneo, Sumatra, and Java were often located in narrow straits between islands. This made interdiction easier for American submarines than for their German counterparts in the Atlantic. To build up the numbers of submarines, they were mass-produced during the war by American shipyards, just as escort destroyers and Liberty and Victory merchant ships were. For the Pacific, specially designed big submarines, nearly twice the size of German U-boats, were developed to carry greater fuel and torpedo loads for long-distance patrols against the Japanese.

The Japanese, on the other hand, never placed much emphasis on their submarine fleet. Their subs mainly targeted warships rather than auxiliary and merchant shipping. In general they underestimated the potential of the submarine throughout the war. This philosophy had been reinforced by the poor showing of their submarines at Pearl Harbor and during the early months of the war. Though they had some successes, they were insignificant compared to the effectiveness of the U.S. submarines in the conflict.

Making the situation worse for the Japanese was the fact that their antisubmarine operations were never very successful either. Because of a general lack of escort ships, the Japanese were not able to adopt the convoy techniques that were so successful in the Atlantic against

A Japanese merchant ship heads for the bottom after being torpedoed by a U.S. submarine during the Pacific war. This photo was taken through the periscope of the successful attacker.

the German U-boats, and they never developed radar. Consequently, by mid-1943 Japanese merchant shipping losses to submarine attacks were very heavy. The essential raw materials could not be delivered from the Southern Resources Areas to support Japanese war industry or military forces. Altogether in the Pacific war, U.S. submarines sank over 1,100 merchant vessels, totaling over 5 million tons. In addition, U.S. subs sank some 200 naval ships. The submarine was in many ways the naval weapon that won the war for the United States in the Pacific.

BYPASSING RABAUL

The Casablanca Conference in January 1943 decided on a movement through the remaining Solomon Islands toward the giant Japanese base at Rabaul. Admiral Yamamoto realized the importance of defending the Melanesian and Australasian approaches to Rabaul, so he reinforced his airfields with fleet carrier air wings and launched major raids on Ironbottom Sound. Heavy losses were inflicted on American ships, but in the process the Japanese carrier air wings suffered additional severe losses.

In an effort to boost morale, on 18 April Yamamoto and his staff set out on an inspection trip to Japanese bases in the Solomons. Because coded messages that outlined his itinerary had been broken by U.S. naval intelligence, American long-range fighters from Henderson Field were able to intercept his plane over Ballale Island near Bougainville and shoot it down, killing Yamamoto. This was a major blow for the Japanese, for they had lost their most able commander.

For the next twelve months into March 1944, the campaign against Rabaul progressed on two fronts: through the Solomons and on New Guinea. During that time the U.S. Fleet fought in no less than forty-five major naval battles and seventeen invasions in the Solomons and Southwest Pacific. The successful campaigns by MacArthur on eastern New Guinea were made possible by the Solomons operations, which tied up the Japanese navy. Since the Japanese could not concentrate on all fronts at the same time, the Allied advance toward the Philippines moved steadily onward.

By mid-March Rabaul was encircled, and 125,000 Japanese troops—90,000 in Rabaul itself—were bypassed, surrounded by the advancing Americans without hope of relief or escape. There was now no need for the Americans to capture Rabaul. It became a backwater as the war progressed westward along the northern New Guinea coast and northward toward the Philippines.

In the last phase of the campaign against Rabaul, a pattern developed that came to characterize much of the remainder of the Pacific war. The Allies would mount no frontal attacks against strongly entrenched Japanese forces if they could avoid it. Moreover, they would not capture every island in the path across the central Pacific. Rather, they would advance in greater leaps, limited only by the range of available land-based air cover, or the availability of carrier-based air support. Thus, the Allies bypassed and isolated major strongholds such as Rabaul, effectively taking them out of the war without the Allies having to invade and conquer them.

LEAPFROG ON NEW GUINEA

By early 1944 the rapidly growing Fifth Fleet was capable of supporting invasions far beyond the reach of land-based aircraft. The next move in the two-pronged attack across the Pacific would be by MacArthur's forces, leapfrogging along the northern New Guinea coast. Units of Task Force 58 were called on to assist in these amphibious landings.

The Japanese thought the New Guinea movement was the single line of advance toward the Philippines. When MacArthur moved farther to the Wakde Islands and then threatened the island of Biak in May, the Japanese decided that they had to stop this advance. Biak had three airfields that were essential to the Japanese defense plan. The new Japanese Combined Fleet commander, Admiral Soemu Toyoda, decided to make an all-out attempt to hold Biak.

The Japanese first took much of their central Pacific air strength and sent it to New Guinea to attack the newly won Allied air bases there. Then they made three reinforcement attempts by sea toward Biak, where MacArthur's forces had become stalemated by the strong Japanese defenses.

The first two attempts turned back after being sighted by Rear Admiral Thomas Kinkaid's Seventh Fleet. The third attempt was to be supported by the finest ships in the Japanese Navy, including the superbattleships *Yamato* and *Musashi*.

On 11 June, however, just as they were about to make their run on Biak, 1,000 miles to the northeast the U.S. Fifth Fleet attacked the Mananas in preparation for an invasion of Saipan.

Toyoda immediately suspended the Biak operation and ordered Vice Admiral Ozawa northward to join the main body of the Mobile Fleet, east of the Philippines. MacArthur was now able to proceed unmolested by Japanese reinforcements. He wrapped up the New Guinea operation by the end of July.

SAIPAN

June 1944 found United States forces engaged in arguably the greatest military effort in history. At the very time the Normandy landings were taking place in Europe, the United States was about to send a huge amphibious force against Saipan in the central Pacific. The mammoth task of projecting 127,000 troops on 535 ships some 3,000 miles from Pearl Harbor, and providing them with fast carrier task force support against the entire Japanese Fleet, was just as complex as the D Day invasion in Europe.

As the amphibious task force proceeded toward its objective, Army planes from the newly won bases in the Marshalls and Navy carrier planes from Task Force 58 struck Japanese bases in the Marianas and in the Carolines. A bombardment by U.S. battleships began on 13 June. It continued until the fifteenth, when two Marine divisions crossed the coral reef through passages blasted by underwater demolition teams and hit the beaches.

Heavy casualties were sustained, but by the end of the day 20,000 marines were ashore. Reinforcements were put ashore, and by 17 June the American offensive had captured the main airfield and begun to push the Japanese back. By this time the Japanese Combined Fleet was approaching the operating area, and Admiral Mitscher had to steam out to place himself between it and the forces on Saipan.

BATTLE OF THE PHILIPPINE SEA

Maneuvering went on for two days as the two forces searched for each other. Mitscher was always mindful of his primary orders: "Capture, occupy, and defend Saipan, Tinian, and Guam." On the afternoon of 18 June Admiral Ozawa's scout planes discovered Task Force 58.

Ozawa's main body had 6 carriers surrounded by cruisers and destroyers in two circular formations. One hundred miles ahead of the main body was Vice Admiral Takeo Kurita with the main Japanese surface force of battleships and cruisers, and 3 carriers. Facing the Japanese Mobile Force of 9 carriers, 5 battleships, 13 cruisers, 28 destroyers, and 430 carrier aircraft was Task Force 58 with 15 carriers, 7 battleships, 21 cruisers, 69 destroyers, and 891 carrier aircraft. From Japan, Admiral Toyoda radioed Ozawa that "the fate of the Empire depends on the issue of this battle; let every man do his utmost!"

Ozawa had counted heavily on getting air support from the Marianas bases. He felt that this land-based air support would more than equalize the opposing task forces. Unfortunately for Ozawa, he did not know that only thirty operational planes remained after the devastating American raids made earlier, and that many of his carrier pilots had returned from the Biak operations sick with malaria. Not aware that the odds were heavily against him because of these factors, he moved to close with Task Force 58.

Alerted to the impending attack, Mitscher and Spruance put more than 450 planes in the air to meet the challenge. New combat information centers with the latest radar equipment guided TF58's Hellcats to approaching enemy planes from advantageous altitudes and directions. The superbly trained American pilots, at peak efficiency after a year of successful combat experience, were ready for the battle.

In eight hours of furious air warfare, 330 Japanese planes were shot down in what historians came to call the "Marianas Turkey Shoot." At the same time, the American submarine *Albacore* torpedoed Ozawa's new carrier flagship, the *Taiho*, and the submarine *Cavalla* put three torpedoes into the carrier *Shokaku*. Both carriers exploded a few hours later with great loss of life. But Ozawa and his staff survived and transferred to the carrier *Zuikaku*.

Ozawa ordered a general retirement to refuel, intending to resume battle the next day—even though he had only 100 carrier planes left. He believed erroneous reports from his surviving pilots that TF-58 had been crippled.

Mitscher, in the meantime, had received no information on Ozawa's movements and chose a course that

The Battle of the Philippine Sea, sometimes called the "Marianas Turkey Shoot." This photo shows a Japanese bomber plunging toward the sea after being hit by antiaircraft fire during the battle.

separated the forces well beyond his optimum operating radius. Late the next day a scout plane located the Japanese formation. Taking a calculated risk, Mitscher launched 200 planes against the Japanese when they were just within maximum operating range. Then came a shock: the Japanese were 60 miles farther away than originally reported. Mitscher decided to let his planes continue, while steaming full speed toward the Japanese in order to reduce the return flight distance.

Just before sunset the Americans found the Japanese force and attacked it, sinking two oilers and a carrier and damaging two other carriers, a battleship, and a cruiser. Ozawa managed to get seventy-five of his fighters into the air. Only ten survived, and the crippled Mobile Fleet sailed away with only thirty-five planes left. Japanese naval air capability had been destroyed, and the Marianas invasion was able to continue, opposed only by the Japanese garrisons on the islands.

During the night after the final engagement, Admiral Mitscher daringly turned on the carrier lights to guide back the returning pilots. Still, many planes were lost. They had to ditch in the sea when out of fuel. But of 209 aviators who had engaged the enemy that day, all but 49 were recovered, either on the flight decks or from the water by destroyers and float planes.

With the Mobile Force defeated and out of the area, TF-58 was able to concentrate on providing full assistance to the invading forces on Saipan and succeeding invasions of Tinian and Guam. Now sustained shore bombardment could be brought to bear before the troops landed, greatly reducing casualties. Both Saipan and Tinian were secured by the end of July, and organized resistance ceased on Guam by 10 August.

Japan had lost her direct air route into the Carolines. The United States had acquired logistic bases for additional steps toward the Philippines, advance submarine bases for attacks on Japanese communications and sealanes to the Indies, and air bases from which the new long-range B-29s would soon be bombing the industrial cities of Japan.

This was the beginning of the end for Japan. The emperor and other high officials now knew that they would have to surrender. The Tojo government fell and was succeeded by a cabinet to which the emperor made known his desire for early peace negotiations. But the Japanese military ethic was still so strong that no official would initiate steps to end the war for yet another year.

RETURN TO THE PHILIPPINES

The next series of invasion plans had yet to be decided when Spruance and other senior naval commanders returned to Pearl Harbor to rest and plan their future operations. The Fifth Fleet was redesignated the U.S. Third Fleet under Admiral Halsey, with Vice Admiral Mitscher

remaining in command of the Fast Carrier Task Force, now called Task Force 38.

In its two drives across the Pacific, both of which exemplified throughout the military principles of maneuver, economy of force, surprise, and massing of force, the Allied forces had arrived in mid-September 1944 at the threshold of their strategic objective, the Luzon–Formosa–China coast triangle. In seven months MacArthur's forces had moved nearly 1,500 miles from the Admiralties to the island of Morotai. In ten months Nimitz's forces had advanced over 4,500 miles from Hawaii to the Palaus. The time had now arrived when a final choice had to be made of the main objective in the target area.

Knowing that the Palau Islands, Yap, and Morotai were probably the next objectives, Halsey joined TF-38 in his flagship, the USS *New Jersey,* and carried out air strikes against the central Philippines. The results were astounding. TF-38 destroyed 200 enemy airplanes and sank a dozen freighters and a tanker. Convinced that the central Philippines were weakly defended, Halsey sent Nimitz an urgent message recommending that the Palaus and Yap be bypassed and that ground forces for these operations be turned over to MacArthur, at his urging, for an invasion of Leyte Island in the central Philippines. Until this time there had been some indecision among the Joint Chiefs between Formosa and the Philippines as the objective of the central Pacific campaign, but now the choice seemed clear. Because of the weaknesses discovered by Halsey in the central Philippines, the Allies would follow his and MacArthur's advice and take the Philippines—first Leyte in October, then Luzon in December. Nimitz would then invade Iwo Jima and Okinawa early in 1945. The Joint Chiefs directed Nimitz and MacArthur to combine forces for the invasion of Leyte on 20 October 1944, after securing Morotai and Peleliu in the Palau Islands.

Morotai was captured in one of the easiest conquests of the war, but overcoming Peleliu's defenses cost the marines the highest combat casualty rate (40 percent) of any amphibious assault in American history. A new Japanese strategy was put into effect. The old strategy called for the defenders to meet the invasion on the beaches, but this obviously had not worked in the face of devastating shore bombardment. The new strategy called for a "defense in depth." The defenders were to have prepared positions well behind the beaches, taking full advantage of the natural terrain. Resistant fortifications were to be constructed, and there were to be no useless banzai charges.

More than 10,000 Japanese had carefully prepared Peleliu in accordance with the new strategy. After three days of naval bombardment, the marines landed on Peleliu on 17 September and quickly made good their beachhead and captured the airfield. But then they ran into the interior defenses, and from then on progress was costly and slow. It was not until February 1945 that the island was cleared of Japanese defenders. By that time the marines had suffered 10,000 casualties, including nearly 2,000 dead.

Long before February, however, the airfields and the anchorages in the Palaus were brought under American control. Had they remained in Japanese hands, they would have been a threat to the Leyte invasion and later operations in Luzon.

In preparing for the Leyte invasion, the Third Fleet conducted heavy attacks on Formosa and Okinawa to destroy potential land-based air support for the Japanese forces in the Philippines. Just before the landings took place, they attacked Formosa again, destroying most of the torpedo bombers that had been sent from the home islands. Over 350 Japanese land-based aircraft were destroyed between 11 and 15 October. This ensured control of the air over the Leyte beaches.

More than 60,000 assault troops were landed ashore on Leyte by sunset on D day, 20 October. From then on it was a tough fight in the interior of the island. General MacArthur waded ashore a few hours after the first landing, accompanied by President Sergio Osmena of the Philippines. In a radio broadcast MacArthur announced his return to the islands and called for Filipinos to rise and strike the Japanese at every opportunity.

By late December MacArthur's Sixth Army had secured the most important sections of the island, those required for air and logistical bases. Japanese troops in the mountains continued organized resistance well into the spring of 1945. While the fighting for Leyte continued, MacArthur's forces moved on to Luzon only slightly behind schedule. In mid-December two Army regiments captured an air base in southwestern Mindoro, 150 miles south of Manila. The invasion of Luzon itself started on 9 January 1945, when four Army divisions landed along the shores of Lingayen Gulf. The Japanese were incapable of naval intervention at Lingayen Gulf, their most significant reaction being kamikaze (suicide plane) attacks against Admiral Kinkaid's supporting naval forces and Mitscher's fast carrier force, now redesignated TF-58. Army units reached Manila on 3 February. It took them a month of bitter building-to-building fighting to root out the Japanese. By mid-March Manila Bay was open for Allied shipping. Except for a strong pocket of resistance in the mountains of central Luzon, organized Japanese resistance ended by late June 1945.

BATTLES FOR LEYTE GULF

Between 23 and 26 October 1944 the Japanese made their greatest challenge to the Leyte landings. Admiral Toyoda knew that if the Japanese lost the Philippines they would lose everything. The lifeline between Japan and the In-

dies would be cut and the Mobile Fleet would be divided, without fuel and ammunition. The Fleet could then be defeated piecemeal and Japan would be blockaded. Toyoda knew he was outnumbered, but this would be the last chance for the Imperial Navy to stop the American advance. Accordingly, he directed nearly every Japanese warship still afloat to attack the enemy at Leyte.

In the four-day action there were four major battles: the Battle of the Sibuyan Sea on 24 October, and, on 25 October, the Battle of Surigao Strait, the Battle off Cape Engano, and the Battle off Samar. These battles were the largest and most complex naval engagements in history. When the battles were over, the Imperial Japanese Navy had lost most of its remaining carriers, plus most of its remaining surface forces.

With the Japanese surface navy ruined, its carriers sunk and pilots lost, the United States proceeded with the reconquest of the Philippines. Eighteen amphibious assaults were conducted between the landings on Leyte and the final landings in March 1945 on the islands of Mindanao and Panay. It was during these actions at Leyte Gulf, however, that another new threat appeared for the first time in the Pacific war—the kamikaze suicide planes. (The word *kamikaze* meant "divine wind." This referred to a typhoon, which reputedly saved Japan in 1281 by destroying a Mongol fleet that was sailing to invade the islands.) From then on until the Philippine Islands were secured, U.S. naval forces suffered increasing damage and sinkings from these planes. The worst of this type of attack was yet to come, however.

IWO JIMA

The conquest of the Marianas had provided bases for the large B-29 bombers to make devastating air raids on the Japanese industrial cities. But between the Marianas and Japan was the volcanic island of Iwo Jima. As long as the Japanese held the island, the home islands' defenses were alerted when bombers were en route, and fighters were scrambled to intercept them.

The 3,000-mile round trip was much too far for Allied fighters to accompany and defend the bombers. Damaged bombers were often lost in the sea on the return trip because they would not hold up for that distance. The Americans determined to put an end to this dangerous situation. In U.S. hands the island's airfields could be improved to handle emergency landings for the big bombers, and to provide a base for fighter planes to escort them over Japan.

The Japanese, fully aware of the importance of the island to their defenses, expected an assault. They removed the civilians and reinforced the garrison to 23,000 troops. They proceeded to transform the island into the strongest fortress in the Pacific. Iwo Jima was an

8-square-mile island of lava cut into hills and ravines, overlooked by 550-foot Mount Suribachi, an extinct volcano. The Japanese tunneled into the volcanic rock and made interconnecting passageways between 400 concealed pillboxes and concrete blockhouses. Their artillery was placed in caves on Mount Suribachi, where it could sweep the beaches.

When the invasion force arrived, heavy naval bombardment on the island was able to be conducted for only three days of the ten requested by the marines, because of the accelerated timetable decreed by the Joint Chiefs of Staff. This was to prove grossly inadequate.

D day at Iwo Jima was set for 19 February 1945. Five hundred landing craft carrying eight battalions of marines moved to the line of departure. Meanwhile, more than a hundred of TF-58's planes attacked the island with rockets, machine guns, and general purpose and napalm bombs. Naval guns shifted from slow, destructive fire to fast, neutralizing fire to drive the defenders underground. When the assault waves approached the beach, the support ships shifted fire again to provide a barrage of fire ahead and on the flanks of the advancing marines. More than fifty rocket-firing amphibious ships advanced to give the marines close support.

Despite all this preparatory fire, the assault waves quickly piled up on the beach because the amphibian tractors were unable to climb the crumbling volcanic ash. Many landing craft broached (turned sideways in the surf) or ran into earlier boat waves. The marines, stranded on the steep beach, soon were hit by withering machine-gun, mortar, and heavy gunfire from weapons that had withheld their fire earlier so they would not reveal their positions. Through this holocaust the marines inched forward, isolating Mount Suribachi and reaching

the edge of the nearest airfield. Of 30,000 marines who hit the beach that first day, 2,400 became casualties.

The fighting continued through the night, and the next day the airfield was captured. The assault on Mount Suribachi then began. After three days of blasting and burning out pillboxes and sealing up caves with grenades, flamethrowers, rockets, and demolition charges, the mountain was surrounded and a patrol reached the summit and raised the American flag. By good fortune the flag raising was photographed by a war correspondent. A life-sized sculpture later made from the photo immortalized the moment and has provided inspiration ever since to the American people. The sculpture is now located in Washington, D.C.

While the vicious fighting was in progress on Iwo Jima, the supporting naval forces of TF-58 and the Amphibious Support Force were hit by numerous kamikaze attacks. The carrier *Saratoga* was badly damaged, and the escort carrier *Bismarck Sea* sank after a tremendous explosion that blew off her stern.

The Iwo Jima Monument near Arlington National Cemetery in Washington, D.C., immortalizes the capture of Mount Suribachi by the U.S. Marines in February 1945.

Some of the more than 500 amphibious craft en route to the assault beaches at Iwo Jima. Mount Suribachi looms in the background.

Instead of taking five days as originally planned, the conquest of Iwo Jima took over a month. It wasn't until 25 March that the last Japanese troops made their final attack. Only 200 Japanese were captured; all the rest were killed. For the first time casualties among the assault forces exceeded those of the Japanese defenders. Over 19,000 marines and sailors were wounded and nearly 7,000 were killed. Admiral Nimitz said the marines on Iwo Jima made "uncommon valor a common virtue."

THE BATTLE OF OKINAWA

The war was now closing in on the home islands of Japan. From the middle of February, carrier aircraft began striking the Japanese cities with high explosives and incendiaries. On 25 February, even before Iwo was secured, fighters from TF-58 supported 200 B-29s in a massive raid on Tokyo, burning out 2 square miles of the enemy capital and destroying 150 Japanese aircraft. Afterward, TF-58 steamed past Okinawa, bombing the island's airfields and taking intelligence photographs. The final gigantic amphibious assault and battle of the Pacific war was about to begin.

Weeks of heavy raids and softening-up attacks on Japanese bases on Kyushu and Okinawa preceded the assault landings on Okinawa. On 1 April a force of 1,300 ships carrying 182,000 assault troops arrived off the island, having come from bases all over the Pacific. Over 100,000 Japanese defenders awaited their attack from well-prepared positions, as on Iwo Jima and Peleliu. The Japanese troops on Okinawa knew that they were the last obstacle to an Allied invasion of the Japanese home islands. Many had pledged to fight to the death to prevent the island from falling.

Almost from the beginning, elements of the invasion fleet were subjected to fierce kamikaze attacks. On the morning of 6 April, however, the Japanese began their last major counterattack of the war. Over 350 Japanese kamikazes came out of Kyushu to strike the fleet. Meanwhile, the last surviving Japanese surface force, made up of the huge battleship *Yamato*, the light cruiser *Yahagi*, and eight destroyers, sailed south from the Inland Sea, propelled by the last 2,500 tons of fuel oil in Japan. It was to be a one-way trip, for both aircraft and ships. Since the ships did not have enough fuel to return, their mission was to drive through the invasion fleet, causing as much damage as possible. They planned to beach themselves at the invasion site, firing until all their ammunition was expended or until they were destroyed.

The kamikazes sank several U.S. picket destroyers, but not before warnings had been radioed by the sinking ships. Met by combat air patrol fighters from TF-58, 150 planes were shot down. The remaining 200 made it to the Okinawa area. There they were mostly destroyed by

A Japanese kamikaze suicide plane comes in to attack the USS *Missouri* during the Okinawa invasion. The plane caused only minor damage; it can be seen coming in over the port antiaircraft batteries.

fighter planes and intense antiaircraft fire. Meanwhile, the *Yamato* force was allowed to proceed far enough southward so it would not be able to retreat to safety. Then Admiral Mitscher struck with the full force of his carrier aircraft. Only two destroyers survived the attack and made it back to base.

For the next three months the carrier task forces and other ships of the U.S. Fifth and Third Fleets suffered hundreds of kamikaze attacks as they supported the Okinawa action and thrust their power into the Japanese home islands. On 21 June 1945 Okinawa was declared secure after the defending Japanese general and his chief of staff acknowledged defeat by committing suicide. During the battle for the island the Navy had endured the loss of 68 ships and over 4,000 sailors—more than either the marines or the Army suffered in the hard going on the island.

But the U.S. Navy stayed, and Okinawa was secured. The battle had cost the Japanese 100,000 men and 7,000 airplanes. Okinawa was the end of the fighting for the Japanese. Emperor Hirohito told his Supreme War Council on 22 June that they must find a way to end the war. Fire-bombing raids were turning Japanese cities into ashes, and their Navy and Air Force were gone. The Soviet Union had informed the Japanese that they would not renew their Neutrality Pact in April, and since Germany had surrendered in May, entrance of the Soviets into the Pacific war was imminent.

An invasion beach on Okinawa. In the background, part of the huge invasion force is busy off-loading supplies to support the forces ashore.

THE FINAL DAYS

Bringing an end to the war was not easy. There were still powerful factions in the Japanese military forces who favored a fight to the bitter end. The Japanese people would never accept a surrender that would not preserve the emperor and imperial system. The Japanese made peace gestures to the Soviets during their negotiations for extension of the neutrality pact. But the Soviets remained silent—so silent that Stalin did not even tell the United States or Britain about the peace initiatives during their meeting in Potsdam, Germany, in late July.

However, the United States knew about the peace initiatives because U.S. intelligence was reading the messages between the Foreign Ministry in Tokyo and the Japanese ambassador in Moscow. On 26 July the Potsdam Declaration spelled out the terms of surrender for Japan, specifying that unconditional surrender would pertain only to the military forces and that possessions except the four home islands—Hokkaido, Honshu, Shikoku, and Kyushu—would have to be given up. No

provisions concerning the emperor were made, since the Allies had not yet decided on this question. This omission caused much concern in Japan.

As the Soviets stalled and the Japanese procrastinated, the Americans and British were actively planning an invasion of the home islands of Japan, code-named Operation Downfall. Events were moving faster than governments, however. On 16 July the United States successfully exploded the first atomic device at Alamogordo, New Mexico. Within hours atomic bombs were en route to the Marianas bomber bases. And during the next three weeks the combined U.S. and British fleets, the most powerful ever assembled in history, ranged freely up and down the Japanese coast, shelling and bombing the cities virtually at will.

After a thorough assessment of projected casualties to both sides that would result from the planned invasion of Japan, versus the casualties and damage anticipated from dropping the atomic bomb, President Harry Truman decided to use the A-bomb in an attempt to end the war without the necessity of an invasion.

Nagasaki, Japan, after the atomic bomb explosion. Only a few steel and concrete buildings remain standing.

On 6 August 1945 a B-29 carrying an atomic bomb left Tinian and headed for Hiroshima, an industrial city on the Inland Sea. The weapon utterly destroyed the city. The Soviets then realized that the end had arrived and that they had to get into the Pacific war immediately if they were to get in on the victory. On 8 August the Soviet Union declared war on Japan and moved its forces into Manchuria and Korea, sweeping the Japanese before them. Despite the destruction at Hiroshima and the dropping of leaflets warning of the consequences of further delay, the Japanese military elements in the government refused to consider unconditional surrender. So on 9 August another U.S. aircraft dropped a second atomic bomb on the industrial port of Nagasaki.

Faced with this ultimate destruction, Emperor Hirohito advised his Supreme Council to accept the Potsdam Declaration. The cabinet agreed, but only on the condition that the imperial system remain. The U.S. secretary of state, speaking on behalf of the Allied governments, accepted the condition subject to stipulations that the emperor must submit to the authority of the supreme allied commander during the occupation of Japan, and the Japanese people should decide on the emperor's final status in free elections at a later date. The cabinet, on the advice of the emperor, agreed to these stipulations on 14 August. The next day, with one carrier raid already flying over Tokyo, the Third Fleet received the order to "cease fire."

In the next two weeks the Allies converged on Tokyo Bay. On Sunday morning, 2 September 1945, the Japanese foreign minister and representatives of the Imperial General Staff boarded the USS *Missouri* at anchor in Tokyo Bay and signed the surrender document on behalf of the emperor, the government, and the Imperial General Headquarters. General Douglas MacArthur signed the acceptance as supreme allied commander for the Allied powers. Fleet Admiral Chester Nimitz signed as representative for the United States. Following him were representatives of the United Kingdom, China, the Soviet Union, Australia, Canada, France, the Netherlands, and New Zealand. Shortly thereafter, General MacArthur moved into his Tokyo headquarters to direct the occupation of Japan. World War II was over.

The Japanese surrender delegation boards the USS *Missouri* for the final ceremony that formally ended World War II. This was the first time the Japanese had surrendered to a foe in more than 2,000 years.

Chronology

July 1941	U.S. halts oil sales to Japan
7 Dec. 1941	Japan bombs Pearl Harbor
11 Mar. 1942	MacArthur leaves Philippines
18 Apr. 1942	Doolittle raid on Japan
8 May 1942	Battle of Coral Sea
4 June 1942	Battle of Midway
7 Aug. 1942	Marines land on Guadalcanal
9 Feb. 1943	Guadalcanal secured
Aug. 1943	Aleutians recaptured
Mar. 1944	Rabaul bypassed
15 June 1944	Saipan landing
18 June 1944	Battle of Philippine Sea
July 1944	New Guinea secured
20 Oct. 1944	MacArthur invades Philippines
23–26 Oct. 1944	Battle for Leyte Gulf
19 Feb. 1945	Iwo Jima landing
1 Apr.–21 June 1945	Battle of Okinawa
6 Aug. 1945	Atomic bomb dropped on Hiroshima
8 Aug. 1945	Soviets declare war on Japan
2 Sept. 1945	Japan surrenders

Study Guide Questions

1. After the United States restricted the sale of oil to Japan in 1941, where was their only remaining possible source of supply?
2. What did the Japanese do to cause the United States to declare war on Japan?
3. A. What targets were successfully attacked by the Japanese at Pearl Harbor?
   B. What key land assets were missed?
4. What three miscalculations did the Japanese make about Pearl Harbor?
5. What were Nimitz's orders at the start of the Pacific War?
6. What was the name of the war plan for the Pacific War that had been developed and refined at the Naval War College?
7. What was the ABDA defense alliance?
8. What American general was ordered to leave the Philippines in March 1942?
9. Where was there a gap in the Japanese defense perimeter?
10. What were the Japanese hopes for the conduct of the war in 1942?
11. What was the Doolittle raid on Japan in April 1942?

12. A. What battle was the first great combat of the Pacific War between carrier forces?
    B. What was the result of the battle?
13. How did Nimitz know about Japanese intentions at the Battle of Midway?
14. Why is the Battle of Midway regarded as the turning point of the Pacific War?
15. On what island in the Solomons did the Japanese and Allied forces converge to determine the outcome in the southwestern Pacific?
16. Where were "Ironbottom Sound" and "the Slot" located?
17. What name was given to the Japanese operations that attempted to reinforce Guadalcanal?
18. What was the fundamental difference between the submarine wars in the Atlantic and the Pacific?
19. What happened to the Japanese commander Admiral Yamamoto in April 1944?
20. What central Pacific island was the target of one of the greatest military efforts in history in June 1944?
21. What was the principal effect of the Japanese defeat in the Battle of the Philippine Sea?
22. What was the new Japanese defense strategy put into effect on Peleliu in late 1944?
23. When and where did General MacArthur make good on his promise to return to the Philippines?
24. What did the Japanese see as the consequences if they lost the battles for Leyte Gulf in October 1944?
25. A. What were the kamikazes?
    B. Where did they first appear?
26. Why was it necessary for Allied forces to secure Iwo Jima?
27. Why did the Japanese mount a fanatical defense of the island of Okinawa?
28. To whom did the Japanese make their initial "peace feelers" to end the Pacific War?
29. What three events in early August 1945 made it imperative for the Japanese to accept the Potsdam Declaration for their surrender?
30. When and where did the Japanese sign the surrender document?

Vocabulary

Tokyo Express	scout plane
defense in depth	calculated risk
kamikaze	Bataan Death March
pillboxes	fire bomb

10

The Cold War Era, 1945–1991

Even before the surrender of Japan, the American public had begun to bring pressure on Congress to dismantle the greatest military force ever assembled in human history and "bring the boys home." Knowledgeable Americans knew that the United States had acquired worldwide responsibilities by becoming a superpower. The country could not retreat into isolationism as it had done after World War I. Nevertheless, the rush to demobilize was so swift that the American armed forces were soon rendered almost impotent.

From a wartime Navy of nearly 3.5 million, within a year barely 500,000 remained. Of an army strength of over 8 million, only 1 million remained a year after the war ended, and that deterioration continued to a low of only 600,000 by 1950. This drastic reduction in strength made it difficult at times to man even the smaller numbers of ships left in commission. Nearly all naval construction was halted, and 2,000 vessels were decommissioned. Many of these were laid up in "mothballs" for future use in an emergency, with their engines, hulls, and guns covered with protective coatings.

The American public had become complacent. There appeared to be no remaining enemies in the world, and besides, the United States had a monopoly on the atomic bomb. It was assumed by many that the newly created United Nations could solve any disputes that might arise in a peaceful manner.

In the face of this attitude, the Soviet Union quickly resumed the offensive in its war against capitalism. It soon demonstrated that its strategic long-term goal of a Communist-dominated world remained unchanged. The wartime alliance with the West had been only a temporary tactical maneuver.

THE COLD WAR BEGINS

While Americans pinned their hopes on the United Nations, sped their demobilization, and slashed the defense budget, the Soviets made only a token demobilization. By mid-1946 the Soviet Union had consolidated its wartime military gains and subjugated all the nations of Eastern Europe because the United States was unable to effectively contest this action. The U.S. Army was too weakened, and these areas were beyond Navy range.

America had only two options: make a diplomatic protest or use the atomic bomb. The former could accomplish nothing without any power to back it up, and American public opinion was solidly against war—especially atomic war—even in the face of blatant Soviet aggression in territories adjacent to the USSR.

President Truman, top officials in his government, and United States military commanders soon became aware of the Soviet intentions. Soviet annexation of eastern Poland and the Baltic countries; installation of Communist governments in Eastern Europe; meddling in the internal affairs of Iran, Turkey, and Greece; aiding Mao Tse-tung's Communists in the Chinese civil war; and the creation of Communist puppet governments in East Germany and North Korea left no doubt.

To arouse Americans who were again seeking a "return to normalcy," in March 1946 President Truman invited Winston Churchill to make a speech at Westminster College in Fulton, Missouri, in which he would issue a strong warning concerning the USSR. In this speech Churchill stated, "From Stettin in the Baltic to Trieste in the Adriatic an iron curtain has descended across the continent. . . . From what I have seen of our Russian friends and allies during the war, I am convinced that there is nothing they admire so much as strength, and there is nothing for which they have less respect than for weakness, especially military weakness." Thus was born the term given to the barrier between the West and communism: the *iron curtain.*

The American public was startled, but it was not moved toward significant action. When Truman proposed universal military training (the draft) as a means of rebuilding the services, Congress eventually responded with a Selective Service Act full of loopholes for those who wished to avoid military service. The weak-

The demobilization of the fleet progressed rapidly in the years following World War II, as indicated by this aerial view of some of the mothballed ships at San Diego, California, in 1950.

ening of the services continued. Ships sat alongside piers with half crews, unable to get under way.

UNIFICATION OF THE SERVICES

Along with demobilization came a reappraisal of the entire U.S. defense structure. Under the slogan of "unification," many in government and in the Army and its Air Corps component proposed a centralized military establishment that would, they hoped, make the shrinking peacetime defense budgets stretch further. The Navy came under special criticism. Several loud voices stated that the Navy was extravagant and unnecessary because there was no naval power anywhere in the world to oppose us.

The Army Air Corps sought independent status as the U.S. Air Force. They pointed to their strategic bombing role in Europe and Japan, and the fact that only they had the ability to deliver the atomic bomb, since Navy planes were not large enough. Some Air Corps generals questioned the need for a Navy at all, arguing that any future wars, unlikely as they were, could be won cheaply and quickly by bombing. They saw the proposed Air Force as the nation's new first line of defense.

Fleet Admiral Nimitz, by now the chief of naval operations, took a more realistic view. He felt that no one weapons system would be adequate to provide for all aspects of national defense or to protect the nation's growing world interests, most of which were dependent upon

free use of the seas. Various Navy spokesmen such as Nimitz and Secretary of the Navy James Forrestal did not foresee a major world war in the immediate future. Instead, they saw the dangers of takeovers in countries bordering the Soviet Union and Communist-inspired insurgencies in many underdeveloped nations. The countries threatened were the ones most closely associated with the West and most dependent upon logistic and tactical support from the sea. Furthermore, Forrestal opposed the idea of a single chief of staff over all of the armed forces because that would almost certainly result in an emphasis on one of the services at the expense of the others.

Despite the general Navy opposition to unification, there were many things to be said for it. Unified command in large combat areas could be a significant advantage, improving overall battle coordination. Also, it might help to eliminate some waste and duplication, which none of the services could afford with their austere peacetime budgets.

After long debate, Congress finally passed the National Security Act (NSA) in July 1947. The new law created the Department of Defense, headed by a secretary of defense, with subordinate Departments of the Army, Navy, and Air Force, and the Joint Chiefs of Staff. Under the terms of the NSA, the secretary of defense became a member of the president's cabinet, while the secretaries of the services did not have cabinet rank. It established the Air Force as a separate service and gave it responsibility for strategic bombing and for combat operations in support of land armies. The Navy retained its carrier aviation and its land-based reconnaissance wing, as well as the Marine Corps. The Army kept its traditional roles. Secretary Forrestal became the nation's first secretary of defense.

Under the same act, the National Security Council, with permanent members including the president, vice president, secretary of state, and secretary of defense, became the nation's top national security policy body. The National Security Act also provided for the creation of the Central Intelligence Agency (CIA).

THE TRUMAN DOCTRINE AND THE MARSHALL PLAN

Several events that occurred during the months before approval of the National Security Act made a significant impact on the congressional decision to maintain a strong Navy–Marine Corps team with all of its component forces. The post–World War II Soviet moves into the Balkan and Baltic nations had gone unopposed, but when the Soviets tried to expand into Iran and the countries bordering the eastern Mediterranean, President Truman took steps as commander in chief that caused Congress to become more aware of the danger. Strong pressure in the United Nations by the United States caused the Soviets to back down and get out of northern Iran.

In 1946–47 George Kennan, a prominent American diplomat stationed in Moscow, published his view that "the main element of any United States policy toward the Soviet Union must be that of a long-term, patient but firm and vigilant containment of Russian expansionist tendencies." This policy of *containment* became the cornerstone of U.S. cold war foreign policy for the next four decades.

In the spring of 1947 President Truman applied this containment policy to counter Soviet moves toward Greece and Turkey. In Greece, there had been civil war since the closing days of World War II, with Communists supported by the Soviets seeking to overthrow the legitimate government that had returned to power there after the war. The Soviets had been threatening Turkey since the war as well, because Stalin wanted access to the Dardanelles, through which Soviet ships from Black Sea ports had to transit to reach the Mediterranean.

In March 1947 in a speech before Congress, President Truman enunciated the Truman Doctrine, thus formalizing the containment policy. Truman stated, "It must be the policy of the United States to support free peoples who are resisting attempted subjugation by armed minorities or by outside pressures. . . . We must assist free peoples to work out their own destinies in their own way." In support of the doctrine, Congress voted sub-

stantial economic aid to both Greece and Turkey. U.S. military bases were established in both countries, and they are still there today. U.S. Navy units were sent to the Mediterranean as a diplomatic show of force. Soviet expansion toward the Mediterranean was thus checked.

This was the beginning of the permanent deployment of the U.S. Sixth Fleet in the Mediterranean Sea. Truman said that U.S. policy was "to support the cause of freedom wherever it was threatened." Thus the Navy found itself projecting American foreign policy at the same time as it was struggling in the halls of Congress for its very existence.

In June 1947 Secretary of State George Marshall announced Truman's plan to provide economic aid for reconstruction of European countries. This plan, formally named the European Recovery Program, became known as the Marshall Plan. Its purpose was to restore the economies of the war-ravaged countries in Europe and, in the process, make it more difficult for the Soviets to make more inroads there. Although the Soviet Union was invited to participate, it refused to do so, and it prohibited any of its new satellites from accepting the American assistance. The Soviet leaders denounced the plan as American economic aggression. Thus began an era of contention between the Western democracies headed by the United States and the Communist bloc dominated by the USSR that would extend over much of the next forty-five years. The cold war had started in earnest.

THE NORTH ATLANTIC TREATY ORGANIZATION (NATO)

As American political and economic policy began to assert itself, several Soviet actions solidified Western determination. In 1948 the Communist party executed a sudden coup d'état in Czechoslovakia, seizing complete control of the country and causing the death of the Czech president. Many Americans and Europeans now began to see how aggressive the forces of Soviet-backed communism really were.

The next incident was the Berlin Blockade in June 1948. The Soviets clamped a blockade on all materials entering or leaving the occupied city of Berlin by road, rail, or canal. This action was an attempt to cut off the army garrisons of the western Allies—Britain, France, and the United States—in the city and starve West Berlin into capitulation to the Soviets and their East German satellite. The Allies responded with a massive airborne supply operation called the Berlin Airlift, which lasted eleven months. During this time, over 2 million tons of supplies were flown into the city, one-fourth of it carried by Navy planes.

In response to the growing Soviet menace, the United States, Canada, and their West European allies agreed in 1949 to create the North Atlantic Treaty Orga-

In 1949 the United States, Canada, and their western European allies created the North Atlantic Treaty Organization (NATO), a military alliance designed to enhance the security of the Western democracies.

nization (NATO). In this treaty, all agreed that "an armed attack against one or more of them . . . shall be considered an attack against them all." The nations that signed this military alliance were Belgium, Britain, Canada, Denmark, France, Iceland, Italy, Luxembourg, the Netherlands, Norway, Portugal, and the United States. Turkey and Greece became members in 1951, the Federal Republic of Germany joined in 1955, and Spain joined in 1982. France withdrew from military participation in 1966, though it still participates in political affairs. The former Soviet satellite countries Hungary, Poland, and the Czech Republic joined in March 1999. NATO headquarters today is located in Belgium.

On the Communist side, in 1949 the Soviets established the Council for Mutual Economic Assistance as the economic organization of Communist-bloc countries. In 1955 the Eastern European Mutual Assistance Treaty, more commonly referred to as the Warsaw Pact, created the military counterpart to NATO. The former organization died with the demise of the Soviet Union in 1991.

Throughout the balance of the cold war from the early 1950s on, Soviet turboprop Bear and supersonic Badger reconnaissance aircraft continually monitored U.S. and NATO maritime exercises throughout the Mediterranean Sea and Atlantic Ocean areas. In the 1980s some of these aircraft were based in Cuba. From there, they often flew surveillance missions all along the Atlantic seaboard of the United States. Often they were intercepted and escorted by U.S. and NATO fighters, keeping tension high throughout these years.

THE FAR EAST

In the Far East the end of World War II and the defeat of Japan fanned the flames of smoldering nationalism and anticolonialism into major insurgencies trying to take control of weak governments. Communist backing was often a major factor in these revolutions.

The government of Nationalist China, headed by Chiang Kai-shek, was driven from the mainland to Taiwan by Mao Tse-tung's Communists in December 1949 after five years of civil war. The vacuum left by British and French withdrawals from Southeast Asia in the early 1950s stimulated insurgencies in Burma, Thailand, Malaya, and Indochina. Indochina erupted into open warfare. The Dutch were forced to leave the East Indies after a revolution by the Indonesian people. The British granted independence to India, Pakistan, and Ceylon.

In Korea after World War II, the Potsdam Conference had decreed that this former Japanese possession would be temporarily divided, with the Soviets occupying the part north of the thirty-eighth parallel and the United States occupying the southern part of the country. The Soviets quickly established a puppet Communist regime and trained a large North Korean army. In May 1948 they established the People's Democratic Republic of Korea, with its capital in Pyongyang.

In the south, the United States and the United Nations helped establish the Republic of Korea (ROK). In free elections, the South Koreans elected Syngman Rhee as first president and set up their capital at Seoul in July

1948. Not until U.S. forces began their evacuation did an American advisory group start to train an ROK army. This was still ill-equipped and poorly organized when the last of the American garrison forces departed in June 1949. American lack of resolution had set the stage for another war involving American servicemen. A year later, on 25 June 1950, the North Korean army crossed the thirty-eighth parallel in a full-scale invasion of South Korea.

THE KOREAN WAR

The North Korean invasion of South Korea in June 1950, backed by the Soviet Union and the Chinese Communists, had two main purposes. The first was to unify Korea into a Communist state. The second purpose was to establish a geographic dagger pointed at the center of Japan, where General MacArthur's occupation rule prevented Communist subversion from gaining a foothold. U.S. State Department spokesmen had suggested that Korea was not important to American strategic defense. This implied that the United States would not oppose an invasion, and undoubtedly encouraged the North Korean leaders to try open aggression.

As soon as President Truman learned of the invasion, he directed the U.S. delegate to the United Nations Security Council to call an emergency meeting. The USSR was boycotting the council, and with no Soviet veto to hurdle, the Security Council condemned the North Korean act as a breach of world peace and ordered military sanctions. The United States undertook the direction of military operations. President Truman ordered the Joint Chiefs of Staff to take any action necessary to aid South Korea and repel the invasion. The Joint Chiefs named General MacArthur commander in chief, Far East. He was later named supreme commander of United Nations forces.

The UN Security Council called on other member nations to come to the aid of South Korea and to assist the United States with military forces. Eventually fourteen other countries—Great Britain, Canada, Australia, New Zealand, France, Brazil, Greece, Turkey, Norway, Sweden, the Netherlands, Thailand, Colombia, and the Philippines—sent military and naval contingents, and many others sent medical and material aid.

The South Koreans were soon overrun by fifteen well-equipped North Korean divisions. Seoul fell only three days after the invasion, and the "Reds," as the Communists were called, proceeded southward with little opposition. General MacArthur committed three of the four American occupational divisions in Japan to stem the tide and gain some time for UN forces to build up strength through the port of Pusan. U.S. general Walton Walker and the remnants of the ROK army fought hard but retreated steadily. By late July only an area about 25 miles west by 80 miles north of Pusan remained in allied hands. This was called the Pusan Perimeter.

Fortunately, at this point American reinforcements and equipment began pouring into the Pusan Perimeter. Aided by naval bombardment, air strikes, and U.S. marines, the defenders began to inflict severe casualties on the attacking North Koreans. By the third week of August, after being stalled for three weeks on the Pusan Perimeter, the North Korean drive started to lose steam, and General MacArthur began plans for possibly the most daring amphibious assault ever conceived.

OPERATION CHROMITE: INCHON

By September 1950 General Walker had consolidated the Pusan Perimeter and made it nearly impossible to penetrate. A stalemate had been reached. The UN forces were growing ever stronger and could undoubtedly have broken through the weakening North Korean lines but at great cost. General MacArthur did not want to incur those losses, so he proposed an exceptionally complex amphibious assault on Inchon, the port of Seoul. The objective was to capture Inchon and Seoul, and thus cut the North Korean supply line to their armies on the Pusan Perimeter. This would isolate over 90 percent of the North Korean army and, for all practical purposes, destroy North Korea's capability for making war.

The proposed landing at Inchon, however, presented extreme difficulties. The only approach to the port was through the Flying Fish Channel, a tortuous 30-mile run through mud flats that became visible each day at low tide. The range of tide at Inchon is one of the greatest in the world—29 feet on the average, and sometimes as much as 36 feet. It was this tide, however, that made the landing feasible, for it allowed the LSTs to go right up to Inchon's waterfront to disembark troops and vehicles. The troops, though, would have to use ladders to scale a seawall. Worst of all, if the landing were unsuccessful, not only the troops but also the LSTs would be lost, since the ships would later be trapped, sitting high and dry on the tidal mud flats.

D day for the Inchon landing was set for 15 September, because it was only on the three days beginning 15 September that the tides would meet amphibious requirements. The Marine brigade, a key force in General Walker's successful defense of the Pusan perimeter, was withdrawn to form the nucleus of the First Marine Division, which would spearhead the landing.

Vice Admiral Arthur Struble, commander of the Seventh Fleet, was in overall command. Carrier air support was provided from three U.S. carriers in Task Force 77. The First Marine Division was to make the first landing, followed by the U.S. Seventh Infantry Division, an airborne regiment, and a South Korean marine regiment. These ground forces made up the X Corps, commanded by Major General Edward Almond, USA.

A cruiser-destroyer force threaded its way up the Flying Fish Channel on 13 September to bombard the North Korean fortifications on the islands of Wolmi-do and Sowolmi-do, which protected the harbor and city. There was a spirited exchange of fire during which three destroyers were hit, but the shore and air bombardment on 13–14 September was sufficient to enable the landing to proceed on schedule the following morning.

At 0630 on the fifteenth, the first waves stormed ashore at Green Beach on Wolmi-do. The island was se-cured in thirty-one minutes. Sowolmido followed quickly, thanks to 40-mm fire from one of the support ships. The main landing followed in the late afternoon. Red Beach was in downtown Inchon, the only place heavy equipment such as tanks, bulldozers, and trucks could be landed. Blue Beach was on the southern out-skirts of the city on a muddy, narrow beach too soft to take heavy equipment.

At 1730 the first wave hit Red Beach. Not until the fourth wave landed did the defenders commence any

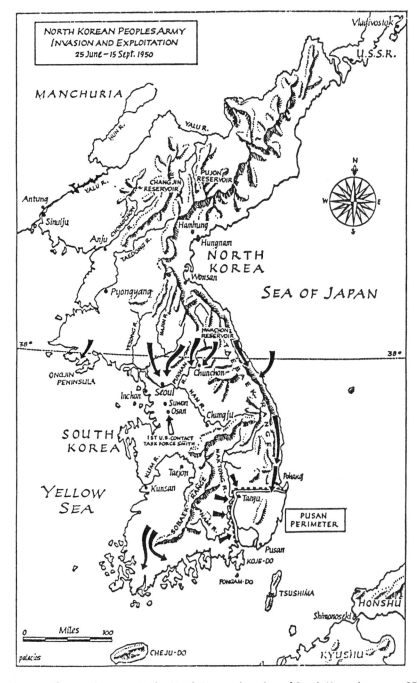

The Korean theater of operations, 1950. The North Korean invasion of South Korea began on 25 June 1950.

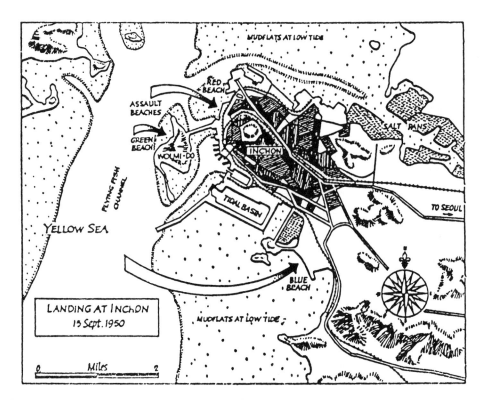

A schematic drawing of the Inchon landing, showing Green Beach on Wolmi-Do, Red Beach on the seawall of the city, and Blue Beach to the south. Blue Beach became the main logistics beach after the initial landings.

serious opposition, but by that time the troops ashore were securing enemy strong points and advancing toward their first objective line, 1,000 yards inland. By 2000 they had moved beyond their objective. The landings went on during the night and the next day, as bulldozers tore down the seawall to facilitate landing heavy equipment. The marines at Blue Beach landed against light resistance and seized the main rail line to Seoul, but their LST support did not arrive until the following morning's high tide.

Twenty-four hours after the landings at Inchon started, the marines shifted their command post ashore and declared the landing phase of the operation concluded. Before the enemy could regroup, Kimpo Airfield outside Seoul was captured on 18 September, and the marines were closing in on Seoul. The Inchon operation proved to be one of the most successful amphibious assaults in military history. "The Navy and Marines have never shone more brightly," General MacArthur remarked.

BREAKOUT AT PUSAN

On the day after the Inchon landing, General Walker and his Eighth Army began a major offensive to break out of the Pusan Perimeter. The North Koreans were now in an untenable military situation. With their main supply route through Seoul severed and their only other supply route along the east coast road under steady naval bombardment, the North Koreans had no means of logistic support. When the Inchon invasion force turned southward and met the Eighth Army coming north from Pusan on 26 September, for all practical purposes the war in South Korea was over. On the twenty-eighth Seoul fell. All fighting had not ceased, but the North Koreans had no hope of victory. All that remained was "mopping up." In that process, over 125,000 North Korean soldiers were taken prisoner.

After much debate in the United Nations, that body authorized General MacArthur to proceed north of the thirty-eighth parallel to destroy the remnants of the North Korean forces. While the Eighth Army advanced against heavy opposition toward Pyongyang, the ROK army, now reorganized, reequipped, and trained in the hardships of war, roared 100 miles northward in ten days along the east coast against little opposition.

Another major amphibious assault behind North Korean lines was planned to assist the ROK forces by cutting off the enemy's route of escape and to hasten the fall of Pyongyang. MacArthur embarked the X Corps in amphibious ships for transportation from Inchon to the east coast of North Korea for an assault on Wonsan. The concept was similar to the Inchon landing. The retreating North Koreans would be encircled, and their capability to resist would be reduced even more.

Marines climbing the seawall at Red Beach during the Inchon landings.

The timetable was interrupted, however, by a huge Communist minefield at Wonsan Harbor. Instead of taking five days to sweep the mines clear as planned, the job took fifteen. The minefield had caused the allies to lose command of the sea. The delay enabled the North Koreans to retreat in some semblance of order. The amphibious landing became an "administrative" operation, taking place after the ROK forces had already captured the city. In the meantime, the Eighth Army captured Pyongyang on 19 October.

CHINESE INTERVENTION

Despite warnings that his invasion of Communist North Korea would bring Chinese Communist intervention, MacArthur's forces continued to drive northward toward the Yalu River boundary with Chinese Manchuria. MacArthur's intelligence officers did not believe the Chinese would enter the war in force. They believed that if they were going to do it at all, they would have done it when the allies had their backs to the sea at Pusan. Thus MacArthur sent the Eighth Army north from Pyongyang and the X Corps north from Hamhung. On 26 October elements of the ROK army arrived at the Yalu.

There was an 80-mile gap between the two northward-moving UN forces because of no east-west com-

munications and roads. Chinese forces began to advance southward into this gap. Elements of the ROK army met the Chinese in several heavy encounters in late October and early November. On 2 November, Chinese forces attacked units of the Eighth Army near Unsan.

MacArthur warned the Joint Chiefs on 6 November that if the movement of Chinese forces across the Yalu continued, his army faced destruction. On 24 November MacArthur gave the order for his forces to begin a drive to the Yalu. That same day, the first U.S. elements reached the Yalu at Hyesanjin. Then on 25 November 1950 200,000 Chinese, called Volunteers of the People's Liberation Army, launched a major offensive, sweeping the allies before them and cutting off a large group of marines at the Chosin Reservoir north of Hungnam.

The next two weeks saw the United Nations forces fight their way back southward in full retreat, even as the cold and snow of the Korean winter closed in. In temperatures as low as 25 degrees below zero, marines and other allied forces were often forced to fight their way out of surrounded positions. Navy and Marine planes pounded the Chinese forces in the hills. Under this umbrella, the marines finally reached the coastal city of Hungnam on 9 December. During the next two weeks, 105,000 troops, 90,000 Korean refugees, thousands of vehicles, and tons of bulk cargo were combat-loaded in

A mine claims a South Korean minesweeper in Wonsan Harbor during the Korean War. It took fifteen days to complete the sweeping of mines from Wonsan, a delay that enabled the North Korean army to escape following the Inchon landing.

orderly manner on waiting amphibious vessels in the greatest "amphibious operation in reverse" ever conducted. During the entire time, naval gunfire and carrier air strikes kept the Communist forces back. This created a no-man's-land around the Hungnam defense perimeter that the Chinese could not penetrate. On Christmas Eve 1950, the last troops departed and the Navy's Underwater Demolition Teams blew up all port facilities before leaving.

The forces evacuated from Hungnam were sped southward and reintroduced into the fighting below the thirty-eighth parallel, where the bulk of United Nations forces had retreated by 15 December.

General Matthew Ridgway took command of the Eighth Army on 26 December following the death of General Walker in a jeep accident. The Eighth Army slowed its retreat but could not stop the Chinese advance before losing Seoul again on 4 January 1951. In late January Ridgway began a slow advance toward the Han River south of Seoul, a methodical drive that culminated in the recapture of the South Korean capital on 15 March. UN forces made more advances in the succeeding months, particularly along the east coast, where they reached a point about 50 miles north of the thirty-eighth parallel. But there the war bogged down for both sides.

DISMISSAL OF MACARTHUR

General MacArthur had hated the limitations placed upon him after the Chinese intervened. He particularly wanted to be allowed to follow Chinese aircraft in "hot pursuit" over the Yalu River into Manchuria and to bomb Chinese staging bases on the north bank of the river. The Western European allies put great pressure on the United States to forbid such action. They feared that the war would escalate and eventually involve the Soviets on the basis of the Sino-Soviet Mutual Defense Treaty. This opinion was shared by the U.S. State Department, and their view prevailed with the president.

When he was unable to persuade President Truman to accept his recommendations, in March 1951 General MacArthur sent a letter attacking the president's policies to Joseph Martin, the minority leader of the House of Representatives. When Martin made the letter public, President Truman relieved MacArthur for insubordination, replacing him with General Ridgway.

In his letter, MacArthur pointed out that "Europe's war against the Communists was being fought in Asia with arms, while the diplomats there still fight it with words; that if we lose the war to Communism in Asia the fall of Europe is inevitable; win it and Europe most probably would avoid war, and yet preserve freedom. . . . There is no substitute for victory."

TRUCE TALKS

By June 1951 the severe casualties inflicted on the Chinese began to make an impression. The USSR's ambassador to the United Nations suggested that armistice talks might be held, and the United Nations leaders agreed. Thereafter began over two years of almost fruitless negotiations at Panmunjom, a small village along the thirty-eighth parallel. Meanwhile, fierce fighting continued, although neither side attempted a major offensive to capture territory.

During the negotiations, the Chinese Communists showed no willingness to compromise. To them, a concession was a sign of weakness and an invitation for the other side to make additional demands. Negotiating with the Communists was clearly shown to be another battlefield, with the weapons being steadfastness of policy, infinite patience, and complete firmness.

Dwight Eisenhower was elected president in November 1952. A major promise of his campaign was to bring an end to the Korean War. This stimulated new efforts in the truce talks, and finally, after more than two years of negotiations, an armistice was signed on 27 July 1953. The agreement divided the two Koreas along a frontier near the thirty-eighth parallel, but based on the existing cease-fire line. South Korea kept its freedom,

General of the Army Douglas MacArthur, commander in chief of U.S. forces during the first nine months of the Korean War. He was relieved by President Truman in April 1950 because of disagreements over war strategy. Lieutenant General Walker, commander of ground forces in Korea during the first part of the war, is riding in the rear.

gaining in the process about 1,500 square miles of territory at a cost of 70,000 South Korean, 34,000 American, and 5,000 other UN casualties on the battlefields. In addition, several million Korean civilians are believed to have died during the course of the war.

A major issue in the truce talks concerned prisoners of war (POWs). Many North Koreans and Chinese taken prisoner in the south refused to go back to their countries. Furthermore, after American prisoners were returned, they brought with them many tales of inhumane treatment in North Korean prison camps and failure to comply with international conventions concerning treatment of POWs. The issue of North Korean treatment of American POWs would continue to be a topic of discussion between U.S. and North Korean representatives at Panmunjom for years to come. Both the North Koreans and the United Nations still keep representatives at Panmunjom. They meet periodically to conduct negotiations on many military incidents that have occurred over the years since the armistice ending the war.

NAVAL CONTRIBUTIONS

Although only a few insignificant naval actions took place at sea during the Korean War, sea power made major contributions. The role of the Navy in supplying and defending the Pusan Perimeter, and in the invasion at Inchon, has already been discussed. In addition,

throughout the war naval forces under Admiral C. Turner Joy conducted shore bombardment of coastal roads, naval air attacks on strategic targets and lines of communications, and close air support of troops in the field. This naval power was indispensable to the allied effort. Close air support of ground forces provided by Navy and Marine pilots and planes was so effective that the North Koreans eventually gave up all daylight offensive actions. Allied ground forces were never harassed by North Korean air power, because Navy, Marine, and Air Force pilots controlled the air, attacking North Korean air bases and shooting down any North Korean aircraft that ventured forth.

KOREAN WAR AFTERMATH

Encouraged by the outcome in Korea, Communist guerrillas led by Ho Chi Minh intensified their war against the French in Indochina. In 1954 the French were defeated in battle at Dien Bien Phu. This event resulted in the partition of Indochina into North and South Vietnam, Laos, and Cambodia. The victory emboldened the Chinese Communists, who threatened to invade Taiwan and the Nationalist-held islands of Quemoy, Matsu, and the Pescadores. But in November the United States signed a treaty to guard Taiwan and the Pescadores from Communist invasion, and the Chinese shifted their attention to insurgencies in Indonesia, Thailand, and Malaya.

In 1955 the Communist Chinese threatened the Nationalist-held Tachen Islands and invaded one of them. President Eisenhower did not want to get into a war with China, but he was committed to the defense of Taiwan. Consequently, he asked Congress to grant him the authority to use military force as necessary to accomplish such defense, and it was granted. Since the Tachens themselves were indefensible, the Navy undertook to evacuate all the inhabitants to Taiwan, an operation that was conducted successfully.

Two post–Korean War events during the summer of 1958 illustrated the value of sea power in stabilizing a threatening situation and preventing potential war.

Following a revolt in Iraq that toppled the pro-Western government in July, Lebanese president Camille Chamoun requested U.S. military assistance to protect his country from a similar event. Within a few hours, the Sixth Fleet carrier striking force was in position off Lebanon. The Amphibious Ready Group began landing marines on the afternoon of 15 July on the beaches near Beirut Airport. The American forces were met by bikini-clad girls and ice cream vendors selling Popsicles. No insurrection took place, the situation calmed, peaceful elections were held, and the Americans withdrew.

President Gamal Abdel Nasser of Egypt and his Soviet supporters did not overlook the significance of the landing, even though many Americans missed the point. The Soviets were forced to back down on their promises to Egypt to support coup d'état attempts in the Middle East. As a consequence they lost much prestige among the Arab nations. The Lebanese operation demonstrated that the U.S. Sixth Fleet was a force-in-being capable of decisive action. That the Soviets did not have such a capability caused them to embark upon a significant naval shipbuilding program designed to remedy their weakness in the Mediterranean Sea.

At the same time the Lebanese operation was attracting so much attention—and probably not by coincidence—the Communist Chinese made new preparations to attack Quemoy, an island still held by the Nationalists near the port city of Amoy. Siege guns subjected the island to constant bombardment. Admiral Burke, the CNO at the time, anticipated a confrontation with the Chinese in Asia at the very time that the Sixth Fleet was committed in Lebanon. He placed the entire Pacific Fleet on alert and sent units of the First Fleet to reinforce the Seventh Fleet in supporting Taiwan. When the Lebanese plot was defused by the swift U.S. naval action there, the Chinese became discouraged, backed off, and relaxed tensions.

This was very short-lived, for on 23 August another ferocious artillery barrage opened up on Quemoy. The United States dispatched six carriers and their supporting forces to the area, prepared to do all in their power to defend the Nationalist islands. With such support, the Nationalist air force took on the Chinese air force using new American-built planes equipped with heat-seeking Sidewinder missiles. They quickly drove the Communists from the sky. U.S. Navy planes then joined the Nationalists in patrols over the Taiwan Straits. The Navy ferried supplies in to the defenders of Quemoy on amphibious craft. By September the Navy had 150 ships operating in the Taiwan area.

The demonstrated fighting capability of the Nationalists and the heavy American naval force were decisive in causing the Chinese Communists to reconsider their planned invasions. Admiral Nimitz wrote that "the quick assembly of the U.S. Navy's Pacific power was the factor most responsible for averting a general war."

Unfortunately, provocative behavior on the part of the North Koreans did not end with the Korean War armistice. In the years since many incidents have occurred that have shown their continued willingness to test the resolve of South Korea and the United States. One of the worst of these took place in January 1968, when a U.S. intelligence-gathering ship, the USS *Pueblo* (AGER-2), was attacked and captured by the North Koreans 15 miles off Wonsan Harbor. As had been common practice for some time, the ship was conducting routine intelligence-gathering operations in international waters off the coast of North Korea. On 23 January the lone ship was suddenly approached by several North Korean torpedo boats and a subchaser. After several attempts to get away, during which she was continually fired upon, she was boarded and her crew was rounded up at gunpoint. Then the ship was forced into Wonsan Harbor, where the crew was removed to a detention site.

For the next eleven months her crew of 82 officers, enlisted men, and civilians were held as prisoners by the North Koreans. They were often subjected to beatings to try to make them admit that they were in North Korean waters when they were captured. Only after agreeing to a false confession (which was later repudiated) was the U.S. negotiating team at Panmunjom finally able to obtain their release. The ship itself is still on display as a tourist attraction at Wonsan. This incident marked the first time in over 150 years that a U.S. warship had been captured on the high seas by a foreign power.

NEW NAVAL CAPABILITIES

Although the Korean War did not bring peace to a troubled world, it had some positive consequences for the U.S. Navy. The prewar contention by some that naval warfare was obsolete was largely discredited. The Korean War had shown that naval shore bombardment, carrier air strikes, close air support, amphibious landings, and logistic support from the sea were all necessary parts of any military operations. Congress thereafter authorized the building of six large *Forrestal*-class aircraft carriers, and plans for new classes of amphibious and mobile logistics ships were drawn up.

On 1 November 1952 a new threshold in nuclear warfare was crossed with the test explosion of the first U.S. hydrogen bomb on Eniwetok Atoll in the Pacific. In August 1953 the Soviet Union detonated its version of the super-explosive bomb. As President Eisenhower expanded U.S. military power to cope with the growing Soviet cold war threat, there was a greater spirit of cooperation among the Joint Chiefs of Staff. They now realized that all components of the U.S. armed forces had a definite role in limited war, as well as in deterring possible nuclear war with the Soviet Union. This new cooperative spirit would show itself many times in various crises throughout the remainder of the cold war and thereafter, when joint forces from all services would many times be called upon to protect U.S. interests around the globe.

Approval of the new carrier construction program won for the Navy its battle to be a part of the nation's nuclear striking force. The *Forrestal* class was designed to launch planes capable of carrying nuclear bombs. The difficulty of locating and neutralizing mobile nuclear-equipped carrier forces was certainly a deterrent that any aggressor would have to consider seriously.

While the new carriers were being built, an even more far-reaching naval technical development occurred. Under the direction of the Navy's hard-driving Captain (later Admiral) Hyman G. Rickover, the world's first nuclear-powered submarine, the USS *Nautilus* put to sea in January 1955. It was soon followed by a fast-growing fleet of nuclear attack submarines. During the remainder of the twentieth century, nuclear power would become as significant to the Navy as the shift from sail to steam had been during the Civil War.

The next significant development was an intermediate-range nuclear-tipped ballistic missile named the Polaris, which could be launched from a submerged submarine. Simultaneously a new class of submarines that could launch it was built. The USS *George Washington* went into commission in 1959 as the first of the new fleet of ballistic missile submarines. These new submarines, and the succession of improved missiles they would carry, would join with the Army's land-based ICBMs (intercontinental ballistic missiles) and the Air Force's manned bombers to become a significant leg of the nation's *triad* of strategic deterrence for the balance of the century. Several classes of nuclear-powered aircraft carriers and other surface warships followed.

For much of the next three decades, U.S. nuclear attack submarines would play a major (and only recently revealed) role in the cold war at sea. Specially equipped submarines were often sent on extended secret spy missions to monitor Soviet military communications only miles off the Soviet coasts. Others frequently secretly followed Soviet missile subs on their patrols, ready to sink

Vice Admiral Hyman G. Rickover. When considering the contributions of naval leaders since World War II, one would be hard pressed to find anyone who had a more profound effect than Admiral Rickover. Always controversial and often irascible, his dedication and perseverance earned for him the title "Father of the Nuclear Navy." For forty years he almost singlehandedly led the Navy's postwar development of probably the most sophisticated weapon system the world has ever known—the nuclear submarine.

them before they could launch their deadly cargo should war have ever broken out during these years.

During the 1960s, a whole new generation of mobile logistic ships designed for underway replenishment (UNREP) joined the fleet. These had the capability of servicing whole task groups at sea at speeds up to 20 knots. Improvement in large helicopters added the new dimension of vertical replenishment (VERTREP) to mobile logistics. Both the Sixth Fleet in the Mediterranean and Seventh Fleet in the West Pacific receive the bulk of their stores in UNREP and VERTREP operations today.

Similarly, in the 1960s and 1970s new ships transformed the amphibious squadrons of the Atlantic and Pacific Fleets into 20-knot operational groups capable of landing a fully equipped marine battalion on an enemy beach. The advent of nuclear weapons required the modification of amphibious doctrine, emphasizing mobility and dispersal. The helicopter made a major impression on amphibious warfare also, with the tactic of vertical envelopment, which is the airlift of troops and equipment to landing areas behind the selected assault beach. There, they can prevent enemy reinforcements from opposing the landing and the later delivery of logistic support.

THE CUBAN MISSILE CRISIS

As potentially explosive as the incidents between the U.S. and communism in the late 1940s and 1950s were, the 1962 Cuban missile crisis was the most dangerous of all cold war crises to that date. It was a direct confrontation between the United States and the Soviet Union.

On 14 October 1962 high-flying U-2 reconnaissance aircraft on photographic intelligence missions positively identified Soviet ICBM launching pads under construction in Fidel Castro's Cuba. Earlier photographs had shown surface-to-air missile batteries being erected and Soviet-flag freighters laden with electronic gear, construction equipment, and even suspected crated missiles being unloaded in Cuban ports. With proof of the ICBM sites confirmed, it became obvious that the Soviets were trying to overcome the superiority of America's Polaris missile submarines by placing the majority of American cities well within the 2,200-mile range of Soviet missiles.

President Kennedy had only two choices: do nothing, and make the United States vulnerable to Soviet nuclear blackmail, or force the Soviets to remove the missiles, even at the threat of nuclear war. After an agonizing appraisal of the alternatives, the president called upon the U.S. Navy to establish a quarantine (a type of selective blockade) of Cuba. Having made the decision, the president told Admiral George Anderson, then CNO,

"Well, it looks as if everything is in the hands of the Navy."

Admiral Anderson replied, "Mr. President, the Navy will not let you down."

The next evening, 21 October, the president went on national television and told the American people and the world that the Soviet Union had placed missiles in Cuba. He announced that "a strict quarantine of all offensive equipment under shipment to Cuba is being initiated," and that any ship bound for Cuba carrying such cargo would be met by the U.S. Navy and turned back. By 24 October over 180 Navy ships were involved in the operation, establishing a quarantine line on an arc 500 miles to the east of Cuba. Naval vessels and aircraft continuously conducted reconnaissance missions over and around the island.

Soviet Premier Nikita Khrushchev branded the U.S. charges as lies and warned that if America carried out any act of "piracy," the Soviet Union would react accordingly. Work on the missile sites continued. Thirty thousand U.S. marines embarked in amphibious ships near Cuba made preparations to invade the island. Intelligence reported that twenty-five Soviet ships were on their way to Cuba and nearing the quarantine line. The question was, would they turn back, would they have to be boarded and captured, or would they have to be sunk? Tension rose. War seemed only hours away.

A Navy patrol plane and destroyer intercept a Soviet merchant ship during the Cuban quarantine in 1962.

On the afternoon of 24 October word was received that many of the Soviet ships had either stopped or turned back. Secretary of State Dean Rusk is reported to have remarked, "We're eyeball to eyeball, and I think the other fellow just blinked." On 26 October a Soviet charter ship was stopped, boarded, and searched and allowed to proceed when found not to be carrying any contraband. This established the right to stop and search suspected quarantine violators.

Later that day, President Kennedy offered to end the quarantine and promised not to invade Cuba if the Soviets would remove their missiles. Unwilling to challenge the superior American sea power, Khrushchev capitulated. Nuclear holocaust was averted, and the world breathed easier. Khrushchev's attempt to overcome American nuclear superiority had failed. Determined leadership coupled with sea power had preserved the peace; the Navy had indeed not let the nation down. President Kennedy summed it up clearly: "Events of October 1962 indicated, as they have all through history, that control of the sea means security . . . peace . . . [and] victory. The United States must control the seas if it is to protect our security."

Khrushchev and the Soviet Union had been checked, but as a result, the buildup of Soviet sea power that had begun after the setback in Lebanon was given top priority. It moved forward with great momentum under the leadership of the Admiral of the Fleet of the Soviet Union, Sergei G. Gorshkov. By the 1970s, that momentum would give the Soviets a navy second only to that of the United States, with a powerful Mediterranean squadron, the world's largest submarine force, an aircraft carrier with vertical-takeoff planes, an amphibious force with naval infantry embarked, and impressive new merchant, oceanographic, and intelligence collection fleets as well.

In the aftermath of the Cuban missile crisis, the United States and the Soviet Union agreed in 1963 to establish a direct communications link—the famous "hotline"—between the two governments for use in the event of a future crisis. In 1972 President Nixon and Premier Brezhnev signed the Strategic Arms Limitation Treaty (SALT I), the first of several such treaties. One provision contained an antiballistic missile (ABM) defense system agreement (henceforth called the ABM Treaty). Under this treaty, no further antiballistic missile systems could be developed by either country. Another provision froze the numbers of land-based and sea-launched ballistic missiles (ICMBs and SLBMs) at then-existing levels.

THE VIETNAM WAR

Vietnam had been a part of French Indochina since the mid-1800s, when France had acquired control of the area now comprising Vietnam, Laos, and Cambodia as a result of imperialist expansion into the region. During World War II Vietnam was occupied by the Japanese. It declared its independence following the Japanese defeat in 1945. The French, however, tried to reassert their control in a war that lasted from 1946 to 1954. In that year the French suffered a major defeat by Communist forces led by Ho Chi Minh at Dien Bien Phu, leading to complete French withdrawal two years later. After the French defeat a Geneva accord established a demilitarized zone (DMZ) along the seventeenth parallel between North and South Vietnam, just as was done in Korea following World War II. The Communists under Ho Chi Minh were given control of North Vietnam, and South Vietnam, initially placed under French control, soon came under the control of anti-Communist Nationalists led by Bao Dai. The partition was supposed to be temporary until free elections would unify the country two years later.

In 1955 a new leader, Ngo Din Diem, was chosen by Bao Dai. He organized the government into the Republic of Vietnam and declared himself president. He was backed by U.S. President Dwight Eisenhower and the Southeast Asia Treaty Organization.

Communist China and the Soviet Union poured assistance into North Vietnam. Fearing that this would soon lead to expansion southward by North Vietnam, President Eisenhower offered South Vietnam military aid, including 700 advisors, and economic assistance in the amount of $200 million a year. Initially this American aid brought great prosperity to South Vietnam. However, Diem ran a corrupt and dictatorial government, composed largely of politicians and military officers who had earlier sided with the French. They carried with them a legacy of defeat and were never fully supported by the population. Ho Chi Minh, on the other hand, was regarded as a hero by most Vietnamese, both in the North and the South, because of his role in the defeat of the French. These facts would bear heavily on the eventual outcome in the embattled country.

When it came time for the 1956 elections to determine national unification and type of government, Diem, fearful of defeat at the polls, refused to allow them. Civil war flared immediately. Communist rebels in the South, called the National Liberation Front (NLF), or Vietcong, received the support of Communist North Vietnam. They resorted to massacre and terrorization of the peasantry to force support of the NLF. When he took office in 1962, President John Kennedy, following the advice of the Joint Chiefs and Secretary of State Dean Rusk, decided to increase the number of American military advisers in South Vietnam to 23,000 by the middle of 1963. They soon were piloting helicopters and returning Vietcong fire. The NLF, now reinforced by thousands of troops from North Vietnam, were spreading their control over the countryside, murdering about 500 village leaders, teachers, and businessmen each month. In response to this deteriorating situation, in November 1963 South Vietnamese military leaders staged a coup. They assassinated Diem and seized control of the government.

THE TONKIN GULF INCIDENT

Open involvement of the United States in the war began in August 1964, during the presidency of Lyndon Johnson. The destroyer USS *Maddox* was patrolling in the Gulf of Tonkin off the North Vietnamese coast on an intelligence mission. The ship was outside of the 3-mile limit then recognized by the United States but within the 12-mile limit claimed by North Vietnam. On 2 August the *Maddox* was attacked by three NVN patrol boats, which fired torpedoes and machine guns at her. In the ensuing battle, one of the patrol boats was left dead in the water.

President Johnson ordered the destroyer to resume its patrol in the gulf as an expression of American rights to freedom of the seas. The following night, during stormy weather, another North Vietnamese torpedo attack was reported by the *Maddox* and the destroyer *C. Turner Joy,* though later evidence seemed to indicate the alleged attack may never have occurred. In any event, the president ordered aircraft from the carriers *Constellation* and *Ticonderoga* to bomb North Vietnamese patrol boat bases and an oil storage depot in retaliation. Two days later, Congress passed the Tonkin Gulf Resolution, which gave the president a free hand to employ necessary measures to "repel any armed attack" or "prevent further aggression." This resolution, along with subsequent congressional financial appropriations, formed the legal basis for America's escalating involvement in the Vietnam War.

In February 1965, after heavy American casualties were sustained in a Vietcong mortar attack on the Pleiku Air Base, President Johnson retaliated with carrier air attacks on barracks and port facilities in North Vietnam. A terrorist attack three days later killed twenty-three Americans in an enlisted men's hotel. The president now ordered the U.S. Marines to land at DaNang to protect a major air base located there, and to develop and defend additional bases in the northern part of South Vietnam to prevent North Vietnamese incursions across the DMZ. The marines landed on 8 March and shortly thereafter joined South Vietnamese forces in "search and destroy" missions against the Vietcong.

With the commitment of the marines, the general U.S. buildup began. Amphibious assaults and combat air support from the Seventh Fleet steadily grew in size and strength. Army combat troops arrived and took over the Chu Lai base in April 1967, while the marines, now numbering more than 70,000, operated from a series of bases from DaNang north to the DMZ. The marines were supported by 26,000 U.S. Navy Seabees in the northern area. They fought regularly against regiment-sized North

Vietnamese units and thousands of Vietcong. An example of this fighting was the siege at Khe Sanh in which surrounded marines inflicted heavy casualties on the enemy for over six months.

The U.S. Navy involvement was massive. The Seventh Fleet had as many as five carriers operating off "Yankee Station" in the Tonkin Gulf continuously for the next five years. Their movements were often monitored by one or more Soviet intelligence-gathering trawlers (AGIs) operating in the Gulf. Over sixty amphibious assaults were made on South Vietnamese beaches, in missions designed to eliminate pockets of Vietcong and North Vietnamese forces that had been located by intelligence. By 1968 President Johnson had committed more than half a million American servicemen to South Vietnam. B-52 bombers flew hundreds of massive "Rolling Thunder" bombing raids against enemy targets from bases in Guam and Thailand.

In addition to these activities, the Navy also became involved with all kinds of sea-launched commando, river, and coastal patrol operations. A whole new "Brown Water Navy," named the Mobile Riverine Force, was created. It consisted of armored monitors, armored troop carriers, and a variety of patrol and minesweeping craft. Riverine patrols roamed through the numerous canals and rivers of the Mekong Delta south and west of Saigon. Air-cushion vehicles patrolled the coastal sounds, the Plain of Reeds, and many rivers. Thousands of armed helicopters and helicopter gunships zipped through the air to strike known and suspected enemy concentrations. Navy "swift boats" and Coast Guard cutters interdicted attempts by the North Vietnamese to infiltrate troops and supplies by sea in Operation Market Time. Special Forces, SEAL teams, UDTs, and Sea Commandos conducted hundreds of raids and ambushes against the elusive enemy. (Sea Commandos were highly trained Vietnamese with SEAL and U.S. Marine advisers.)

RESTRICTIONS HINDER VICTORY

In spite of the increased American involvement, however, the war dragged on for several years. There was no declaration of war by Congress, and political indecision in Washington made effective military prosecution of the war difficult if not impossible. Many bombing restrictions in North Vietnam and prohibitions against mining North Vietnamese waters were imposed, mainly out of concern over provoking a reaction from the Soviet Union or China.

Continuous attacks by carrier- and land-based aircraft along the famous Ho Chi Minh Trail, the overland Communist supply route through the Laotian and Cambodian jungles, could not stop a steady flow of combatants and material from North Vietnam. There rarely was

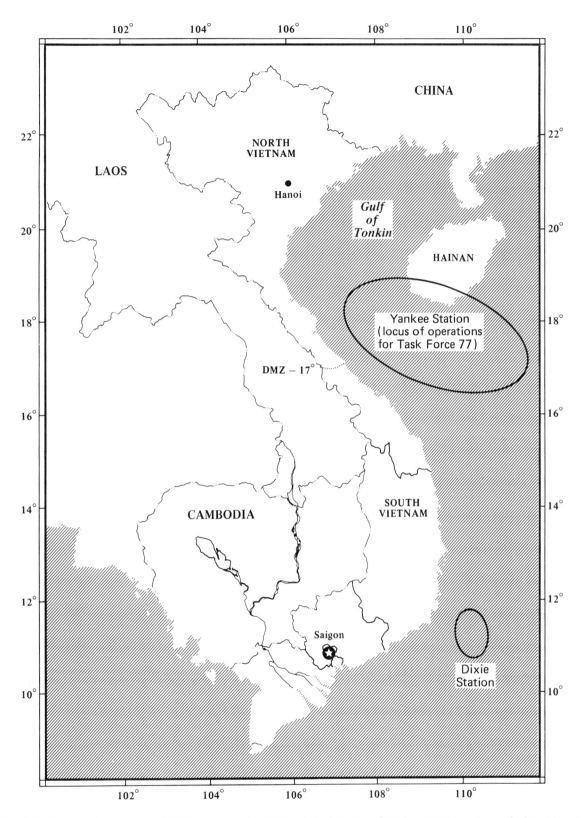

North and South Vietnam as they were until 1972, showing the DMZ and the location of Yankee Station in the Gulf of Tonkin, where many ships of the U.S. Navy were deployed during the war.

A Navy swift boat speeds up a Vietnamese river to attack the Vietcong during the Vietnam War.

anything resembling a battlefront. Instead, guerrillas popped up from jungles, villages, and rice fields where only moments before peaceful-looking farmers had tended their crops.

The Chinese, Soviets, and other Communist-bloc nations kept their North Vietnamese allies amply supplied with weapons, ammunition, and equipment, mainly through the port of Haiphong. U.S. ships and aircraft were under strict orders not to fire on any "third country" shipping, even when it was observed off-loading cargo to the enemy, again out of concern over provoking the Soviets or the Chinese.

For a time in late 1967, it began to look as though the Communists were being beaten in the field. Then on 30 January 1968, during Tet, the Buddhist New Year, they struck at major cities all across South Vietnam. They created havoc in Saigon and held the provincial capital of Hue for twenty-five days.

This "Tet Offensive" was eventually beaten back. The North Vietnamese and Vietcong suffered many casualties and gained no Communist battlefield objectives. But the offensive stimulated a peace movement in the United States, supported by many college students and all kinds of leftists and liberals. The president found his administration under increasing pressure to get out of the Vietnam War due to the rising toll of casualties and material costs, as well as the growing protests at home. Finally, President Johnson announced a unilateral bombing halt of North Vietnam and invited Hanoi to peace talks in Paris. He announced at the same time that he would not seek reelection.

VIETNAMIZATION

As the peace talks dragged on through 1969, newly elected President Nixon began withdrawing Americans from Vietnam. He insisted that America still sought the original objective, to ensure that the South Vietnamese had the right to choose and maintain their own form of government. He believed the way to attain that was to help the Vietnamese take over all aspects of their government and military operations.

So, a massive training program called Vietnamization was undertaken to prepare the South Vietnamese to administer their affairs and operate in an effective manner. In the civilian area, training was given to local government officials, civil servants, teachers, dock managers, builders, farmers, industrialists, medical personnel, and police forces. An effort called Civic Action helped in nearly every conceivable way to make the South Vietnamese self-supporting. Good roads, bridges, airports, and harbor facilities were built by the Seabees and U.S. Army and civilian engineers, financed by American tax dollars. One of the best internal transportation systems in Asia was created for the struggling nation.

By the end of 1970 some 93 percent of South Vietnam's population had been brought under government control from a low of only 42 percent three years before. A succession of weak governments after Diem's assassination had been replaced by a stable and freely elected government headed by President Nguyen Van Thieu, which appeared to be in control of the nation's destiny.

On the military side, the years of training of the officer corps and noncommissioned officers by American advisers were beginning to yield results. Many elements of the South Vietnamese forces had been transformed into efficient fighting organizations. Navy, sea commando, and air force elements were considered the best, but there also were excellent army units. A fine system of military bases and facilities, fuel dumps, communications equipment, and a huge supply system had been developed and gradually turned over to the South Vietnamese. Almost all of the riverine and patrol craft were turned over to the South Vietnamese navy. American forces had been reduced by half by the middle of 1971, and less than 150,000 were still in Vietnam by the end of that year. The Seventh Fleet started to reduce the number of ships on station.

While Vietnamization appeared to be going well, fighting flared up again in early 1972, despite the Paris peace talks that had been going on fruitlessly for nearly three years. In response to the North Vietnamese attacks, President Nixon authorized renewed bombing of North Vietnam, including Hanoi. The Communists were thrown back with heavy losses, but the fighting continued. Finally, the president authorized the mining of Haiphong Harbor. Within a week, the enemy was desperate for supplies because Communist-bloc ships were unable to proceed into the harbor from the Gulf of Tonkin for off-loading. Two dozen ships were trapped in the harbor, unable to depart. The Communists stopped all significant military action and came back to the peace table. On 27 January 1973 all parties to the war signed an accord ending the fighting and providing for the peaceful withdrawal of the remaining American advisers by March 1973.

THE FALL OF SOUTH VIETNAM

The United States made promises to support the South Vietnamese government and military forces. However, many of these promises were dependent largely on President Nixon himself. But the president, though notably successful in foreign affairs, had become embroiled in the Watergate scandal. As the Washington political scene became more and more confused, congressional interest in virtually everything other than the domestic political situation waned. Any connection with Vietnam had come to be regarded as a political liability by congressmen after the revelations of the My Lai Massacre in 1969 and the Pentagon Papers controversy in 1971. This feeling, plus the terrible cost of American involvement in the war—some 150 billion dollars and over 56,000 deaths, as well as the widespread internal political turmoil—left little support in Congress for South Vietnam.

President Nixon finally chose to resign in August 1974, rather than face the possibility of an impeachment

A U.S. Navy lieutenant works with his South Vietnamese counterpart during the Vietnamization program.

trial over the Watergate affair with the further disruption of governmental functions that would cause. President Gerald Ford took over the reins of government, hoping to heal the wounds of the controversy. In this atmosphere, any proposal to maintain the necessary level of financial and military aid to South Vietnam met with very limited response from Congress and the American people.

America's preoccupation with domestic political affairs encouraged the Vietcong and North Vietnamese to violate all provisions of the cease-fire agreement. They began bringing in massive reinforcements through the northern provinces of South Vietnam. In March 1975, two years after American withdrawal, South Vietnam's ability to withstand Communist pressure collapsed. By the end of April, the whole country had capitulated to North Vietnam and the NLF. Two weeks earlier, the American-supported Cambodian government had fallen to the Khmer Rouge, a fanatical Communist insurgent group in that country. Laos was taken over by the Communist Pathet Lao in early December. Communism had triumphed in Indochina, after nearly thirty years of constant warfare.

VIETNAM WAR AFTERMATH

After the Vietnam War, massive cutbacks took place in the numbers of Navy ships and personnel. Total active fleet ships dropped from about 650 in 1972 to about 450 by 1978. During these same years, numbers of Navy personnel dropped from about 600,000 to some 525,000, and Marine Corps personnel from around 200,000 to 190,000. These downward trends continued until the early 1980s, when worldwide events such as the Falklands War, the Iran-Iraq conflict, and the rise of international terrorism caused the trend to be reversed at least for a while.

Even before the U.S. withdrawal from Vietnam, sweeping changes were being planned in personnel policy, administration, technology, and weapons in the Navy. The old Navy bureau organization was changed to five material systems commands in the interest of improving efficiency and keeping up with the rapid pace of technological advances. These commands—Air Systems, Sea Systems, Electronics Systems, Supply Systems, and Facilities Engineering—were placed under the chief of naval material. That chief, along with the chief of naval personnel and the chief of the Bureau of Medicine and Surgery, reported directly to the chief of naval operations.

In the early 1970s a program to update many personnel administrative practices was initiated by Admiral Zumwalt, who was, at the age of forty-nine, the youngest CNO in the history of the Navy. He made many changes, promulgated by means of a series of directives called "Z-Grams." Beards, more liberal hairstyles, civilian clothes on liberty, motorcycles on bases, and other departures from tradition excited many of the younger people and worried older hands. In some instances the rapid changes instituted by the new CNO caused confusion, necessitating more moderate courses of action to be adopted by later CNOs. Efforts were instituted to make the Navy more attractive to women and minorities, and these met with much success after some initial setbacks.

Admiral Elmo Zumwalt, chief of naval operations from July 1970 to July 1974. Perhaps more than any other post–World War II CNO, he modernized the Navy and brought it in line with modern organizational theory.

THE *MAYAGUEZ* INCIDENT

A month after the last Americans left South Vietnam, on 12 May 1975 a disabled American merchant ship, the SS *Mayaguez,* was seized in international waters off Cambodia by the Khmer Rouge, who had seized power in that country a few weeks earlier. The exact reason why they did this has never been determined. They then began towing the ship toward Kompong Som on the mainland. When President Gerald Ford was told of the developing incident, he was determined that this would not become another hostage situation similar to the *Pueblo* incident in 1968. He ordered the carrier *Coral Sea* and the destroyers USS *Henry B. Wilson* and USS *Holt* to steam at full speed to the Gulf of Thailand to rescue the ship and its crew. Meanwhile the ship was spotted anchored off Kho Tang Island, 40 miles from the Cambodian shore. The *Holt* was directed to proceed there to seize the ship, while a force of marines airlifted from Okinawa would rescue the crew, believed to be held on the island.

On the morning of 15 May the first of an eventual 250 marines were landed by helicopter on Kho Tang. They immediately began to encounter heavy resistance from Khmer Rouge troops there. While this fire fight was in progress, planes from the *Coral Sea* bombed targets on the mainland. This action apparently convinced the Khmer Rouge that they had underestimated U.S. resolve. Soon a fishing boat was seen approaching the destroyer *Wilson* flying a white flag. Aboard were the thirty-nine crewmen of the *Mayaguez.* At almost the same time, a boarding party from the *Holt* boarded the deserted *Mayaguez* and towed her to safety. That night the last of the Marine attack force was successfully airlifted off the island by Air Force helicopters. Altogether eighteen marines and airmen were killed or missing in action during the assault and withdrawal from Kho Tang. Another twenty-three were killed in a helicopter crash on their way to the operation. At a time when its resolve was in doubt following the debacle in Vietnam, the incident showed the world that the United States would pay whatever price was necessary to protect its citizens and preserve its national honor.

THE FALKLANDS WAR

In early 1982 a major maritime event took place in the South Atlantic off the coast of Argentina, when the Falkland Islands, long the subject of an ownership dispute between Britain and Argentina, were taken over by an Argentine occupation force on 2 April. In response, the British, whose colonists had occupied the islands since 1833, gathered an invasion force consisting of two ski-jump carriers, several amphibious ships, five submarines, and about thirty escort, auxiliaries, and support ships. They sailed in groups from England across the

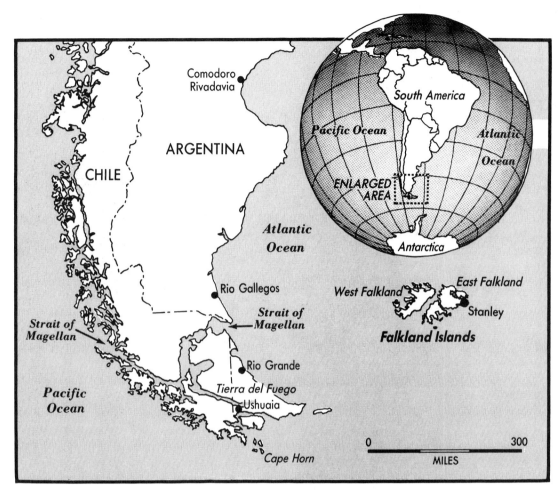

The area of operations during the Falklands War of 1982.

South Atlantic, arriving off the Falklands in late April. For the next two months the battle for control of the Falklands raged, involving nearly all elements of modern naval warfare. The Argentines finally capitulated on 4 June, but not before the British had lost several ships, including two frigates and a transport ship, to air-launched Exocet missiles fired from Argentine A4 attack planes. Several others were damaged. One of the Argentines' few capital ships, the cruiser *General Belgrano,* was torpedoed and sunk by a British nuclear attack submarine.

Though not directly involved, the U.S. Navy benefited greatly from the lessons learned by the British during the war, many of which caused dramatic changes to be implemented in our Navy. Even though they were not as capable as our large-deck carriers, the two British carriers, HMS *Hermes* and HMS *Invincible,* and their Harrier jump-jet air groups, played a major role in taking control of the air from the Argentines, without which victory would have been impossible. The action effectively quieted many skeptics in Congress who had begun to question the need for maintaining fifteen carriers and their as-

sociated support ships. It contributed to this force level being kept unchanged throughout the 1980s. Also, the 1950s and 1960s had seen a trend toward the use of aluminum vice steel plate in the construction of most U.S. and British warships as a means of compensating for the increased weight of habitability features and new electronic gear. One of the major problems on many of the British warships hit during the Falklands campaign, however, was uncontrollable burning of their aluminum structures. Most U.S. warships built since have incorporated steel plate wherever possible, and fire-retardant, shrapnel-resistant insulation is applied to any remaining aluminum plating used.

Finally, of course, the Falklands War demonstrated once again the value of naval power projection capability at a time when the new Reagan administration was pushing for funds to revitalize the U.S. armed forces (to reverse the post-Vietnam decline). Funding for defense, particularly the Navy, would not be a significant problem throughout the rest of the 1980s, due in no small measure to the British success in the Falklands War.

Many lessons were learned about the survivability of modern warships during the Falklands War. Here, HMS *Avenger* aids HMS *Plymouth* after the latter was hit by Argentine bombs.

GRENADA

In late October 1983 in response to a takeover of the Caribbean island nation of Grenada by Cuban-backed Communist forces, a joint U.S. task force with elements of all services conducted a major amphibious operation and took control of the island in three days. Forces from several nearby Caribbean allied island governments also took part in the operation. In the process, about 600 American citizens, mostly students attending medical school there, and 80 foreign nationals were evacuated to safety. Later, U.S. forces helped the Grenadians reestablish their representative government and rebuild damaged buildings and other facilities.

PANAMA

Relations between the United States and Panama steadily deteriorated throughout the 1980s. By 1988 the country had become a major staging area for drug smuggling to the United States, and its dictator, General Manuel Noriega, was indicted on drug-trafficking charges by a U.S. federal grand jury. In response, the Noriega government became increasingly belligerent toward U.S. interests there, causing the United States to impose economic sanctions in retaliation. In May 1989 a national election voted Noriega out of power, but he refused to accept the result and had the vote annulled.

In December 1989 following a series of incidents that culminated in the killing of a U.S. Marine lieutenant by Panamanian Defense Force (PDF) troops, the Noriega government declared that a state of war existed between the United States and Panama. Early in the morning hours of 20 December 1989, President Bush sent a combined invasion force of 12,000 U.S. Army, Navy, Air Force, and Marine Corps troops to remove Noriega and return the country to the control of the officials who had

Part of the huge cache of Soviet-made arms and ammunition recovered during the Grenada operation in October 1983. Note the Cuban Economic Office label on this crate of 7.62-mm ammunition.

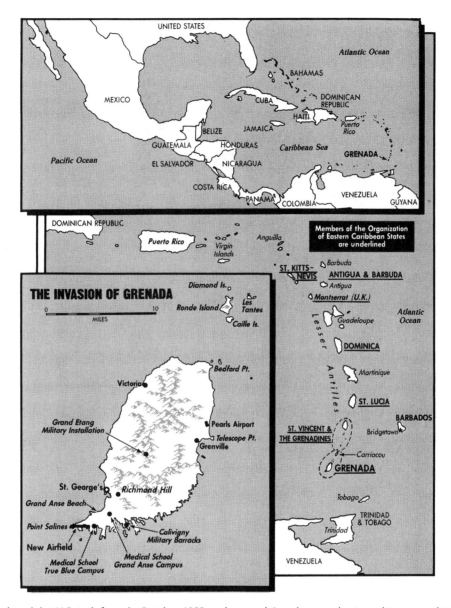

The invasion of Grenada by a joint U.S. task force in October 1983 underscored American resolve to resist communist takeovers of democratic governments in the Western Hemisphere during the 1980s.

been lawfully elected in May. These forces joined another 12,000 U.S. military personnel, mostly Army, already stationed in the Panama Canal Zone.

The intervention, called Operation Just Cause, was the largest U.S. military operation in the 1980s. Some fierce fighting occurred at times, but rapid envelopment by coordinated airborne and armored U.S. forces quickly overcame most PDF strongholds. By the end of the day, most military objectives had been achieved, and only scattered pockets of resistance remained. Noriega himself managed to elude capture and sought refuge at the Vatican's diplomatic mission in Panama City. He eventually surrendered to U.S. authorities in January 1990. He was later transported to the United States, where he is presently serving a prison sentence after being convicted on drug-trafficking charges.

The successful intervention restored democracy to Panama, and, despite many protestations by neighboring Central American countries at the time, U.S. interests in the region have been more secure since.

TERRORISM

One of the more unfortunate trends that marked the 1980s was the rise of terrorism worldwide, especially in connection with events in the Middle East. Principal among these events was the Iran-Iraq War, which lasted most of the decade. Of only slightly less importance was

U.S. Marines patrolling a street in Panama during Operation Just Cause in 1989.

the issue of a homeland for the Palestinian Arabs, which caused almost continuous strife between Israel and neighboring Arab states. Many of the more extreme Arab groups involved in both struggles, unable to challenge Israel and the Western nations with military interests in that area, turned to international terrorism to advance their causes. Since many of the terrorist acts involved U.S. allies or U.S. citizens or both, our armed services, especially the Navy and Marine Corps, were asked to respond to several of the crises—but not always with beneficial results. One of the most tragic events occurred after a Marine force was asked to join the UN peace-keeping effort in Lebanon in 1983. On 23 October a sui-

There was not much left of the U.S. Marine headquarters in Beirut following the terrorist bombing in 1983.

cide bomber driving a truck full of explosives attacked the headquarters building at Beirut Airport housing some of the peacekeeping force. This resulted in the deaths of 241 marines and naval personnel in the building at the time.

Other terrorist actions during the 1980s included the taking of civilian and military hostages of U.S. and several other Western nationalities, car bombings, assaults against civil facilities such as airports and train stations, and airliner bombings and hijackings. In the early part of the decade, a number of these actions were shown to have been directly sponsored by Libyan leader Colonel Muammar Qaddafi, who had established several terrorist training bases within Libya. In the mid-1980s Qaddafi began to make threats concerning freedom of navigation in the Gulf of Sidra in the Mediterranean off Libya's northern shore. There were several incidents involving U.S. naval air and surface forces, during which Libyan fighters were shot down and Libyan patrol boats were sunk.

Finally, on 15 April 1986, in retaliation for the continuing threats and several Libyan-sponsored terrorist acts against U.S. citizens in Europe, and with the agreement of most of our European allies, a combined attack was carried out against Libyan terrorist support bases. Air Force F-111s based in England struck army barracks and an airport near Tripoli and the port of Sidi Bilal. Carrier-based A-7s and F/A-14s attacked other barracks at Ben-

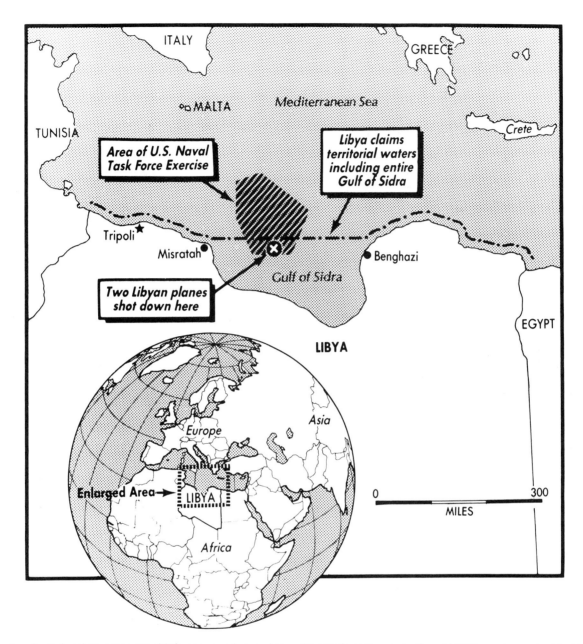

Libya, under its ruler Colonel Muammar Qaddafi, sponsored several terrorist attacks in Europe in the mid-1980s, and provoked incidents with the U.S. Sixth Fleet, ultimately resulting in a retaliatory attack on Libyan terrorist bases in April 1986.

ghazi and an airfield at Benina. Qaddafi himself narrowly missed being killed during the course of these raids, in which only two U.S. Air Force F-111 crewmen were lost. The attack had a dramatic effect on reducing Libyan-sponsored terrorism throughout the world.

Unfortunately, it has often proven difficult to take much effective action against acts of terror, especially in the Middle East. Perpetrators from these countries are often elusive, and they operate from ever-changing bases of operation, so it is hard to target effective reprisals directly against them. Many times in the 1980s and since Americans and other Western hostages have been used

as pawns in the power struggles of many of these terrorists. Death threats, threats of future hostage taking, and threats to reduce or cut off oil exports to offending nations have been routinely made to counter any suggestion of reprisal attacks against the terrorists' sponsor countries.

This situation prompted what came to be known in the United States as the *Iran-Contra* affair in the mid-1980s. In this incident a series of illegal arrangements was secretly made by several naval and other government officials that had the effect of supplying arms to Iran in exchange for help in obtaining the release of

A Soviet-built Libyan guided missile corvette burns in the Gulf of Sidra after a clash with U.S. Navy aircraft in March 1986.

several American hostages. Some of the profits from the deal were then used to provide arms for the U.S.-favored Contra revolutionaries in Nicaragua. A key figure in this affair was Marine Colonel Oliver North, who was later found guilty of, essentially, overstepping the bounds of his authority in the matter.

THE PERSIAN GULF

In September 1980 a war began between Iran and Iraq that would progress through several phases until August 1988, when a truce was negotiated that would end most of the open warfare. Though the proximate cause of the war was a longstanding border dispute, there had also been many years of previous political and ethnic tension between the two countries. The first years of the war turned into a war of attrition, during which neither side was able to achieve significant inroads into the territory of the other, despite many casualties on both sides. During much of the conflict from the mid-1980s onward, the war erupted into much of the Persian Gulf, with each side trying to disrupt the oil tanker trade of the other and thereby gain economic advantage. Soon tankers of all na-

tions transiting the gulf, especially the Strait of Hormuz, were subject to air and mine attacks by both nations. Because of our political posture in the area—the United States has generally assumed the role of peacemaker—and perhaps also because we are somewhat less dependent on Middle Eastern oil than most other Western nations and therefore less vulnerable, the United States played a major role in keeping the Persian Gulf open for transit by oil tankers of all nations during the latter stages of the Iran-Iraq War. Throughout 1987 and 1988 U.S. frigates and cruisers served as convoy escorts, accompanying and protecting tankers transiting the gulf.

These operations were not conducted without cost. In May 1987 the frigate USS *Stark* (FFG-31) was attacked and hit by two Exocet missiles launched from an Iraqi aircraft while the ship was on radar picket duty in the gulf. In April 1988 the USS *Samuel B. Roberts* (FFG-58) was almost cut in two by a mine but was saved by the damage-control efforts of her crew. Then, in July 1988, an unfortunate incident demonstrated the limitations of even the most modern equipment in this type of situation. The Aegis cruiser USS *Vincennes* (CG-49), in the middle of a battle against Iranian gunboats in the Strait of Hormuz, mistakenly shot down a civilian Iranian airliner that approached the ship in a seemingly threatening manner over the strait. All 290 people aboard the plane died.

Many mine warfare ships, mainly in our Naval Reserve fleet, engaged in mine-clearing operations following the end of hostilities in the gulf. These operations continued until early 1990, at which time all the mines released by both sides during the war were considered to have been neutralized.

THE DEMISE OF THE SOVIET UNION

The Soviet economy, never very strong since World War II, had been suffering more and more from both low productivity and lack of modern technology in the 1980s.

The USS *Fox* provides escort to the tanker *Gas Prince* during the Iran-Iraq War in the Persian Gulf, July 1987.

Much of this state of affairs resulted from restrictive Communistic policies concerning private property and the accumulation of personal wealth and an emphasis on military spending. These, in conjunction with years of cold war military posturing and provocative foreign policy had severely limited any infusion of money and technology from the West.

Both as a means of internal economic reform and to try to win favor with Western nations, soon after he came to power in 1985, the Soviet Premier Mikhail Gorbachev initiated a series of liberal reforms and policies collectively called *glasnost* (new openness in foreign relations) and *perestroika* (internal political and economic reforms). In 1987 an important bilateral arms-reduction agreement called the INF (Intermediate-range Nuclear Forces) Treaty was negotiated between the United States and USSR that reduced many tensions. It eliminated intermediate-range nuclear missiles (those with ranges between 300 and 3,400 miles) in Europe. Relations with Western nations were also improved by many state visits, summit meetings, and further arms control negotiations conducted throughout the late 1980s, and by a loosening of controls over the satellite states of Eastern Europe that had been dominated by the Soviet Union since World War II.

In 1991 the first of several important strategic arms reduction agreements between the United States and the Russians was signed. Called the Treaty on the Reduction and Limitation of Strategic Offensive Arms, or START I Treaty, it cut total numbers of strategic nuclear warheads in both countries by 25 to 35 percent. Later that year President Bush announced a unilateral withdrawal of all U.S. land-based tactical nuclear weapons from overseas bases and all sea-based tactical nuclear weapons from U.S. ships, submarines, and aircraft.

All of Gorbachev's domestic reforms, however, proved to be insufficient to hold back a rising tide of

democracy that, once set in motion, rapidly engulfed the Soviet Union. The populations of the satellite states took advantage of the erosion of Soviet control to press forward successful self-determination movements. These eventually resulted in complete independence of all the former satellite states by 1990. Perhaps the most important and surely the most emotional symbol of the new European order occurred in November 1989 with the demolition of the Berlin Wall. It had divided East and West Berlin in Germany for thirty years and symbolized the repression of the satellite nations behind the so-called iron curtain. Germany itself was formally reunited a year later. The Warsaw Pact alliance between the USSR and the former satellite nations was disbanded in February 1991.

But most amazing to most Western analysts was the rapid rise of the democratic movement within the Soviet Union itself. Simultaneously with the loss of the satellite states, people in most of the republics making up the Soviet Union staged their own demonstrations for self-rule. Quickly rising to the foremost position was the Russian republic, led by Boris Yeltsin, who only a few years earlier (1988) had been thrown out of the Soviet Politburo

One of the most emotional symbols of the end of the cold war era was the demolition in November 1989 of the Berlin Wall, which had divided the city since 1961.

Soviet premier Mikhail Gorbachev and his wife Raisa during a state visit to the United States in May 1990.

Following the demise of the Soviet Union, Boris Yeltsin of the Russian Federation emerged as the most powerful of all the leaders of the former Soviet states.

for urging Gorbachev to proceed more quickly with the liberalization program.

Things came to a head in August 1991, when the remaining old-line Communists in the Politburo attempted to stage a coup. They arrested Gorbachev and detained him and his family for three days at his vacation home on the Crimean Peninsula on the Black Sea. The Soviet Army, however, declined to support the coup and refused to attack the Russian parliament building in Moscow, from which Yeltsin was leading the opposition to the coup. The overwhelming support for both Yeltsin and Gorbachev from the people of Moscow, and indeed the whole Soviet Union, proved decisive. Within days the situation was fully resolved. Gorbachev was returned to Moscow, and the coup leaders were themselves arrested.

Yeltsin had now become the most powerful leader in the disintegrating Soviet Union. In early December he made the dissolution official by proclaiming the existence of a new Commonwealth of Independent States made up of the former Soviet republics. On Christmas Day 1991, Gorbachev resigned and the Soviet Union was formally dissolved. The red, white, and blue pre-revolutionary Russian flag was raised over the Kremlin.

The cold war was over. The Western democracies, led by the United States, had successfully prevailed against almost fifty years of challenge from Soviet communism.

Chronology

1945	World War II ends
1946	Churchill "Iron Curtain" speech
1947	Unification of U.S. forces
1947	Truman Doctrine and Marshall Plan
1949	NATO created
1950–53	Korean War
1955	Warsaw Pact created; *Nautilus* launched
1958	China attacks Quemoy
1962	Cuban missile quarantine
1964–73	Vietnam War
1968	*Pueblo* incident
1975	*Mayaguez* incident
1980–88	Iran-Iraq War
1982	Falklands War
1983	Granada invasion
1986	Attack on Libyan terrorists
1989	Panama invasion
1991	Cold War ends; USSR disbanded

Study Guide Questions

1. What happened to the U.S. armed forces after World War II ended?
2. What were the only two possible American response options to Soviet takeovers of Eastern European nations following World War II?
3. What term was originated in 1946 by Winston Churchill to describe the conflict of interests between the West and the Soviet Union?
4. What was the objective of postwar "unification" of the U.S. armed services?
5. What was the final result of congressional deliberations on armed forces unification?
6. What events caused the beginning of the U.S. Sixth Fleet deployments to the Mediterranean?
7. What was President Truman's plan for reconstruction of war-torn Europe?
8. A. What two Soviet actions in the late 1940s caused the Western democracies to create a formal alliance to counter the spread of Soviet communism?
   B. What was this alliance called?
   C. What Soviet-sponsored military alliance was formed in response?
9. What happened in China in 1949?
10. A. Where did the Potsdam Conference draw the boundary line between North and South Korea?
    B. Which major nations aligned themselves with North and South Korea?
11. What were the objectives of the North Korean invasion of South Korea?
12. Who was the supreme commander of UN forces in Korea?
13. What made the landing at Inchon so risky?
14. What happened on 25 November 1950 that changed the whole complexion of the Korean War?
15. Why was General MacArthur relieved by President Truman?
16. Where were the Korean truce talks held?
17. What was the historical significance of the *Pueblo* crisis in 1968?

18. What new kinds of submarines became part of the U.S. fleet in the 1950s?
19. A. What was the American response to the discovery of Soviet intermediate-range missiles in Cuba in 1962?
    B. What was the result?
20. What did the USSR do as a result of the Cuban confrontation?
21. Where was the dividing line between North and South Vietnam after 1954?
22. What triggered civil war in South Vietnam in 1956?
23. What controversial event brought the United States into the war on a major scale?
24. What official and common names were given to the Communist South Vietnamese insurgents?
25. What was the "Brown Water Navy" and where did it operate?
26. What restrictions were placed on the conduct of the war by U.S. civilian leadership?
27. What result did the Tet Offensive of 1968 have in the United States?
28. What was the final outcome of the Vietnam War?
29. What did the resolution of the *Mayaguez* incident show the world in 1975?
30. What effects did the Falklands War of 1982 have on the U.S. Navy?
31. What happened on the island of Grenada in 1983?
32. Why did the United States take military action in Panama in 1989?
33. Why did the United States conduct an attack against Colonel Qaddafi's Libya in 1986?
34. What was the role of the U.S. Navy during the Persian Gulf warfare in the 1980s?
35. What profound change took place in the early 1990s that brought an end to the cold war?

Vocabulary

superpower
demobilization
cold war
iron curtain
the draft
Warsaw Pact
geographic dagger
armistice
repatriation
demilitarized zone (DMZ)
Brown Water Navy
third-country shipping
ski-jump carrier

Joint Chiefs of Staff
"mothballs"
Marshall Plan
coup d'état
NATO
Communist bloc
hot pursuit
range of tide
quarantine (blockade)
Yankee Station
helicopter gunship
Vietnamization

11

The 1990s and Beyond

The end of the cold war in 1991 brought with it a greatly diminished threat of nuclear warfare between superpowers. Still, there were many serious issues that would concern the U.S. Navy and the other U.S. armed services for the remainder of the decade and into the new millennium. On the international scene, these issues included the problem of the nuclear stockpile of the former USSR; continuing conflict in the Middle East, southern Europe, and elsewhere; proliferation of nuclear weapons among third world nations; the international illegal drug trade; and world terrorism, much of it directed against U.S. forces and interests. On the domestic scene there was concern over internal strife caused by the post–cold war downsizing of the services and the increasing role of women in the military; drug trafficking within the United States; and domestic terrorism, especially following the terrorist attacks on the Pentagon and New York's World Trade Center in September 2001.

THE FORMER SOVIET UNION

Immediately upon taking over the leadership of the former Soviet states that comprised the new commonwealth, President Boris Yeltsin found himself faced with several very serious problems. Most important were the issues of revitalizing the economies of Russia and the other former Soviet states, what to do with the armed forces, and how to control of the formidable Soviet nuclear arsenal.

In pursuit of economic support for his new commonwealth, Yeltsin immediately established friendly working relations with Western heads of state. After assurances that he now controlled the nuclear weapons, the United States and other Western nations started sending much aid in various forms.

In January 1993 President Bush and Yeltsin signed the second Strategic Offensive Arms Reduction and Limitation Treaty (START II), considered the broadest disarmament pact in history. Its terms called for both sides to reduce long-range nuclear arsenals to between 3,000 to 3,500 warheads within a decade and for the complete elimination of land-based multiple-warhead missiles. Many nuclear missiles on both sides have since been dismantled and destroyed, and the process was still ongoing into the new millennium. In late 1996 Yeltsin announced that from that time on, no Russian-controlled nuclear missiles would remain aimed toward any of the Western states. In early 1997 President Clinton announced that several of the former Soviet satellite states would soon be permitted to join the North Atlantic Treaty Organization (NATO). The Czech Republic, Hungary, and Poland did so in 1999. Only a few years earlier such an idea would have seemed incredible to most in the West.

THE MIDDLE EAST

The peace in the Persian Gulf area following the end of the Iran-Iraq War in 1988 unfortunately proved to be short-lived. With his forces no longer engaged in the war with Iran, Iraq's leader Saddam Hussein was free to attempt other more aggressive military adventures to the south.

OPERATIONS DESERT SHIELD AND DESERT STORM

In August 1990, suddenly and without warning, Iraqi forces under the command of Iraq's leader Saddam Hussein staged a brutal invasion of neighboring Kuwait. That country was captured quickly, along with thousands of Western civilian oil-field workers and their families, who were then detained and used as hostages against Western reprisal. Saudi Arabia, fearful of becoming the next victim of Hussein's aggression, quickly appealed to the United Nations and especially to its ally, the United States, for help. In an unprecedented show of unanimity against such aggression, the UN passed a trade embargo against Iraq, restricting movement and sale of all goods, including oil and food products, into and out of Iraq. Simultaneously, the United States embarked upon Operation Desert Shield, deploying the largest U.S. military and naval force assembled since the Vietnam War to Saudi Arabia.

By the end of 1990, about 450,000 U.S. military personnel and 100 U.S. Navy ships were engaged in operations in support of Desert Shield. Forces from many other nations also joined U.S. forces there to form the so-called UN coalition. U.S. and allied ships patrolled in the Persian Gulf, Arabian Sea, and Red Sea, enforcing the UN trade embargo against Iraq. Among the forces deployed in the Saudi desert were thousands of U.S. marines. Navy hospital ships largely staffed with Naval Reserve medical personnel deployed off the Saudi coasts ready to handle any casualties. And maritime sealift transported the bulk of the heavy equipment and supplies needed to sustain the operation.

The UN Security Council imposed a deadline of 15 January 1991, by which time Hussein had to move all of his forces out of Kuwait or face military action. Hussein did not leave Kuwait. On 16 January a massive air assault on every target of military significance in Iraq and

Kuwait turned Operation Desert Shield into Desert Storm. Tens of thousands of air sorties (attack missions) were launched by U.S. Navy, Army, and Air Force planes and helicopters and those of other coalition forces. The coalition soon achieved air superiority and quickly shot down any offensive-minded Iraqi aircraft that managed to get airborne.

On 23 February the allied ground offensive into Kuwait and southern Iraq began, under the overall command of General H. "Stormin' Norman" Schwarzkopf, U.S. Army. The United States and coalition forces made short work of the now demoralized Iraqi troops, most of whom had been heavily bombed and cut off from all resupply of food and munitions by the air campaign. By 26 February Kuwait City was secured, and on the evening of 27 February President Bush announced a cease-fire, which became permanent on 8 April. Victory for the coalition forces was complete, thus ending the largest air and ground offensive fought since World War II. The Iraqis lost tens of thousands of troops killed as the result of air and ground attacks, and many thousands more became prisoners of war. U.S. losses were amazingly low

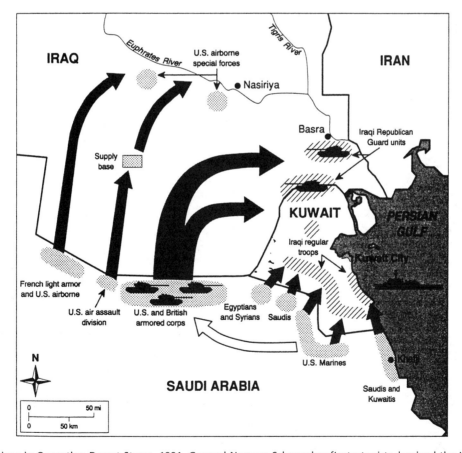

The theater of operations in Operation Desert Storm, 1991. General Norman Schwarzkopf's strategists deceived the Iraqis into believing the main thrusts into Kuwait would come north from Saudi Arabia and via an amphibious assault near Kuwait City. Actually, most of the coalition forces engaged in a swift flanking movement to the west into southern Iraq, cutting off the Iraqi forces in Kuwait from any hope of escape or resupply. *Facts on File*

by any measure: 89 combat deaths, 38 missing in action, and 212 wounded. Ultimately more than 527,000 U.S. military personnel were in the theater of operations, including 82,000 U.S. Navy men and women and 94,000 marines.

AFTERMATH OF DESERT STORM

Following the end of hostilities in Operation Desert Storm in Iraq in February 1991, Iraqi leader Saddam Hussein devoted much effort to reestablishing control over his country. Part of this effort involved the suppression of ethnic Shiite Moslems in southern Iraq.

In August 1992 U.S., British, and French warplanes began enforcing a UN-imposed *no-fly zone* (an area over which hostile aircraft are prohibited from flying) over the southern part of Iraq, designed to protect the Shiites from further attacks by Hussein. This no-fly zone continued to be enforced into the new millennium, along with economic sanctions and trade embargoes. The purpose of both was to try to force Hussein to treat the Iraqi people better and to force him to comply with terms of the 1991 cease-fire agreement regarding UN inspections of suspected munitions plants and CBR (chemical, biological, radiological) weapons sites. Access for these inspections had been a persistent problem.

In August 1996 there was much concern over a threatening movement of some 45,000 troops and 300 tanks toward UN-protected Kurdish-held territory in northern Iraq. In response President Clinton ordered a joint U.S. Navy–Air Force strike against Iraqi air defense systems and bases in the southern part of the country. On 3 and 4 September some forty-four land-attack Tomahawk cruise missiles (TLAMs) were launched from four surface ships and an SSN in the Persian Gulf, and two B-52 bombers from Guam. The bombers also launched thirteen air-launched cruise missiles (ALCMs). All Iraqi air defense targets were hit, but no target was completely destroyed. Nevertheless, Hussein appeared to have "gotten the message," and the troops and tanks were withdrawn shortly thereafter. Hussein, however, continued to order occasional threatening troop movements, and provocative behavior within the no-fly zones, throughout the rest of the 1990s and beyond. In response to several of the latter incidents, coalition forces conducted several small-scale air attacks on various Iraqi airdefense sites, using planes from Navy carriers operating in the area.

CONFLICT IN THE BALKANS

Unfortunately, after the demise of the Soviet Union, conflict broke out in several of the countries formerly under its control. In 1991 a civil war began in the Baltic country of Yugoslavia, which was once a client state of the Soviet Union. Yugoslavia's six republics—Slovenia, Croatia, Bosnia-Herzegovina, Serbia, Montenegro, and Macedonia—began to break apart for two reasons: (1) economic

A Tomahawk cruise missile is launched by the cruiser USS *Shiloh* (CG 67) operating in the Persian Gulf as part of Operation Desert Strike against Iraqi air-defense installations in September 1996.

Yugoslavia and its six republics as of 1991.

ued. Economic sanctions against Serbia and Montenegro were imposed the following May, also with little effect. By the end of 1992 the situation had deteriorated to the point that Yugoslavia ceased to exist for a time as a separate nation.

In October 1992 the UN established a no-fly zone prohibiting flights of military aircraft over Bosnian air space, which was extended to cover all types of aircraft in early 1993. The UN also proclaimed so-called safe areas around several cities, including the nearly leveled city of Sarajevo in southeastern Bosnia, control of which had been a strategic objective of both sides in the conflict. Air Force planes and Navy ships and carrier- and land-based aircraft helped NATO forces enforce the embargo, no-fly zones, and safe areas, but President Clinton was reluctant to introduce ground troops into the conflict. Instead, he preferred diplomatic pressure. Beginning in 1992, at least one Navy carrier battle group and a Marine amphibious ready group were continually stationed in the Adriatic Sea, both to support Navy operations and as a show of force.

Fighting continued for two more years until late 1995, when the United States joined other NATO forces under the auspices of the United Nations to try to bring a halt to the conflict by a heavier application of force. In August and September 1995 in Operation Deliberate Force, Navy and Marine Corps planes from the carrier *Theodore Roosevelt* joined with NATO aircraft from an air-base at Aviano, Italy, to conduct air strikes against Serb military positions south and east of Sarajevo. These strikes were in retaliation for the Serbs overrunning the UN-protected cities of Srebrenica and Zepa and mortar attacks on Sarajevo that killed and wounded more than eighty civilians. Altogether 3,500 sorties were flown

difficulties caused by the end of Soviet aid, and (2) long-standing friction between ethnic groups in its population. In June 1991, after Croatia and Slovenia declared their independence from the former Yugoslavia, fighting broke out between ethnic Serbs in Croatia who claimed part of that republic for Serbia, and the Croat militia. Soon the conflict broadened into Bosnia-Herzegovina, between Serbs who claimed part of that republic as well, and Muslims and Croats, who claimed the rest.

After months of bloody fighting that included atrocities on both sides, in late 1991 the UN imposed an oil, trade, and weapons embargo against Yugoslavia (which was supplying troops and arms to the Serbs) and Serbia in an attempt to end the fighting. The embargo had little effect, however, and the fighting and atrocities contin-

A British inspection team drops to the deck of a merchant ship to inspect its cargo during NATO arms embargo enforcement operations in the Adriatic Sea in August 1993.

against 350 separate targets. Finally, in December 1995, the presidents of Bosnia-Herzegovina, Serbia, and Croatia signed a treaty to end the war. It was negotiated in Dayton, Ohio, with much involvement of the U.S. State Department. The pact divided Bosnia into two largely autonomous parts. NATO agreed to deploy some 60,000 troops, including 20,000 U.S. Army troops, in Bosnia for at least a year to maintain the peace. Many of these troops, including the Americans, were still there as the year 2001 ended.

OTHER PROBLEM AREAS

Problems broke out in other areas of the world as well. In January 1991 a civil war erupted in the former Soviet-aligned African state of Somalia after the cessation of aid from the former Soviet Union, when several clan-led rebel armies forced longtime president Mohammed Siad Barre to flee the country. In his absence several of these groups began battling among themselves for territory, soon resulting in widespread anarchy and famine. The situation was particularly acute because nearly every adult male in the country possessed at least one firearm due to the supply of weapons remaining there from the old Soviet Union.

In December 1992 28,000 U.S. troops, including 1,800 marines, took part in the UN-sponsored Operation Restore Hope, which was intended to bring in food supplies and restore some order to the country. Assisted by units of the French Foreign Legion, the marines patrolled the streets of Mogadishu, the country's capital. They deployed from four ships that had sailed there from the U.S. Navy base at Diego Garcia in the Indian Ocean, and were joined by a covering carrier battle group from the Persian Gulf.

Although clan warlords signed a peace accord in March 1993, much sporadic violence continued, and finally in October, following a gun battle between U.S. soldiers and clan members that left eighteen dead and approximately seventy-five wounded, President Clinton set March 1994 as the date by which all remaining U.S. forces would leave the country. About 2,000 marines were kept offshore for several months thereafter as potential cover for the remaining UN troops.

In mid-1996 Navy–Marine Corps amphibious ready groups were called upon on two occasions to assist in evacuation of U.S. nationals and other noncombatants from the African nations of Liberia and the central African Republic of Bangui, both of whom were experiencing outbreaks of ethnic violence, famine, and disease. The marines also reinforced the U.S. embassy in Monrovia, Liberia, during that crisis.

In the spring of 1998 much apprehension arose over the issue of nuclear weapons proliferation when India and Pakistan each exploded nuclear test devices in response to the other doing so. Escalating conflict between the two nations that might have led to a regional nuclear war was halted only by the diplomatic efforts of the Clinton Administration acting in conjunction with the United Nations. Fortunately both nations were deterred from continuing on a course that could have led to nuclear destruction of both sides. The issue of nuclear nonproliferation continues to be a major international concern.

In April 2001 a U.S. Navy reconnaissance aircraft flying a mission over international waters in the South China Sea suffered a midair collision with a Chinese fighter jet that came too close. Following the collision the Chinese plane crashed into the sea, killing its pilot. The American plane made an emergency landing on China's Hainan Island south of the mainland. Its crew of twenty-four men and women was held for the next eleven days until they were released into U.S. custody. They received a hero's welcome when they returned to the United States a few days later. The plane was later dismantled and returned in pieces to the United States in early July.

DRUG TRAFFICKING

Throughout the 1990s and beyond all services within the U.S. Defense Department and the Coast Guard have been called upon to support both international and domestic efforts to suppress the illegal drug trade. In the 1990s drug producers in South America increasingly transported their drugs to the United States by way of Central America. Traffickers used boats, low-flying aircraft, and tractor-trailers hauling legal cargo to smuggle drugs bound for American markets. In response, all services have lent support with their various intelligence agencies worldwide. They also have conducted joint drug-interdiction training exercises with host nation forces, particularly in Central and South America. Ground radar and airborne surveillance assets of the Navy and other services have also been used to track and intercept boats and aircraft suspected of drug smuggling. On the domestic scene all services conduct extensive drug awareness and testing programs designed to discourage the use of all illegal drugs and other substances by service personnel.

INTERNATIONAL TERRORISM

In early August 1998 U.S. embassies in Kenya and Tanzania were virtually destroyed by terrorist car bombs. These attacks were determined by U.S. intelligence services to have been masterminded by a wealthy exiled Saudi Arabian terrorist named Osama bin Laden, who had proclaimed a holy war against the United States for its part in the action against Iraq in the early 1990s. In retaliation for these bombings, on 20 August 1998 President Clinton ordered cruise missile attacks to be carried out against two targets: terrorist training camps run by bin Laden in Afghanistan and a factory in Sudan believed to be involved in manufacturing chemical weapons for him. Over seventy Tomahawk missiles were fired during the attacks by U.S. Navy ships in the Persian Gulf and in the Red Sea. Though he was thought to have been present at the Afghanistan site at the time of the attack, bin Laden escaped injury and continued to be a major terrorist threat against the United States and its interests.

In August 2000 the guided missile destroyer USS *Cole* (DDG-67) while in port in Aden, Yemen, for a routine fuel stop, had a large hole blown in her port side by a bomb-laden boat crewed by two suicide bombers. Seventeen U.S. Sailors were killed and thirty-nine others were injured in the blast. The terrorists conducting the attack were subsequently linked to bin Laden. The damaged ship was transported back to the Ingalls Shipyard in Pascagoula, Mississippi, aboard a civilian transport ship. There the ship was repaired and relaunched in September 2001, ironically in the same week as the terrorist attacks on the World Trade Center and the Pentagon.

DOMESTIC EVENTS

The 1990s proved to be somewhat turbulent times at home as well, both for the Navy and other armed services. In response to the end of the cold war threat, a downsizing and consolidation of forces among all U.S. armed services began, which was still in progress into the new millennium. Added to the natural pressures caused by this were several unfortunate incidents of both actual and alleged sexual misconduct that were brought to national attention by the news media. Chief among these were allegations of harassment of female junior officers and civilians by over 100 male naval aviators attending an annual convention sponsored by the Tailhook Association at the Las Vegas Hilton in September 1991 and incidents of fraternization with and harassment of female trainees by male drill instructors that surfaced at an Army training base at Aberdeen, Maryland, in late 1996. The tension caused by these and other scandals involving sexual harassment was felt throughout the military services. The issue of how best to fully integrate women into the U.S. armed services has yet to be completely resolved, though much progress has been made in recent years.

In April 1995 the threat of domestic terrorism was again highlighted when a powerful bomb exploded in front of the Federal Building at Oklahoma City, Oklahoma, killing and maiming scores of innocent people. In July a year later, a bomb detonated at the 1996 Olympic Games in Atlanta, Georgia, killing one person and injuring several others. In the same month came the explosion of TWA Flight 800 off the coast of Long Island, New York,

A Navy dive team prepares for a descent during the grim search and recovery operations at the site of the TWA flight 800 crash off Long Island, New York, in July 1996.

which killed all 230 passengers and crew. Navy divers participated in a salvage operation that lasted until late fall 1996 and eventually resulted in the recovery of most of the bodies of those killed and most of the wreckage of the plane. The wreckage was assembled and analyzed to try to determine the cause of the explosion. At first it was thought that terrorism may have played some part in the incident, but it was later determined that the most likely cause of the explosion was an electrical discharge into a vapor-filled fuel tank.

As the nation entered the new millennium, ominous signs began to appear that the threat posed by terrorism would continue to assert itself, as evidenced by the bombing of the USS *Cole* in August 2000. Then, on the morning of 11 September 2001 the unthinkable happened. Both of the two World Trade Center towers in New York City were hit and set afire by hijacked airliners. A short time later a third hijacked plane hit the Pentagon in Washington, D.C. A fourth plane, presumably headed toward targets in Washington, D.C., crashed into the countryside in western Pennsylvania, most likely as the result of a scuffle between its hijackers and the passengers and crew.

Both Trade Center towers collapsed later that morning, causing a loss of life of nearly 3,000 people. As a result of the attack on the Pentagon, 189 people were killed. President George W. Bush immediately called the terrorist attacks an act of war. He vowed to retaliate against the terrorist organizations responsible for them (Osama bin Laden and his al-Qaida terrorist organization were prime suspects). The Navy immediately deployed ships of the Atlantic and Pacific Fleets off the East and West Coasts to help guard against further terrorist attacks. Air National Guard planes flew combat air patrols over New York, Washington, D.C., and other large cities throughout the country. Within a few weeks, some 50,000 reservists of all services were given mobilization orders to augment Air National Guard units, help guard U.S. airports, and provide other support. This homeland defense effort was designated Operation Noble Eagle.

In the days following the 11 September attack, plans were made to retaliate against bin Laden's al-Qaida organization and any countries that supported him, beginning with the Taliban government in Afghanistan. When the Taliban would not give up bin Laden, the United States deployed military assets to the region in preparation for a large military confrontation there. These deployments included the aircraft carriers *Theodore Roosevelt, Carl Vinson,* and other carriers and support ships in the Arabian Sea, over 100 Air Force fighter-bombers, and a large contingent of U.S. special operations forces. Many other nations pledged to support the American effort.

On 8 October 2001 Operation Enduring Freedom began with air strikes by Navy and Air Force planes on strategic targets throughout Afghanistan. These were accompanied by humanitarian airdrops of food to relieve the suffering of the Afghan population. Much of the ground fighting was left to the Northern Alliance, a loose coalition of rebel Afghans in northeastern provinces who had long been fighting Taliban control of the country.

By late November the Northern Alliance, supported by relentless air attacks by U.S. Navy and Air Force planes, and by about 300 American special forces personnel on the ground, had gained control of most of the country from the Taliban. Several key al-Qaida officials had been killed, but bin Laden himself remained at large.

Meanwhile, at home there were several instances of contamination of news organization offices in Florida and New York by letters containing anthrax disease spores. These were followed by additional anthrax letters sent to offices of the State Department and to key members of the Senate. The letters also contaminated several postal facilities while en route, eventually resulting in the deaths of several postal workers and others who came into contact with the spores. It has yet to be determined who sent these letters and whether or not they are directly connected to international terrorist organizations.

It remains to be seen as of this writing what the long-term outcome of these events will be.

A LOOK BACK—AND AHEAD

The last decades of the twentieth century were very challenging ones for our Navy. In the Vietnam years of the sixties and seventies, the Navy had nearly 1,000 ships and 600,000 people in uniform; by the year 2000, the number had dwindled to a figure of just over 300 ships and 370,000 people. Joint operations with the other services are now the rule rather than the exception. Technology continues to drive toward new concepts in weapons and equipment at an ever-increasing pace. And several events in the 1990s showed that there remains a lot still to be done to better integrate women into all the armed services, including the Navy.

The Vietnam experience forced us to accept the facts that even the most powerful Navy on Earth has its limitations and that we cannot expect to prevail in every confrontation. Events such as the Iran-Contra affair, the *Vincennes* incident, and the Tailhook scandal have reminded us that even the best-intentioned people can make mistakes. Increasing budgetary constraints following the demise of the Soviet Union and the end of the cold war have forced us to realize that we cannot always acquire every new weapon or program we may want and all the new ships we may need. The international drug trade, and terrorists at home and abroad, have shown that our modern enemies are not always easily identifiable, and often cannot be directly attacked, at least not by traditional means.

In spite of all this, our Navy continues to perform its mission with distinction, meeting every challenge both at home and abroad. Many trying times surely lie ahead as we continue to try to deal with the tragic events that have afflicted our country, but there is no doubt that each generation of Navy men and women will do their best to continue to protect America and our way of life from all enemies, both foreign and domestic.

Chronology

Aug. 1990	Iraq invades Kuwait
Jan. 1991	Operation Desert Storm
June 1991	War in Bosnia begins
Aug. 1992	Iraqi no-fly zone imposed
Dec. 1992	Operation Restore Hope
Apr. 1995	Oklahoma federal building bombed
July 1996	TWA Flight 800 salvage
Sept. 1996	Missile attack on Iraq
Aug. 1998	Attack on bin Laden terrorist base
Aug. 2000	Attack on USS *Cole*
Sept. 2001	Terrorist attack on World Trade Center and Pentagon

Study Guide Questions

1. What were the main provisions of the START II disarmament treaty signed by the United States and the Russian Commonwealth in 1993?
2. A. What action caused the United States to engage in massive military operations in the Persian Gulf area in 1990–91?
   B. What were these operations called?
   C. What was the outcome?
3. What was the purpose of the no-fly zone imposed by the UN over southern Iraq in 1992?

4. What provocative actions did Hussein carry out in Iraq throughout much of the 1990s?
5. A. What major terrorist actions against the United States occurred in Africa in 1998?
   B. Who masterminded these?
   C. What was the U.S. response?
6. Where in Europe did fighting break out in 1991?
7. What other trouble spots in Africa involved the U.S. Navy and Marines in the 1990s?
8. What event in 1998 caused much concern over nuclear nonproliferation issues?
9. What major incidents occurred in 1991 and 1996 that caused much internal tension in the U.S. armed forces?

10. What incident of domestic terrorism took place in Oklahoma in 1995?
11. A. What terrorist attack against America took place in September 2001?
    B. What military action took place as a result of the attack?

Vocabulary

no-fly zone
holy war
nuclear weapons proliferation

mastermind
economic sanctions

Glossary

ABM TREATY—Anti-Ballistic Missile Treaty negotiated between the United States and the USSR in 1972.

ALLIANCE—a formal pact among nations in a common cause.

AMMUNITION DUMP—storage facility for military ammunition and other munitions.

AMPHIBIOUS INVASION—an attack launched from the sea by naval forces embarked in ships or craft.

ANCHORAGE—an area assigned for anchoring ships.

ANTISUBMARINE WARFARE (ASW)—older term for all methods used against enemy submarines. Now called *undersea warfare* (USW).

ANZAC—the military forces of New Zealand and Australia.

ARMISTICE—a temporary cessation or suspension of hostilities by mutual consent.

ARTILLERY BARRAGE—a series of projectiles fired at a target area, usually on land, from large-caliber land guns such as howitzers and cannons.

ATTRITION—a gradual diminution in number or strength due to the application of constant stress.

BANZAI CHARGE—a desperate, suicidal attack used by Japanese troops in World War II.

BARRAGE—heavy curtain of artillery fire placed in front of friendly troops to screen and protect them.

BEACHHEAD—the initial objective of an amphibious assault. A section of enemy coast, which, after capture, will be used for the continuous landing of troops and equipment in an amphibious operation.

BELLIGERENT—an opponent or nation engaged in warfare against another.

BLITZKRIEG—a swift, sudden military offensive, usually by combined air and land forces.

BLOCKADE—a naval operation wherein ships are prevented from entering or leaving certain ports or areas.

BOYCOTT—to abstain from using, buying, or dealing with, as a protest.

BRIDGEHEAD—a military position established by advanced components of an enemy force on one side of a bridge, river, or pass.

BROADSIDE—simultaneous firing of all main battery guns on one side of a warship.

CALIBER—in naval guns up to three inches in diameter, the diameter of the bore in inches or millimeters; in guns larger than three inches, the length of the gun in inches divided by the bore diameter.

CAMPAIGN—a series of military operations undertaken to achieve a specific objective within a given geographic area.

CEASE-FIRE AGREEMENT—an agreement to suspend active hostilities; a truce.

COALITION—an alliance, especially a temporary one, of factions, parties, or nations.

COLLIER—a ship designed to replenish coal-burning ships.

COMBINED OPERATIONS—military operations involving the use of several branches of one military service acting together, such as ground, air, and seaborne.

COMMANDO—a small fighting force especially trained for making quick, destructive raids against enemy-held areas.

COMMISSION—to put a ship into active service; a military rank granted by action of the national government.

COMMUNISM—a social-governmental system characterized by an absence of classes and by common ownership of the means of production.

CONVOY—a group of merchant ships or naval auxiliaries, or both, usually escorted by warships and aircraft.

COUNTERATTACK—a return attack against an enemy.

COUNTERBATTERY—shore battery fire directed at an attacking warship.

COUP D'ÉTAT—a violent takeover of a government by force.

CRISIS—an incident or situation involving a threat to the United States, its territories, and its possessions that rapidly develops and creates a condition of such diplomatic, political, or military importance to the

U.S. government that the commitment of U.S. military forces and resources is contemplated to achieve national objectives.

D DAY—term used to designate an unnamed day on which a military operation begins; debarkation day for an amphibious assault. Days following are designated by plus numbers, as in "D +7."

DEMILITARIZED ZONE (DMZ)—a region, defined by diplomatic or political agreement, wherein military forces and installations may not be established.

DEMOBILIZATION—dismissal or release from active military service or use; disbandment of a military unit.

DEMOLITION—destruction by means of explosives.

DEMORALIZE—to undermine the confidence or morale of a target group.

DEPLOYMENT—a cruise in foreign waters.

DEPTH CHARGE—a USW explosive dropped from ships, as opposed to depth bombs, dropped from airplanes.

DETERRENCE—measures taken by a state or alliance of states to prevent hostile action by another state.

EMBARGO—a government-ordered stoppage of foreign trade in a particular type of goods or commodity.

FIGHTER PLANE—an aircraft intended primarily for engaging in combat with other aircraft or airborne weapons.

FORAY—a sudden raid or military advance.

GARRISON—a military post, or troops stationed at such a post.

GLASNOST—a Russian word for relaxation of secrecy and other liberal reforms in governmental foreign policy.

GUN EMPLACEMENT—a mounting or protected site for the mounting and operation of a gun.

H HOUR—a term used to designate the time, usually on D day, for an operation to commence.

HOME PORT—port or air station at which a ship or aircraft is normally based.

HUNTER-KILLER GROUP—in World War II, a naval force consisting of an ASW carrier, associated aircraft, and escort ships.

ICBM—intercontinental ballistic missile.

IMPERIALISM—the policy of extending a nation's authority by territorial acquisition or by establishing political or economic control over other nations.

IMPRESSMENT—the forcing of a person to act as a crew member of a ship, especially a warship, against that person's will.

INCENDIARIES—munitions causing or capable of causing fire.

INFILTRATE—to sneak into enemy territory, or to enter a target group or location by use of stealth.

INF TREATY—Intermediate-range Nuclear Forces Treaty, eliminating intermediate-range nuclear missiles from Europe.

INSURRECTION—an act of open revolt against civil authority or a legal government.

INTELLIGENCE—any information of possible military value about an enemy.

INTERDICTION—destruction of roads, bridges, railroads, tunnels, and the like to prevent the support of enemy forces.

INTERIOR LINES OF COMMUNICATIONS—means or routes within a country or other land area over which supplies and messages can travel.

INTERNATIONAL WATERS—waters external to any nation's territorial seas or internal waters, open to free use by the ships of all nations.

ISOLATIONISM—a national policy of remaining aloof from political, economic, or military entanglements with other countries.

JOINT OPERATIONS—military operations involving more than one military service.

KAMIKAZE—a World War II Japanese pilot trained to make a suicidal crash attack in a plane loaded with explosives.

LEE—the side of a ship or shore away from the direction from which the wind is blowing.

LETTER OF MARQUE—a document issued by a nation allowing a private citizen to equip a ship with arms in order to attack or seize enemy ships and goods.

LIBERATE—to free from oppression or foreign control.

LIMITED WAR—a war in which limited means short of total war are used to achieve a defined objective, usually well short of total victory.

LOGISTICS—the science of planning and carrying out the movement and maintenance of military forces.

MAGAZINE—a compartment aboard ship or ashore fitted for the stowage of ammunition.

MAIN BATTERY—the largest or most powerful armament of a ship or plane.

MAINMAST—the second mast of a ship with two or more masts, except when the first is taller.

MILITIA—a citizen army, as distinct from a regular army of professional soldiers.

MINE BARRAGE—a field of mines sowed in a water area to discourage the passage of shipping through the area.

MISSION—the objective or purpose of a military organization or operation.

MONITOR—a heavily armored warship with a low, flat deck and one or more raised gun turrets.

MONROE DOCTRINE—the U.S. policy of opposition to outside interference in the Americas, named after a foreign policy statement made in 1823 by President James Monroe.

MUNITION—war material, especially weapons and ammunition.

MUTINY—rebellion against constituted authority aboard ship.

NATO—North Atlantic Treaty Organization.

NAVAL GUNFIRE SUPPORT—gunfire from ships in support of a land operation.

NEUTRALITY—the state of nonparticipation in a war.

PACIFIST—one who believes that all disputes between nations can and should be settled peacefully, excluding military means of resolution.

PARAPET—low protective wall along the edge of a fortification, intended to protect soldiers from enemy fire.

PERESTROIKA—a Russian word for liberalization of domestic economic and social policies.

PILLBOX—a roofed concrete emplacement for a machine gun or other weapon.

PINCERS MOVEMENT—a military maneuver in which the enemy is attacked from two flanks and the front at the same time.

PORT—seagoing term for left; an observation window on a vessel.

PREDREADNOUGHT—any capital ship built between the end of the American Civil War and the launching of the British battleship *Dreadnought* in 1907.

PRIVATEER—a private commerce raider who attacks enemy shipping for personal gain, similar to a mercenary in land warfare. Traditionally commissioned by a *letter of marque* by the sponsoring government.

PROTECTORATE—a relationship of protection and partial control assumed by a superior power over a dependent country.

PROTOTYPE—an original model on which all subsequent designs are based.

QUARANTINE—similar to a blockade, except that only ships with designated contraband are prevented from entering or leaving a designated port or area.

RADAR—*ra*dio *d*etection *a*nd *r*anging; an instrument for determining, by radio frequency echoes, the presence of objects, and their range, bearing, elevation, and more recently, course and speed.

RAID—a surprise attack, such as one made by a commando force.

RANGE OF TIDE—the vertical distance between high and low tide levels in a body of water.

REBELLION—an uprising or organized forceful opposition intended to overthrow an existing government or ruling authority.

REPRISAL—retaliatory action for an injury or attack.

RIFLING—spiral grooves cut inside a bun bore to impart a spin to a projectile being fired.

SABOTAGE—damage inflicted by enemy agents, or those sympathetic to the enemy, so as to obstruct the productivity or normal functioning of a target installation, facility, or ship.

SALT TREATIES—Strategic Arms Limitation Treaties signed by the United States and the USSR beginning in the 1970s.

SALVAGE—to save or recover material or ships that have been wrecked, sunk, or damaged.

SCUTTLE—to sink a ship deliberately, usually to avoid capture by an enemy.

SEA-LANE—a route of travel across an ocean or other large body of water. See also *sea lines of communication*.

SEA LINES OF COMMUNICATION—the sea routes of travel, supply, and transport between two points on an ocean or other large body of water. See also *sea-lane*.

SEA POWER—the ability of a country to use and control the sea, and to prevent its use by an enemy.

SHOAL WATER—shallow water.

SHOW OF FORCE—a public display of military power designed to influence the outcome of an event of international interest, often political.

SHRAPNEL—shell fragments from a high-explosive shell.

SILHOUETTE—an outline of something with no detail visible in the interior, usually filled in with black in the case of a drawing.

SKI-JUMP CARRIER—an aircraft carrier, usually of medium size, fitted with an inclined bow ramp to expedite the takeoff of V/STOL aircraft.

SKIRMISH—a minor encounter in war between small groups of troops, often as part of a larger engagement.

SNORKEL—a device used by a submarine to enable it to draw air from the surface while submerged; to operate submerged with just the snorkel showing.

SONAR—*so*und *n*avigation *a*nd *r*anging; underwater sound equipment for the detection of submarines and for navigation.

SORTIE—to depart; the act of departing, as from a port; an airstrike.

SPRING LINE—a mooring line at an acute angle to a ship.

STALEMATE—a deadlocked situation in which further action by either of two opponents is impossible or useless.

STARBOARD—seagoing term for right.

START TREATIES—Reduction and Limitation of Strategic Offensive Arms Treaties negotiated between the United States and the USSR in the 1990s.

STOCKPILE—a supply of material accumulated and stored for future use.

STRATEGIC TRIAD—a scheme of unclear deterrence based on potential use of land-based ICBMs, ballistic-missile submarines, and manned bombers.

STRIKING FORCES—forces intended to carry out an offensive attack against an enemy.

SUBVERSION—the act of undermining the character, morale, or allegiance of a target group.

SUMMIT MEETING—a meeting of the highest level of government officials of two or more nations.

SURVEILLANCE—close observation of a person or group, often undercover.

SWEEP—a mine-clearing operation on land or sea; a military patrol through an area to rid it of enemy forces.

TACTICS—the employment of a military unit or units in battle.

TIMETABLE—a schedule listing the times at which certain events are planned to take place.

TRENCH WARFARE—a type of land warfare common during World War I, typified by assaults and counterattacks against entrenched enemy positions or fortifications.

TRIANGULATION—the location of an unknown position or target by forming a triangle having the unknown location and two known angles as the vertices.

TURBINE—a multibladed rotor, driven by steam or other hot gases or a liquid, which, in turn, drives a propeller or compressor.

UDT—underwater demolition team.

UNCONDITIONAL SURRENDER—a surrender with no preconditions.

UNDERSEA WARFARE (USW)—a term encompassing all aspects of warfare beneath the sea, including but not limited to antisubmarine warfare (ASW), mine warfare, and UDT operations.

UNDERWATER DEMOLITION TEAM (UDT)—a team of specially trained personnel who do reconnaissance and demolition work along the beaches prior to an amphibious assault.

UNDERWAY REPLENISHMENT (UNREP)—replenishment by use of other ships while the receiving ship is under way.

UNRESTRICTED SUBMARINE WARFARE—use of submarines to attack any type of enemy target shipping, usually without prior warning.

U.S. FLAG SHIPS—merchant ships registered in the United States and operating under the American flag on the high seas.

VIETNAMIZATION—name given to the process wherein the conduct and control of all military operations in South Vietnam were turned over to the armed forces of that country upon the withdrawal of U.S. troops in the early 1970s.

WARHEAD—forward section of a torpedo or missile that caries the explosive charge.

WAR MATÉRIEL—the equipment, apparatus, and related supplies of a military force engaged in warfare.

WAR OF ATTRITION—a lengthy war in which both sides concentrate on reducing the other's forces rather than capturing territory.

WATERLINE—the line on a vessel's hull to which it sinks when in the water.

Nautical Sciences

Maritime Geography

Geography is the study of where things are on the earth. It is also more than that. It is about the relationship of things in a given area—natural resources, land, climate, soils, people, governments, and economics, among other things. For naval science students, an important part of geography has to do with the location of important places and the transportation routes between them, by both land and sea. Also of particular interest are the relationship of geography and politics (called geopolitics) and a field of study called military geography.

In the next two chapters, we will talk about many of these aspects of geography, especially the seas. We will call our approach to this subject *maritime geography.* During this study, it would be very helpful if you refer to a large globe or world map to find the places we will talk about.

WHY STUDY GEOGRAPHY?

Geography has been considered an important subject for study since ancient times. A knowledge of geography is needed if you want to be a good citizen of your country and the world. Only by knowing your own country will you be aware of its strengths and needs. Geography helps supply such knowledge.

Citizens today need to know about more than just their own country. We are all citizens of the world, as well. An intelligent citizen must be concerned about problems in other lands. Only by understanding other people and their needs can we hope to create a peaceful world. Not all nations are blessed with great resources. We need the resources other countries can provide to maintain our standard of living.

We also must be aware of the dangers posed by possible enemies. Our nation wishes to maintain its independence and security. But it is clear that some other nations do not have such good intentions. They seek to change governments and bring nations under their control. And their objectives are not just political and social. Their actions are geared to world geography. They want

to control the world from geographic strongpoints so they can spread their economic, political, and military control across the globe. All U.S. citizens should understand these *geopolitical* goals.

Understanding geography requires the use of maps. In geography, a map is the most basic tool. In this unit you will learn where important countries and places are located. And you will learn about the oceans and seas around these places. To assist in the correct pronunciation of place names, the more difficult ones in the following two chapters are followed by syllabic pronunciation guides.

THE WORLD OCEAN

When we speak of the *world ocean,* we mean the 71 percent of Earth's surface covered with salt water. If you were to add freshwater surfaces to those of salt water, you would find that barely one-fourth of Earth's surface is land. Since nearly three-fourths of our world is water, it is clear that the seas are of great importance to life on Earth. The science of oceanography deals with this vital aspect of all life.

The world ocean is the political, economic, and military lifeblood of much of the world. It carries raw materials, food, and manufactured products throughout the world. It provides the people of the world protein-rich seafoods. It is also becoming an important source of minerals.

The continents are large islands in this vast ocean. They divide the world ocean into six major ocean *basins.* Still smaller, partially enclosed subdivisions of the oceans are called *seas.* The six ocean basins, listed in order of size, are the South Pacific, North Pacific, Indian, North Atlantic, South Atlantic, and Arctic.

There are many "seas" that are really only part of these oceans. Some of the more important from the standpoint of location and natural resources are the Mediterranean Sea, Caribbean Sea, North Sea, Baltic Sea, Black Sea, Red Sea, Arabian Sea, South China Sea,

Sea of Japan, Barents Sea, and Bering Sea. There are a number of important *gulfs*, or pockets of the seas that reach into the continents. Most notable of these are the Gulf of Mexico, the Persian Gulf, and the Gulf of Aden. You should be able to locate all of these on a world map or a globe.

A similar body of water to a gulf but usually though not always smaller is a *bay*, defined as a large body of water opening into a sea. Examples are the Chesapeake Bay on the U.S. East Coast, and San Francisco Bay on the West Coast. A *sound* is similar to a bay, except that it connects between two or more inlets or parts of a sea, like Long Island Sound off New York.

Only in the last hundred years or so have the scientific instruments been available for making accurate charts and maps of the ocean floor. These show that the ocean floor is just as varied as the land surfaces. Submarine (underwater) geography shows deep sea ridges like mountain ranges, sea mounts like mountain peaks on land, basins and plains like valleys and surface plains on land, and great trenches even deeper than the Grand Canyon. These features fall within the study of oceanography, which is covered in unit 2.

On the edges of the oceans are the world's seaports and naval bases from which ships sail forth. Seaports are harbors, towns, or cities having access to the sea, and containing facilities for cargo handling and ship maintenance of all kinds. A naval base may or may not be located at a seaport. It has facilities for sustaining naval warships and auxiliary vessels. The routes these ships travel are the strategic waterways of the world.

MILITARY GEOGRAPHY

From ancient days until World War II, military geography was largely a matter of opposing armies finding places to fortify and defend. It might have also involved finding terrain that would be helpful in fighting the battle—hills, rivers, forests, and so on. At sea, the ancients looked for sheltered coves or the leeward side (side away from the wind) of islands where seas were calm. Here their oarsmen might be more effective in ramming enemy vessels. Narrow channels with shoals made defense easier for those familiar with the area.

In World War I military geography began to be considered. By World War II, every aspect of geography became important in military planning. Global warfare had begun. Planners had to think about fighting and supporting armies in deserts, jungles, polar regions, mountains, and islands around the world. Supply lines, routes of communications, and transport became crucial. Manmade features such as cities, roads, railroads, bridges, airfields, and harbors often decided success or failure. In the Korean and Vietnam Wars the geopolitical effects were worldwide. The same is true of the turmoil in the less-developed nations of Africa, Asia, and Central America since then.

Natural resources of all kinds have become necessary for military victory. Vital materials must be shipped over long sea-lanes (routes across the sea) from distant places. Soils have to grow enough food to support millions of personnel overseas as well as the home population. Increasing amounts of water, coal, and petroleum are needed to support industry and fuel military vehicles. Raw materials, transportation, and distance have become crucial to victory in war and to national survival.

Today, as in World War II, every aspect of world geography is taken into account by military planners. Because we depend on foreign sources for many natural resources, as well as overseas bases and alliances, the maritime aspects of military geography are very important. Sea communications routes, through geographic choke points such as straits, island groups, and canals, are more important than ever before.

1

Maritime Geography of the Western Seas

The sea-lanes of the Atlantic are the most traveled in the world ocean. The main shipping lanes go between the East Coast of the United States and Western Europe, the two most industrialized regions of the world. The heaviest bulk cargo traffic is carried in huge tankers between the Persian Gulf–area oil fields and Western Europe, traveling the long route around the Cape of Good Hope in South Africa. (The jumbo tankers are too large to go through the Suez Canal, the route taken by smaller tankers and general cargo ships on their way to both U.S. and European ports from Asia.) The United States imports a large percentage of its total oil needs, and much of that comes across Atlantic sea-lanes—from the Persian Gulf, Venezuela, and Nigeria.

The Atlantic also provides the water routes between Europe and South America and the Caribbean, and between Gulf of Mexico and East Coast ports and Latin America.

The most important military sea-lanes are those between the United States and its Western European NATO (North Atlantic Treaty Organization) allies, and those to the oil countries of the Middle East. The North Atlantic sea-lanes are the only way aid could be delivered from North America to Western Europe in time of war. The United States, on the other hand, is greatly dependent on oil from the Middle East and strategic minerals from Africa and South America. We also need European, South American, and African markets for U.S.-manufactured products and agricultural produce.

ATLANTIC OCEAN

The Atlantic Ocean consists of two basins roughly separated by an underwater mountain range called the Mid-Atlantic Ridge. The western basin lies between North and South America, and the eastern basin is between Europe and Africa. The total ocean has an area of about 31,660,000 square miles. Its average depth is about 10,930 feet. The deepest spot in the North Atlantic is in the Puerto Rico Trench, 28,374 feet deep. In the South Atlantic it is the South Sandwich Trench, 27,113 feet deep, about 400 miles east of South Georgia Island, off Argentina. The mid-ocean floor is dominated by the Mid-Atlantic Ridge. Only a few islands emerge above sea

level along the ridge, most of which crest one to two miles beneath the surface. These islands are Iceland and the Azores in the North Atlantic, and Ascension Island and Tristan da Cunha in the South Atlantic.

Minerals. Few mineral deposits in the Atlantic Ocean's floor can be worked profitably at this time. Those that are mined are located in the shallow waters of the continental shelves (the extension of the continents out to a water depth of 600 feet). The largest mining operations in the Atlantic are for sands and gravels along the Atlantic seaboard of the United States.

The largest single offshore mining operation in the world is based on Ocean Cay in the Bahamas. *Aragonite sands,* composed mostly of calcium carbonate, are dredged up. They are used in the manufacture of cement, glass, and animal feed supplements. A cement industry also is operated in Iceland, based on shell-sands. Phosphates for fertilizers are mined in a number of spots along the shores of all continents facing the Atlantic.

The most important mining operations in the Atlantic are the oil wells in the Gulf of Mexico off the coasts of Texas, Louisiana, and Mexico. Also, there is much oil production in the North Sea between Great Britain and Norway.

Fishing. The North Atlantic has been the scene of major commercial fishing for more than a thousand years. On both sides of the ocean there are major fisheries. Cod, haddock, flounder, and ocean perch are found in the Grand Banks off the Canadian province of Newfoundland and the northeast coast of the United States. Lobsters are a high-value harvest from the New England coast, the Caribbean, Brazil, and South Africa. Herring, sardines, and anchovies are caught in the North Sea's Dogger Bank and in the Norwegian Sea in the far north. Tuna is caught along the African coast and in the Caribbean. The Atlantic has some of the most heavily fished areas in the world.

Ports and Naval Bases. The major U.S. Atlantic ports are Boston, New York, Baltimore, Norfolk, and Charleston. There are many other ports of lesser importance from the standpoint of annual volume. These ports, however, are also very important to coastal shipping and the general prosperity of the nation.

The major naval bases on the East Coast of the United States are Newport, Rhode Island; New London, Connecticut; Norfolk, Virginia; King's Bay, Georgia; and Mayport (near Jacksonville), Florida. A major naval shipyard is located at Portsmouth, Virginia. Large commercial shipyards that handle major naval shipbuilding programs are located at Bath, Maine; Quincy, Massachusetts; and Newport News, Virginia. On the eastern side of the Atlantic, the U.S. Navy maintains an important naval air station at Keflavik, Iceland, and a much-used naval base at Rota, Spain. The major ports of Britain are Liverpool, London, and Southampton. The largest and busiest Atlantic port of Western Europe is Antwerp, Belgium. Other important Western European ports are Rotterdam, Holland; Bremerhaven and Hamburg, Germany; Le

Havre, France; Copenhagen, Denmark; Oslo, Norway; and Lisbon, Portugal. Almost all direct support for U.S. forces in Germany comes through Antwerp or Bremerhaven. You should know the location of these ports. They all figure prominently in U.S. trade, and all are vital to the defense and economies of Western Europe.

On the western side of the South Atlantic are some important South American ports. A large amount of bauxite ore for making aluminum is exported from Georgetown, Guyana, to the United States and other industrialized nations. Tropical woods, quinine, and natural rubber are exported from Belém, near the mouth of the Amazon River in Brazil. The great Brazilian cities of Rio de Janeiro and São Paulo-Santos export iron ore and import U.S.- and European-manufactured products used

The Port of New York. Manhattan is to the upper left, with the Hudson River and its wharves on the left and the East River to the right. Courtesy Port of New York Authority

in that huge country. Buenos Aires, Argentina, and Montevideo, Uruguay, export beef to the United States and export beef and wheat to Europe. They also import manufactured products from the United States and Europe.

West African ports of special trading interest to the United States include Casablanca, Morocco, for lead and cobalt; Monrovia, Liberia, for iron ore; Lagos, Nigeria, for oil; Accra, Ghana, for cocoa and gold; and Cape Town, South Africa, for gold, diamonds, platinum, and chromium, among other strategic minerals.

Strategic Geography. When we use the word *strategic* with geography, we are referring to areas on Earth's surface that are important from a military standpoint. The Atlantic side of the European coast has a number of strategic waterways. The two most important of these are the Strait of Gibraltar and the Danish straits Skagerrak (Skăg'-e-răk) and Kattegat (Kät'-e-gät) (see fig. 1-3B).

The Strait of Gibraltar is the western entrance to the Mediterranean Sea. It also is the door to the Atlantic Ocean for Russian Black Sea and Mediterranean Squadron naval vessels. Under control of Britain, Gibraltar is also vital to allied interests in southern Europe and North Africa.

Russian naval vessels from the Baltic Sea Fleet must go through the Danish straits to get into the North Sea and North Atlantic. The main Russian naval bases and shipbuilding cities on the Baltic Sea are St. Petersburg and Kaliningrad. Other important East European ports are Riga, Latvia, and Gdynia (Ga-din'-ē-a) and Gdansk (Ga-dänsk'), Poland.

Another strategic area from the standpoint of defending allied shipping in the North Atlantic is known as the Greenland–Iceland–United Kingdom (G-I-UK) gap. This is a wide expanse of water between Greenland, Iceland, the Faeroe Islands, and northern Scotland. It is through this seaway that Russian naval warships and submarines from their northern fleet based at Murmansk, on the Barents Sea, and Archangel on the White Sea, have to proceed to gain access to the Atlantic Ocean.

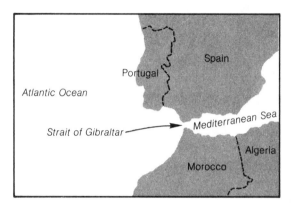

The Strait of Gibraltar.

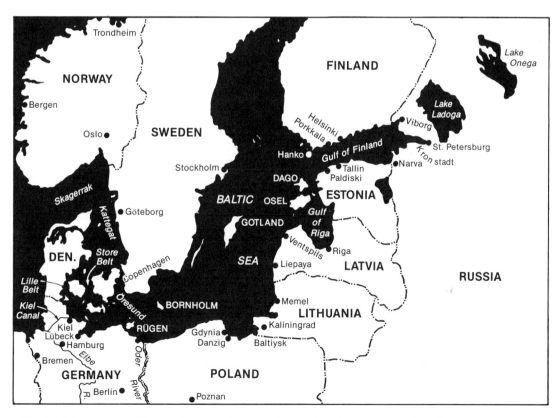

The Baltic Sea ports and bases. The strategic straits Skagerrak and Kattegat are the only access in and out.

A major objective of the United States and its NATO allies in the event of future war with any of the Russian states would be to try to keep their submarines out of the North Atlantic shipping lanes by blocking their passage through the Strait of Gibraltar and the G-I-UK gap.

Some of the most significant events in modern times—ones that have had profound and continuing effects on military strategy in northern Europe and throughout the world—were the democratization of the former Soviet satellite nations of Eastern Europe in the late 1980s, the reunification of Germany in 1990, and the fall of the Soviet Union in 1991. More on these events and their effects is presented in the history section of this text.

CARIBBEAN SEA AND GULF OF MEXICO

The Caribbean has an area of 1,020,000 square miles, with two deep basins separated by the underwater Nicaragua Rise. The rise runs from the hump of Honduras and Nicaragua in Central America northeastward past Jamaica to Haiti. This shallow rise, only 200 to 1,000 feet deep, takes up almost one-fourth of the Caribbean Sea area. To the north is the Yucatán basin with the Cayman Trench, the deepest part of the sea at 25,216 feet. The southern and western half of the sea, extending from Costa Rica to Haiti, and then eastward to the islands of the Lesser Antilles, is as deep as 16,400 feet.

The Lesser Antilles, small islands bordering the eastern limits of the Caribbean, are on a ridge of very active volcanoes. Mount Pelée, on the island of Martinique, killed 30,000 people during a violent volcanic eruption in 1902. More recent but less damaging volcanic action has occurred on several of these islands since then.

Currents from the equatorial Atlantic flow into the Caribbean from the southeast along the coast of northern South America. Part of this current continues north into the Gulf of Mexico before moving eastward again between Cuba and Florida, and then up the East Coast of the United States. The prevailing winds, which to a large extent follow the currents, bring strong hurricanes into the area and up the East Coast in the late summer and fall of the year. Almost every year these huge storms cause great property damage and loss of life somewhere in the Caribbean islands, on the Gulf Coast, or along the eastern seaboard of the United States.

The Gulf of Mexico has an area of 598,000 square miles and an average depth of 4,960 feet. From the Yucatán Peninsula of Mexico in the south, around the gulf clockwise to the southern tip of Florida, the continental shelf extends far to sea. In the north it has been broadened even farther by silt carried out to sea by the Mississippi River.

Minerals. The Caribbean in general has fewer mineral resources than other ocean basins. The exception to this is the Venezuelan oil fields on Lake Maracaibo (Mär-ä-ki′-bō). This offshore drilling operation makes that country the world's fifth largest producer of petroleum. Venezuela is one of the top exporters of oil to the United States.

The Gulf Coast of Louisiana and Texas is also rich in oil produced from offshore rigs. Oil and natural gas fields are also being developed along the Mexican coast near Tampico. One of the worst oil-pollution catastrophes to date occurred in the Mexican field in 1979–80 when an underwater well exploded. Millions of barrels of oil escaped into the gulf, spreading an oil slick all the way to Texas beaches.

Fishing. A great deal of fishing is done by the people of the many Caribbean islands. Most of this is small scale—that is, catches are brought ashore and consumed fresh. The most important commercial fishing operations are for shrimp and menhaden in the Gulf of Mexico. There is a large shrimp catch along the U.S. and Mexican Gulf Coasts. This is where almost all of the shrimp consumed in the United States is caught.

Menhaden fishing is the most mechanized. Small boats pump their catch into larger carrier vessels. The fish are then brought ashore and processed into fish meal for export, mostly to less developed countries. Fish meal is a high-protein product used for fish cakes, seafood sauces, and the like.

There also are large numbers of delicious Caribbean lobsters, called *langusta,* caught around all the islands. Some are frozen into packages of expensive lobster tails. Langusta differ from Maine lobsters only in that they do not have large claws. Excellent blue crabs are also caught along the U.S. Gulf Coast, some for canning but most for the fresh market.

Ports and Naval Bases. Houston, Texas, and New Orleans, Louisiana, are the major U.S. ports on the Gulf Coast. Other important ports are Galveston and Port Arthur, Texas; Mobile, Alabama; and Tampa, Florida. Veracruz is the most important Mexican port. Barranquilla (Bär-räng-ke′-yä), Colombia, and Maracaibo and La Guaira (La Gwī′-ra) (port of Caracas), Venezuela, are important in those nations. The capital cities in the Greater and Lesser Antilles are the major ports of each of those islands. The largest and most important of these cities is Havana, Cuba. The island of Aruba, in the Netherlands Antilles, not far from Lake Maracaibo, is a major oil-refining site. Much asphalt is exported from Port of Spain, Trinidad.

The Antilles are a favorite area for luxury passenger cruise ships. To escape the winter, Americans cruise out of Port Everglades (Miami), Florida, and San Juan, Puerto Rico, on pleasure voyages to exotic Caribbean ports such as St. Thomas, Jamaica, and Barbados.

The United States has no major naval bases on the Gulf Coast, but there are small naval stations with home-port facilities at Pascagoula, Mississippi, and Ingleside,

Texas. A large commercial shipyard that hosts major naval shipbuilding programs is also located at Pascagoula. In addition there is a naval support activity at New Orleans, Louisiana, and important naval training and development centers at Gulfport, Mississippi, and Panama City and Key West, Florida. There is a major naval air base complex at Pensacola, Florida, and other naval air facilities are in the Corpus Christi, Texas, area. Important U.S. naval bases in the Caribbean are at Guantánamo (Gwän-tä'-na-mō) Bay, Cuba, and Roosevelt Roads, on the eastern end of Puerto Rico.

Strategic Geography. Certainly the most important strategic spot in the Caribbean is the Panama Canal. Splitting the Central American peninsula in the Republic of Panama, the canal is the main route for most ocean traffic between the Atlantic and Pacific. The Canal Zone was run by the United States for most of the last century, but it was turned over by treaty to Panama in 1999.

The Panama Canal has always been vital to U.S. interests. From the naval standpoint, it has been the best way to transfer all but the largest ships of the Atlantic and Pacific fleets rapidly back and forth in the event of tension or war. There is no question of its importance as a choke point of international trade. While the canal is probably not as important to U.S. defense as it once was, its loss to an enemy power would severely harm U.S. and Western Hemisphere security and economic interests.

Cuba. Cuba has been a major problem in the Caribbean for the United States for the past forty years. Under communist dictator Fidel Castro, Cuba became an ally of the former Soviet Union. Cuba has served as a base of operations for revolutionaries throughout the Caribbean and Latin America. There is a base to support submarines at Cienfuegos in southern Cuba. A large number of gunboats are based in various small ports around the island. A number of interior airfields base

fighter squadrons that fly modern fighter and attack aircraft.

For three decades prior to the demise of the Soviet Union, a constant stream of Soviet ships and aircraft supplied Soviet goods to Cuba. With the cargo came military equipment and advisers that made the Cuban armed forces one of the largest and best-equipped military forces in the Western Hemisphere. Cuban forces supported communist forces fighting in several African and Central American revolutions throughout the 1970s and 1980s.

The United States broke diplomatic ties with Cuba in 1961 when Castro openly embraced communism and announced his alliance with the Soviet Union. A low-key relationship was resumed in 1977, but there have been no serious moves to reopen embassies or exchange ambassadors since.

When relations were broken, the United States made sure that the treaty granting the United States a naval base at Guantánamo Bay, in far southeastern Cuba, stayed in effect. "Gitmo," as naval personnel call it, is the Navy's main training base for the U.S. Atlantic Fleet. It has a fine harbor and good facilities. Except for an occasional hurricane in the fall, the weather is excellent most of the year for all types of fleet training, including aircraft operations and missile firing. The U.S. Marines maintain a force at Gitmo for defense of the base.

Cuba is only about 90 miles from Florida, and it is directly in the path of the major sea-lanes between the United States, Central America, northern South America, and the Panama Canal. This communist presence is a constant threat to the peace and security of the Caribbean area, and to the security of the southeastern United States.

Following the demise of the Soviet Union in the early 1990s, all Russian aid to Cuba stopped, throwing it into a

The Panama Canal.

Aerial view of the U.S. naval base at Guantánamo Bay, Cuba.

state of severe economic depression that has persisted to the present day. This has led several times in the past, most recently during the summer of 1994, to large-scale attempts at illegal immigration into the United States by its population. During these incidents several thousand Cuban refugees used makeshift watercraft of all imaginable descriptions to try to make it across the Straits of Florida to land in the southern part of that state. Most of them were stopped and rescued from their often overcrowded and unseaworthy craft by U.S. Coast Guard and Navy ships and patrol boats. They were then taken to temporary camps at the Guantánamo Naval Base pending eventual return to Castro's Cuba.

Additional incidents of a similar nature can almost certainly be expected in the future, as long as Cuba continues to be an economically unstable force for unrest in the area.

THE ARCTIC OCEAN

The Arctic Ocean is the smallest of the major oceans. It has an area of 4,700,000 square miles with an average depth of 3,250 feet. The deepest part of the ocean is the Abyssal Plain running across the North Pole at a depth of 15,091 feet. The Arctic basin is divided by three major submarine ridges that separate four large undersea plains and a number of smaller plains. The continental shelf north of Alaska, Canada, and Greenland extends about 50 to 125 miles from shore. However, the continental shelf north of Asia extends from 300 to 600 miles

During several summers in the mid-1990s thousands of Cubans tried to cross the Straits of Florida in rickety seacraft to try to immigrate illegally into the United States. U.S. Coast Guard photo

toward the pole. That portion of the Asiatic continental shelf under the Barents Sea north of Russia and Scandinavia extends more than 1,000 miles to sea, past Spitsbergen (Spĭts'-bûr-gan) and Franz Josef Land.

Minerals. Along the Asian side of the Arctic Ocean are five seas: Chukchi (Chŏŏk'-chē), East Siberian, Laptev, Kara, and Barents. Much geologic exploration for minerals has been done there in the last few years. Large oil and natural gas deposits probably exist in the Laptev Sea north of Siberia.

The continental shelf off Alaska has also been the scene of much oil drilling. Major oil discoveries were made in the late 1960s and early 1970s in Prudhoe Bay.

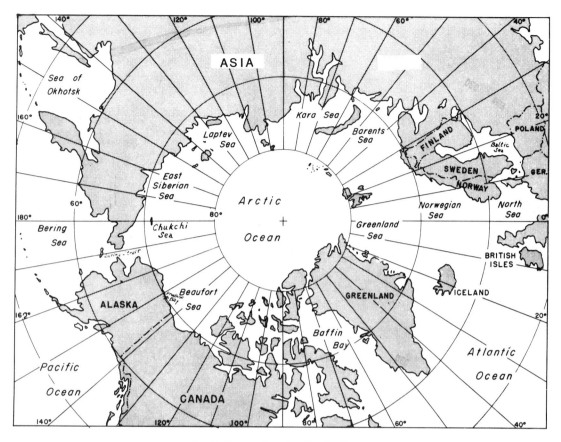

Arctic Ocean, showing the Arctic seas.

The 800-mile trans-Alaska pipeline was completed in 1977 at a cost of $8 billion. More than a million barrels of oil now flow south daily from Prudhoe Bay to Valdez (Val-dëz'), Alaska, where tankers take it on board for delivery to West Coast refineries.

In March 1989 the largest oil tanker spill in U.S. history occurred when one of these tankers, the 987-foot *Exxon Valdez,* carrying 1,260,000 barrels of crude oil taken on at Valdez, ran aground on a reef in the Gulf of Alaska some 25 miles south of that port. Ultimately the resulting oil slick from 260,000 barrels lost in the mishap spread some 470 miles into the gulf. Many formerly clean Alaskan beaches and tidal basins were covered with inches of black sludge. A two-year multimillion-dollar effort was mounted to try to clean up the worst of the spill, but the accident nevertheless killed some 10 percent of the area's bird population, along with thousands of sea otters and seals. The cause of the accident was later determined to be incompetent navigation by the tanker's captain and crew.

Large oil deposits have also been found in the continental shelf off the Beaufort (Bō'-furt) Sea coast of Canada, some 400 miles east of Prudhoe Bay. Large natural gas deposits are now being tapped in the area of Melville Island in the Queen Elizabeth Islands.

Getting oil out of the Arctic is not very easy. The frigid cold, prolonged gale-force winds, and icing and freezing of lubricants and equipment make oil drilling extremely expensive and hazardous. The Arctic Ocean itself is almost always covered with constantly moving *ice floes.* Engineers have created artificial islands built from seabed sand and gravel dredged up during the brief summer melt, sometimes poured through holes cut in the 7-foot-thick ice. Much of the year the crude oil must be heated in order to flow satisfactorily through the pipelines and drilling rigs, because of the extreme cold. But the demand for oil in the world is so great that no effort is spared to solve the problems.

Fishing. Only in the Barents and Norwegian Seas can commercial fishing take place. There, huge catches of cod, haddock, redfish, and halibut are made annually for the fresh-fish markets in Europe and the former Soviet states. Annual catches average over 2 million tons. There is evidence of overfishing in these Arctic seas, so quotas have been set by the fishing nations. Some whaling is done in the area by a small Icelandic whaling fleet.

Ports and Naval Bases. Only Murmansk, Russia, and Narvik, Norway, are important ports in the Arctic. The former we have already identified as a naval base for the

The *Exxon Valdez* oil spill was one of the worst environmental disasters in history. The tanker is shown top left, grounded atop Bligh Reef in the Gulf of Alaska.

Russian northern fleet. The latter is an important fishing port and a loading place for high-grade iron ore from Swedish mines at Kiruna (Kir′-u-nä) about 125 miles inland.

Strategic Geography. There are no significant commercial sea routes across the Arctic ice ocean at this time. In 1969, a specially built 150,000-ton icebreaker-tanker, the SS *Manhattan,* made a successful trip through the pack ice in the Northwest Passage. The route was from Davis Strait through Baffin Bay and Melville Sound to Prudhoe Bay and Barrow, Alaska. Though the route proved possible, the costs involved were so high that pipelines are probably a more satisfactory way to move oil south from Alaska.

Before its demise, every year since the 1950s a Soviet surface force of icebreakers, naval vessels, and merchant ships tried to transit the northern seas from the Atlantic to the Pacific. They were often successful, but it was always a great effort. The force resupplied many of the tiny settlements started by the Soviet government on the seacoasts.

In 1958 the American nuclear submarine USS *Nautilus* became the first vessel ever to reach the North Pole under the ice. Since then, U.S., Soviet, and, more recently, Russian nuclear submarines have made many patrols under the ice. Engineers occasionally propose having submarine tankers cross the Arctic Ocean under the ice, cutting thousands of miles off the surface routes between U.S. and Canadian Beaufort Sea oil fields and northern Europe. Since the great circle routes across the Arctic are the shortest distance between Asia and the United States for both submarines and aircraft, the region would almost certainly be a major operational area in the event of war.

MEDITERRANEAN SEA AND BLACK SEA

The Mediterranean Sea is a shallow, long, landlocked sea about 1,145,000 square miles in area. Its average depth is 4,921 feet, but there are some deep basins west and south of Italy. The Hellenic Trough, south of Greece, is the deepest area, more than 16,700 feet deep. The sea lies in a broad trench between the European and African continents. It stretches about 2,500 miles from the Strait of Gibraltar on the west to Israel on the east. The word *Mediterranean* comes from the Latin words *medius,* meaning "middle," and *terra,* meaning "land"; together they mean the sea "in the middle" of the lands (of Europe, Asia, and Africa).

The Mediterranean is divided into two basins, east and west of the Strait of Sicily. The continental shelves are very narrow around the Mediterranean, though most of the Adriatic Sea and Gulf of Gabes (Gä′-bes), off Tunisia, have sea floors that are actually continental shelves. Great sediment beds extend far to sea from the mouths of the Nile River in Egypt, Rhone (Rōn) River in France, and Ebro (Ē′-bro) River in Spain.

The Mediterranean basin is one of the most active volcanic areas in the world. There are at least eleven active volcanoes in the Aegean (I-jē′-an) Sea, in a belt from Athens to Rhodes. Four of these are islands, and the others are submerged. Many more underwater volcanoes are in the western Mediterranean, to the north and west of Sicily, and around the Balearic (Bal-ē-ar′-ik) Islands and Corsica. The whole Mediterranean area, and especially Greece, Turkey, and Yugoslavia, often has large earthquakes. The pressures between the Eurasian and African geological plates push in on the sea from both sides. Volcanic lava from the interior of the earth wells up with huge pressure, causing volcanoes and earthquakes at the *fault line* where these plates meet.

The Black Sea is located above Turkey on the eastern end of the Mediterranean, between Europe and Asia. It has an area of about 180,000 square miles, with maximum depths of slightly over 7,000 feet. It connects with the Mediterranean through the Turkish straits and the Sea of Marmara. In many respects it is a landlocked saltwater lake, whose mineral content has gotten so high that it supports little life except in the surface layers. Some scientists have speculated that it was formed by overflow from the Mediterranean when the ice melted after the last ice age some 10,000 years ago. Its formation may have given rise to the story of the great flood in the Bible, and perhaps to the legend of the sinking of Atlantis. Recent photography of the bottom by remote-controlled submersibles has found evidence of ancient land-based habitation.

Minerals. No readily accessible mineral deposits have been located in the Mediterranean. Far below the sediments on the sea floor, however, drillers have found large beds of rock salt, sulfur, potash, and gypsum. All would be valuable for the chemical and fertilizer industries. At the present time these minerals can be mined only from deposits on Sicily and other islands.

Oil wells are being drilled offshore along the Adriatic coast of Italy, in the Gulf of Gabes off Tunisia, and off the Nile delta in Egypt. Although geologic studies seem to indicate that there is oil and natural gas along much of the Mediterranean coastline, there is no equipment at present that can reach the depths necessary to get it.

Fishing. The Mediterranean basin supports a fishing industry twice as valuable as that of any ocean. Catches bring high prices because most Mediterranean peoples consider fish a luxury food, like steak. Thousands of small fishing boats bring in small catches. Hake, sole, red mullet, and many other species of fish have a recorded catch in excess of a million tons each year. The total catch is probably much larger, since many local fishermen do not report an accurate number.

There is danger of large-scale pollution in the Mediterranean. This pollution threatens to destroy the balance of life in the sea. Overfishing is likewise making some kinds of fish scarce in some areas. The manmade pollution is worsened by the fact that this sea is almost totally landlocked. It loses by evaporation almost three times as much water as it gets from rainfall and runoff from land. Only the flow of water from the Atlantic keeps the sea at the same level over time. There is also a small flow from the Black Sea through the Turkish straits.

An example of humans' effect on the ecology of the eastern Mediterranean can be seen by looking at the changes that have taken place there since 1970. In that year, a high dam was completed across the Nile at Aswan (A-swan′), Egypt. This stopped the seasonal flood of fresh water and plant food into the sea by way of the Nile. Because of this, a fishing industry that had existed since the dawn of Western civilization has now almost ceased to exist near the mouth of the Nile.

Ports and Naval Bases. The Mediterranean was the cradle of Western civilization. For nearly seven thousand years, there has been recorded history in the eastern Mediterranean. Egypt, Crete, Phoenicia (Fi-nish′-e-a), Greece, and finally Rome led the parade of culture and trade across the sea in ancient times. The Romans called the Mediterranean *Mare Nostrum,* which means "our sea."

During the Middle Ages, Christian and Muslim cultures clashed in the Crusades. The clash ended in what can be thought of as a geographic compromise: Christians settled to the north and west in Europe, and Muslims settled to the south and east in Africa and Asia.

The Mediterranean Sea has always been very important to the countries around it. It is still so today. Great port cities are located in all of the countries bounding the Mediterranean coast: Barcelona and Valencia in Spain; Marseilles (Mar-say′) in France; Genoa, Naples, and Venice in Italy; Piraeus (Pi-rē′-as), the port of Athens, Greece; Istanbul (Is-tan-bōōl′), Turkey; Beirut (Ba-rōōt′), Lebanon; Haifa (Hi′-fa) and Tel Aviv (Tel′ a-vēv′), Israel; Alexandria, Egypt; Algiers (Al-jirz′), Algeria; Odessa (O-děs′-a) on the Black Sea arm in Ukraine; and a host of others.

The ports and countries around the Mediterranean are familiar places to sailors, world politicians, and tourists. There are many naval bases in the Mediterranean. The main Spanish base is at Barcelona, a favorite port of call for U.S. naval ships. The principal French base is at Toulon (Tōō-lon′), near the beautiful Riviera cities of Nice (Nēs) and Cannes (Kăn), also favorite places for U.S. Sixth Fleet sailors. The Italian navy's headquarters is at La Spezia (La Spā′-tsyä), and its fleet's biggest southern base is in Taranto (Tä′-rän-tō).

The Southern Command of NATO has its headquarters near Naples, with another important base at Izmir (Iz-mir′), Turkey. The homeport of the flagship of the

The harbor at Naples, Italy. The twin cones of the volcano Mount Vesuvius are in the background.

U.S. Sixth Fleet is at Gaeta (Gä-â'-tä), Italy, about halfway between Rome and Naples.

The Ukrainian Black Sea fleet headquarters is located at Sevastopol on the Crimean Peninsula. Major shipyards for merchant and naval surface ships are located at Nikolayev (Nik-a-lä'-yaf), near Odessa, which is where Russian aircraft carriers are built.

Strategic Geography. We have talked about the Strait of Gibraltar as the doorway to the Atlantic Ocean from the Mediterranean Sea. There are two other key choke points of navigation associated with the Mediterranean area: the Turkish straits, called the Bosporus (Bos'-per-as) and the Dardanelles (Därd-n-elz'), and the Suez Canal.

In peace the Turkish straits are open to all ships by international agreement. In war, however, the straits may be closed to any nation at war with Turkey. Turkey is a member of NATO. Russian and Ukrainian naval vessels from Black Sea ports freely use the straits to support and relieve the ships in the Mediterranean.

The Suez Canal is a vital waterway for the allies. On this narrow water path through the Egyptian desert, most surface cargo between Europe and Asia passes. As was proved in the Arab-Israeli wars in 1967 and 1973, the canal can be blocked quickly with mines or a few sunken ships.

Farther to the west, during the late 1970s and early 1980s the North African country of Libya, and its dictatorial ruler Muammar Qaddafi, became a growing sponsor for terrorist activity throughout the Mediter-

ranean basin. This continued until 1986, when in retaliation for several Libyan-sponsored terrorist attacks, the United States launched a retaliatory attack against Qadhafi's terrorist bases. The area has been relatively quiet ever since.

The Turkish straits consist of the Bosporus and the Dardanelles, the only access between the Mediterranean and the Black Sea.

Study Guide Questions

1. What are the most important military sea-lanes in the Atlantic for the United States? Why?
2. A. What are the two Atlantic basins?
   B. Where is the deepest spot in the North Atlantic? The South Atlantic?
3. What are the principal mineral and mining industries of the Atlantic and its gulfs and seas?
4. Where are the major fishing areas of the Atlantic?
5. What are the major naval bases on the U.S. Atlantic coast?
6. Which two European ports handle most of the support traffic for U.S. land forces in Germany?
7. What are some important trade goods the United States imports from Africa?
8. A. What does strategic geography mean?
   B. What are the choke points of navigation leading to and from the Atlantic basins?
9. Why is the Greenland–Iceland–United Kingdom gap important to the allies?
10. What severe storms occur each fall season in the Gulf of Mexico and Caribbean Sea?
11. A. Which two minerals are the chief resources of the Gulf of Mexico and Caribbean areas?
    B. Where are these minerals being mined?
12. Where are the major naval air and surface bases in the Caribbean and Gulf of Mexico?
13. A. What is the vital navigational choke point of the Caribbean area?
    B. What is the principal importance of this waterway to the United States?
14. Which Caribbean nation and government is a great worry to the United States? Why?
15. Why is the naval base at Guantánamo Bay important?
16. Where is the deepest part of the Arctic Ocean?
17. What valuable resource is being obtained from the continental shelf off Alaska and Canada in the Arctic Ocean?
18. Why would the Arctic probably become a major operational area in event of a war between the United States and any Asiatic country?
19. How has the high dam on the Nile River at Aswan, Egypt, affected the ecology of the eastern Mediterranean?
20. A. What are some famous and important ports of the Mediterranean?
    B. Where are some of the important naval bases in the Mediterranean?
21. A. What are the names of the important Turkish straits?
    B. Why are these straits important to the NATO allies—and to the Ukrainians?
22. Why is the Suez Canal important to western Europe?

Vocabulary

Lake Maracaibo	jumbo tanker
Dogger Bank	exports
Suez Canal	imports
Latin America	lobster, langusta
Strait of Gibraltar	ice floe
Skagerrak Strait	fault line
Kattegat Strait	Dardanelles, Bosporus
Yucatán Peninsula	Turkish Straits
Prudhoe Bay	

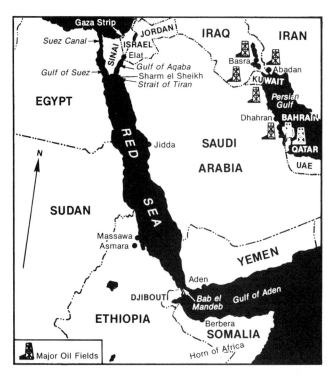

Maritime Geography of the Eastern Seas

Oil—its source and the sea routes over which it travels—dominates most trade in the seas south of Asia. From the Persian Gulf and Arabian Sea, the routes go westward to the Red Sea and Suez, and eastward through the Strait of Malacca and the seas around China to Japan. The trade moves from eastern Africa, India, Indonesia, and western Australia to Suez. It moves from China, Japan, Indonesia, and the islands of the Pacific to the West Coast of the United States and South America. Suez to Singapore, the most important British lifeline of past years, still is the scene of trade and travel between the Orient and the West.

Because of the strategic importance of the Middle East—its warm-water ports; its oil; and its hundreds of millions of people, many trying to survive with weak governments and poor environments—U.S. naval forces operate routinely in the Indian Ocean. The U.S. Fifth Fleet flagship has its homeport in Manama, Bahrain. The United States tries to maintain friendships in the region despite political and economic unrest. Third World nations are trying to improve the lives of their people, and must look to the seas to do so.

THE RED SEA AND GULF OF ADEN

The Red Sea is a warm, very salty sea stretching some 1,300 miles southeast from the Egyptian port of Suez to the Strait of Bab el Mandeb. It is only 90 to 200 miles wide, with an area of 169,000 square miles. The Axial Trough in the very middle of the narrow sea is the deepest at 9,580 feet near the Saudi Arabian port of Jidda (Jid'-a).

Minerals. The Red Sea has no known oil deposits. It is a possible future source of valuable metals, however. Pools of boiling hot brine are found in the Axial Trough. These waters are rich in *dissolved metals,* including zinc and copper, in the seabed muds. Someday it may be possible to mine these minerals.

Fishing. There is not much fishing in the Red Sea. Many kinds of fish are caught, but except for sardines near the Gulf of Suez, there is no major fishery. Lights are used to attract fish to the nets, since coral reefs make bottom trawling risky and expensive.

Ports and Naval Bases. The port of Suez is important because it is the southern anchorage for ships waiting to go through the canal northward to the Mediterranean Sea. Port Said (Sä-ēd') on the northern end of the canal is important for the same reason. Mesewa (Me-sä'-wa) is the only port and naval base in Ethiopia. Jidda, a seaport in Saudi Arabia, serves as a port of entry for the Moslem holy city of Mecca, about forty miles inland.

Djibouti (Jŏ-bōō'-tē), the capital city and port in the nation of the same name, is the major African port on the Horn of Africa, on the Gulf of Aden. It not only serves its own country but also is the main port for shipment of Ethiopian imports and exports. The major port of the area is Aden, capital of Yemen (Yem'-an).

Strategic Geography. The Red Sea is a strategic waterway. Along with the Suez Canal and Gulf of Suez to its

Suez, the Red Sea, the Gulf of Aden, and the Horn of Africa. The southern entrance to the Red Sea is controlled by the Strait of Bab el Mandeb. The oil fields of the Persian Gulf are at the upper right.

north, and the Gulf of Aden to the south, the Red Sea is the main waterway between Europe and Asia. The northern access is the Suez Canal. The choke point in the south is the Strait of Bab el Mandeb. (The Arabic word *bab* means "gate" or "strait.") Less than 20 miles wide, the strait separates Yemen on the Arabian Peninsula from Ethiopia and the Republic of Djibouti in Africa.

THE PERSIAN GULF AND GULF OF OMAN

The Persian Gulf area is the leading oil-producing area in the world. The gulf is bounded by Iran on the north, Kuwait and Iraq at the northwest end, Saudi Arabia on the west, and the Arab sheikdoms of Bahrain (Ba-rän') island, Qatar (Kät'-ar), United Arab Emirates (UAE), and Oman on the south and southeast. All of these countries

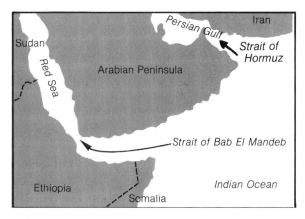

The Strait of Bab el Mandeb.

are major oil producers. The gulf itself has been divided for oil drilling by these nations, since much of the oil is gotten by offshore rigs.

Minerals. Though oil was known to be present in the region since ancient days, the drilling of oil wells there is a fairly recent development. The first wells in Iran were not drilled until 1935, and those in Kuwait did not start up until 1946. World War II caused a major increase in drilling in both Iran and Saudi Arabia. In the past twenty years, the wells and offshore rigs there have become very important. Today, about a third of the total oil production of the world comes from the Persian Gulf. The United States, Western Europe, and Japan have come to depend on Arab oil in large part. The United States imports about 40 percent of its annual oil needs from the area, Western Europe about 70 percent, and Japan more than 90 percent.

Ports and Naval Bases. The major oil-exporting ports are Ras Tannura (Ta-nur'-a), Saudi Arabia; Abadan and Kharg (Karg) Island, Iran; Sitra, Bahrain; Das Island, UAE; and, Mina Abdulla, Mina Shauiba, and Mina Al-Ahmadi, Kuwait.

Fishing. The entire Persian Gulf is shallow. Half of it is less than 120 feet deep, and all but a few spots less than 200 feet. Because it is so shallow, sunlight can reach the bottom in most places, causing lots of plankton to live there. *Plankton* are tiny animals and plants that provide food for small fish. Since there is much plankton, a large variety of fish live in the gulf. Sardines, anchovies, mackerel, and barracuda are the main kinds caught by local fishermen. In the waters controlled by Qatar and the UAE are valuable pearl fisheries.

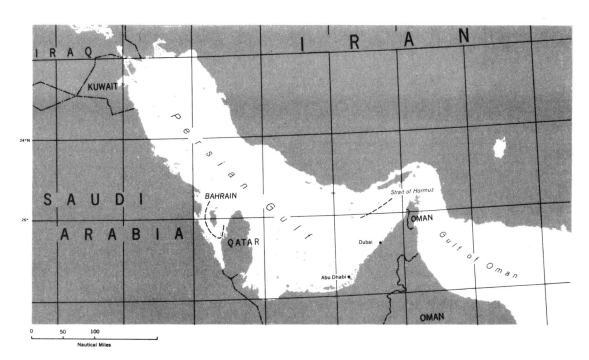

The Persian Gulf and Gulf of Oman. The Strait of Hormuz is a key choke point for all ships entering or leaving the Persian Gulf.

Strategic Geography. While oil is the big strategic resource, the political and strategic geography of the gulf is also important. Acquiring a warm-water port on the Persian Gulf has been a major goal of Russia and the states of the former Soviet Union for the past hundred years. A major political goal of Western nations over the same period has been to prevent this from occurring. Before the fall of the shah of Iran in 1979, that country was an ally of the United States and the West. The United States had sold much military equipment to the shah's army and navy and had trained thousands of Iranian military personnel. Aside from selling oil to the West and even helping to "keep a lid" on the price, the shah also kept peace and security in the Persian Gulf and Gulf of Oman, and he blocked the Soviet Union's attempt to gain a foothold in this area. The United States had helped to build two new Iranian naval bases, one at Bandar Abbas on the Strait of Hormuz and the other at Chah Bahar (Chä Ba-här') on the Gulf of Oman.

After the fall of the shah, however, armed uprisings of various Islamic fundamentalist factions in Iran put the country in chaos, as exemplified by the U.S. hostage situation in 1979–81, followed by a very destructive war of attrition with Iraq that did not end until 1988.

Peace in the area was short-lived, however, because with his forces no longer engaged in the war with Iran, Iraq's leader Saddam Hussein was then free to pursue far more serious military actions two years later, when he invaded neighboring Kuwait. In response the United States and other United Nations (UN) coalition forces conducted Operations Desert Shield and Desert Storm that ultimately forced Hussein's troops out of Kuwait in late February 1991. Ten years later, UN-imposed no-fly zones are still being enforced over northern and southern Iraq, and Hussein has continued to engage in provocative actions that pose an ongoing threat to peace and stability in this area.

INDIAN OCEAN

The Indian Ocean is the third largest in the world. It has an area of 28,400,000 square miles with an average depth of 12,760 feet. Maximum depth is 24,442 feet in the Java Trench southwest of the Indonesian islands of Sumatra and Java on the eastern edge of the ocean.

The main feature of the Indian Ocean floor is a great mid-ocean ridge system, which is shaped like an upside-down **Y**. The Southwest Indian Ridge goes around southern Africa and joins the Mid-Atlantic Ridge. The Mid-Indian Ridge continues south of Australia to join with the Mid-Pacific Rise. Many volcanoes lie along the submarine ridges of the Indian Ocean. Many of the islands in the ocean were formed by active and inactive volcanoes.

Two of the world's greatest river systems, the Indus River of Pakistan and Ganges-Brahmaputra (Găn-jēz' Brä-ma-pōō'-tra) of India, have built huge *submarine fans* into the Arabian Sea and Bay of Bengal. These fans are made up of sediments carried from the Himalaya (Him-a-lā'-a) Mountains in those two countries.

Minerals. Mining in the Indian Ocean floor is becoming more important. Tin ore is mined off the shores of Thailand, Malaysia, and Sumatra in the Strait of Malacca. Deposits of sands rich in rare heavy minerals such as monazite, zircon, and magnetite are mined off Sri Lanka (Srē Län'-ka), the Indian state of Kerala (Kĕr'-a-la), the east coast of South Africa, and near Perth in western Australia. A major oil field also lies off western Australia. Rich beds of manganese chunks have been found on the Indian Ocean floor. Methods are being developed to mine these valuable clusters of manganese, nickel, copper, titanium, and lead.

Fishing. The fishing industry in the Indian Ocean is small, but growing rapidly. It now exceeds four million tons annually. Tuna and shrimp are the main catches at this time, off the coast of India. Japanese, Korean, and Taiwanese vessels are now combing the ocean for these species. Most of the shrimp are canned and sold on the U.S. market. Lobsters are caught off South Africa and western Australia for the U.S. market too. The Indian Ocean catch will continue to grow in value, as fishing and canning techniques improve and the demand for fish protein increases.

Ports and Naval Bases. The United States has built a small communications station and air base on Diego Garcia in the mid–Indian Ocean to support naval communications and deployed Indian Ocean forces.

Strategic Geography. We have already discussed two of the main sea routes in the Indian Ocean. They are the oil routes from the Persian Gulf through the Red Sea to Suez, and along the east coast of Africa and around the Cape of Good Hope. The other major sea-lane is past Singapore at the tip of the Malay Peninsula, through the Strait of Malacca, and across the Indian Ocean to Suez. The Strait of Malacca is a main route between Asia and Europe, and is the route Japanese oil tankers follow from the Persian Gulf to Japan. This strait is one of the key strategic choke points of navigation in the world.

In the spring of 1998 much apprehension over nuclear weapons proliferation in the region arose when India and Pakistan each exploded nuclear test devices. There followed a period of escalating tension between the two nations that might have led to a regional nuclear war but for American intervention in conjunction with the United Nations. The issue of nuclear nonproliferation continues to be a major concern in the area.

In the late 1990s the issue of support of terrorist activities in this region became of great concern, particularly in regard to Afghanistan. Bordered by Pakistan to the south and east, Iran to the west, and in the north and northeast by Russia and China, this poverty-stricken and rugged country became the adopted home of one of the foremost terrorist organizations of modern times, led by a wealthy exiled Saudi Arabian named Osama bin Laden. In the fall of 2001 the country became the scene of Operation Enduring Freedom, in which U.S. and allied military forces joined with Afghan rebels to rid the country of bin Laden's al-Qaida terrorist organization and the repressive Taliban government that supported him.

Principal navies of nations around the Indian Ocean are those of South Africa, India, and Australia. Pakistan has a small but efficient navy. The French also have a naval force in the ocean, based at Réunion, to protect their Indian Ocean interests.

PACIFIC OCEAN

Covering nearly one-third of Earth's surface, the Pacific Ocean is by far the largest of the world's oceans. It covers an area of 64,000,000 square miles with an average depth of 14,050 feet. The deepest part of the ocean is the Marianas Trench, which at 36,161 feet at its maximum depth is also the deepest spot on Earth.

The western half of the Pacific sea floor is complex, with thousands of volcanic peaks, trenches, ridges, and submarine plateaus. Many of the volcanoes are no longer active and are in various stages of erosion from sea and weather action. The tops of these volcanic peaks are the beautiful Pacific islands one dreams about. There are many coral reefs, which teem with colorful marine life. The most famous and largest reef is the Great Barrier Reef, which runs more than 1,250 miles along the coast of northeastern Australia.

The Hawaiian Islands and the Society Islands, which include Tahiti and Bora Bora, are beautiful places. They are the classic South Sea islands of waving palms and white beaches. Many other South Sea islands, however, especially in the Southwest Pacific, are deadly jungles with disease, stifling heat, incessant rains, and few natural resources.

Minerals. Not much mining is done in the Pacific yet, but many large mineral deposits have been located in coastal areas and on the ocean floor. Some tin is mined off the Indonesian island of Sumatra; iron ore has been mined for years off Japan; and mineral sands (titanium, zircon, and monazite) are mined off the coast of Queensland, Australia. There are small working oil fields between Australia and Tasmania and off New Zealand's North Island. Other oil drilling is taking place off the coast of southern California and in the Cook Inlet of Alaska. Phosphates are mined along the coasts of Chile, Peru, and Baja California in Mexico.

There are vast fields of manganese chunks in much of the Pacific. An especially heavy belt extends from Baja California to Hawaii, and from there to the islands of Palau and northward to Japan. It is estimated that this area, nearly 1.35 million square miles, is literally paved with manganese! A number of companies are working to find a cheap way to mine this vast undersea resource.

Fishing. The annual catch of fish and shellfish from the Pacific greatly exceeds that taken in any other ocean. More than half of all the world's catch of marine fish, shellfish, and *crustaceans* (crabs and lobsters) comes from the Pacific each year.

Most fisheries are located within 150 miles of the coasts. The exception to this is tuna fishing, which is carried on throughout the high seas. There are large fisheries for cod, pollock, flounder, rockfish, sea bass, and red snapper all over the Asiatic continental shelf—in the eastern Bering, Okhotsk (Ō-kŏtsk'), Japan, and Yellow and South China Seas. Fisheries for sardines and anchovies lie off Peru, California, northern Japan, and Korea. Pollock and salmon are fished in the Gulf of Alaska and off the coasts of Washington and Oregon states.

There are very important fisheries for shrimp, crabs, lobsters, and squid in the waters across the northern Pacific. Giant shrimp, called prawns, are caught in the Yellow and South China Seas, off northern Australia, and in the Gulf of Alaska. The largest of all crabs, the Alaskan king crab, is taken in the Gulf of Alaska along the Aleutian (A-lōō'-shan) Islands and in the Sea of Okhotsk. These huge crabs sometimes grow to more than three feet from claw to tail. Huge lobsters are caught around most of the islands of the Pacific.

Ports and Naval Bases. The most impressive thing about the geography of the Pacific is its size. Some examples: the distance from the Panama Canal to Yokohama (Yō-ka-hä'-ma), Japan, is 7,680 miles, and to Singapore (Sĭng'-ga-pôr), 10,529 miles; from San Francisco to Manila, Philippines, 6,299 miles, to Melbourne, Australia, 6,970, to Hong Kong, 6,044, to Singapore, 7,350, and to Honolulu, Hawaii, 2,091 miles. From Yokohama to Singapore through the Taiwan (Ti'-wän') Strait is 2,880 miles. Distance, then, is certainly an important factor to consider when discussing Pacific strategy.

In addition to the ports mentioned above, there are many others of importance: Seattle and Los Angeles in the United States; Calleo, the port of Lima, Peru; Santiago, Chile; Wellington and Auckland, New Zealand; Sydney and Brisbane, Australia; Jakarta, Indonesia; Singapore; Bangkok, Thailand; Canton and Shanghai, China; Kobe and Osaka, Japan; Taipei (Ti-pā'), Taiwan; Haiphong (Hi-fŏng'), Vietnam; and Vladivostok (Vlăd-a-vŏs'-tŏk), Russia.

The major U.S. naval base on the West Coast is San Diego, California. Smaller operating bases are located at Seattle. There are U.S. naval shipyards at Bremerton, Washington, and Mare Island, California. Civilian shipyards with major naval ship contracts are in Seattle, San Francisco, Los Angeles, and San Diego.

U.S. naval bases in the Pacific are located at Pearl Harbor, Hawaii, and Yokosuka (Yō-ka-sōō'-ka), Japan. The U.S. Third Fleet has its headquarters at Pearl Harbor. The U.S. Seventh Fleet flagship is based in Yokosuka, where there is a large ship-repair facility with drydocks. There is a large naval air facility at Atsugi, near Tokyo, which is the primary base for support of U.S. naval aviation in the western Pacific. Although most ships in the Seventh Fleet deploy from homeports on the U.S. West Coast, a carrier battle group has maintained its homeport in Yokosuka, Japan, for over thirty years.

The Russian Pacific Fleet has its headquarters at Vladivostok. Other naval bases are located in Nakhodka (Na-khôt'-ka), Sovetskaya Gavan (Sa-vet-ski-ya Gä'-van), and Petropavlosk (Pe-tra-pav'-lofsk). A submarine-building yard is located far up the Amur River at Komsomolsk (Kŏm-sa-môlsk').

The Chinese navy is small but growing in strength. It has bases in a number of Chinese ports, including Amoy, Shanghai (Shăng-hi'), Tsingtao (Ching-dou'), and Dairen (Dī-ren'). The Indonesians have a naval base at Surabaja (Sur-a-bi'-a); the Taiwanese at Kaohsiung (Gou'-shyoong'); the South Koreans at Pusan; and the Thais at Sattahip (Sä'-ta-hēp). The Japanese have a small Maritime Self Defense Force, which is capable of limited operations around the home islands.

Strategic Geography. The U.S. Navy has two main tasks in event of a war in the Pacific: (1) protect the long supply lines to our forces and (2) keep the sea-lanes open to our allies, especially Japan, South Korea, the Philippines, Thailand, Australia, and New Zealand.

Japan is the key to U.S. foreign policy in Asia and the principal nation to be defended in the Far East. Japan's industries and hardworking people make that country the most prosperous in the area. At the same time, the World War II peace treaty prohibits Japan from having armed forces with an offensive capability. The United States, by treaty, is obligated to defend Japan from foreign attack.

Treaties also commit U.S. forces to help our other Pacific allies in the event of aggression. We have strong mutual defense ties with Australia and New Zealand. The United States keeps a U.S. Army force permanently deployed in South Korea. There is always some North Korean threat against this ally, including in recent years the capability to build nuclear weapons. U.S. forces were supposed to be withdrawn in the early 1980s, but this withdrawal has been delayed indefinitely by the North Korean threat.

After the Vietnam War U.S. relations with China steadily improved. Establishment of full diplomatic relations, including exchange of ambassadors, occurred in 1979. A reversal occurred in mid-1989, however. Chinese army tanks and troops brutally attacked students demonstrating for democratic reforms in Tiananmen (Tie-nan'-men) Square in Beijing (Be-jing'). Thousands of the students were killed or wounded; many were later jailed or executed as criminals. The Chinese government later tried to deny that the crackdown ever took place. The incident caused renewed concern over the issue of human rights in China that has persisted to this day.

In April 2001 a U.S. Navy reconnaissance aircraft flying a mission over international waters in the South China Sea suffered a midair collision with an intercepting Chinese fighter jet. Afterward the American plane made an emergency landing at China's Hainan (Hi'-nän') Island south of the mainland. Its crew was detained for the next eleven days until they were released into U.S. custody. This incident caused U.S.-China relations to sink to a new low, but some improvement has occurred since. The military threat posed by China in the region, and the poor record of the Chinese on human rights, will undoubtedly be of ongoing concern to the United States for some time to come.

On behalf of the United Nations, the United States administers the Trust Territory of the Pacific Islands in the central Pacific. The biggest island groups in the territory are the Marshall Islands, Caroline Islands, and Mariana Islands. These islands were taken from the Japanese during World War II. A number of major air bases were built by the Japanese and Americans during the war, but all have been either shut down or reduced to a small size.

In general, the Pacific has been calm in recent years. Smoldering difficulties remain in most Asian nations, however. The United States has to keep alert in the area by having naval forces deployed there at all times.

ANTARCTIC SEAS

The seas around Antarctica are *circumpolar;* that is, they surround the south polar continent of Antarctica. In area they total about 13.5 million square miles. More than half, about 8 million square miles, freezes over each winter, and 1.5 million square miles are frozen year around.

The water and ice boundaries are determined by water movement. There is a rather well-defined zone in which southward-flowing warm water rises over the column of cold Antarctic waters flowing northward. The cold-water portion of the water column is called the *polar front,* and the warmer surface zone is called the *Antarctic convergence.* This convergence is the northernmost boundary of the Antarctic seas, generally about 55 degrees south latitude.

The continental shelf of Antarctica is very narrow. Oceanic basins 13,000 to 16,500 feet deep lie beyond the steep continental slope. The northern edge of these basins is the mid-ocean ridge system that separates the Antarctic from the Atlantic, Indian, and Pacific Ocean basins.

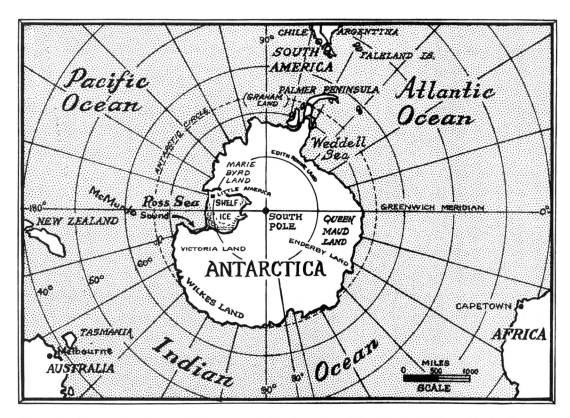

The continent of Antarctica. The continent is completely surrounded by the waters of the Atlantic, Pacific, and Indian Oceans and by the Ross and Weddell Seas.

Minerals. Modern drilling and infrared photography have found many minerals in Antarctica and its surrounding seas, but these deposits are currently too expensive to mine.

Fishing. Whaling was a thriving business in the Antarctic for a hundred years until the early 1930s. Then modern floating factory ships and fast whalers with harpoon guns nearly wiped out the whale population. Only about one-tenth of the original whale population still survives, and a number of species are nearly extinct. The market for whale products has dropped a lot, though, so the demand for whales has decreased. Iceland and Japan still engage in some whaling, under some control by the International Whaling Commission.

There is some harvesting of krill, a name given to small shrimp-like animals that abound in some Antarctic waters during certain seasons of the year. This is of only limited commercial value.

Ports and Naval Bases. The U.S. Navy has a naval research base at McMurdo Sound in Antarctica. It has been manned since the International Geophysical Year explorations in the 1960s. Australia and New Zealand have research sites in other areas of the continent.

Strategic Geography. Antarctica is out of the mainstream of the world's air and sea-lanes. There is little interest in it at the present time, either for resources or for strategic reasons. Exploration and cold-weather equip-

Penguins climb on the ice shelf near the Antarctic peninsula, near the U.S. scientific station at Palmer.

ment testing are now the main activities there. Also, basic research is being conducted on marine life and the weather. Studies indicate that south polar weather and currents have a great effect on many areas of both the Southern and Northern Hemispheres.

Study Guide Questions

1. A. What is the narrow strategic sea located at the southern approaches to the Suez Canal?
   B. What is the key strait at the southern end of this sea?

2. Why is the Persian Gulf important to the United States and its allies?

3. What is the key strait at the southern entrance to the Persian Gulf?

4. What occurred in the Middle East in late 1990 that caused U.S. and allied UN forces to go to war with Iraq?

5. A. List the three main sea routes in the Indian Ocean.

   B. Which one is the main route between Asia and Europe?

6. Which country in the Indian Ocean region received worldwide attention in 2001 because of the 11 September terrorist attack on the United States?

7. Where has the United States built an important base in the Indian Ocean area?

8. A. Which ocean is the largest in the world?

   B. Where is the deepest spot in this ocean, and what is the depth there?

9. A. What formations are found on much of the western half of the Pacific sea floor?

   B. What often forms around the rims of volcanic islands in the Pacific?

10. A. Where is the major naval base on the West Coast of the United States?

    B. Where are major naval shipyards located?

11. Where are the major U.S. naval bases in the mid- and western Pacific?

12. Where does the Russian Pacific fleet have its headquarters?

13. What are the two main tasks of the U.S. Navy in the event of war in the Pacific?

14. Which country is considered the key to U.S. foreign policy in the Pacific? Why?

15. What are present U.S. relations with China?

16. A. Who administers the Trust Territory of the Pacific Islands?

    B. What are its main island groups?

17. What is meant by the term *circumpolar ocean* when referring to the Antarctic seas?

18. A. What valuable Antarctic resource has now been nearly wiped out?

    B. Which two countries still engage in this industry?

19. Where does the United States have a naval research station in Antarctica?

Vocabulary

Strait of Hormuz	krill
Bab el Mandeb	prawns
Strait of Malacca	circumpolar
Marianas Trench	titanium
crustacean	war of attrition
manganese	plankton
Horn of Africa	

UNIT 2

Oceanography

The Navy defines oceanography as the "application of the sciences to the phenomena of the oceans, including the study of their forms and their physical, chemical, and biological features." Simply stated, oceanography is the scientific study of what happens on, in, and under the world's oceans.

Greater attention is now being given to the oceans by nearly all nations, including the United States. Some reasons for this are:

- *Social.* The coastal regions of our nation, which include estuaries, mouths of inland rivers, and the Great Lakes, are major population and job centers. More than 40 percent of the U.S. population lives and works near the nation's seacoasts. The coasts extend some 5,400 miles along the Gulf of Mexico and the Atlantic and Pacific Oceans, another 2,800 miles along the shores of the Great Lakes, and over 2,000 miles along the beaches of Hawaii, Guam, Puerto Rico, and the Virgin Islands.

- *Economic.* The oceans are rich with natural resources, food, and fuel. They are the "last frontier" for many vital materials on Earth.
- *Political.* The oceans link the continents. The world ocean covers nearly 71 percent of Earth's surface. It is a field for much competition between industrialized nations. It provides the sea lines of communication over which commerce between the United States and many foreign nations takes place.
- *Strategic.* The oceans are vital to U.S. defense. The fleet ballistic-missile submarines that operate in them and their intercontinental missiles give the nation its most important deterrent against aggression by nuclear-armed nations around the world.

In this unit, some of the many features of oceanography are discussed. Oceanography spans the past, the present, and the future of our world. It is especially important to a maritime nation such as the United States.

Earth's Oceanographic History

Our study of oceanography will begin with a discussion of the origin of Earth and its seas. Where did it all begin—how and why? A basic idea of how our planet Earth began is essential in our study of the life-giving seas. More about the scientific theory of the formation of the universe and the solar system is given in the astronomy unit (unit 4) of this text.

FORMATION OF THE OCEANS

Modern science has given scientists a good idea of how Earth began. This study is a part of astronomy called *cosmology,* the science concerned with the nature of the universe and its origin. Scientists who study cosmology are called *cosmologists.*

Cosmologists believe that what is now our solar system (the Sun, the planets, and their moons) began about 4.5 billion years ago as a large cloud of gas and dust. Gradually, gravity and centripetal forces caused this cloud to spin and take the shape of a huge disk, with the infant Sun in its center. From time to time, eddies, swirls, and collisions occurred in this disk, causing a number of smaller clusters of materials to separate and whirl in orbits around the large cluster forming the Sun. One of these swirling masses became the planet Earth.

After millions of years of increasing pressure and temperature, metallic crystals of iron and nickel melted and sank toward the core, or center, of the earth. Because of the intense heat created within the earth by compression, molten rock (magma) called *lava* often broke through the surface, either in large cracks in the earth's crust or in active volcanoes that expelled gases and solid materials. The hydrogen molecules, other gases, and water vapor that escaped from the earth gradually rose. The Sun's rays acted on the released gases and soon distributed them around the new planet to form an atmosphere. Meanwhile, the earth continued to contract into a more solid mass, developing what is now the planet's crust.

The intense heat created by the compression of the earth continued to cause thousands of volcanoes to bring lava and water vapor to the surface. Radiation from the Sun also continued to form Earth's atmosphere by breaking up water molecules into separate atoms of hydrogen and oxygen. Because the hydrogen was lighter, much of it escaped into space, while the heavier oxygen atoms were retained in the atmosphere by gravity. Gradually, poisonous ammonia and methane gases in the atmosphere were dissipated by the Sun as both it and Earth cooled. Slowly, the atmosphere cooled enough to cause the water vapor in the air to condense and return to the surface in the form of rain. Falling on Earth's hot surface, some water hissed into steam, joined with new water vapor brought to the surface by volcanoes, and rose to be condensed and fall again and again as rain and, later, as snow.

This continuous precipitation (rain and snow) probably went on for thousands, maybe millions, of years. Finally, about 4 billion years ago, Earth had cooled to about its present size and temperature. Lighter granite (granitic rocks) had risen to higher elevations on the surface, and the heavier basalt (basaltic rocks) sank, creating high and low areas. Eventually most of the low spots in the crust filled with rainwater. These gigantic water pools eventually formed the world ocean—not in the same geographic shape we see the oceans today but, nevertheless, covering about 70 percent of Earth's surface.

The cycle of evaporation and condensation continues today, though now only a small percentage of the vapor ascending into the atmosphere comes from volcanoes and other cracks in the earth. Most of the water vapor today comes from the ocean surface and trapped groundwater, which is heated and recycled by the Sun. Over millions of years, the oceans have overrun some coastal edges of the early continents as the result of wind and water erosion, earthquakes, and landslides in those areas. At the same time, the buildup of polar icecaps has kept an almost constant amount of water in the seas. Ours is a continually changing geologic world. However, these changes happen too slowly to be seen in the lifetimes of humans, except in instances of violent natural change, such as volcanic eruption or massive earthquake.

THE EARTH'S CRUST: CONTINENTAL DRIFT

Earth is made up of several "shells," somewhat like a golf ball. Earth's *core* consists of two parts: a solid inner core of nickel and iron with a diameter of about 860 miles, and a molten outer core of these metals about 1,300 miles deep. Above this is about 1,800 miles of dense rock called the *mantle.* The uppermost layer of the mantle, several hundred miles thick, is called the *asthenosphere.* It is composed of molten rock called magma. The rigid outer crust, the *lithosphere,* "rides" or "floats" on

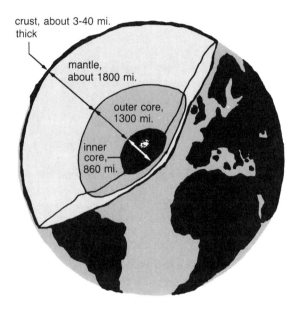

Scientists divide the planet Earth into the crust, mantle, outer core, and inner core. The uppermost layer of the mantle, called the asthenosphere, is composed of magma, or molten lava. The outer, rigid crust is called the lithosphere.

this molten part of the mantle. The crust is Earth's surface, the only part we can easily see. It consists of our continents and ocean basins. With an average depth of about 20 miles under continents, Earth's crust may be as much as 40 miles deep beneath mountains. Under the oceans, however, it is only 3 to 10 miles thick.

The lithosphere, or Earth's crust, is divided into six major *plates* and about a dozen smaller ones. The major plates are the American, African, Eurasian, Indo-Australian, Antarctic, and Pacific plates. Most of Earth's volcanic eruptions and earthquakes occur on the boundaries or *margins* of these plates.

It is not known how many times our planet's plates have separated, come together, and separated again over the 4.5-billion-year geologic history of our planet. This movement of landmasses is known as *continental drift.* This theory was first seriously proposed about 1912. Many studies and modern oceanographic and geologic instruments have, in general, tended to confirm it. In the late 1960s the theory was modified to take into account all major geological structures of the earth. The new theory is known as *plate tectonics.*

Let us trace the probable geologic history of our Earth based on the continental drift theory. After millions of years of pressures and strains, some 65 million years ago Africa and South America had drifted apart. The Atlantic and Indian Oceans had formed, and North America and Europe were about to split, leaving Greenland to stand between them in the Northern Hemisphere. India moved rapidly (relatively) across the Indian Ocean on its 5,500-mile, 180-million-year trip. It would collide with

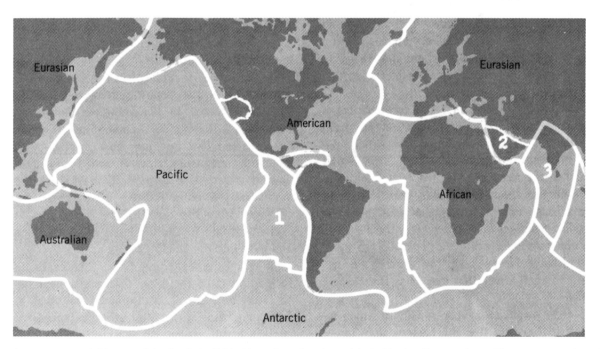

The lithosphere, or outer rigid crust of the Earth, is divided into six major plates, labeled in the diagram above. There are a number of smaller plates also, three of which are numbered in the diagram: *(1)* the Nazca Plate, *(2)* the Arabian Plate, and *(3)* the Indian Plate.

southern Asia and push up the world's highest mountain range, the Himalayas. Australia began to break away from Antarctica and move northward, while the latter continent moved toward the South Pole. The African plate crashed into the Eurasian plate south of Europe and pushed up the Pyrenees mountain range between Spain and France, the Alps in France and Switzerland, and the Apennines of Italy. On the other side of the globe, the Pacific plates pushed up the Andes in South America, the Sierras along the West Coast of North America, and the islands of Japan.

In time the continents gradually took the places on the globe that are familiar to us today. The major ocean basins and numerous seas—once a single ocean mass with one giant continent—now provide the vital sea lines of communication and commerce between the widely separated continents. The globe as we know it today is the result of a geologic process that has taken billions of years and continues even now.

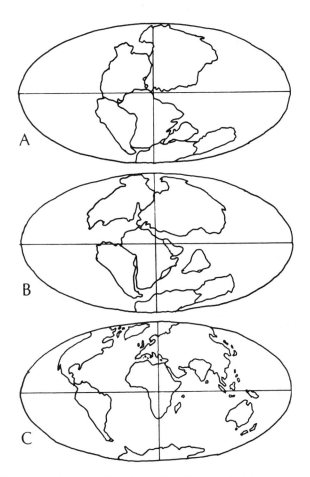

The progression of continental drift. *(A)* The original supercontinent Pangaea, 200 million years ago. *(B)* The world 135 million years ago. Pangaea has split into Laurasia, to the north, and Gondwanaland, to the south. *(C)* Our world today. India has collided with Eurasia, and Australia has split from Antarctica; North and South America have joined in Central America.

THE EARTH'S CRUST TODAY

The evolutionary process just discussed created a global jigsaw puzzle of segments known as *geological plates.* The plates drift over the uppermost, semimolten layer of Earth's mantle like giant chunks of ice, moved by the churnings in the interior. Where these plates come together, Earth and its inhabitants experience the awesome energy of earthquakes and volcanoes. *Seismographs,* modern instruments that measure the intensity of earthquakes, have helped to locate the boundaries of the plates, called fault lines. Also along these boundaries, mountains rise and fall and volcanic islands push up from the sea. The energy released in the explosion of a nuclear bomb is small compared with these huge geologic forces.

Earthquakes. The great earthquake belts that lie along the plate margins are extremely important to sailors and people who live on seacoasts and in harbors. Volcanoes have created new islands and island chains—the Hawaiian Islands, some Aleutian and Japanese islands, and islands in the Caribbean and Mediterranean Seas, among others. In the United States, the entire West Coast is in an earthquake "belt." The best-known feature of this belt is the San Andreas Fault, which runs through the center of California and close to San Francisco. In fact, some geologists predict that all of Baja California and much of the present state of California may someday break away from the North American continent and drift toward Alaska, arriving there in about 50 million years!

But not all such catastrophes will happen in the distant future. In fact, many earthquakes occur daily. Tokyo, Japan, for example, often experiences two to three tremors each day. Fortunately, few are ever felt by people, though sensitive seismographs do record several hundred of them each year. In 1902 Mount Pelée, a volcano near St. Pierre on the Caribbean island of Martinique, erupted with an earthquake and superheated gases that killed 30,000 people within seconds. In 1906 San Francisco was almost totally destroyed by a large quake on the San Andreas Fault. Within the past ten years, devastating quakes have killed thousands of people in Italy, Iran, Yugoslavia, Turkey, Greece, Guatemala, Nicaragua, Mexico, and the former Soviet Union. Another less serious but widely reported quake disrupted the baseball World Series in October 1989 in San Francisco, causing much damage and at least sixty-three confirmed deaths. The largest disaster of all time from a single earthquake occurred in 1976 in Tangshan, China, when almost 700,000 people were reported to have been killed.

Tsunami. When an earthquake happens near or under the sea, ocean waves radiate from the quake's source in ever-widening circles. There may be little movement detected on the open sea, but as these waves reach shallow waters along coastlines, the waves slow down and pile up in huge crests, sometimes more than 100 feet high. These huge waves are called *tsunami,* a Japanese word that means "surging walls of water." These fantastic walls of water can race across the deep oceans at jet-plane speeds of 450 miles per hour (mph) but then slow to 25–30 mph in coastal waters. Tsunami are often incorrectly called tidal waves, but they have no relationship to the tides at all.

The Hawaiian Islands, Alaskan coast, and western Pacific areas are periodically lashed by tsunami that have caused great loss of life. The worst tsunami in the history of the world followed the eruption of the volcano Krakatoa between the islands of Java and Sumatra in Indonesia in 1883. The volcanic explosion blew off 5 cubic miles of rock and sent dust and ash as high as 50 miles into the air. The debris from Krakatoa orbited Earth for several years, sometimes falling as "brown snow" or "dirty rain" (rain or snow contaminated with dirt particles carried aloft by volcanoes or other large explosions). The resultant tsunami, as high as 120 feet, destroyed all life on many nearby islands, and 36,000 people died on Java and Sumatra alone. Another terrible tsunami killed 27,000 people and wrecked 7,000 fishing boats in Japan in 1896, and 5,000 died in the Philippines in a 1976 tsunami.

Study Guide Questions

1. What is oceanography?
2. Why does our government maintain an active program of oceanographic research?
3. What is the scientific theory explaining the origin of the world ocean?
4. How much of Earth's surface is covered by water?
5. Describe the "construction," or makeup, of Earth, listing and describing the major layers from the center outward.
6. What are the names of the six major *plates* of the lithosphere?
7. A. Explain the theory of continental drift.
   B. When did the most recent sequence of geologic events leading to the present continental locations begin?
8. Where is the most famous earthquake belt in the United States?
9. A. What is a *tsunami?*
   B. What events could cause a tsunami?

Vocabulary

oceanography	erosion
cosmology	mantle (of Earth)
asthenosphere	thermonuclear fusion
lithosphere	eddy, eddies
lava	plate tectonics
evaporation	geological plates
condensation	fault line
basalt	seismograph
granite	tsunami
continental drift	earthquake
dirty rain	magma

Undersea Landscapes

For many centuries people believed that the sea floor was simply a deep, smooth basin with a bottom covered with oozy mud. In fact, until the twentieth century, most knowledge of the ocean floor came from the ancient method of heaving a lead-weighted line overboard in shallow water and looking at the mud, weeds, and sediments that clung to the weights when retrieved. People thought that this ooze covered the bottom and "swallowed up" everything—even sunken ships and lost civilizations. It was not until echo sounders and hydrophones were invented by a U.S. Navy scientist to search for submarines during World War I that oceanographers really began to understand that the ocean bottom has just as varied a geography as the land surface. From that time onward, an intense effort to chart the sea floor has taken place.

RELIEF OF THE EARTH

The *relief* of the earth refers to the different elevations and form of its surface, called its *topography*. A *relief map*, for instance, shows the different heights of a part of the earth's surface by use of shading, colors, or numbered *contour lines* (lines along which the elevation is constant).

There are two main levels in the relief: the continents, or continental terraces, including their submerged zones, called the *continental shelves,* and the deep ocean floor. The *deep ocean floor* is also called the *deep sea,* the *deep ocean basin,* or the *abyss.* The deep sea floor is described in terms of the individual features comprising it, such as abyssal plains, oceanic ridges, sea floor fractures, deep-sea trenches, islands, and seamounts. It has an average depth of about 12,000 feet (about 2 to 2½ miles), but there are regions over 7 miles deep. Though 71 percent of Earth's crust is covered by water, just two-thirds of that is truly deep oceanic basin.

Echo sounders (sometimes called fathometers) provide a rapid means of finding the depth of water over which a vessel is traveling. They measure the time it takes sound pulses to travel from the vessel on the surface to the ocean floor and return as echoes. Echoes that bounce back quickly indicate a shallow bottom or per-

haps the top of an undersea mountain. Echoes that take longer indicate deeper water, such as a deep mid-ocean trench. On average, sound travels 4,800 feet per second in water. If an echo takes two seconds to return, then the sound has traveled two times 4,800 feet, or 9,600 feet. Since it is a round trip, half that distance would be the depth of the water—in this case, 4,800 feet.

THE OCEAN FLOOR

Echo soundings have determined that the ocean floor is divided into three distinct areas: the continental shelf; the deep ocean basin, or abyss; and lying between them, the continental slope.

The *continental shelf* borders on continental land areas. Actually, the margins of the continents are under water. The sea, it can be said, spills over the brims of the ocean basins, covering the continental shelves with relatively shallow water. Most maritime nations of the world have agreed that, in a legal sense, the continental shelf is a part of the land out to a depth of 200 meters (about 656 feet). In that shelf area the rights of exploration and use of resources belong to the adjacent continental nation according to international law.

The continental shelf is a gradually sloping sea bottom surrounding all continents on Earth. The shelf generally drops about 7 to 10 feet every mile until approaching the 75-to-100-fathom curve (450–600 feet), and then the slope becomes very steep downward toward the abyss. The average width of the continental shelves is about 42 miles. Off parts of North Carolina the shelf extends out to about 75 miles. In the Barents Sea off the Arctic coast of Russia it extends 800 miles, and off the coast of California it is less than a mile in width. Off parts of Peru and Japan, the plunge begins almost immediately.

The shelves are not always smooth, gradual slopes. They vary from smooth plains to irregular, rough terrain. Many sediments, such as rocks, sand, mud, silt, clay, and gravel, cover the shelves. The most common material is coarse sand, consisting mainly of particles carried away from the continental landmass and deposited by rivers, currents, ice, and wind during the ice age.

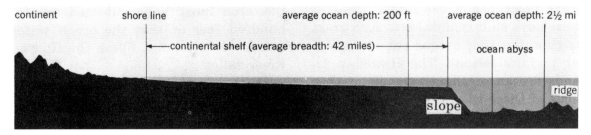

The continental shelf topography as it generally appears off the continental shores. There is some variation in width and smoothness throughout the world. Submarine canyons often cut through the shelf.

Biologically, the continental shelves are sunlit areas that support most of the sea vegetation and saltwater fishes and animals on Earth. Even today, our knowledge about the ocean is mostly limited to the continental shelf regions. It is here that most fishing is done. Exploration for, and production of, oil and other minerals is done almost entirely on the continental shelves. It is here that nations are most liable to confront each other as their growing populations increase their demands for fuels, minerals, and food.

Beyond the continental shelf, no matter how far from the land, the bottom drops off suddenly. This is where the continental crust of granitic rocks ends and the bottom drops off to the sediments on the ocean floor, which has a base of basaltic rock. The sharp descent is called the *continental slope.* Here is where the deep sea truly begins. Oceanographers and geologists have found that the continental slopes generally drop from 100 to 500 feet per mile, but with increasing depth they tend to flatten out and merge into the deep ocean floor.

Humans find this area a bleak and uncomfortable world. There is no light and no plant life. The pressure, cold, and silence increase as one descends. The bottom sediments are mainly mud and clay, with small amounts of sand and gravel. There may be rocks in areas with active volcanoes. In some areas the steepness of the slope is dramatic, as along the western coast of South America, where there is an 8-mile descent from the top of the Andes Mountains to the bottom of the Peru-Chile Trench in a horizontal distance of less than 100 miles.

The continental slopes have some of the most rugged features on Earth. They are scarred with spectacular features like submarine canyons, steep cliffs, and winding valleys. Some places have terraces and plateaus, while others have sheer drop-offs of several thousand feet.

Submarine canyons in the continental slope are similar to canyons found in the southwestern United States. They are often carved out of the shelf and slope by past glaciation, tidal currents, other underwater currents, and landslides. Rapidly moving underwater currents carrying debris and sediments are called *turbidity currents.* They scour the canyon walls much like river or wind erosion does on continental surfaces.

Some submarine canyons are much larger than the Grand Canyon of Arizona. The Hudson Canyon in the western North Atlantic, for example, extends from waters with a depth of 300 feet at the canyon head, 90 miles southeast of New York Harbor, to a depth of 7,000 feet some 150 miles offshore. The 50-mile-long canyon is 4,000 feet deep in places and has a number of big tributaries entering it. It cuts through the continental slope and joins a low spot in the continental shelf that marks the entrance of the Hudson River channel off New York Harbor. The Hudson Canyon is continuously scoured by currents containing large amounts of silt coming out of the Hudson River. The silt is eventually deposited on an enormous plain of mud called a *submarine fan.* Similar fans extend hundreds of miles out to sea from the mouths of other great rivers of the world, notably the Mississippi, Indus, and Ganges.

The ocean floor lies at the foot of the continental slope and is the true bottom of the ocean. The *deep ocean floor* extends seaward from the continental slope and takes up one-third of the Atlantic and Indian Oceans and three-quarters of the Pacific Ocean. They are the last large areas to be explored, truly the "last frontier" on Earth.

Oceanographers have determined that most of the Pacific deep ocean basin consists of hills forming a rough topography, while plains are widespread in the Atlantic. All these plains are connected by canyons or other channels to sources of sediments on land. These sediments are transported by turbidity currents down the slope to be deposited on the plains.

Ocean Ridges. Every deep ocean floor has impressive mountain ranges called *ridges.* The great Mid-Atlantic Ridge soars more than 6,000 feet above the nearby sea floor in some places, and rises above the surface to form islands such as the Azores and Iceland. It extends from north of Iceland to below the tip of South Africa. It continues around Africa and joins the Mid-Indian Ocean Ridge coming down from the Arabian Peninsula. The Mid-Indian Ridge continues eastward south of Australia and New Zealand, joining the East Pacific Rise.

The East Pacific Rise is the main underwater feature in the southern and southeastern Pacific Ocean. Located

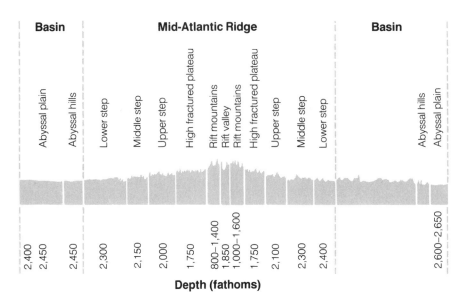

A profile of the Mid-Atlantic Ridge.

about 2,000 miles from the west coast of South America, it runs northward to the peninsula of Baja California. The whole 40,000-mile-long mountain chain is sometimes given a single name, the Mid-Ocean Ridge, although it is somewhat off center in the Pacific. Many underwater earthquakes occur in a *rift* running down the ridge's centerline. Large portions of the major plate margins of Earth's surface lie along the centerline of the Mid-Ocean Ridge.

Ocean Islands, Seamounts, and Guyots. All true *oceanic islands* are volcanic in origin. They differ from island fragments that have broken away from continental masses, such as New Zealand, New Guinea, and Greenland. Almost all of the small islands of the Pacific are

oceanic islands—the tops of former volcanic mountains. When erosion has worn away much of a volcanic peak in the ocean, a strand of coral islands is left around the old volcanic rim. This formation is known as an *atoll*. The central *lagoon* of the atoll is what remains of the old volcanic crater.

In some cases, these coral islands continue to subside and finally disappear beneath the sea surface, leaving what is known as a *seamount.* Many strings of seamounts dot the floor of the central Pacific, the ancient remains of former islands. They are found in all oceans but are most common in the Pacific Ocean.

Scattered underwater mountains with peaks that never reached the surface retain the name seamounts,

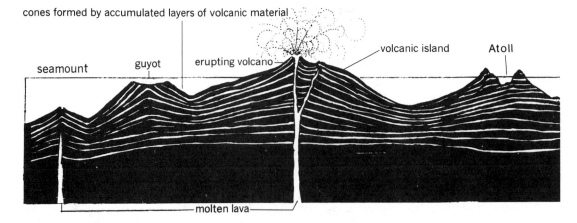

The development of oceanic islands from submarine volcanoes. At the center, the drawing shows a volcanic island with its active volcano. At left is a seamount, an underwater volcanic peak that has become extinct or inactive before reaching the surface. At the far right, the decaying volcanic island has eroded to become an atoll with the crater now a lagoon surrounded by coral-covered island fragments of the crater's rim. To the right of the seamount is a guyot, once an island or submerged peak that had its top eroded away by sea action.

Eruption of Myojin Reef Volcano, 170 miles south of Tokyo, Japan. The lava from this underwater volcano has pushed above the surface of the Pacific to form a new island.

but those with flattened tops are called *guyots*. They have been found in the Pacific but not in the Atlantic or Indian Oceans. The stacking of lava from repeated volcanic eruptions is believed to have created these guyots. Their smooth, flat tops indicate that they were probably leveled off by wave action. It is believed that the great weight of the guyots caused them to sink into the sea floor at the same time as the level of the ocean was rising.

The Hawaiian Islands are a volcanic island chain. Spectacular lava eruptions are regular occurrences from a number of famous volcanoes in the islands. Kilauea and Mauna Loa on the big island of Hawaii are two of the world's most active volcanoes. Mauna Loa lifts its head 13,677 feet above the blue waters of the Pacific. But this is less than half of its real height, for from its base on the sea floor to its lava-covered summit, Mauna Loa measures more than 31,000 feet. Other island chains of this type include the Caroline, Gilbert, Samoan, and Society Islands.

Sediments of the Deep Ocean Floor. The sediments of the ocean floor consist of three general types of materials: oozes, clays, and land-derived muds. The oozes are found in warm, shallower waters and are composed of marine shells and skeletons of minute animals. Equatorial areas and the Atlantic Ocean have concentrations of these oozes. A dark brown or reddish clay is found in the deep, cold parts of the ocean basin. It is made up of airborne, volcanic, and meteorite dusts. Most of the North Pacific floor is covered by this reddish clay. The land-derived muds consist of materials brought down by rivers that flow into the oceans and spread over the abyssal plains by turbidity currents.

Sediment that builds up on the ocean floor does not always remain stationary. On the continental slopes, great underwater landslides occur, especially in earthquake zones. In some areas, slow bottom currents move clay particles for hundreds of miles. Physical obstacles, such as the continental shelf, mid-ocean ridges, submarine canyons and trenches, and seamounts cause channeling and eddying of water flow. These actions result in scouring in some areas on the edge of the abyssal plains and deposits of great thickness in others.

The rate of buildup of the fine sediments on the deep seabed is very slow—about an inch every 2,500 years. Yet in some places the upper levels of the sea contain so much microscopic plant and animal life that the seabed beneath is blanketed with thousands of feet of sediment (ooze) from their remains. Underwater volcanic eruptions spread sediments for miles. Volcanic ash and dust from eruptions on the surface may circle the globe for years before falling again to Earth's surface. Icebergs also deposit sediments in the ocean. River ice and ice formed along the shore will entrap *detritus* (loose material) that gradually sinks to the bottom as the ice melts. Seismic measurements indicate that there is 1,000–1,200 feet of undisturbed sediments in areas of the deep oceans that have a minimum of underwater currents.

Mineral crystals often solidify or encrust around tiny objects on the sea bottom, forming *nodules,* or lumps of metal. The most valuable of these are manganese nodules, which are also rich in copper, nickel, and cobalt. These lumps of almost pure metals have grown over millions of years and literally pave the ocean bottom over wide areas. Some of these manganese nodule beds stretch for thousands of miles across the mid-latitude oceans. They are especially abundant in very deep water in a broad band from California to Midway Island, in a triangular area southeast of Japan, in the Baltic Sea, off the U.S. East Coast, and in a band from Brazil to South Africa.

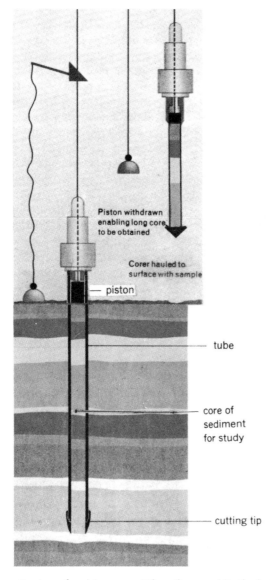

A schematic view of a piston corer. When the corer hits the bottom, the piston stops. The momentum of the tube carries it into the sediment. The piston creates a partial vacuum in the tube so that up to 60 feet of sediment core may be obtained. As the corer is raised to the surface, the sediment sample is held in by clamps that close automatically over the end of the tube.

Research has been under way for years to try to develop an economical means of retrieving this wealth from the deep ocean bed, but because of the great depths involved (12,000 or more feet), it is a difficult task. Those who figure out how to do it will be able to gain untold wealth and much-needed resources for the world.

Coring the Seabed. Most deep seabed samples are taken by coring. *Coring* is done by dropping a weighted tube vertically into the seabed so a cylinder of sediment is trapped inside. It can then be pulled to the surface.

Studying the cores and the shells of tiny animals in the ooze and sediments tells a great deal of the history of that part of the ocean. Fossils give clues about the geological age of the strata of sediments in which they are found. Animal and plant fossils indicate the temperatures of the sea when these living things existed.

The standard piston coring tube cannot penetrate beyond 100 feet into the sediments, and 50–60 feet is the norm. To get greater core lengths, hollow rotary drills are now being used in advanced oceanographic research. The rotary drills can drill in deep water and obtain cores thousands of feet long (in segments).

Deep-water drilling has told us much about the history and composition of the oceans and their sea floors, as well as about the continents of Earth. Such drilling showed that the North Atlantic began to form about 200 million years ago and the South Atlantic about 150 million years ago. Mineral and oil deposits beneath the ocean floor have also been located by deep-water drilling. Deep-ocean cores have confirmed the theory that Earth's surface is made up of moving plates.

Study Guide Questions

1. How did Navy hydrophones open a whole new area of study for oceanographers?
2. What are the two main levels in the relief of the earth?
3. What are other names for the deep ocean floor?
4. A. How does an echo sounder determine the depth of water?
   B. If it takes 5½ seconds for an echo to return to an echo sounder, how deep is the water in that spot?
5. What are the three distinct divisions or areas of the ocean floor?
6. Under international law, to what water depth does a maritime nation have the right to explore and exploit?
7. What is the *continental slope?*
8. Why are the continental shelves the most valuable part of the ocean floor today?
9. What is a submarine fan, and how does it develop?
10. What are the major segments of the Mid-Ocean Ridge?

11. Describe the geologic sequence of events in the "wearing down" process of an oceanic island.
12. What is the difference between a *seamount* and a *guyot?*
13. A. What are the three general types of sediments found on the ocean floor?
    B. Why do sediment thicknesses vary widely from one part of the ocean floor to another?
14. A. How do metallic nodules form on the ocean floor?
    B. What is the engineering problem that must be solved regarding the "mining" of these nodules?
15. A. What is the purpose of a coring tube?
    B. How does it work?

Vocabulary

sediment	submarine fan
ooze	echo sounder
ocean ridge	topography
atoll	relief map
seamount	contour line
lagoon	continental shelf
guyot	continental slope
volcanic eruption	terrace
glaciation	nodules (metallic)
turbidity current	coring tube
submarine canyon	detritus
chasm	abyss

3

Seawater: Its Makeup and Movements

Why is the ocean salty? What elements are in water and in the "salts" of the sea? How do waves, currents, and tides move, and why?

People have asked these questions for centuries. Matthew Fontaine Maury of the U.S. Navy, who is regarded as the founder of modern oceanography, greatly increased our knowledge of the oceans through his studies of navigational charting and of currents, winds, and storms from 1842 to 1861.

Since then, much has been learned about the oceans, but with each new bit of information, more questions arise. The seas are not only beautiful and interesting but also absolutely essential to the very existence of mankind. In addition to the untold wealth beneath their surface and within their seabeds, the seas make possible life itself on our planet.

WHAT IS WATER?

Water is one of the most abundant, widely distributed, and essential substances on the surface of the earth. It is an essential requirement for the cells of humans, other animals, plant life, and even crystals of many minerals. Water has many forms. Ice is water in solid form, clouds (and steam) are water in vapor form, and water in liquid form can be found in any lake, river, or ocean.

Snow is probably the purest natural source of water. Rain is next in purity, although both snowflakes and raindrops are formed with a tiny nucleus of salt or dust. Pure water is a compound of two parts hydrogen and one part oxygen. In chemical terms, this is expressed as H_2O. Only when water is between the temperatures of 32 degrees and 212 degrees Fahrenheit (0 to 100 degrees Celsius) at standard atmospheric pressure is it a liquid.

PHYSICAL BEHAVIOR OF WATER

In large part, the special characteristics of water make life on Earth possible. For instance, most materials expand when heated and contract when cooled. Water, however, contracts until cooled to about 4 degrees C (39.2 degrees F) but then expands rapidly as it freezes, increasing in volume about 9 percent. A milk carton filled with water and placed in a freezer will expand greatly and may split, for instance. A glass bottle will shatter as the ice expands.

If this unique expansion did not take place, ice would sink in water, causing water to freeze from the bottom up. As we all know, however, ice cubes float. More important, ice floats on the surface of the ocean, a lake, or a pond, serving as an insulating barrier and holding the heat in the water below. If this were not so, much of Earth's oceans would probably be mostly ice most of the time, and life as we know it might have evolved very differently.

Another quality of water is its ability to store heat. Only ammonia has a greater heat storage capacity than water. Land, on the other hand, absorbs and loses heat quickly. If the globe were all land, like the Moon, it would be scorching hot every day and freezing cold every night. Not many life forms could survive under these conditions. The vast world ocean, however, acts as an enormous heat-controlling thermostat. It absorbs and loses heat more slowly than the land nearby. Also, because of the great currents in the sea, the ocean can absorb heat in one area and then transfer it to other areas where some of that heat is released.

Those who live near the seacoasts, or the Great Lakes, are well aware of this characteristic of water. In summer weather air temperatures are cooler near the coast than farther inland, where the Sun quickly heats the ground. In winter, because the water retains heat longer, the exact opposite happens: it is warmer near the coast and colder farther inland.

Except under extreme pressure, such as at great ocean depths (or under laboratory conditions), water is not compressible. That is, a given amount of water cannot be made smaller in cubic volume. On the other hand, this liquid can be stirred or mixed easily, and the molecules will readily associate with each other, retaining its liquid form. This means that water can "turn over," allowing the heat from the surface to move into deeper depths, colder water to move to the surface, and water to evaporate from the surface, aided by wind and wave action. These processes of absorption and evaporation are vital to the pattern of world climate and to the transfer of heat from equatorial to polar regions.

Water affects sound and light in important ways, too. The speed of sound in water, for example, is very much greater than in air and increases with temperature, pressure, and salinity (salt content). Of these factors, temperature is by far the most important in affecting the velocity of sound. The optical properties (ability to transmit light) of seawater are of fundamental importance to life in the oceans.

There are many other fascinating facts about water. Besides being essential to all animal and plant life, it is also widely used in science and industry as a solvent, as a blending agent, and even as a standard for certain physical properties. The reference points of most thermometers, for example, are the freezing and boiling points of water. Water is also used as a coolant, a dilutant, a cleansing medium, and in the production of heat and power.

SALTS OF THE SEA

Chemically, seawater is a very pure substance. It is more than 95 percent water, that is, hydrogen and oxygen. About eighty elements are found in solution or suspension in the remaining 5 percent. The two basic elements in this remaining portion are sodium and chlorine, which combine to become common table salt. The most significant of the other elements in seawater in concentrations greater than one part per million, or one milligram per liter, are sulfate, magnesium, calcium, and potassium. The remaining elements are present in extremely small amounts.

The total salt in seawater is expressed in parts per thousand. Ocean salinity varies between 32 and 37 parts per thousand (3 to 4 percent by volume), with open ocean waters usually about 35. (That is, if a seawater droplet were divided into 1,000 tiny parts, there would be 965 parts of water and 35 parts of salt.) The enclosed basins and seas have higher salt concentrations. For example, the Mediterranean Sea has about 38.5, and some areas in the Red Sea, particularly during the summer months, have salinities as high as 41, the highest salinity values in the world ocean. Landlocked lakes that serve as basins for water running off surrounding land, like the Great Salt Lake of Utah or the Dead Sea of Israel, with salinities of 250 and 350, have the highest salt content of any bodies of water on Earth.

How did the ocean water get salty? The early world ocean probably was much less salty than today's ocean, since most of the water came from rains caused by the condensation of steam from escaping water vapors of the developing Earth. But for millions of years, rain and melted snow have been running over the land, dissolving various minerals and carrying them down to the sea.

In fact, the salts of the ocean are the result of over 2 billion years of wearing away of the rocks of Earth's crust. Those materials that are soluble (can be dissolved) remain in the ocean water. Insoluble materials fall to the bottom and form sediments and clays that may eventually turn into sedimentary rocks. Though the process continues, much of the material that runs into the ocean now is from sedimentary rocks that have gone through the cycle before. For this reason, the concentration of salts in the sea is fairly stable now, having changed very little for millions of years.

During all this time, the water of the oceans has been passing through continuous cycles of evaporation and condensation. Every year about 80,000 cubic miles of seawater are drawn off by evaporation. Of this huge quantity of water, about 24,000 cubic miles return to the continents as rain, sleet, and snow. Most of the rest returns directly to the ocean as rain, but 1 or 2 percent remains in the atmosphere as water vapor. Gusty surface winds carry aloft salt from ocean spray, dust, volcanic ash, and even smokestack pollutants that become nuclei for rain or snow. The moisture in the atmosphere is attracted to these foreign bodies. Droplets form and gradually grow until they become so heavy that they fall to the surface as raindrops during the warm months and snowflakes during the cold months.

Water that has evaporated from the surface of the ocean finally returns to it carrying a microscopic pollutant or mineral. This round trip of evaporation, condensation, and return travel to the sea by way of precipitation is called the *hydrologic cycle* (water cycle). (See diagram.) Plants on land also add to the amount of water vapor entering the air by the process called *transpiration*. This is a special term used to identify the evaporation process through plants and trees.

There are nearly 329 million cubic miles of seawater on our globe. The dissolved minerals carried to the ocean in the hydrologic cycle represent fantastic amounts of every known element. In only 1 cubic mile of seawater, it is estimated that there are nearly 165 million tons of dissolved minerals, as shown in the following list:

Sodium chloride (common salt)	128,000,000 tons
Magnesium chloride	17,900,000 tons
Magnesium sulfate	7,900,000 tons
Calcium sulfate	5,900,000 tons
Potassium sulfate	4,000,000 tons
Calcium carbonate (lime)	578,832 tons
Magnesium bromide	350,000 tons
Bromine	300,000 tons
Strontium	60,000 tons
Boron	21,000 tons
Fluorine	6,400 tons
Barium	900 tons
Iodine	100–1,200 tons
Arsenic	50–350 tons
Rubidium	200 tons
Silver	up to 45 tons
Copper, lead, manganese, zinc	10–30 tons
Gold	up to 25 tons
Uranium	7 tons

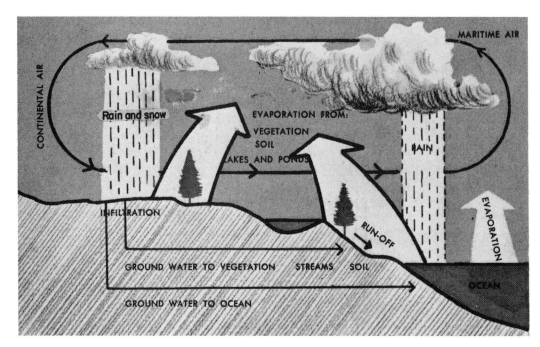

The hydrologic cycle is the continuous movement of moisture by evaporation into the atmosphere, where it condenses and falls back to Earth as precipitation and then returns to the sea. During its journey over Earth's surface, the water dissolves minerals and carries them either suspended or in solution back to the ocean. This explains how the oceans became salty.

Only magnesium and bromine are presently taken from the ocean water commercially. This is because the supply of most of the other minerals is still plentiful from land mining sites, and it would cost too much to extract them from seawater. Much of the magnesium used in the manufacture of lightweight alloys for airplanes and satellites now comes from the sea, however. The bromine is used in the manufacture of antiknock gasoline and other chemicals. Research is constantly being done to try to develop profitable methods of extracting dissolved minerals from the sea. This is an area of oceanography and metallurgy (the extraction of metals from ore or seawater) that will undoubtedly expand as continental mineral resources are used up.

WATER TEMPERATURE

Upper ocean water temperature varies from about 32 degrees F (0 degrees C) in the polar regions to a high of about 85 degrees F in the Persian Gulf. The salinity of seawater lowers its freezing point. We know that fresh water freezes at 32 degrees F; seawater has a freezing point of about 28 degrees F (–2.2 degrees C). On the deep ocean bottom, however, the cold, dense water stays at a uniform temperature of about 4 degrees C (39.2 degrees F) all the time in all latitudes.

An instrument called a *bathythermograph,* commonly called an XBT, can be dropped from ships to check water temperatures at various depths (*bathy* means "depth," *thermo* stands for "temperature," and *graph* stands for

"record"). Most Navy combatants have an XBT to take readings for continuous monitoring of the ocean for undersea warfare.

Ocean water samples can be taken in *Nansen bottles,* named for a Norwegian oceanographer, Fridtjof Nansen. The Nansen bottle is a metal cylinder with automatic closing valves on each end. These valves are linked by levers so they work together. The bottles are attached upside down on a long wire. During lowering, water flows straight through the bottle until it reaches the desired depth. At sampling depth, a weight called a messenger is sent down the wire, releasing the first bottle, which overturns, its valves closing to secure the sample. Another messenger weight, formerly resting on that bottle, then slides down to repeat a similar action on the next bottle below.

As the Nansen bottles capture the water at each desired depth, the mercury column in a thermometer fastened to the outside is automatically fixed. This records the exact temperature of the water when the bottle turned over. In this way, temperatures at any depth in the ocean can be measured. When brought to the surface, the water sample can also be tested for salinity, other chemical content, minute marine life, and so on.

THE COLOR OF WATER

In shallow places, the ocean's water appears light green, while in deeper areas it seems to be blue, gray, or dark green. These are colors seen when the water does not contain silt or mud near shore or the mouths of rivers. The colors change depending on whether the day is cloudy or sunny. Actually, the water itself has no color. What we see as its color is caused by the reflection of the sky or scattering of light in the water. Some ocean bodies have been given their names because they are colored at times by plant or animal life in them, or by colored silt flowing into them. The Red Sea, for instance, is so named because of the red phytoplankton in the water. The Yellow Sea is so named because of the yellow clay silt carried into it by the rivers of northern China.

We know that the main source of energy for life is the Sun. Its radiant energy reaches us after traveling about eight minutes and some 93 million miles through the void of space. Sunlight consists of a range or *spectrum* of different wavelengths of energy. These include infrared, visible, ultraviolet, and x-rays. The different colors of the visible spectrum can be seen by using a *prism,* or they can be seen in a rainbow. The atmosphere serves as a giant filter, keeping out most of the dangerous ultraviolet (above violet) rays. Much infrared light is absorbed by the water vapor and carbon dioxide in the atmosphere. This atmospheric blanket acts like a big greenhouse, keeping in the warmth that helps to sustain life on Earth.

Some of the visible light striking the surface of the ocean is reflected back, but some goes down into the water. As it descends, it changes in quality and quantity. The water acts as a filter also, gradually scattering various wavelengths of light, starting at the red end of the spectrum. Therefore, the deeper one goes into the water, the greater the amount of blue light. The color of the watery world below about 90 feet (30 meters) is a dark zone of blues, violets, grays, and blacks, and nothing else. The depth to which light penetrates varies according to the position of the Sun and the turbidity (suspended materials) in the water.

The oceans can be divided into three environments on the basis of light. The topmost is the *lighted zone,* which ranges in depth from a maximum of about 330 feet (100 meters) in the open, clear sea to about 3 feet (1 meter) in muddy estuaries. Next is the *twilight zone,* which is very dark violet, with only the slightest light penetration. No effective plant production takes place here; this layer ranges from about 260 to 655 feet (80 to 200 meters). Below the twilight zone is the area of total and eternal darkness called the *dark zone.* This is a very thick layer in which no plants grow and animal life consists of carnivores and detritus (particles of plant or animal matter) feeders. This area has no light at all except that which is created by an object or animal itself.

WAVES

Waves in a liquid are caused by any energy source that disturbs the water surface. The energy transmitted by ocean waves can be very great. Blocks of stone weighing more than 1,300 tons have been moved by waves.

Any disturbance, even a raindrop in a puddle, will create ripples of tiny waves. The tsunami waves caused by an erupting undersea volcano, a submarine landslide, or an earthquake can travel all the way across the ocean. Wind, however, is the most common cause of ordinary sea waves. Sailors often call wind-driven waves "sea," or the *state of the sea.* A *swell* is a long, smooth wave coming from a distant storm center. Swells may indicate an approaching storm, and they are common in advance of hurricanes.

As the wind begins to blow over a smooth ocean surface, a certain amount of wind energy is imparted by friction and pressure on the underlying sea surface, causing waves to be formed. Wave height depends on three main factors: wind speed, duration of the wind, and the length of the *fetch* (the distance the wind blows over the water). The longer the fetch and the stronger the wind, the higher and longer the wave will be. At about 13 knots of wind, whitecaps will begin to form. Sea waves 12 to 15 feet high are not uncommon during a strong sea. Waves 25 to 30 feet high or more form during severe storms or hurricanes.

Waves in excess of 50 feet in height are very unusual, although a few are occasionally reported. Years ago the Navy tanker USS *Ramapo* reported a 114-foot wave. What may have been seen and measured by eye in that incident, however, could have been the spray associated with a large, unstable wave. Another huge wave that capsized a fishing vessel was immortalized in the summer 2000 movie *The Perfect Storm.* One of the major difficulties in estimating wave height is the lack of reference points. There is also another factor: the perception of the observer. For example, a small frigate operating with an aircraft carrier will frequently report larger waves than those reported by observers on the carrier.

The storm area of the sea over which wind blows to create waves may extend over more than 2,000 square miles on the open ocean. The larger the wave, the more easily the wind can add more energy to its crest. There is a limit to a wave's growth, however. At the edge of the fetch—that is, where the wind effect on the waves ceases—the waves gradually change into smooth swells.

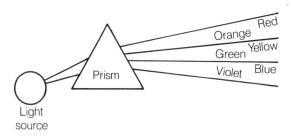

The visible spectrum of sunlight.

Waves are normally described by certain terms. The top of a wave is called the *crest,* while the lowest part, usually between two waves, is called the *trough.* The height of a wave is the vertical distance between the crest and the trough, while the length of the wave (the *wavelength*) is the horizontal distance between two successive crests. The length of time it takes for a complete wave (successive crests or troughs) to pass a given point is called the *period* of the wave. Normally wind waves have short periods, ranging from 2 to 5 seconds. Swells far in advance of a major storm may have a period of from 12 to 15 seconds. The period of a tsunami wave ranges from 10 minutes to as much as an hour.

BREAKERS AND SURF

Waves that break (fall over) when they hit bottom in shallow water are called *breakers.* A line of breakers along a shore is called a *surf,* or *surf line.* There are three kinds of breakers. The kind is determined by the slope or *gradient* of the bottom.

A *spilling breaker* develops where there is a mild, gradual, almost flat bottom shape. The breaker is slight and can be seen advancing as a line of foam toward the beach.

A *plunging breaker* occurs where there is a steep bottom slope, such as occurs with a coral reef a mile or so offshore. Such a gradient creates the often huge surfs off Australia, South Africa, and Hawaii that are the joy of surfers. The plunging breaker creates an advancing vertical wall of water called *surf.*

A *surging breaker* occurs where there is a very steep bottom slope with sudden rock formations such as along the coasts of Alaska, Chile, Norway, Maine, and much of California. These formations are very close to the continental landmass. The waves crash into the bottom rocks, and the breaker explodes in a surge of foaming, turbulent water. It is extremely dangerous to be near such a coastline in bad weather, and it is rarely safe to swim in such areas. Many people are swept into the sea by sudden surging breakers and drowned each year.

Knowledge of sea waves, swell, and surf conditions is crucial to naval and marine amphibious operations. Surf conditions must be predicted accurately in order to determine when troops and vehicles from amphibious landing craft can be safely landed. A four-foot surf is considered to be the "critical" height for normally safe amphibious landings on an average beach. Above that height, boats may *broach*—that is, turn broadside to the beach after grounding. Broaching can cause damage to propellers and bring sand into engine intakes.

BEACH AND COASTLINE EROSION

Coastal landforms owe their shapes to the action of waves, tides, and currents on coastal rocks and sedi-

The state of the expected surf is always an important consideration in the planning of an amphibious assault. Beaching a landing craft properly is difficult when the surf is heavy.

ments. Such wearing down and changing of the coastal outline and makeup is called *erosion.* Repeated ocean action against exposed rocky headlands, and especially sandy shores, constantly remodels beaches and topography near the shore.

In some cases the waves may lift up huge rocks bodily, break off rocky outcroppings, and throw them ashore. At other times the steady grinding of erosive sands wears away sediments and soil, creating cliffs that may eventually crumble. Occasionally whole sand beaches may be washed to sea or moved and deposited elsewhere. People who have had the misfortune of having a beach cottage undermined or washed away on the eastern seaboard or on the Gulf of Mexico during gales and hurricanes know what this means.

Waves and currents produced by waves cause most major shoreline changes. It is estimated that shorelines of the United States are being worn away at the rate of about 1 foot each year. Cape Cod, Massachusetts, may be eroded away completely in about five thousand years if the present rate of erosion by waves continues, for example.

On the other hand, waves and currents cause sediments to accumulate in other places. The great Mississippi River Delta continues to grow into the Gulf of Mexico from sediments carried down the river from interior North America. This endless struggle between construction and destruction of the surface of the earth is one reason that geology and oceanography are so interesting.

In addition to the pounding of water itself against the shore, small fragments of rocks and sand carried by the waves also scour away beaches and wear down the shoreline. Seaward of breakers, fine grains of sand and pebbles constantly move back and forth like sandpaper on a tabletop, in a continual grinding action. Often, this erosion effect is concentrated more in one area of the shore than in another. For example, a line of incoming ocean waves that encounters an island or a landmass jutting out into the sea tends to change its direction of forward motion. The waves align themselves with the bottom contours as well as conform to the general slope of the coastline. When one part of the line develops drag and changes direction or bends because of shallower water, this response is called *refraction*. Such information is very important when an amphibious assault is being planned.

Engineers must also know the way water waves are bent so they can take advantage of natural phenomena when designing structures to protect shorelines and harbors. They must know where the natural energy is concentrated and where it is weaker so they can build for greatest effect and economy.

The most common structure built to protect harbors is the *breakwater*. A breakwater is a line of big rocks, sometimes strengthened by steel-reinforced concrete. It may be a single structure protecting a harbor entrance, or a series of segments that actually create and protect a harbor or an anchorage. In the latter case, there will normally be two or more harbor entrances and exits for shipping. A breakwater is designed to protect ships at anchor or alongside piers in a harbor from waves, swells, or surf.

Another common structure along inhabited seacoasts is the *groin*. Usually built in a series of two or more, groins are walls of stone or wooden pilings built at right angles to a shoreline to prevent erosion by *longshore currents*. Longshore currents are part of the water movement associated with incoming ocean waves. Since water from these waves is continually moving shoreward, there must be some way for this water to return to sea. In many beach areas, this results in some of the water mov-

ing parallel to the beach in a definite flow and speed. Such currents carry scouring sediments to and from the beach out to deeper water. In the process, they may destroy the beach and make real estate along that area nearly worthless. They also sometimes create *bars* that become navigational hazards. Groins serve as dams to stop the movement of sediments by these currents. They may protect a given beach, but such interference with natural processes may also result in more erosion farther down the beach from waves. Careful surveys must be made before such structures are built.

Rip Currents. Rip currents are strong, seaward-moving currents that occur along some shores. They return excess water that has been pushed ashore by strong waves. They occur when a longshore current moving in one direction parallel to a beach hits another longshore current moving in the opposite direction. The result is a strong movement of water outward to the breaker line and even beyond.

Rip currents are often incorrectly called *undertow* (the seaward and downward thrust of a wave as it breaks). But these currents do not actually pull swimmers or waders *down*. They may upset a wader and will pull a swimmer *out* from shore to deep water. Some rip currents are fast, moving at speeds of up to 2 miles an hour.

Rip currents can be very dangerous to those who do not swim or to the swimmer who tries to fight the rip. Even a good swimmer may tire quickly trying to swim against such a current. If caught in a rip, you must not fight the current. Rip currents are rarely more than 100 feet wide, so the best advice is to swim parallel to the

An aerial view of the harbor entrance for Port Everglades, Florida, the port of Miami. Breakwaters of rocks protect the harbor entrance and also serve as groins to keep shifting sands from filling the channel.

shore or breakers until you have gotten past the current. In other words, you should try to swim across the current, getting help from the rip, and using just enough strength to avoid being pulled out to deep water beyond the breaker line. By swimming across the current, you should be able to quickly get out of the main pull of the rip and swim back to shore. You must not panic or struggle and overexert yourself.

OCEAN CURRENTS AND GYRES

The study of ocean currents can be complex. Like everything else in oceanography, new discoveries about the movements of ocean water are being made all the time. The effect that ocean currents have on people, the food cycle, and the weather of the world is profound. We can only introduce this subject here and hope that some students will want to explore this fascinating area of oceanography more on their own.

The movements of the atmosphere (winds) and oceans (currents) are linked to each other. A significant factor in these movements is the rotation of the planet on its polar axis. Earth's rotation, or spin, creates an invisible force called the *Coriolis effect,* or *Coriolis force.* This force deflects moving particles to the right (clockwise) in the Northern Hemisphere, and to the left (counterclockwise) in the Southern Hemisphere.

Two other important factors affect global movements of wind and water. These are (1) wind acting on the water surface, and (2) the boundary effects of the continents. Because of the continents, no major ocean current runs all the way around the world.

The heating of water in the equatorial region causes surface water there to rise and then to spread out and flow "downhill" over the surface toward the poles. (The water level of the Sargasso Sea in the mid-Atlantic east of Florida is actually about 3 feet higher than the water level along the west coast of the North Atlantic basin.) As it drifts toward the poles, this water cools and sinks, pushing the water below it toward the equatorial regions. This kind of circular flow, caused by heat differences within the water, is called *convection.* The more important factor affecting global water movements, though, is surface wind. Combined with the landmass placement, surface wind produces a different system. The resulting surface water movements—ocean currents—are a combination of these two flows.

The prevailing winds in the Northern Hemisphere blow from the northeast in the latitude belt from 0 to 30 degrees. These are the *trade winds,* which drive the ocean surface waters to the west. The prevailing winds in the belt from 30 to 60 degrees north blow from the southwest. These are the *prevailing westerlies,* which drive the waters back toward the east. From 60 degrees north to

the North Pole, the *polar northeasterlies* blow mainly from the northeast, causing surface current movement toward the west (see the global winds diagram).

The combined effect of these winds is to create broad circular currents in the ocean basins in both the Northern and Southern Hemispheres. The movements in the Southern Hemisphere are opposite from those in the Northern Hemisphere because of the Coriolis effect. These circular systems of currents are called *gyres.* (Keep in mind that winds are named by the direction from which they are blowing, while currents are described in terms of the direction in which they are flowing.)

While these major currents are well defined, they continuously mingle with other currents, especially in the subpolar regions. Also, there is a constant exchange of Atlantic Ocean water with the Mediterranean Sea through the Strait of Gibraltar. This is due to the difference in salinity of these two bodies of water, which causes lighter Atlantic water to flow into the Mediterranean basin, while the heavier, saltier water flows out beneath it.

The Gulf Stream. The Gulf Stream is the most important current affecting the United States and its entire Atlantic seaboard. The Gulf Stream system flows in a clockwise motion in the North Atlantic. In the center of this moving water mass is the legendary Sargasso Sea. This is a vast area of floating plants, thought to be true natives of these waters, which float near the surface by means of air bladders. This is not a thick mass of seaweed that traps ships as is so often pictured in mystery stories of the sea. On the average about 3 miles deep, this oval area is about 2,000 miles east and west by 1,000 miles north and south. The blue waters of the Sargasso Sea form one of the oceanic deserts, and the plant species that inhabit this region are adapted to this environment.

The North Equatorial Current carries warmer waters northwestward along the West Indies on the eastern rim of the Caribbean Sea. Part of the current breaks off and enters the Gulf of Mexico. The bulk of it rushes northward to form the Gulf Stream that moves along the Florida, Georgia, and Carolina coasts, and then begins to spread out and turn eastward in the North Atlantic Drift. The water flows northward at about 3 to 4 miles an hour. The stream becomes wider and breaks off into *meanders* (different streams) in the northern latitudes. As it goes along the Grand Banks of Newfoundland, it parallels the southward-moving, cold Labrador Current. The Labrador Current brings icebergs that have *calved* (broken away) from the western Greenland glaciers and drifted into the North Atlantic shipping lanes. Here they meet the Gulf Stream's warm water and eventually melt.

In wintertime the warming effect of the Gulf Stream and North Atlantic Drift make the climate along the eastern seaboard of the United States and Canada, Iceland,

The major ocean currents and gyres.

Great Britain, and Western Europe much warmer than other regions in the same latitude. In the late summer and early fall, the southern side of the Sargasso Sea is the spawning ground for hurricanes, which are severe storms with winds greater than 75 mph. These storms, driven by winds higher in the atmosphere, often follow the Gulf Stream into the Caribbean and the Gulf of Mexico or up the East Coast of the United States. They often leave a trail of destruction before dissipating in the high latitudes of the North Atlantic.

The Kuroshio Current. The Kuroshio or Japan Current originates from the greater part of the (Pacific) North Equatorial Current. Like the Gulf Stream, which flows northwestward on the Atlantic side of the state of Florida, the Kuroshio Current flows northwestward from Japan's Ryukyu Islands.

During the year there are on average twenty typhoons in the western Pacific. Typhoons are the Pacific equivalent of hurricanes. Spawned in the region of the North Equatorial Current, just north of the equator, they often roar along the track of the Kuroshio, particularly during the late summer months, when high-level hemispheric winds flow in a similar pattern. During the cooler months, the typhoon track is through the

The Atlantic Ocean, showing the Gulf Stream–North Atlantic Drift and the Sargasso Sea. The North Atlantic gyre is clearly shown. The cold Labrador Current to the west of Greenland brings down icebergs that have calved (broken away) from western Greenland's glaciers.

Philippines and into the South China Sea and eventually into Vietnam. As the warm Kuroshio Current spreads out north of Japan, it passes south of but close to the cold Oyashio Current coming out of the Bering Sea. The Kuroshio Current travels eastward across the North Pacific and splits into two branches. One of these branches is the Alaskan Current, which travels counter-clockwise around the Gulf of Alaska and westward south of the Aleutian Islands. The other branch becomes the California Current, which travels southward along the west coast of the United States.

Subsurface or Countercurrents. While the frictional force of Earth's winds sets the major surface currents of the world in motion, a counterforce caused by gravity and the Coriolis effect, particularly in higher latitudes, often creates an opposite motion in the deeper water layers.

Near the equator, the deepest water may be moving exactly 180 degrees (opposite) from the surface flow. This amazing phenomenon was discovered in 1952 by Townsend Cromwell, a scientist working with the U.S. Fish and Wildlife Service. He was experimenting with deep-sea fishing techniques.

Letting down long lines into the South Equatorial Current in the Pacific Ocean, a west-flowing current, Townsend discovered that the lines drifted eastward. This indicated the existence of a strong undercurrent. Later research showed that this undercurrent, or *counter-current*, proceeds 3,500 miles to the Galapagos Islands off Ecuador, carrying 30 million tons of water eastward every second.

In 1955 oceanographer Henry Stommel theorized that a countercurrent flowed beneath the Gulf Stream. In 1957 the combined United Kingdom–United States International Geophysical Year (IGY) investigation proved that Stommel's theory was correct.

The oceanographers used in their investigations a floating underwater device called the *Swallow buoy.* Invented by Dr. John Swallow, this equipment can be made to free-float while remaining at any chosen depth. It carries a simple "beeper" or "pinger" that sends out electronic signals that can be picked up by a receiver aboard ship. Using Swallow buoys at different depths, oceanographers found that the Gulf Stream surface current moves about 100 miles a day northeastward, while at depths from 1,350 to 1,500 fathoms, countercurrents move in the opposite direction about 1½ to 15 miles per day. Just above the ocean floor at 1,750 fathoms, the countercurrent was found to move 2½ miles a day in the opposite direction.

The different directions of motion and speed of the surface and the countercurrents create a turbulence between the two layers of water, resulting in considerable vertical mixing. This mixing is particularly strong at the equator, where the two currents travel in nearly opposite directions. As a result, there is an upward transfer of rich nutrients, which is responsible for large numbers of fish in these regions. These distinct layers of water also influence the transmission of underwater sounds, an important consideration in undersea warfare.

TIDES

Earth's nearest neighbor in space, the Moon, is the main cause of the rise and fall of ocean tides. Anyone who has lived by or visited an ocean shore has seen the ebb and flow of the tide twice daily. The ancient Greeks first recognized the relationship between the tides and the Moon's monthly movement around Earth. It was not until Sir Isaac Newton (1642–1727) worked out his theory of gravity in 1687, however, that this relationship could be explained.

Science has determined that everything in the universe exerts a gravitational force or pull on everything else. The pull of gravity is very small for small objects, but for a planet, moon, or star, the force is enormous, tending to pull every other object into its own center of gravity. The mass (amount of material) of the body and the distance it is from the other object or body determine the gravitational effect. It is gravity that holds the planets in their orbits around the Sun and keeps the Moon and Earth "tied" together as companions in space.

The pull of the Moon's gravity causes the oceans on the Moon's side of Earth to bulge out toward it. The gravitational pull, however, is not the same everywhere. The points of Earth closer to the Moon are pulled more strongly, and those farther away are pulled less. This effect, in addition to an outward centrifugal force on the far side of Earth caused by the rotation of the Earth-Moon system about their common center of gravity, causes the water on the far side of Earth to bulge outward as well, though not as much as on the near side.

The Sun also causes tides, but this effect is only about two-fifths as strong as that caused by the Moon. Though it is of course much more massive than the Moon, the Sun's effect on tides is smaller because it is 390 times farther away.

The variations in position of the Sun and Moon in relation to Earth produce the high and low ranges of tides. At times of the new and full moons, the tides are highest and lowest because the forces of the Moon and Sun are working together. The result is *spring tides.* (The term has nothing to do with the spring season.) Halfway between the new and full moons, when we see the half moon during the first and third quarters, the tidal forces of the Moon and Sun are opposed. At this time the difference between high and low tides is much less. These are called *neap tides.*

The *ebb* of a tide is the fall of the tide, that is, the moving of the tide away from the shore. The *flood* of the tide

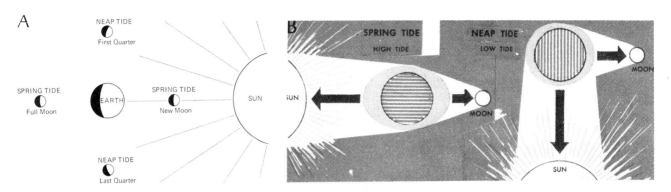

In diagrams *A* and *B* the positions of the Sun and Moon are illustrated when they exert maximum and minimum forces on Earth's tides. When the Sun and Moon are in line with each other, their combined gravitational pull results in the largest tidal ranges, known as spring tides. When the Sun and Moon are at right angles in relation to Earth, their combined gravitational pulls tend to reduce tidal ranges to a minimum, resulting in neap tides.

is the rise of the tide, or the flowing of the tide toward the shore to its highest point. The ebb and flood of tides vary widely around the world. They are affected not only by basic gravitational forces but also by the location of the continents and mid-ocean ridges, the shape of the shoreline, the frictional drag between the water mass and the seabed, and the Coriolis force created by Earth's spin. Each tidal system is restricted to its own ocean basin by the continents.

Time and Tides. High tides occur twice a day in most parts of the world because, as mentioned earlier, when it is high tide on the side of Earth nearest the Moon, there is also a lower high tide on the opposite side of the Earth. Knowing that Earth turns on its axis once in twenty-four hours, we might presume that these high tides would be exactly twelve hours apart. However, the Moon and Earth are not in a fixed position relative to each other. The Moon revolves around Earth once in about twenty-seven days, in the same direction as the Earth rotates. Because of this motion, it takes twenty-four hours and fifty minutes for a given location on Earth to again be directly opposite the Moon. Therefore, there are twelve hours and twenty-five minutes between high tides.

Because these facts are known precisely, *tide tables* for each harbor on Earth can be accurately predicted for many years in advance. The National Ocean Service (NOS), a division of the National Oceanic and Atmospheric Administration (NOAA), publishes *Tide Tables* and *Current Tables* to assist mariners sailing in most parts of the world. Times of high and low tides figured from these tide tables normally are published daily in the *plan of the day* aboard ship and at naval bases. This information is important in port because responsible officers and the deck department can use it as a guide when providing for slack in a ship's mooring lines. The ship's navigator must also be aware of tidal changes in harbors and channels because variations in water depths may be ex-

treme. If tidal currents are strong, boat officers and coxswains must take such information into account when planning boat runs and schedules.

Height and Speed of Tidal Currents. The tides in mid-ocean are measurable only with scientific instruments and may have a height of only a few feet. On the shorelines, however, the effect of tides is usually easy to see. In Boston, the range is about 12 feet, in Norfolk less than 6, and in the Mediterranean only a few feet. In some areas of the world, though, tidal effects are extreme. This is especially so in the high northern latitudes. The highest tides in the world are experienced in the Bay of Fundy, between Nova Scotia and the Canadian mainland, where the spring tide often exceeds 50 feet. Another very high tide occurs at the island of Mont-St.-Michel, France, on the English Channel. This island is surrounded by 10 miles of sands at low tide, but when the 41-foot tide rises, the water moves toward the shore at a rate of 210 feet per minute and completely surrounds the island. Very high tides are also experienced in Alaska, northern Europe, and the northeastern coast of Asia. The harbor at Inchon, Korea, for instance, must enclose its piers with *graving basins* or *docks.* This is a system of locks that hold in the 40-foot tidal waters during low tide, thereby keeping ships alongside the piers afloat. Were it not for the graving docks, the ships would hit bottom and be damaged severely.

Tidal Currents and Bores. In areas where a high tide is common, a *tidal bore* or *tidal surge* is often a twice-daily event where the tide sweeps up a river whose mouth opens directly on the sea. The world's highest tidal bores sweep up the Amazon River in Brazil and the Hangchow (Tsientang) River in China. These bores rise from 15 to 25 feet and speed up the rivers at 10–16 mph. The Amazon tidal bore affects the river more than 300 miles inland. Many rivers in Scotland, England, Norway, and Alaska have tidal bores. The River Severn in England has a

3-foot bore that travels 21 miles inland. The Petitcodiac River in Nova Scotia, Canada, has a bore wave 5 feet high that travels 50 miles inland.

Dangerous *tidal currents* occur in places where there are big inlets with narrow entrances. This occurs with some fjords (long narrow inlets from the sea) in Greenland, Norway, Alaska, and Chile. Currents rushing past at 8 or 10 knots make it much too dangerous for boats and ships to attempt passage during much of the day. Tidal currents surge at speeds up to 10 knots through channels in the Great Barrier Reef northeast of Australia. The meeting of tidal currents and winds of the Atlantic Ocean and the North Sea in the Pentland Firth between northern Scotland and the Orkney Islands creates a bore sometimes 10 feet high.

Many sailors have lost their lives in the Pentland Firth bore (called the Swelkie by local Scots) since the days of the Vikings. The firth is said to be haunted by the ghosts of the drowned, who howl and call out with the strong northwest winds to sailors passing by on dark winter nights.

TIDAL ENERGY

Tidal energy is one of the oldest forms of energy used by humans. A tidal mill built in the Deben *estuary* (a wide part of a river where it joins the sea) in Great Britain was mentioned in records as early as 1170 and is still in operation. Creative engineering has resulted in a large number of schemes that make the tides a reliable source of energy.

Tidal energy requires large capital investments, but once built, tidal power installations may last much longer (with small maintenance costs) than thermal or nuclear power stations. Favorable tidal conditions for such power plants exist at many locations in France, and in Brazil, Argentina, Australia, India, Korea, Canada, China, Russia, and some other countries. The French built the world's most highly successful tidal plant near St. Malo at the mouth of the Rance River estuary. A dam containing turbines spans the estuary. As the tides rise and fall, they spin turbines that drive banks of generators. The idea is simple: dam in a basin, which fills with the incoming tide, then, at low tide, release the water through sluice gates (regulated-flow channels or gates) so it can spin turbines and generate electricity.

The Dutch have worked for centuries reclaiming land from the sea with dikes and pumps. Their biggest project was the enclosure of the Zuyder Zee. Another was the Delta Estuary Plan across estuaries of the Rhine, Meuse, and Scheldt Rivers, completed in 1978. One part of this system generates electricity by tidal flow. At the same time, the project creates freshwater lakes for recreation, reduces and protects the amount of shoreline di-

rectly exposed to the storm waves of the North Sea, reclaims land from the sea, and creates a coastal highway system that connects many previously isolated islands in southern Holland.

Study Guide Questions

1. Who is the founder of modern U.S. Navy oceanography?
2. What is unique about the cooling and freezing of water?
3. How does the ability of water to store heat make life possible on Earth?
4. A. What are the four main elements in seawater?
   B. What is the percentage of salt in open ocean water?
5. A. What are the saltiest bodies of water in the world ocean?
   B. In landlocked lakes?
6. How did the ocean water get salty?
7. Describe the *hydrologic cycle.*
8. What two minerals are extracted from seawater on a commercial basis?
9. A. What is the freezing point of seawater?
   B. What is the constant temperature of water in the deep sea?
10. What determines the color of water (as seen by the human eye)?
11. What is the most common cause of ocean waves?
12. Upon what three things does wave height depend?
13. What are the parts of a wave?
14. What are the three kinds of *breakers*, and what determines each?
15. A. Why are surf and swell so important to amphibious operations?
    B. What is meant by "critical" height of surf?
16. A. What water actions reshape coastal landforms?
    B. What is such action called?
17. What is the main type of structure built to protect harbors from the sea called?
18. A. What is a *longshore current?*
    B. What type of structure is built to prevent erosion from these currents?
19. A. What is a *rip current,* and how may it affect swimmers?
    B. How should a swimmer move to get out of a rip current?
20. A. What force, caused by Earth's rotation, affects the major currents of the world ocean?
    B. In what direction does this force deflect major currents north and south of the equator?
21. What very important current affecting the United States originates on the southern border of the Sargasso Sea?

22. A. Which current brings icebergs into the North Atlantic shipping lanes?
    B. How does the Gulf Stream affect icebergs?
23. A. What important current in the North Pacific has many similarities with the Gulf Stream in the North Atlantic?
    B. What severe storms originate in the same general area as does this current?
24. A. How do deeper water layers often move in relation to the major surface currents?
    B. What are these subsurface currents called?
25. A. What is the main cause of the ocean tides?
    B. How does the Sun affect the tides?
26. When are tides highest and lowest, and what are these tides called?
27. A. How do naval personnel find out about the tidal situation in their port of call?
    B. Which persons aboard ship are particularly concerned about the tides? Why?
28. Where do the world's highest tides occur?
29. A. What is a *tidal bore*?
    B. Where do the highest tidal bores occur?
30. What is the general theory of operation of a tidal power plant?

Vocabulary

thermostat
absorption
suspension
broach (boat)
refraction
breakwater
longshore current
groin
soluble
hydrologic cycle
transpiration
bathythermograph
Nansen bottle
spectrum
prism
ultraviolet
infrared
graving basin
crest (wave)
trough (wave)
fetch (wave)
surf

wavelength
salinity
breakers
rip current
Coriolis effect
gyre
Gulf Stream
calving (iceberg)
Sargasso Sea
countercurrent
Swallow buoy
tide
spring tide
neap tide
ebb and flood tides
tidal bore
swell
period (wave)
fjord
estuary
turbine
sluice

4

Life in the Seas

So far in this unit we have talked about some physical, geological, and chemical aspects of oceanography. There is a fourth major scientific area: biology. *Marine biology* deals with the living, or organic, content of the sea—its plants and animals.

There are many separate areas of study within modern marine biology, and we cannot explore them all in this text. One important field is biological oceanography, or marine *ecology*. This field is concerned with marine organisms and their environment. It is directly related to (1) human use of the sea for food and employment, and (2) the effect of marine life on naval operations. This latter includes how marine organisms affect ships, installations, and equipment; the ability of people to live and work on and under the sea; the effectiveness of sonar equipment; and many other important things.

PLANKTON, START OF THE LIFE CYCLE

Plankton, both plant and animal, are those billions of tiny floating organisms that wander with the ocean currents or drift in the uppermost layers of the sea. The plankton provides the "ocean pasture" for the smallest animals and fish. Materials in suspension in the sea, including decayed plant and animal life, provide the nutrients plankton need.

Phytoplankton are microscopic marine plants that start the food chain, an ecological system in which almost every form of life becomes the food for another, usually higher, form of life. Next are the *zooplankton,* tiny animals and larvae of larger sea life. Finally there is a whole range of larger fish and sea animals, which extends from fishes and crabs to the giant blue whale, the world's largest mammal.

To show how small plankton are—and to see if enough could be gathered for a meal—explorer Thor Heyerdahl dragged a plankton net behind his balsawood raft, *Kon-Tiki,* for many hours across the southern Pacific in 1947. He managed to gather a small amount of edible plankton, which he made into a sort of fish paste. He found it to be very salty. Studies have now proved that this material is almost pure protein. In fact, the sea is be-

lieved to contain a large percentage of the world's total protein supply.

Upwelling, El Niño, and La Niña. Upwelling is the movement of deeper layers of water toward the surface. This happens when prevailing winds along a shore cause movement of upper water layers away from the coast. The Coriolis force is also a factor in this process. The resultant vertical circulation from great depths brings decayed materials high in nitrogen and phosphates to the surface. Upwelling occurs near the steepest gradient of the continental slope.

The most remarkable upwelling occurs along the Peruvian coast between the shoreline and the northward-flowing Humboldt Current. The nutrients and minerals nourish plankton, which, in turn, attract great numbers of fishes, large and small, to the area. Great flocks of seabirds feed on these fish, and the islands on which the birds nest are covered with tons of their droppings, called *guano.* Over 330,000 tons of guano are "mined" annually for high-grade fertilizer. Fishermen catch up to 100,000 tons of anchovies and sardines and the larger fish that feed on them each year.

Every now and then, for reasons not yet fully understood but probably related to reduced trade winds, the Humboldt Current meanders from its normal course or actually disappears, allowing warmer currents to come along the coast and make the surface layers of water warmer than usual. This stops upwelling, and without the life-supporting nutrients, fish begin to die. Additionally, millions of sea birds may die in such famines. The hydrogen sulfide from the decaying bodies of both fish and birds is so thick that ships' hulls are turned black. This occurrence is locally called the *Callao Painter,* named after the nearby port of Callao, Peru. The phenomenon that causes upwelling to stop is called *El Niño* ("little boy" in Spanish). The El Niño effect results in unusually warm surface waters in the Equatorial Pacific. For marine life, it is one of the most destructive oceanographic conditions in the world. It can also cause dramatic climatic changes in Central and North America and elsewhere.

The most recent and severe episodes of the El Niño effect occurred in the winter of 1997–98. During this time sea life in the area off western South America was reduced by about 20 percent. Severe flooding occurred across South America and the southern United States, and Australia and parts of the central United States experienced hotter conditions and severe drought.

A related effect called *La Niña* ("little girl" in Spanish) usually follows when the El Niño subsides. The La Niña effect results in unusually cold surface waters in the Equatorial Pacific. Resulting global climate changes tend to be opposite those associated with El Niño. In the continental United States, during El Niño years temperatures in the winter are warmer than normal in the North Central States and cooler than normal in the Southeast and the Southwest. During a La Niña year, winter temperatures are warmer than normal in the Southeast and cooler than normal in the Northwest.

The Red Tide and Black Sea. In the Red Sea, atmospheric and sea conditions similar to El Niño occasionally occur. There, when the upwelling of cool water stops, the surface layers become heated and bring about a population explosion (or bloom) of tiny red-colored phytoplankton called *dinoflagellata*. They become so numerous that the water takes on a reddish color, giving it the name *Red Tide* (and giving the Red Sea its name). The Red Tide clogs the gills of fish, causing them to suffocate and die. Millions of dead fish are washed ashore, and the resulting stench carries for miles. A similar event occurs, more rarely, along the east coast of Florida. Some years ago, many resorts and bathing beaches had to close down until the Red Tide passed and the dead fish were cleared away.

The Black Sea is essentially a very large saltwater lake. Its only opening is through the Turkish straits (Bosporus and Dardanelles) to the Aegean Sea. The straits are very shallow, so there is little exchange of water between the two seas, and no chance for upwelling or the introduction of dissolved oxygen in the Black Sea. As a result, the Black Sea is stagnant. The residue of marine life in the surface layers sinks to the bottom and remains there to decay.

The decay of animal and vegetable matter uses up whatever oxygen is available and creates hydrogen sulfide gas. Over thousands of years, this gas and lack of oxygen have completely destroyed bottom life in the Black Sea. The hydrogen sulfide layer begins about 200 feet below the surface and continues to the bottom. There is no life in this "black zone," which has given its name to the sea.

For navies, the Black Sea poses a special problem. Hydrogen sulfide gas, when mixed with water, has a corrosive effect on metals. Recall the *Callao Painter* turning the sides of ships black. A submarine operating for long periods of time in the hydrogen sulfide zone would run a serious risk of ruining her hull fittings, thereby endangering the boat and her crew.

THE FOOD CYCLE IN THE SEA

Life in the ocean may answer many of the questions about the origin of life and its historical past, as well as help solve the problems of improving human life in the future. The life cycle in the sea is of great importance to everyone. Marine biologists are the scientists who are working to find the answers to some of these questions.

The life cycle is the chain of natural events in which organic plants and animals take in foods and chemicals, release wastes during their lifetimes, and then die and decompose. Bacterial, current, wave, and solar (Sun) energy rotate this material from the bottom of the sea, bringing it back into the sunlight where the process of photosynthesis regenerates new life.

In the sea, as on land, sunlight supports the life cycle. It does so through the process of *photosynthesis*, the manufacture of food in a green plant. In the sea, floating chlorophyll-bearing (green-colored) phytoplankton are the basic food producers of the sea. They provide the proteins, starches, and sugars necessary to support the sea's smallest life. Phytoplankton are the food for the zooplankton, tiny animals of many shapes, which are either free-floating or self-propelled. The zooplankton—which also include the eggs and larvae of some larger fishes—are the food for small flesh-eaters (carnivores) of the ocean. In turn, the small carnivores are eaten by larger ones. Death and decay complete the cycle. The organic material of both plants and animals decays as the result of bacterial action, thereby releasing again the

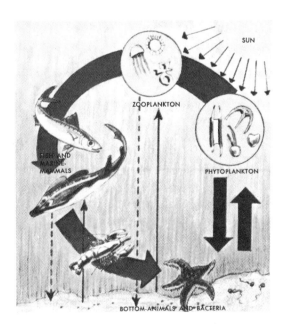

The life and food cycle in the ocean. Beginning with the phytoplankton, which live on the nutrients and decayed matter from the sea bottom that upwell into the lighted zone, the cycle moves around to where dead animals drop to the bottom, providing the matter upon which phytoplankton live, to begin the cycle anew.

nutrient raw materials—carbon, phosphorus, and nitrogen—needed to start the process of photosynthesis over again. Since the organic material sinks, most of the decay occurs in deep water. Upwelling currents eventually return the nutrients to the lighted zone in the upper 15–20 fathoms of water where this life cycle can begin again.

Though phytoplankton can live only in the lighted zone, usually in the upper 90 feet, zooplankton and larger animal life have been found in all parts of the ocean, including at the bottom of the deepest part of the 35,800-foot-deep Mariana Trench. Animals that live in these great depths are generally small, ferocious carnivores. They have very soft, scaleless bodies with a wide variety of shapes. They are often snakelike with narrow fins and very pliant bones, and most are black in color because of the dark environment. Many have developed long, needle-sharp teeth and huge mouths. Others are blind because they have no need for eyes in the pitch-black world of the abyss. Still others have large bulging eyes, and many have luminescent spots and devices that glow in the dark. This natural luminescence (light) is believed to attract prey, their mates, or both. Much has yet to be learned about these strange deep-sea animals.

At the shoreline, creatures of the sea live under very difficult conditions. They are subject to the extremes of drying, flooding, baking, and freezing if they are exposed when the tide rises and falls. Waves and currents may also wash them up on the beach to die. And, of course, there are many predators that can get them when they are exposed. Many sea animals that live on the edge of the sea are small, flat, or streamlined, and many have suction-type devices that hold them tightly to rocks. Starfish have hundreds of such suction cups on their five arms. Barnacles attach to underwater surfaces and excrete a chemical that acts as a cement to keep them in place the rest of their lives.

Other marine life is found in tidal pools and hollows of rocks and coral where they are sheltered from predators, and yet have life-sustaining water around them even when the tide is out. In this category are some corals, sponges, sea anemones, sea cucumbers, and sea urchins. Others live on the beaches and burrow into the sand for protection when the tide is out. Able to remain in the air from one high tide to the next, this type includes some crabs, clams, sandworms, and sand dollars, among many others.

LIFE IN THE SHALLOW SEA

Most sea animals live in the relatively shallow water seaward of the low tide level above the continental shelf. Over much of the continental shelf, marine plant life (phytoplankton) is able to float, or in some instances to attach itself to the bottom and remain within range of sunlight. The plants vary in size from microscopic single cells such as algae and diatoms to huge seaweed plants called *kelp,* which may be 150 feet long. Algae are the most common of all plants. They are a number of different colors; some float, and others attach themselves to rocks. There are also some grasslike plants. In general, however, the sea does not have the wide variety of plants found on land or the advanced members of the plant family like trees or flowering shrubs. Much of the sea and the sea floor, in fact, is barren.

Where plants exist, however, there will normally be an abundance of animal life. The smallest animals of the zooplankton group are the one-celled *protozoans.* Jellyfishes are the largest form of zooplankton. These are beautiful, transparent creatures composed of many white, blue-green, and blue cells, but they often have stingers by the thousands on their lacy tentacles that can cause extreme pain, convulsions, and, if one panics, even death. Others in the group of tiny animals that live off phytoplankton are the larvae (young forms) of oysters, snails, and sea worms. More developed animals are the crabs, shrimps, lobsters, clams, oysters, squid, mussels, octopi, and scallops. These animals eat the smaller species of zooplankton and graze upon phytoplankton. Starfish and sea urchins dine on shellfish such as oysters and clams.

MARINE ANIMALS

There are two major divisions of marine animals: those that do not have jaws, and those that do.

Only two types of jawless fish exist—the hagfish and the lampreys. Their mouths are circular and are used to attach to their prey. The hagfish feeds on dead or dying animals, but lampreys attach themselves to living fish, using their rasping tongues to make open sores from which they feed on blood and tissue. The sea lampreys in the Great Lakes have caused great damage to the lake trout and whiting fisheries, but in the oceans they are insignificant. The lampreys entered the Great Lakes via the St. Lawrence Seaway, illustrating how human endeavors can in some instances upset an ecological system.

Jawless fish. A sea lamprey attacking a lake trout in the Great Lakes. Lampreys attach themselves to living fish, using their rasping tongues to make open sores from which they feed on their host's blood and tissues. Courtesy Great Lakes Fishery Commission

There are four groups of marine animals that have jaws: fish, reptiles, birds, and mammals. Fish range throughout the seas, but most live in the shallow, warmer seas. Within this group are five subgroups: (1) bottom-living fishes of both shallow and deep seas, which have large heads and whip tails; (2) large carnivorous fishes with tough, leathery skins and sharp cutting teeth, such as the sharks and rays; this group includes the largest fish—the whale shark, basking shark, and manta ray; (3) sturgeons, which have bony plates on the skin and are commercially valuable for their eggs, called caviar; (4) the largest group, which includes most commercial fishes, such as cod, herring, turbot, salmon, tuna, mackerel, flounder, bass, and many others; and (5) lungfish, three of which are freshwater types, and one called the *coelacanth*. This oddity, once thought to have died out some 50 million years ago, was found in the Indian Ocean in 1938. An occasional specimen has been caught from time to time since.

The reptile group has only a small number of species that live in the sea today—a far cry from the Age of Reptiles, when they were the dominant form of life in the world ocean. Reptiles are cold-blooded. That means they cannot regulate their temperatures as mammals do, so they usually inhabit warm tropical seas. There are four groups of living marine reptiles: turtles, marine iguanas, sea snakes, and a few ocean crocodiles.

Sea turtles grow to a huge size. The rare leatherback sometimes exceeds 6 feet in length and weighs over half a ton. Turtles swim with flippers. They come ashore to lay their eggs in holes dug in the sand. There, they are at the mercy of many different kinds of predators. Few of the young make it back to the sea before being eaten by seabirds.

Marine iguanas live only in the Galapagos Islands of Ecuador, off the west coast of South America. They are the only marine lizards. They live in large herds on the rocks near shore and feed on seaweed.

Sea snakes are poisonous, some related to cobras and kraits. They have paddlelike flat tails so they can swim. They inhabit sheltered coastal waters, especially near river mouths, and some live in brackish water upstream. There are nearly fifty species of these poisonous snakes living in the tropical Pacific and Indian Oceans. They range from East African waters throughout southern and Southeast Asia, Oceania, Australia, and in the warm Japan Current all the way north to Japan and Korea. A few species exist along the Pacific coast of Central and South America. Although sea snakes are poisonous, they do not disturb swimmers and are said not to bite unless forcibly restrained. They feed on fish, mostly at night. This makes them dangerous to fishermen who may net them when they are attracted by schools of fish and the lights of fishing boats. Asian fishermen are said to throw them from their nets with bare hands. There are a number of deaths caused by sea snakes each year.

The seabird group includes a number of different species. The waders live and feed along the shallows, in estuaries of rivers affected by tides, in ponds, and in mangrove swamps. Birds of the open sea, such as the albatross and petrel, live most of the time in the open ocean, coming ashore only to breed. The emperor penguin lays its eggs on sea ice in Antarctica. It is the only bird that never comes ashore. There are many other varieties of penguins, all of them in the Southern Hemisphere. Seabirds feed mainly on fish. As penguins cannot fly, they catch fish by diving and swimming. Pelicans and gannets catch them by diving. Gulls and terns spot and then pounce on their prey from the air.

The mammal group has a limited number of marine species, but they are some of the world's most interesting animals. They include the polar bear and sea otter, which are similar in most characteristics to land animals but are adapted to the sea. The polar bear has extra-long legs, which makes it a powerful swimmer, and a thicker coat, which insulates it against the icy waters and winds of the Arctic. There are only about 2,000 polar bears living in the wild today because of overhunting.

The sea otter has webbed feet and is well adapted to life in the sea. It inhabits only the coastal regions of California and Alaska, where it feeds in the giant kelp beds on abalone and sea urchins. The sea otter spends most of its life at sea, sleeping, eating, and even giving birth to its young among the kelp. It was almost exterminated for its valuable pelt by the early 1900s, but strict hunting regulations have allowed it to make a good natural recovery.

Other marine mammals, however, have changed a great deal from the form they once had on land. There are three groups: the sea cows, the seals, and the whales.

A mother Adelie penguin and recently hatched chick at Mammoth Penguin Rookery on Mount Bird, Ross Island, Antarctica. Penguins cannot fly but are excellent swimmers.

The sea cows include the manatees of Florida and the jungle rivers of South America. The sea cow eats lily pads. It is cigar shaped with front flippers and a flat tail but no hind flippers.

There are three groups of seals: the earless, or true, seals; the eared seals, or sea lions; and the walrus. They are all fish-eaters and have streamlined bodies and limbs modified to be flippers. They are fast, expert swimmers and can easily catch their prey in the water. They have a layer of thick blubber beneath the skin to protect them from the cold. The fur seals of Alaska have luxuriant pelts much prized for coats. After many years of over-hunting, they are now carefully protected and "harvested" for their pelts, a valuable natural resource. The California sea lion is the most common performer in zoos. The walrus has long ivory tusks and is found only in Arctic waters.

Whales, dolphins, and porpoises are all air-breathing mammals that bear their young alive, nurse them, and maintain a constant body temperature. They spend their lives entirely in water and breathe through openings called *blow-holes*. Movement is aided by horizontally flattened *tail flukes*. There are two subgroups of whales: the baleen, or whalebone, whale and the toothed whale.

Instead of teeth, the *baleen whales* have a fine mesh sieve with up to 800 or more plates of baleen or whalebone that hang like a curtain from the upper jaw. When feeding, the whale opens its jaws. When the jaw closes, the baleen allows the water to flow out but keeps any col-lected marine life in. The main foods of the baleen whale are plankton and krill (a shrimplike animal that grows up to 2–3 inches long and is found in large numbers in Antarctic waters). Baleen whales range in size from the minke (just over 30 feet) to the blue whale, which often grows to 90 or 100 feet in length and weighs 100 tons. The giant blue whale, the largest mammal that has lived on the Earth, weighs 2 to 3 tons at birth, doubles its weight in its first week of life, and seven months later weighs about 24 tons! The largest blue whale on record was 108 feet long. From a world population of about 40,000 in 1930, there are now only a few thousand left. Some conservationists fear it is close to extinction be-cause its death rate may soon exceed its reproductive rate.

Unlike baleen whales, *toothed whales* have teeth after birth. These teeth number from just a few in some species to as many as 250, although some may be concealed be-neath the gum. The narwhal has a single long, tusklike tooth in the upper jaw. Toothed whales have one blow-hole, in contrast to the baleen, which have two. This group includes the animals commonly called dolphins or porpoises, as well as sperm whales. The sizes in this class range from the porpoise, which is about 5 feet long, to the sperm whale, which is up to 68–70 feet long. They eat fish primarily, but the sperm whale also likes giant squid found at great depths. Records of sperm whales being entangled with submarine cables at depths to 3,700 feet indicate that some of the squid on which they feed are browsing on the bottom.

LIFE IN THE OPEN OCEAN

Beyond the shallow waters of the continental shelf, there is much less sea life because there is little plant life. Food is scarce. The animals of the region come to the surface to feed on the limited zooplankton and smaller fish, but in general, food is hard to find.

Giant 1½-ton elephant seals bask in the sun on an Antarctic beach. Ungainly on land, they are fast swimmers in the water, able to catch fish to eat.

A blue whale comes up for air in the Queen Charlotte Strait off the Pacific coast of Canada. This species is the largest mammal on Earth.

We talked earlier of the Sargasso Sea in the central Atlantic. Here there is a great deal of floating *sargassum weed,* which gives the area its name. This weed floats near the surface in clumps, plainly visible to sailors traversing the area. With the exception of this weed, the water of the Sargasso Sea is about the purest and clearest salt water in the world. In fact, as sea life goes, there is little life other than the tiny shrimp, fish, and crabs that live among the tangle of sargassum. Limited phytoplankton live in the area because there is almost no upwelling of nutrients from the deep sea bottom.

On the edges of the currents of the sea live many of the great game fishes of the world, such as marlin, sailfish, tuna, and sharks. Especially good fishing grounds for these fish are on the fringes of the Gulf Stream along the eastern seaboard and on the Mexican coasts in both the Atlantic and Pacific. Tuna species are found throughout the world ocean as they follow the plankton communities and migrate to central ocean spawning grounds.

There are places on a continental or island shelf where the ocean floor rises much closer to the surface in high underwater plateaus. These areas have an abundance of marine vegetation for fish to feed on. These plateaus are called *banks.* They are the best fishing grounds in the world: the Grand Banks off Newfoundland, Georges Bank off Massachusetts, the Dogger Bank in the North Sea, and in the Pacific near Japan and Alaska.

THE FISHING INDUSTRY

According to a recent United Nations report, some 3.8 million vessels of all sizes and 30 million people are engaged in some phase of the marine fishing industry worldwide. The annual worldwide consumption of fish and fish products from all sources is some 120 million tons. Of this, some 20 percent comes from aquaculture (fish farming). The remaining 80 percent comes from fishing in the world's oceans and inland waters. Of this, about 55 percent comes from the Pacific, 20 percent from the Atlantic, and the rest from the other world oceans and inland waters.

The amount of seafood eaten annually in different parts of the world is related to eating habits that people have developed over centuries and the local standard of living. For example, in a recent year in the United States, each person ate an average of only about 15 pounds of fish and other seafoods. In Japan in the same year, the average person consumed over 80 pounds. Many other people, especially in underdeveloped countries, may eat more than that, usually in the form of fish-meal cakes purchased from major commercial fishing nations.

The history of the fishing industry is part of the evolution of world commerce and the never-ending search for food. Since the beginning of the twentieth century,

Japanese fishermen take aboard a load of fresh-caught Alaskan king crabs in the Bering Sea north of the Aleutian Islands. The U.S. Coast Guard Bering Sea Patrol enforces the North Pacific fishing treaties within 200 miles of the Alaskan coast.

many improvements in fishing vessels, nets, and preservation methods have occurred. Progress made in fishing methods since 1930 alone has been greater than that made in the previous three thousand years. Three main types of new vessels have been developed: the giant *purse seiner,* a vessel that uses sonar equipment to locate and entrap schools of fish; the oceanic *long-liners,* which can fish for tuna throughout the tropical oceans; and the *factory trawlers.*

The large purse seiners were designed by Americans to pursue tuna on the high seas. They are based in California but cruise the world. Their large nets can catch a whole school of tuna at one set. Many of the larger ships can carry 1,500 tons of frozen fish in their holds.

The long-liners originated in Japan and South Korea. These vessels lay out from one to three floating longlines, each more than 20 miles long and bearing baited hooks every few feet. They seek mainly to catch marlin, sailfish, and tuna.

The trawler fleets of the world have greatly increased, especially under Eastern European and Asian flags, and they fish the continental shelves throughout the world. Trawlers generally stay at sea for several months and bring in a catch of up to 250 tons of fish that have been automatically cleaned and stored in ice. The Japanese and Russians have developed huge fish-factory ships that process and can the catch at sea. They serve as "mother ships" to a fleet of trawlers. They deliver their products directly to foreign markets at prices that cannot be matched by fishermen with less sophisticated equipment.

AQUACULTURE

The oceans are a good source of food now, but their potential is even greater. The seas alone could provide

A U.S. Coast Guard helicopter inspects a Russian fish-factory ship operating in the Gulf of Alaska.

enough protein for the entire world population of more than 6 billion people. At the present time, however, only about 1 percent of the protein in the human diet comes from the sea. A change in people's eating habits, careful conservation and harvesting practices, and cultivation of selected kinds of marine plant and animal life could increase food production from the sea. We must be very careful, however, not to deplete the breeding stock of fish or to overfish given areas. If we do, the disaster of extinction that has occurred with some land animals may be repeated.

A term used today to identify marine "farming" is *aquaculture,* the cultivation or raising of marine plants and animals for food. Sea farming has existed for many centuries. The ancient Romans in the Mediterranean and the Chinese and Japanese have raised oysters for more than 2,000 years. Oyster bed cultivation remains one of their main commercial marine projects. Today most of the world's oysters come from such beds.

An adult oyster can produce as many as 100 million eggs at one laying! But only a few oysters per million eggs survive in their natural environment. Each egg develops into a zooplankton larva and floats about for two to three weeks before settling down on a rock or other surface. People have traditionally cultivated oysters by providing old oyster shells for the larvae to settle on; these old shells are called the *clutch.* Predators, such as starfish, are cleared out, and the area is fenced off. In a few years the oysters are ready to be harvested.

This method has been improved upon, however, because it was too slow. Previously, only the food that fell to the bottom could be eaten by the growing oysters. Now most oyster beds have been replaced by *suspension cultures* in which the clutch is hung from ropes attached to floating frame rafts, or to stakes driven into the bottom. This way, the oysters have access to plankton floating by in all depths, and they are safe from their bottom-dwelling enemies. Using this method, it is possible to harvest 6,400 tons of oyster meat per square kilometer in about two years. French oyster farms near Bordeaux produce 500 million oysters annually for the European market. The Japanese have increased productivity of oysters from 600 pounds per acre under natural conditions to well over 30 tons per acre under culture.

Even more productive is aquafarming the common mussel. Mussel cultivation near Vigo, Spain, on the Atlantic Ocean, nets an unbelievable 27,000 tons of mussel meat from each square kilometer of floating farms!

Fish farming has had a high record of success for centuries in Southeast Asia, the Philippines, Indonesia, and China. The raising of milkfish in shallow fish ponds filled with brackish water has reaped some 200 tons per square kilometer using commercial fertilizers and more than 500 tons using human sewage as the nutrient fertilizer. In the open ocean, 7 tons is the natural production. The United Nations has figured that, in Southeast Asia alone, there are at least 5,500 square kilometers of shallow sea that could be turned over to milkfish production. Such production could supply most of the annual protein requirements of Asia.

Over a thousand years ago the Chinese developed a complex ecological fish farming system that they still use today. They place six different kinds of carp into a single deep pond, knowing that each species occupies a different habitat (water depth) and consumes different food. The grass carp consumes the surface vegetation. There are two mid-water dwellers, one that eats zooplankton, the other phytoplankton. Finally, there are three bottom feeders that eat mollusks, worms, and the feces of the grass carp. This is an extremely efficient ecological system that even serves to eliminate "pollution." The system is ancient, but it is naturally organic—and it works.

Woods Hole Oceanographic Institute in Massachusetts has worked out a similar system involving algae, oysters, seaweed, abalone, sand worms, and flounder, after which clean water is returned to the sea. The main crop is oysters, with abalone and flounder as secondary crops. It is a natural sewage treatment plant. The sewage is used to grow plankton algae, which in turn provide food for oysters. The waste from the oysters is consumed by seaweeds, which is then fed to abalone. The remainder that falls to the bottom of the tank is eaten by sand worms, which are then circulated to a neighboring tank to serve as food for flounder. The system is designed to produce 1 million pounds of seafood meat annually from a one-acre production facility of fish and shellfish holding tanks, and a fifty-acre algae farm using sewage from a community of 11,000 people.

In Southeast Asia, in addition to the milkfish farming described above, the people also harvest mullet, shrimp, and crabs in ponds constructed by clearing mangrove swamps and diking them with mud. These are extremely productive. The small fry are first fed in a nursery pond, while algae, bacteria, worms, and other plankton are raised naturally in production ponds with the addition of fertilizer. When the fry get to fingerling size, they are transferred to the production ponds. There they literally gorge themselves, growing to mature size in just a few months. The average yield of such ponds is about 500 pounds per acre.

Aquaculture is not limited entirely to fish. Along the Pacific coast of Asia, people have been supplementing their diets with a variety of seaweeds for ages. It is mixed in rice dishes and used as greens and seasoning. It is highly nutritious and excellent tasting. Some giant algae have been used for centuries as fertilizer for farm crops and as cattle food. Giant kelp plants of the Pacific are processed for iodine, medicines, and a variety of other products that are used in cosmetics, textiles, ink, paper, paints, drugs, and food preservatives.

Woods Hole has estimated that if only one-tenth of the 1 billion acres of available coastal wetlands worldwide (100 million acres) were converted to aquacultural development, the potential yield would equal the maximum considered naturally possible from the world's oceans—100 million tons each year.

Freshwater commercial fish farming in the United States has become more and more popular and successful since World War II. The varieties most commonly raised in ponds or basins are trout, walleyed pike, perch, and catfish. Most freshwater fish now seen in the frozen fish counters of supermarkets are products of these fish farms. Most of the pike are raised in Canada, Upper Michigan, and Wisconsin. Trout are raised throughout the country, but mostly in the mountain areas and northern part of the country. Catfish and perch are raised in the South and Southwest. Aquaculture is currently the fastest-growing sector of agricultural production in the United States.

SEA NOISES

An interesting biological phenomenon in the oceans is the "deep scattering layers." Discovered in World War II, these layers have become increasingly important to mariners and oceanographers. Scientists experimenting with marine sound detection gear recorded echoes from layers some distance above the ocean floor. During daylight hours there are usually three distinct layers that remain at depths from 700 to 2,400 feet. At night they rise almost to the surface and diffuse, or they may merge into a broad band as much as 500 feet thick.

After some years of research, oceanographers deduced that there seemed to be a close parallel between the layers and the daily vertical migrations of certain marine animals. Today, this theory has generally been accepted, though there is still much to be learned about the phenomenon. It is believed that huge concentrations of tiny planktonic animals rise toward the surface to feed on phytoplankton, and then, at daybreak, seek the dark depths for protection from sunlight and predators. It appears that the layers are composed of a wide variety of zooplankton, including tiny fish, shrimplike animals, lantern fish, fish with bladders or gas-filled bubbles, and tiny jellyfish with gas-filled floats. Biologists consider the layers to be important in explaining the distribution of life within the sea.

These deep scattering layers create horizontal sound-reflecting bands at various depths over broad stretches of the world's oceans. Until the phenomenon was identified, it caused confusion to operators of echo-sounding devices and sonar equipment. In addition, many marine animals have sound-emitters that create a wide assortment of noises beneath the sea. A person on the surface does not hear the noises because of the frequencies and sound level at which they are transmitted, but they can become a constant clangor over hydrophones. Such noises must be contended with in naval operations, in particular anti-submarine operations. Hydrophone reception can be seriously hampered, as some noises are very similar to the sound transmitted by naval surface and underwater vessels. Such noises can also be psychologically stressful to sonar operators. Therefore, the Navy began a program to record and identify biological and mechanical sounds so sonar operators could be trained to distinguish between them. The Navy also started a continuing research program to design equipment that could filter out as much of this biological noise as possible.

The problem of identification is complicated by the fact that the recorded sound differs according to the number of animals making noises. One croaker fish makes a drumming noise, but a dense shoal of croakers sounds like a pneumatic drill tearing up a pavement, completely drowning out the noise of any ship's propeller. The tiny snapping shrimp makes a sharp snap with its claw, but a large number of them sound like radio static.

In recording marine animal noises, scientists identified the sounds by comparing them with more familiar land animals. They learned, for example, that porpoises and whales whistle, click, bark, and moan; barnacles slurp; black mussels crackle; toadfish croak, growl, and whistle; weak-fish and perch produce a rapid, raspy croak; the northern puffer squeaks and coughs; and the sea robin makes a sound like fingernails being scraped over a drum.

The animals also use different means to make their sounds. Crustaceans make percussion noises with their claws. Fish usually make noises with their swim bladder, the size and species of fish determining in which way it is vibrated. Some fish also make grinding noises with their teeth or fins. It is still not known why these animals make these noises, but they probably are related to breeding, spawning, and defensive actions, among other purposes. Through their study of these noises, marine biologists hope to learn more about the behavior of these animals. Such information could be used to help improve commercial fishing practices.

BIOLUMINESCENCE

Luminescence means "light created or emitted at low temperatures, not as a result of burning heat." In nature, there are at least four sources of such light: (1) mineral phosphorus (phosphorescence), (2) radioactive minerals that respond to or reflect certain wavelengths of light, (3) cool gases that can be activated by electricity (fluorescent light), and (4) *bioluminescence,* that is, light created by insects (fireflies), certain fishes of the abyss, and microscopic marine *dinoflagellata,* a single-celled phytoplankton. It is this fourth source of natural light that we shall talk about here.

The luminescence of the sea at night is one of those common, yet curious, sights of the sea. It is a bluish-green, often sparkling, glow seen in waters disturbed by bow waves, wakes, and cresting waves. In some areas of the world this luminescence is very bright, to the extent that agitation of the sea by a passing vessel can briefly produce enough light on topside to read. When these organisms are stimulated by waves, their rhythmic reaction looks like a swirling movement of light, like a pinwheel. In calm conditions, the orbital movement of the seawater creates horizontal streaks where the dinoflagellata tend to concentrate. Oceanographers are constantly expanding their study of such natural bioluminescence in the sea.

For the Navy, this luminosity of seawater is more than just an interesting natural wonder. Observed from the air or from the bridge of a large ship, the luminous wake of a ship or periscope traveling at even moderate speed can be detected for some distance. It can clearly reveal the vessel's position and, roughly, its course and speed. During World War II amphibious landings and other naval movements were, on several occasions, given away by bioluminescence in the warm waters of the Pacific. Naval oceanographers generally know where heavy luminescence regularly occurs and can forecast periods of this phenomenon in areas where naval operations are planned.

FOULING AND DETERIORATION

Of the many important problems with which marine biology is concerned, none has greater economic significance to the Navy and commercial maritime interests than the control of marine fouling and deterioration. The effects of marine growth on ships' hulls, their saltwater intakes, valves, and piping are costly. Important also is the damage by marine organisms to the wood, plastics, metal, and concrete of shore installations. For the U.S. Navy alone, the protection and maintenance of ships, waterfront structures, and offshore equipment against biological deterioration and fouling costs many millions of dollars annually. More importantly, such uncontrolled fouling and deterioration can reduce the combat readiness of naval ships and shore facilities.

Constant scientific research has developed chemical agents that have successfully protected hull surfaces for as long as twenty-four months. The problem is far from solved, however. New naval equipment constantly requires the development of better antifouling agents.

Biological fouling impairs sonar gear by weakening sound transmissions. In some areas of the world, such fouling can make sonar gear unfit for use in just a few months. The problem is complicated by the need to develop an antifouling agent that will not itself degrade the acoustic qualities of the equipment.

The growing use of underwater optical instruments, such as fixed television and camera lenses, has created further problems. Such lenses can be fouled in a very short time. Some kind of transparent protective coating must be developed before planned submerged television monitoring stations can be installed.

Large stationary structures built on the continental shelf for both military and commercial projects have additional fouling problems. Offshore oil-drilling platforms, lighthouses, radar stations, and oceanographic research stations are generally intended to be permanent structures. Fouling and deterioration by bacteria, fungi, and marine animals are serious threats to such platforms.

Submarine cables containing telephone and electric power, and underwater pipelines, have been attacked by shrimplike animals called *gribbles.* They have gnawed through wooden pilings and rubber and plastic insulation. The famous *teredo,* or "shipworm," can destroy wooden pilings, burrow into rocks and cement, weaken stone seawalls, and destroy insulation on cables. They have even drilled through solid lead sheathing of submarine power cables laid as deep as 7,200 feet!

DANGEROUS MARINE LIFE

People generally think of danger at sea as attack by fearsome animals. Actually, animal life in the sea is usually more helpful than harmful. Nevertheless, there are two categories of marine species that can be very dangerous to humans: carnivorous and poisonous or venomous.

Carnivorous Animals. Sharks are the leading carnivores of most marine ecosystems. Of the 300 species identified, the larger species are the top predators in their environment. Although infrequent, shark attack remains a significant threat for bathers along the world's seacoasts and for people who work in the marine environment.

The danger of being attacked by a shark is exaggerated in the minds of many people. The degree of hazard depends both on the location and on the numbers and condition of the individuals in the water. Sharks are unpredictable and curious and will investigate any object in the water. They are likely to attack the dead or the wounded. They have an exceptional ability to detect a disabled or wounded animal at long range. Blood in the water attracts and excites them through their sense of smell.

The largest of all fish in the ocean is the tropical whale shark, which may reach 70 feet and weigh several tons. Basking and white sharks, found in temperate and tropical waters, reach more than 40 feet in length, while the tiger shark averages about 18 feet but may reach as much as 30 feet in length.

Sharks have become an increasing threat to swimmers in recent years. The danger of shark attack is greatest in tropical and subtropical areas, but shark attacks have been recorded along all coasts of the United States, especially off Florida. The white shark, above, is the most dangerous of all.

Sharks are found in all oceans from 45 degrees north to 45 degrees south latitude. The danger of shark attack appears to be greatest in tropical and subtropical areas between latitudes of 30 degrees north and 30 degrees south. The most dangerous areas are Australia, South Africa, Cuba, and the Pacific coast of Panama. In recent times, however, an increasing number of shark attacks have occurred on all coasts of the United States, especially off Florida beaches. No one knows for sure why the numbers of these shark attacks is rising. One possible cause is that the supply of fish in offshore areas upon which the sharks normally feed may be decreasing because of pollution and overfishing. Although shark attacks can result in serious injury, they are seldom fatal except when the victim is small.

The sharks considered most dangerous to people are the great white shark, most dangerous of all; the tiger shark, probably the most common of tropical sharks; the sand shark, most dangerous in East Indian waters; and the hammerhead shark, found throughout the oceans in both tropical and temperate zones.

When sharks are present, people should not dangle arms or legs in the water. Injured swimmers should be removed from the water quickly. Any flow of blood should be stopped as quickly as possible. Dark clothing and equipment are safest for swimmers. All movements should be slow and purposeful to avoid attracting sharks; if they appear, swimmers should remain perfectly still. Some sharks have departed when struck on the snout, but this should be done only as a last resort because it could aggravate them.

Barracuda are extremely dangerous. They may reach 6 to 8 feet long. They have knifelike canine teeth and, being swift swimmers, strike rapidly and ferociously. They are feared more than sharks in some areas of the West Indies. Found off the Florida coasts and in the Indian and Pacific Oceans, they are attracted by almost any bright or colored object in the water and attack quickly. Because of the poor visibility, they can be especially dangerous in murky coastal waters, where they will attack at the slightest movement.

Killer whales are found throughout the oceans, from the Arctic to the Antarctic. They are nearly fearless. They reach a length of 15 to 30 feet. In packs, they often attack much larger whales. They are very swift swimmers, seeking out seals, walruses, and penguins as prey. Despite their name, attacks against people are rare and are thought to be the result of confusion with their natural prey. The only defense against the killer whale is a hasty retreat from the water.

Moray eels have narrow, powerful jaws with knifelike teeth. They may reach a length of 10 feet. They can inflict severe cuts or may hold a bulldog-like grip until death. They dwell mostly in crevices and holes under rocks and coral in tropical and subtropical seas. Morays seldom attack unless provoked, so it is very wise not to poke around in places where they may be lurking. They are common along the California coast.

The *giant devil ray* or *manta ray* may reach a spread of 20 feet and a weight of 3,500 pounds. They have a wide range in the topical seas. They are very curious and may investigate air bubbles of divers, getting entangled in the air hose. They have a very coarse skin, which will produce severe abrasion on contact. Otherwise, they usually do not attack humans.

Stinging Animals. Poisonous marine invertebrates that inflict injury by stinging are divided into four main groups:

- Corals, sea anemones, hydroids, and jellyfish
- Mollusks, including octopi and certain shellfish
- Bloodworms and bristleworms
- Sea urchins

Corals and *sea anemones* have stinging cells that are used to capture food or as a defense against enemies. These cells inject a paralyzing drug into the victims, causing illnesses common among skin divers, sponge fishermen, and other marine workers. This group includes the elk horn coral of the West Indies and rosy sea anemones of the Atlantic.

Coral cuts and stings are very painful, slow to heal, and often become ulcerated. The wounds should be promptly cleaned and any particles removed. Bed rest, elevation of the limb, and packing with a mustard pack will help. When you are walking on a coral reef, heavy shoes, gloves, and wet suits are recommended.

The *hydroids* include poisonous invertebrates like the *Portuguese man-of-war,* often wrongly called a jellyfish. The Portuguese man-of-war floats on the surface of all tropical oceans and the Mediterranean Sea. Its tentacles trail many feet into the water and can give painful stings. The *fire coral,* a false coral that is sometimes called stinging coral, is found among true corals in the warm waters of the tropical Pacific, Caribbean Sea, and Indian Ocean.

Most *jellyfish* look like big, white, wispy mushrooms. They swim by water jet propulsion at many depths in the oceans. The *sea wasp* of the tropical seas, and especially those of the Australian, Philippine, and Indian Ocean areas, are extremely dangerous. Oftentimes they are seen in huge numbers in the South China Sea.

Swimmers who brush against the Portuguese man-of-war and jellyfish may be stung by their threadlike tentacles. Sting symptoms may vary from a mild prickly sensation to a throbbing pain that can render the victim unconscious. Pain may remain in the area of the sting or radiate to the armpit or abdomen. There may be redness and swelling, blistering, or small skin hemorrhage. There are no specific antidotes, but washing with diluted ammonia or alcohol and swabbing with mineral oil or baking soda may help.

The sea wasp jellyfish is very venomous. It can cause death in three to eight minutes. Symptoms are almost immediate shock, muscular cramps, loss of sensation, nausea, constriction of the throat, paralysis, convulsions, and, finally, death.

There are two members of the *mollusk* group with a venomous sting or bite: (1) those with spirally twisted single shells, such as snails, and (2) those with no shell, such as the octopus and squid.

Those with cone-shaped shells are potentially dangerous. They have a head with one or two pairs of tentacles, and a flattened fleshy foot. *Cone shells* are favorites of shell collectors. There are some 400 species, and most have a fully developed venom apparatus. They are found in tropical waters of the Pacific and Indian Oceans and in the Red Sea. They are common on the beaches of the Pacific islands.

The venom apparatus of the cone shell lies near the shell opening. The round teeth at the end of a tubelike appendage are thrust into the victim, and the venom is forced under pressure into the wound. The sting usually produces numbness and tingling, which quickly spread, becoming especially noticeable about the lips and mouth. Paralysis and coma may follow, with death as the result of heart failure.

Cone shell wounds must be quickly cleaned and suction applied to remove poison. Antibiotics may be desirable. The patient should be kept warm. Stimulants may be required, and hospitalization is recommended.

The *octopus* has eight arms or tentacles, the *squid* and *cuttlefish* ten, around a muscular central body mass. They have parrotlike beaks and well-developed venom apparatus. They can move rapidly underwater by water-jet propulsion.

Fortunately, these perilous-looking animals are timid. Octopi hide in holes in the coral and among rocks of the continental shelves. They are curious but very cautious. The danger of the octopus is its bite, and a small one can cause as much venom damage as a large one. The fear of being grabbed by eight choking arms is unfounded. Bites usually occur when captured specimens are being handled. Bleeding from a bite is profuse, indicating that clotting is retarded by the venom. A burning sensation, nausea, and swelling are likely. The victim usually recovers, but at least one death has been reported from the bite of a small, unknown variety of octopus.

Bloodworms and *bristleworms* have tufted, silky bristles in a row along each side. These bristles can penetrate the skin in the same manner as cactus spines. Their strong jaws can also inflict a painful bite. The bristles and bite of a bloodworm result in a pale area that becomes hot, swollen, and numb or itchy. Bristleworm irritation may last several days. Bristles are best removed with a forceps or by placing adhesive tape over the bristles and pulling them out. Scraping will break them off and may

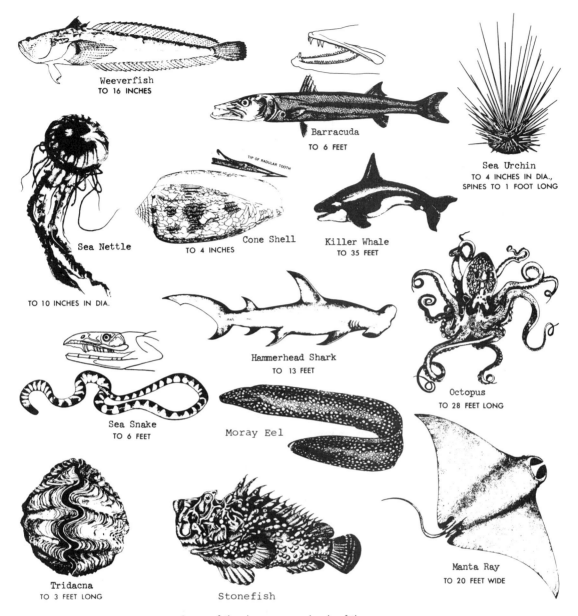

Weeverfish
TO 16 INCHES

Barracuda
TO 6 FEET

Sea Urchin
TO 4 INCHES IN DIA.,
SPINES TO 1 FOOT LONG

Sea Nettle

TIP OF RADULAR TOOTH

Cone Shell
TO 4 INCHES

Killer Whale
TO 35 FEET

TO 10 INCHES IN DIA.

Hammerhead Shark
TO 13 FEET

Octopus
TO 28 FEET LONG

Sea Snake
TO 6 FEET

Moray Eel

Tridacna
TO 3 FEET LONG

Stonefish

Manta Ray
TO 20 FEET WIDE

Some of the dangerous animals of the seas.

cause infection. The wound should be rubbed with alcohol to soothe discomfort.

Sea urchins occur in large numbers in coastal waters. They have a round body covered with needle-sharp spines, many of which are poisonous. They are a real danger to swimmers, waders, and divers. The spines, poisonous or not, can inflict deep puncture wounds. Those with poison are long, slender, sharp, and hollow, enabling them to penetrate deeply into the flesh. They are extremely brittle and are likely to break off. The tip of the spine has tiny pincers and a sense bristle that releases the venom. This apparatus will continue to inject poison into the victim for several hours after parting from the sea urchin.

Penetration of the skin produces an immediate burning sensation. Redness, swelling, and generalized aching are likely to follow, and deaths from muscular paralysis have been reported.

Vertebrate marine animals that have venomous stings include a number of fishes and sea snakes. Sea snakes were discussed earlier in this chapter. The fishes fall into a number of species: (1) the stingrays, (2) catfish, (3) weeverfish, and (4) scorpionfish.

Stingrays are a much-feared flat fish found in warm coastal waters. They may grow to weigh several hundred pounds. They are a serious menace to waders. They lie on the bottom, largely concealed by sand and mud. Stepping on one will result in the ray driving a venomous barbed tail into the foot or leg with great force. The spines may be driven completely through a foot or well into the leg bone of the victim. The stingray wound causes immediate shooting pain. The wound area will swell and become gray and, later, red. Severe stings by large specimens can be deadly.

There are about a thousand species of *catfish* in the world. Some of the salt-water catfish are venomous. Their venom glands are located in the sheath of the dorsal and pectoral spines. Some species have curved barbs on the ends of the spines, which make venom absorption more certain. Some freshwater catfishes are delicious to eat, but salt-water catfishes are not often eaten. They usually inhabit rivers, open reef areas, estuaries, and large sandy bays. They are common all along the eastern seaboard, the Gulf of Mexico, India, the Philippines, and Indonesia.

A wound from a catfish spine results in instant stinging and throbbing. The pain may radiate or remain local, numbing an arm or leg. Asian catfish can inflict a violently painful wound that may fester for forty-eight hours and then result in gangrene and death. There are no known antidotes for catfish and other poisonous fish stings.

Weeverfish are very venomous animals of the temperate zone. They are aggressive, small marine fishes less than 18 inches long. They inhabit sandy or muddy bays. They bury themselves in the mud with only their heads exposed. With little provocation, they will dart out with poisonous fins erect and strike with unerring accuracy, driving their spines into the victim.

There is instant stabbing pain after being struck. Within thirty minutes, the pain becomes so severe that the victim may scream and thrash about wildly, then lose consciousness and die. The venom attacks both the nervous and blood systems. Immediate first aid and treatment by a doctor may save the patient's life. Recovery time takes several months, depending on the condition of the patient and the amount of venom received. There is no antivenom.

The great weever is found along western Africa, in the Mediterranean Sea, and around the British Isles and Norway. The lesser weever inhabits the North Sea, southward along the European coast, and the Mediterranean.

The *scorpionfish family* comprises the most poisonous of all fishes. There are three main groups: (1) zebrafish, (2) scorpionfish, and (3) stonefish. The sting of any of these fish will produce serious results. The deadliness of some of the stonefishes may be ranked with that of the cobra.

The *zebrafish,* also called *lionfish,* is a beautiful shallow-water fish of tropical and temperate seas. They live around coral reefs, spreading their fanlike, lacy fins like peacocks. They are usually found in pairs. Beneath the beauty are hidden as many as eighteen long, straight, needle-sharp fin spines. Each spine is equipped with lethal venom. These fish are a real menace to anyone exploring tropical coral areas.

The *scorpionfish* inhabits shallow water bays and reefs in the Pacific Ocean. These fishes conceal themselves in crevices among debris, under rocks, or in seaweed. They have nearly perfect protective coloration that makes them almost invisible. When alerted or removed from the water, they erect poisonous spines like zebrafish do.

Stonefish of the Pacific Ocean are found in tide pools and shoal areas. They are hard to see because they usually lie motionless and partly buried in the mud or sand. They are not afraid of any intrusion in their area, making them a danger to anyone with bare feet. The fish is a mud-brown color and warty like a toad. It has thirteen dorsal, three bottom, and two pelvic spines, all short and heavy with enlarged venom glands.

Symptoms produced by all of the scorpionfish family may vary in degree, but the pain is immediate, sharp, and radiates quickly. Pain may cause a victim to thrash about in a wild manner, scream, or lose consciousness. The immediate wound area may be pale, surrounded by a zone of redness, swelling, and heat. Paralysis of an entire arm or leg may result. Death is the usual result of an encounter. A sting should be treated like a snake bite. In some cases the victim may recover after months of treatment, but with impaired general health.

Persons swimming where scorpionfish live must be alert to the danger and absolutely avoid touching them. Since the species are generally fearless, one should not aggravate them as they will attack. A direct encounter with any of the scorpionfish is an invitation to disaster.

UNDERWATER RESEARCH

In order to see firsthand what goes on in the sea, oceanographers for years have been seeking ways to observe the depths. The lack of air, tremendous underwater pressure, utter darkness, and the cold have all combined to prevent researchers from descending into the deep ocean and remaining there for an extended time. Only in recent years have people succeeded in exploring the sea in meaningful ways. New individual diving gear and methods and advanced undersea research vehicles have been developed and successfully operated. It is a whole new scientific frontier.

The traditional rubber-canvas suit with metal helmet and lead-filled shoes has been used successfully in depths up to 600 feet. Movement underwater is slow, and the diver is tied to a lifeline and air hose to the surface. More recently, the self-contained underwater breathing apparatus (SCUBA) has been developed. A qualified scuba diver can carry his or her own compressed air

The research bathyscaphe *Sea Cliff*. It is a free-moving underwater research vessel used to take photos, collect samples with mechanical arms, and stay at great depths for extended periods of time.

tanks and swim freely, if extremely careful, into water up to 200 feet deep. A diver usually uses a wet suit, flippers, and mask, especially for deeper descents and for extended underwater periods.

For much deeper human exploration, oceanographer Auguste Piccard developed the *bathyscaphe* in 1948. The name comes from two Greek words, *bathy* meaning "deep" and *scaph* meaning "boat." The bathyscaphe is a free-moving underwater research vessel that is somewhat like a submarine. When under the sea, scientists in bathyscaphes can look through ports at an underwater world lighted by powerful waterproof lights. They can take photos, collect samples with mechanical arms, and stay down at great depths for long periods of time.

Another very interesting vessel is the FLIP (floating instrument platform) ship. This research platform can flip from a horizontal position to a vertical one. The bow, carrying a marine laboratory, remains 50 feet in the air, while the stern, containing various measuring and sounding instruments, is plunged 300 feet below the surface. All of the furniture and equipment in the laboratory section is mounted on gimbals, so it stays upright and level during the flip operation.

Another Navy project has been the development of a deep submergence rescue vessel (DSRV) to be used in case of submarine accidents.

The Navy has also conducted extensive underwater living experiments. These have included *underwater habitats*—living and research quarters—where underwater scientists called *aquanauts* have learned to live for long periods at great depths.

In recent years increasing use has been made of remote-controlled self-propelled exploration vehicles fitted with TV cameras, lights, and a variety of other sensors and grappling devices. Many are capable of operation at great depths, have produced amazing video shots, and have recovered artifacts of sunken ships such as the famous passenger ship *Titanic* and the German battleship *Bismarck*.

THE THREAT OF POLLUTION

Human beings are consumers of vast quantities of raw materials and fuels. A tremendous amount of waste material results from this use—individual, societal, industrial, and accidental. A large part of this waste finds its

The Navy's oceanographic FLIP (floating instrument platform) ship is one of the most unique in the world. It is towed out to a research site at sea, then "flipped" into a vertical position by flooding the front end, as shown here. The ship consists of a 350-foot-long cylindrical tube with many instruments to take measurements of temperature, salinity, and currents. The crew's quarters in the stern remain above water, and all equipment and furnishings inside are on swivels so they remain horizontal regardless of the ship's inclination.

way into the sea. Fortunately, only a small percentage of this consists of pollutants. *Pollutants* are substances that damage marine processes or cause loss or the restricted use of an ocean resource. Some pollutants interfere with the life processes of marine organisms and reduce biological productivity of the oceans. Others, including oil and litter, are dangerous to people, interfere with recreational activities, or detract from the beauty of the seascape.

It is impossible to completely stop pollution of the oceans. It may be possible to stop pollution of some inland lakes and rivers and to significantly reduce it in others. But the mere fact that people use raw materials makes it impossible to eliminate waste materials. The real issue is what level of pollutants society is willing to accept. This depends directly on the amount of money, research, and effort people are willing to put into reduction and control of individual and industrial waste.

Seven main groups of pollutants presently affect the marine environment and cause international concern: (1) petroleum; (2) heavy metals; (3) radioactive materials; (4) chemical and synthetic fuels, solvents, and pesticides; (5) litter; (6) domestic sewage; and (7) biological pollutants.

Petroleum. The worldwide "energy crunch" came into focus in the 1970s and will continue for the foresee-

A Navy trainer attaches a special harness to Tuffy, an Atlantic bottle-nosed dolphin. Instruments attached to the harness measure Tuffy's heartbeat, respiration, and temperature during tests off California. The dolphin was trained to work with the Navy's Sealab underwater habitat program.

able future. Since the early 1970s, millions of tons of crude oil, gasoline, and other petroleum products have crossed the oceans in thousands of tankers. Each year, it is estimated that more than 6 million tons of this petroleum enters the oceans. Much of it is oil washed out of fuel tanks and bilges when they are pumped, but some of

One of the ten most serious pollution accidents in the past fifty years was the breakup of the American tanker *Torry Canyon* after going aground off Land's End, England, in 1967. The 61,263-ton ship spilled more than 120,000 tons of oil on the sea and beaches of southwestern England.

it is the result of ship collisions and groundings. Oily waste from land areas can run off into the sea. Additionally, there have been terrible spills from undersea oil rigs in the North Sea, the Gulf of Mexico, the California coast, and elsewhere. During Operation Desert Storm in early 1991 crude oil was intentionally dumped into the Persian Gulf by Iraqi forces in Kuwait. These catastrophes dumped thousands of tons of oil per day into the water, creating oil slicks that covered thousands of square miles.

Oil slicks on the high seas can kill plankton in the surface zone, but in general it will dissipate over a period of time. Often it gathers in tarlike balls that eventually sink to the bottom. While such "oil litter" can do no good, it probably does not do much permanent harm either. On the other hand, when such an oil slick reaches shore or collects in harbors, coves, or bays, the results are disastrous for the seabirds, mollusks, and other shallow-water life. Also, an oil spill will devastate the economy of a beach resort area.

The Navy's major pollution problem in harbors, ports, channels, and U.S. waters is the discharge of oils and oily wastes. The Navy has an active program to eliminate all such pollution and works closely with the Environmental Protection Agency and the Coast Guard in this effort.

Heavy Metals. The sea's main heavy metal pollutants are mercury and, to a lesser extent, barium. These metals are discharged in the effluent from chemical plants, cement works, and other manufacturing processes, doubling their natural accumulation in the sea. As a result, increased traces of mercury have been found in shellfish and other fish species throughout the world, including the Arctic Ocean and the Great Lakes. Sea life, especially shellfish, absorb the mercury. Fish, oysters, and clams retain it, and it continues to build up, never being cast off. In certain coastal areas near where the pollution enters the water, deadly concentrations occur in the fish. This has occurred in Minimata Bay at Kyushu Island, Japan. Many people have become severely crippled and mentally ill from eating mercury-poisoned seafood caught in the bay.

Radioactive Materials. Since World War II, many countries have begun to develop nuclear power stations and fuel-processing plants to help solve their energy shortages. In theory such plants can be made safe from leaks so they will not contaminate nearby land and water environments. The fact is that the cost for so doing is very high, and accidents have occurred. Increasing amounts of radioactive pollutants have found their way into the water.

In recent years much concern has arisen over radioactive waste products and reactor parts dumped into the seas over the years. In some cases old sunken sealed drums of radioactive wastes have corroded and leaked, causing contamination of local fish populations. Most countries with nuclear capabilities have agreed to dispose of future wastes in land dumps as the result of international accords dealing with this issue.

Chemical and Synthetic Compounds. Chlorine, fluorine, bromine, and iodine are proving very dangerous to marine life. These compounds fall into two main groups: (1) pesticides, such as DDT and other chemical weed and insect killers; and (2) the biphenols, such as aerosol propellants, solvents, refrigerants, and cleaning agents.

DDT is known to cause reproductive problems in some marine birds. The brown pelican, for instance, is an endangered species in some areas now. When the pelicans eat fish that have absorbed DDT from field and river runoff into coastal bays, their eggs have flimsy shells that break in the nest.

Most of the adult fish in the Great Lakes have absorbed pesticide and herbicide runoff from farmlands along the rivers that drain into the lakes. Pesticides often kill the eggs and small fry, so they have greatly reduced the natural reproduction of game fish in streams, rivers, and ponds, especially in the upper Midwest and in the Great Lakes states. As a result, these states now have to restock their waters annually from fish hatcheries in order to sustain fish populations.

Pesticides running off from farmlands can eventually find their way into drinking water. In some recent studies more than sixty agricultural pesticides were found in the drinking water of people in fourteen states in the mid-Atlantic and southeastern regions. Especially high concentrations were found in parts of Maryland and Virginia that border on the Chesapeake Bay. Prolonged exposure to such contamination can cause cancer in humans.

Litter. Marine litter is solid waste of society and ships at sea. It is trucked, barged, and dumped into rivers and into the oceans at a rate of more than 6 million tons each year. The ocean floor and coastal areas are littered with this debris; much of it consists of packing materials—plastic, aluminum, wood, and glass—all of which may take centuries, at best, to be broken down by the salts of the sea. In recent years various types of medical refuse have become of particular concern. Much of this litter is not *biodegradable.* In other words, it will never decay and break down. Beaches all over the world are cluttered with this trash, some of which floats to the farthest corners of Earth. It is unsightly, it is a hazard to swimmers and small craft navigation, it clogs harbors, and it may destroy the natural habitat of shorebirds and animals.

On the sea bottom, however, some of this trash actually helps create habitats for plant and animal life. Derelict ships, car bodies and tires, and cement blocks, among other things, have been used to make artificial reefs that are eventually covered by marine growth. The vegetation brings fish, and a flourishing cycle of sea life is created where previously there may have been none. This beneficial result of litter, however, is unique and differs greatly from its usual effect on the environment.

Sewage. The organic pollutants from sewage are especially troublesome in enclosed water areas. They contain high levels of nutrients that promote rapid plankton growth, in both fresh and salt water. This great increase in plankton population uses up the available oxygen, upsetting the natural *ecosystem.* Some 8,000 tons of sewage sludge is dumped daily from barges into the Atlantic Ocean off New York City. Many coastal areas, especially along the shores of the Mediterranean, have been contaminated by unprocessed sewage flow. Coastal wetlands have become "dead" areas, choked with algae and filled with disease-bearing bacteria. When such areas are destroyed, either by raw sewage or by draining, filling, or reclamation projects, a devastating blow is struck to the natural reproductive capacity of marine wildlife.

To help prevent pollution of inland waterways and harbors, Navy ships are equipped with two types of sewage systems: (1) marine sanitation devices (MSDs), which enable sewage to be treated before it is discharged from the ship; and/or (2) collection, holding, and transfer systems (CHTs), which collect and hold sewage until it can be transferred ashore in port or pumped overboard in unrestricted waters beyond the territorial limits (at least 12 miles from shore). Many commercial ships and most U.S. pleasure craft are fitted with similar equipment.

Biological Pollutants. Besides the foregoing types of sewage pollution, in recent years various kinds of biological pollutants have also caused concern. These include both animal and plant organisms that find their way into bilge and ballast water of ships visiting foreign ports, which is then discharged into coastal and inland waters of the United States. Once released into our waterways, these organisms can grow and spread without bound owing to the lack of any effective control mechanisms that may be present in their native environments. Two such instances of great concern in recent years have been the introduction of the Zebra mollusk into the Great Lakes and various rivers such as the upper Mississippi and Susquehanna by ships arriving from Europe, and a type of sprawling marine weed called hydrilla that chokes out native vegetation in the Chesapeake Bay.

WHAT IS THE ANSWER?

One thing is very clear. If ocean pollution continues at its present pace, instead of the sea becoming the aquaculture garden of the future, it could become a biological desert. This would have grave consequences for a world that is going to become increasingly dependent on the sea for food and mineral resources. Instead of becoming a living and recreation area for millions, it could become a polluted, stagnant pool. Wastes that are disposed of in the sea must be treated before dumping so they will not pollute. We must learn to recycle wastes. We must pass effective and practical laws and then enforce them. Life on Earth is dependent on the sea and will increasingly continue to be so.

There is still much hope. People are gradually learning about the importance of our relationship with the sea and the ecological balance that exists between the sea, the land, and all plant and animal life. All nations together must develop an international policy that will protect the common heritage of humanity.

Study Guide Questions

1. What is marine biology?
2. In what areas does marine biology have a direct impact upon naval matters?
3. What are the two basic families of plankton in the seas?
4. A. What is *upwelling?*
   B. What is the effect of El Niño?
5. What oceanographic phenomenon has given the Red Sea its name?
6. Why has the Black Sea been so named?
7. Describe the steps in the marine food cycle.
8. What are some of the unique characteristics of marine animals that live in the deep sea (abyss)?
9. What are some special characteristics of sea animals living at the edge of the sea?
10. A. What are the smallest animals of the zooplankton group?
    B. The largest?
11. How has the St. Lawrence Seaway affected the ecological environment of the Great Lakes?
12. What are the four groups of marine animals with jaws?

13. A. What are the four groups of living marine reptiles?
    B. Where are the most dangerous of these animals found?
14. What part of the world is the penguin's native habitat?
15. A. What are the three groups of seals?
    B. Which are protected by hunting laws?
16. A. What are the two main groups of whales?
    B. What is the main difference between the two groups?
17. A. Why is the Sargasso Sea so named?
    B. Why is this area almost a "desert" in the sea?
18. What are three things that can help increase food production from the sea?
19. To date, what types of ocean fish or shellfish have proved to be most successful in aquafarming?
20. A. How do the *deep scattering layers* affect naval operations?
    B. What causes these layers?
    C. Because of biological noises in the sea, what special training did the Navy begin for sonarmen?
21. A. What does bioluminescence mean?
    B. What causes it?
    C. How can this phenomenon affect naval operations?
22. What is the most serious effect of marine fouling and deterioration for the Navy?
23. What are the two categories of marine species that can be dangerous to people?
24. What are the four groups of stinging marine animals that can injure humans?
25. What are the four species of poisonous fish that are particularly dangerous to people?
26. A. What does *SCUBA* mean?
    B. Before divers use scuba gear, what qualifications should they have?
27. What is the purpose of a bathyscaphe?
28. What are the seven main groups of sea pollutants?
29. A. What are the main causes of petroleum pollution in the sea?
    B. Where is the most damage caused by an oil spill?
30. What is the particular danger of heavy metal pollution?
31. How does pollution by synthetic compounds affect natural reproduction of seabirds and animals?
32. How do radioactive pollutants affect marine life and humans?
33. A. How does domestic sewage upset the natural ecosystem in enclosed water areas?
    B. What must be done to sewage before it can safely be returned to rivers, lakes, or the ocean?
34. What are two forms of biological pollution that have found their way into U.S. waters in recent years?

Vocabulary

marine biology	aquaculture	predator	dorsal
zooplankton	oyster bed clutch	kelp	scorpionfish
larva, larvae	habitat	algae	SCUBA
nutrients	deep scattering layer	diatoms	bathyscaphe
decompose	upwelling	protozoan	aquanaut
protein	marine fouling	lamprey	pollution
guano	teredo worm	brackish water	pesticide
hydrogen sulfide	gribbles	flukes	radioactive
Callao Painter	mollusks	baleen whale	biphenols
El Niño	sea anemone	endangered species	biodegradable
Red Tide	hydroid	purse seiner	ecosystem
food cycle	jellyfish	stingray	litter
chlorophyll	sea urchin	ballast water	bioluminescence
carnivore	vertebrate		

Meteorology

The men and women who "go down to the sea in ships" fight a continuous battle with the elements. At sea the safety of a ship and her crew can depend on evasive action taken to avoid the full fury of a storm. Extra measures are taken well in advance of approaching bad weather to minimize damage to the ship, her gear, and her cargo.

We have all heard the statement "Everybody talks about the weather, but nobody does anything about it." In the past, this statement may have been true, but it is not today. Meteorology—the science of weather—is helping to make our lives safer and easier. Storm forecasts and weather warnings are much more accurate than they have been before. A network of weather stations provides information for safe commercial and military flights.

Today weather satellites in orbit above Earth provide worldwide meteorological information used in weather prediction and scientific research. Agricultural weather services help farmers plan for planting, harvesting, and marketing. Meteorology enables aircraft to take advantage of air currents, and this improves fuel conservation and flight time. There have even been successful experiments in causing rain. Also, meteorologists are exploring ways to break up dangerous tropical cyclones and tornadoes before they can reach populated areas. Yes, something is being done about the weather!

METEOROLOGY AND HISTORY

The importance of weather in history cannot be overemphasized. Weather has influenced the struggles of humanity, in peace and war, since earliest times. Most people are well aware of the damage weather can do to the economy, transportation, and housing. The study of any war will show that the weather has been critical in major battles and campaigns, on both land and sea. Some examples of the influence of weather on warfare are listed below; many more could be given:

- The defeat of the Spanish Armada in 1588 by Sir Francis Drake's small fleet was helped greatly by a bad storm in the English Channel.
- The brutal Russian winter was instrumental in defeating Napoleon's invasion of that country in 1812 and Hitler's invasion during World War II.
- In 1941 gales and poor visibility in the North Pacific helped the Japanese fleet move unobserved to within striking distance of Pearl Harbor.
- The D Day landings on Normandy's coast in June 1944 were delayed due to storm warnings. Whole artificial harbors were created to protect ships that were off-loading supplies from the fury of storms expected during the early phases of the invasion.
- The wet and dry monsoons of Southeast Asia determined, to a large extent, the active military operational areas during the Vietnam War.
- The dry and rainy seasonal patterns in Iraq, Kuwait, and Saudi Arabia greatly influenced the timing and conduct of Operations Desert Shield and Desert Storm in 1990–91.

The first meteorological instrument, developed by Leonardo da Vinci in the 1400s, was a crude hygrometer, which measured moisture in the air. Galileo Galilei, an Italian scientist, invented the first simple thermometer in the late 1600s. This invention may be regarded as the first step in the development of meteorology as a science. Later in the 1600s, barometers, wind-measuring devices, and improved thermometers and hygrometers were developed.

A major advance in meteorology occurred in 1854–56. During this time a French astronomer named U. J. Leverrier developed a system for organizing weather observations in the Black Sea area. He found that he could locate and trace various storms from one map to another, predict their future positions, and thus make a weather forecast. This was the forerunner of

Those who go down to the sea in ships fight a continuous battle with the weather. A Navy destroyer noses into a heavy sea in the central Pacific.

synoptic meteorology (a general view of the weather). It is our modern system of observing and collecting weather data.

Significant advances in the science of meteorology were made during the two world wars. A Norwegian meteorologist, Vilhelm Bjerknes, developed the air-mass and polar-front theories of weather. These theories are the basis for many of the forecasting rules used today. A network of reporting stations was established, and so the means of collecting data were greatly improved. As aviation advanced, air-mass frontal forecasting became highly developed. This increased knowledge became critical for safe commercial, passenger, and military flights.

Great progress has been made in meteorology during recent years, but much remains to be learned. Considerable amounts of money and a great deal of research time are spent every year on the weather. Today, the weather satellite is an indispensable tool of meteorologists. From its vantage point high above Earth, it sends back accurate photographs of cloud cover and storm fronts, and it records temperature, humidity, and other weather phenomena.

Our Atmosphere

It is not possible to understand much about weather without having a fundamental knowledge of the atmosphere around us. Actually, we live at the bottom of a vast ocean of air that completely covers the earth. This atmosphere has major layers up to about 1,000 miles above Earth's surface, though it is believed that traces of gaseous elements, such as helium, are present as far out as 18,000 miles.

Our atmosphere is a mixture of different gases. Near the surface of the earth, the air is made up of approximately 78 percent nitrogen, 21 percent oxygen, and 1 percent argon and other gases such as carbon dioxide, hydrogen, and neon. Within the atmosphere is scattered about 1 percent water vapor, called *humidity.* The amount of water vapor is greater in equatorial regions and less in the polar regions.

It is rather interesting to compare the water ocean with the air "ocean." Water, for instance, is nearly incompressible. A cubic foot of surface water weighs about the same as a cubic foot taken from the bottom of the Marianas Trench. But this is not the case with a cubic foot of air taken from different altitudes. The higher one goes, the lighter the air becomes, and consequently the more easily compressed it is.

The atmosphere thins so rapidly that over half of the total atmosphere by weight is in the first 3½ miles of atmosphere. It is within this 3½-mile "air envelope" that almost all of Earth's weather occurs. By the time a balloon has ascended to 20 miles, 99 percent of the atmospheric weight and gases lie below. Beyond 45 miles, only helium and hydrogen are present, in very tiny amounts. Within the air envelope, then, lies the tempestuous air ocean, constantly churning and mixing the gases we breathe. Here are all the winds, clouds, rains, and storms that make the weather.

The atmosphere consists of five principal layers. From the earth's surface outward into space, they are the troposphere, stratosphere, mesosphere, thermosphere, and exosphere. There are also transition zones of vital importance between some of these layers. The tropopause lies between the troposphere and the stratosphere; the chemosphere or ozone layer lies mainly between the stratosphere and mesosphere. The ionosphere is the whole area encompassing the mesosphere and the thermosphere. We will talk about each of these important layers and transition zones.

TROPOSPHERE

The *troposphere* is the ocean of air immediately above the earth's surface. It extends to a height of about 11 miles above the equator, about 7½ miles in the temperate zones, and only about 5 miles above the poles. Currents, storms, and waves occur in this air ocean, much as in the seas. Air in the troposphere is constantly turning over. In fact, *tropos* is a Greek word meaning "changing" or "turning." In the troposphere, the temperature and composition of gases change rapidly.

Nearly all clouds are in the troposphere, so it is here that weather occurs. Air heated by the earth rises, in a process called *convection,* and is replaced by cooler air descending from higher altitudes. As the hot air rises, the pressure decreases, and the air expands to become less dense. When it rises, if it cools sufficiently, it will condense into clouds and then perhaps into rain or snow. The whole process is determined by the simplest of the laws of gases: expansion is a cooling process, while compression generates heat.

The average temperature of the air at sea level is about 56 degrees F. At the top of the troposphere the temperature is about –85 degrees F. The air automatically cools about 5½ degrees for each 1,000 feet it travels upward; the reverse occurs in descent. This automatic temperature change in rising or falling air is called *adiabatic* warming or cooling.

Air circulation in the troposphere is of great importance to us because the circulation of air masses determines our weather. As a result, accurate weather prediction is dependent upon a thorough understanding of air movement in the troposphere. Intense study of the atmosphere in recent years has proved that the swift movement of cold-air masses about the vast Antarctic continent is a major factor in determining the world's weather. This is one of the main reasons that several nations, including the United States, have had a continuing interest in Antarctic research.

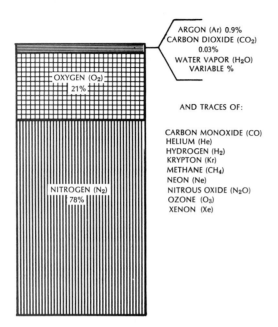

What we call the "air ocean" is really a mixture of gases. By volume it is composed of about 21 percent oxygen and 78 percent nitrogen, with the remaining 1 percent made up of carbon dioxide, hydrogen, helium, and traces of the rare gases such as neon, argon, krypton, and xenon.

TROPOPAUSE

The *tropopause* is that transitional zone between the troposphere and the near void of the stratosphere. It starts just above the troposphere, at altitudes of from 5 to 11 miles, and it is divided into three overlapping areas: tropical, extratropical, and Arctic tropopauses. The area between 20,000 and 40,000 feet is of importance to air navigation. This is where the jet stream is located, a current of air that moves swiftly from west to east around the earth. The jet stream is most prominent above the extra-tropical and Arctic tropopause overlaps.

The jet stream was discovered in World War II, when B-29 bombers flying about 4 miles high found great assistance from westerly winds of up to 300 mph. Planes were able to get into this stream and increase ground speed, shorten air time, and conserve fuel. Staying out of these currents on the return trip also saved time and fuel.

The jet streams have now been charted seasonally as well as geographically. It has been found that these winds are strongest over Japan and the New England states. Three major jet streams move over the North American continent in winter. One of them nearly blankets the United States. Information on the jet streams is especially significant to commercial airlines, which use the information in plotting their flight paths.

There is a direct relationship between the jet streams and lower atmospheric air masses. Meteorologists have found that the jet streams move with the cool air masses

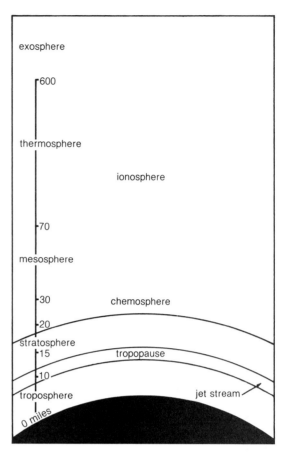

The atmosphere consists of five principal layers. Each layer has unique characteristics. Their exact boundaries are indistinct. The numbers shown here represent average heights.

near the earth's surface. Thus in winter the streams are over the temperate zones, where U.S. and Eurasian pilots can take advantage of them. However, in summer the jet streams move much farther north, out of most of the main commercial air lanes.

STRATOSPHERE

The *stratosphere* lies just above the tropopause and extends to an altitude of about 30 miles. There is almost no weather here because the air is too thin to create clouds. The temperature in the stratosphere drops much more slowly than in the lower layer. In fact, the temperature averages a fairly constant –40 degrees F to –50 degrees F and actually begins to get warmer in the upper limits. By the time a pilot has reached the stratosphere, about three-fourths of the weight of the air is below the aircraft. Modern commercial aircraft seek to fly in the stratosphere when not using the jet streams because there is so much less air resistance. This makes much better fuel mileage possible. Pilots also favor this flying level because there is no turbulence and they can fly at top speeds.

IONOSPHERE

Above the stratosphere lies an area of electrically charged particles called *ions.* This *ionosphere* begins perhaps as low as 30 or 40 miles up and extends to about 500 miles. Disturbances on the Sun, such as sunspots, change the ionosphere's form, and it is turbulent with magnetic and electrical storms. It is in the ionosphere that the Northern Lights create their colorful display.

It is possible to send ordinary radio waves around the world by bouncing them off ionospheric layers. In other words, the ionosphere will reflect radio waves of certain frequencies. By determining the best frequencies and times of day to transmit them, communications are greatly enhanced. This phenomenon is one with which every Navy and ham radio operator is familiar.

The *mesosphere,* the lowest level of the ionosphere, extends from about 30 to 50 miles above the earth. This layer is one of extreme temperature changes. At the lowest part of the layer the temperature may be as high as 32 degrees F. But it will drop to below –100 degrees F at the mesosphere's upper limits. It will then start to rise again above 70 miles, as one moves into the thermosphere.

The *thermosphere* is the highest level of the ionosphere. The air is extremely thin and the particles are ionized, or electrified, by loss of their electrons. This ionization is caused by the constant bombardment of cosmic rays from outer space. It is in the thermosphere that the principal radio-reflecting layers of the ionosphere are located. Extremely high temperatures exist in this layer. Recent information shows that temperatures in the thermosphere can approach 1,700 degrees F at a 300-mile altitude.

Another very important transition zone within the broad ionospheric region, but actually starting well below it, is the *chemosphere* or ozone layer. Beginning at an altitude of about 15 miles, this layer shields Earth from the harmful ultraviolet rays of the Sun. Ozone, a gas composed of three atoms of oxygen per molecule (rather than the two in a normal oxygen molecule), absorbs the ultraviolet rays.

There has been much concern in recent years that the ozone layer is being slowly depleted by fluorocarbon gas reacting with the ozone. Fluorocarbons have been widely used as propellants in aerosol cans for such products as hair spray and spray paint, and also as refrigerants in air conditioning systems in cars, homes, and businesses. As a result of this danger, many spray can and air conditioning manufacturers in the United States and elsewhere have switched to other substances, but these alternatives tend to be more expensive. Fluorocarbons are also released by the burning of styrofoam.

EXOSPHERE

The topmost layer or outer fringe of the atmosphere is called the *exosphere.* It begins about 500 miles above the earth's surface and continues out to about 18,000 miles. Only the light hydrogen and helium atoms exist in the area—in atomic form because of the intense cosmic radiation. Temperatures may be as high as 4,500 degrees F in daylight and may drop to near absolute zero (–460 degrees F) at night.

Within the exosphere are the intense radiation areas called the *Van Allen radiation belts.* These belts encircle Earth in two segments. One is about 400–3,400 miles above Earth, while the outer belt extends from about 8,000–40,000 miles out. The inner belt contains high-energy protons, and the outer belt contains high-energy electrons. Manned space missions are intentionally flown well beneath the lower limits of the Van Allen belts, and satellites operating in these regions must be shielded against the radiation encountered there. The exosphere is the end of our air ocean. Beyond it is outer space.

ATMOSPHERIC PRESSURE

The layer of atmosphere that surrounds us exerts a pressure of nearly 15 pounds per square inch (14.696 psi, or about 1×10^5 Pascals) at sea level. The weight of the atmosphere varies from place to place, depending on the amount of water vapor present, the temperature, and the height above Earth's surface. Variations in atmospheric pressure are measured by a *barometer.*

The Navy uses two types of barometers: mercurial and aneroid. Usually the aneroid type is employed aboard ship. The mercurial type consists of a calibrated glass tube filled with mercury. It is used at shore activities to check aneroid barometers for accuracy. The aneroid, or dry, barometer contains a small metallic cell that contracts when atmospheric pressure increases and expands when pressure decreases. The cell is connected

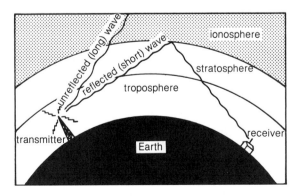

The ionosphere is a radio reflector for shorter wavelengths. They rebound from it and make long-range radio communication possible. Longer radio waves are not reflected by the ionosphere and pass through it.

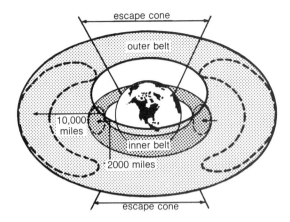

The Van Allen radiation belts encircle the earth somewhat like doughnuts, with radiation-free "escape cones" over the poles. The most intense radiation in the inner belt is about 2,000 miles up, and in the outer belt, about 10,000 miles.

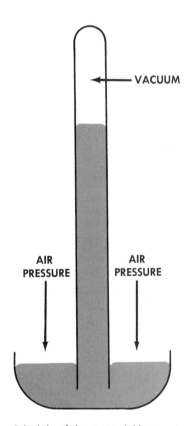

Principle of the mercurial barometer.

The aneroid barometer has a cell that expands or contracts with the decrease or increase of air pressure.

to a needle, which points to a graduated scale around the face of the barometer. As the cell expands or contracts, the needle indicates the atmospheric pressure on that scale.

Barometers may be graduated in either inches of mercury or millibars. Both inches and millibars are measurements of the height of the mercury column supported at a given time. One "atmosphere" equals 14.696

psi, the pressure at sea level; a bar equals about 0.98 atmosphere, and a millibar equals 1/1,000 of a bar. The average atmospheric pressure at the earth's surface is 29.92 inches, or 1,013.2 millibars. You will often hear the barometric pressure readings given in inches of mercury on TV weather forecasts. Millibars, however, are normally used on weather charts.

An *air mass* is a large body of air with the same temperature and humidity. An air mass takes on the characteristics of the surface over which it forms. Thus, cold-air masses originate in the cold polar regions, and warm-air masses originate in the tropics. The tropical or polar air masses can develop over either continental or maritime surfaces. These two surfaces give their names to the different kinds of air masses. Since land and sea reflect the Sun's radiation differently, the two kinds of air masses have different characteristics.

It takes more heat to change water temperature than soil temperature, and in seawater, that heat is absorbed to depths in excess of eighty feet. However, only a few top inches of soil will absorb radiation. This means that oceans are slower to warm up, and slower to cool down, than are land or continental surfaces. Maritime air, therefore, will tend to bring moderate temperatures, neither too hot nor too cold, as it moves over land areas.

In the winter, the United States is swept by continental air masses from the cold Arctic. In the summer, it is swept by warm, moist maritime air masses from the Gulf of Mexico, the Caribbean Sea, and the Pacific Ocean off the Mexican coast.

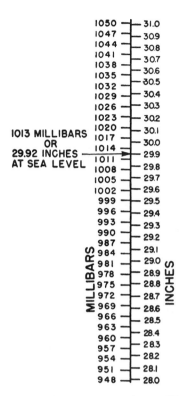

Inches of mercury and the corresponding millibar scale used for measuring barometric air pressure.

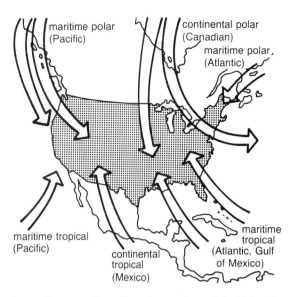

The primary air masses that affect the weather of the United States.

When warm- and cold-air masses touch, the boundary between them is called a *front*. There will usually be cloudiness and precipitation in a frontal area. A *warm front* is formed when a warm-air mass moves over a cold-air mass; when the reverse occurs, it is called a *cold front*. When neither mass advances on the other, a *stationary front* is said to exist.

Violent frontal weather systems can be predicted from a chart showing atmospheric pressures. Weather charts usually illustrate barometric pressures as *millibar reading points*. The lines in the figure, drawn through points of equal pressure, are called *isobars*. Isobars never join or cross. Some may run off the chart, but others may close, forming irregular ovals. Reporting stations send in their barometric readings to a central weather bureau, where weather charts are made. Isobars also give a rough indication of the amount of wind in an area. The closer that the isobars are to one another the stronger the wind in that area.

WHAT MAKES THE WEATHER?

Weather is the condition of the atmosphere. Changes in weather are caused by changes in the air's temperature, pressure, and water vapor content; wind causes the weather to move. It can be said, therefore, that weather is the condition of the atmosphere, expressed in terms of its heat, pressure, wind, and moisture.

It is heat, and the transfer of heat, that makes weather. This heat, of course, comes from the Sun. Heat causes the weather changes. Without it there would be no winds, varying air pressures, storms, rain, or snow. All weather changes are caused by temperature changes in different parts of the atmosphere.

There are some fundamental natural laws that determine these changes. Warm air is lighter in weight and can hold more water vapor than cold air. Cold air is heavier and has a tendency to flow toward the rising warm air, replacing it on the earth's surface. As this air moves, wind is created, thus beginning the complex forces that cause the changing weather.

Our main source of energy, the Sun, bombards Earth with 126 trillion horsepower each second. The Sun's energy is transmitted as electromagnetic waves, or radiation, traveling at 186,300 miles (3×10^8 meters) per second. The solar radiant energy is referred to as *insolation* (*in*coming *sol*ar radi*ation*). About 43 percent of the radiation reaching our planet hits the earth's surface and is changed into heat; the rest stays in the atmosphere or is reflected into space.

Clouds and other atmospheric influences absorb some of the incoming radiation, but they reflect much of it. A typical cloud reflects back 75 percent of the sunlight striking it. Since Earth's average cloudiness is 52 percent, about 36 percent of the total insolation never reaches our planet. Dense forests absorb up to 95 percent of the sunlight striking them, and water reflects 60–96 percent, depending upon the angle at which the light hits the surface.

Over a long period of time, the earth's temperature remains fairly constant, despite the constant inflow of solar radiation. This tells us that the earth is also giving off heat at about the same rate. The earth's cloud cover

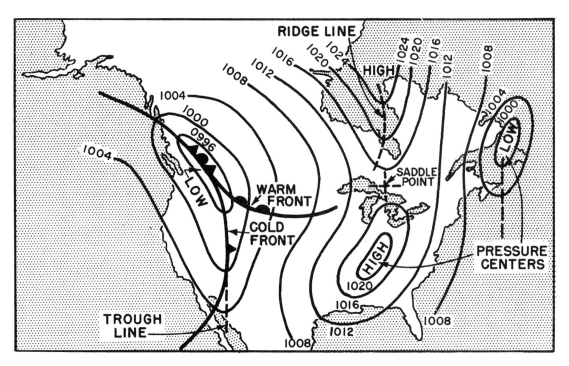

A sample weather map showing frontal systems outlined by lines called isobars, drawn through points of equal pressure. Isobars never join or cross. Some may run off the chart, and others will form irregular ovals that define areas of high and low pressure. When the lines are close together they represent areas of higher wind intensity, with the direction of the wind from high- to low-pressure areas.

acts like the glass on a greenhouse. It lets the short solar rays pass through; the earth absorbs these and then reradiates the heat as long heat waves. But these long heat waves cannot all get through the atmosphere because they are absorbed by the water vapor. So they stay within the "greenhouse" in a continual cycle. You will notice this especially on hot, overcast summer nights when the humidity is high.

The atmosphere thus acts almost like an automatic thermostat in controlling the earth's heat. It screens out the dangerous solar radiation and reflects some of the excess, and it acts as an insulator to keep most of the heat from escaping at night. Without the atmosphere, the earth would be like the Moon—with boiling temperatures during the day and subfreezing temperatures during the night.

MEASURING TEMPERATURE

A thermometer is an instrument for measuring temperature. It is a narrow glass tube filled with alcohol or mercury. The liquid rises and falls within the bore as the rise and fall of the temperature causes the liquid to expand and contract. A temperature scale is marked on the tube.

The Navy and most civilians in America usually use thermometers with a *Fahrenheit* (F) scale. On that scale, the freezing point of water is 32 degrees and the boiling point is 212 degrees. Temperatures in meteorology and most other sciences, however, are usually expressed ac-

cording to the *Celsius* (C) scale, in which the freezing point of water is 0 degrees and its boiling point is 100 degrees.

The Celsius scale is in the metric system, which one day is supposed to be the principal measurement system used in the United States, as it is already in most of the rest of the world. It is likely, however, that for a good many years conversion of temperatures from one scale to the other will be a common necessity.

There are 5 degrees of Celsius temperature for every 9 degrees of Fahrenheit. Since 32 degrees F is equivalent to 0 degrees C, to change a Fahrenheit reading to Celsius you subtract 32 degrees and then multiply the remainder by 5/9 (formula: $C = 5/9[F - 32]$). Let's say you want to change 59 degrees F to Celsius. Subtracting 32 degrees from 59 degrees leaves 27 degrees. Multiply 27 degrees by 5/9 and you get 15 degrees C.

To change a Celsius reading to Fahrenheit, the process is reversed. Simply multiply the Celsius temperature by 9/5, and add 32 degrees (formula: $F = 9/5 C + 32$ degrees). Using the figures from the previous example, to change 15 degrees C back to Fahrenheit, first multiply it by 9/5, which gives you 27 degrees; then add 32 degrees. You are now back to the original 59 degrees F.

Most inexpensive house thermometers are filled with red-dyed alcohol. If you compare a mercurial thermometer with a red-alcohol one you will note that the top of the column of liquid is in the shape of a curve, called a *meniscus*. Because of the different characteristics

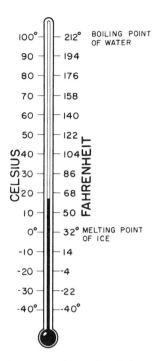

The Celsius and corresponding Fahrenheit temperature scales.

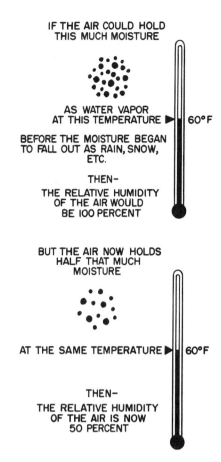

An illustration of the concept of relative humidity.

of the liquids involved, the accurate reading for an alcohol thermometer is at the *bottom* of this curve; for a mercury thermometer it is at the *top.*

MEASURING RELATIVE HUMIDITY AND DEW POINT

The atmosphere always contains water in the form of vapor. Nearly 71 percent of Earth's surface is covered by water. Heat causes the evaporation of millions of tons of water from these surfaces daily. In a process called *transpiration,* additional huge amounts of water enter the air from the green leaves of plants. As this warm, moist air rises, it expands and cools, eventually reaching its saturation level—100 percent relative humidity. Then the vapor condenses into a liquid. The water droplets form into clouds, and precipitation (usually rain or snow) will occur. This water cycle of evaporation, condensation, and precipitation, referred to as the hydrologic cycle, is continually in process.

We already have mentioned that the amount of water vapor the atmosphere can hold varies with the atmosphere's temperature. The *relative humidity* is the amount of water vapor the air is actually holding, expressed as a percentage of the amount that air, at that temperature, can hold. When the air contains all the water it can hold at a given temperature, humidity is at the 100 percent saturation point. If it contains half of what it could hold at that temperature, the relative humidity is 50 percent. Since warm air can hold more water

than cold air, the relative humidity goes up when air with a given amount of water vapor cools, and it drops when that air is heated. It follows, then, that as air rises, it cools and the water vapor condenses, eventually falling as some form of moisture.

The *dew point* is the temperature to which air must be cooled—at constant pressure and constant water vapor content—to reach saturation (100 percent relative humidity). When air is cooled to its dew point temperature, small water droplets condense on objects. Dew is formed. At higher altitudes, this simply means that the air has been cooled sufficiently to cause a cloud to begin losing water vapor. If conditions are right, these cloud droplets will fall as rain or snow.

Relative humidity and dew point are measured by using a *psychrometer.* A psychrometer is simply two ordinary thermometers mounted together on a single strip of material. The bulb of one is covered by a water-soaked wick, from which the moisture is allowed to evaporate. The moisture will evaporate until the amount of water in the wick equals the amount of water vapor in the surrounding atmosphere. Since evaporation is a cooling process, the reading on the wet bulb will be lower than on the dry bulb—unless the humidity is 100 percent, at which time both readings are the same. The difference between the wet-bulb and dry-bulb readings is applied to tables developed for that purpose. From the table, the relative humidity and dew point can be read easily. Aboard ship, *sling psychrometers* are often used to speed up the process of getting accurate wet- and dry-bulb readings. A handle and chain are attached to a psychrometer and the apparatus is whirled around in order to rapidly bring the wet bulb into contact with a greater volume of air. Using a steady, slow swing, the whirling is continued until no further change can be detected in the wet-bulb reading. Then the table is referred to.

Study Guide Questions

1. What are the two main elements in our atmosphere and the approximate percentages of each?
2. What changes occur to the air as one ascends into the atmosphere?
3. Where does most of Earth's weather occur?
4. What are the five principal layers of Earth's atmosphere?
5. A. In what layer of the atmosphere are most clouds found?
    B. What are the laws of gases that apply to the development of clouds?
6. Why have the United States and several other countries studied Antarctic air masses in recent years?
7. A. What is the tropopause?
    B. Why is it so important to commercial aviation?
8. What are some of the current studies concerning the jet stream, and why are these studies important?
9. Why do modern commercial aircraft prefer to fly mostly in the stratosphere?
10. What visual phenomenon occurs in the ionosphere over the polar regions?
11. What is the importance of the ionosphere to communications?
12. A. What is the average air pressure at sea level?
    B. What instrument measures air pressure?
13. What are two types of barometers used by the Navy?
14. What is weather?
15. What three things cause changes in the weather?
16. What is the "greenhouse effect?"
17. A. What are the two most widely used temperature scales?
    B. What are the freezing and boiling points of each?
18. What is the water cycle?
19. What is the dew point?
20. What instrument measures relative humidity and dew point?

Temperature Conversion Problems

1. Do the following conversions:
    A. 122 degrees F = ____ degrees C
    B. 86 degrees F = ____ degrees C
    C. –4 degrees F = ____ degrees C
    D. 104 degrees F = ____ degrees C

2. Do the following conversions:
    A. 60 degrees C = ____ degrees F
    B. 20 degrees C = ____ degrees F
    C. –10 degrees C = ____ degrees F
    D. 35 degrees C = ____ degrees F

Vocabulary

atmosphere	ionization
humidity	barometer
troposphere	millibar
stratosphere	isobar
tropopause	air mass
ionosphere	precipitation
chemosphere	insolation
mesosphere	Celsius
thermosphere	Fahrenheit
exosphere	relative humidity
ozone layer	psychrometer
convection	jet stream
dew point	

2

Clouds and Fog

Water is always present in the air, in greater or smaller amounts. It can be present in three states: solid, liquid, and vapor. In chapter 1 we discussed water vapor in the air, called humidity. Relative humidity was defined as the percentage of the amount of vapor the air can hold at a given temperature. In this chapter we will discuss how water vapor is formed into clouds, and what kind of weather the various kinds of clouds may foretell. This information is vital to meteorologists, but it can also be both helpful and interesting to the average person.

DEFINITION OF A CLOUD

Tiny particles of dust, sand, pollen from plants, factory smoke, and salt particles from oceans are always present in the air. These fragments of matter are called *hygroscopic nuclei*, a term meaning "particles that readily absorb moisture." A cloud is a mass of hygroscopic nuclei that have soaked up moisture from the water vapor in the air.

The heat generated by the Sun's energy causes earthbound moisture to evaporate into the sky in the form of water vapor. This water vapor rises, since it is lighter than air. If the air it passes into is cold enough, the vapor condenses—in other words, it turns back into moisture. The water droplets that result from this process cling to the hygroscopic nuclei. Bunched together, these water-soaked nuclei form a cloud. Fog is formed the same way; it is a cloud very close to the ground.

As these droplets ride air currents, one of three things can happen, depending upon the temperature and wind. They may reevaporate and rise further into the atmosphere; they may rise and freeze into ice crystals, sometimes in sufficient amounts to form ice crystalline clouds; or they may collide with other nuclei and form larger drops that become heavy enough to fall as rain, snow, or sleet.

Changes in atmospheric conditions account for the many different shapes of clouds, and for their presence at various altitudes. Cloud formations give a clue concerning the forces at work in the atmosphere. Navy and civilian meteorologists must keep accurate records of clouds and must account for cloud cover in their periodic weather reports. Such information is important in forecasting.

CLOUD CLASSIFICATIONS

There are three basic cloud types: *cirrus* (wispy), *cumulus* (heaped-up), and *stratus* (layered). In addition to the three basic types, there are other types having names that are combinations of these with the word *nimbus* (meaning "rain") or the prefix *alto-* (meaning "high"), identifying clouds in the middle altitudes. Another prefix, *fracto-*, is often used to describe fragmented or windblown clouds.

Clouds are often classified in accordance with the altitudes at which they most frequently occur. The altitude classes are *high, middle,* or *low*. Sometimes a fourth class, *towering,* is used to identify an exceptionally high cloud with its base in the low-altitude area. Altitudes associated with each of these classes are (1) low: surface to 7,000 feet; (2) middle: 7,000 to 20,000 feet; and (3) high: above 20,000 feet.

Middle clouds seldom attain heights greater than 13,000 feet in the polar regions, though they may reach 23,000–45,000 feet in the temperate and tropical zones.

Clouds are usually named according to their appearance. Appearance, though, is largely dependent upon the altitude in which they are found. Grouped by appearance and altitude, there are ten general cloud types.

Low Clouds. Low clouds are of five main types:

1. *Stratus* clouds, the lowest cloud type, are often like a gray layer with a uniform base. They may cause drizzle, but never rain. Fog becomes stratus when it lifts.
2. *Nimbostratus* are dark, shapeless, rain-laden clouds, often blanketing the sky. They are true rain clouds and "look wet" because they often have streaks of rain extending to the ground beneath them. They are often seen in the summer at the base of thunderheads. In the winter they bring steady, heavy snow.
3. *Stratocumulus* are irregular, rounded masses of clouds spread out in puffy or rolling layers. These

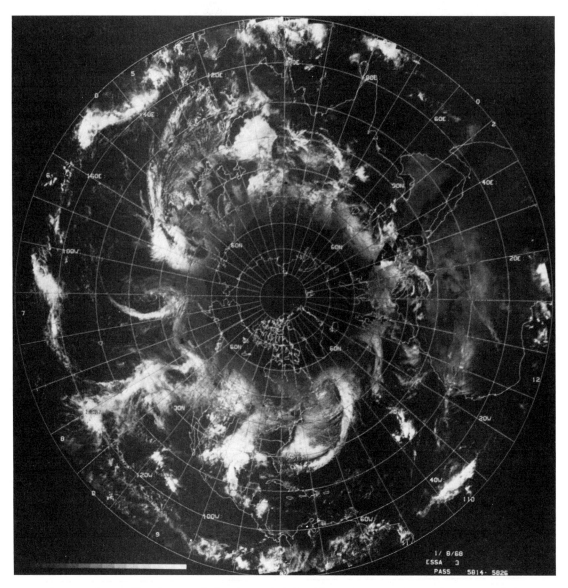

A composite satellite photograph showing typical cloud formations over the Northern Hemisphere.

large clouds are usually gray with darker spots or shading. They do not produce rain, but they sometimes fuse at the base and change into nimbostratus. They usually precede bad weather.

4. *Cumulus* clouds are dense, puffy clouds with a beautiful, cauliflower-like appearance. On summer days they look like giant cotton balls in the sky. They rise by day in warm air and usually disappear at night. Fleecy cumulus clouds usually mean fair weather ahead—unless the puffs begin to pile up and the dark edge of a nimbus rain cloud starts to form at the base.

5. Thunderheads start at almost any altitude and sometimes extend to heights of as much as 75,000 feet. *Cumulonimbus* is the name given to these clouds. They are very dense clouds of the tower-

ing variety. The base of the cloud is the dark nimbus rain cloud. Severe thunderstorms and destructive tornadoes may come from these clouds, which normally are seen only in the summer.

Middle Clouds. Middle clouds are basically stratus or cumulus but with bases beginning about 10,000 feet. They are denoted by the prefix *alto-*:

1. *Altocumulus* are gray or whitish layers of puffy, fleecy clouds. These roll-like clouds are made of water droplets, sometimes laid out in parallel bands. The Sun will sometimes produce a pale blue or yellow corona through altocumulus clouds. The presence of these clouds means that rain will probably occur within twenty-four hours.

Stratus clouds.

Cumulus clouds.

Nimbostratus clouds.

Cumulonimbus clouds.

Stratocumulus clouds.

Altocumulus clouds.

2. *Altostratus* clouds are dense sheets of gray or blue, sometimes looking like ridges of frosted glass, or flattened vapor trails. The Sun or Moon will glow dimly through altostratus, but without a halo or corona. Light rain will probably occur within twenty-four hours.

High Clouds. High clouds are composed almost entirely of tiny ice crystals. There are three basic types:

1. *Cirrus* clouds are thin, wispy clouds composed mainly of ice crystals. They are often called "mare's tails." In scattered patches, they normally indicate clear, cold weather. But if they are in parallel lines across the high sky, it usually signals a violent change in the weather within thirty-six hours. Spring ice storms, hurricanes, typhoons, or other severe storm conditions will generally appear soon—even if the day when you see the parallel cirrus is beautiful and sunny.

2. *Cirrostratus* clouds may nearly cover the sky with a filmy cloud. They often have a curly appearance at their edges. Because they are made of ice crystals, these clouds form large halos around the Sun and Moon. They indicate that clear and cold weather can be forecast.

3. *Cirrocumulus* clouds are thin, patchy clouds that often form in wavelike patterns. These clouds do not leave shadows on the earth. Precipitation will usually follow them within twenty-four hours.

CLOUDS AT SEA

Clouds have been leading lost seamen, navigators, and explorers to land since the days of the earliest hardy sea voyagers. Fleecy white clouds on the horizon that are seemingly stationary usually indicate that an island is close by. Clouds form above islands for the same reason

Altostratus clouds.

Cirrus clouds.

Cirrostratus clouds.

Cirrocumulus clouds.

that they do above any land: moisture rises from vegetation, meets cooler air aloft, and condenses into clouds. In the tropics, these clouds often reflect the colors of sandy beaches or coral reefs below. Overhanging clouds may also warn seamen of rocks, reefs, or shoals surrounding islands.

PRECIPITATION

Precipitation (rain, snow, sleet, and hail) cannot occur without clouds. The fact that there are clouds, however, does not necessarily mean that the moisture in them will fall as a form of precipitation. Temperature and the presence of hygroscopic nuclei or ice crystals will determine whether or not there will be precipitation and what form it will take.

Raindrops are formed when moist air is cooled to the point where the moisture condenses into heavy drops. Normally, droplets move about in the cloud somewhat like dust blowing. Cloud moisture droplets are very tiny—only 1/2,500 of an inch in diameter—and are too light to fall to Earth. Only if the droplet grows to a diameter of 1/125 of an inch or larger will it fall from the cloud. The average raindrop, then, is a million times larger than a cloud droplet. Cloud droplets grow to a size large enough to fall as rain or snow by combining with one another—a process called *coalescence.*

Coalescence occurs in two known ways. First, bigger droplets move about slowly in the clouds, eventually bumping into other droplets and combining with them. This is usually the case when rain falls from a nimbostratus or other low cloud. Second, the more important kind of coalescence occurs when, in higher-altitude clouds (such as the middle layer of cumulonimbus), ice crystals and water droplets form near each other. The droplets evaporate, and the resulting vapor collides with the ice crystals and condenses into snow or ice pellets that fall toward Earth, melting into rain as they pass through warmer air at lower altitudes.

RAINMAKING

Rainmaking has been a concern of humans since the most ancient times. Rain dances, sacrifices, drums, cannons, and smoke have all been used to try to make rain, especially when the land was parched with drought. None of these methods worked, of course. But modern rainmaking techniques, based upon the known facts of coalescence, have been successful in causing rainfall.

In modern rainmaking techniques, an aircraft drops dry-ice crystals or silver-iodide crystals into potential rain clouds. This process is called *seeding* the cloud with artificial nuclei. It has been found that one pound of frozen carbon-dioxide (dry-ice) crystals spread by airplane can start a shower from a large cumulus cloud. Silver iodide can also, using special generators, be sent up from the ground in the form of a gas—a less expensive method. Both methods cause water droplets to form around the foreign substance and then fall as rain.

Seeding, however, is not successful unless conditions are nearly right for natural rainfall. Seeding can make rain come a bit earlier and may cause more rain to fall than might have occurred naturally. It might also cause rain to fall from a cloud that, under natural conditions, would never have produced raindrops. But seeding cannot cause rain to fall from fair skies or from fair-weather cumulus clouds. Nor is it possible to cause rain to fall over a large area.

SNOW, SLEET, HAIL, AND FROST

Sleet occurs when rain that has formed in relatively warm air falls through a layer of freezing air. The air is not quite cold enough to cause the falling rain to freeze—until that rain comes into contact with a bit of dust. The dust will cause the raindrops to freeze, at least partially, into a super-cooled mush, which freezes when it hits the ground, trees, or telephone wires. Such a sleet or ice storm can cause power lines to collapse, or tree branches to break and fall on power and telephone lines, roofs, and roads.

Hail usually occurs in the summertime. It begins as frozen raindrops in high levels of cumulonimbus thunderheads. The ice pellets may grow if updrafts of air push them upward one or more times after they are coated with water from lower cloud layers. They will eventually fall when they are too heavy to be lifted by an updraft. They may grow even more during their descent by picking up moisture that then freezes. Most hailstones are smaller than marbles, but people and animals have been killed or severely injured by hailstones as large as baseballs. Hail can destroy a growing crop in minutes.

In wintertime, when the upper air is very cold, water vapor will condense into ice crystals. What we call *snow* is the result. Water vapor will also crystallize around hygroscopic nuclei floating in the air, where the cloud's temperature ranges from −4 degrees F to +10 degrees F.

Dew and frost do not fall from the skies as do rain, sleet, and snow. *Dew* is water vapor that condenses on objects that have cooled below the condensation point of the air around them. *Frost* is similar to dew, but it forms at temperatures below freezing. The water vapor changes directly into ice crystals on contact with the object, without first changing into dew.

FOG

What we call fog is really a low-lying cloud that is near or touching the surface of the earth. It is formed when cool air moves in and mixes with warm air having a high relative humidity. When the temperature falls below the dew point, fog is formed. Each water droplet has a particle of dust or smoke as its central nucleus.

Fog formation thus requires the presence of moisture, a gentle breeze, and a combination of warm and cold temperatures. A cool breeze passing over warm waters will create fog, and so will warm air passing over a stretch of sea. The breeze will spread the fog out over the surface, and it will lie in lower areas such as valleys and swamps.

Fog is hazardous to aviation because it limits both "ceiling" and visibility. Similarly, fog at sea—near offshore islands, along coasts, and in bays, inlets, harbors, and river mouths—is a continual hazard. Although aircraft and ships have radar to assist them in foggy conditions, the eyes of alert pilots and ship lookouts are necessary for safe navigation. Indeed, the nautical "rules of the road" explicitly require that lookouts be stationed aboard ship. And many an airplane flight has been delayed, either in landing or taking off, because of poor visibility.

Fog at Sea. Fog at sea is frequently formed through a process known as *advection* (moving forward). When warm air that has passed over warm water moves to an area of colder water, fog is likely to develop. Because seawater temperatures are fairly uniform within a large area, fog often lasts for many days and nights once it develops in a given area.

The great fog banks of the North Atlantic and those of the northern Pacific around the Aleutian Islands of Alaska demonstrate what happens when two adjacent bodies of water have greatly different temperatures. In the vicinity of the Grand Banks of Newfoundland, warm air that has passed over the warm Gulf Stream quickly turns to fog when it strikes the current of very cold water that flows southward from the Arctic. Off Alaska, the same situation exists. The air over the warm Japanese Current comes in contact with the cold, southward-flowing waters of the Bering Sea.

Advection Coastal Fogs. Advection fog is the name given to air-mass fog produced by air in motion or to fog formed in one place and transported by wind to another. These fogs occur when the wind moves warm, moist air from a warm ocean surface to a colder land surface—or vice versa. These fogs will normally dissipate each day, since the winds carrying the air will change direction when the Sun rises.

Every sailor is fully aware of the fogs that can blanket the harbors and coastlines near Newport, Norfolk, New York, San Diego, Los Angeles, San Francisco, and Puget Sound. Many a ship has spent hours listening to fog signals when faced with "pea soup" in harbor. It is even more difficult, however, to listen for fog signals when under way. Lookouts covering all quarters peer into gray nothingness, while the junior officer of the deck never takes his or her eyes off the radar repeater on the bridge.

Steam Fog. This is a type of advection fog formed by air saturation. It occurs when cold air moves over warm water. When this happens, water evaporating from the warm surface easily saturates the cold air, thus producing the steam fog. You can produce this same effect by setting a pan of warm water out in freezing cold air. This type of fog occurs often in the far north, where it is called "sea smoke." It can be seen in the late fall or winter when a river or pond "steams" as frigid air cools the water until it begins to form a coating of ice.

Radiation Fog. This fog is caused by the heat that the earth radiates. It forms only at night, over a land surface. This is a common type of fog, and it may cover a large area; but it usually lifts before noon, having been "burned" away by the Sun's rays. After sunset, the earth receives no more heat from the Sun, but the ground continues to radiate heat. The surface begins to cool, and layers of air close to the surface are cooled by conduction. If the air is sufficiently moist, it will chill to its dew point and form fog. This type of fog can be extremely hazardous for drivers. Fog patches may suddenly develop in low areas, drastically reducing visibility.

Frontal Fogs. Although weather fronts are discussed in chapter 5 of this unit, *frontal fog* should also be mentioned here. This fog is caused by the movement of cold-air masses. It most commonly occurs under the frontal surface of the cold-air mass and is caused by the evaporation of falling precipitation. Such a circumstance is common in December or January when a warm front (the midwinter thaw) is caught between the normal cold weather of winter and a new cold front, which pushes the warm air ahead of it over cold ground. In the upper Midwest this results in "case weather" with very heavy, wet fog dampening the air, melting snow, and causing extremely dreary days.

Study Guide Questions

1. Of what is a cloud made?
2. What causes earthbound moisture to evaporate?
3. What are the three basic guidelines used to determine which kinds of clouds are in the sky and how they may affect weather prediction?
4. What are the names of the three basic cloud types?
5. What are the two means of classifying clouds?
6. What are the ranges of altitude for low, middle, and high clouds?
7. What type of weather is associated with these types of clouds?
   A. stratus   D. cumulus
   B. nimbostratus   E. cirrus
   C. cumulonimbus   F. altocumulus
8. How were early navigators often able to find previously uncharted islands?
9. What is precipitation?

10. A. How do raindrops form?
    B. What is coalescence, and how does it happen?
11. What two techniques are used in modern rainmaking?
12. A. What is sleet?
    B. What causes it to occur?
13. What is hail, and how are hailstones formed?
14. What is fog, and how is it formed?
15. A. Where are the two most famous natural sea-fog areas located?
    B. Why do they have such frequent fog?

Vocabulary

hygroscopic nuclei
cirrus
cumulus
cumulonimbus
coalescence
silver-iodide crystals
cloud "seeding"
"ceiling"
"sea smoke"
visibility

fog
stratus
nimbus
nimbostratus
drought
thunderhead
hailstone
advection fog
frontal fog
advection

3

Wind and Weather

Air in motion is called *wind*. Winds blow because they are attempting to achieve a balance in atmospheric pressure. The unequal distribution of atmospheric pressure is caused by the unequal heating of Earth's surface. Winds blow from high-pressure areas to low-pressure areas. The strength of these winds depends on the distance of the high from the low and the difference in pressure (the gradient) between the two areas. Since various places on Earth's surface receive more heat than others, temperatures and strengths of winds differ from one area to another.

There is a continual flow of wind over the face of the earth as the result of this uneven heating. From about 2½ to 3 miles above the surface to the tropopause, winds are westerly in direction at all degrees of latitude, from the equator to the poles. At the surface, a band of easterly winds called the *trade winds* extends from the equator to 30 degrees, both north and south. Between 30 degrees and 60 degrees, in both the Northern and Southern Hemispheres, there are the *prevailing westerlies*. Finally, between 60 degrees and both poles there are winds called the *polar easterlies*.

Why are there so many different wind directions, and why are there differences in wind circulations in the Northern and Southern Hemispheres? The answers to these questions come from our knowledge of the motions of Earth itself.

WIND AND THE EARTH'S ROTATION

Two motions of Earth affect the weather. The movement of Earth around the Sun accounts for the seasonal changes on Earth. We will talk briefly about this a bit later. The other motion is the rotation of Earth on its axis. This rotation causes night and day, with the consequent heating and cooling effects on the atmosphere. It also produces the major wind belts of Earth.

If Earth did not rotate, the warmer air over the equator would rise and move north and south toward the poles, high above Earth's surface. The air would cool and sink as it moved toward the poles. Later, it would move back toward the equator at a steady speed and direction. However, the Coriolis effect discussed in unit 2 causes the direction of the wind to curve to the right in the Northern Hemisphere and to the left in the Southern Hemisphere. This curving or deflection effect continues until a balance with other forces is reached.

At this point, we must again bring in the factor of atmospheric pressures in order to explain why there are different belts of prevailing primary winds on Earth.

We know that air rises at the equator and begins moving northward at high altitudes. It eventually sinks and accumulates near the surface, forming a high-pressure area. This sinking and accumulating takes place in the area of 30 degrees north and south latitudes. These areas are called the Horse Latitudes.

Air must always flow outward from the center of a high-pressure area; this is called *divergence*. Conversely, air flows in toward the center of a low-pressure area; this effect is *convergence*. It follows that when both high and low pressure areas are present, air flows from the high to the low pressure area, thus creating *wind*.

PREVAILING WINDS

The Doldrums. The equatorial belt of light and variable converging winds is called the doldrums. They vary in position and tend to move north and south of the geographic equator with the Sun. In the doldrums the temperatures are high and excessive precipitation occurs. Days go by without a breath of wind; thus, in the days of sail, ships avoided this area, if possible. Severe tropical storms begin here.

Trade Winds. At the surface and on the pole-ward sides of the doldrums there are bands of easterly winds

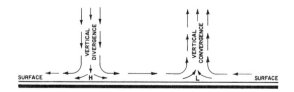

An illustration of vertical convergence and divergence. Unequal heating of the earth's surface results in unequal distribution of pressure. Warm air rises or converges above lows, and colder air falls or diverges around highs.

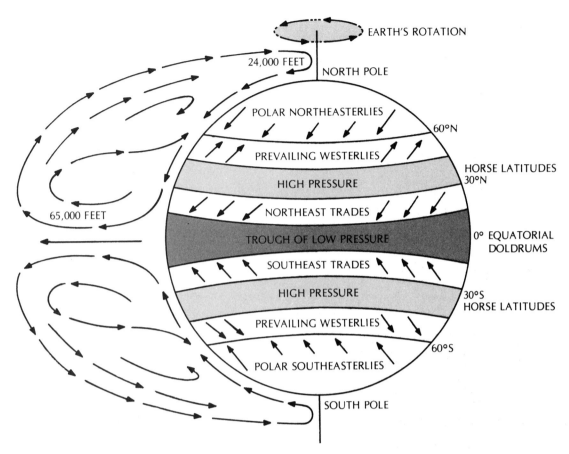

The general circulation pattern of air over the rotating Earth.

called the trade winds. The northeast trades were a popular route for sailing vessels, and aircraft traveling west in the Northern Hemisphere are favored with a tail wind and clear skies if they fly near 30 degrees north latitude. The winds come from the southeast in the Southern Hemisphere, and thus are called the southeast trades.

Subtropical High-Pressure Belt. These are the Horse Latitudes. Because of sinking wind from aloft and diverging winds at the surface, these areas generally have fair weather. The diverging winds cause the trade winds found on the equatorial side of this high-pressure belt. The Horse Latitudes tend to be cloudless and calm, with weak, undependable winds. The term "Horse Latitudes" comes from the fact that, in the days of sail, ships carrying horses from Europe often were becalmed here. When this happened, the horses died for lack of food and water, so the dead animals were thrown overboard to prevent the spread of disease.

Prevailing Westerlies. These winds are found on the pole-ward side of the subtropical highs and are created by the diverging winds of these highs. They blow from the southwest in the Northern Hemisphere and from the northwest in the Southern Hemisphere. The prevailing westerlies provide most of the air flow over the United States.

Polar Front Zone. The belt of low pressure known as the polar front zone lies in the area of 60 degrees north and south latitudes. In the north it is called the Arctic Semipermanent Low, and in the south it is called the Antarctic Permanent Low. These two areas are noted for their bad weather because the westerlies and the polar easterlies converge in them.

Polar Easterlies. This is a zone of poorly developed surface winds created by outflow from the high pressure at the poles. They have a northeasterly direction in the Northern Hemisphere and a southeasterly direction in the Southern Hemisphere.

WIND AND THE EARTH'S REVOLUTION

We have discussed in some detail the effects of the rotational movement of Earth on weather, and particularly its effect on winds. Another important movement is the revolution of our planet around the Sun. This movement, combined with Earth's inclination, causes the seasons.

Earth is inclined at an angle of 23½ (23.5) degrees from the perpendicular to the plane of its orbit of revolution, called the plane of the ecliptic. This simply means that Earth tips at this angle all the time, like a top as it

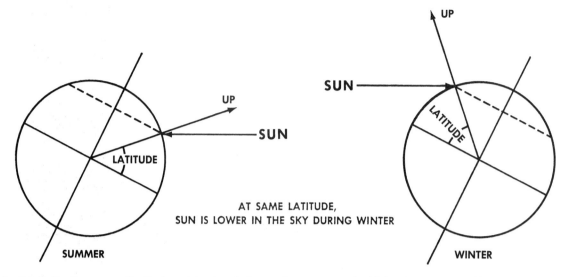

AT SAME LATITUDE,
SUN IS LOWER IN THE SKY DURING WINTER

Earth's inclination causes the Sun's position in relation to the equator to be higher in summer and lower in winter.

begins to slow down. Because of this fact, the part of Earth receiving the most direct rays from the Sun will vary over a year from 23.5 degrees north (tropic of Cancer) to 23.5 degrees south (tropic of Capricorn), as Earth proceeds in its orbit around the Sun.

Our seasonal weather variations are the result of the angle with which the Sun's rays strike Earth as it revolves around the Sun, not the nearness of Earth to the Sun. In summer, because of Earth's inclination, the Sun's rays in the Northern Hemisphere are more direct, even though at this time Earth is farther away from the Sun. Thus, the rays are more concentrated and deliver more energy per unit area, making the weather warm. In winter in the Northern Hemisphere, Earth is actually closer to the Sun, but sunlight hits this hemisphere at a greater angle. Thus, the same amount of sunlight is spread over a larger area, delivering less energy per unit area, so it gets cooler. The reverse of this process happens in the Southern Hemisphere.

SECONDARY WIND CIRCULATION

We have discussed the primary circulation of winds on Earth. It is the unequal heating of the planet between the equator and the poles that causes north-south winds. The rotation of Earth turns these winds east or west depending upon the hemisphere in which they occur. But winds are also affected by the topography of the land and the currents of the seas.

We know that nearly three-fourths of Earth's surface is water. But not many people realize that three-fourths of the world's land surfaces are in the Northern Hemisphere. In the summer these land surfaces heat very rapidly, while the water areas heat very slowly. In winter, the land cools rapidly and the water cools comparatively

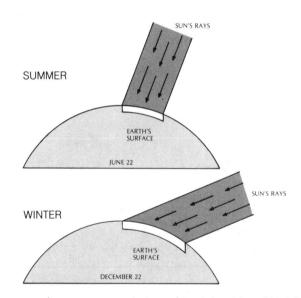

The seasonal temperature variations of Earth in mid- and high latitudes are a result of the angle at which the Sun's rays strike the surface. Note the difference in the surface areas struck by the same amount of sunshine in summer and winter. Because the amount of energy per unit area is higher in summer *(top)*, it gets hotter than in winter, when the energy per unit area is lower *(bottom)*.

slowly, because the water retains part of the heat it gained during the previous summer. For this reason, water areas are cooler than land areas during the summer and warmer during the winter. The daily variation of temperature over open water is seldom more than 2 or 3 degrees, but 300 miles inland, it is rarely less than 15 degrees.

The difference between the land and sea temperatures causes the pressure belts of the primary wind circulation to be broken up into enclosed high- and low-pressure areas, called *centers of action*. We see, therefore, that the geography of the continents and seas can also influence the wind and weather.

HIGHS (ANTICYCLONES)

In the Northern Hemisphere, air flows in a clockwise manner around high-pressure centers of action (also called anticyclones). Air subsides (sinks) in the center and diverges (blows outward) from the center of the high-pressure area. Subsiding currents are warmed adiabatically, so few clouds are formed. Generally fair weather prevails, either warm or cold, depending upon the season.

Local high-pressure areas will develop anyplace where air cools, compresses, and subsides. The Horse Latitudes and the polar highs are good examples of this. But high-pressure areas can develop anywhere. When a high develops, the clockwise anticyclonic spiral of air develops and air begins flowing to surrounding lower-pressure areas.

Major high-pressure areas exist near the poles. They produce very cold air, dependent on the seasons. A high-pressure area exists over Greenland all the time because of the vast icecap there. Subtropical highs can usually be found southwest of California and near the Azores in the Atlantic. The high associated with the North Polar zone repeatedly creates icy polar fronts, which every winter sweep over most of North America east of the Rockies. This area is called the North American High. A similar high-pressure area exists in Siberia, where the temperate zone's coldest temperatures have been recorded. The North American and Siberian Highs are continental highs.

LOWS

The only "permanent" low-pressure area on Earth is the Doldrum Belt near the equator. The Aleutian Low off Alaska is a low-pressure cell associated with the Polar Front and influenced by the Japanese Current. It is intense during the winter but ill-defined in summer. Another low-pressure area lying near Iceland is called the Icelandic Low. The Gulf Stream influences this low.

Traveling low-pressure cells are frequently found in the area of the Polar Front. These are formed by the interaction of the polar air to the north and the maritime tropical air to the south. These lows are called *migratory lows*. Migratory storms may also move into lower latitudes from the Polar Front. Such storms often occur in the south-central United States and on the U.S. East Coast near Cape Hatteras.

Local lows often form directly below large thunderhead clouds. Heat lows form over deserts and other intensely hot areas; a low-pressure area lasts most of the summer over the Arizona and California deserts. Lows sometimes form on the leeward side of mountain ranges and cause rushing winds to "pour" down from the nearby mountains. These lows are common just east of the Rocky Mountains in Colorado.

MOUNTAIN WINDS

We have just mentioned the lows that sometimes form on the lee side of mountain ranges. These winds are so persistent and predictable in some areas that they have earned their own names. Topography is a major factor in the formation of such winds, but temperature differences and the rotation of Earth also contribute.

As warm air rises on one side of the mountains, it cools and loses its moisture as rain or snow. The dry, cooler air then rushes down the opposite side, heating the air and pushing it into the low. Famous mountain winds are the Chinooks of the Rockies, the Santa Anas of southern California, and the foehns of the Swiss and French Alps. These winds sometimes reach gale force and, in the western United States, often become dust storms.

VALLEY WINDS

Probably the most famous valley wind system is the Mistral of southern France. This is a cold, dry wind that rushes down the Rhône Valley toward the low-pressure system that often develops over the Mediterranean Sea. Sometimes reaching whole gale and storm force over 60 mph, this wind is one the U.S. Sixth Fleet must be on the alert for when involved in western Mediterranean operations.

MONSOONS

Monsoons are seasonal winds characteristic of South and Southeast Asia, though they occur elsewhere with less intensity and regularity. The monsoon is a very persistent wind that blows on predictable seasonal paths and with definite seasonal characteristics.

Summer (Southwest) Monsoon. As continental Asia begins to warm in the spring, the water area over the Indian Ocean remains relatively cool. The warming effect gradually creates a continental low over the central Asian plateaus and desert. This low draws cooler air from the south. As the moisture-laden Indian Ocean air pushes northeastward over the land, it begins to cool and condense. The rains begin to fall in southern India in mid-May and continue to build up in intensity as the continent warms. The wet air rushes into the southern slopes of the Himalaya Mountains and dumps astounding amounts of rain on the southern Asian countries. It is common for the southeast Burmese coast to have 200 inches of rainfall during the period between mid-May

Beaufort no.	Speed in knots	Descriptive terms	Sea criterion	Approximate equivalent sea disturbance scale in open sea		
				Sea state no.	Description	Mean height of waves (in feet)
0	Less than 1	Calm	Sea like a mirror.	0	Calm (glassy)	—
1	1–3	Light air	Ripples with the appearance of scales are formed, but without foam crests.	1	Calm (rippled)	½
2	4–6	Light breeze	Small wavelets, still short but more pronounced. Crests have a glassy appearance and do not break.	1	—	1
3	7–10	Gentle breeze	Large wavelets. Crests begin to break. Foam has glassy appearance. Perhaps scattered whitecaps.	2	Smooth (wavelets)	2½
4	11–16	Moderate breeze	Small waves, becoming longer. Fairly frequent whitecaps.	3	Slight	5
5	17–21	Fresh breeze	Moderate waves, taking a more pronounced long form. Many whitecaps are formed (chance of some spray).	4	Moderate	9
6	22–27	Strong breeze	Large waves begin to form. The white foam crests are more extensive everywhere (probably some spray).	5	Rough	14
7	28–33	Moderate gale	Sea heaps up and white foam from breaking waves begins to be blown in streaks along the direction of the wind. (Spray becomes heavy).	6	Very rough	19
8	34–40	Fresh gale	Moderately high waves of greater length. Edges of crests break into spray. The foam is blown in well-marked streaks along the direction of the wind.	7	High	25
9	41–47	Strong gale	High waves. Dense streaks of foam along the direction of the wind. Sea begins to roll. Spray may affect visibility.	7	—	31
10	48–55	Whole gale	Very high waves with long, overhanging crests. The resulting foam in great patches is blown in dense white streaks along the direction of the wind. On the whole the surface of the sea takes on a white appearance. The rolling of the sea becomes heavy and shocklike. Visibility is affected.	8	Very high	37
11	56–63	Storm	Exceptionally high waves (Small- and medium-sized ships might for a long time be lost to view behind the waves.) The sea is completely covered with long white patches of foam lying along the direction of the wind. Everywhere the edges of the wave crests are blown into froth. Visibility affected.	9	Phenomenal	45 or more
12	Above 64	Hurricane and typhoon	The air is filled with foam and spray. Sea completely white with driving spray. Visibility very seriously affected.	9	—	—

The Beaufort Wind Scale and Correlative Sea Disturbance Scale.

and late September. At the foothills of the Himalayas, 500 inches of rain in the same period have been recorded almost every year. The greatest rainfall ever recorded occurred at Cherrapunji, India, during the monsoon: 1,041.78 inches. Squalls and typhoons occur over the Bay of Bengal during this time.

Winter (Northeast) Monsoon. As the cold season of the Northern Hemisphere approaches, the continental high over Siberia regenerates and begins to dominate the air circulation over South and Southeast Asia. The wind now reverses itself and blows from the northeast. The rains of the summer season cease. A warm, low-pressure area now exists over the Indian Ocean. The cooler, dry air from central Asia now blows southwestward across the continent over the Himalayas and into the southern countries. The northeast wind persists from late September until April, when the humidity begins to rise for the next summer monsoon.

During the winter monsoon there is little rain, and by the time January and February arrive, the soil is parched and cracked, leaves have curled and died, and dust lies thick over much of the countryside. Dust in Upper Burma around Mandalay is often 4 to 6 inches thick along roads and in villages.

WINDS AND THE BEAUFORT WIND SCALE

Meteorologists must always be aware of wind velocity and wind direction. Wind speed is always given in knots, according to international agreement. The instrument used to measure wind speed is called an *anemometer.* Wind blows into metal cups, which are attached to arms. The whirling cups turn a spindle, the speed of which is calibrated into wind speed. A vane atop the anemometer aligns itself with the direction of the wind. A dial on the instrument readout indicates the apparent wind velocity and direction.

In addition to wind-measuring equipment, the Beaufort Wind Scale with Correlative Sea Disturbance Scale can also be used to estimate wind speed. This scale is based on careful observation of sea conditions. Admiral Sir Francis Beaufort of the British Royal Navy developed the scale in 1805 to estimate wind speeds from their effect on sails. His table numbered the winds from 1 to 12, in order of increasing severity. It compared them to the Sea Disturbance Scale, which describes sea state and mean height of waves on a scale of 1 to 9. Descriptive terms identify the winds and their counterpart waves. The Beaufort Wind Scale enables the shipboard weatherman or sailor to estimate wind speeds merely by looking at the sea state and then comparing the two scales.

By convention, wind direction is specified according to the compass direction or geographic point of origin from which the wind blows.

Study Guide Questions

1. A. What is a simple definition of wind?
   B. Upon what does the strength of wind depend?
2. What are the three primary wind belts in the Northern Hemisphere?
3. A. What two motions of Earth affect the weather?
   B. Which of these motions causes the major wind belts?
4. How does the Coriolis effect cause winds to deflect in the Northern and Southern Hemispheres?
5. A. How does atmospheric pressure affect the primary wind belts?
   B. What are the principal high-pressure belts on Earth's surface?
6. What determines the directional name of a wind?
7. Explain each of the world's prevailing wind and pressure belts.
8. A. What movement of Earth causes the seasons?
   B. What is meant by Earth's "inclination"?
9. What names are given to the 23.5 degrees north and 23.5 degrees south latitude lines?
10. What are the principal causes of secondary wind circulation?
11. What is the effect of the geography of the continents and seas on the primary wind belts in the Northern Hemisphere?
12. How does air "act" in a high-pressure area?
13. Over what countries in the Northern Hemisphere do "permanent" high-pressure areas exist?
14. A. Where do the principal low-pressure areas exist on Earth?
    B. Where do seasonal lows usually develop in the United States?
15. A. What are the most famous mountain winds, and where do they blow?
    B. What type of weather do these winds bring?
16. What valley wind is of particular concern to the Sixth Fleet?
17. A. What are monsoon winds, and where are they most common?
    B. Describe the generation of the southwest and northeast monsoons.
18. A. What instrument is used to measure wind velocity?
    B. What dialed instrument indicates wind speed and direction to the ship's bridge watch and navigator?
19. A. What is the Beaufort Wind Scale?
    B. How is the Correlative Sea Disturbance Scale used with the Beaufort Wind Scale?

Vocabulary

gradient	Tropic of Capricorn
Coriolis effect	migratory lows
anticyclone	Chinook winds
doldrums	foehn winds
trade winds	Santa Anas (winds)
Horse Latitudes	monsoon
prevailing westerlies	anemometer
Beaufort Wind Scale	Tropic of Cancer

4

Fronts and Storms

Mariners have much to fear when they are threatened by a severe storm. A North Atlantic gale can strain rigging, spring seams, bend plates, smash equipment, and tear loose topside equipment, even on aircraft carriers or bulk petroleum tankers. Winds of 100 knots and waves of sixty feet or more are respected by an experienced seaman. The prudent mariner will maneuver to stay clear of storms whenever possible.

An experienced mariner should be able to see when weather disturbances are coming. One should observe the sky and sea and carefully assess readings of the meteorological instruments aboard. Also, today's radio communications provide regular weather summaries. The mariner at sea will carefully plot such weather information and compare it with the vessel's position and where she is heading.

DEVELOPMENT OF FRONTS

Fronts develop when air masses of different temperatures collide; air masses rarely fuse unless they are very similar in temperature and moisture content. Fronts are weather systems that are sometimes called *waves*, as in the term "cold wave."

Along the meeting edge or boundary of two dissimilar air masses, a battle for supremacy is fought. Usually the colder of the two masses, being heavier, predominates and forces the warmer air upward. A *cold front* displaces the warm air ahead of it upward, while a *warm front* moves upward over a retreating cold-air mass.

When a cold front moves faster than a warm front, it overtakes the warm front, forcing the warmest part of the air mass upward, but leaving the cooler air below. By the time the cold front meets or *converges* with the cooler mass ahead of the warm front, the warm air has been pushed above both masses. The convergent frontal mass that remains is called an *occluded front*. Regardless of the type of front—cold, warm, or occluded—the frontal weather is either unsettled or stormy. Fronts always bring bad weather.

A cold front or warm front may extend for hundreds of miles. But the area in which frontal weather disturbances occur is usually a band 15–50 miles wide for a cold front and up to 300 miles wide for a warm front. The point where the cold and warm fronts converge is frequently the center of a low-pressure area.

FRONTAL ZONES

The world's primary frontal zones are the Intertropical Convergence Zone, Arctic Frontal Zone, and Polar Frontal Zone. The convergence of the northeast trade winds of the Northern Hemisphere and the southeast trade winds of the Southern Hemisphere causes a band of unstable weather encircling Earth in the doldrums. This is called the *Intertropical Convergence Zone* (ITCZ). It varies in position, largely due to the seasons. This is a storm development area, but the storms themselves usually move pole-ward before they become severe. Brief, violent windstorms called *squalls* occur when the warm air rises, resulting in sudden, intense rainfall of short duration. There normally is good visibility between these squalls. In tropical seas it is often possible to see multiple separate rain squalls in progress, and several rainbows, all around the horizon.

The *Arctic Frontal Zone* develops between the arctic air of the far north and the polar maritime air of the North Atlantic and Pacific Oceans. This frontal zone may disappear as it moves northward during the summer, when it meets similar cold air.

The *Polar Frontal Zone* is formed by the convergence of the air that flows toward the equator from the Polar Easterlies and the Prevailing Westerlies—in other words, the temperate zones. This polar front is very significant, since it greatly influences the weather in the temperate zones. The polar fronts move toward the poles during the summer and toward the tropics in the winter. This is why people in the temperate zones often experience a series of cold waves or snaps—because the colder polar easterlies often break through the warmer band of westerlies.

COLD FRONTS

When a cold front is coming, the first change you notice is a darkening of the horizon to the west and to the north.

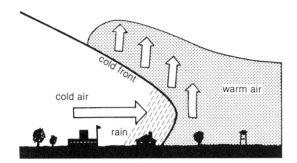

A cold front is formed when a cold-air mass moves into a warm-air mass, causing the warm air to rise.

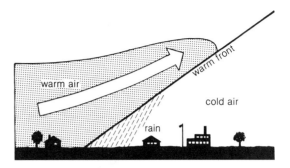

A warm front is formed when a warm air mass rises over a cold-air mass.

Very soon thereafter, the cloud ceiling lowers, and rain begins. A fast-moving cold front, which may move as much as 700 miles in a day, with cumulonimbus clouds preceding it, brings sudden, violent showers or thunderstorms. Rainfall probably will be steady if cumulonimbus clouds are not ahead of the front.

Passage of a cold front is usually marked by a wind shift, a drop in temperature, a rise in pressure, a rapid clearing of the sky, and good visibility. Squall lines often precede the cold front; these are often violent, causing flash floods from downpours, cloudbursts, and extremely turbulent winds.

WARM FRONTS

A warm front will be preceded by cirrus clouds in parallel; then, in order, will follow cirrostratus, altostratus, nimbostratus, and finally stratus. Visibility is poor in advance of a warm front. Frequently fog forms, and steady rain or drizzle prevails. Thunderstorms may develop ahead of this front.

When the frontal line is passing, a definite shift occurs in the wind direction, and the temperature rises sharply. Gradual clearing will take place, and pressure remains steady or falls slowly. A warm front moves much more slowly than a cold front, normally less than 15 mph. Cloud sequences will begin as much as forty-eight hours in advance, often with rain. Cloud sequences may occur 1,000 miles in advance of the front itself.

OCCLUDED FRONTS

This is an unstable frontal cyclone with a rapidly moving cold front. It will overtake warmer air masses. The cold front in this cyclone will always move so rapidly that it will force the whole overtaken warm front aloft. This type of occlusion is called the cold-front type.

The cold front that remains on the surface is called the *occluded front*, and the warm front that is raised aloft is called the *upper front*. Most occlusions of this type occur on the eastern portions of continents. Heavy

frontal precipitation with thunderstorms occurs, though of less intensity than with a regular cold front.

A warm-front type of occlusion occurs when the air ahead of the warm front is colder than the air behind the cold front. When this occurs, the cold front rides up over the warm frontal surface. The warm front, in this case, remains on the surface and is called the occluded front, while the cold front lifted aloft is called the upper front. This type of occlusion occurs chiefly in the Pacific Northwest. Severe icing and precipitation may occur in the area just behind where the cold front starts to rise.

THUNDERSTORMS

The thunderstorm occurs within clouds with vertical development, such as cumulus and cumulonimbus. These storms are characterized by loud thunder, flashes of lightning, very heavy precipitation, strong gusts of wind, and occasional hail or tornadoes. Because the thunderstorm is local in nature and relatively short in duration, it is difficult to forecast.

A thunderstorm develops in three rapid stages. The first stage is an updraft of warm, moist air into the atmosphere. The water vapor cools and condenses into clouds, and the clouds grow taller and taller as the updrafts continue. This first stage of development is called the *cumulus stage.*

The second stage, called the *mature stage* of thunderstorm development, is characterized by both updrafts and down-drafts within the storm-producing cloud. The cooler the upper part becomes as it towers into the atmosphere, the faster raindrops and even hail will begin to form and fall. Downdrafts are caused by the raindrops falling. There is frictional drag between the raindrops and the surrounding air, so that the air is pulled down with the raindrops. The mature cell usually extends above 25,000 feet. The downdrafts do not extend that high, however, because there is insufficient moisture at the higher altitudes.

The final stage is called the *dissipating* or *anvil stage.* As more and more air is brought down by raindrop

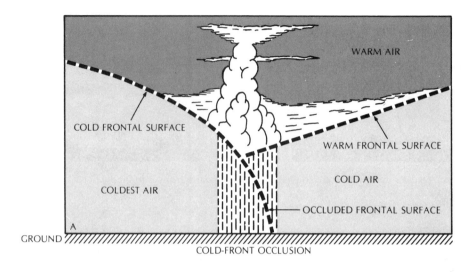

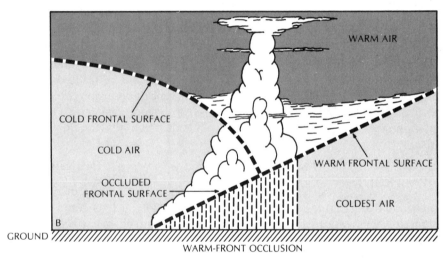

Two types of occluded fronts. In the upper drawing of a cold-front occlusion, the cold air behind the cold front is colder than the cold air ahead of the warm front, pushing the warm front aloft. In the warm-front occlusion on the bottom, the cold air ahead of the warm front is colder than the cold air behind the cold front, forcing the cold front aloft. From Kotsch, *Weather for the Mariner*, 133

friction, these downdrafts take the place of updrafts and spread out. The entire lower portion of the cloud becomes downdraft, and the high winds in the upper altitudes flatten the top of the cloud into an anvil shape. Rain is now falling heavily on the ground, but the storm will dissipate in a short time.

WEATHER PHENOMENA WITH THUNDERSTORMS

Rain is found in every thunderstorm. Some of this rain will form in regions below freezing level. Hail will form if the updrafts carry melted or partially melted raindrops into the higher, colder altitudes. Snow and ice crystals also may be in any thunderstorm, winter or summer, though in summer they will melt into rain when nearing the earth.

A thunderstorm is most turbulent in the area of heaviest precipitation. Icing will often occur just above the freezing level, making this a very hazardous area for aircraft.

The leading gust of wind, sometimes called a microburst, is one of a thunderstorm's dangers. This gust occurs just prior to the passage of the storm. The strong winds at the surface are the result of the horizontal spreading-out of the storm's downdraft currents as they approach the surface of the earth. The speed of the first gust usually is the highest recorded during any thunderstorm and can blow in any direction—even in opposition to the surface wind that is "pushing" the storm. Such conditions can result in "wind shear," which is very dangerous to aircraft in the process of taking off or landing.

Surging air currents in the thunderhead cloud create static electricity, the source of *lightning*. This process is

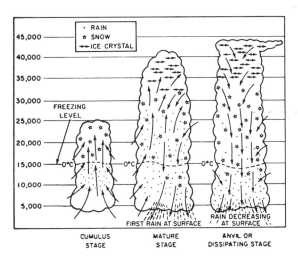

Life cycle of a thunderstorm cell.

not completely understood, but it is generally believed that lightning is caused by the breaking-up of large water droplets into positively and negatively charged particles. Positive charges develop near the top of the cloud, and negative particles accumulate in the lower reaches. An electrical discharge occurs when these charges reach sufficient strength to overcome the electrical resistance between them. The lightning, then, is nature's way of neutralizing the charges between the two electrical regions.

The buildup of electricity in a thunderhead may reach millions of volts. The lightning may flash within the cloud, jump to other clouds, jump from the clouds to the ground, or even jump from the ground up to the cloud.

Lightning occurs in two steps. First, a *leader* of electrified (ionized) air runs between the two oppositely charged regions. This establishes the "circuit" for the second stroke, which leaps along the leader to complete the circuit. This second stroke is the one you see, and consequently, the one that causes the thunder you hear. The lightning generates terrific heat, causing an explosive expansion of glowing hot air and producing the audible thunder.

Lightning follows the shortest route between a cloud and the ground. Thus, high points such as trees, telephone poles, TV antennas, ship and boat masts, and the like are the places most likely to be struck by lightning.

Lightning also follows the easiest route to ground after striking, so it will follow electrical wires, plumbing pipes, sailboat rigging, and even drafts of air in its attempt to reach the ground. It is very unwise to be on or near bodies of water during a thunderstorm; never be out in an open boat. Mountainous areas also should be avoided during an electrical thunderstorm, especially crevices or rushing mountain streams.

A fundamental rule for airplane pilots is never to fly under or through a thunderstorm. It is safest to fly around the storm. If a pilot must fly through one, it should be penetrated at an altitude of about one-third its height.

TORNADOES

The most intense and violent of localized storms is the *tornado*. It is usually associated with violent thunderstorm activity and heavy rain. Tornadoes are wind whirlpools of such violence that houses in their path will disintegrate like matchsticks, brick buildings will be destroyed, and trains will be derailed. Feathers and straws may be propelled by the swirling wind with the force of power-driven nails.

Tornadoes are of very small diameter, usually 300–400 feet; but they may continue on an erratic path for more than 100 miles. Winds in the *vortex*—the whirlwind causing the funnel—often exceed 300 mph. But the speed of the storm moving over the earth's surface is comparatively slow, usually 25–40 mph. The duration over any given spot may be only seconds—but in that short time the devastation can be almost total.

Tornadoes build up only during severe thunderstorms. Fortunately, only about one thunderstorm out of a thousand develops a tornado. A tornado forms as a funnel cloud on the forward edge of a fully developed cumulonimbus cloud. Rising air causes a swirling at the base of the parent cloud. As the swirl increases in size and speed, the funnel drops out of the cloud, like an elephant's trunk dangling toward the surface. When it touches ground the funnel is called a tornado; if it forms over water, it is called a *waterspout*.

Tornadoes are most common in the temperate zone (the midlatitudes between 23.5 degrees and 66.5 degrees north and south), probably because of the greater atmospheric-temperature contrasts there. The midwestern United States is the most tornado-ravaged area of the world. Usually these storms hit in the late spring or early summer. But they can occur at almost any time.

The extreme low pressure in the vortex of a tornado causes closed homes and barns to explode outward from the normal pressure of air trapped inside. There is a 100–200 mph updraft in the center of the funnel, which can suck up all manner of dust and debris, houses, cars, animals, and even people.

TROPICAL CYCLONES

A *cyclone* is a circular area of low atmospheric pressure around which winds in excess of 74 mph blow. These winds are counterclockwise in the Northern Hemisphere and clockwise in the Southern Hemisphere. The so-called tropical cyclones are subdivided into three categories: (1) tropical depression—maximum wind less than 34 knots, (2) tropical storm—maximum wind 34–63 knots,

The funnel of a tornado spins with such force that it can destroy everything in its path. Tornadoes are a local weather phenomenon, often difficult to forecast. Whenever severe thunderstorms are present, a tornado is a possibility. Most tornadoes occur in the summer.

and (3) hurricane or typhoon—maximum wind 64 knots and up.

Large tropical cyclones occur in many places throughout the world and are called by various names. They form over all tropical oceans except the South Atlantic, but they do not form over continents. They are common in the West Indies, often ranging up the East Coast of the United States and into the Gulf of Mexico, where they are called *hurricanes*. Tropical cyclones occurring east of the International Date Line in the Pacific have also become known as hurricanes. In the Western Pacific, off the coast of China, they are called *typhoons*. Off the west coast of Australia they are called *willy-willies,* and off the Philippines they are called *baguios.*

Hurricanes and typhoons are given women's and men's names, alternating up the alphabet in the order in which the storms appear each season. Before 1978, all these storms were named after women.

Although the velocities associated with these tropical cyclones are less than those of a tornado, they cover hundreds of times the area and last much longer. The tropical cyclone is the most destructive of all weather phenomena, and the one that is of greatest concern to the oceangoing sailor.

A famous waterspout that appeared near Martha's Vineyard off Massachusetts in 1896. This huge waterspout was calculated to be 3,600 feet in height and 240 feet wide at the base.

LIFE OF A HURRICANE

The birth of a hurricane often occurs in that region near the equator where trade winds meet to form the Intertropical Convergence Zone (ICZ). Tropical cyclones, however, never occur right on the equator because they require the twisting Coriolis forces of Earth's rotation to start them spinning, which are not present there.

A hurricane is born in a hot, moist air mass over the ocean. The rotating low at the ICZ pushes air toward its center, forcing the hot moist air to lift. The lifting causes the moisture to condense. As this moisture condenses, it heats the rotating air more, causing it to rise even more swiftly. As more moist tropical sea air sweeps in to replace this rising air, more condensation takes place, and the cycle intensifies. That is why hurricanes are so violent—because of the tremendous energy released by the continuous condensation and an inexhaustible source of moisture. All the while, the Coriolis effect keeps the air turning more and more rapidly, until it is a giant wheel of swirling winds.

Although their tracks cannot be predicted individually, in general in the Northern Hemisphere hurricanes move westward from their point of origin, then curve to the northeast. In the Southern Hemisphere they start out westward and then curve southeastward. They vary in diameter from 60 to 1,000 miles. They have moderate winds at their outer edges, increasing toward the center, where velocities higher than 175 knots (200 mph) have been recorded. At the center is an area called the *eye* of the storm, which averages about 14 miles in diameter.

This area is relatively calm, with light winds and clear or moderately clear skies and a little drizzle.

An Atlantic hurricane, then, starts as a tropical low, grows into a storm, and eventually matures into a hurricane when its winds exceed 75 mph. While it is moving along its track, it is growing in intensity. By the time it begins to curve to the northeast, it comes over cooler waters and into cooler air. Cooling reduces its internal action, until it finally dissipates into an extratropical low, usually ending as a gale or storm over the North Atlantic or North Sea.

The elements of wind, temperature, pressure, humidity, and rain vary little in the different quadrants of a tropical cyclone. Winds increase from the outer limits to the edge of the eye. The temperature rises and the humidity falls at the center. Precipitation is in the form of showers at the outer limits. It becomes heavier toward the center, and is heaviest in the right front quadrant.

Hurricanes are usually associated with great wind-caused tides called storm surges that inundate the land areas they approach, and cause more damage than do the wind and rain of the storm itself. The doldrums, with their baffling winds and frequent rain squalls and thunderstorms, is the breeding place of most tropical cyclones.

HURRICANES, TYPHOONS, AND THEIR TRACKS

Hurricanes occur most frequently in September and October, but they can happen anytime from June to December. A typical hurricane that originates in the doldrums

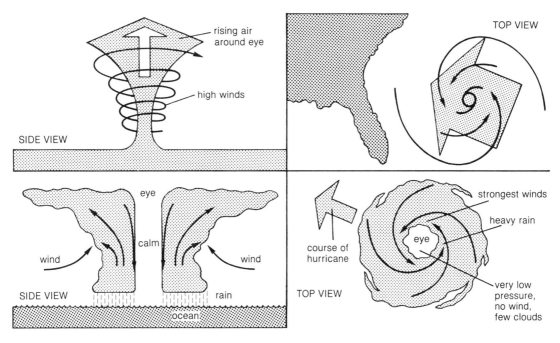

Anatomy of a hurricane. *Upper left:* Hurricane winds rise in a counterclockwise spiral around an eye of calm air. *Lower left:* A cross section shows the shape of the hurricane cloud layers. *Upper right:* The whole hurricane system moves toward the southeast coast of the United States. *Lower right:* Seen from above, the hurricane has a circular shape with a central eye.

The eye of Hurricane Gracie, September 1959. The picture was taken from a "hurricane hunter" aircraft that was tracking the storm.

east of the West Indies will follow a curving track northeastward from the Greater Antilles. It then hits the east coast of Florida and turns north, spreading destruction along the eastern seaboard of the United States, sometimes as far north as New York. Such an East Coast hurricane will usually cause heavy rains from Philadelphia northward into New York, Connecticut, Rhode Island, and Massachusetts. It will also cause tidal flooding from Georgia to Virginia, even if the main brunt of the storm never actually hits the coast.

With somewhat less frequency, but often with greater violence, a hurricane originating in the same area will move south of Cuba and swing into the Gulf of Mexico, where, like a captured tempest in a bathtub, it will wreak havoc throughout the Gulf Coast. A Gulf Coast hurricane often will dissipate in the Mississippi Valley, with heavy rainfalls extending as far north as Tennessee, Kentucky, and Illinois.

The southwestern part of the North Pacific has more tropical cyclones than any other place on Earth. These generally are born between the Marshall Islands and the Philippines and move toward the east coast of China, then northeastward over the Philippines, Taiwan, Oki-

nawa, and Japan. The typhoon may veer into the Asian continent almost anywhere along its east coast. When it does, it is usually accompanied by terrible storm surges. These sweep deep inland along the low-lying coastal plains and up the numerous rivers, causing widespread destruction and loss of life. And, just as a hurricane may move into the Gulf of Mexico, a typhoon may sweep south of the East Indies (Indonesia) into the Bay of Bengal. It then hits the coast of southern Asia.

In probably the greatest natural catastrophe of history, a typhoon swept over the Bay of Bengal in 1737. The storm pushed a forty-foot surge of water inland, killing 300,000 people. A hurricane that hit Galveston, Texas, in 1900 killed 6,000 people. A terrible hurricane struck New England in 1938, causing 600 deaths and property damage exceeding $250 million. The entire boardwalk at Atlantic City, New Jersey, has been swept away on several occasions. The whole city of Belize, British Honduras, was destroyed in the late 1960s; the survivors rebuilt on a new site further inland on higher ground. The strongest hurricane ever recorded in the Western Hemisphere was Hurricane Gilbert, which came west across the Atlantic and lower Gulf of Mexico in September 1988. It hit the

TYPE OF WARNING	DAYTIME SIGNALS	NIGHT SIGNALS	EQUIVALENT WIND SPEEDS	
			KNOTS	MPH
SMALL CRAFT			UP TO 33	UP TO 38
GALE			34–47	39–54
STORM			48–63	55–73
HURRICANE			64 OR GREATER	74 OR GREATER

Storm warning signals.

Yucatán Peninsula with winds of 175 mph and a record low pressure of 26.13 inches of mercury, killing 500 people and rendering 500,000 homeless as it swept across Latin America.

Cyclonic winds in the Northern Hemisphere circulate in a counterclockwise direction; those in the Southern Hemisphere circulate clockwise. Mariners must know this if it becomes necessary to maneuver out of a hurricane's path.

If you face in the same direction the storm in the Northern Hemisphere is moving, winds in the right semicircle are circulating so as to draw a vessel in that area into the path of the storm center. This is called the *dangerous semicircle*. The wind also will tend to carry the vessel along with the storm as it moves along its track. On the other hand, winds in the left semicircle, called the *navigable semicircle*, tend to drive the vessel out of the path of the storm and help her to get behind it.

Maneuvering a vessel in a hurricane consists mainly of determining whether she is in, or approaching, the dangerous semicircle, and if she is, finding the best method of working out of that undesirable position.

STORM WARNING SIGNALS

Flags and pennants hoisted at the National Weather Service and other shore stations indicate the presence or fore-cast presence of unfavorable winds. These signals are now flown over most major marinas on the Great Lakes, other major recreational lakes in the nation, ocean beaches, coastal harbor marinas, and Coast Guard stations:

- *Small craft warning.* One red pennant displayed by day, and a red light over a white light at night, indicate that winds of up to 38 mph (33 knots) and sea conditions dangerous to small craft are forecast in the area.
- *Gale warning.* Two red pennants displayed by day, and a white light above a red light at night, indicate that winds ranging from 39 to 54 miles an hour (34–47 knots) are forecast.
- *Storm warning.* A single square red flag with a black center displayed during daytime, and two red lights at night, indicate that winds of 55 mph (48 knots) and above are forecast.
- *Hurricane warning.* Two square red flags with black centers displayed by day, and a white light between two red lights at night, indicate that winds 74 mph (64 knots) and above are forecast for the area.

HURRICANE WARNING SYSTEM

The U.S. Hurricane Warning System was set up in 1938 as a cooperative effort of the National Weather Service, the Navy, and the Army Air Corps. Up to that point, hurricanes struck with almost no previous warning. Reconnaissance airplanes equipped with radar and weather instruments were sent to scout suspected storm areas.

In more recent years, weather satellites supplemented by reconnaissance aircraft are used to supply data on these storms. Bulletins are issued every few hours, giving the latest information on the storm, its intensity, and its present location and probable path, thus furnishing timely warning to all who may be in danger. Ships and aircraft can change course to avoid the storm; people have time to secure their property to reduce damage, and evacuate from areas expected to bear the brunt of the storm.

Study Guide Questions

1. A. How do weather fronts develop?
   B. What usually happens when a cold front meets a warm-air mass?
2. What kind of weather does a front usually bring?
3. What are the three types of frontal systems?
4. A. What are the names of the world's primary frontal zones?
   B. Where is the Intertropical Convergence Zone (ITCZ), and why is it of particular importance?
5. What are squalls, and what are their characteristics?
6. Why is the Polar Frontal Zone important to those who live in the temperate zones?
7. What are the first signs of an approaching cold front?
8. What are the signs of an approaching warm front?
9. What weather is associated with occluded fronts?
10. What are the three stages of a thunderstorm, and what happens in each stage?
11. What weather phenomena occur within a thunderstorm?
12. Why should aircraft avoid flying through a thunderstorm?
13. What is lightning, and what causes it to happen?
14. A. What is meant by the statement "Lightning follows the easiest route"?
    B. What causes thunder?
15. A. Where do most tornadoes occur?
    B. What name is given to a tornado over water?
16. A. What are the three categories of tropical cyclone?
    B. What is the established minimum wind velocity for a tropical cyclone?
17. How are the names given to tropical cyclones around the world chosen?
18. How does a hurricane develop, and why is it so violent?
19. What are the two most usual tracks or paths of a North Atlantic hurricane?
20. What is the "eye" of the hurricane, and what is unusual about this part of the storm?
21. What aspect of a hurricane usually causes the most damage and casualties?
22. When is "hurricane season"?
23. Explain the "dangerous" and "navigable" semicircles of a hurricane.
24. What are the four categories of signals for unfavorable winds in the vicinity of harbors and beaches in the United States?
25. What means are used to locate and track hurricanes?

Vocabulary

warm front	tornado
cold front	tropical depression
occluded front	hurricane
Intertropical Convergence Zone	typhoon
squall	willy-willies
waterspout	baguio

5

Weather Forecasting

Weather forecasting has developed into a full-time activity of the U.S. government, the armed services, and many commercial meteorological enterprises. This chapter will discuss some of the procedures used by the National Weather Service and the Naval Meteorological and Oceanography Command to forecast the weather.

NATIONAL WEATHER

The principal weather agency in the United States is the National Weather Service. It is part of the National Oceanic and Atmospheric Administration (NOAA), which is a part of the Department of Commerce. The National Weather Service reports the weather of the United States and its territories and provides weather, hydrologic (water effects), and climate forecasts and warnings to the general public. It issues warnings about such destructive weather conditions as hurricanes, tornadoes, and floods. It provides special weather services in support of aviation, marine activities, agriculture, forestry, urban air-quality control, and other activities that are sensitive to the weather.

The National Weather Service is composed of a headquarters at Camp Springs, Maryland, near Washington, D.C.; five national operating centers; and six regional offices that support field activities throughout the continental United States, Puerto Rico, Alaska, Hawaii, and other islands in the Pacific Ocean. It receives weather data from about 12,000 substations, many of which are maintained by volunteers.

Chief among the five national operating centers is the National Centers for Environmental Prediction, actually a group of nine different specialized centers that each focus on one aspect of the overall national warning and forecasting process. They include the Aviation Weather Center at Kansas City, Missouri; the Climate Prediction Center at Camp Springs, Maryland; the Space Environment Center at Boulder, Colorado; the Storm Prediction Center at Norman, Oklahoma; the Tropical Prediction Center (better known as the National Hurricane Center) at Miami, Florida; and four other centers.

The National Weather Service employs thousands of people twenty-four hours a day, seven days a week. It operates some 400 weather facilities throughout the fifty states, and it also has facilities in overseas locations and on ships worldwide. Each day it receives and processes 12,000 synoptic (general) and 25,000 hourly reports from surface observation stations; 1,400 reports from ships; 1,500 atmospheric soundings; 2,500 reports from aircraft; and all available cloud, temperature, and other data from weather satellites.

The service provides weather information to newspapers, radio and television stations, and other media for the general public. It makes studies of climate and conducts basic and applied research for the purposes of improving future forecasts and services and advancing the science of meteorology.

Much of the National Weather Service's everyday activity is geared to the service of aviation through its Aviation Weather Center in Kansas City, Missouri. It makes available up to the minute flight condition forecasts to all parts of the aviation community.

THE NAVAL METEOROLOGY AND OCEANOGRAPHY COMMAND

Because the National Weather Service must serve so many interests in so many ways, it cannot gear its activities to the special needs of the armed services worldwide. Each of the services must maintain its own weather agency. For the Navy, this is the mission of the Naval Meteorological and Oceanography Command headquartered at Stennis Space Center, Mississippi. It provides global forecast services to meet Navy and other Department of Defense needs throughout the world. It includes elements of the operating forces, shore establishment, and Navy Department, and cooperates fully with all national, regional, and international weather agencies. It is also an active participant in the World Meteorological Organization (WMO).

Navy weather units are maintained with all major aviation units, major combatant and auxiliary vessels, fleet flagships, and most naval shore activities. Trained enlisted aerographer's mates and meteorological officers are assigned to these weather units. On ships that do not carry aerographers and meteorologists, weather observa-

A Navy quartermaster plots the course of his ship and nearby storms. The quartermaster serves as aerographer on smaller ships.

tions and reporting are carried out by the ship's navigator, assisted by trained quartermasters.

There are six U.S. Naval Meteorological and Oceanographic Centers (NMOCs) located around the world where they can serve the operating forces within their regions. The NMOCs are located at Norfolk, Virginia; San Diego, California; Rota, Spain; Pearl Harbor, Hawaii; Yokosuka, Japan; and Bahrain in the Persian Gulf. The NMOCs use the basic information acquired from various sources, compile it into weather broadcasts and warnings, and transmit this information to the operating forces within their areas of responsibility.

FORECAST SERVICES

The National Weather Service publishes many kinds of weather forecasts. Among these are twenty-four-hour detailed forecasts, five-day forecasts, thirty-day general outlooks, twelve-hour aviation forecasts, and special bulletins, weather maps, and storm and frost warnings.

Newspaper, TV, and radio weather reports rely on many of these services. For air safety, complete weather reports are given to pilots by the Federal Aviation Agency, in cooperation with the National Weather Service. Pilots also get frequent updates of weather information while flying. It is common for commercial airline passengers to hear their captain, just a few minutes after the plane takes off, reporting the weather conditions expected at the destination of the flight.

The two kinds of weather reporting are local and long-range forecasting. The long-range study is more

concerned with an overall view of the climate, and with predictions for a year or more in the future. Publications called *almanacs* provide long-range weather predictions for the year ahead; these are based on average weather reported for years past.

Local weather is predicted up to a month or so in advance. The accuracy of these predictions is dependent upon timely readings taken at many reporting stations—on land and by weather ships, balloons, and weather satellites. While forecasting is becoming much more accurate, it still is not an exact science, due to the wide variety of local atmospheric uncertainties.

In the Navy elements of the Naval Meteorological and Oceanography Command prepare several types of forecasts, each for a specific purpose and containing specific information.

Area forecasts are prepared by major units afloat and ashore. The area covered is the "operating area" of the major units. Area forecasts will include a synopsis of weather conditions in the forecast area. They will report all pressure systems and their associated weather, including the system's position, intensity, and direction of movement. Intensity will include wind direction and velocity, visibility, and weather types. Position will always be reported by latitude and longitude.

Local forecasts are prepared by ships or stations and are used in planning local operations. These reports will include a brief summary of the synoptic pressure situation, fronts, severe weather, fog, and so on. They normally cover a thirty-six-hour prediction period. Specific details affecting operations (such as flying conditions, temperatures, precipitation, sea conditions, icing, ceilings, visibilities, and turbulence) are all included in the local forecasts.

Route, flight, and *terminal forecasts* are prepared for a flight operation and are issued by the station or ship involved in the operation. The *route forecast* refers to weather conditions along a specific route. The *flight forecast* pertains to the weather conditions on successive stages of a flight. The *terminal forecast* provides landing and takeoff conditions at fields on the way.

Storm warnings are included in scheduled broadcasts to both the fleet and the merchant marine. Warnings are issued by the NMOC responsible for the area in which the storm is located. Storms reported are thunderstorms, tornadoes, local wind storms, and major cyclonic storms. Special warnings are issued for tropical cyclones.

WEATHER SATELLITES

Weather satellites are the newest forecasting tool available to the meteorologist. Early weather satellites began with the TIROS (TV and Infrared Observation Satellite) in 1960. Since then, improved systems have been developed and placed in orbit.

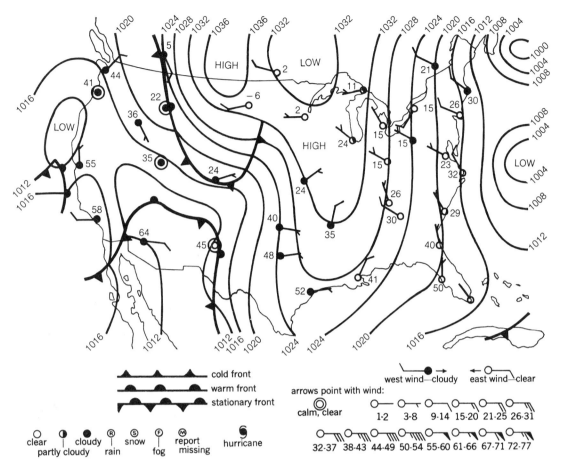

A simplified weather map similar to those issued daily by the National Weather Service. Temperatures are in degrees Fahrenheit and pressure isobars are labeled in millibars. Arrows indicate wind direction and velocity in miles per hour (mph).

The newest satellites are equipped with cameras that transmit pictures of the cloud formations on the earth's surface, either by day or by night. Other sensors relate surface temperatures and fronts, storms, snow, sea ice, and cloud heights. Orbiting at a height of about 900 miles, these satellites circle Earth every 115 minutes and view the entire planet three times a day.

Geosynchronous satellites, hovering 22,300 miles at a fixed location above the equator, photograph an entire hemisphere every half an hour. Spectacular pictures of whole hurricane systems and frontal weather patterns are now a regular part of weather forecasting.

WEATHER MAPS AND CHARTS

Weather maps are printed and distributed each week by the National Weather Service. Each packet contains the weather maps for each day of the week in pamphlet form. All symbols used on the maps are explained in map legends, so even the novice can obtain considerable information from them. Isobaric forecasting is possible by careful reading of the weather maps, since all frontal zones are carefully charted, along with wind direction.

Study Guide Questions

1. What is the purpose of weather forecasts?
2. Which U.S. government agency is responsible for providing weather forecasts and accurate meteorological information?
3. What is the purpose of the Naval Meteorological and Oceanography Command?
4. What is the principal difference between long-range and local forecasting?
5. What is an area forecast?
6. What weather information is transmitted back to Earth by weather satellites?

Vocabulary

National Weather Service
geostationary satellite
almanacs (weather)
weather forecasts

World Meteorological
  Organization
Naval Meteorological and
  Oceanography Command

Astronomy

Astronomy is the study of the universe—in particular, the study of the stars and other heavenly bodies, and their composition, motion, position, and size. You might ask, "Why delve into the mysteries of the universe? What does an astronomer produce or achieve?" The product of astronomy is a greater knowledge and understanding of the universe. True, much of this knowledge has not yet been used directly. However, the study of astronomy led to the discovery of the fundamental laws governing all modern technology. Astronomy is directly responsible for the scientific age, which has fundamentally altered our lives.

The universe is the most awesome concept in the human imagination. The size of the universe is beyond our comprehension. Earth-based and space-based telescopes have found 1 million galaxies in the Big Dipper alone, and they have observed light coming from distant galaxies and other objects over 12 billion light years away.

ORIGIN OF THE UNIVERSE

There are many theories about the origin of the universe. Ever since ancient peoples first began to study the world around them, scientists and philosophers have wondered how Earth and the universe came to be. Although we certainly know more than ancient thinkers did about the origin of things, many questions remain unanswered. Astronomers and other scientists that speculate on the nature of the universe and try to answer these questions are called cosmologists, and their science is called cosmology.

The modern scientific theory of the origin of the universe is called the "Big Bang," or expanding-universe, theory. It was first proposed in 1927 by the Belgian astronomer Georges Lemaître. His theory has since been supported by many other scientists and a growing body of scientific data. Lemaître postulated that all matter in the universe was originally concentrated in an incredibly dense mass. Packed inside was all the material of today's universe at a temperature greater than 100 trillion degrees C.

According to this theory, creation began about 13 billion years ago when a huge explosion sent dust and gas hurtling through space in all directions. As this exploding fireball expanded, particles destroyed one another, releasing high-energy radiation. Today scientists believe that this expanding motion will never cease. Indeed, studies of the movements of other star groups indicate that all are moving away from us at fantastic speeds.

Because of the extremely high temperatures, all the matter in this early central core was separated into protons, neutrons, and electrons. Just after the explosion, however, the temperature dropped enough so that particles could combine. Elements with high atomic weight were created when protons captured large numbers of neutrons. But these elements were unstable and quickly decayed into atoms of lesser mass. Slow neutron capture produced more stable elements, with low atomic weight. This accounts for the high percentage of hydrogen and helium in the universe and the small amounts of heavier elements.

In May 1992 scientists analyzing data on microwave radiation gathered by an orbiting Cosmic Background Explorer (COBE) satellite announced that they had been able to verify the existence of slight temperature variations in space that would have resulted from the Big Bang. This discovery has given further support to the theory—so much so that several prominent cosmologists called it the greatest scientific discovery of the last century.

Cosmologists believe that what is now our solar system (the Sun, the planets, and their moons) began about 4.5 billion years ago as a large cloud of gas and dust from the Big Bang. This cloud consisted of the "cosmic mix" of molecules found everywhere in the universe—90 percent hydrogen, 9.7 percent helium, and .3 percent heavier elements such as carbon, oxygen, iron, and others. Small eddies developed within the cloud as it turned in space like a giant whirlpool. A large eddy at the center contracted more rapidly than the rest of the cloud and formed the "proto-Sun."

In the cold depths of the cloud surrounding the proto-Sun, certain gases combined to form compounds such as water and ammonia. Solid dust and metallic crystals appeared. Gradually, forces in the spinning cloud flattened it into the shape of an enormous disk. At a great distance, this disk would have looked somewhat like a gigantic revolving phonograph record, with the proto-Sun at the center.

Within this whirling disk, eddies and swirls continued to appear. Some were torn apart in collisions, while others were broken up by the growing gravitational pull of the proto-Sun. As this battle continued in the wheeling system, some local swirls gained material and others lost it. Finally, a number of these swirls became swirling disks large enough to hold together under the strength of their own gravitational fields. Each was a proto-planet, moving through space around the Sun and sweeping up material left over from the original cloud.

As the proto-Sun's mass was pulled together, collisions, compression, and radioactivity heated the mass until temperatures at the center reached millions of degrees C. In a process called *thermonuclear fusion,* hydrogen atoms fused (combined under great pressure and temperature) to form helium. This process is the source of the energy that has kept the Sun ablaze ever since.

The thermonuclear fusion at the core of the proto-Sun released large amounts of energy and caused the proto-Sun to shine. At first a dull red, in time it became the golden yellow star that we see today. Because it was about 100 times larger in diameter than the largest of the proto-planets, it became a star instead of a planet. Its gravitational pull was strong enough to trap light hydrogen atoms in its interior. These atoms fueled the thermonuclear fusion process.

Proto-Earth and the other proto-planets were born as whirling clouds of ice particles and solid fragments—each a cosmic dust storm. Later this material collected into balls. Gradually these proto-planets grew by the accumulation of cold dusts from the region of space near them. (Even today, planets continue to sweep up dust and meteorites.)

In time radioactive elements and the compressive action within the cold Earth began to give off heat. After millions of years the temperature became high enough to melt the materials at Earth's center. The iron, nickel, and other heavy metals spread throughout the ball then began to sink, forming the molten core of the planet. Later, molten rock outside the core (magma) broke through fissures to the surface. This allowed molecules of hydrogen, water vapor, and other gases to escape, creating an atmosphere above the planet's surface. The oceans were formed when the water vapor released into the atmosphere began to condense and precipitate. The lighter gases, especially hydrogen, did not stay in the atmosphere long. They left behind a high concentration of the heavier, rare elements of the universe—elements essential for the formation of rocks, plants, and our own bodies.

There are other theories of the creation of the universe and the solar system, of course. The foregoing scientific theory is the one accepted by most modern-day cosmologists. Perhaps with more numerous and better satellite-based telescopes, exploratory sites on the Moon and beyond, and further explorations in outer space, one day we will be able to shed more light on this fascinating topic.

1

Astronomical Observations

Until the twentieth century, observations of the heavens were made visually from Earth's surface, either with the naked eye or, after the Middle Ages, with an optical instrument called the *telescope*, a device that magnifies the image of distant objects. But Earth-based observations of celestial bodies with an optical telescope, however large and refined it might be, are hindered by Earth's atmosphere. Sometimes the atmosphere makes observations impossible, as on a cloudy night. Even at the best of times, it will cause distortion of the incoming light from the body, making it impossible to observe very detailed surface features of even the nearest bodies, like the Moon and the planet Mars.

Fortunately, twentieth-century technology has provided methods of observation of the heavens that are far better than the Earth-based optical telescope. These include the spectrograph, radiotelescopes, balloon and spacecraft-borne telescopes, and, since the 1960s, manned spacecraft. Each of these will be discussed below.

THE TELESCOPE

Because of its wide availability and relatively low cost, the traditional telescope will always have a place in astronomy. There are many different sizes and types of optical telescopes. They range from portable models designed for the amateur, a few inches in diameter and a couple of feet in length, to giant reflecting telescopes with computer-driven aiming machinery mounted in buildings called *observatories*. These are used primarily by professional astronomers, who make most of their observations by means of time-exposure photography, rather than visual sightings.

If we were to take a trip to an observatory during "working" hours, it would be at night. We probably would have to drive up a high hill or even a mountain to get there. The large research observatories are located in remote places away from the lights, smoke, and smog of the cities. On the mountaintop the air is thinner and clearer, eliminating as much atmospheric haze as possible. Ideally, the observatory is built in a location where

the weather affords a maximum number of clear nights with "steady atmosphere."

The distinguishing feature of an observatory is its great revolving dome. Through a slit-like opening in this dome, the telescope peers into the night sky. Except for the hum of motors and the click of switches, all is quiet as the astronomers direct the telescope at the desired spot in the heavens. The whole dome can be made to turn to point the telescope at stars or planets anywhere in the sky.

The environment in the dome must be exactly as it is outside. It must be dark, so that the time-exposure photography will not be interfered with in any way. The temperature in the dome must be the same as outdoors, with no extra heat, since any such warm air would affect the telescope's lenses and mirrors, blurring the photography. Thus in winter the astronomer must wear heavy clothing as protection from the cold.

Today the telescope and its fine cameras are usually operated by computers. The astronomical photographs are taken on sensitive photographic glass plates instead of on film. Glass plates do not curl and can be stored and handled with greater ease. Time exposures are used because the plate must store up the feeble light received from the stars, perhaps for hours. Such time exposures reveal the movement of the planets, asteroids, meteors, and comets against a background of stationary stars.

The astronomer is much more than a mere "stargazer." When working with optical equipment in an observatory one must be an electronics technician, photographer, and computer operator. During the day the astronomer must be a mathematician, physicist, chemist, mechanic, research analyst, and office manager. The library of the observatory maintains a filing system of photographs and written records. Research and laboratory work goes on every working day, and in observatory shops new astronomical instruments are continually being developed.

TYPES OF TELESCOPES

The telescope is the most important object in the observatory. There are two principal types of telescopes: the *re-*

The U.S. Naval Observatory's installation at Flagstaff, Arizona. The building shown houses a sixty-one-inch reflecting telescope.

fracting and the *reflecting* telescopes. Both types can be fitted with spectrographs to photograph the color spectrum of incoming light.

The magnifying power of a telescope is important only in observing nearby celestial bodies, since the stars cannot be magnified. In observing the stars, the light-gathering power of the telescope becomes all-important. The amount of light a telescope can collect depends entirely on the area of its main lens or mirror. The larger the lens or mirror, the brighter the star will appear.

The *refracting telescope* uses two lenses. There is a single convex (outwardly curved) lens called the *objective lens* at the end of the telescope. This lens forms a reduced, inverted image of the celestial body being viewed called

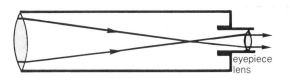

A refracting telescope.

the objective image. The *eyepiece lens* then magnifies this image, making the object appear closer and enlarged.

The largest refracting telescope in the world is located at the Yerkes Observatory at Williams Bay on Lake Geneva, Wisconsin. Operated by the University of Chicago, this refractor has an objective lens with a diameter of 40 inches (102 centimeters).

Because a lens can be supported only around its edge, the size and weight of the lens itself produces unavoidable distortions in the shape, which in turn affect the image. The 40-inch Yerkes refractor thus represents the practical upper size limit for this kind of telescope. To get around this limitation the *reflecting telescope* was developed. Sir Isaac Newton is credited with developing the first one in 1672. This type telescope uses an *objective mirror* in place of the objective lens. This slightly concave (inwardly curving) mirror forms an image which is then reflected by a secondary mirror to where the eyepiece magnifier is mounted.

There are two types of reflecting telescope. In the *Newtonian reflector,* a flat secondary mirror reflects the light and brings it to a focus at the side of the telescope.

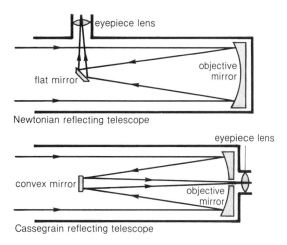

Reflecting telescopes may be either Newtonian or Cassegrain. A Newtonian reflector has a small, flat secondary mirror that focuses the image to the side, while the Cassegrain has a convex secondary mirror that focuses the image to the bottom of the telescope.

In the *Cassegrain reflector,* the secondary mirror causes the light to focus behind the objective mirror. Thus the objective mirror must have a hole in the center to allow light to pass through. The eyepiece is then placed at the bottom of the telescopic tube. Cassegrain reflectors are much more expensive than Newtonian reflectors and are specially designed for telescopes with large mirrors.

The world's largest conventional reflecting telescope with a single primary mirror is the 327-inch (830-centimeter) Subaru telescope at the Mauna Kea Observatory in Hawaii. To lower the cost and solve the technical problems associated with making such large mirrors, several innovative designs have been developed in recent years. In one of these, a group of thirty-six separate mirrors called segments are joined together to form a gigantic 394-inch (1000-centimeter) primary reflecting mirror. Each segment is individually controlled by computer to within one-millionth of an inch. Two of these telescopes are located at the Mauna Kea Observatory.

In another technique called optical interferometry, the signals from two or more smaller telescopes at separate locations are combined so that the resulting image is equal to that which would be created by a very large telescope. The largest of these is under construction at the European Southern Observatory in Chile. When completed in 2002, it will combine the optics of four fixed telescopes and several mobile ones to provide the total light-gathering ability of a 630-inch (16-meter) conventional reflecting telescope.

THE SPECTRUM

By gathering light from celestial bodies and analyzing the colors it contains, astronomers can determine the amount of hydrogen, helium, and other elements in the body. These light rays, though sometimes very weak, carry with them the complete story of their birth. This story is told by their *spectrum,* the rainbow of colors that can be produced from white light by a prism. The *spectrograph,* which is attached directly to a telescope, breaks up incoming light into its component wavelengths or colors to be photographed. It filters light through a prism, which divides light into the separate colors of the spectrum.

The electromagnetic spectrum, arranged in order of increasing wavelength, ranges from gamma rays on the short end of the scale through x-rays, ultraviolet rays, visible light, infrared light, and radio waves. Visible light is only a small part of the total spectrum. Except for certain radio waves, most of the other types of electromagnetic radiation cannot penetrate Earth's atmospheric shield.

The photograph that records the color bands in the spectrum is called a *spectrogram.* When analyzed, it tells scientists which elements produced the light. Each chemical element gives off its own pattern of colors. Light from vaporized iron gives out one pattern, while hydrogen, helium, oxygen, and the others each emit different patterns. These color patterns are clearly visible in the spectrum of incoming light from celestial bodies. This is one way the astronomer can tell that the Sun, planets, and stars are made of the same elements that we find here on Earth.

THE RADIOTELESCOPE

In the early 1900s, astronomers discovered that in addition to radiation in the visible light spectrum, many celestial bodies also emit radiation in the radio-frequency portion of the electromagnetic spectrum. This discovery gave rise to the development of *radiotelescopes.* In a radiotelescope, a dishlike antenna is used to gather the radio waves from space—much like an objective mirror gathers light waves in a reflecting telescope. Astronomers can thus measure and record the characteristics of incoming radio waves.

Radiotelescopes must be very sensitive in order to detect faint radio waves from space. Also, because the wavelength of radio waves can be thousands of times longer than those of light waves, radiotelescopes must be very large. Since radio waves are so long, however, radio reflectors do not require the precision of optical telescopes. The mirror on the Hale telescope, for instance, is polished to one-millionth of an inch, the tolerance for light waves. But a radio reflector for long radio waves can be made of iron mesh, with a tolerance of half an inch.

The world's largest steerable radiotelescope is the Robert Byrd radiotelescope at Green Bank, West Virginia.

Its dish is oval-shaped, 328 by 361 feet. Other very large ones are at Eifel Mountain near Bonn, Germany, 328 feet; and Jodrell Bank in Cheshire, England, 250 feet in diameter. The world's largest stationary radiotelescope, with a diameter of 1,000 feet, is near Arecibo, Puerto Rico.

In recent years, it has been found that an array of several radiotelescopes can work together to form a giant radiotelescope. Such an array of about thirty receivers at the National Radio Astronomy Observatory at Socorro, New Mexico, can produce images of the radio sky that rival optical telescopes in precision.

Because some celestial bodies are too far away or too cold to radiate visible energy, the radio "star map" or radio source map of the sky does not correspond with an actual map of the stars. Radio astronomers have found many huge regions of high-speed gases and the remnants of celestial supernovae explosions. Sunspots also give off radio waves, as does the corona of the sun. Radiotelescopes have discovered *quasars*. These objects look no larger than a single star, but they emit hundreds of times more energy than most galaxies. They have also discovered *pulsars*, which are bodies that radiate energy at regular intervals. Once thought to be artificial beacons, they are now considered to be rapidly rotating compressed stars in the last stages of stellar life.

Special Uses of the Radiotelescope. While radiotelescopes normally are used only to receive radio waves, it is possible to modify these devices for other purposes. The radiotelescope can direct powerful radio beams at a celestial object and then receive them when they rebound toward Earth. Radiotelescopes equipped with such transmitters are often called *radar telescopes.* Because radio waves travel at the speed of light, radar telescopes can furnish accurate data about the distance of celestial bodies near Earth. By using various wavelengths, information about the composition of these bodies can be obtained.

Radiotelescope technology has also showed that not all radio waves from space come from swirling, excited gases and celestial bodies. A particular kind of wave was found to be emitted by the cool, quiet hydrogen clouds strewn throughout space. Mapping these hydrogen radio signals has enabled astronomers to pierce the dusty regions of space through which light rarely passes. Such maps told them that our Milky Way galaxy is shaped like a pinwheel, and that it rotates, carrying the Sun and the planets with it. Until the radiotelescope, scientists could only speculate that this was the case, as it is with many other galaxies.

The same radiotelescope techniques have also found molecules in space. Amino acids, the basis of all living things, were found all through space by means of the radiotelescope. No optical device could have accomplished this feat.

The spectroscopes and radiotelescopes have found that hydrogen and helium account for more than 99 percent of all matter in the universe. It is believed that 93 percent of all the atoms in the universe are hydrogen, accounting for 76 percent of its mass. Almost 7 percent are helium atoms, totaling 23 percent of the mass. All the rest of the elements add up to only a fraction of 1 percent of the total.

No matter where astronomers have searched in space, the universe appears to be made up of the same elements. This is a very important fact. It tells us that if life exists elsewhere in the universe, such life almost certainly would consist of the same elements we have on Earth.

Recently, radiotelescopes have also been used to control and receive data from spacecraft exploring our solar system. In the controlling mode, they send very strong signals radiated at high power levels (300,000 to 400,000 watts) to reach the distant spacecraft, then listen for the faint replies and data transmissions, which are often only a few fractions of a millionth of a watt strong.

In October 1992 the National Aeronautics and Space Administration (NASA) began using radiotelescopes in a systematic search for any possible radio signals being broadcast in the microwave band by extraterrestrial life in our galaxy. Federal funding for the program was terminated by Congress in 1993 due to budget pressures, but a private group called the SETI (an acronym for Search for Extraterrestrial Intelligence) Institute was able to obtain enough funding to keep the project going. Called Project Phoenix, its goal is to scan the 1,000 closest stars for all frequencies in the microwave region between 1.0 and 3.0 GHz (gigahertz) that might indicate intelligent origin. Currently over half the candidate stars have been examined, but no transmissions of possible intelligent origin have been identified yet. This search represents the most exhaustive effort yet to provide an answer to the question of whether or not we are alone in the universe.

BALLOON OBSERVATORIES

The atmospheric shield that protects Earth from radiation also distorts the light that gets through to our telescopes on Earth. In order to gain more accurate knowledge of the universe, we have to go beyond our atmosphere. For this purpose, astronomers use high-altitude balloon observatories that can go up to about 20 miles above the surface. In these balloons, they are above 99 percent of the atmosphere.

Although relatively new, balloon astronomy is playing a great part in the study of the universe. Balloons are much cheaper than spacecraft and can easily carry people aloft in their gondolas. They also can carry up to two

Scientists of the Office of Naval Research launch a plastic high-altitude balloon from a Coast Guard ship. The balloon's apparatus will measure cosmic radiations near the northern magnetic pole.

that orbited between 1986 and 2001, and most recently the *International Space Station,* have been manned. The astronomical data and new knowledge gained by these spacecraft during the last forty years has greatly exceeded the total knowledge acquired by all previous earthbound observations since the dawn of history.

The study of our solar system by manned and unmanned spacecraft has been done in three distinct phases since 1957:

- The *reconnaissance phase* consists of flybys, photography, and, more recently, TV imaging.
- The *exploration phase* involves the use of orbiter and probe (exploratory) spacecraft to do detailed mapping and measurement.
- The *intensive study phase* uses manned and unmanned landers and space probes for closeup examination and experimentation.

A summary of the more significant of these efforts to date follows.

THE EXPLORATION OF THE SOLAR SYSTEM

The *Explorer I* satellite was followed by about fifty additional Explorer reconnaissance spacecraft, which collectively provided a wealth of information about Earth and its region of the solar system, including the following:

- The nature and effect of the solar wind
- The nature, extent, and behavior of Earth's magnetosphere (Earth's magnetic field)
- A detailed survey of the space between Earth and the Moon
- The nature and density of Earth's upper atmosphere

Between 1962 and 1975 a total of eight orbiting solar observatories (OSOs) were launched into orbit around Earth to study the Sun. Their instruments returned much data on solar flares, the Sun's corona (outer atmosphere), and solar activity in the gamma ray, x-ray, and ultraviolet bands of the electromagnetic spectrum.

Skylab, mentioned earlier, contained a group of eight solar observation instruments and cameras. During the time it was manned, between May 1973 and February 1974, about 150,000 observations of the Sun were made. These produced many spectacular photos of solar flares and sunspots. The *Skylab* and OSO data "rewrote the book" on solar physics, our understanding of how and why the Sun functions, and the effects the Sun has on terrestrial weather and communications.

While these spacecraft were investigating the nature of near-Earth space, a series of eleven Pioneer spacecraft began a reconnaissance of the remainder of the solar system, including the Sun, the other planets, their satellites, and the space between them. *Pioneer 10* and *Pioneer 11,*

tons of telescopes, spectrographs, and other instruments. The pictures and other findings can be brought directly down to Earth, rather than sent by radio transmission, as from satellites.

Though balloons have their advantages, they also have several disadvantages. They are difficult to stabilize, they are not self-propelled, and the upper atmosphere causes observational distortions. Consequently, astrophysicists and astronomers in recent years have found the space-based platforms discussed in the following section far more useful.

SATELLITES AND EXPLORATORY SPACECRAFT

The true beginning of the space age was 4 October 1957, when the first artificial satellite, *Sputnik I,* was successfully launched by the Soviet Union. *Sputnik I* was followed four months later by the first U.S. satellite, *Explorer I.* Since then there has been a steady procession of artificial satellites and other spacecraft sent into space on scientific astronomical missions.

Explorer I was fitted with a device designed to map Earth's magnetic field by measuring the energies of incoming charged particles at different levels of the outer atmosphere. Although it failed at this, it succeeded in providing a count of charged particles trapped in previously unknown bands around Earth far above the upper atmosphere—the now familiar Van Allen radiation belts.

Since that time, many astronomical spacecraft have been launched into space by NASA, by the former Soviet Union, and by several other nations. Some of these, including the Apollo missions of the late 1960s, the American *Skylab* orbited in 1973, the Russian *MIR* space station

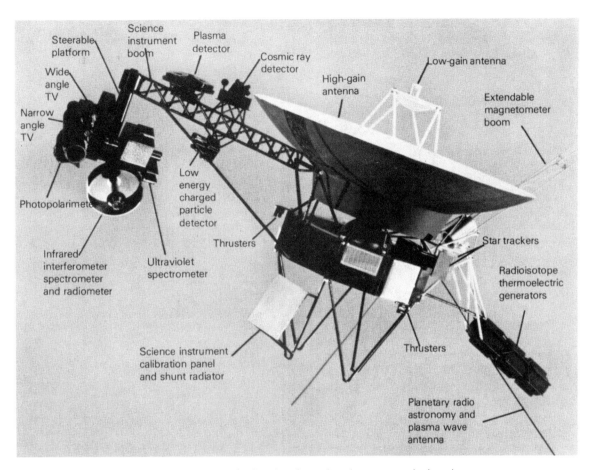

The Voyager spacecraft, showing the various instruments deployed.

launched in 1972 and 1973 to fly by and photograph Jupiter and, in the case of *Pioneer 11*, Saturn, are now the most distant artificial objects from Earth.

Pioneer 10 crossed the orbit of Pluto, the outermost known planet, in 1986, becoming the first artificial object to escape the solar system. It is now about 6 billion miles from Earth, and it is expected to continue transmitting useful data for some time to come. *Pioneer 11*, which followed a different path in order to fly by Saturn in 1979, passed Pluto in 1994. To date, neither has registered any gravitational disturbances that would tend to indicate the presence of a tenth planet, which some astronomers have theorized exists. They, and two follow-on Voyager spacecraft launched in 1977, all returned telemetry data (instrumentation readings) from the outer regions of our solar system. More will be said about their discoveries in chapter 4 of this unit.

Mariner reconnaissance spacecraft conducted orbital surveys of Mars in the late 1960s and of Venus in the early 1970s. Two Viking landers made soft landings on the Martian surface in the mid-1970s. They sent back hundreds of pictures of the Martian terrain and conducted experiments to try to determine whether microbial life-forms exist in the soil. Several Soviet probes fitted with parachutes penetrated the atmosphere of Venus in the 1970s and 1980s and radioed back some pictures of the surface and data on temperatures and pressures until they overheated and shut down. A pair of Soviet reconnaissance probes conducted a close flyby of Halley's comet during its 1986 swing through the solar system, confirming among other observations that the head of the comet is composed primarily of dirty ice.

In 1989 a Magellan spacecraft fitted with an advanced radar imaging device was launched to produce a detailed map of the surface of Venus. It arrived in orbit over the planet in 1991 and began its task, which ended in 1994 with an intentional plunge into the Venusian atmosphere. Its spectacular results are summarized in chapter 4 of this unit. Also in 1989 a *Galileo* spacecraft was launched as a follow-on to the Voyager mission to Jupiter conducted in 1979. On its way it passed close by the asteroids Gaspra and Ida, and it sent back several pictures of them. *Galileo* arrived at Jupiter in December 1995 and began a mission to take detailed observations of the planet and its moons. It also relayed back telemetry from a probe that it released months before that plunged into the Jovian atmosphere. More on its discoveries is given in chapter 4.

A close-up picture of the Martian surface furnished by one of the two Viking landers that successfully landed on Mars in July 1978.

In April 1990 the Hubble Space Telescope was placed in orbit around Earth by a space shuttle mission. Although its telescope system proved flawed and had to be repaired during a shuttle mission in 1993, since then its many new discoveries have revolutionized astronomers' views of the universe and our solar system.

In September 1992 a *Mars Observer* spacecraft was launched to do detailed photographic mapping of the Martian surface, but unfortunately all contact with it was lost as it approached Mars in August 1993. Two more exploratory spacecraft were launched to Mars by the United States during 1996. They arrived in July and September 1997. Several more were either launched or planned during the next several years. More about them is presented in chapter 4 of this unit.

In addition to the foregoing unmanned exploratory efforts, in the 1960s the United States made a determined effort to put an astronaut on the Moon by the end of that decade. The effort began with several Mariner and Surveyor spacecraft that conducted orbital mapping of the lunar surface in the early 1960s, and ended with the successful landing of *Apollo 11* on the Moon's surface in 1969. Five additional manned lunar landings and explorations were conducted, the last being *Apollo 17* in late 1972.

In February 1986 the Soviet Union launched the first components of a small space station called *MIR* into an elliptical orbit between 300 and 400 kilometers high. Though originally intended to last only about seven years with an intermittent crew of two cosmonauts, additional modules to enlarge it and extend its life were added, and it was more or less continually manned by Russians and occasional visitors from other nations, including the United States from 1989 until it was brought down from orbit in 2001.

In 1998 the first components of a new *International Space Station* were launched, with parts to be eventually contributed by sixteen nations. Two years later, in November 2000, the first crew of one American and two Russians arrived at the station, and it has been permanently manned since then. Additional components are continually being added, which will bring its total mass in orbit to about 453 metric tons when complete sometime in the next several years.

THE FUTURE

The next few years should be exciting ones in the field of space exploration. Many additional missions to the planet Mars are planned over the next decade, perhaps culminating in a manned mission sometime before the year 2020. A new mission to Saturn, the *Cassini* spacecraft, was launched in late 1997, to arrive at that planet in 2004. A mission to explore the planet Pluto is a possibility. And it has been proposed that other satellites be placed in low orbits around the Sun to monitor its activities. Further amazing observations and photographs of the heavens by the Hubble Space Telescope are sure to continue.

The search for extraterrestrial life in the solar system and beyond will be an ongoing quest for the foreseeable future. In addition to the previously mentioned radio astronomy search for extraterrestrial radio signals, astronomers have also recently reported irregularities in the emissions and motions of certain nearby stars. This would be explainable by the presence of planets in orbit around them. Claims of discovery of nearly twenty such planets have been made to date. If it could be shown that the formation of planets is a fairly common occurrence in the universe, statistics would then indicate that the probability of at least some form of life existing elsewhere in our universe is fairly high. Such a discovery would rank among the greatest scientific achievements of all time, with great consequences for humankind.

Study Guide Questions

1. What is an observatory, and what is it used for?
2. Where are observatories usually located, and why?
3. Why are most observations made in an observatory recorded on glass photographic plates?
4. What are some of the things an astronomer must be able to do, besides making celestial observations?
5. Name and describe the two main types of telescopes.
6. What does a radiotelescope do?
7. Why is a map of the radio sky different from a visual map?
8. What are quasars?
9. What are pulsars?
10. What is the main advantage of making astronomical observations from a high balloon?
11. When and with what event did the space age begin?
12. What are the three main phases of the study of the solar system by spacecraft?
13. What kinds of studies have the Explorer series of spacecraft done?
14. What was the main work of *Skylab* in 1973–74?
15. A. What was the mission of the *Pioneer 10* spacecraft?
    B. Where is it now?
16. A. How many Apollo manned Moon exploration missions were there?
    B. During what period of time did they occur?
17. What important exploratory missions to Venus and Jupiter were conducted during the 1990s?
18. What new space station is currently being constructed in Earth's orbit?

Vocabulary

observatory	radiotelescope
spacecraft	quasars
space probe	pulsars
refracting telescope	corona
reflecting telescope	telemetry
cosmologist	astrophysicist
electromagnetic spectrum	*Sputnik I*
spectrograph	magnetosphere
radioactivity	space station
SETI	extraterrestrial life
Hubble Space Telescope	*International Space Station*

2

The Moon

At one time most scientists thought that the Moon and Earth were probably formed at the same time and in about the same way. But analysis of lunar sample material brought back by the Apollo missions showed surprising differences between the compositions of the Moon and Earth. The Moon is iron-poor, with a density about the same as Earth's mantle.

Consequently, the favored theory now is that shortly after Earth cooled, it was struck a glancing blow by a large object. The impact spewed material from Earth's mantle, which eventually came together to form the Moon. To settle the question, more on-site research needs to be done, perhaps using a base camp that might one day be established on the lunar surface.

The Moon's diameter is 2,160 miles, roughly a third that of Earth. The Moon is generally said to be about 239,000 miles away from Earth; this, however, is an average distance. The distance actually varies from about 226,000 miles at the closest to 252,000 miles at the farthest.

The Moon circles Earth every 27⅓ days. It also completes one rotation about its axis in the same time period, which accounts for the fact that the Moon always has the same side facing Earth. In other words, the Moon rotates once on its axis and revolves once around Earth in the same length of time.

The Moon has no atmosphere. Thus, there is no gradual daily temperature change from hot to cold, as on Earth. On the Moon, a person partially in the sunlight and partially in the shade would feel extreme heat and cold at the same time. The Moon's surface temperature in sunlight may get as high as 243 degrees F. In the dark of the lunar night, it goes down to –261 degrees F.

Because there is no atmosphere on the Moon, there is no sound either. Also, since there are no obscuring atmospheric effects, a person on the Moon can see twice as many stars in the sky as on Earth's surface.

MOON GEOLOGY

Erosion on the Moon takes place very slowly because there is no rain or wind. However, our astronauts learned that the spray of the *breccia*—broken rocks from crashing meteorites—causes extensive erosion. The constant stream of atomic particles coming from the Sun also causes a steady wearing away of the Moon's surface rocks.

Among the lunar rocks returned to Earth was one that scientists labeled *igneous*. This means that the rock was once molten, but later became solidified. This indicates that the Moon, like Earth, has (or once had) a hot interior and volcanoes.

Some scientists believe it possible that the Moon is both hot *and* cold. They believe it has a cold exterior shell or crust, perhaps 250–625 miles deep, surrounding a warm belt of rock, and possibly even a molten core. This would make it much like Earth—except that Earth's outer crust, called the *lithosphere*, is only about 15 miles thick.

The surface walked on by the Apollo astronauts was covered by breccia. There also is a layer of dust made up of tiny glass *tektites*. These little spheres are no bigger than sand granules, and some are microscopic in size. They are multicolored, with hues ranging from dark brown to yellow to clear. Tektites make up one-quarter to

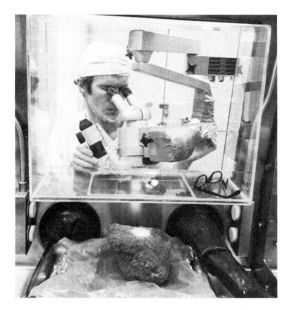

A test director at the Lunar Receiving Lab looks at basketball-sized Moon rocks through a microscope.

one-third of the lunar dust. Many scientists believe that the beads are congealed rock droplets, formed when meteorites blasted the Moon and sent out a spray of fine molten particles. The lunar dust layer, called the regolith, covers the entire surface of the Moon to a depth ranging from a few centimeters to 100 meters or more. Various lunar landers and the Apollo astronauts found that it is rather loose on top and compacted underneath.

The Lunar Receiving Laboratory of NASA in Houston carefully examined all the lunar dust and rock samples brought back by the Apollo expeditions. Some rocks appeared to be rich in magnesium; others sparkled with colorful crystals. When scientists burned a sample of Moon soil and studied its spectrograph, they found about sixty elements. The Moon rocks appear to be rich in titanium, but with less than one-third of the sodium and potassium found in comparable igneous rocks on Earth.

THE SURFACE OF THE MOON

The surface of the Moon is pockmarked with craters. The larger circular craters, easily seen through binoculars, have been visible for centuries. There are also smooth plains and mountain ranges on the Moon's surface. Galileo mistook the plains for bodies of water and called each one a *mare* (plural, *maria*), the Latin word for "sea." The craters have been named in honor of scientists and philosophers. The mountain ranges are named after mountain ranges on Earth.

The great black maria are younger than the rest of the Moon. They cover up older craters and show fewer signs of meteorite bombardment. Radioactivity measurements of rocks from the Sea of Tranquility show that they were made 3.6 billion years ago—1 billion years later than the Moon or Earth.

Some maria have definite magnetic fields. This was discovered when Mariner reconnaissance spacecraft orbiting the Moon experienced a greater pull of gravity over certain maria. Probably a massive body, such as an iron asteroid, lies under such maria. It is thought that the "seas" welled up when the lunar crust was punctured by a swarm of asteroids, about 2–3 billion years ago.

These buried super-heavy magnetic concentrations beneath the lunar surface have been named *mascons.* Mascons are much too heavy to remain on the surface of a molten body. But they are known to be near the Moon's surface, because of the extra gravitational pull they exert on spacecraft in lunar orbit. This lends strength to the belief that the Moon's crust is strong and very thick. If this were not so, the mascons would have sunk into the deepest core of the Moon—especially if the Moon were a soft, molten body.

There are about twenty maria, and they cover about half of the Moon's surface. Most are on the near side of

A photo of the Moon's back side, taken from the *Apollo 10* command and service module from an altitude of 60 nautical miles.

the Moon. The term *maria* has been retained, though now they are known to be filled with lava or volcanic ash, not water. Through a telescope the maria look much darker than the craters or mountains. This is because the lunar plains have a lower reflectance. An object that reflected all light would have a reflectance of 100 percent, while one that absorbed all light would have 0 percent. The Moon is actually a rather poor reflector, with a reflectance of only about 11 percent. The Moon gives off no light of its own, but reflects the Sun's light; moonlight, therefore, is reflected sunlight.

CRATERS

It is still not known how the Moon's craters were formed. One theory says they were formed by the impact of huge meteorites. This theory is supported by the fact that craters on the Moon look much like craters formed by meteorite collisions on Earth. Another theory states that craters were formed by volcanoes. If so, these volcanoes had to be far bigger than any on Earth. Another theory suggests that the craters were formed by the bubbling action of the molten Moon as it cooled.

A seemingly infinite number of craters cover the Moon's surface. The largest on the near side is Bailly, 183 miles in diameter, but several unnamed ones on the far side are larger than 200 miles in diameter. The craters are the most striking formations on the Moon, and they are present in all sizes. The typical crater has a surrounding ring, which is from 1,000 feet to 20,000 feet high.

Many smaller craters are almost certainly the result of early volcanic activity, as gases and dusts escaped from the Moon's interior. Some of these can be compared to volcanic craters on Earth, formed when the surface of the earth collapses into an underlying cavity from which lava has flowed. (Often a central peak remains in the center of such craters—for example, the island in Crater Lake, Oregon.)

The most conspicuous crater is Tycho, in the Moon's southern hemisphere. It is easily seen when the Moon is full. Tycho has a great system of rays, which radiate as far as 1,500 miles out from the edges of the crater. The crater Copernicus has a similar system. Rays are thought to be fine surface material that was splattered out of the most recent impact craters when they were formed. Some rays are chains of small craters, created by the explosive ejection of material during the formation of the main crater.

In late 1996 a spectacular discovery of possible water ice on the Moon was announced by U.S. scientists. Radar signals originated by a Defense Department satellite called *Clementine* indicated the presence of the ice in a large shady crater near the Moon's south pole, where the temperature is about –387 degrees F (–197 degrees C). The ice is thought to have been deposited there by a comet impact in the distant past. If it does in fact exist, the ice could be used by future human explorers as a source of both potable water and fuel. The *Clementine* satellite was the first U.S. Moon exploration effort since the last Apollo mission in 1972.

As a follow-up to *Clementine*, the *Lunar Prospector* satellite was placed in orbit around the Moon in January 1998. It was equipped with a neutron spectrometer that could detect the presence of hydrogen plus nine other elements including iron, titanium and aluminum. It did in fact detect large amounts of hydrogen at the Moon's poles, thus supporting the possibility of water there. After completing its mission in July 1999 it was intentionally crashed into a crater at the lunar south pole, to try to kick up enough material to prove the presence of water. However, scientists observing the crash site from more than twenty observatories around Earth and the Hubble Space Telescope could not detect any signs of the impact. Scientists are presently drawing up a detailed mineral map of the Moon's surface based on the data gathered by *Lunar Prospector*.

MOON MOUNTAINS AND RILLES

The Moon's mountain ranges lie in great arcs bordering the circular maria. Some of their peaks are as tall as the highest Earth mountains. They are concentrated in the Moon's southern hemisphere. With peaks sometimes rising more than 20,000 feet above the plains, lunar moun-

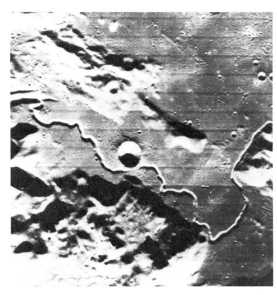

Rilles are cracks in the lunar surface similar to shallow, meandering river beds on the western deserts of the United States.

tains are very rugged, since they are not eroded by wind, water, or ice.

A large telescope will also show that the Moon's surface is covered with many cracks, called *rilles*. They are similar to shallow, flat-bottomed river beds on Earth. There seems to be no connection between rilles and other surface features because they sometimes extend hundreds of miles, uninterrupted by mountains, valleys, or craters.

MOONQUAKES

The *Apollo 11* astronauts set up a moonquake detector at the Sea of Tranquility. This detector was an instrument called a *passive seismometer,* a device that transmits reports of tremors on the Moon's surface. Scientists had expected the Moon to experience quakes similar to our earthquakes. But they found out that a moonquake causes the Moon to vibrate in an entirely different way. Earth tremors are severe only for seconds: beyond the rather small area of the quake, only the finest instruments can record them. Moonquakes, however, cause the whole Moon to vibrate for extended periods.

In only three weeks after its placement, the Tranquility Base seismometer registered twenty-five different tremors on the Moon's surface. Fourteen of them were from avalanches of lunar rocks falling down the slopes of crater walls. When the *Apollo 12* lunar module was purposely crashed back on the surface of the Moon in 1969, the shock set the whole Moon vibrating for nearly an hour. It will take many years and many seismograph stations to explain this and to find out how the interior of the Moon is structured.

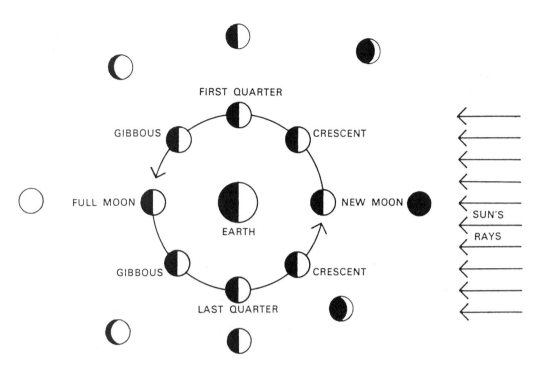

The phases of the Moon. The inner circle shows the Moon's position in relation to the Sun and Earth at various points in its orbit. The outer circle shows how the Moon looks from Earth at these times.

PHASES OF THE MOON

The Moon's motion in its orbit causes its phases. Since the Moon shines only by reflected sunlight, the relative positions of the Moon, Earth, and Sun determine how much of the Moon we can see at a given time. At new moon, the Moon is between Earth and the Sun, with the dark side facing Earth. A day or so later the Moon is seen as a thin, bow-shaped figure called a *crescent*. As the lighted part grows in size, the Moon is said to *wax* to full moon. At full moon, the entire illuminated side is turned toward Earth, since it is exactly opposite the Sun in the sky.

The full moon rises in the east as the Sun sets in the west; thus, we can see it all night. Sometimes it is so bright it can be seen well into the morning hours after sunrise. When the Moon is halfway between the new moon and the full moon, one-half of the Moon is bright and it is in its first quarter; this means that the Moon is a quarter of a circle (90 degrees) away from the Sun. After full moon, the lighted part gets smaller, and the Moon is said to *wane*. It goes through its last quarter and back to new moon again. When more than half of the Moon is visible, between the first and last quarters, it is called *gibbous*.

Because Earth and the Moon are both solid bodies illuminated by the Sun, they both cast cone-shaped shadows in space. Occasionally, the Moon passes through the conical shadow of Earth. This event is known as a *lunar eclipse*. Such an eclipse can be either

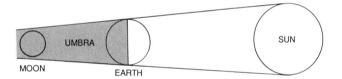

Diagram of a lunar eclipse. Such an eclipse occurs when the Moon passes into the shadow cast by Earth, called its umbra.

partial or total, depending on how much of the Moon enters Earth's shadow.

WHY EXPLORE THE MOON?

Although spacecraft have been studying the Moon for nearly a half century, many scientific questions still remain about its origin, how it formed, what it is made of, and how it has evolved over time. Less than a quarter of its surface has been mapped in detail. Data from the *Lunar Prospector* mission of 1998–99 has answered some of these questions, but others will probably remain unanswered until further explorations take place.

There are many practical reasons to explore our Moon. It is conceivable that people someday will be able to mine its mineral wealth. The Moon can also serve as a laboratory for further exploration of the solar system and the stars. It would be an ideal place to train space explorers and to provide them a base of operations for further exploration of the solar system.

Astronomical laboratories and observatories on the Moon would be unhindered by the atmosphere of Earth. They would be able to probe greater distances into space. Communications relays or missile and transportation control stations could serve in a wide variety of constructive ways. Military applications are sure to be developed also, though one hopes that the steps of humanity into outer space will be devoted to peaceful purposes.

Study Guide Questions

1. What is currently the most widely accepted theory of how and when the Moon was formed?
2. Why do we on Earth always view the same side of the Moon?
3. Why is there no gradual daily temperature change on the Moon?
4. What causes erosion on the Moon's surface?
5. What is breccia?
6. What are the maria, and how did they get that name?
7. A. What are mascons?
   B. How were they discovered?
8. What is "moonlight"?
9. What probably caused most Moon craters?
10. What significant discovery about the Moon was made in 1996?
11. What are rays and rilles on the Moon?
12. Explain the basic difference between a moonquake and an earthquake.
13. A. What are the phases of the Moon?
    B. What does "gibbous" mean?
14. What causes a lunar eclipse to occur?
15. What are some practical reasons for exploring the Moon?

Vocabulary

astronaut	reflectance
moonquake	crater
seismometer	gibbous
erosion	sidereal month
breccia	synodical month
lithosphere	eclipse
igneous rock	wax, wane
mare, maria	

3

The Sun

Earth has been warmed by the light of the Sun for 4.6 billion years. All life is maintained by the solar energy that is converted into chemical energy by plants. Moreover, the power from all fossil fuels, water, and winds can be traced back to the Sun. The Sun, therefore, is the source of most of the world's energy. (The only exceptions are nuclear energy, lunar tidal energy, and the heat produced in the interior of the earth and released by volcanoes and hot springs.)

The Sun actually contains 99.86 percent of all the matter in our solar system. An "average" star, it is considered by astronomers to be medium-sized. It is composed of luminous gases. The Sun's weight is about 1 million times that of Earth. The Sun's gravitational attraction is 270 times that of Earth; consequently, a 100-pound keg of nails would weigh 27,000 pounds on the Sun!

The average distance from the Sun to Earth (that is, Earth's average orbital radius) has been calculated to be 92,870,000 miles—nearly 93 million. This average distance is known as an *astronomical unit,* a huge unit of measure often used in describing distances in outer space. The Sun has a diameter of about 865,000 miles—about 109 times that of Earth.

It is not possible for us to look directly at the Sun without first protecting our eyes. Any attempt to do so will cause temporary blindness, unless some sort of filter or special fogged lens is used. The best way to see the Sun is through a telescope—but *only* if using special precautions. Use this method: hold a piece of white cardboard a foot or so behind the eyepiece, and focus the scope until the Sun's edge appears sharp. *Never* look directly at the Sun through a telescope or binoculars. The Sun's rays will burn the retina of your eye, causing permanently impaired vision, or even blindness.

COMPOSITION OF THE SUN

Spectrographic evidence shows that the Sun consists of gases at very high temperatures. The majority of these are concentrated under great pressures in the interior, possibly in a "core." Energy released by thermonuclear reactions in the core makes its way outward to the *photo-*

sphere, the light-giving surface of the Sun. The photosphere blends into the next layer, the *chromosphere,* which is the lowest layer of the Sun's atmosphere.

Composed mainly of hydrogen and gaseous calcium, the chromosphere has an average depth of 8,000–10,000 miles, with flame-like prominences (huge jets of hot gas) often shooting far higher. The chromosphere is visible only during eclipses of the Sun, or by using a *coronagraph,* a telescope that uses a black disk to hide the Sun's brightness.

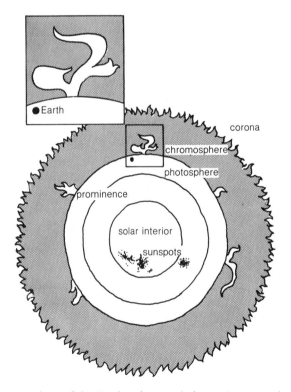

The atmosphere of the Sun has three main layers. Innermost is the photosphere, the 200-mile-thick layer from which visible light is emitted. Outward from this is the chromosphere, a layer of hydrogen and helium that extends from about 6,000 to 10,000 miles above the photosphere. Solar flares and prominences are often seen shooting from the chromosphere. Beyond the chromosphere is the Sun's corona, a vast region of low-density gas extending millions of miles into space. The inset shows the size of Earth relative to a typical solar flare.

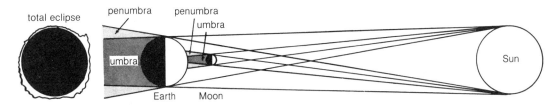

A solar eclipse. The umbra is the darkest part of the shadow of the Moon on the Earth's surface; the penumbra is the outer, or lighter, part of the shadow.

It happens that the Moon has almost the same visible size in the sky as the Sun. Consequently, when the Moon passes between Earth and the Sun, the bright photosphere is sometimes completely covered, creating the glorious spectacle of a total eclipse of the Sun, or *solar eclipse.*

From the chromosphere, shock waves carry the energy through a transition zone to the *corona,* the outermost layer of the Sun's atmosphere. It is very large and very faint and can be seen only in a total eclipse. The corona has been seen out to a distance of 7 million miles from the Sun, and it is certain that traces of the corona extend at least to Earth. Its low density, however, makes it invisible beyond the 7-million-mile limit.

SUNSPOTS

Sunspots are whirling fountains of hot gas that have come out of the interior of the Sun. Hotter than the surrounding gases of the photosphere, these fountains of gas rise through the chromosphere, expanding and then cooling. When cooling, they appear darker than the hotter and brighter environment behind them—thus earning the name "sunspots."

Sunspots may often be seen projecting well beyond the chromosphere as a *prominence.* An eruptive promi-

nence extending more than 400,000 kilometers above the surface of the Sun was photographed in 1973 by the Naval Research Laboratory's telescope mounted on *Skylab.* Sunspots may last only a few minutes or as long as a year and a half. There are times when few are seen, and other times when there are many. There seems to be a sort of sunspot cycle, with the greatest number occurring about every eleven years.

It is believed that the sunspots are responsible for the beautiful and spectacular Aurora Borealis visible in the higher northern latitudes. Similar polar lights, the Aurora Australis, appear in the southern hemisphere. Here is how these lights are created. The radiation pressure of the Sun pushes some of the hot sunspot material completely away from the chromosphere. These gases are electrically charged, since they came from the Sun's interior, where atomic nuclei and electrons are separated. Some of these particles are drawn into Earth's atmosphere near the magnetic poles. There they form an electric field. When elements of oxygen and nitrogen collide with hydrogen, or reform into complete atoms, radiation in the form of light is produced. This causes an aurora.

Sunspots create electrical and electronic disturbances on Earth. The great hydrogen flares erupting from the spots send x-rays and atomic particles racing thousands

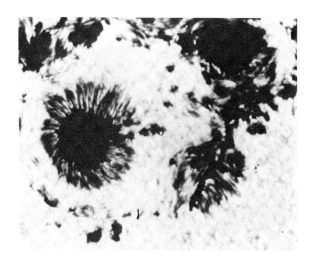

Sunspots photographed by a Navy balloonist from an altitude of 80,000 feet. The black spots are dark cores of relatively cool gases embedded in a strong magnetic field. Sunspots produce magnetic storms and major disturbances in radio broadcasts on Earth.

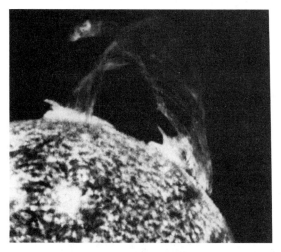

A photograph of the Sun taken on 19 December 1973 from NASA's *Skylab 4.* This shows one of the most spectacular solar flares ever recorded, spanning more than 367,000 miles across the solar surface.

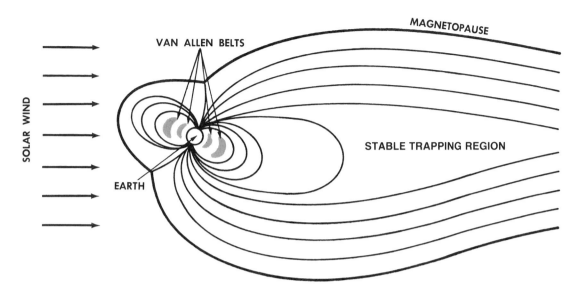

The magnetosphere is formed by the Sun's effect on Earth's magnetic field. The outermost boundary of the magnetosphere is the magnetopause. Notice the location of the Van Allen radiation belts.

of miles beyond the planets of our solar system. This barrage is called the *solar wind.* This wind erodes the lunar surface, creates comet tails, and even causes erratic changes in compass readings and the weather. It also affects the height of the ionosphere, causing fading and static in shortwave radio transmissions.

THE MAGNETOSPHERE

The outermost layer of Earth's atmosphere is the *exosphere,* which extends to about 18,000 miles from the planet's surface. Surrounding or overlapping the exosphere is the *magnetosphere.* The magnetosphere is formed by the Sun's effect on Earth's magnetic field.

Earth acts as a huge magnet, surrounded by a magnetic field. But this magnetic field does not dissipate into space. It is confined within the magnetosphere by the solar winds, which rush by at up to 900,000 miles per hour. The boundary of the magnetosphere is called the *magnetopause.* It is 40,000 miles from Earth's surface on the sunward side and is drawn out into a huge comet-like tail, between 3 and 4 million miles long, on the side away from the Sun. The magnetosphere changes its shape daily as the strength of the solar wind varies. This causes changes in the areas closer to Earth and affects radio transmission and the weather.

Inside the magnetosphere are huge numbers of charged particles that have been trapped by Earth's magnetic field. These particles circle Earth in four doughnut-shaped regions, one artificial and three natural. Earth is in the doughnut hole, and there are no trapped particles above or below the north and south poles. These rings are the narrow *Starfish ring* caused by a U.S. hydrogen bomb exploded at a height of 250 miles in 1962; the inner

and outer Van Allen radiation belts; and the *stable trapping region,* which contains lower-energy particles. This last region extends almost the whole length of the magnetosphere. The magnetosphere, then, is the region overlapping the exosphere, within which Earth's magnetic field is confined by the solar wind.

THE SUN'S ENERGY

The Sun produces gigantic amounts of energy. It can cause temperatures in excess of 100 degrees Fahrenheit at a distance of about 93 million miles—as we well know on a hot summer's day. And consider this: Earth actually receives less than one *two-billionth* of the Sun's energy. The rest is lost in space. The Sun's energy passes through space by the process of radiation. It is this energy that warms us, grows our crops, and gives us our seasons, winds, and weather.

The Sun actually is its own fuel. It literally is eating itself up at the rate of millions of tons of hydrogen each second. But it contains enough hydrogen to keep going at this rate for at least 6 billion more years.

The 10,000-degree C heat on the surface of the Sun will melt, and then vaporize, any known substance. For every mile below the surface of the Sun, the temperature rises about 22 degrees C. At the core, the temperature is 15 *million* degrees C. In that swirling cauldron, hydrogen is being transformed into helium, and some of the helium may be fusing into heavier elements.

This process is called *nuclear fusion.* In the process, some of the hydrogen is destroyed; that portion reappears, with a tremendous burst of energy, as radiation. The radiation eventually becomes visible sunlight, after escaping from the Sun's surface. A process similar to the one going on in the Sun was used to develop the hydrogen bomb.

SOLAR ENERGY: ANSWER TO THE WORLD'S ENERGY PROBLEM?

The direct use of the Sun's energy is of great and immediate importance. Most of the world's energy needs are still being met through the use of water power, coal, and petroleum. These sources, however, are not plentiful enough to keep pace with the rapid increase in the demand for energy.

We will one day run out of coal and petroleum. Nuclear energy is assisting to a limited, but growing, degree. But there are problems with this form of energy—such as the dangers of radioactive contamination and the difficulties in disposing of radioactive wastes. Uranium fuel itself is not in abundant supply on Earth. Thus, alternative sources of energy must be found and developed.

Many scientists in government and industry are looking for ways to use the Sun's power. By harnessing even a small fraction of this virtually inexhaustible source of power, we could supply the world's total energy needs. Solar furnaces, batteries, and motors, solar water heaters, and solar heating of buildings and houses have been tried successfully, though only on a limited scale, because of the high costs. When the problems of solar energy are solved in a cheap and practical way, the standard of living of the entire world is certain to rise. The opportunities for astronomers and scientists in the area of solar power and energy development are unlimited. Along with the oceanographic development of the seas and the conservation of our natural and human resources, research in solar energy will certainly play a major part in our future.

SOLAR EXPLORATION

In recent years as mentioned in the introductory chapter of this unit, several spacecraft have been launched with missions of further observation of the Sun. The most advanced of these to date was the probe *Ulysses*, a joint project of the European Space Agency and NASA. It was launched in October 1990 by the space shuttle *Discovery*. Its mission was to explore the regions over the Sun's north and south poles. In order to reach the speeds needed to achieve this orbit, it had to get a gravity boost from the planet Jupiter, which it encountered in February 1992. It passed over the Sun's south pole in the fall of 1994 and over its north pole in the fall of 1995. It completed a second orbit of the Sun in December 2001. Like the Jupiter probe *Galileo*, it also photographed the impact of comet Shoemaker-Levy with Jupiter in July 1994.

The Hubble Space Telescope has also been used for several investigations involving observations of the Sun since that spacecraft's launching in 1990.

Study Guide Questions

1. What is the source of most of Earth's energy?
2. How far is Earth from the Sun?
3. Why is it so dangerous to look at the Sun through any kind of lens?
4. What is the composition of the Sun? List and describe each succeeding major layer.
5. A. What is the corona?
   B. What is a coronagraph?
6. What is the importance of sunspots to Earth?
7. What is the magnetosphere? Explain the effect that the solar winds have on the magnetosphere.
8. How does the Sun's energy get to Earth?
9. How is the Sun its own fuel?
10. Is solar energy the answer to the world's shortage of fuels for energy?
11. What are the major problems in the use of nuclear energy for power?
12. What spacecraft has been conducting observations of the Sun's north and south poles since its launching in 1990?

Vocabulary

solar energy	aurora
astronomical unit	solar eclipse
photosphere	transition zone
chromosphere	exosphere
coronagraph	sunspot

4

The Planets

There are nine known planets in our solar system. In order outward from the Sun, they are Mercury, Venus, Earth, Mars, Jupiter, Saturn, Uranus, Neptune, and Pluto. Planets circle the Sun in regular orbits, and in that respect they are similar to Earth. Venus and Mars have some additional similarities to Earth, but the other planets are quite different. Mercury scorches under the intense rays of the Sun. The outer planets are strange cold worlds, surrounded by poisonous atmospheric gases and chemicals uncommon on Earth.

The planets are wanderers in the sky; the word "planet" actually means "wanderer." They are called that because they are constantly moving about the Sun in their orbits. Since they are moving, it is difficult to keep track of them without some sort of chart. A chart that serves as a timetable for the movement and location of the planets is called an *almanac* or an *ephemeris.*

The planets all orbit the Sun in the same direction and generally in the same plane. Earth's orbit about the Sun, called *the plane of the ecliptic,* is the usual reference to which all the other orbital planes are compared. The planets' orbits around the Sun are each in the shape of an ellipse (an egg shape), just a slight variation from a circle. The Sun is located at one focus point of these ellipses. The gravitational pull of the Sun keeps the planets in their orbits. Were it not for this gravity, the planets would continue moving in a straight line. You might compare the orbital plane to an old phonograph record—the Sun is at the center, and each planet's orbit falls into its own groove outward from the center.

As the planets travel in their elliptical paths, they sweep out equal pie-shaped areas in their orbital planes with equal times. Thus, when the planets are closer to the Sun, they are traveling faster in their orbits. When they are farther away, they are traveling slower.

Although planets are much smaller than stars, they are also much closer to us, so that a telescope can magnify them. Five planets can be seen without a telescope: Mercury, Venus, Mars, Jupiter, and Saturn. Uranus is just at the limit of visibility, and Neptune and Pluto can be seen only with a telescope.

The planets Venus, Mars, Jupiter, and Saturn are sometimes called the "Big Four" because they are so eas-ily visible. Since its orbit is nearer the Sun than Earth's orbit, Venus can only be seen in the western sky just after sunset or in the eastern sky before sunrise, because it is always near the Sun as we look at it. It is thus called the *evening star* or *morning star.* Mars, Jupiter, and Saturn have orbits that lie outside that of Earth. Thus they can be seen all night. The Big Four are brighter than any of the stars and do not twinkle as stars do. Because of their relative nearness, they appear as discs instead of points of light. The planets, like our Moon, shine only by reflected sunlight.

The time it takes a planet to go around the Sun is called its *orbital period.* Sometimes the planets, as seen from Earth, seem to go backward in their orbits—that is, east to west. This backing up, or *retrograde motion,* is easily explained. The best example of observable retrograde motion is with the planet Mars. Mars travels slower than Earth does, since it is farther from the Sun. So when Earth comes along on its orbit, it catches up to Mars and overtakes it, like a car passing another on a highway. Mars then seems to be moving in retrograde motion (backward) as viewed from Earth.

Mercury and Venus do not have satellite moons. All other planets except Earth and Pluto have two or more, with additional ones being continuously discovered in recent years. At last count, Jupiter has twenty-eight, Saturn thirty, Uranus twenty-one, and Neptune eight. Galileo discovered the first four of Jupiter's moons in 1610 after he developed one of the first telescopes. Several of Jupiter, Saturn, and Neptune's moons were photographed from close range by Pioneer and Voyager spacecraft during flybys in the 1980s, and by the Galileo spacecraft in the 1990s. These spacecraft also discovered several previously unknown moons orbiting these planets. The Hubble Space Telescope has discovered many more since it has been in orbit.

MERCURY

Mercury is the smallest of the inner planets in the solar system. Its temperature is so high on the sunny side that it has no atmosphere. The temperature is 800 degrees F

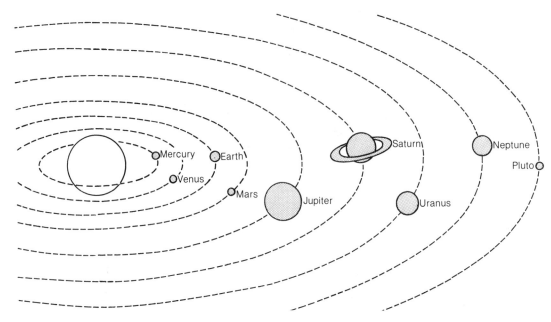

The planets of our solar system. The planets orbit the Sun in the same direction and in generally the same plane. The plane of Earth's orbit is called the Plane of the Ecliptic. Each planet's orbit is in the shape of an ellipse (oval), which varies in most cases only slightly from a circle.

on the lighted side and –300 degrees F on the dark side. Since there is no atmosphere, there is no erosion.

TV cameras mounted on the *Mariner 10* spacecraft observed Mercury in 1974 and 1975. It has a heavily cratered, dusty surface like that of the Moon and a large core of iron somewhat like Earth's. Mercury has a series of cliffs, some extending up to 2 miles high, which cut across the surface for hundreds of miles. They probably formed about 4 billion years ago when cooling of the planet's core crumpled the crust.

Mercury was named for the speedy messenger of the gods in Greek mythology. It has the shortest period of revolution about the Sun—88 days. Because it is so close to the Sun, the planet is difficult to observe. It is best seen just after sunset in March and April and just before sunrise in September and October.

VENUS

It was once believed that Venus was almost a twin sister of Earth, because the two planets are so nearly alike in size, mass, and density. Astronomers of the seventeenth and eighteenth centuries believed Venus to be very warm, but with plentiful water and lush vegetation, and probably peopled by small, dark-skinned people.

Since 1962 about twenty Soviet and U.S. spacecraft have explored Venus. Several of a series of Soviet Venera landers launched from the late 1960s to the early 1980s successfully penetrated the Venusian atmosphere and reported its density and pressures before landing on the surface. They recorded surface temperatures of 900 de-

grees F and returned pictures of a barren, lunarlike landscape. These observations, plus others by American spacecraft, have shown that the planet is a very unlikely place for life of any kind.

There is no water and no free oxygen on Venus. The surface temperature of 900 degrees F is hot enough to melt lead and zinc. The atmosphere is even less friendly. A deep layer of carbon dioxide, 100 times heavier than Earth's atmosphere, would bear down on an inhabitant with the weight of the ocean at a depth of 3,300 feet. The great heat on Venus is caused by what is commonly called the "greenhouse effect." The heavy layer of carbon dioxide traps entering sunlight and prevents the escape of heat energy. The dense atmosphere keeps the intense heat evenly distributed around the planet, with little variation between day and night or from pole to pole. Vision in this atmosphere of carbon dioxide would be limited to a few hundred feet, since only 2 percent of the Sun's light breaks through the cloud layers to the surface.

The thick cloud cover makes it nearly impossible to observe any surface features. However, the areas in which the Soviet Venera spacecraft landed appeared to be composed of loosely packed granite.

Earth turns once on its axis every day, but Venus turns only once in 243 Earth days. Because of its orbit around the Sun, a solar day on Venus is 117 days from one sunrise to the next, but because of the super-refractivity (extreme bending of light rays by the ultra-dense atmosphere), no one on the Venusian surface could tell the difference. Unlike most planets, Venus spins clockwise, opposite to its orbit around the Sun.

	planetary diameters	distance from Sun	orbital period	number of moons
	Mercury 3000 miles	4/10	1/4(88 days)	0
	Venus 7526 miles	7/10	3/5(225 days)	0
	Earth 7918 miles	1 = 93,000,000 miles	1 = 365 days	1
	Mars 4200 miles	1-1/2	1-9/10(687 days)	2
	Jupiter 85,500 miles	5	12 years	16 (+12)
	Saturn 71,400 miles	9-1/2	29 years	18 (+12)
	Uranus 29,850 miles	19	84 years	16 (+5)
	Neptune 31,250 miles	30	165 years	8
	Pluto (1430) miles	39	248 years	1

Sun
864,000 miles

A planet table (data current as of April 2002). Distances from the Sun are given as multiples of Earth's mean distance from the Sun (called an astronomical unit), and orbital periods are given in Earth days and years. The numbers in parentheses in the "moons" column refer to recently discovered "irregular" satellites that orbit outside the plane of the other known moons.

Photographed by *Mariner 10* on its way to Mercury and *Pioneer 12*, as well as by cameras aboard the *Galileo* spacecraft on its way to Jupiter in 1991, the clouds above Venus race at more than 200 miles per hour from east to west. These clouds lie up to 40 miles above the huge, shallow craters that have been detected on the surface. Above the clouds, a haze extends another 15 miles. Findings sent back so far do not reveal the composition of the inner cloud layers. The tops, however, seem to consist mainly of fine sulfuric-acid droplets—a mist that is thought to be more corrosive than automobile-battery acid.

While the missions to Venus described above were certainly important, all the data they accumulated was dwarfed by the latest U.S. space probe to visit the planet, the *Magellan* spacecraft. Launched in 1989, it reached Venus in 1991 and began an extended radar survey of the planet in strips 10 to 17 miles wide. This effort enabled scientists to view details the size of a football field in razor-sharp detail. Magellan showed that the surface was full of enormous lava flows, unexpected pancake-like structures, and large impact craters up to 120 miles in diameter. Large areas of the surface, however, are relatively smooth, with very few small craters, indicating that the surface is probably only about 400–800 million years old, relatively young on a geological time scale. The absence of small craters indicates that the planet has had a thick atmosphere for at least that long.

Magellan's radar maps show no signs of past major water bodies such as shorelines or ocean basins. Unlike Earth, there is no evidence of plate tectonics (movements of crustal mass), which may indicate it lacks an

A photograph of a densely cratered region of the planet Mercury, taken by a TV camera aboard *Mariner 10* in 1974. The photo was taken from a range of about 47,000 miles above the planet's surface.

asthenosphere between its crust and mantle. The distribution of volcanoes is also interesting. On Venus hundreds of thousands, perhaps millions, of them appear to be randomly distributed around its surface, rather than distributed in groups such as in the "Ring of Fire" around Earth's Pacific rim.

With its power supplies nearly depleted, Magellan's mission ended with a dramatic plunge into the Venusian atmosphere in October 1994, the first time an operating planetary spacecraft was intentionally destroyed. The purpose of the maneuver was to gather data on Venus's atmosphere before Magellan ceased to function.

So Venus, named for the Roman goddess of beauty, is in fact a grim and lifeless inferno hidden behind its clouds. But to us on Earth, Venus is often the brightest object in the sky, besides the Moon and Sun. Venus shines most brightly when it is between us and the Sun, even though the sunlight falls on the side away from us, for the planet is closest to us at that time.

MARS

Of all the planets in our solar system, Mars, the fourth from the Sun and the next one beyond Earth, has aroused the greatest interest. Named after the Roman god of war, it is often called the "red planet." It is not as easily recognized as Venus or Jupiter because it is not as bright. But Mars's red color and its rapid movement from west to east among the stars make it stand out in the sky.

The best time for viewing Mars is when it is nearest to Earth in August and September. In those months it sometimes comes as close as 30 million miles. In February and March it is over 60 million miles away and much less easily viewed. It is best seen when in direct opposition—in other words, when Earth is directly between the Sun and Mars.

Many scientists of the past thought Mars capable of supporting some kind of life. The Italian astronomer Giovanni Schiaparelli announced that he had observed a series of intersecting lines on the Martian surface in 1877. He called them *canali,* Italian for "channels" or "canals." Many people believed that the canali must have been made by intelligent beings because they were so straight. Or they thought that perhaps they were created by free-flowing water, indicating that Mars could be capable of supporting life. But subsequent observations and extensive photography from the Mariner and Viking series of space probes definitively proved the canali to be an illusion.

In 1969 and 1970 *Mariner 6* and *Mariner 7* made six-month-long journeys to photograph Mars, looking specifically for life on the planet. They found no sign of living things or an environment that could support them. The landscape appeared barren, and there was no evidence of water.

Mariner 9, by extensive photography of the Martian surface, revealed that large amounts of water must have once washed over the planet to form great canyons, meandering hundreds of miles across the surface. Today, however, Mars has a grim, lunarlike landscape, pockmarked with craters.

The Martian atmosphere contains small amounts of oxygen and water vapor, but not enough to sustain life as we know it on Earth. It is mostly carbon dioxide, and only about 1 percent as dense as Earth's—about the same as our atmosphere 20 miles up. Thin white clouds occasionally appear in the Martian atmosphere, and a veil of

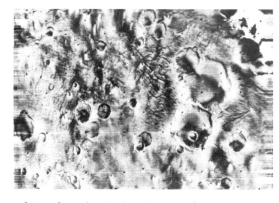

A view of Mars from the *Mariner 9* spacecraft. Several theories have been proposed to account for the channels in the middle of the picture, but final determination of their origin will probably have to await a manned exploration mission.

haze rises above each polar region during the winter seasons. The polar regions grow and shrink during the winters, which appear to be similar to Earth seasons. The Martian polar ice is thought to be composed of frozen carbon dioxide and frozen water vapor.

Fierce seasonal Martian winds whip up huge dust storms of the pinkish-colored iron oxide that covers about three-fourths of the Martian surface. The windstorms may rage for months, at speeds of up to 300 miles per hour, covering much of the planet with swirling reddish and yellowish dust clouds. The dust of Mars is extremely fine, something like fine talcum powder. This dust sometimes is carried 35 miles above the planet's surface.

Huge inactive volcanoes are present on the Martian surface. Nix Olympica (Snow of Olympus) is the size of the state of Nebraska. It rises 15 miles above the surrounding terrain and has a main crater 40 miles in diameter. A volcano named South Spot has the largest volcanic crater on Mars, measuring 75 miles across.

Temperatures on Mars range from near 32 degrees F in summer in the early afternoon to –135 degrees F just before sunrise. The surfaces of the darker areas may be 40 degrees warmer due to absorption of the Sun's rays. But because of the thin atmosphere, the air a few feet above the ground may be as much as 80 degrees cooler than the surface itself. The daily temperature range of about 170 degrees would be extremely uncomfortable, if

A close-up of the great Martian volcano Nix Olympica. This volcanic mountain rises 15 miles above the surface and is more than 370 miles wide at its base.

not fatal, to Earth's higher organisms. The polar regions seem to have fairly constant temperatures of about –190 degrees F.

Mars is about twice the diameter of the Moon and about half that of Earth. While Earth has a surface area of 197 million square miles, Mars is only about one-quarter that size, 55½ million square miles. Mars' gravity is only about one-third (0.38) of Earth's. That means a person weighing 150 pounds on Earth would weigh only about 57 pounds on Mars.

Two NASA Viking spacecraft landed safely on Mars in 1976. Carrying cameras, sensors, and radio-controlled arms, one Viking retrieved and analyzed samples of Martian soil and rocks in a series of on-board chemical tests. The analyses were sent back to Earth. In what has been the most detailed search for life on Mars so far, the results were generally considered inconclusive. Interestingly, one of the many pictures sent back from the Viking orbiter contained an eerie image of what seemed to some to be a human face carved out of a hill. It has appeared periodically in many tabloid newspapers ever since.

In 1996 NASA scientists reported that they had discovered fossilized evidence of ancient Martian bacteria in an Antarctic meteorite determined to have originated on Mars some 3 billion years ago. Their findings were based on chemical, mineral, and structural evidence found in the interior of the meteorite. The discovery was immediately hailed as one of the most important in the last century by many scientists interested in the possibility of extraterrestrial life. Later, however, other scientists disputed these claims, stating that the alleged "bacteria" were in fact products of chemical reactions.

Suffice it to say that these events sparked much renewed interest in the possibility of present or past life on Mars. In response, several new missions to Mars were planned to shed further light on the possibilities. The most successful of these to date was *Mars Pathfinder*, launched in December 1996. It made a cushioned landing on the Martian surface on the Fourth of July 1997. Carried aboard was a 22-pound solar-powered, wheeled vehicle called Sojourner. It was designed to roam around to collect and send back information obtained through black-and-white and color photos and an alpha proton x-ray spectrometer. For the next two months *Pathfinder* returned many high-quality images of the planet and other scientific data.

Several follow-on missions to Mars have been either launched or planned for the future. The first of these, called *Mars Odyssey*, achieved low orbit around the planet in late 2001 and sent back preliminary data indicating that large amounts of hydrogen are present in the northern polar region. This may indicate the existence of extensive water ice in the Martian surface at this location. Some of the later missions may eventually be capable of returning samples of the Martian surface to Earth. Exten-

Mars Pathfinder's twenty-five-inch-long rover *Sojourner* was the first vehicle of its kind to be landed on the surface of an extraterrestrial body. Here, it has been photographed by its base station alongside a rock dubbed "Barnacle Bill." A larger rock named "Yogi" awaits exploration at the upper right. A portion of the ramp leading to the surface from the base station appears at the lower left. JPL/NASA photo

sive analysis could then be done to try to definitely settle the question about former or current life on the planet. A mission sending astronauts to Mars may be a possibility sometime in the next twenty years.

JUPITER

Jupiter is the fifth planet from the Sun. Larger than all the other planets put together, its diameter is more than ten times that of Earth. It orbits about 484 million miles from the Sun and never comes closer to Earth than 367 million miles. Despite its great distance, it usually outshines everything in the night sky except the Moon and Venus.

Named after the king of the Roman gods, Jupiter remained an almost complete mystery until NASA's *Pio-*

neer 10 passed within 82,000 miles of its cloud tops in December 1973. *Pioneer 11* moved to within 27,000 miles a year later to find out more.

Two U.S. Voyager spacecraft with more advanced instruments flew by Jupiter and several of its moons in March and July 1979. Many superb color pictures of the planet and its four major moons, Io, Europa, Callisto, and Ganymede, were transmitted back to Earth. Several spectacular new discoveries were made, including sulfur and sulfur dioxide vulcanism on Io and water ice on Callisto and Ganymede.

Jupiter can easily retain all kinds of gases in its atmosphere, especially hydrogen and helium. The whirling planet rotates so swiftly that a day is only ten hours long. The force of Jupiter's gravity is such that a

A photo of part of the surface of Mars taken from the *Mars Pathfinder*'s Carl Sagan base station, showing landmarks named the "Twin Peaks" on the horizon. The appearance of the rocks has led scientists to conclude that the area was once washed by a huge flood, with enough water to fill the Mediterranean basin on Earth, a billion or more years ago. There is much speculation about the origin of this water and where it all went. JPL/NASA photo

150-pound man would weigh 350 pounds at the equator and 425 pounds at either pole.

Travel to Jupiter by astronauts is beyond the most advanced space technology today. The twenty-one-month trip itself would be beyond the capability of present life-support systems. Also, communications would have a forty-five-minute lag because of the distance to it. Temperatures above the planet's cloud layer are about –200 degrees F, and much higher temperatures, possibly in the thousands of degrees, exist closer in. The chief peril, however, comes from Jupiter's radiation belts. Lethal doses of radiation, a thousand times more

than a human being could stand, were sustained by *Pioneer 10* for several hours prior to its point of closest approach. It seems possible that Jupiter is surrounded by radiation belts similar to Earth's Van Allen belts.

The atmosphere of Jupiter is made up mostly of hydrogen and helium. There also are small but extremely important amounts of methane, ammonia, and water. Wide, circling bands of white, yellow, brown, and gray make up much of Jupiter's face. Inside these belts of clouds there is much turbulence, and jet streams race through the area. Farther in, after an area of relatively clear atmosphere, there is a darker cloud deck. It consists of dark yellow, orange, and brown clouds, composed mainly of icy particles of ammonium hydrosulfide. The innermost layer of clouds is a massive, thick band of liquid-water droplets suspended in the hydrogen-helium atmosphere, with ice-crystalline, cirrus-like clouds on top.

A view of the planet Jupiter from *Pioneer 10* shows the cloud tops and the famous Red Spot. The spot is 25,000 miles wide, about three times the diameter of Earth, and may be a permanent storm in the upper atmosphere.

Beneath this deep cloud deck, about 125 miles below the tops of the outermost cloud layer, pressures approach 100 times that of Earth's atmospheric pressure at sea level (14.6 pounds per square inch). The temperature can reach 800 degrees F here.

We do not yet know for sure what is within the cloud layers. But according to current theory, there is no solid surface as on the other planets. Instead, the hydrogen is gradually squeezed into a dense, hot fluid under increasing pressure. Finally, about 1,800 miles down, a crushing gravitational force (equal to 100,000 Earth atmospheres) and temperatures of 12,000 degrees F change the hydrogen and helium into a substance so dense that it behaves like a liquid. Some 12,000 miles down, under a pressure of 3 to 5 million "atmospheres" and at a temperature of 18,000 degrees F, the hydrogen becomes a metal, in a form unknown on Earth. Jupiter may also have a core of iron and other heavy elements, probably no larger than Earth.

While Jupiter's atmosphere is kept constantly churning by its interior heat, one feature of the planet remains almost unchanged. That is the mysterious Red Spot in the southern hemisphere. The Red Spot is some 17,000 miles long by 8,500 miles wide. It drifts slowly around the planet, staying generally in the same latitude. Its color sometimes fades to a gray and then returns to its red-orange state. Some scientists think the Red Spot is a long-lived storm that will eventually disappear. Others

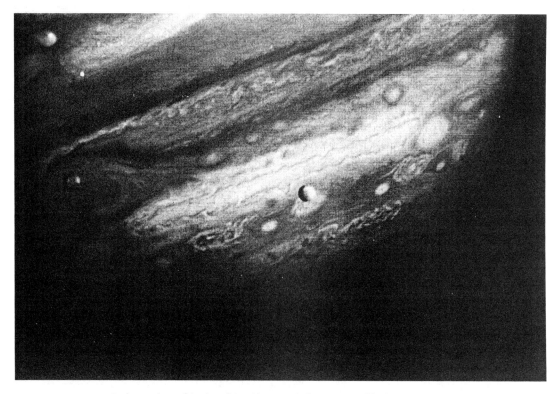

A closer view of Jupiter from *Voyager 1* shows two of its larger moons.

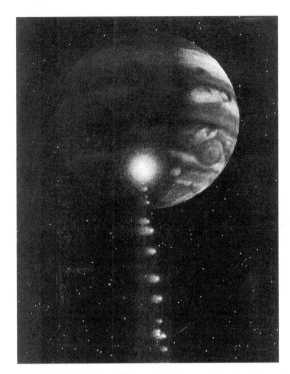

A photo of the 1994 impact of fragments of comet Shoemaker-Levy on Jupiter, taken by the *Galileo* spacecraft. NASA photo

think that it is a concentration of methane, ammonia, and hydrogen—the characteristic gases of Earth's earliest atmosphere.

In October 1989 the Galileo spacecraft was launched from the space shuttle Atlantis with a dual mission to launch an exploratory probe into the Jovian atmosphere and thence to orbit the planet for at least two years in order to conduct an extensive survey of the planet and its four major moons, called the Galilean satellites in honor of their discoverer. While on its way it passed near the asteroid belt, close enough to get detailed pictures of two asteroids, and discover a small moon orbiting around one of them. In July 1994 another spectacular series of pictures was made of the impact on Jupiter of fragments of comet Shoemaker-Levy. Additional photos of this amazing encounter were made by other spacecraft, including the Hubble Space Telescope and probes *Ulysses* and *Voyager 2*. Impact speeds of the fragments were estimated to be 130,000 miles per hour. Huge fireballs and plumes of dust and gas were observed, followed by black and brown discolorations, some of which were as large as planet Earth.

Galileo entered orbit around Jupiter in December 1995, the same day as its probe released months earlier slammed into the Jovian atmosphere at a speed of about 106,000 miles per hour (47 kilometers per second). The probe incorporated experiments to measure temperature and pressure along the descent path, locate major cloud decks, and analyze the chemistry of atmospheric gases.

The probe also attempted to detect and study Jovian lightning both by looking for optical flashes and by listening for the radio static they generate. It traveled to between 130 and 160 kilometers below Jupiter's cloud tops before the extreme atmospheric pressure there rendered it inoperable. Although Galileo's mission was originally planned to last only two years, it is still sending back information about Jupiter and its four Galilean moons as of this writing.

The new discoveries about Jupiter and its moons to date by the Galileo orbiter and probe include the following:

- Jovian wind speeds in excess of 400 mph (600 kph), with speeds increasing with depth
- Far less lightning activity (about 10 percent of that found on Earth) than anticipated
- Helium abundance in Jupiter very nearly the same as the Sun (24 percent compared to 25 percent)
- Extensive resurfacing of the moon Io's surface due to continuing volcanic activity since the Voyager flybys in 1979
- Evidence of liquid water beneath the moon Europa's frozen surface

The last discovery has been particularly intriguing to scientists because if Europa does in fact have liquid water, it would be the first place other than Earth in the solar system known to have it, and it might well harbor some forms of, at least, microscopic life.

Undoubtedly, many more amazing discoveries about Jupiter and its moons await in years to come.

SATURN

Named for the Roman god of time, the beautiful ringed planet Saturn is the solar system's second-largest planet. Saturn's rings are made up of billions of tiny solid particles. They extend outward from 7,000 miles to 171,000 miles above the planet's surface. They are on the plane of the planet's equator, tipped to the orbit at an angle of 26.8 degrees. The rings rotate about the planet, the inside ring moving at a faster speed than the outer ones.

It is believed that Saturn's interior is composed of a core of rock covered by a mantle of ice. This in turn is surrounded by a dense atmosphere of compressed hydrogen, topped with clouds of methane and ammonia. At 886 million miles from the Sun, Saturn has extremely low temperatures. It is probable that there is no solid surface for thousands of miles under the cloud layers. In this respect, Saturn may be quite similar to Jupiter.

The *Pioneer 11* spacecraft that flew by Jupiter in late 1973 was redirected to make a flyby of Saturn in September 1979, while *Pioneer 10* continued outbound. There was some concern that its instruments would not continue to function for the Saturn encounter, as they had

A spectacular view of the shadowed side of the planet Saturn returned by *Voyager 1*.

been designed to last only for the Jupiter mission, but in the end most worked perfectly, and continued to do so for years thereafter.

The two more capable Voyager spacecraft flew by Saturn and several of its moons in late 1980 and August 1981. A tremendous amount of new knowledge about the planet, its rings, and its moons was gained as a result, including dozens of spectacular high-resolution color pictures.

The total of all the data on Saturn gathered by *Pioneer 11*, *Voyager 1*, and *Voyager 2* has revealed that Saturn is a planetary system unlike any other in our solar system. Indeed, with its multiple rings and some thirty known satellites, Saturn is a kind of solar system in miniature. It displays many of the fundamental physical processes connected with the formation and early evolution of our planetary system. The continued study of Saturn may shed much light on how the solar system was formed. The exploration of Saturn by the Pioneer and Voyager spacecraft is considered to be among the greatest achievements of science in the last century.

Following their encounters with Saturn, *Voyager 1* continued on a path out of the solar system, and *Voyager 2* was redirected toward eventual flybys of Uranus in January 1986 and Neptune in August 1989. Having completed its "grand tour" of the outer planets, *Voyager 2* is

now following its sister out of the solar system. It will continue to return data on interstellar space until its power supply is exhausted sometime around the year 2018. Both will eventually overtake *Pioneer 10* and *Pioneer 11*, which were launched earlier, because the Voyagers are proceeding at higher speeds.

An exploratory spacecraft to study Saturn and its moons called *Cassini* was launched in October 1997, for a planned arrival at the planet in 2004. A joint venture of NASA, the European Space Agency, and the Italian Space Agency, *Cassini* is the largest and most sophisticated spacecraft ever built to explore a planet. It will explore the Saturn system in detail for over four years in orbit and drop a parachuted probe called *Huygens* to study the atmosphere and surface of the moon Titan.

URANUS

Uranus, named for the Greek god of the heavens, was discovered by Sir William Herschel in 1781. It is located almost 1.8 billion miles from the Sun. The methane, ammonia, and hydrogen that make up the planet are primarily in a solid state, due to the –300 degrees F temperature.

The planet has sixteen known small moons, plus another five that may be fragments of others that broke

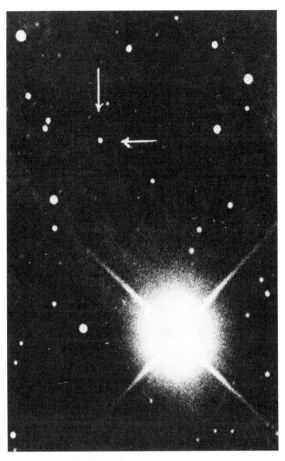

Variations in the orbit of Uranus (perturbations) led astronomers to believe that it was being influenced by the gravitational pull of an unknown planet beyond it. In 1930 Clyde Tombaugh discovered the ninth planet after examining a series of telescope photographs. This photo shows Uranus as viewed from the twenty-four-inch telescope at Lowell Observatory, Flagstaff, Arizona.

apart in the distant past. Uranus appears greenish when seen through the telescope, probably because of its atmospheric methane. In March 1977 scientists at Cornell University and Arizona's Lowell Observatory observed what seemed to be a system of rings in the space between the planet and its five larger moons.

Voyager 2 flew by Uranus on 24 January 1986 and verified the presence of the rings. It assessed them as composed of small gravel-like rocks and stones. It also discovered ten more small moons, unobservable from Earth. Another significant discovery about the planet was that its magnetic axis is inclined about 65 degrees with respect to its spin axis, which was thought to make it unique among the planets of our solar system until *Voyager 2* found a similar situation at Neptune in 1989.

NEPTUNE

Uranus and Neptune are often called the twin planets, even though the latter is more than 1 billion miles farther from the Sun. They are similar, though, in size (roughly 30,000 miles in diameter) and composition.

When it was discovered that Uranus did not travel in its regular orbit at all times, astronomers figured that there had to be some object whose gravity pulled Uranus off its path. Astronomers calculated the probable position of such an object—and thus found the planet Neptune in 1848.

Much of what we now know about Neptune and its satellites was discovered by Voyager 2 when it passed about 2,900 miles above the planet's north pole on 25 August 1989. Neptune's orbital period around the Sun is 165 years. Voyager's spectroscopy readings showed that Neptune's atmosphere is mainly hydrogen, with some helium and about 2 percent methane, which gives it a blue color. The interior is probably rock and water ice. Violent winds as high as 1,250 miles per hour were observed. Voyager's magnetometer discovered that Neptune's magnetic axis is tilted 47 degrees from the planet's rotational axis, similar to Uranus. Why these phenomena exist at both planets remains a matter of scientific speculation.

Voyager also found three rings of dark, carbon-like material surrounding the planet and six previously unknown small moons circling it.

Following its encounter with Neptune, *Voyager 2* went on to pass close to its largest moon, Triton. Voyager revealed even more amazing facts about this satellite. Its surface temperature was found to be −391 degrees F, making it the coldest body in our solar system, only 69 degrees F above absolute zero. Surface features strongly suggest the possibility of large-scale water-ice volcanism, making it unique in this respect in the solar system.

PLUTO

The *perturbations* (variations in the regular orbit) of Uranus were not completely explained by the discovery of Neptune. Therefore, astronomers looked for further explanation in the form of another planet. Finally, in 1930 an American astronomer, Clyde Tombaugh, discovered the ninth planet after examining a series of telescopic photographs.

Pluto was selected as the name for the "newest" planet because Pluto was the Roman god of darkness and the underworld. The planet Pluto is very dark indeed. It orbits at an average distance of 3.67 billion miles from the Sun.

This faraway, mysterious world is an oddity in the solar system. Its orbit is inclined to the plane of the rest of the planets and is also highly elliptical, so that for 20 years of each of its 248-year journeys around the Sun, Pluto is actually inside the orbit of Neptune. This occurred most recently between 1979 and 1999.

Mass and density calculations indicate Pluto is composed of rock and methane ice. Pluto and its satellite,

Charon, discovered in 1978, form a so-called binary planetary system. Charon orbits Pluto at a distance of only about 10,600 miles, and it is fully half the size of the planet. It orbits Pluto in 6.4 days, exactly matching Pluto's rotation rate, so that like Earth's moon, Charon always shows the same face to the planet.

Because of its unique orbital characteristics, scientists have speculated that perhaps Pluto is a comet or asteroid captured by the Sun's gravity, or even a satellite of Neptune thrown deeper into space by a close encounter with Neptune's large moon Triton. NASA is planning to launch a spacecraft to investigate the planet sometime in the next twenty years. Attempts to photograph the planet using the Hubble Space Telescope have been made, but because of the extreme distance, not much detail is observable.

Study Guide Questions

1. Name the nine planets in order from the Sun.
2. What gravitational force keeps the planets in their orbits?
3. What type of timetable is used to keep track of the movement and location of the planets?
4. What is an orbital period?
5. Why do some planets appear at times to be going backward in their orbits?
6. Which two planets are closest to Earth?
7. What information did *Mariner 10* provide us about Mercury?
8. What have recent space probes revealed about Venus?
9. When do we usually see Venus best, and what do we call it at these times?
10. What planet is called the "red planet"?
11. A. What are the canali?
    B. What happened to the canali theory?
12. How far from the Sun is Mars?
13. Compare Mars with Earth as to diameter, atmosphere, and other environmental factors.
14. What important discovery about Mars was allegedly made on Earth in 1996?
15. Which planet is the largest of our solar system?
16. Why is space travel to Jupiter by astronauts not possible in the foreseeable future?
17. What is the probable composition of Jupiter?
18. A. What is the Great Red Spot of Jupiter?
    B. Why is the Red Spot of particular interest to scientists?
19. What were the significant discoveries made about Jupiter by the *Galileo* spacecraft and probe in the 1990s?
20. Why were the explorations of Saturn by *Pioneer 11* and the two *Voyager* spacecraft of such importance?
21. How were the planets Neptune and Pluto discovered?
22. What is unique about the magnetic fields of Uranus and Neptune?

Vocabulary

planet
plane of the ecliptic
almanac (celestial)
ephemeris
ellipse
retrograde movement

orbital period
perturbation
Nix Olympica
ice volcanism
Galilean satellites

5

Asteroids, Comets, and Meteors

Between the orbits of Mars and Jupiter there are a multitude of small bodies referred to as *asteroids*. The area in which they orbit the Sun is called the *asteroid belt*. They have irregular orbits, but all revolve around the Sun in the same direction as the larger planets. Approximately 2,000 of these asteroids have been discovered by astronomers so far, and many have been given names. Some scientists believe there may be 25,000 or more such bodies.

Astronomers long wondered why the large distance between Mars and Jupiter seemed to be without a planet. After several hundred years of looking, in 1801 the first and largest asteroid, Ceres, was found. Orbiting at a mean distance of 257 million miles from the Sun, Ceres is only 480 miles in diameter. Other asteroids are considerably smaller. Many have diameters of less than 1 mile.

Some astronomers think the asteroids are material that was left over when the solar system was formed about 4.6 billion years ago. Others believe that they are leftovers from a collision of two relatively small planets at some time in the distant past. Still others believe that they are the remnants of a small planet that exploded for some unknown reason.

None of the asteroids have any kind of atmosphere. They appear to be little more than irregular chunks of rock and metallic substances.

A close-up photo of the asteroid Gaspra, taken by the *Galileo* spacecraft while on its way to Jupiter in 1991. NASA photo

As has been previously mentioned, while the Galileo spacecraft was on its way to Jupiter, it passed close by the asteroids Gaspra in 1991 and Ida in 1993, photographing them and in the process discovering a small satellite named Dactyl orbiting the latter. In June 1997 a Near Earth Asteroid Rendezvous (NEAR) spacecraft launched in 1996 came within 750 miles of the carbon-rich asteroid Mathilde while on its way to a year-long encounter with the asteroid Eros, which it reached in February 2000. In February 2001 it landed on Eros' surface, after having transmitted some 200,000 detailed pictures of the asteroid back to Earth. The pictures reveal a surface strewn with boulders, craters, and mysterious bright spots. Eros is considered a geologic relic from the formation of the solar system about 4.5 billion years ago.

COMETS

Comets appear as bright streaks of light, sometimes visible without the aid of a telescope. They are the most plentiful bodies in our solar system, perhaps numbering more than 100 billion. They are the travelers of the solar system. Comets wander in huge elliptical orbits, out of the plane of the ecliptic, far beyond the planet Pluto, but still revolving around our Sun.

Most comets have little mass. They are believed to be composed of a nucleus of frozen gases and dustlike particles composed of such elements as carbon and sodium, rather like a dirty snowball. When a comet approaches the solar system, radiation from the Sun begins to heat it, causing particles of material and vapor to begin to be released from its surface. These form a halo around the nucleus called a *coma*. The nucleus and coma together form the *head* of the comet.

As the comet comes closer, pressure from sunlight causes the vapor and dust particles in the coma to fan out from the head in a direction opposite the Sun. This causes a luminous *tail* to appear as sunlight is reflected from it, and the comet becomes visible from Earth. Tails more than 200 million miles long have been observed. As the comet swings around the Sun, its tail appears to continually change direction, since it always points away from the Sun. As the comet moves away from the Sun, its

This photograph of the comet Kohoutek was taken by members of the Lunar and Planetary Laboratory photography team at the University of Arizona's Catalina Observatory on 15 January 1974. Kohoutek will not reappear for another 75,000 years.

tail is pushed in front of the head. Eventually the tail either disintegrates or is collected again by the nucleus. The comet will then return to the darkness of outer space.

Every trip around the Sun causes comets to lose some of their matter. Eventually they may break up completely, leaving debris all along the path that was once their orbit. Sometimes Earth crosses a part of a former comet path. The tiny particles then collide with our atmosphere, producing a *meteor shower.*

A comet is usually named for the first person to report its discovery. Probably the most famous comet is Halley's comet. The British astronomer Edmund Halley computed the orbit of the great comet in 1682. In the process, he discovered that it had the same orbit as comets recorded by astronomers in 1531 and 1607. Halley suspected that all three were the same comet, which he calculated had a predictable orbital cycle of about seventy-five years.

This prediction proved to be correct when the comet reappeared in 1758. Sightings of Halley's comet have continued into more recent history. It was sighted in 1834 and again in 1910. It reentered our solar system in 1986 and was photographed from close up by two Soviet Vega spacecraft and a European Space Agency probe called *Giotto.* They reported its composition to be mainly dirty water ice. Its nucleus appears to be potato-shaped, rather than spherical as had been expected.

There are about 600 cataloged comet appearances going back to Halley's appearance in 87 B.C. Of them, about 500 are "long-period" comets that will not return for 200 years or more, if at all. Of the remaining "short-period" comets, 65 have been seen more than once. Based on observations made by the Hubble Space Tele-

scope, scientists now believe that there may be more than 1 million of these bodies in orbits far beyond that of Pluto, in a region called the Kuiper Belt, stretching as much as a fifth of the way to the nearest star.

METEOROIDS, METEORS, AND METEORITES

A *meteoroid* is a chunk of rock or metal orbiting in outer space. Meteoroids by the countless thousands orbit the Sun. Some are tiny particles of dust that eventually drift down through Earth's atmosphere. Others weigh anywhere from a few ounces to many tons. Meteoroids are invisible because of their relatively small size—until, by chance, they are drawn into the Earth's gravitational field. Then, as the meteoroid rushes through the atmosphere, it heats up from friction with the air. This causes it to sparkle brilliantly as it streaks across the sky toward Earth.

When this happens, the meteoroid becomes a *meteor.* Meteors are usually seen only below a 100-mile altitude. Most of these little bodies burn up long before reaching Earth and arrive as tiny cinders of dust. The streak of light called a meteor or "shooting star" is actually the fiery death of a meteoroid.

Occasionally the meteoroid is large enough that it does not burn up completely before it hits the earth. As soon as it hits the ground, it is called a *meteorite.* An extremely large and bright meteor is called a "fireball." Fireballs often end up as large meteorites, landing somewhere on Earth.

There are two main kinds of meteorites: stony meteorites called *aerolites* and iron and nickel ones called *siderites.* Aerolites are much like the stones on Earth, composed of oxygen, silicon, magnesium, and some iron. The siderites, however, are about 90 percent iron, 8 percent nickel, and a mixture of other minerals. Of the meteorites that have been found, aerolites outnumber siderites two to one.

Astronomers believe that most meteorites are the fragments of a shattered planet within the asteroid belt. Thus an analysis of them can tell us a good deal about the relative abundance of elements in the other planets. The stony meteorites probably came from the former planet's crust, while the iron ones came from the planet's core. Such study has convinced most astronomers and cosmologists that Earth's core is composed of iron and nickel.

As mentioned in the previous chapter, in 1996 quite a stir was raised in scientific circles when it was announced that a meteorite discovered in Antarctica and believed to have originated on Mars as the result of a comet or asteroid impact there appeared to contain fossilized evidence of ancient bacteriological life on Mars.

The largest meteorite ever found in the Western Hemisphere was discovered in Greenland by Admiral

Robert Peary in 1894. It weighs thirty-four tons and presently is kept in the American Museum of Natural History in New York. A sixty-ton siderite has been found in southwest Africa, but it still lies where it landed. The largest meteorites found thus far are siderites.

A third kind of meteorite called a *tektite* has been found in widely scattered parts of the globe. This small meteorite usually weighs between an ounce and a pound. It is composed of a glassy compound having high silicon content, along with oxides of aluminum, magnesium, iron, calcium, sodium, and potassium. Some are nearly transparent, while others come in various shades of green, amber, and brown. Tektites do not resemble any rock or glass substance on Earth. They may have come from the interior of a destroyed planet where materials were subjected to extremely high temperatures. Considerable research is being devoted to tektites, for they may help solve many mysteries concerning the origin of the solar system.

There has been much concern in recent years about the effect a very large meteoroid, asteroid, or comet would have if it were to strike Earth. Some scientists speculate that such an impact may have already occurred in the past off the Yucatán Peninsula in Central America, raising a planetary dust cloud that caused the extinction of dinosaurs in prehistoric times about 65 million years ago.

Study Guide Questions

1. How is it thought that the asteroids originated?
2. Where are the asteroids located in the solar system?
3. Of what are comets composed?
4. What causes a comet to be visible?
5. In what respect are comets like planets?
6. Of what are the tails of comets composed?
7. What happens when a comet breaks up, leaving debris that eventually enters Earth's atmosphere?
8. A. What is the name of the most famous comet?
   B. How often can it be seen from Earth?
9. Which recent comet gave astronomers their most up-to-date comet information?
10. What causes a meteor to be a "fireball"?
11. What happens to most meteors?
12. What are the main kinds of meteorites?
13. A. What are tektites?
    B. Where did they probably originate?

Vocabulary

asteroids	meteors
comet	aerolites
nucleus	siderites
meteor shower	tektites
Halley's comet	meteorites
meteoroids	

6

The Stars

The stars are distant suns in space. The closest star, of course, is the Sun. But the universe contains literally billions upon billions of stars. The Sun is 93 million miles away. The next closest star is Alpha Centauri, about 26.46 *trillion* miles distant. It readily becomes apparent that we are talking of distances that are mind-boggling. Miles or kilometers are useless in measuring such vast spaces. Thus, the *light-year* has been adopted as the common unit of astronomical distances.

A light-year is the distance that light travels in a year. This distance is, for practical purposes, nearly 6 trillion miles. Remember that a light-year is a unit of *distance* and not a unit of *time*, even though the word "year" is used. It is a bit like when you describe the distance to some location as a "twenty-minute drive" or a "fifteen-minute walk." When astronomers say a star is "ten light-years away," they mean that it takes light ten years to travel from the star to their observatory.

Even when using light-years to measure cosmic distances, the numbers can become huge. Modern telescopes can see out to distances of billions of light-years. This means, in fact, that astronomers are looking back "into time." They see distant stars and galaxies as they were millions or billions of years ago, since it has taken their light that long to arrive on Earth. The light that is leaving the stars tonight will not reach here for countless centuries. Since radio waves and light waves travel at the same speed, any "communication" directed at beings in distant galaxies would not be received for at least that many years.

STARS CLASSIFIED

The nature of a star can best be determined from its spectrum (wavelengths emitted), though other information is also necessary. Because of the stars' spectral differences, scientists classify them according to their temperature and color. This information, along with data on brightness and distance, has enabled astronomers to develop a *spectrum-luminosity diagram*. This diagram divides the stars into distinct groups according to their color (spectrum) and their magnitude or stellar brightness (luminosity). The term *luminosity* refers to the brightness of a star as compared to the brightness of the Sun.

The spectrum-luminosity diagram, then, shows the relationship between the color and the magnitude of a star. In general, blue stars are large and bright. Red stars are usually smaller and dimmer, though there are a number of well-known giant and supergiant red stars. Colors range from blue through white, yellow, orange, and red. The Sun, a yellow star, is an average star in brightness and temperature.

The *apparent magnitude* of a star is its brightness as it appears to an observer on Earth. The *absolute magnitude* is the brightness that a star would have at a standard distance from Earth of 10 parsecs—32.6 light-years (a *parsec* is 3.26 light-years). First-magnitude stars are about 100 times brighter than those of sixth magnitude. The ratio of 2.51 for a difference of one magnitude (2.51 multiplied by

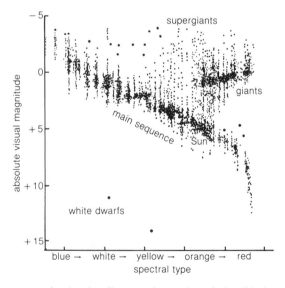

The spectrum-luminosity diagram shows the relationship between the color and magnitude of a star. White dwarf stars are cooler and less bright than our own Sun and are found beneath the "main sequence" stars. The main sequence comprises 98 percent of all stars. As helium builds up in the centers of stars, they reach their hottest and most brilliant point and become blue giants. As they age, blue giants cool and move off the main sequence to become red giants, supergiants, and finally white dwarfs.

itself five times is approximately 100) is the base of the magnitude scale used in modern astronomy. Stars fainter than the sixth magnitude can be seen from Earth only through a telescope.

Our Sun has an absolute magnitude of +5. The giant stars are given an absolute magnitude of 0, thus making them 100 times brighter than the Sun. There are even brighter stars called *supergiants,* which are as much as 1 million times as bright. Their absolute magnitudes would therefore be negative.

The most interesting class, however, is the one called *white dwarfs.* These stars are at least 100 times fainter than the Sun but are much hotter. They have about the same mass as the Sun, but they are smaller in size. The white dwarfs have densities much greater than any substance on Earth. A cubic inch of material from one of these stars could weigh as much as a ton. An ordinary finger ring would weigh 75 pounds on a white dwarf. Of the more familiar stars, Rigel, Polaris (the North Star), and Antares are supergiants; Arcturus and Capella are giants. Vega, Altair, and the Sun are medium-sized stars in the group called the *main sequence* on the spectrum-luminosity scale. The main sequence comprises 98 percent of all stars presently observed by astronomers.

CEPHEID STARS

One way astronomers can determine a star's brightness is by using nearby cepheid stars as a reference. These bright stars expand and contract with a definite rhythm, and thus they are called *cepheid variables.* They are sometimes referred to as the "lighthouses of space." The cepheid variables are hottest when they are at maximum brightness and coolest when they are at minimum brightness. Their variations in brightness are usually about one magnitude. There also are changes in the spectrum radiations as the star's brightness varies.

When the star contracts, its internal pressure and temperature increase. The star must expand in a sort of explosion. Once the star has expanded, the balance is again upset—so the star contracts again, under its gravitational attraction. Another name for the cepheid variable, because of this alternating phenomenon, is *pulsating star.*

The discovery that there is a constant relationship between the period of variation and the brightness of cepheid stars has enabled astronomers to use them not only as brightness references but also as a means of measuring distances in space. By noting how many days it takes the star to grow bright and dim, they can deduce the absolute magnitude of the star, and consequently how far away it is. Thus, when other methods of determining distances are not practical because of extreme distance, cepheid variables provide a valuable method for calculating star distances.

LIFE CYCLE OF STARS

A star begins as a huge, cold, dark sphere of gas and dust. Where or how this original star material was formed is not known. Some astronomers believe it came from the ashes of stars long gone; others say it had been present since the "beginning." No one knows when the beginning was, of course, and there are those who think that the universe did not have a beginning but has always existed. Cosmologists are still trying to find the answers to these questions.

But we do know that stars are being born today out of the gas and dust of the Milky Way, our galaxy of stars. The Hubble Space Telescope has provided many spectacular photos of this process taking place. Because of advances in astronomy and nuclear physics, the major stages in the life of a star have been fairly well determined.

The main factor determining what kind of star will be born is how much gas and cosmic dust become locked together by gravity in that particular area. If there is a lot of material available there, the star will probably end up as a brilliant blue giant. If it is like most stars, it will become a yellow star like our Sun, with a much longer "life" than a blue giant. With even less dust and gas, it will become an orange dwarf that will live on for billions of years.

It perhaps seems somewhat odd that the brighter stars have a shorter life. This is rather easily explained. The more fuel there is to burn, the greater the heat and the consumption rate; so, comparatively speaking, the brighter star is burning itself out faster. The rate of fuel consumption is set at the beginning and does not vary. Once the hydrogen-to-helium fusion cycle begins, it will continue until the hydrogen is exhausted.

In the introduction to this unit, we described the probable birth of the Sun. Thus we need not explain the entire cycle of the birth of a star again. By way of review, though, we know that the radiation pressure eventually builds up toward the center of the gas-dust ball. As the temperature and pressure increase, the ball begins to glow. When the nuclear furnace starts working full time, the whole swirling gas ball glows, sending its energy out into space in the form of visible light and other electromagnetic radiation.

Most astronomers believe there is a "normal" evolution of stars. As the helium content builds up in the center, leftover hydrogen accumulates, upsetting the internal balance of the star. To compensate, the star increases in size and luminosity, until about one-eighth of the original hydrogen has been transformed to helium. The star continues to increase in size, finally becoming a red giant. As a giant, the star consumes fuel at a tremendous rate, until its hydrogen is used up.

The helium produced in stellar fusion actually represents the star's "ashes." But the helium ashes also fuse as the pile grows, gradually changing into heavier elements. Eventually, after a final burst in size and brilliance, the star either collapses or explodes and disintegrates, depending on its size.

Most of the bright stars we can see in a clear evening are stars in the giant or supergiant stages, edging closer to their last burst of glory. A few are bright new ones, and others are ordinary ones that are close enough to appear very bright.

NOVAE

Sometimes a star appears in the sky for the first time in recorded astronomical history. These stars have been called *novae* (plural form of *nova,* the Latin word for "new"). Even more rarely this new star is a *supernova,* which blazes forth with a luminosity as much as 1 million times that of an ordinary star.

Records of these "new stars" appear in accounts as far back as 134 B.C., when the ancient Greek astronomer Hipparchus observed one in the constellation Scorpius. Chinese records tell of a brilliant star appearing in the daytime sky in A.D. 1054. Tycho Brahe, a German astronomer, found one in the constellation Cassiopeia in 1572 and observed it until it disappeared in 1574. Others have been observed throughout history, including one in 1987.

Since these stars appear suddenly and disappear relatively quickly—after only a few days for supernovae, and a year or two for other novae—they are now more correctly called "temporary stars." Novae really are not new stars at all. Actually, they are stars in the very last stages of life. Due to the instability that develops in their nuclear core in the end of their life as giants, their nuclear furnace finally explodes. After the explosion, it is thought that the star returns to about its original state, but with a loss of mass. It becomes a huge expanding gas

and dust cloud surrounding a small dense core. This atmosphere remains lighted by the core embers. After a year or two, it often can be photographed through a large telescope as a gaseous cloud, called a *planetary nebula* (plural, nebulae).

NEBULAE

Some nebulae are easily visible through a telescope; thus, they can be studied very minutely through the spectrograph. Nebulae are among the most beautiful of all astronomical phenomena.

There are three kinds of nebulae. The *bright nebula* glows and is easily visible because there is a bright star nearby that illuminates it. A *dark nebula* is composed of the same gas and dust as the bright nebula, but it is visible only because it is silhouetted against the stars behind it; there is no illuminating star in the region of a dark nebula.

The third kind is the *planetary nebula;* this is actually a nova or temporary star with a large cloud of particles surrounding it as the result of the stellar explosion. These nebulae show considerable surface detail, even though they are much less dense than planets.

BINARIES AND STAR CLUSTERS

Stars have a tendency to cluster together due to gravitational attraction. Pairs of stars are called *binaries,* or *double stars.* Larger groups of stars are referred to as *star clusters.*

The Whirlpool Nebula, a bright spiral nebula.

A globular cluster named Messier 3. Globular clusters contain thousands of stars. Clusters form systems nearly spherical in shape.

Clusters are classified both by their appearance and their "population." A *moving cluster* contains a few stars that travel in parallel lines. *Open clusters* are loosely grouped stars, often found in areas where there are glowing masses of dust and gas. Most open clusters are found in the Milky Way, so they often are called galactic clusters. *Globular clusters* contain thousands of stars—too many to count, even with the best photography. They may contain as many as 100,000 stars. *Star clouds* are clusters in which the stars are so thick that they look like glowing clouds.

GALAXIES

On a clear night you can see what appears to be a wispy cloud extending across the northern sky. It is in fact a vast band of stars called the Milky Way—our own *galaxy.* A galaxy is a huge collection of stars, star clusters, dust, and gas, all held together by gravitation.

The Milky Way is shaped like a giant disc or pinwheel, with more stars in the center than at the edges. It is estimated to be 80,000–100,000 light-years from one edge to the other. From top to bottom it is 10,000–15,000 light-years thick. The Milky Way contains over 100 billion stars revolving about a common center in the constellation Sagittarius. These stars revolve at fantastic speeds.

Our Sun is located about two-thirds of the distance from the center of the galaxy to its outer rim. The Sun and the rest of our solar system revolve around the center of the galaxy, moving at a speed of about 150 miles per second. Still, it takes about 225 million years for us to complete one circuit.

The galaxy looks much like a spiral nebula. In fact, earlier astronomers thought the Milky Way was a nebula. But modern telescopes clearly show that the galaxy is composed of billions of stars too far away to be distinguished as separate points of light. The Milky Way is best seen on a clear summer night, running across the sky from north to south.

As crowded as the stars in the Milky Way appear, we see only a fraction of the actual number because of the huge amount of gas and dust fogging up the space between the stars. Most of the stars in the center of the galactic swirl are thus blocked from view.

All the stars in our galaxy can be placed in two distinct groups. These groupings are called *Population I* and *Population II.* The basis of these classifications is their location in the galaxy. Population I stars are found in regions where there is a great deal of dust and gas. These are young stars that are still forming, growing, and adding mass. The stars in the neighborhood of our Sun belong to Population I, as do the open clusters.

Population II stars are older stars, located in regions essentially free of dust and gas. They have used up the available supply of raw material from space and are, relatively speaking, near the end of their lives as luminous stars.

In May 1997 scientists analyzing data from a gamma ray observatory satellite orbiting in 1991 announced the discovery of a giant antimatter cloud of positrons some 3,000 light-years wide near the center of the Milky Way galaxy. When such positrons merge with normal electrons they annihilate each other, releasing energy in the process. The density of the cloud, however, is so thin that it would pose no danger to anything in the galaxy that it might encounter.

There is a large number of other galaxies, each containing billions of stars. Each galaxy is separated from neighboring galaxies by oceans of space. Many of the galaxies have cepheid variables in the outer regions of their formations, as well as temporary stars and some supernovae. The cepheids enable astronomers to calculate roughly how far distant these galaxies are from us. Galaxies may be classified, according to their shapes, into three different groups (1) *ellipsoidal galaxies,* which have rather clearly defined, symmetrical shapes, ranging from spheres to ellipsoids; (2) *spiral galaxies,* which have a distinct nucleus with one or more spiral arms; and (3) *irregular galaxies,* which have no regular shape.

Recent Hubble Space Telescope observations have led astronomers to conclude that there are massive *black holes* in the centers of most galaxies, including our own. A black hole is a theoretical concentration of mass so great and so dense that not even light can escape its gravitational pull. Astronomers believe that black holes might be formed from imploding remnants of dying supergiant stars. The masses of black holes are proportional to the masses of the galaxies containing them. The one in the center of our galaxy may have a mass equal to 2 million times our Sun.

Study Guide Questions

1. What are the stars?
2. After the Sun, what star is closest to Earth?
3. A. What is the most common unit of astronomical distance?
   B. In miles, what distance does it represent?
4. Why is communication with distant galaxies impractical at the present time?
5. A. How are stars classified?
   B. What are the principal star colors?
6. What is the difference between apparent and absolute magnitude of stars?
7. A. What is the "main sequence" of stars?
   B. What is the spectrum-luminosity diagram?
8. What is unique about white dwarf stars?
9. What are cepheid stars?
10. What is believed to be the sequence in the life cycle of a star?

11. What is the principal factor determining what kind of star will be "born"?
12. Why do brighter stars have shorter lives?
13. What is thought to be the normal evolution of stars?
14. What are novae?
15. A. What is a nebula?
    B. What are the three kinds of nebulae?
16. What are binaries?
17. How are star clusters classified?
18. A. What is a galaxy?
    B. To which galaxy does our solar system belong?
19. What is the shape of the Milky Way?
20. What is the difference between the two population groupings in our galaxy?

21. A. How are galaxies classified?
    B. What are the three classifications?

Vocabulary

light-year	nova
luminosity	nebula
apparent magnitude	supernova
absolute magnitude	binaries
cepheid variable	galaxy
main sequence star	Milky Way
constellation	spiral galaxy
black hole	ellipsoidal galaxy

Physical Science

Since the dawn of recorded history humankind has sought to make sense of the world around us. In seeking to gain this understanding, we have made much progress in almost every field of human endeavor. Broadly speaking, *science* is the search for relationships that can be used to explain and predict how and why people, animals, and things behave as they do. When these relationships are applied to devices designed to assist us in satisfying our everyday needs and goals, this gives rise to *technology.*

There are many branches of science. One branch consists of the biological sciences, which deal with the study of living things. Another branch is collectively referred to as the physical sciences, concerned with matter, forces, and energy. Two of the main topics in the physical sciences are physics and chemistry. Physics is the study of how forces, matter, and energy in various forms interact. Chemistry is the study of matter and how it changes under various conditions. Other topical areas included in physical science are geology, the study of the earth's structure; meteorology, the study of the atmosphere; and oceanography, the study of the oceans. These and other applied physical sciences used in the study of the earth are nowadays often referred to as the "earth sciences." While they are often studied individually, all the physical sciences are ultimately related and are often dependent on one another. For example, an oceanographer must know about the chemistry of water, and a chemist must know about the physics of atomic structure.

Those who engage in the search for scientific truth are called *scientists.* Although some important scientific discoveries are made by chance, most are the result of prolonged work over time, called *research.* Doing research involves generating ideas, creating *hypotheses* (possible explanations), performing experiments to verify or sometimes disprove the hypotheses, and then publishing the results so others in the scientific community can carry the progress forward.

Scientists use many methods and techniques in their investigations, but all use some form of a systematic approach called the *scientific method.* It involves some or all of the following steps: (1) making observations, (2) forming questions, (3) forming hypotheses or explanations, (4) conducting experiments to test the hypotheses, (5) collecting data and analyzing the results, and (6) drawing conclusions. As the result of their applications of the scientific theory, scientists form theories and laws to help make predictions concerning the future. A *theory* is a reasoned explanation of observed events, while a *law* is a statement that describes and predicts the future outcome of these events. Many times scientific theories and laws are expressed as mathematical equations that may be used to predict outcomes of natural events.

In this unit we will take a brief look at several of the physical sciences subjects of key importance to today's Navy that have not already been covered in other units of this text.

Motion, Force, and Aerodynamics

The riddle of how and why things move has fascinated humankind since ancient times. About 2,300 years ago, Greek philosophers studied motion. As they observed the world around them, it seemed to them that all matter should be at rest or motionless in its normal state. Things that they observed to be in motion always seemed to tend to slow down and eventually stop. To their way of thinking, in order to keep moving an object had to have some unbalanced force acting on it. In the absence of such a force, a moving object would slow down and eventually stop.

The famous Greek philosopher Aristotle (384–322 B.C.) concluded from this that the speed of an object depends entirely on the force being applied to it and the resistance it meets. Aristotle's law, however, was later proven to be inaccurate.

In the sixteenth century the Italian scientist Galileo Galilei (1564–1642) observed that an object in horizontal motion would continue to move at the same speed with no additional force. Later in the same century this statement was accepted by Sir Isaac Newton, and with some elaboration, it became the basis of the first of his now-famous three laws of motion.

NEWTON'S LAWS OF MOTION

Newton based his laws of motion largely on observation and experimentation. Like all theoretical laws, Newton's laws were originally based upon what Newton saw around him, and then with some brilliant insight, he expanded his results to include new phenomena and possibilities.

Newton's first law of motion states that a body at rest tends to remain at rest, and a body in motion tends to remain in motion in a straight line, unless an outside force acts on the body. This law is sometimes called the law of inertia.

Newton's second law of motion states that the acceleration of a body is directly proportional to the force acting on it, and inversely proportional to the mass of the body, and is in the same direction as the applied force. Mathematically this is often expressed by the formula $F = ma$.

Newton's third law of motion states that whenever one body exerts a force upon a second body, the second exerts an equal but opposite force back upon the first. Stated another way, for every action there is an equal but opposite reaction.

As an example of Newton's laws, suppose you want to take a trip in your car. When you first get in you are at rest (motionless), because no unbalanced forces are acting on you. Then when you press on the accelerator, the car's engine exerts a force on it and everything in it, including you. You therefore accelerate forward, along with the rest of the car. Within the car, your seat pushes forward on you, and you in turn push back on the seat with an equal but opposite force for as long as the car is accelerating. Eventually you reach cruising speed—say, 30 miles per hour—and ease up the pressure on the accelerator. Though the engine is still running, at this cruising speed the forward force of the engine is exactly matched by opposing forces such as air friction, thus producing a state of no net or unbalanced forces acting on either you or the car. Therefore you stay at a steady speed of 30 miles per hour. Then when you want to slow down you apply the brakes, thus generating a net force on the car in a direction opposite to its motion. It begins to slow down. Meanwhile, you tend to keep moving forward inside, unless you are restrained by your seat belt and friction with the seat. While the seat belt restrains you, you and the seat belt each exert an equal but opposite force on each other. Eventually you and the car stop, where once again no net forces are acting on either you or the car.

Taken together, Newton's three laws describe the relationships among force, mass, acceleration, and velocity for all bodies in motion at relatively low speeds as compared to the speed of light, 3×10^8 meters per second or 186,000 miles per second. Such motion is often called *Newtonian motion*. Fortunately, most motion on Earth falls into this category. We can therefore easily use Newton's laws to make all manner of predictions about things undergoing Newtonian motion. Sometimes, however, bodies in space can travel much faster. For them, time, mass, and length become distorted, and different rules devised by Albert Einstein (1879–1955) apply. These rules are collectively called Einstein's *theory of relativity,* which he formulated early in the last century.

FORCES

Let us take another look at Newton's second law of motion. How do we define acceleration? *Acceleration* is the change in velocity per unit of time, normally one second. *Velocity* is the rate of motion in a given direction. In the example above, the velocity was expressed in terms of miles per hour. Other widely used units are feet per second, and in the metric system, meters per second or kilometers per hour. *Force* can be defined as power or energy exerted against a body in a given direction. Its units are pounds in the English system and newtons (N) in the metric system. *Mass* is the quantity of material contained in a body. In the metric system the unit of mass is the kilogram. In the English system the pound is often erroneously used to indicate mass, although it is really a force unit.

The *weight* of a body is an expression of the amount of the force of gravity on it at a given location. Thus, the weight can change, depending on location, while mass does not. For example, the force of gravity on the Moon's surface is about one-sixth that of Earth. Thus, a person weighing 120 pounds on Earth would weigh only 20 pounds on the Moon. While on the way to the Moon, in space where gravity is minimal, the person would have almost no weight. The person's mass, however, would be the same at all three locations.

One kind of force that must be dealt with for all moving earthbound objects is *friction.* Friction is caused by contact between the moving object and other substances around it. The amount of the friction is dependent on the nature of the materials in contact, the force between them, and sometimes their velocity relative to each other. Solids moving against each other generate *contact friction.* Bodies moving through fluids such as water or air (considered a fluid in these cases) generate *fluid friction,* which increases with the speed of travel through the fluid. This type of friction is often called *drag.* Friction always acts in a direction opposite to the direction of motion. The energy generated by friction is usually dissipated in the form of heat.

WORK, ENERGY, AND POWER

When a force acts through a distance, *work* is said to have been done. In the English system the units of work are foot-pounds, and in the metric system, newton-meters. One newton-meter is called a joule. Doing work on a body increases its level of *energy.* It may gain height, velocity, or temperature, or sometimes all three. Under the proper conditions a body may be able to transform some

of its energy back into work, thus losing energy. There is, therefore, an equivalence between work and energy, indicated by the fact that they have the same units: foot-pounds in the English system and joules in the metric system.

The rate at which work is done or energy is gained or expended is *power.* In the English system the unit of power is the horsepower, and in the metric system it is the watt. There are 746 watts in one horsepower. For example, if 10 newtons of force acted over a distance of 10 meters for 5 seconds, the power generated would be (10 × 10)/5, or 20 watts (equivalent to about .013 horsepower). A larger unit of power called the kilowatt (KW), equivalent to 1,000 watts, is commonly used, especially in connection with electrical power consumption. If the United States ever fully adopts the metric system, all products such as automobile engines will be rated in kilowatts instead of horsepower. Most American-built marine engines used on boats already use kilowatts as their standard power units.

THE PHYSICS OF FLIGHT

The path of a body in flight is determined by Newton's laws of motion, according to the forces acting upon it. Some of these forces are natural, and others are manmade. Various combinations of these forces produce different effects on the flight path. *Aerodynamics* is the science that deals with the motion of bodies moving through air and other gases. Missiles and aircraft use aerodynamic forces to maintain their flight path. The surface of a body in flight is called its *airfoil.* The aerodynamic forces acting on a moving airfoil are thrust, drag, gravity (weight), and lift. Other factors that can affect a body in flight are the *angle of attack* between the airfoil and the airstream, and in the case of a body flying in a curved path, centripetal force.

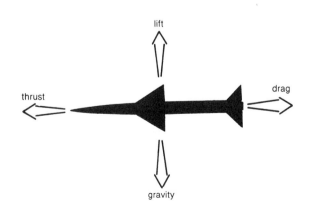

The aerodynamic forces acting on a moving airfoil such as a missile are thrust, drag, gravity, and lift. The combination of these forces produces a resultant force that will determine where the missile goes.

Each of the forces described above is a *vector quantity*, meaning something that has both magnitude (length or size) and direction. All forces acting on a body can be mathematically combined by adding their vectors to form the resultant or net force. The net force determines the motion of the body, in accordance with Newton's laws.

In the 1700s Daniel Bernoulli (1700–1782) postulated that since the total energy in any isolated system remains constant, if one element in any system of streamlined fluid flow is decreased, another must increase to counterbalance it. This is called *Bernoulli's principle.* Air flowing past the fuselage or over the wing of a guided missile or aircraft forms a system to which this theorem can be applied.

When air passes over the streamlined convex wing of an aircraft, it must travel a greater distance than air passing under it. Since the two parts of the airstream reach the trailing edge of the wing at the same time, the air that flows over the wing must move faster than the air that flows under it. According to Bernoulli's theorem, this results in a lower pressure on the top than on the bottom surface of the wing. This pressure difference tends to force the wing upward, thereby giving it lift. Since most missiles use flat wings rather than the curved wings of conventional aircraft, they must get the necessary lift entirely from the angle of attack.

Here is an example. Consider an airplane taking off from a runway. Before it starts rolling, its speed is zero,

and there is no drag. When its brakes are released, the force of thrust developed by its engines at full power is unbalanced, and as a result, the plane begins to accelerate rapidly down the runway, in accordance with Newton's second law. As its speed increases, the lift force grows rapidly by Bernoulli's theorem.

As its takeoff run progresses, the plane's forward acceleration gradually decreases while speed increases, because the opposing drag force increases steadily. When the nose rises off the runway, the angle of attack also increases, adding still more upward force. Soon the total lift force overcomes the downward weight produced by gravity, and the plane lifts off. Shortly after takeoff the plane's forward acceleration may fall off to zero as increasing drag matches thrust. The plane continues at a steady speed by Newton's first law, until it decreases drag by raising the landing gear plus its wing flaps. Now the plane can accelerate once again as it climbs to cruising altitude and attains cruising speed.

Should the propulsive force be decreased for any reason, such as to slow down for landing, the force of drag will exceed the thrust. The plane will slow down until the forces are again in balance.

In aerodynamics, acceleration is often measured in terms of the standard acceleration of gravity, abbreviated by the letter "g". A freely falling frictionless body is attracted to the earth by a force equal to its weight, with the result that it accelerates at a constant rate of approxi-

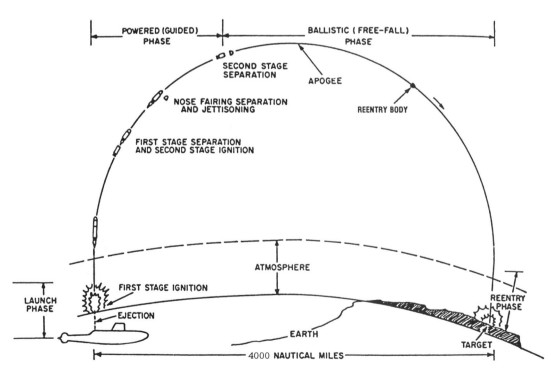

Typical trajectory (flight path) of a sea-launched ICBM. A ballistic missile is affected by several aerodynamic forces during its flight phases through Earth's atmosphere. While in space it is subject primarily to gravitational and inertial forces.

mately 32 feet (9.8 meters) per second each second (written as 32 ft/sec^2 [9.8 m/sec^2]). Its acceleration while in free fall is thus said to be 1 g. Bodies making rapid turns will experience other accelerations, and therefore forces, due to centripetal force (which can be many times that of gravity), often expressed as multiples of g's. As an example, if a jet fighter making a tight turn experiences a sideways force of 5 g's, there is a sideways force on it equal to 5 times its weight.

A missile or aircraft is designed to withstand only a certain number of g's, and if that is exceeded, damage to its structure, its payload, or its instruments may occur. In the case of manned aircraft, its pilot may black out (become unconscious).

MACH NUMBERS

Speeds of missiles and high-performance aircraft are often expressed in terms of Mach numbers, rather than in miles per hour or knots. The Mach number is the ratio of the body's speed to the speed of sound in that particular part of the atmosphere. For example, if an aircraft is flying at a speed equal to one-half the local speed of sound, it is said to be flying at Mach 0.5. If it moves at twice the local speed of sound, its speed is Mach 2.

The speed expressed by the Mach number is not a fixed quantity, because the speed of sound in air varies directly with the square root of air temperature. Because of air temperature changes in the atmosphere with increasing altitude, the speed of sound decreases from 770 mph (344 meters per second) at sea level on an average day when the air is 68 degrees F (20 degrees C), to 661 mph at the top of the troposphere. The speed of sound remains constant between 55,000 feet and 105,000 feet, then rises to 838 mph, reverses, and falls to 693 mph at the top of the stratosphere.

Study Guide Questions

1. A. According to ancient Greek philosophers, what keeps an object in motion?
   B. According to Isaac Newton, what keeps an object in motion?
2. State Newton's three laws of motion.
3. A. How fast is light speed?
   B. What theory describes the motion of bodies with speeds near light speed?
4. What are the units of force
   A. In the English system of units?
   B. In the metric system?
5. A. Is the weight or the mass of an object subject to change?
   B. How is the weight of an object determined?
6. What kind of force must be reckoned with for all earthbound objects in motion?
7. What are the four aerodynamic forces on bodies in flight?
8. According to Bernoulli's theorem, how is lift developed by a curved wing?
9. What is meant by g-forces?
10. How are Mach numbers derived?

Vocabulary

Newton's laws of motion	centripetal force
Newtonian motion	vector quantity
acceleration	free fall
net force	velocity
resultant force	Mach numbers
metric system	g-force
mass	friction
drag	aerodynamics
lift	thrust
angle of attack	work
power	energy
joules	watts

2

Buoyancy

Why does a metal ship float? How can a submarine hover at a desired depth? To answer questions such as these it is necessary to know something about a type of force called the *buoyant force.*

Over 2,000 years ago the Greek scientist Archimedes (287–212 B.C.) found that an object immersed in a fluid is pushed up with a force that equals the weight of the fluid it displaces. This force has come to be called the *buoyant force,* and the principle that describes it is named *Archimedes' law* in honor of its discoverer. For purposes of Archimedes' law, it does not matter whether the "fluid" is a liquid or a gas. The law applies equally to both.

WHY OBJECTS FLOAT

Suppose that a stone with a volume of half a cubic meter weighs 9,800 newtons in air. When it was submerged in water, by Archimedes' law it would feel an upward force equal to the volume of water displaced, or 4,900 newtons in this case, since the weight of a cubic meter of water is 9,800 newtons. The *apparent weight* of the stone in the water—its weight in air minus the buoyant force— would now be 4,900 newtons and it would sink.

Now let us suppose that instead of a stone, we had a hollow iron boat also weighing 9,800 newtons. We place the boat in the water and it begins to sink. As it does so, it begins to displace some of the water, so again by Archimedes' law it begins to feel an upward force equal to the weight of the water being displaced. After it has sunk into the water to the point at which a cubic meter of water has been displaced, it feels an upward force exactly equal to its weight, 9,800 newtons. At this point the upward buoyant force exactly equals the downward weight, so there is no longer any net downward force on the boat. By Newton's first law, described in chapter 1 of this unit, objects with no net force on them tend to remain at rest. Thus, our boat would now float, assuming there were still some part of it above water, called the *freeboard.* The line around the boat where the surface of the water meets it when it floats is called the *waterline.*

Now suppose a hole were drilled in the hull of our boat below the waterline, allowing the water to flow in.

As it fills, the combined weight of the boat plus the water inside would be always greater than the weight of the water being displaced, no matter how far down it sinks. Thus in this situation the boat would eventually fill completely and sink to the bottom, just as in the example of the stone above. So it really does not matter what material is used to construct the boat. A hollow boat will always float as long as there is still some part of it above water when it has sunk to a depth at which its weight is matched by the upward buoyant force provided by the water being displaced.

Density is a scientific term used to describe how much of a material is present per unit of its volume. It is usually specified using the metric system, in kilograms per cubic meter or sometimes grams per cubic centimeter. Anything with a density less than that of water, such as wood, will always float, since when it sinks into water it will always achieve equality of the upward buoyant force with the downward weight before it is totally submerged. Solids having a greater density than water will always have a greater downward weight than upward buoyant force, so they will always submerge completely.

Gases as well as liquids exert upward buoyant forces. Instead of a boat model, suppose we experiment with a small rubber balloon. If we blow up the balloon with air at the same or lower temperature than the air surrounding it, by Archimedes' law an upward force will begin to act on it equal to the weight of the outside air being displaced. But the weight of the balloon's skin plus the air inside it will be greater, thus causing the balloon to fall to the floor, just as the stone in water sank to the bottom.

But now suppose we blew hot air, or a light gas such as helium, into the balloon. Heated air and light gases like helium are less dense than regular air, so they weigh less per unit volume. If we inflate our balloon to the same size as before, the same upward force as before would be felt by it. But the downward weight force would be less. The balloon, therefore, would rise into the air, since there is an unbalanced upward net force on it. In the case of a large balloon launched into the atmosphere, as the balloon rises the air gets thinner, so eventually at some altitude the upward buoyant force decreases

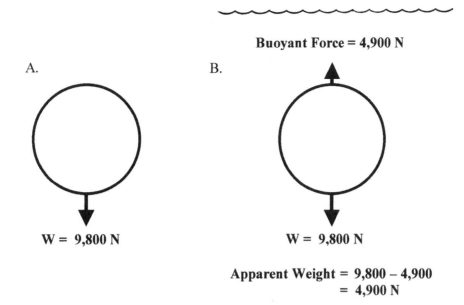

Buoyant Force = 4,900 N

A.

B.

W = 9,800 N   **W = 9,800 N**

Apparent Weight = 9,800 – 4,900
= 4,900 N

A stone with a volume of half a cubic meter that weighs 9,800 N in air (A) has an apparent weight of 4,900 N in water (B) because of the upward buoyant force on it equal to the weight of the water displaced.

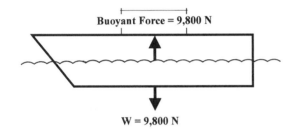

A hollow boat weighing 9,800 N will sink into the water until it displaces an equal weight of water, whereupon it floats at that level.

to the point that it equals the downward weight, and the balloon floats at this altitude.

THE SUBMARINE

When cruising on the surface of a body of water, a submarine acts just like the boat model described above. It will sink only partially into the water, to a depth at which its weight is balanced by the upward buoyant force of the water it displaces. For most submarines this happens when the hull is about two-thirds submerged.

Now suppose that the submarine wants to submerge completely. To do this, it needs more weight to compensate for the upward buoyant force exerted on it by the weight of the water displaced by its totally submerged hull. To provide the weight, submarines are fitted with fillable water tanks inside their structure called *ballast tanks*. When water is pumped into these tanks, their weight plus the structural weight of the submarine now combine to weigh more than the upward buoyant force,

so the submarine dives. To level off at some desired depth, the submarine adjusts the amount of water in the ballast tanks until the downward weight and upward buoyant force are roughly in balance. The propulsion system of the submarine plus its diving planes can now keep the submarine at the desired depth, like an airplane flying at some level in the atmosphere. If the weight and buoyant force were *exactly* matched, the submarine would be able to hover at the desired depth without any forward propulsion, much like the balloon hovering in air.

To surface from a submerged depth, the submarine forces water out of the ballast tanks with compressed air until the upward buoyant force is once again greater than the downward weight. At this point the submarine will surface, aided by its propulsion system. Thus, a submarine in water acts much like a balloon in air, even though the densities of the media in which they operate are much different.

SHIP STABILITY

One of the considerations in ship design is that it should be stable in a wide variety of sea conditions and if damaged. The stability of a ship is dependent on the location of its center of gravity and its center of buoyancy at various angles of inclination or roll. The *center of gravity* is defined as the center of mass of the ship, around which the ship seems to move. The center of gravity does not change position as the ship moves. The *center of buoyancy* is the geometric center of the portion of the ship's hull that is underwater. It tends to move in an arc as the ship rolls. For good stability a ship should have its center of gravity as low as possible in the hull, so that there is a large amount of horizontal distance between the downward force through the center of gravity and upward force through the center of buoyancy. This will generate torque (force of rotation) that will tend to right the ship whenever it rolls. If the center of gravity rises because of either intentional or unintentional addition of weight high in the ship, this righting torque will tend to decrease, and the ship's stability may be impaired to the point that it might capsize if it rolls too far.

Because of the foregoing, if a lightly loaded ship is operating in heavy weather, it will sometimes take on additional water in tanks near the keel (bottom), or fill empty fuel tanks with water, in order to lower its center of gravity as low as possible. In this condition it will be less likely to experience dangerous rolls in stormy seas. The additional water is called *ballast*.

Study Guide Questions

1. Who is credited with discovering the law of buoyant force?
2. State the principles of Archimedes' law.
3. What is the apparent weight of an object in water, and how is it computed?
4. How can a boat constructed from a material more dense than water float?
5. What is density, and how is it computed?
6. Why does a hot-air balloon tend to rise in the air, while one filled with cold air does not?

7. With what equipment is a submarine fitted to allow it to submerge?
8. Upon what factors is a ship's stability dependent?
9. What might happen if excessive weight is added high in a ship?
10. What will a ship sometimes do to lower its center of gravity in stormy seas?

Problems

1. A steel cube with a volume of 1 cubic meter and a density of 7,800 Kg/m^3 is submerged in water (density 1,000 Kg/m^3). If each kilogram weighs 9.8 newtons,
   A. What is the weight of the cube in air?
   B. What is the upward force on the cube when it is completely submerged?
   C. What is the apparent weight of the cube in water?

2. A wooden cube of density 600 Kg/m^3 is floating in water.
   A. How much water in m^3 will it have to displace in order to float?
   B. What percentage of its volume will be above water when it floats?
   C. How deep into the water will it sink?

Vocabulary

buoyant force	density
Archimedes' law	ballast
apparent weight	ballast tanks
freeboard	center of gravity
waterline	center of buoyancy

3

Basic Electricity

The study of electricity began with the ancient Greeks. They discovered that by rubbing a mineral called *amber* with a cloth, they could create a mysterious force of attraction between the cloth and the amber. They also observed that after they rubbed two different ambers with two different cloths, the two cloths would repel one another—as strongly as they were attracted to amber. These forces were called *electric* (from the Greek word for amber), and the cloths and ambers were said to be *electrically charged.*

Although the Greeks discovered electric force, they could not explain it. In fact, it was not until the atomic theory of matter was developed that the true cause of electricity was found. When scientists discovered that atoms were composed of negatively charged particles (electrons) that orbit around positively charged particles (protons), they could explain electrical charge. Normally there is a balance between the negative charge of electrons and the positive charge of protons. Therefore, under most conditions, an atom will have no charge. But if the number of electrons is increased, the atom will become negatively charged. On the other hand, if electrons are taken away, the atom will have a positive charge. Charged atoms are called *ions.*

One of the fundamental laws of electricity is that like charges repel each other, and unlike charges attract each other. In the atom, the electrons are held in their orbit by the attractive force between them and the protons in the nucleus. In the Greeks' experiments with amber, the cloth picked up electrons from the amber, thus becoming negatively charged. This left the amber with a positive charge—and unlike charges attract one another.

CONDUCTORS AND INSULATORS

An electric charge can move through a material if it has a large number of *free electrons*—that is, electrons that can easily move from atom to atom in the material. Substances that permit the free motion of a large number of electrons because of their atomic structure are called *conductors.* Silver, copper, and aluminum wire, in that order, are the best conductors. But copper and aluminum wire are the most commonly used because they are least ex-

pensive. Electrical energy is conveyed at the speed of light through conductors by the free electrons. As the electrical energy passes, each electron moves a very short distance to the neighboring atom, where it replaces one or more electrons by forcing them out of their orbits. The replaced electrons repeat the process in other nearby atoms.

Some substances have very few free electrons and are therefore poor conductors. These substances, such as rubber, glass, or dry wood, are called *insulators.* Good conductors such as wire are used to carry electricity, and they are covered by insulating material to prevent the electricity from being diverted from the conductors.

VOLTAGE

The force that causes electricity to move in a conductor is called *voltage* or *electromotive force* (E). There are six basic ways to generate voltage:

1. *Friction.* Voltage can be produced by rubbing two materials together. *Static electricity* is the most common name for this type. It occurs frequently in dry climates or on days of low humidity.
2. *Pressure.* Voltage can be produced by squeezing crystals such as natural quartz or, more usually, manufactured crystals. Compressed electrons tend to move through a crystal at predictable frequencies. Crystals are frequently used in communications equipment.
3. *Heat.* Voltage can be produced by heating the place where two unlike metals are joined. The hot junction where the moving electrons from the two different metals meet is called a *thermocouple.* The difference in the temperature of the two metals determines the amount of voltage. As a result, thermocouples are often used to measure and regulate temperature, as in a thermostat.
4. *Light.* Voltage can be produced when light strikes a photosensitive (light-sensitive) substance. The light dislodges electrons from their

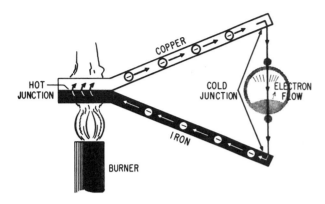

Voltage produced by heat.

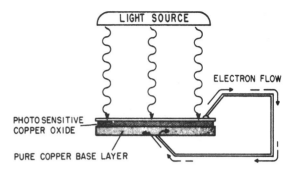

Voltage produced by light.

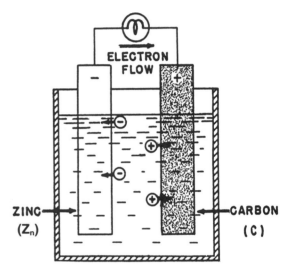

Simple one-cell battery.

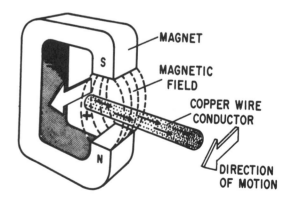

Voltage produced by magnetism.

orbits around the surface atoms. Voltage produced in this manner is called *photoelectric*. The *photoelectric cell* is the device that operates on this principle. A plate coated with compounds of silver or copper oxide, which are extremely sensitive to light, can also produce a flow of electrons. Light is used to generate voltage in devices requiring extreme precision—such as television cameras, automatic processing controls, door openers, and burglar alarms.

5. *Chemical action.* Voltage can be produced by chemical reactions, as in a battery cell. The simple voltaic battery consists of a carbon strip (positive) and a zinc strip (negative) suspended in a container with a solution of water and sulfuric acid. This solution is called the *electrolyte*. The chemical action that results from this combination causes electrons to flow between the zinc and carbon electrodes. Batteries are used as sources of electrical energy in automobiles, boats, aircraft, ships, and portable equipment.

6. *Magnetism.* Voltage can be produced when a conductor moves through a magnetic field, or vice versa, in such a manner as to cut the field's lines of force. This is the most common source of electric power; it is the method used in electric generators. Usually, a copper-wire conductor is moved back and forth through the magnetic field created by a **U**- or **C**-shaped electromagnet.

An instrument designed to measure voltage in an electrical circuit is called a *voltmeter*.

CURRENT

The flow of electricity through a conductor is called *electric current*. Electric current is classified into two general types: direct current and alternating current. *Direct current* flows continuously in the same direction, while an *alternating current* periodically reverses direction. An *ampere* (or *amp*) is the unit used to measure the rate at which current flows. The symbol for current flow is "I."

An instrument designed to measure current in an electrical circuit is called an *ammeter*.

Every material offers some resistance or opposition to the flow of electric current. Good conductors offer very little resistance, while insulators or poor conductors offer high resistance. The size and composition of wires in an electric circuit are designed to keep electrical resistance as low as possible. A wire's resistance depends on its length, diameter, composition, and temperature.

Manufactured circuit elements that provide a definite specified amount of resistance are called *resistors*. Resistance is measured in *ohms* (symbol: Ω, the Greek letter *Omega*). One ohm is the resistance of a circuit element (or circuit) that permits a steady current of one ampere to flow when a potential difference of one volt is applied to that circuit.

An instrument designed to measure resistance in an electrical circuit is called an *ohmmeter.*

BATTERIES

A battery consists of a number of cells assembled in a common container and connected to function as a source of electrical power. A cell is the fundamental unit of a battery. A *simple cell* consists of two electrodes placed in a container holding the electrolyte.

The *electrodes* are the conductors by which the current leaves or returns to the electrolyte. In a simple cell, they are carbon and zinc strips, placed in the electrolyte. In the *dry cell* there is a carbon rod in the center and a zinc container in which the cell is assembled. The electrolyte may be a salt, an acid, or an alkaline solution. In the automobile storage battery the electrolyte is in liquid form. In the dry cell battery, the electrolyte is a paste.

A *primary cell* is one in which the chemical action eats away one of the electrodes, usually the negative. Eventually the electrode must be replaced or the cell discarded. In the case of the common dry cell, as in a flashlight battery, it is usually cheaper to buy a new cell.

A *secondary cell* is one in which the electrodes and the electrolyte are altered by the chemical action that gener-

ates current. These cells may be restored to their original condition (recharged) by forcing an electric current through them in the opposite direction to that of discharge. The automobile storage battery is a common example of a battery composed of secondary cells.

THE ELECTRICAL CIRCUIT

Whenever two unequal charges are connected by a conductor, a pathway for electrons and thus current flow is created. An *electric circuit* is a conducting pathway consisting of the conductor and the path through the voltage source. For example, a lamp connected by wires to a dry cell's terminals forms a simple electric circuit. The electron current flows from the negative (–) terminal of the battery through the lamp to the positive (+) battery terminal, and continues by going through the battery from the (+) terminal to the (–) terminal. As long as this pathway is unbroken, it is a closed circuit and current will flow.

When electrical experiments were first conducted in the 1800s, the electron was as yet undiscovered, so it was assumed that current was a flow of *positive* charges from the positive to the negative terminals of a source in a circuit. This idea became so widespread that still today for many applications electrical current is said to proceed from positive to negative terminals. In the scientific community however, the idea of an *electron current* flowing from negative to positive is more prevalent, and

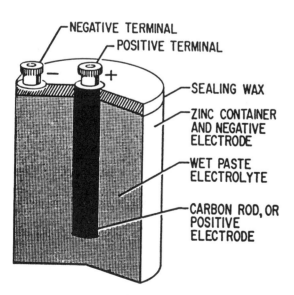

Dry cell battery, cross-section.

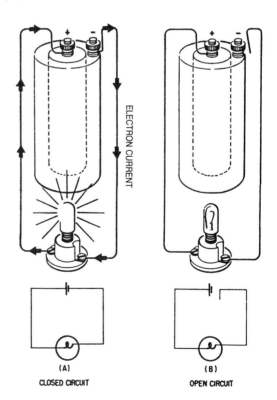

(A) Simple electric circuit (closed); *(B)* Simple electric circuit (open).

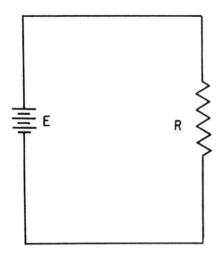

Schematic diagram of a basic circuit. A battery is designated by the symbol E; a light bulb is the resistance, labeled R.

probably easier to understand, so that is the concept used herein for our discussion of electricity.

A *schematic* is a diagram in which symbols are used for a circuit's components, instead of pictures. These symbols are used in an effort to make the diagrams easier to draw and easier to understand. Schematic symbols aid the technician who designs or repairs electrical or electronic equipment.

OHM'S LAW

In the early 1800s, George Simon Ohm proved that a definite relationship exists among current, voltage, and resistance. This relationship, called Ohm's law, is stated as follows: The current in a circuit is directly proportional to the applied voltage and inversely proportional to the circuit resistance. Ohm's law may be expressed as an equation: $I = E/R$ (Equation A).

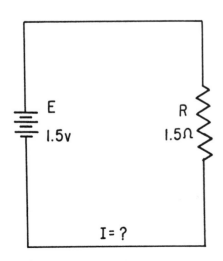

Circuit 1. Determining current in a simple circuit.

I = current in amperes
E = voltage in volts
R = resistance in ohms

If any two of the quantities in the equation are known, the third may be easily found.

Example: Circuit 1 contains a resistance of 1.5 ohms and a source voltage of 1.5 volts. How much current flows in the circuit?

Solution: $I = E/R = 1.5\,V/1.5\,\Omega = 1$ ampere

In many circuit applications, the current is known, and either the voltage or the resistance will be the unknown quantity. To solve a problem in which current and resistance are known, the basic formula for Ohm's law must be transformed to solve for E. Multiplying both sides of the equation by R, the formula for finding voltage is: $E = IR$ (Equation B).

Similarly, to transform the basic formula when resistance is unknown, multiply both sides of the basic equation by R and then divide both sides of the equation by I. The resulting formula for resistance is: $R = E/I$ (Equation C).

POWER

Electrical power refers to the rate at which work is being done. *Work* is done whenever a force causes motion. Therefore, since voltage makes current flow in a closed circuit, work is being done. The rate at which this work is done is called the *electric power rate*, and its measure is the *watt*—the basic unit of power. Power is equal to the voltage across a circuit, multiplied by the current through the circuit. Using P as the symbol for electrical

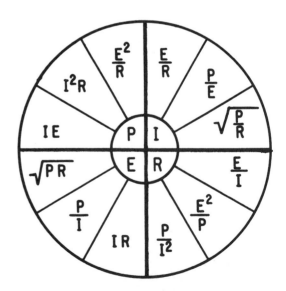

Summary of basic formulas for Ohm's law and for power. In each quadrant of the circle are three formulas. Each formula can be used to find the unknown factor whose symbol appears in the adjacent quadrant of the central circle.

power, the basic power formula is: P = IE (Equation D). As an example, when E is 2 volts and I is 2 amperes, P becomes 4 watts.

When voltage is doubled and resistance remains unchanged, power is doubled *twice*. This occurs because the doubling of voltage causes a doubling of current (see Equation A), which therefore doubles both of the factors that determine power. In other words, the rate of change of power, in a circuit of fixed resistance, is the *square* of the change in voltage. Thus the basic power formula P = IE may also be expressed as $P = E^2/R$ (Equation E), or $P = I^2R$ (Equation F). (These equations can easily be derived by simple substitution from Equations A and B.)

Study Guide Questions

1. What are the positive and negative charged particles in an atom?
2. What force keeps the electrons of an atom revolving in regular orbits?
3. How is electricity conveyed?
4. A. What substances are the best conductors of electricity?
   B. Why?
5. What is an insulator?
6. What is the fundamental law concerning electrical charges?
7. What unit is used to measure electromotive force?
8. What are the six common methods of producing voltage?
9. What is a thermocouple?
10. Where is the photoelectric cell used?
11. What is the most common source of chemically created electricity?
12. What is the unit of measure for current?
13. What is the unit of measure for resistance?
14. What factors determine the amount of resistance in a conductor?
15. What is an electrical circuit?
16. How does electricity flow in a circuit?
17. What is a schematic diagram?
18. A. Describe Ohm's law.
    B. What does it enable us to find?
19. What is the unit of measure for power?
20. What are the three formulas for electrical power?

Simple Circuit Problems

1. A simple circuit consists of one 60-watt bulb and a standard 120-volt source of electricity.
   A. What is the current I in amperes?
   B. What is the resistance R in ohms?
2. A simple circuit powered by a 115-volt battery has 200 ohms of resistance in it. What is the current I in amperes?
3. A simple battery-powered circuit has .75 ampere running through one 150-ohm resistor. Using this information, find the voltage of the battery.

Power Problems

1. What power in watts is being dissipated in a resistance of 100 ohms if 2 amperes of current are flowing through it?
2. What is the resistance of a 100-watt light bulb connected to a 120-volt power supply?

Vocabulary

electricity	battery
conductor	schematic
insulator	Ohm's law
electromotive force	ohm
voltage	resistance
thermocouple	ampere
photoelectric	current
voltmeter	ammeter
ohmmeter	

4

Electronics

There are a great many devices used in modern life in general and in the Navy that are based on electricity and the electromagnetic wave. Some of these include the computer, audio equipment of all kinds, radio, television, radar, and sonar. Chapter 3 of this unit covered the subject of basic electricity. In this chapter we will discuss the nature of the electromagnetic wave upon which all of the devices mentioned above are based.

In general there are two kinds of waves by type: mechanical and electromagnetic. *Mechanical waves* require some sort of material in which to travel or propagate (spread). Many of these can be felt and seen. Examples of this type of wave would be water waves through water, sound waves through air, or vibrations along a taut string. The other type of wave is called *electromagnetic,* so called because these have both an electrical and a magnetic component. This type of wave is non-material and cannot be directly felt or seen. This type of wave often travels best in a complete vacuum, in which there is no material present. Examples of this kind of wave would be radio, TV, radar, light, and infrared (heat) waves. The material or space through which waves travel is called the *medium.*

Regardless of the type of wave, all need some sort of energy source to originate. Waves can be thought of as nature's means of dissipating energy from this source. They will continue to propagate until the energy level in the surrounding medium is the same as the energy at the source location. There are also two kinds of waves classified by their form. *Longitudinal waves* cause the medium through which they travel to be displaced back and forth along the path of the wave, like a spring bouncing back and forth. Sound is a wave of this kind. *Transverse waves* cause the medium to be displaced perpendicular to the direction of travel of the wave in a pattern often called a sine wave. An example of this kind of wave is that produced in a stringed instrument when the string is plucked.

ELECTROMAGNETIC WAVES

All electronic devices use electromagnetic waves as the basis of their operation. Very briefly, an electromagnetic wave is produced by a rapidly expanding and collapsing magnetic field, which is in turn produced by alternately energizing and deenergizing an electronic circuit especially designed to generate such waves. In electronics, such a generating circuit is often referred to as an oscillator. For many applications an amplifier of some type is used to boost the power of the oscillator output, and an antenna is used to form the outgoing wave.

An electromagnetic wave, because of the methods by which it is propagated, always resembles a sine wave in appearance. The wave can be described by its wavelength, frequency, and amplitude. In the figure, one complete electromagnetic wave or cycle is shown, and the terms used to describe it are defined as follows:

- A *cycle* is one complete sequence of values of the strength of the wave as it passes through a point in space.
- The *wavelength,* abbreviated in electronics by the Greek letter λ (lambda), is the length of a cycle expressed in distance units, usually either meters or centimeters.
- The *amplitude* is the wave strength at particular points along the wave. It is a measure of the energy contained in the wave. Large amplitude waves convey more energy than do those having small amplitude.

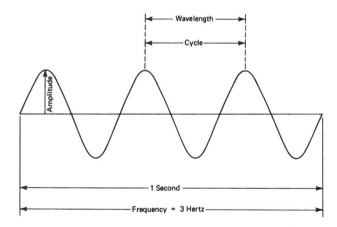

Characteristics of a radio wave with a frequency of 3 hertz.

- The *frequency*, abbreviated as f, is the number of cycles repeated during 1 second of time. If the time frame shown in the figure were 1 second long, for example, it could be said that the frequency of the wave shown is 1 cycle per second.
- The *period*, abbreviated by the Greek letter τ (tau) is the time required to complete one cycle of the wave. In the example above, the period would be 1 second. Period and frequency are related by the formula τ = 1/f.

In the vacuum of space, an electromagnetic wave is theorized to travel at a velocity approaching the speed of light, or 3×10^8 meters per second (186,000 miles per second). Frequency and wavelength of an electromagnetic wave are related by the formula $\lambda = 3 \times 10^8 / f$, where λ is the wavelength in meters and f the frequency in cycles per second. Thus, every specific electromagnetic frequency is radiated at a specific wavelength.

In recent years, the term *hertz*, abbreviated Hz, has come to be used in place of cycles per second, in honor of the German pioneer in electromagnetic radiation, Heinrich Hertz (1857–1894). One hertz is defined as one cycle per second. Frequency is expressed in terms of numbers of thousands (kilo), millions (mega), or billions (giga) of hertz. For example, 10,000 cycles per second is expressed as 10 kilohertz, abbreviated 10 kHz; 2.5 million cycles per second would be 2.5 megahertz, or 2.5 MHz.

The behavior of an electromagnetic wave is dependent upon its frequency and corresponding wavelength. For descriptive purposes, electromagnetic frequencies can be arranged in ascending order to form a "frequency spectrum" diagram. Electromagnetic waves are classified as *audible-frequency* waves (20–20,000 Hz) at the lower end of the spectrum, *radio* waves from about 5 kHz to 30 GHz, and *visible light* and various kinds of *rays* at the upper end of the spectrum.

Though electromagnetic wave frequencies within the range of 20 to 20,000 Hz are called the audible frequencies, it must be remembered that to be heard such waves must be transformed into mechanical sound waves through devices called *speakers.*

PROPAGATION EFFECTS

The medium through which radio waves travel will affect their path. Weather or atmospheric conditions can cause variation from the straight path that the waves might otherwise take in a vacuum. These variations are called refraction, reflection, diffraction, and trapping.

Refraction (bending) occurs when there is a change in the density or the atmosphere in which the wave is traveling. Take for example a radio wave transiting the atmosphere. Because the atmosphere gradually decreases in density with altitude, the wave is refracted, or bent downward. This increases the horizontal distance the wave will have to travel to get out of the atmosphere.

Refraction also causes bending of radio waves over the horizon. Low-frequency waves are bent more readily than high-frequency waves, so low frequency waves are used for long-range radars and long-distance radio communication.

Radio waves are *reflected* from the ionosphere, which is generally from 30 to 250 miles above Earth. The distance between the transmitter and the point where the reflected sky wave returns to a ground receiver is called the *skip distance.*

Diffraction causes spreading of radio waves behind obstructions. It results from the generation of secondary waves by the primary wave.

Trapping occurs when a temperature inversion in the atmosphere traps cold air close to Earth's surface. Under those circumstances radio signals may be reflected from the warmer air above back to Earth a number of times. This will increase the range of the transmitted signal. This trapped cold air is called a *duct.*

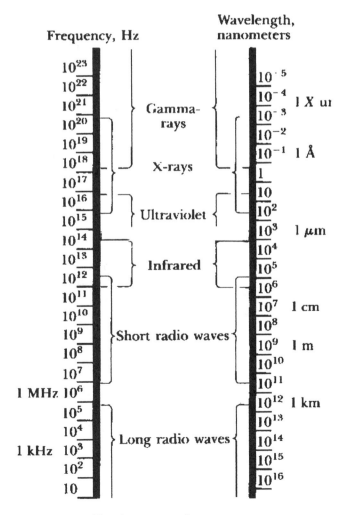

The electromagnetic spectrum.

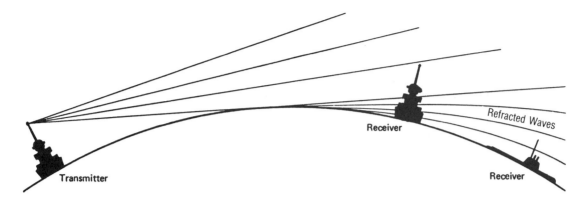

Refraction is the bending of radio waves over the horizon, extending their range to receivers beneath Earth's curvature.

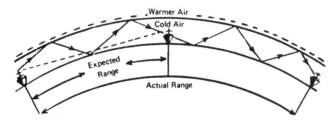

Trapping. The duct acts as a wave guide.

RADIO

As mentioned above, radio waves are electromagnetic waves transmitted in the range from about 5 kHz to 30 GHz. On Earth most of these waves are intentionally generated by electronic devices such as radio and TV transmitters, though some are byproducts of other electronic gear. There are also a number of natural radio transmitters, such as interstellar gas and star systems in space. Artificial radio transmissions use a series of electromagnetic waves transmitted at constant frequency and amplitude called continuous waves. Because an unmodified continuous wave cannot convey much information, the wave is normally modified or *modulated* in some way. When this is done, the basic continuous wave is referred to as a *carrier wave.*

In practice there are three methods by which a carrier wave may be modulated to convey information. These are amplitude, frequency, and pulse modulation. In *amplitude modulation,* abbreviated AM, the amplitude of the carrier wave is modified in accordance with the amplitude of a modulating wave, such as voice or music. In the radio receiver the signal is demodulated by removing the modulating wave, which is then amplified and related to the listener by means of a speaker. This type of modulation is widely used in the commercial radio broadcast band, with carrier wave frequencies in the kHz range.

In *frequency modulation,* abbreviated FM, the frequency of the carrier wave instead of the amplitude is altered in accordance with the frequency of the modulat-

ing wave. This type of modulation is used for FM commercial radio broadcasts and the sound portion of television broadcasts, with carrier wave frequencies in the MHz range.

Pulse modulation is different from either amplitude or frequency modulation in that there is usually no impressed modulating wave. In this type of modification, the continuous wave is broken up into very short bursts, or "pulses," separated by relatively long periods of silence during which no wave is transmitted. This is the type of transmission used by most types of radars.

RADAR

Radar (short for *r*adio *d*etection *a*nd *r*anging) was developed originally as a means for detecting and ranging on targets in warfare. But it has also been adapted to an increasing number of other applications ranging from speed detection devices to storm tracking. Radar is based on the principle that electromagnetic waves can be formed into a beam, and that part of waves so transmitted will be reflected back if the wave encounters an object in its path.

Navy radars are grouped in three general categories: search, fire control, and special. *Search radars* are of two categories: air search and surface search. These are used for early warning and general navigation. Search radars detect targets at maximum range, while sacrificing some detail. *Fire control radars* are important parts of gun and missile fire control systems. They are used after a target has been located by search radar. *Special radars* are used for specific purposes, which include ground-controlled approach (GCA) radar at airfields, carrier-controlled approach (CCA) radar, and height-finding radar.

Radar operates very much like a sound wave or echo reflection. If you shout in the direction of a cliff, you will hear your shout return from the direction of the cliff. What actually takes place is that the sound waves generated by the shout travel through air until they strike the cliff. There they are reflected, and some return to the originating spot, where you hear them as an echo. There is a time interval between the instant you shout and when you hear the echo. The farther you are away from the cliff, the longer the interval before the echo returns. The distance to the cliff is proportional to the length of the time interval. If a directional device is built to transmit and receive this echo, it can be used to determine the direction and distance to the cliff, since we know the speed of sound.

Radar equipment works on the same principle. Pulse-modulated radio waves of extremely high frequency are beamed out, and the radar set is programmed to receive its own echo. This out-and-back cycle is repeated up to 4,000 times per second. If the outgoing wave is sent into clear space, no energy is reflected back to the receiver. But if the wave strikes an object—such as an airplane, a ship, a building, or a hill—some of the energy comes back, at the speed of light, as a reflected wave.

In the case of a search radar, the echoes received by the radar receiver appear as marks of light on a cathode ray tube (CRT), a device similar to a TV screen. It is commonly called a "scope" or PPI (plan position indicator).

The scope is marked with a scale of yards or meters, miles or kilometers (1,000 meters), and degrees. It provides a bird's eye view of the area covered by the radar, showing the transmitter in the center of the screen. Each time a target is detected it appears as an intensified spot on the scope. Thus an observer watching the PPI can tell the range and bearing to the target. Other radars can tell the altitude of incoming aircraft and missiles.

RADAR IN THE NAVY

Radar has many uses in today's Navy. Surface search and navigational radars are used extensively to assist Navy ships in navigating through constricted waters and during times of poor visibility and stormy weather, as well as tracking other shipping in the area. Air search and height-finding radar is used to track both friendly and potentially threatening aircraft, and fire control radars of various kinds are used to guide shipboard weapons to their targets.

The information gathered by most shipboard search radars is presented and analyzed in a shipboard space called the Combat Information Center (CIC); in some more advanced surface warships this space is called the Combat Direction Center, or CDC. Quite often on today's ships during general quarters the commanding officer (CO) assumes a battle station in the CIC or CDC and leaves the executive officer as the senior officer on the bridge. As the head evaluator of the information coming into the center, the CO must decide which targets to engage and with what means—aircraft, guided missiles, or radar-directed gunfire. The CO must also decide how to

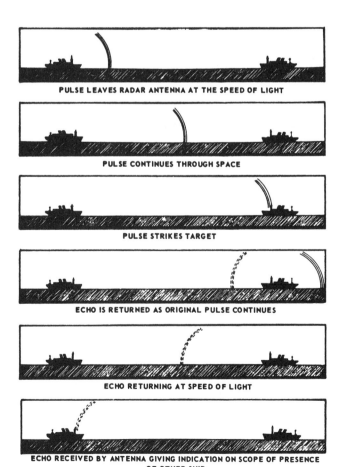

PULSE LEAVES RADAR ANTENNA AT THE SPEED OF LIGHT

PULSE CONTINUES THROUGH SPACE

PULSE STRIKES TARGET

ECHO IS RETURNED AS ORIGINAL PULSE CONTINUES

ECHO RETURNING AT SPEED OF LIGHT

ECHO RECEIVED BY ANTENNA GIVING INDICATION ON SCOPE OF PRESENCE OF OTHER SHIP

The principle of radar operation.

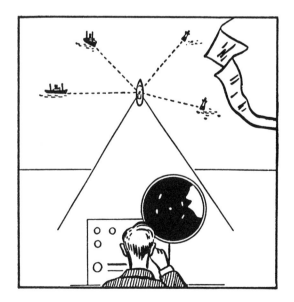

A PPI (plan position indicator) scope presentation. On this scope targets appear as white dots called pips. Here the inset shows the PPI scope presentation of the physical targets shown above it.

maneuver in order to escape or engage enemy ships, submarines, and aircraft.

ELECTRONIC WARFARE

Electronic warfare (EW) uses highly sophisticated electronics to counter the enemy's radiated electromagnetic waves and to ensure the proper and effective use of our own. The electronic warfare systems include (1) collection of information regarding the enemy without its being aware, and without divulging our presence; (2) hindering or rendering the enemy's electronic spectrum useless by jamming circuits with electronic countermeasures (ECM), now referred to as electronic attack (EA) measures; and (3) electronic counter-countermeasures (ECCM), now called electronic protection (EP), which ensure the proper use of our electronic spectrum—in spite of the enemy's attempts to direct EA at our unit.

Study Guide Questions

1. A. What are the two types of waves?
   B. What are the two forms these waves can take?
2. A. What is the standard unit of measurement of frequency?
   B. What does this measurement represent?
3. What is the audible frequency range?
4. What four variations from the straight wave path are caused by atmospheric or weather elements?

5. Define the following wave terms:
   A. Cycle
   B. Wavelength
   C. Amplitude
   D. Period
6. What range of frequencies in the electromagnetic spectrum comprise radio waves?
7. What is the fundamental principle of radar?
8. What are the three general categories of U.S. Navy radars?
9. What are the two categories of search radars, and what are they used for?
10. What is the "scope" or PPI presentation for a search radar?
11. What are the functions of EA and EP?

Vocabulary

electromagnetic wave
  radar
amplitude
wavelength
cycle
frequency
hertz
refraction
diffraction
trapping

fire control radar
Combat Information Center
  (CIC)
Combat Direction Center
  (CDC)
electronic warfare
electronic attack
electronic protection
jamming
electronic countermeasure

Sound and Sonar

In chapter 4 of this unit we described the different forms that wave energy can take. Classified by type, these are material and electromagnetic waves. Sound is a material wave. Like all waves, it originates at a source of energy, which in the case of sound causes matter to vibrate. These vibrations are passed along into the material surrounding the source—the *medium*—in the form of a series of longitudinal (in the directional of travel) pressure waves. Each wave carries with it a certain amount of energy imparted to it by the source as it vibrates. Once started, if the medium through which it travels is of uniform temperature and density, the individual waves spread through the medium in the form of expanding three-dimensional spheres, much like ripples expanding over a two-dimensional water surface from the point of impact of a stone.

Because the available energy in the wave is spread over an ever-increasing area as each sphere expands, with the area of a sphere being $4\pi r^2$, the energy per unit area falls off rapidly as the distance (the radius r) from the sound source increases. The amount of energy or power in a sound wave at any given location is called the *sound intensity*. It is expressed in terms of watts per square centimeter or per square meter. In order for a human to hear a sound, it must hit the eardrum with an intensity of at least 10^{-12} watts per square meter. Anything less will not deflect the eardrum sufficiently for the sound to be heard.

A human's ability to hear a sound also depends on the frequency of the sound, or the number of times per second that a sound wave passes by. As was stated in chapter 4 of this unit, the audible frequency range for the human ear is 20 to 20,000 Hz. Sounds in the extreme high and low ends of this frequency range require more power per unit area to be heard than do sounds in the mid-range.

THE PHYSICS OF SOUND

Because sound is a material wave, it stands to reason that the more material there is per unit volume in the medium, the better sound will travel through it. Because of the increase in molecular motion within a material as temperature increases, temperature of the medium also affects sound transmission. Sound travels better within a given material if its temperature is higher as opposed to when its temperature is lower. The table below gives the speed of sound in meters per second at sea level for different materials at different temperatures:

Material	Speed of sound (m/sec)
Air at 0 degrees C	332
Air at 20 degrees C	344
Air at 100 degrees C	392
Kerosene at 25 degrees C	1,324
Water at 25 degrees C	1,498
Wood (oak)	3,850
Steel	5,200

Sound waves have the same general behavior as other types of waves. They can be reflected by media having a greater density than the medium they originate in, as for example when a sound wave traveling through air hits the wall of a room. The reflected sound is called an *echo*. They can be bent or *refracted* as they pass from one medium to another, if the densities are not too dissimilar. Sound waves can also be *diffracted*, spreading after they pass through a narrow opening. They obey the formula

$$v = f\lambda$$

where v is the velocity of the wave, f its frequency, and λ is the wavelength. Thus, if we know the speed of sound for a given medium, and either the frequency or wavelength, we can easily calculate the unknown quantity. When a sound wave is reflected from an object creating an echo, one can easily compute the distance to the object if the speed of sound in the medium containing it is known, using the simple formula

$$\text{Distance} = \text{rate} \times \text{time}$$

For instance, if the speed of sound in air were 344 m/sec, and it took 4 seconds for an echo to return to a source, then the one-way distance would be (4 sec ÷ 2) × 344 m/sec = 688 meters. Besides specifying the intensity of a sound in terms of its power per unit area, as described above, there is another widely used measure of sound intensity relative to the quietest sound the ear can hear. This measure, called *relative intensity* or *noise level*, is calculated in units called *decibels*. A sound having 0 decibels is equal in intensity to the lowest that can be heard, 10^{-12} watts per square meter. On the decibel scale a sound of 100 decibels would be 10^{10} times as intense as a sound of 0 decibels. A sound of 120 decibels is the loudest sound that the ear can stand without pain as the eardrum begins to tear. Sound decibel levels that are negative indicate a sound that is too faint to be heard without amplification, as for example, distant fish sounds in the ocean.

THE PHYSIOLOGY OF SOUND

Without a human ear to hear a sound wave there would be no sound, only noise. The sound waves are gathered and funneled by the outer ear into an opening through the skull called the *ear canal.* At the inner end of the ear canal is a very thin sensitive membrane called the eardrum. Its extreme sensitivity is indicated by the fact that it can detect sound intensities of 10^{-12} watts per square meter, equivalent to a pressure of only 2×10^{-5} newtons (the metric unit of force) per square meter! It is obvious that you should be very careful to protect your eardrums from loud or highly focused sound, such as that produced by highly amplified music or earphones.

Beyond the eardrum is the *middle ear.* Here three delicate bones called the hammer, anvil, and stirrup transmit the sound from the eardrum to the *inner ear,* where a liquid-filled structure called the cochlea is located. Sound vibrations in the liquid are sensed by special cells that translate the mechanical vibrations to electromagnetic nerve impulses. These impulses travel through the auditory nerve to the brain, where the person interprets them as sound.

Some animals such as bats and dogs have ears that are sensitive to sounds above the 20,000-Hz upper frequency limit that humans can hear. Sounds in this region are called *ultrasound.* Bats use these high intensities to navigate by means of echoes returned from objects around them, and dog owners may use ultrasonic dog whistles to call their pets.

THE DOPPLER SHIFT

You may have noticed the apparent change in frequency or pitch of a train whistle or automobile horn as the train or auto approaches, passes, and departs. Actually, there is no change in the frequency emitted by the source. There is, however, a change in the frequency reaching the ear, because of the relative motion between the source and you. As the train or auto approaches, the effect is an increase in frequency caused by compression of the distance between waves. When the source is opposite you, you hear the same frequency as the whistle or horn puts out. When the train or auto moves away, the effect is to increase the distance between waves, thus causing a decrease in the frequency reaching your ear. This phenomenon is known as the *Doppler effect,* named for the Austrian physicist Christian Doppler (1803–1853). The total change between the highest and lowest frequencies heard is called the Doppler shift.

The Doppler shift can be used to determine the speed and direction of motion of a sound's source, such as a submarine in the ocean. It also occurs with electromagnetic waves such as radio and light. By analyzing the Doppler shift in light from a distant star, for instance, astronomers can determine the speed at which it is moving away from us. Radar detectors use the Doppler shift to determine the speed of baseballs and automobiles.

SOUND IN THE SEA

Since Navy ships and submarines operate in the sea, the characteristics of sound in seawater are of special interest to Navy people. The speed of sound waves traveling through seawater is affected by three factors: (1) its temperature; (2) its pressure, a function of depth; and (3) its salinity, or salt content.

Temperature is by far the most important of these factors. The speed of sound changes from 4 to 8 feet per second for every degree of temperature change. The temperature of the sea varies from freezing in the polar seas to more than 85 degrees F in the tropics. It may decrease by more than 30 degrees from the surface to a depth of 450 feet. So temperature changes in the sea have a great effect on the speed of sound in the seawater.

Sound also travels faster in water under pressure, since the density increases somewhat as pressure in-

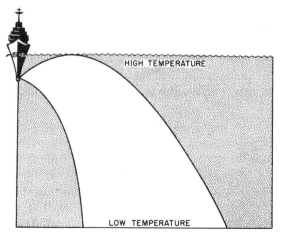

A refracted sound wave in the ocean.

creases. Pressure increases as depth increases, so the deeper a sound wave is, the faster it travels. This pressure effect is smaller than temperature effect, but it cannot be neglected, since it increases about 2 feet per second for each 100 feet of depth.

Seawater has high mineral content or *salinity*. The density of seawater is about 64 pounds per cubic foot; that of fresh water is only about 62.4 pounds per cubic foot. This variation is the result of the salt content in the seawater. The saltier the water, the greater its density, and hence the faster the speed of sound in it. The speed of sound increases about 4 feet per second for each part-per-thousand increase in salinity—a lesser effect than that of temperature, but greater than that of pressure.

SONAR

The principal means of detecting and tracking submarines at sea is called sonar (short for *s*ound *n*avigation *a*nd *r*anging). The earliest sonar device, used in World War I, was a simple hydrophone, which could be lowered into the water to listen for noises generated by submerged submarines. Three ships equipped with this equipment could pinpoint the location of U-boats by triangulation—plotting the bearings of the hydrophone noise from the three ships and seeing where the bearings crossed.

Today's sonar gear is much more sophisticated. It provides highly accurate ranges and bearings to the submerged submarine. Analysis of Doppler data provides accurate courses and speeds for the submarine. The sonar information is normally presented visually on a CRT screen rather than by sound as the early devices did. In addition, very sophisticated sonars for use by helicopters and fixed-wing aircraft have been developed.

There are two basic modes of operation of sonar systems employed for the detection of targets. They are referred to as active and passive.

Active sonars transmit underwater sound pulses that strike targets and return in the form of echoes. The returned echoes indicate the range and bearing of the target. Surface undersea warfare (USW) ships usually employ the active (pinging) mode when seeking out submarines. Active sonar is also used by submarines and ships to analyze shorelines, bottom characteristics, and ocean depths. Submarines can switch to active modes to locate ships or

A frigate fitted with a bow-mounted sonar dome rests in drydock at the Boston Naval Shipyard.

other submarines, but this is rarely done because it would give away the transmitting sub's location.

Passive sonars do not transmit sound. They only listen for sounds produced by the target to obtain accurate bearing and estimated range information. Target detection is achieved at great ranges through the use of highly sensitive hydrophones. Passive sonar is normally used mainly by submarines, but surface ships can employ passive modes in addition to their active sonar. Submarines use passive sonar to analyze the noise of passing ships. USW aircraft, helicopters, and shore stations also use passive sonar.

Until recently most shipboard sonar systems were mounted in domes underneath the ship's bow, and were therefore called *hull-mounted* systems. In the past few years a new type of passive sonar system called a *towed array* has been installed in increasing numbers of USW surface ships and submarines. This consists of a semi-buoyant tube of a length of several thousand feet or more that is fitted with numerous hydrophones. The tube is unreeled and towed behind the ship. Such an array is extremely sensitive and can pick up noise generated by submarines operating many miles away.

Most ships also have aboard a *fathometer* (echo sounder) for determining water depth under the hull. A sound pulse is transmitted toward the bottom, and its echo is received back. The fathometer is normally used as a navigational aid, particularly when entering shallow water. It also is used regularly in oceanographic research to determine the contour of the sea bottom. Most Navy ships keep their fathometer on continuously to have an accurate recording of the water depths on their course. The information can be displayed numerically or automatically recorded by a stylus on a roll of graph paper.

Dipping Sonar and Sonobuoys. Sonar equipment called *dipping sonar* can be used by helicopters to detect submerged submarines. The helicopter can hover and lower a hydrophone or pinging transducer into the sea to a depth of about 400 feet. The sonar searches a 360-degree area. After searching, the helicopter hauls in the cable and goes to another spot quickly. When a submarine is detected, the helicopter can attack it with homing torpedoes or bring in other USW units to assist.

Radio sonobuoys are small, expendable floating hydrophone units that are dropped in the area of a suspected submarine by aircraft. They are usually dropped one at a time in a circular pattern around the contact area. By analyzing the radio signals received from each sonobuoy, the location and direction of movement of the submarine can be determined. It can then be attacked by the aircraft itself or by other available USW forces.

A Navy helicopter lowering a dipping sonar during an undersea warfare (USW) exercise.

Study Guide Questions

1. A. What kind of a wave is sound?
   B. What form do sound waves have?
2. How does sound spread through a uniform medium?
3. A. What is the minimum intensity in watts/m² that a sound must have in order to be heard?
   B. What pressure in newtons/m² does this correspond to?
4. What is the audible frequency range?
5. In what units is relative intensity or noise level measured?
6. Why should people be careful to protect their eardrums against loud sounds?
7. A. What is the apparent frequency shift of a passing whistle or horn called?
   B. What causes this shift?
8. What three factors affect the speed of sound in water?
9. What does the Doppler effect enable a sonar technician to do when analyzing returning sonar echoes from a submarine?
10. What are two modes of operation of shipboard sonar systems?
11. Why do submarines rarely use active sonar?
12. How do helicopters use sonar to detect submarines?

Vocabulary

medium (sound)	Doppler effect
sound intensity	salinity
eardrum	active sonar
ear canal	passive sonar
inner ear	hydrophone
auditory nerve	sonobuoy
fathometer	

Glossary

ABYSS—a very deep area of an ocean.

ACCELERATION—a change in velocity per unit of time.

AERODYNAMICS—the science of how objects move through gases, especially in regard to flight.

AMMETER—an instrument to measure electric current.

AMPERE—the unit of electric current.

ANGLE OF ATTACK—the angle between the chord of a wing and the relative wind.

ARCHIMEDES' PRINCIPLE—an object immersed in a fluid feels an upward force equal to the weight of the fluid being displaced by the object.

ASTEROID—any of a number of small bodies orbiting between the planets Mars and Jupiter.

ASTHENOSPHERE—uppermost layer of Earth's mantle.

ATOLL—a ringlike coral island that encloses a lagoon.

AURORA—a high-altitude multicolored luminosity in an atmosphere.

BALLAST—any material placed low in a vessel or balloon to enhance stability or neutralize buoyancy.

BALLISTIC MISSILE—a missile that goes on a free-falling path after a powered and guided ascent.

BATHYSCAPHE—a small research vessel designed to operate at extreme ocean depths.

BATHYTHERMOGRAPH—a temperature- and depth-sensing device used to record water temperatures at various depths.

BATTERY—a device that converts chemical to electrical energy.

BAY—a large body of water partly enclosed by land but having a wide outlet to the sea.

BERNOULLI'S PRINCIPLE—when a fixed quantity of fluid flows, the pressure is decreased when the flow velocity increases.

BIODEGRADABLE—subject to breaking down or decay by natural forces.

BIOLUMINESCENCE—light created by living organisms.

BLACK HOLE—a region of space surrounding matter so dense that not even light can escape its gravitational pull.

BRECCIA—fine particles of broken rocks.

BUOYANT FORCE—upward force on an object immersed in a fluid.

CENTER OF BUOYANCY—the center of the submerged portion of a body.

CENTER OF GRAVITY—the center of mass of a body; its natural pivot point.

CENTRIPETAL FORCE—a force on a body in curved motion that is directed toward the center of curvature.

CHEMOSPHERE—the region of the atmosphere between 20 and 120 miles in altitude in which photochemical reactions occur.

CONDUCTOR—materials through which an electric charge readily moves.

CONTINENTAL SHELF—the sea bottom from the shore to a depth of 200 meters (100 fathoms).

CORIOLIS EFFECT—a tendency due to Earth's rotation that makes moving objects tend or curl clockwise in the Northern Hemisphere.

CORONA—envelope of gas surrounding the Sun's chromosphere.

COSMOLOGY—the astrophysical study of the origin, processes, and structure of the universe.

CRUISE MISSILE—an air-breathing surface-to-surface or air-to-surface guided missile.

CRYSTAL—a three-dimensional solid structure in which the constituent atoms or molecules are arranged in a precise and repeating pattern.

DECIBEL (db)—unit of sound intensity level.

DETRITUS—disintegrated matter or debris.

DIFFRACTION—bending of waves around an obstacle as they travel.

DIRTY RAIN—rain contaminated with dust or other airborne pollution.

DOLDRUMS—ocean regions near the equator characterized by calms or light winds; the light winds of these areas.

DOPPLER EFFECT—an apparent change in pitch (frequency) of sound or electromagnetic waves caused by relative motion between the source and receiver.

DRAG—fluid friction.

ECHO SOUNDER—a sonic device used to obtain water depths by measuring the time required for a sound pulse to make a round trip to the sea bottom and back.

ECLIPSE—the cutting off of light from one celestial body by another.

ECLIPTIC—the plane of Earth's orbit about the Sun.

ECOSYSTEM—a system of plants and animals and their environment.

ELECTRIC CIRCUIT—a continuous path through which electricity can flow.

ELECTRIC CURRENT—a flow of charged particles.

ELECTROMAGNETIC WAVE—nonmaterial wave consisting of oscillating electric and magnetic fields that move at the speed of light through space.

ELECTRONIC COUNTERMEASURES—the use of electronics to reduce the effectiveness of enemy electronic equipment. Now often called electronic attack (EA) measures.

ELECTRONIC WARFARE—aspect of warfare concerned with the use of electronic equipment and sensors.

ELLIPSE—a closed curve that is formed from two foci or points in which the sum of the distances from any point on the curve to the two foci is a constant.

ESTUARY—an area of the sea that extends inland to meet the mouth of a river.

FATHOM—unit of depth equal to 6 feet.

FAULT LINE—a plane along which geological formations may shift position.

FLUID—a material that flows: liquid, gases, and plasmas.

FREE FALL—the unconstrained motion of a body subject only to a gravitational force.

FREQUENCY—number of occurrences or cycles per unit time.

GEOSYNCHRONOUS SATELLITE—a satellite whose orbital velocity is matched to the rotational velocity of the planet; it appears to hang motionless above one position over the planet's surface.

G-FORCE—an apparent force generated by an acceleration maneuver, either linear or in a curved path, measured in g's, or multiples of the force of Earth's gravity at sea level (9.8 m/s^2 or 32 ft/s^2).

GRADIENT—a rate of inclination or slope.

GULF—a large body of salt water, almost surrounded by land.

GYRE—a circular pattern of ocean current.

HERTZ (Hz)—unit of frequency equal to one cycle per second.

HULL—the body or shell of a ship or seaplane.

ICBM—intercontinental ballistic missile.

IGNEOUS ROCK—rock formed by solidification from a molten state.

INSULATOR—a material through which the flow of electrical charge is greatly impeded.

IONOSPHERE—an electrically conducting set of layers of Earth's atmosphere, extending from about 30 to more than 250 miles above the surface.

JET STREAM—a high-speed wind near the upper troposphere, generally moving from a westerly direction at speeds above 200 mph.

KEEL—central longitudinal beam of a ship from which the frames and hull plating rise.

KILOGRAM—SI unit of mass.

LIGHT YEAR—the distance light travels in a year.

LITHOSPHERE—outer crust of the earth.

MACH NUMBER—the ratio of the speed of an object to the speed of sound in the surrounding medium.

MAGNETIC FIELD—a region of space near a magnetized body where magnetic forces can be detected.

MAGNETOSPHERE—an asymmetric region surrounding a planet in which charged particles are trapped by the planet's magnetic field.

MASS—quantity of material present, measured in kilograms in the SI system.

MECHANICAL WAVE—wave consisting of periodic motion of matter.

MEDIUM—the environment or substance through which a wave travels.

MESOSPHERE—the portion of Earth's atmosphere from about 20 to 50 miles above the surface.

METEOR—the luminous phenomenon seen when a meteoroid enters the atmosphere, commonly known as a shooting star.

METEORITE—a part of a meteoroid that survives through Earth's atmosphere.

METEOROID—a small rock in space.

MILLIBAR—1/1,000 of a bar; the standard sea-level pressure is about 1,013 millibars.

NEBULA—a diffuse mass of interstellar gas or dust.

NET FORCE—vector sum of forces on an object.

NEWTON—SI unit of force, equal to about a fifth of a pound.

NOVA—an exploding star that increases in brightness due to internal explosions.

OHM—SI unit of electrical resistance.

OHMMETER—an instrument to measure electrical resistance.

ORBIT—the path of an object that is moving around a second object or point.

OZONE LAYER—a layer of Earth's atmosphere between 10 and 20 miles in altitude that contains a high concentration of solar radiation–absorbing ozone.

PERIOD—time required for one complete cycle of an event to occur.

PHOTOELECTRIC—electrical effects caused by illumination.

PHOTOSPHERE—the visible surface of the Sun.

PITCH—the frequency of a sound.

PLANE OF THE ECLIPTIC—the plane containing Earth's orbit around the Sun.

POWER—the rate of doing work, expressed in watts in the SI system.

PPI SCOPE—plan position indicator radar scope; a radar screen that presents a chartlike picture of the surrounding land and sea.

PULSAR—any of several very short period interstellar radio sources.

QUASAR—a starlike object, probably clusters of stars, that emit characteristic visible and radio radiation.

RADAR—*ra*dio *d*etection *a*nd *r*anging; an instrument for determining, by radio frequency echoes, the presence of objects and their range, bearing, and elevation.

REFLECTANCE—the ratio of the total light reflected by a surface to the total incident on the surface.

REFRACTION—a change in direction of a wave when passing from one medium to another.

RETROGRADE MOTION—backward movement.

RIP CURRENT—strong, seaward-moving water currents along a seashore.

SATELLITE—an artificial device or natural body in orbit around a larger body.

SEA-LANE—a route of travel across an ocean or other large body of water.

SOUND—a long body of water connecting larger bodies.

SPACECRAFT—a vehicle designed to travel in space.

SPACE PROBE—a one-way, unmanned exploratory spacecraft.

SPECTRUM—a collection of wavelengths.

STRATOSPHERE—the relatively isothermal part of the atmosphere above the troposphere and below the mesosphere.

TELEMETRY—remote transmission of data by radio or wire.

TIDAL WAVE—an unusually high and prolonged wave in the ocean caused by a disturbance such as an undersea explosion or impact of a large body.

TRAJECTORY—the path of a projectile, missile, or bomb in flight.

TROPOSPHERE—the lowest region of Earth's atmosphere, characterized by decreasing temperature with increasing altitude.

TSUNAMI—a tidal wave caused by an oceanic disturbance.

TYPHOON—a severe tropical hurricane occurring in the western Pacific.

ULTRASOUND—acoustic frequencies above the human range of hearing.

UNDERSEA WARFARE (USW)—a term encompassing all aspects of modern warfare beneath the sea, including but not limited to antisubmarine warfare, mine warfare, and UDT operations.

VECTOR QUANTITY—a quantity having both magnitude (size) and direction.

VERTEBRATE—animal having a backbone.

VISIBLE SPECTRUM—the range of electromagnetic wavelengths visible to the eye as light.

VOLTMETER—an instrument to measure voltage.

WATERLINE—the line on a vessel's hull to which it sinks in the water.

WATT—SI unit of power, equal to one joule per second.

WAVELENGTH (λ)—distance between corresponding points on two successive waves.

WEIGHT—force of gravity on an object.

Bibliography

MARITIME HISTORY

Books

American Military History. Washington, D.C.: Center of Military History, U.S. Army, 1989.

Bradford, James C., ed. *Admirals of the New Steel Navy, 1880–1930.* Annapolis: Naval Institute Press, 1990.

——. *Captains of the Old Steam Navy, 1840–1880.* Annapolis: Naval Institute Press, 1986.

——. *Command Under Sail: Makers of the American Naval Tradition, 1775–1850.* Annapolis: Naval Institute Press, 1985.

Cayton, Andrew, Elizabeth Israels Perry, Linda Reed, and Allan M. Winkler. *America: Pathways to the Present.* Needham, Mass.: Prentice Hall, 2000.

Cutler, Thomas. *Brown Water, Black Berets: Coastal and Riverine Warfare in Vietnam.* Annapolis: Naval Institute Press, 1988.

Dull, Paul S. *A Battle History of the Imperial Japanese Navy, 1941–1945.* Annapolis: Naval Institute Press, 1978.

Engle, Eloise, and Arnold S. Lott. *America's Maritime Heritage.* Annapolis: Naval Institute Press, 1975.

Hobbs, Richard R. *Naval Science 1.* 4th ed. Annapolis: Naval Institute Press, 1996.

——. *Naval Science 2.* 4th ed. Annapolis: Naval Institute Press, 1997.

——. *Naval Science 3.* 4th ed. Annapolis: Naval Institute Press, 1998.

Jordan, Robert Paul. *The Civil War.* Washington, D.C.: Special Publications Division, National Geographic Society, 1975.

Luraghi, Raimondo. *A History of the Confederate Navy.* Annapolis: Naval Institute Press, 1996.

Lyon, Jane D. *Clipper Ships and Captains.* New York: American Heritage Publishing, 1962.

Miller, Edward S. *War Plan Orange: The U.S. Strategy to Defeat Japan, 1897–1945.* Annapolis: Naval Institute Press, 1991.

Miller, Nathan. *The U.S. Navy: A History.* 3d ed. Annapolis: Naval Institute Press, 1997.

——. *The U.S. Navy: An Illustrated History.* New York and Annapolis: American Heritage Publishing and Naval Institute Press, 1977.

Morison, Samuel Eliot. *The Two-Ocean War.* Boston: Little, Brown, 1963.

Polmar, Norman, Eric Wertheim, Andrew Bahjat, and Bruce W. Watson Jr. *Chronology of the Cold War at Sea, 1945–1991.* Annapolis: Naval Institute Press, 1997.

Potter, E. B., ed. *Sea Power.* 2d ed. Annapolis: Naval Institute Press, 1981.

Pratt, Fletcher. *The Compact History of the United States Navy.* 3d ed. New York: Hawthorne books, 1967.

Rickover, H. G. *How the Battleship Maine Was Destroyed.* Annapolis: Naval Institute Press, 1976.

Ridgway, Gen. Matthew B., USA (Ret.). *The Korean War.* Garden City, N.Y.: Doubleday, 1967.

Robinson, Charles M., III. *Shark of the Confederacy: The Story of the CSS Alabama.* Annapolis: Naval Institute Press, 1994.

Rodgers, Vice Adm. William L. *Greek and Roman Naval Warfare.* Annapolis: Naval Institute Press, 1964.

Rohwer, Jurgen. *War at Sea, 1939–1945.* Annapolis: Naval Institute Press, 1996.

Rohwer, Jurgen, and Gerhard Hummelchen. *Chronology of the War at Sea, 1939–1945.* Annapolis: Naval Institute Press, 1992.

Shulman, Mark R. *Navalism and the Emergence of American Sea Power, 1882–1893.* Annapolis: Naval Institute Press, 1995.

Still, William N. J. *The Confederate Navy.* Annapolis: Naval Institute Press, 1997.

Stillwell, Paul, ed. *Air Raid: Pearl Harbor!* Annapolis: Naval Institute Press, 1981.

Tarrant, V. E. *Jutland: The German Prospective.* Annapolis: Naval Institute Press, 1995.

Periodicals

Bryam, Lt. Col. Michael J. "Fury from the Sea: Marines in Grenada." *U.S. Naval Institute Proceedings,* May 1984.

Friedman, Norman. "World Naval Developments." *U.S. Naval Institute Proceedings,* May 1997.

Guérout, Max. "The Wreck of the C.S.S. *Alabama.*" *National Geographic,* December 1994.

Nott, John. "The Falklands Campaign." *U.S. Naval Institute Proceedings,* May 1983.

Rohwer, Jurgen. "Naval Warfare Since 1945." *U.S. Naval Institute Proceedings,* May 1978.

Simmons, Dr. Dean, et al. "Air Operations Over Bosnia." *U.S. Naval Institute Proceedings,* May 1997.

Internet

Air Force Magazine: Specialoperations.com. "The *Mayaguez* Incident."

Columbia Electronic Encyclopedia: Infoplease.com. "Vichy Government."

Darren Milford: Worldwar1.co.uk. "World War I Naval Combat."

Encarta Online Encyclopedia: Encarta.msn.com. "Iran-Iraq War."

Federation of American Scientists: Fas.org/start1. "Strategic Arms Reduction Treaty (START I) Chronology."

Henninger, Inc.: Henninger.com. "*Mayaguez.*"

Magazine Web: Magweb.com. "The Confederate Navy, 1861–1865."

Mariners' Museum: Mariner.org. "Monitor Expedition."

Mark F. Jenkins: Ameriteck.net. "Famous Blockade Runners."

Texas A&M University: Tamu.edu.Navtarch. "The *Denbigh* Project."

University of South Carolina: Cla.sc.edu. "*Hunley* Update."

U.S. Army: Army.mil/cmh. "World War II: The War Against Japan."

U.S. Navy: History.navy.mil. Various topics.

USS *Pueblo* Veteran's Association: Usspueblo.org. "The attack."

Yale Law School: Yale.edu. "The Avalon Project at the Yale Law School: The Barbary Treaties."

NAUTICAL SCIENCES

Books

Ballard, Robert D., et al. *The Ocean Realm.* Kingsport, Tenn.: Kingsport Press, by Special Publications Division, National Geographic Society, Washington, D.C., 1978.

Bellamy, David. *The Life-Giving Sea.* New York: Crown Publishers, 1975.

Hobbs, Cdr. Richard R., USNR (Ret.). *Naval Science 1.* 4th ed. Annapolis: Naval Institute Press, 1996.

———. *Naval Science 2.* 4th ed. Annapolis: Naval Institute Press, 1997.

———. *Naval Science 3.* 3d ed. Annapolis: Naval Institute Press, 1998.

Kotsch, Rear Adm. William J., USN (Ret.). *Weather for the Mariner.* 3d ed. Annapolis: Naval Institute Press, 1983.

Leyden, Michael B., Gordon P. Johnson, and Bonnie B. Barr. *Introduction to Physical Science.* Menlo Park, Calif.: Addison-Wesley Publishing, 1988.

Roberson, Patricia Q., and Naomi L. Mitchell, eds. *Aerospace Science: The Science of Flight.* Maxwell Air Force Base, Ala.: Air Force Junior ROTC, 1993.

Sears, Francis W., Mark W. Zemansky, and Hugh D. Young. *College Physics.* 7th ed. New York: Addison-Wesley Publishing, 1991.

Tropp, Harry E., and Alfred E. Friedl. *Modern Physical Science.* Chicago: Holt, Rinehart and Winston, 1991.

Williams, John E., Frederick E. Trinklein, and H. Clark Metcalf. *Modern Physics.* New York: Holt, Rinehart and Winston, 1984.

Zeilik, Michael. *Astronomy: The Evolving Universe.* New York: Harper & Row, 1979.

Zitzewitz, Paul, Robert Neff, Mark Davids, and Kelly Wedding. *Physics: Principles and Problems.* Westerville, Ohio: Macmillan/McGraw-Hill, 1992.

Periodicals, Booklets, and Reports

Achenbach, Joel. "Power of Light." *National Geographic,* October 2001.

Begley, Sharon. "New Search for Life on Mars." *Newsweek,* 6 December 1999.

DiChristina, Mariette, ed. "Five-Year Guide to Space: The Odyssey Begins." *Popular Science,* June 2000.

Fischman, Josh, and Rachel K. Sobel. "Cities in the Sand." *U.S. News and World Report,* 10 July 2000.

Food and Agriculture Organization of the United Nations. Information Division. "The State of World Fisheries and Aquaculture." Rome: United Nations, 1998.

Gore, Rick. "Neptune—Voyager's Last Picture Show." *National Geographic,* August 1990.

Lemonick, Michael D., and Madeleine Nash. "Unraveling Universe." *Time,* 6 March 1995.

Morison, David. *Voyages to Saturn.* Washington, D.C.: GPO, 1982.

Newcott, William R. "Galileo Mission." *National Geographic,* September 1999.

———. "Return to Mars." *National Geographic,* August 1998.

———. "Venus Revealed." *National Geographic,* February 1993.

Newman, Richard J. "A Hole at the Waterline: Attack on the USS *Cole.*" *U.S. News and World Report,* 23 October 2000.

Sawyer, Kathy. "A Mars Never Dreamed Of." *National Geographic,* February 2001.

———. "Unveiling the Universe." *National Geographic,* October 1999.

Smith, Bradford A. "Voyage of the Century." *National Geographic,* August 1990.

Stafford, Edward P. *Sun, Earth, and Man.* Washington, D.C.: GPO, 1982.

Internet

Boeing Corporation: Boeing.com. "International Space Station: Missions Accomplished and Continued Assembly." May 2001.

Columbia Electronic Encyclopedia: Factmonster.com. "Evolution of Telescopes."

Defense Manpower Data Center: Dmdc.osd.mil/sites. "Military Bases." September 2001.

John F. Graham: Space.edu/projects/book/chapter17. "The Space Probes." December 2001.

National Aeronautics and Space Administration: Nasa.gov. "The Planets."

National Oceanic and Atmospheric Administration: nws.noaa.gov/mission. "National Weather Service." October 2000.

———. Pmel.noaa.gov. "What Is an El Niño?"

Project Phoenix: Seti.org. "Allen Telescope Array."

———. Seti.org. "Project Phoenix General Information."

———. Seti.org. "Signal from Pioneer 10."

Space.com, Inc.: Space.com. "Lunar Mission Provokes Mystery." August 2001.

U.S. Navy News Service: Chinfo.Navy.mil. "Navy announces results of investigation on USS *Cole* (DDG 67)." January 2001.

U.S. Navy Surface Warfare Officer School: Fas.org/man/dod. "Stability and Buoyancy Lessons."

Index
Maritime History

Index

Nautical Sciences

The Naval Institute Press is the book-publishing arm of the U.S. Naval Institute, a private, nonprofit, membership society for sea service professionals and others who share an interest in naval and maritime affairs. Established in 1873 at the U.S. Naval Academy in Annapolis, Maryland, where its offices remain today, the Naval Institute has members worldwide.

Members of the Naval Institute support the education programs of the society and receive the influential monthly magazine *Proceedings* and discounts on fine nautical prints and on ship and aircraft photos. They also have access to the transcripts of the Institute's Oral History Program and get discounted admission to any of the Institute-sponsored seminars offered around the country.

The Naval Institute also publishes *Naval History* magazine. This colorful bimonthly is filled with entertaining and thought-provoking articles, first-person reminiscences, and dramatic art and photography. Members receive a discount on *Naval History* subscriptions.

The Naval Institute's book-publishing program, begun in 1898 with basic guides to naval practices, has broadened its scope in recent years to include books of more general interest. Now the Naval Institute Press publishes about one hundred titles each year, ranging from how-to books on boating and navigation to battle histories, biographies, ship and aircraft guides, and novels. Institute members receive discounts of 20 to 50 percent on the Press's more than eight hundred books in print.

Full-time students are eligible for special half-price membership rates. Life memberships are also available.

For a free catalog describing Naval Institute Press books currently available, and for further information about subscribing to *Naval History* magazine or about joining the U.S. Naval Institute, please write to:

Membership Department
U.S. Naval Institute
291 Wood Road
Annapolis, MD 21402-5034
Telephone: (800) 233-8764
Fax: (410) 269-7940
Web address: www.navalinstitute.org